D1410325

The Diffusion of Power

THE DIFFUSION OF POWER

An Essay in Recent History

BY

W. W. ROSTOW

Professor of Economics and History
The University of Texas at Austin

The Macmillan Company

New York, New York

The author gratefully acknowledges the kind permission of the following publishers to quote from the works indicated: Little, Brown and Co. for *The Unheavenly City* by Edward C. Banfield, copyright © 1968, 1970 by Edward C. Banfield; American Political Science Association for "The American People, Viet-Nam and the Presidency" by Albert H. Cantril; The Institute for Strategic Studies, London, for *Strategic Survey 1969,* © The Institute for Strategic Studies 1970; W. W. Norton & Company for *The Communist Collapse in Indonesia* by Arnold C. Brackman; The MIT Press, Cambridge, Mass., for *Sino-Soviet Relations and Arms Control* by Morton Halperin, © 1967 by Massachusetts Institute of Technology; Princeton University Press for *The Sino-Soviet Conflict, 1956–1961* by Donald S. Zagoria, copyright © 1962 by Princeton University Press; The Viking Press, Inc., for *Power in the Kremlin: From Khrushechev to Kosygin* by Michel Tatu, translated by Helen Katel, copyright © 1968 by William Collins & Co., Ltd., London; The Viking Press, Inc., for *De Gaulle and the Anglo-Saxons* by John Newhouse, copyright © 1970 by John Newhouse; Gallup International, Inc., for two charts that appeared in Report Number 43 (January, 1969) and Report Number 52 (October, 1969) of the *Gallup Opinion Index*; Daedelus, the Journal of the American Academy of Arts and Sciences, Boston, Mass., Fall, 1968, for *The Conscience of the City* by Edward C. Banfield.

The Macmillan Company
866 Third Avenue, New York, N.Y. 10022
Collier-Macmillan Canada Ltd., Toronto, Ontario
Library of Congress Catalog Card Number: 72-77654

FIRST PRINTING

Printed in the United States of America

To J. F. K. and L. B. J. in particular;
but, in fact, to all five American postwar Presidents,
who struggled to defend the nation's interests and the
cause of human freedom while preserving the
possibility of civilization in a nuclear age.

Contents

PREFACE *xi*

INTRODUCTION *xv*

1 *Prologue: The Concentration and Diffusion of Power, 1940–1957* *1*

BOOK ONE

FROM SPUTNIK TO KENNEDY

2 *Sputnik and After: The Communist World* *21*

3 *Four Interwoven Crises in Sino–Soviet Relations, 1958–1960* *28*

4 *Three Crises in the Developing World* *40*

5 *The Eisenhower Second Term: The Domestic Scene* *59*

6 *Sputnik, Military Policy, and Space* *68*

7 *Sputnik and the Atlantic Alliance* *74*

8 *Eisenhower's Policy Toward the Developing World* *86*

9 *Crisis in the Middle East* *94*

10 *Crisis in Latin America* *99*

11 *The Crisis in Indian Economic Development* *104*

12 *Crisis in Southeast Asia* *108*

13 *From Eisenhower to Kennedy* *111*

BOOK TWO
THE KENNEDY ADMINISTRATION

14 *Introduction to Book Two* 133

15 *Growth, Price Stability, and the Balance of Payments* 136

16 *The Allocation of Public Resources* 148

17 *The Race Crisis of 1963* 151

18 *The Organization of National Security Affairs, 1961* 160

19 *Military, Arms Control, and Space Policy* 171

20 *Kennedy's Policy toward the Developing World in General* 185

21 *Some Crises in the Developing World* 189

22 *The Bay of Pigs and Latin American Policy* 208

23 *The Nuclear Question: Vienna, Berlin, and the Atlantic Community* 222

24 *The Cuba Missile Crisis: "Khrushchev at Bay"* 251

25 *Southeast Asia* 264

26 *Kennedy as President* 296

27 *Johnson Before the Presidency and at the Beginning: A Personal Impression* 303

BOOK THREE
THE JOHNSON ADMINISTRATION

28 *Introduction to Book Three* 309

29 *Growth, Price Stability, and the Balance of Payments* 313

30 *The Allocation of Public Resources* 327

31 *Problems of Race, 1963–1969* 336

32 *The White Affluent Radicals* 352

33 *The Organization of National Security Affairs* 358

34 *Military Policy and Arms Control* 369

35 *Europe* 391

36 *Johnson and the Developing World* 406

37 *Vietnam: A Race between Two Political Processes* 435

38 *Vietnam, 1964–1969: From Near-Defeat to Near-Nationhood* 438

39 *Vietnam and American Political Life* 477

40 *Southeast Asia, 1963–1969: A Personal View* 504

41 *Johnson as President* 526

BOOK FOUR

THE PRESENT AND THE FUTURE

42 *The Nixon Administration: A Preliminary Sketch* 537

43 *The American Agenda* 577

APPENDIX

The National Interest 605

NOTES 613

INDEX 711

Preface

As my period of public service came to a close in 1968, I decided that one of my early academic tasks would be to carry forward the kind of analysis incorporated in *The United States in the World Arena.* That book, covering the years 1940–1958, is a study of the interplay between American domestic life and the nation's performance on the world scene. Using essentially the same method, the present volume takes the story down to the early days of 1972. Its title, *The Diffusion of Power*, is in fact the one I would have preferred for the earlier volume, but fourteen years ago my publisher felt it would not be easily understood.

I called on personal experience to illuminate some of the main themes of *World Arena.* In the present work I have used such materials more extensively. I have had the benefit of my personal files, covering occasions when I was a consultant to the Eisenhower administration and worked in support of John F. Kennedy's candidacy down through the election of 1960. I also used my files as a public servant in the 1960s to recall the timing and flow of events, the character of the debates, and the mood of the times. (These files are on deposit at the Johnson Library, to which they will be formally transferred in time.)

I had no access, of course, to the classified papers in the Eisenhower or Kennedy libraries, although I am in the debt of the staffs of both institutions for checking dates and, in the latter case, for permitting me to read certain oral history interviews that have already been released. In the case of the Johnson Library, work I did in helping organize the foreign policy papers of the Johnson administration provided valuable background. But, as the reader will perceive, this book makes no direct use of such materials. I neither asked for nor was I offered special privileges by the Johnson Library.

I have occasionally introduced into the text passages from memoranda I wrote as a public servant to President Kennedy, President Johnson, and Secretary Rusk. I have also used a very few passages from other documents in my files. Some of these were classified at the time. I took pains to assure that the extracts used would not complicate American relations with foreign governments or inhibit the conduct of government business in other ways. In addition, I have had the relevant passages examined by appropriate officials in the executive branch to reassure me that their publication would not be contrary to national security. I am grateful to them for taking the time to deal with this matter in an orderly way in the midst of their urgent current duties.

In reviewing the published material on this period, I found a good many references to my alleged views, actions, and advice that I rendered when in government. Much of what has been written about me is inaccurate. Some writers have even felt free to put into direct quotation things I never said, reflecting perspectives I never held. This kind of misrepresentation is normal at times of intense controversy in a democratic society and is not to be taken seriously. It would be an unjustified intrusion on the reader and a distortion of this essay to correct the record here. But my failure to do so should not be taken as confirmation of such passages.

In writing this book, I acquired many debts. The first is to my students at The University of Texas at Austin. In teaching for three terms a course on the years 1940–1971, I presented these materials as they unfolded in successive drafts. As always, I learned a good deal from the give-and-take of seminar, classroom, and the informal discussions they generated.

The typing and retyping of the manuscript was done with good cheer and occasional enlivening comment by Adele Millen, Barbara Roberts, and Pamela Grisham.

The assistance of Lois Nivens in the writing of this book was of critical importance. From the first day to last she shared, as my secretary and right arm, eight years in the Kennedy and Johnson administrations. Her knowledge of my files (perhaps 50,000 pages of typescript) and of the events they reflect was invaluable; and she helped in many other ways as well.

I benefited greatly from the suggestions of those who turned from their current responsibilities to read and criticize portions of the manuscript in draft: McGeorge Bundy, William Franklin, Edward Fried, Robert Ginsburgh, Andrew Goodpaster, Kermit Gordon, William Griffith, Alexander Haig, Robert Hardesty, Walter Heller, U. Alexis Johnson, William Jorden,

Arthur Krim, Thomas C. Mann, Paul Miles, Arthur Okun, Henry Owen, Robert McNamara, Harry Middleton, Robert Rehwaldt, Elspeth Rostow, Dean Rusk, William Westmoreland.

A good many others responded to questions of substance, provided data, or helped check my memory of events where no written record exists or was available: R. W. Argo, Jr., Andrew Brimmer, Joseph Califano, George Carver, Richard Colbert, John Ford, J. K. Galbraith, Arthur Goldberg, William Gorham, Morton Halperin, Edward Hamilton, Charles Haar, Marshall Kaplan, Amrom Katz, Spurgeon Keeny, Robert Komer, Henry Cabot Lodge, Ray Marshall, Edward S. Mason, Melvin Mogulof, Daniel P. Moynihan, Richard Neustadt, John Newhouse, Ithiel Pool, E. V. Rostow, Stanley Ruttenberg, Paul Samuelson, Harold Saunders, Arthur Schlesinger, Jr., Walter Sedwitz, Samuel Sharp, Maxwell D. Taylor, Llewellyn Thompson, Cyrus Vance, Jerome Wiesner, Ella Wolfe, Robert Wood.

Before we left Washington, I told President Johnson of my intention to write this book. As work got under way, I dropped him a note telling him what was afoot. I said I would be grateful if he would read and criticize the chapters in draft; but that I recognized also that he might prefer to see the book for the first time when published. He chose the latter course.

The debt to my wife, Elspeth Davies Rostow, is beyond easy acknowledgment. My perspective on these years, as we lived them and looked back on them, is as much the product of her reflections as my own; although her account, I daresay, would be different and more colorful than mine. Without her support I could have sustained neither the effort to contribute to those years as a public servant nor to give them some shape as a historian.

W. W. ROSTOW

June 15, 1972
Austin, Texas

Introduction

THIS ESSAY IS ONE MAN'S VIEW OF THE YEARS 1957–1972. IT IS A portrait of how the world community and the United States moved through an extraordinary passage, with elements of both continuity and change. As the period ends, anxieties exist that existed also in the late 1950s: What are the Russians up to in Cuba? Will there be another Arab–Israeli war? What of the future of Southeast Asia? Is there a United States–Soviet missile gap and is it dangerous? What about the American balance of payments?

But the changes are even more striking. We have moved from the terrors of nuclear blackmail to the negotiation of the nonproliferation treaty and the SALT talks. We have seen Mao proclaiming that Moscow should lead world communism in a global crusade, then confronting more than forty Soviet divisions on his frontiers, and finally greeting Nixon in Peking. We see, initially, an exuberant Khrushchev, confident that Soviet heavy industry production would exceed that of the United States by 1970 and denying the automobile age as a capitalist aberration; but his successors, in the midst of a somewhat sluggish economy, decide to bring the automobile cheaply and efficiently to the Soviet consumer, with the aid of Fiat and other Western firms. We begin with Eisenhower's complacent America of the mid-1950s at the zenith of high mass-consumption, content to see its excessive gold stocks drain off to build the reserves of others; but even in his latter years, the United States begins to be thrown on the economic defensive by the rise of Western Europe and Japan; and, then, in the 1960s, it is simultaneously challenged and becomes uncertain in the face of the surging internal problems of the search for quality, while still bearing inescapable responsibilities for order and progress in a nuclear age. We move from a time of romantic hopes, revolutionary and otherwise, in the developing nations to more realistic assessments of the possible pace of change and the inescapable constraints of the human condition in politics and diplomacy, power and growth.

All these transitions are part of the dominating theme of this book: the diffusion of power away from Moscow and Washington. They are also part of the final question: Are men capable of organizing this fragile global community of diffusing power in reasonably stable and peaceful ways, or will the diffusion of power lead to more violence and disorder than we already know?

In the end, looking ahead at the American agenda, I offer what answers I can to this ultimate question. The analysis of this period is shaped by concepts I have developed as a historian and social scientist since the 1930s, but it is also influenced by my experiences as a public servant. No two men view the world around them in the same terms. Nor do they see the events in which they participate from the same angle of vision. This is a distinctly personal book, illuminating, inevitably, only part of a complex passage of history.

Its intellectual structure is built on four cornerstones.

First, the national interest of the United States on the world scene. It is dangerous for a historian or social scientist to pretend to an objectivity which does not exist. The best he can do is recognize his presuppositions and make them clear. Any assessment of American policy during these years will reflect the author's view of the national interest. My view is set out in the Appendix so the reader can examine and weigh my judgment of this root matter.

The other three constructs are ones that I have developed elsewhere. They are: the national style (a chapter in *The American Style*, edited by Elting E. Morison, New York, 1958); the stages of economic growth, elaborated in a volume of that title (Cambridge, 1960 and 1971); and a view of politics as an eternal triangle of competing imperatives—security, welfare, and the constitutional balance between justice and order (*Politics and the Stages of Growth*, Cambridge, 1971).

These four themes flow contrapuntally through the book from beginning to end. I have tried not to let them intrude excessively; but the reader should be aware of their influence on how the story is told and on the conclusions drawn from it.

While this book is personal, it is not a personal memoir. If it were, the structure and subject matter would be quite different. Nevertheless, I thought it useful to introduce some of my experiences as a public servant in order to illuminate the main themes of this essay. I should, therefore, briefly note what I did in government over these years.

In the Eisenhower administration I was an occasional consultant. From time to time I was called from academic life to help on an ad hoc basis: for example, at the time of Stalin's death; before the Geneva summit conference of 1955; during the Lebanon–Jordan crisis of 1958; to participate in a NASA committee, in 1959–1960, on manned versus unmanned flight to the moon. These and other episodes, including work on the Soviet Union, Communist China, and foreign aid, provided some insight into how those bearing responsibility in the 1950s saw the world around them and the nation's problems. I met Eisenhower only once as President, on a minor occasion. My knowledge of his mind and method is indirect, as is my knowledge of how he absorbed advice from his senior counselors and made his decisions.

During 1961 I was in a quite different position. I had known and worked regularly with John Kennedy from early 1958. He appointed me initially deputy special assistant for national security affairs, assigning certain regular areas of work and particular tasks. On these matters I reported directly to him and knew his mind well. In addition, I observed Kennedy making decisions over a considerably wider range than my White House assignments of 1961. I would immediately add, however, that no aide to a President, no matter how close or deeply trusted, can know all of a President's mind on a given issue at a given time. A President's responsibilities are so many, and the consequences that flow simultaneously from them so complex, that he is unlikely to communicate all the considerations that bear on a given decision or the weight he gives to each. Indeed, like a sailing ship captain balancing out wind and tides and currents, he may put these considerations through the computer of his mind without articulating them all—even to himself.

From December 6, 1961, to April 1, 1966, I was chairman of the Policy Planning Council at the Department of State and (from May 1964) also the United States member of CIAP (Inter-American Committee on the Alliance for Progress). I worked, in the first instance, for the secretary of state. In scope, the task covered the whole spectrum of foreign policy. It permitted me to work on important issues which never reached the White House for decision; for example, how to manufacture and distribute cheap proteins to children in the developing nations; the anatomy of Latin American inflation and the nature of its remedy; the cause and potential cure for the fragmentation of politics and parties in the developing world; all manner of contingency planning for events, most of which, blessedly, never happened. And virtually no issue reaching the White House was outside the range of the Planning Council. We had our view, and it flowed into the stream of governmental opinion. But I was only occasionally at White House meetings. My knowledge of Presidential decisions over that period of more than four years is, with a few exceptions, either secondary or a by-product of helping to organize President Johnson's foreign policy papers for his Library since 1969. For example, I did not attend a single meeting with the President on Southeast Asia from December 1961 to February 1966, when I accompanied President Johnson to the Honolulu meeting with the South Vietnamese leaders.

After going to the White House in April 1966 as special assistant for national security affairs, I had to help organize the full range of the President's business in foreign affairs. I remained in that post until January 20, 1969.

During the Nixon administration, on the contrary, my knowledge of policy making has been confined almost wholly to the public record.

Clearly, what I learned varied greatly as among these five periods, at different distances from the center of decision, but the material drawn from experience as a public servant to illuminate this essay is not necessarily useful in proportion to personal closeness to Presidents and their final decisions. This is a book about historical processes and the ideas in men's minds, as well as about the usually painful choices Presidents confronted and the decisions they took. Therefore, experience at low bureaucratic levels, as well as reasonably high ones, proved helpful, as did ideas exchanged with colleagues in the Planning Council and with ambassadors as well as with Presidents.

At a few points my experiences have permitted me to add matters of substance to the historical record of the Kennedy and Johnson administrations. I have also summarized my view of the Presidents, including the two with whom I closely worked. But both the character of this book and my view of what is appropriate as among mutually trustful colleagues have led me to exclude observations about personalities and incidents not directly related to the main themes.

No task I have undertaken as a writer puzzled me more than weaving personal materials and memories into this book. It would have been an affectation to have left them out. But, having been introduced, a few blunt words are required to put these passages in perspective.

I do not believe the history of these years would have been substantially different if I had been teaching economic history and never set foot in Washington. Max Millikan's and my crusade for development aid in the 1950s added, perhaps, a distinctive strand to the work of many hands in that direction; my crusade with Kennedy in late 1960 and early 1961 for wage-price guideposts and my talk with Walter Reuther in June 1961 may have helped tip the balance of Kennedy's policy in that direction; my deeply rooted views about regionalism in relation to the long-run American position on the world scene may have strengthened Johnson's strong personal instinct to move in this direction in 1966–1969. And there were, I guess, other more or less definable contributions.

With respect to Southeast Asia, I did, of course, support the policies of both Kennedy and Johnson, although I had a somewhat different notion of an optimum military strategy. I believe they were right to honor our commitments in Southeast Asia and that those commitments represent abiding interests of the United States that we will deny only to our ultimate peril. In supporting their positions, I trust I was helpful to them; but I did not determine their views. If I had not supported their positions, I would have left government. I mention this to underline that the use of personal material in the text in no way reflects a sense of personal importance in the flow of events analyzed.

If this is so, why does one go to work as a public servant? In my case, because I cared greatly about the issues at stake in the 1960s; I shared substantially the perspective and objectives of Kennedy and then of Johnson; and it was, in any case, my generation's turn to take our place on the line in this difficult passage for America and the world community. Once at work, of course, a public servant has a chance to exercise every ounce of talent and experience, knowledge and wisdom at his command; for the problems of the contemporary world are much bigger than the fallible men who must do their best with them.

When I first went to work in Washington in the summer of 1941 to help set up what was to become the Office of Strategic Services, I was invited by an older friend to have lunch at the Occidental Restaurant. I was struck by the photographs that lined its walls to the ceiling—the great and near great, remembered and forgotten. The genius of the American system struck me—drawing a river of talent to Washington from all over the continent, using that talent for a time, and then, as the nation's life flows on, sending them about their business when their time is up, counting none as indispensable. That remains my image of Washington and service in the federal government.

To say that individual bureaucrats rarely leave clearly definable marks on the contours of history does not mean their role is without meaning. It is they who analyze the problems, set out the alternatives, fight the battles for those they prefer, do the first draft of Presidential or other policy statements. They are part of the flow of events. And if the flow would have been only slightly different with others at their posts, still they have had a chance to have their say and to participate in, rather than merely observe, some of the forces shaping their own lives and the life of their nation. My experience of public service confirmed a dictum I permitted myself at a much earlier time: "History seems to be tolerant of the individual if he avoids the larger illusions of grandeur."[1]

The higher one goes in the American bureaucracy, the more likely one is to understand the limits rather than the scale of his contribution. In working for a President, one is impressed by the enormous gap between his responsibility and that of even the highest ranking officers around him. The American Constitution works just the way it should: responsibility comes unambiguously and personally to rest on the man the people elect.

As the President seeks to reconcile the multiple roles he plays under the Constitution, an aide is conscious that, no matter how close he may be, he can perceive only a portion of the President's mind and problems. And if he writes a book, he ought, following the good precedent of Arthur Schlesinger, Jr., keep this quotation from Grace Tully before him at all times: "None of them [White House aides] could know that for each minute they spent with the President he spent a hundred minutes by himself and a thousand more with scores of other people—to reject, improvise, weigh and match this against that until a decision was reached."[2] More than that, an aide becomes conscious of how little, in the end, he can do to help a President.

I was, then, in varying ways a limited participant and limited observer of the scene for a good portion of these years. The major insights generated by those experiences are available to the reader, but they in no way confer authority on my judgments. There is no automatic correlation, direct or inverse, between a man's experience as a public servant and the value of his analytic conclusions. This book stands on its own as an essay in recent history.

The Diffusion of Power

I

Prologue: The Concentration and Diffusion of Power, 1940–1957

THIS BOOK BEGINS WITH AN ARBITRARY BUT USEFUL BENCHMARK: the launching of the first Sputnik on October 4, 1957. The direct and indirect effects of that event accelerated and intensified certain forces at work on the international scene since the early 1950s. In particular, it moved two issues to the center of the world stage where they remain down to 1972: first, the nuclear question; second, the struggle for the destiny of the developing regions—Asia, the Middle East, Africa, and Latin America. In all their ramifications, those two large questions dominate the subject matter of this essay insofar as it deals with American foreign policy. But where the world stood at the time of the first Sputnik cannot be understood without going back to the world situation as it existed at the end of the Second World War.

THE WAR AND AMERICAN POWER

THE course of the Second World War brought the United States to a position of unique but inherently transient preeminence. In part, this result emerged from the defeat of Germany, Italy, and Japan, and from the dependence of Nationalist China, beset with civil war, on the United States. In part, it arose from the economic enfeeblement of Great Britain, France, and the smaller allies of western Europe under the strains of war and occupation. The war also fatally weakened the fabric of their imperial holdings. On the other hand, the United States, which had had 14.6 percent of its working force unemployed in 1940, was able to fight the war to a significant extent by bringing to bear idle men and idle industrial capacity. In constant dollars, the American GNP rose by more than 50 percent between 1940 and 1944; and there was even a slight increase—about 10 percent—in expenditures for personal consumption.

This surge in American economic strength was reinforced by two special developments of the war years. First, there was a massive and systematic harnessing of science and technology to military purposes. Beyond the military hardware produced, which included the atomic bomb, rockets, and turbines, the United States learned how to organize men and institutions to generate military innovations on a regular basis—as a flow, rather than the product of occasional inventiveness.

Second, there was a revolutionary rise in the importance of air power. Despite drastic postwar demobilization, there emerged from this experience a unique Strategic Air Command (SAC). Until intercontinental ballistics missiles emerged, the existence of SAC bombers, at instant readiness, was a minimum condition for national security and a powerful but limited force on the world scene; and it remains to this day a significant component of American military power.

In 1945, then, the United States towered over all others on its continental island, having brought its economy back to full strength at a time when the other major nations had been weakened. It commanded the seas and the air, and it alone had produced atomic weapons.

This combination of economic strength, organized technological capacity, and power to strike over long distances was reinforced by the wartime experience of sustained alliance operations. This experience began formally with Lend-Lease to Britain in 1941; before the end of hostilities, it embraced all the allies fighting in western Europe and included a wide range of generally less satisfactory alliance arrangements in Asia and the Pacific.

THE WAR AND SOVIET POWER

THE rise in power of the Soviet Union was less glamorous than that of the United States. It did not involve a dramatic surge in economic strength, or new weaponry, but it was, nonetheless, real.

As with the United States, the rise of Soviet power stemmed, in part, from the negative fact that the power of Germany, Italy, and Japan was temporarily eliminated. Positively, it derived from the fact that the war was fought in such a way that it ended with Soviet ground forces as far west as the Elbe. Bulgaria, Romania, Hungary, Czechoslovakia, Poland, a part of Austria, and the eastern portion of Germany were under the physical control of the Soviet Union. The war yielded also a communist government in Belgrade, initially allied with the Soviet Union. Moscow was in a diplomatic as well as a military position to accept the Japanese surrender in Manchuria and North Korea. Because of American, British, and French errors of the 1930s, the Second World War was, in George Kennan's words, "essentially and inescapably defensive . . . one in which we in the West were at first the weaker party, capable of achieving only a portion of our aim and of achieving that portion only in collaboration with a totalitarian adversary and at a price."[1]

For Americans, not conscious of this flawed result and surveying the world scene in the wake of "unconditional surrender," there was satisfaction that the war had been won and a deep consensus that the error of not joining the League of Nations must not be repeated, that the United States must play its part, somehow, in maintaining peace. But there was little or no understanding of what would be involved in that commitment—and its price. The underlying national impulse was to get American forces home, dismantle them, and turn back to domestic life. Except for the memory of the First World War and the failure to consolidate the peace, there was little historical resonance for Americans in the panorama of destruction from London to Tokyo.

For men who were both Russian and communist, the scene was quite different. Through their eyes and memories, the moment was incredible: all the powers that had harassed and restrained Russia over the centuries were prostrate or weak: Germany and Japan; Poland and most of the smaller states, once part of the Austro-Hungarian Empire; Britain and France. Stalin, through the sacrifices of the Russian peoples and the exertions of their allies, was in a position to retrieve in Asia all that was lost in 1905; much that was lost in Europe after 1917; and far more than he tried to negotiate with Hitler in 1939, let alone what he achieved. There had been no moment like it in Russian history since the defeat of Napoleon. The conversation Harriman reports with Stalin at Potsdam was understandable as well as ominous:

> The first time I saw him [Stalin] at the conference I went up to him and said that it must be very gratifying for him to be in Berlin, after all the struggle and the tragedy. He hesitated a moment and then replied, "Czar Alexander got to Paris." It didn't need much of a clairvoyant to guess what was in his mind.[2]

Stalin's vision went further than the ground on which the Soviet armies stood. Communist colleagues had triumphed in Yugoslavia. Communist insurgent forces had leverage in Greece. Communist parties had been greatly strengthened in France and Italy, not merely by the elimination of existing wartime rule but by their role in underground movements. There were Koreans trained in Moscow, ready to be installed in power, as well as Poles, Bulgars, Romanians, Hungarians, and Czechs. And there were the

Chinese, awkward to deal with since the Soviet strategy on China had failed in 1927, but still a force in being with uncertain but considerable prospects for the future and ideological brothers of a sort.

As Stalin and his comrades made their dispositions, they felt a duty to make the most of the opportunities that had been opened up by the course of war—as Lenin had done in 1917. In deciding how far they could go, however, they had to answer some fundamental questions: What were the intentions and policies of the United States? How far could Russia go without risking war with the United States? Stalin recognized clearly the power the United States commanded in 1945; he was not about to take his battered but triumphant country into war with America and risk all that was in hand or might be.

The Beginnings of the Cold War

WHILE as early as August of 1941 Roosevelt and Churchill had held out to the world a large vision embracing the Four Freedoms and self-government, there was throughout the war only one clear strand in American policy: this time the United States must join the world peacekeeping organization whose broad outlines were discussed at Teheran and consolidated at Dumbarton Oaks in August–September 1944. The heart of the enterprise was to be continued concord among the three wartime allies. The territorial issue initially addressed was the future of Germany: should it be unified or split? On this matter, there were divided opinions in the American government, with Roosevelt leaning to a split and others warning that this would set up a competitive power struggle among the victors. Roosevelt's initial approach to Germany, however, was not in terms of the postwar relations of the allies but in terms of the narrower question: how could Germany be prevented from making a third bid for European hegemony?

Although prefigured by earlier events, the fundamental postwar issue of Allied-Soviet relations came sharply into focus in the autumn of 1944. The Russian armies were well into eastern Europe; Moscow and the provisional government of Poland in London had broken relations, and the Russians were building an alternative government from the so-called Lublin Committee, organized as early as December 1941; the Western allies were north of Rome and at, but not across, the Rhine. The question inescapably arose: Who, in the short run, shall exercise political power in the occupied nations; and, in the long run, on what political principles should the life of these nations be reconstructed?

In his famous meeting in Moscow of October 9, 1944, when Roosevelt was off electioneering, Churchill tipped the short-run issue by handing Stalin a piece of paper which proportioned political power and responsibility in southern and eastern Europe between Moscow and the West,[3] country by country. Stalin agreed. Churchill protected British interests in Greece, offering Stalin greater authority elsewhere.

Churchill insisted that he regarded this proportioning of power only as a framework for immediate political authority during the war, not as a definitive settlement.[4] In what way could the short run and long run be reconciled? The answer lay in the question of Poland. If Poland were to be, in narrow security terms, militarily neutralized and friendly with the Soviet Union but politically independent, then the possibility of a continuous Soviet political bloc would be broken; a principle and precedent for the handling of eastern Germany along Western democratic lines (despite Soviet occupation) might be established; and Moscow would have to look to the Western Allies for negotiations which would neutralize a united democratic Germany. A disarmed Germany was clearly in the American and British interest in such a Europe; and it was, in fact, offered.

Poland thus became the most important question in Allied diplomacy shaping the outcome of affairs in Germany and eastern Europe.

At Yalta Roosevelt made the issue of free elections in eastern Europe a paramount matter. He succeeded in extracting from Stalin, in the Yalta Declaration on Liberated Europe, a pledge for "the earliest possible establishment through free elections of governments responsive to the will of the people . . ."; in the parallel Declaration on Poland, Roosevelt achieved agreement that a new Provisional Government of National Unity should be formed, including Poles from abroad, which would be pledged to hold "free and unfettered elections as soon as possible on the basis of universal suffrage and secret ballot." But in his opening statement, Roosevelt made what Churchill described as the "momentous" prediction that the United States would not keep a large army in Europe and its occupation of Germany could be envisaged for only two years.

In the weeks that followed, Stalin did not act on the Yalta agreements. He persisted, step by step, in moving to consolidate communist power in eastern Europe; and just before his death, Roosevelt was greatly concerned, in particular, about Stalin's course in Poland.[5] Stalin postponed introduction into the Polish Government of the London Poles, leaving the Lublin group to consolidate power in its hands.

On April 23, eleven days after Roosevelt's death, Truman put the issue of Poland hard to Molotov and despatched Hopkins, desperately ill, to Moscow a month later. Hopkins got Stalin to act on the Yalta agreement on Poland: that a government of national unity be formed, including Mikolajczyk as Vice Premier, with three additional ministries granted to non-Lublin Poles acceptable to Great Britain and the United States. With this and several lesser concessions, the ground was cleared for the Big Three meeting at Potsdam.

At Potsdam the recognition of the reorganized Polish Provisional

Government (granted by the United States on July 5) was confirmed; and agreement was made that this interim government would hold free and unfettered elections on the basis of universal suffrage and secret ballot, with guarantees of access to the world press to report events before and during the elections.

Truman's diplomacy on Poland in the first four months of his administration appeared to have moved the Polish question forward in terms of the Yalta agreement. However, in the year and a half following Potsdam, Moscow-dominated communists took over Poland in successive stages, climaxed by the election of February 1947, carefully rigged so as to avoid a repetition of the disastrously anticommunist outcome of the plebiscite of June 1946; and in the autumn of 1947 Mikolajczyk, long since rendered politically impotent, fled the country to avoid arrest.

This sequence can only be understood in terms of the unilateral demobilization of American military power and the pervasive American view that the fate of eastern Europe and Poland was second-order business.

The State Department's briefing paper for the conference on Poland and the Balkans was distinctly casual:

> It now seems clear that the Soviet Union will exert predominant political influence over the areas in question. While this Government probably would not want to oppose itself to such a political configuration, neither would it desire to see American influence in this part of the world completely nullified.[6]

When Truman met with his advisers on April 23, 1945, just before seeing Molotov, Stimson said "he would like to know how far the Russian reaction to a strong position on Poland would go. He said he thought that the Russians perhaps were being more realistic than we were in regard to their own security."[7]

Later Truman wrote of eastern Europe in terms which lucidly reflect the dilemma he could not resolve:

> I was trying to be extremely careful not to get us mixed up in a Balkan turmoil. The Balkans had long been a source of trouble and war. I believed that if the political situation in the Balkans could be adjusted so that Hungary, Yugoslavia, Rumania, and Bulgaria, as well as Poland and Austria, could all have governments of their own people's choosing, with no outside interference, this would help us in our plans for peace.
>
> I did not want to become involved in the Balkans in a way that could lead us into another world conflict. In any case, I was anxious to get the Russians into the war against Japan as soon as possible, thus saving the lives of countless Americans.
>
> . . . I was trying to get Churchill in a frame of mind to forget the old power politics and get a United Nations organization to work.[8]

In making his case on Poland to Stalin a month later, Hopkins said: "Poland was only a symbol."[9]

Speaking of Byrnes and his attitude when he went to Moscow in December 1945, a contemporary chronicler says, with accuracy: "Obviously the United States did not intend to back up its view of the Yalta Declaration with force."[10] The ultimate unseriousness of American policy towards eastern Europe determined that Stalin would proceed with his preferred solution—the consolidation under his direct control of all of eastern Europe to the Elbe.

With the failure to enforce the Yalta decision promptly and decisively in Poland, the arena of negotiation shifted to Berlin and the question of German unity. Although valiant efforts to move toward German unity were made by the American negotiators in the Berlin Control Council, by the spring of 1946 that initiative too had failed; and in the year that followed, the concept of a desperate continuing struggle along the boundary of a split Germany and Europe was accepted on all sides. All the wartime debates—on "hard" versus "soft" policies toward Germany, on unity versus dismemberment—were lost in the mists. They could have mattered only if American policy had been determined to enforce on Stalin as his best option a politically free Europe held secure for Russia, as well as the United States, by collective arrangements. Lacking such a policy, the tactical arrangements for the occupation of a defeated Germany set the terms for the great continental struggle which persists, in muted form, down to the present. It led immediately and directly to an extreme but transient concentration of power in the hands of Washington and Moscow.

THE REVISIONIST DEBATE ON THE COLD WAR

WRITING in the *Yale Review* of June 1951, Dexter Perkins noted that it is characteristic of Americans, when they feel safe, to think of past wars with "a somewhat guilty conscience"; and reading our long line of "revisionist" historians, one could conclude "that every war in which this country has been engaged was really quite unnecessary or immoral or both." In recent years we have gone through a quite typical phase of revisionism on the Cold War and its origins that has yielded a quite massive literature.

In a useful essay, Arthur Schlesinger, Jr., has paraphrased what he describes as "the orthodox American view"[11] and the revisionist thesis. He takes the orthodox view to be that the Cold War "was the brave and essential response of free men to communist aggression." He states the revisionist thesis in its extreme form as follows:

> After the death of Franklin Roosevelt and the end of the Second World War, the United States deliberately abandoned the wartime policy of collaboration and, exhilarated by the possession of the atomic

> bomb, undertook a course of aggression of its own designed to expel all Russian influence from Eastern Europe and to establish democratic-capitalist states on the very border of the Soviet Union. As the revisionists see it, this radically new American policy—or rather this resumption by Truman of the pre-Roosevelt policy of insensate anticommunism—left Moscow no alternative but to take measures in defense of its own borders. The result was the Cold War.[12]

In its less extreme forms, the revisionist view argues the rationality of Soviet control over the area to the Elbe, given its military history, and chides American policy-makers for trying to prevent it.

Schlesinger then goes on to try to resolve the debate and remove at least some of the satanic motivations imputed by each side to the other. He (and Hans Morgenthau as well) argues that postwar diplomacy was a clash between American "universalism" and a "sphere of influence" approach that was as natural for Churchill as it was for Stalin. American universalism was rooted in the honest hope that the United States and the Soviet Union would work together for the long haul to keep a volatile planet secure, through a global peace organization—the United Nations. But Moscow could not accept this long-run vision. From a Russian point of view there was a minimum requirement that central and eastern Europe not again be a source of danger; from a communist point of view, a "friendly" eastern Europe had to be a communist eastern Europe. In addition, so the Schlesinger thesis runs, there was, simply, nothing in communist thought that would make the notion of United States–Soviet concord a long-run possibility. Thus, the Cold War resulted from a perfectly comprehensible clash between differing visions of the world. One can, if one wishes, throw into the equation (as Schlesinger does) the pathology of Stalin's personality; or, as the revisionists usually do, allied behavior over the Italian surrender, the lost Soviet request for a large American loan,[13] etc. But the Schlesinger–Morgenthau synthesis would lift the issue from the world of demonology and heroics and put it back in the world of ideas and history, which is all to the good.

A Personal View

I BELIEVE the Schlesinger–Morgenthau view oversimplifies the matter and does less than justice to the sublety and complexity of the thought brought to bear in both Washington and Moscow in the critical months when the Cold War crystallized. As the quotation from Truman's memoir indicates, there was surely an important element of universalism in American thought and policy.

It is also true, as revisionists have emphasized, that American behavior on certain occasions during and immediately after the war smacked of spheres of influence rather than universalism: the reservation of regionalism at San Francisco in the United Nations Charter (Articles 52–54), with its implications of a special status for the Western Hemisphere; the character of the Italian surrender; the arrangements for the occupation of Japan which gave Moscow a dilute voice indeed. Undoubtedly men could and did argue in Moscow that Britain and the United States were operating on the principle what-we-have-we-hold, and the Soviet Union had a de facto right to proceed in eastern and central Europe on the same basis.[14]

But in fact, as the Russians above any others would recognize, the future of Germany was the question of questions and had to be looked at in its own terms. It was Germany that twice in a quarter-century had generated world war.

And responsible Americans agreed. They saw clearly, and said clearly, that the Russians had the right to assure, as nearly as men could shape the course of history, that the Soviet Union not again be attacked by Germany. The single statement of the period that best catches the way thoughtful Americans translated a universalist approach into a practical European alternative to confronting blocs is Vandenberg's. It was made in the Senate on January 10, 1945, on the eve of Yalta. He first pointed out, in universalist terms, that the Allies had to choose between alternative ways of living in the postwar world. One way would be based on exclusive individual action in which each nation tried to look out for itself; the other would be one where, on the basis of joint action,

> we undertake to look out for each other. . . . The first way is the old way which has twice taken us to Europe's interminable battlefields within a quarter of a century. The second way is the new way in which we must make our choice. I think we must make it wholly plain to our major allies that they, too, must make their choice.[15]

Then, in a climactic passage, Vandenberg said:

> Russia's unilateral plan appears to contemplate the engulfment, directly or indirectly, of a surrounding circle of buffer states, contrary to our conception of what we thought we were fighting for in respect to the rights of small nations and a just peace. Russia's announced reason is her insistent purpose never again to be at the mercy of another German tyranny. That is a perfectly understandable reason. The alternative is collective security. . . . Which is better in the long view, from a purely selfish Russian standpoint: To forcefully surround herself with a cordon of unwillingly controlled or partitioned states, thus affronting the opinions of mankind . . . or to win the priceless asset of world confidence in her by embracing the alternative, namely, full and whole-hearted cooperation with and reliance on a vital international organization. . . . Well—at that point, Russia, or others like her, in equally honest candor has a perfect right to reply, "Where is there any such alternative reliance until we know what the United States will do?" . . .

> I propose that we meet this problem conclusively and at once. There is no reason to wait. America has this same self-interest in permanently, conclusively and effectively disarming Germany and Japan. . . . I know of no reason why a hard-and-fast treaty between the major allies should not be signed today to achieve this dependable end.[16]

A Germany disarmed by Allied agreement, with full Soviet rights to monitor its provisions, was built into all the drafts for a German treaty and offered, with some drama, by Byrnes on September 6, 1946, in his address at Stuttgart, in the form of a forty-year treaty of German disarmament.

There is not the slightest doubt that Stalin and his colleagues knew they could have a disarmed Germany at the price of free elections throughout Germany. But that kind of Germany would have made difficult, if not impossible, the kind of totally subservient Poland Stalin wanted; that is, a Poland with a Soviet Zone of Occupation in Germany to its west and the Soviet Union to its east. That kind of Germany would have made difficult and, essentially, futile the installation and maintenance of communist governments throughout the rest of eastern Europe.

Stalin's essential decision was not to deny Russia a vague universalist role in the United Nations in favor of an Eastern bloc: it was to deny Russia the security of a disarmed Germany and, in effect, a disarmed Europe; for with the Soviet armies within its borders and Germany disarmed, neither Britain, France, nor the United States would have an interest in a high level of armaments, so far as Europe was concerned.

I can attest that this was the working vision held at the time by a great many of those working on the European problem in the State Department in 1945–1946, as well as the formal policy of the Truman administration. Still in uniform, I went to work at State on German–Austrian economic problems on August 2, 1945, the day the Potsdam communique was issued. We recognized that the Potsdam communique was a schizophrenic document: its agreed principles looked to a unified, disarmed, democratic Germany, but the danger of a split was palpable in the pattern of unilateral policy already at work in the Soviet Zone. Nevertheless, American policy continued to try to move back towards an agreed resolution of the problem of Germany and Europe.

My assessment in early 1946 was that the split of Europe was being accelerated by the judgment of both Soviet and western European governments that the interest of the United States in the structure of Europe was likely to prove transitory and that, therefore, the Soviet Union had merely to await the progressive withdrawal of the United States before consolidating an eastern European base, while the western Europeans increasingly felt that the very best they might look forward to was holding on to the area up to the Elbe and, perhaps, forming a Western bloc.

As Byrnes prepared for the critical peace treaty negotiations in Paris of the spring of 1946, I formulated a proposal which moved up the bureaucratic ladder and found support with Acheson and Clayton, as well as with Jean Monnet, then in Washington. It was presented to Byrnes over the weekend of April 20–21, 1946. It argued that the piecemeal negotiation of the peace treaties would simply consolidate the split of Europe, and that Byrnes should frame the treaty negotiations with proposals that would move the continent toward unity.

The outcome was judged to depend on whether or not the Soviet performance was based on the assumption of future diminished American concern in European affairs. The proposal stated that:

> The U.S.S.R. response to the alternatives of European organization or vigorous U.S. support for the Western bloc cannot be fairly prejudged. [It asserted, further, that the] nature of an alternative to a European organization . . . makes it desirable in the U.S. interest to press for the superior solution, no matter how small the chances of success may initially appear to be. Only after the exhaustion of the line it represents does acceptance of a bloc alternative appear justified.

Byrnes and his personal staff rejected this proposal, put to them by Acheson and Clayton, because it did not fit his pattern of treaty-by-treaty piecemeal negotiation—and probably also because Byrnes at that time already planned to test Soviet intentions with his proposal for a long demilitarization pact in Germany. The senior political officers in the Department of State opposed it, ostensibly on the grounds that such an American initiative was calculated to frighten the Soviet Union and obstruct negotiations then under way but probably also because some had already concluded that a Western bloc was the only attainable goal of American diplomacy in Europe.

The Acheson–Clayton proposal proved not wholly barren. It led directly to the emergence of the Economic Commission for Europe in Geneva and contributed to lines of thought in the bureaucracy which yielded the Marshall Plan proposal some thirteen months later. It was essentially this kind of vision which lay behind Marshall's June 6, 1947, offer to embrace all of Europe to the Urals in the plan he suggested.

In my view, Stalin rejected Byrnes' German disarmament treaty and Marshall's offer for an all-European recovery program nine months later not because he was reacting defensively to American threats or pressure, but because, as he surveyed the scene before him and his prospects in the time ahead, he felt, on balance, that a consolidated eastern Europe dominated by Moscow had a reasonable chance to be the base from which Soviet power might move west.

I do not believe Stalin and his colleagues lightly set aside the proposal for a German disarmament treaty; and we know that there was a period of debate and uncertainty about how to deal with Marshall's 1947 offer. And as Soviet policy towards Finland and, later, Austria indicates, they understood well a policy of separating security issues from domestic political arrangements. I would guess they debated long and hard and with sophistication on the choice before them. In the end, however, the attractions of holding the satellite empire appeared to outweigh the possible advantages of the Byrnes and Marshall proposals.

Would Stalin have made the same basic decision if he knew substantial American forces would remain in Europe not two years but for a generation and beyond, that Germany would be rearmed, that Tito would defect, and that Moscow's satellites would become progressively more assertive and an increasing source of concern? We do not know; but his compulsion to exert total rather than dilute control within the Soviet Union and, where he could, outside makes an affirmative answer still likely. But if the question is put: Who is more responsible for the Cold War, the Americans or the Russians? I am still inclined to feel, as I did at the time, that unilateral American disarmament and the isolationist mood Roosevelt predicted at Yalta were primary factors in determining Stalin's choice. By 1946 there was not a single American Army division ready for combat, nor a single air group. We put Stalin under intolerable temptation. By the time Truman counterattacked in the spring of 1947 with the Truman Doctrine and the Marshall Plan, Moscow was too deeply committed to change course.

Debate on particular issues continued in the Kremlin. The door was not finally shut on a postwar agreement until Molotov left the Paris discussions on the Marshall Plan in July 1947. Stalin evidently decided he could not permit the eastern European nations the advantages of the Marshall Plan without fatally risking their ties to Moscow. And on the primacy of his eastern European empire, I believe Stalin had pretty well made up his mind by the time he delivered his electoral speech of February 9, 1946. Although the struggle in Washington to avoid the worst continued, the response of the West was given a month later in Churchill's "Iron Curtain" speech in Fulton, Missouri. If an operational rather than a rhetorical date for the beginning of the Cold War is to be chosen, it should probably be the breakdown of the Control Council in Berlin in May 1946.

The Unfolding of the Cold War, 1946–1957

In a manner resonant of Russian history, Stalin's effort to exploit the postwar disarray of Eurasia had two phases. He pressed first in the west and, then, when frustrated, turned to apparent opportunities in the east.

During the summer of 1946 Stalin increased Soviet pressure against Turkey by diplomacy and threat, in Greece by supporting substantial guerrilla warfare via Bulgaria and Yugoslavia, and in Italy and France by vigorous Communist party efforts to gain parliamentary power. Meanwhile, the process of stabilizing Germany as two organized entities proceeded. In 1947 Stalin was thrown on the offensive by Truman's counterattack. He responded to the Truman Doctrine and the Marshall Plan by accelerating the movement toward total control in the east, symbolized by the creation of the Cominform in September 1947. He succeeded in Prague (February 1948), but failed in Belgrade, where Tito's defection was announced in June 1948. The communist effort in Greece then collapsed, the election in April 1948 saved Italy, and France found a group of center parties capable of governing, albeit uncertainly, and containing the domestic communist menace. The deadlock in the Berlin Control Council, already two years old, was dramatized by the Soviet walkout on March 20, 1948, which set the stage for the blockade, which began on March 31.

This phase of Soviet consolidation in eastern Europe ended with the effort to expel the West from Berlin, which was defeated by the airlift in the winter of 1948–1949. In the West this interacting process yielded the Brussels Pact (February 1948), NATO (March 1949), and the creation (May 1949) of a Federal Republic of Germany, including, for economic purposes, the western zones of Berlin, which symbolized and confirmed the Western intent to resist further Soviet expansion.

In the course of 1946 the negotiations for a truce in China also broke down. The communists—strengthened with captured Japanese arms furnished by the Soviet Union, with some Soviet weapons, and with Soviet staff assistance—launched an all-out civil war. In 1946 Stalin probably advised against an all-out effort by the communists to seize power;[17] but once Mao was well started, he was backed by Stalin in 1947–1949, mainly through diversionary operations of the international communist movement.

Communist policy in Asia formally changed in the course of 1947, ambitious new objectives being enunicated by Zhdanov at the founding meeting of the Cominform in September. Open guerrilla warfare began in Indochina as early as November 1946, in Burma in April 1948, in Malaya in June of that year, and in Indonesia and the Philippines in the autumn. The Indian and Japanese Communist parties, with less scope for guerrilla action, nevertheless sharply increased their militancy in 1948. As final victory was won in China in November 1949, Mao's political–military strategy was openly commended by the Cominform to the communist parties in those areas where guerrilla operations were under way. Stalin and Mao met early in 1950 and confirmed the ambitious Asian strategy, planning its climax in the form of the North Korean invasion of South Korea, which took place at the end of June 1950.[18]

The American and United Nations response to the invasion of South Korea, the landings at Inchon, the march to the Yalu, the Chinese Communist entrance into the war, and the successful U.N. defense against massive Chinese assault in April–May 1951 at the 38th parallel, brought this phase of military and quasi-military communist effort throughout Asia to a gradual end. Neither Moscow nor Peking was willing to undertake all-out war or even accept the cost of a continued Korean offensive. And elsewhere the bright communist hopes of 1946–1947 had dimmed. Nowhere in Asia was Mao's success repeated. Indonesia, Burma, and the Philippines largely overcame their guerrillas. At great cost to Britain, the Malayan guerrillas were contained and driven back. Only in Indochina, where French colonialism offered a seedbed as fruitful as postwar China, was there real communist momentum. The conventional view is that Ho Chi Minh was finally forced by Moscow and Peking to settle for half a victory at the Geneva Conference of 1954 in the interest of the larger policy of the communist bloc which had begun to shape up in Asia from the summer of 1951. Khrushchev asserts, on the contrary, that the French willingness to grant North Vietnam to the communists, after Dienbienphu, was "the absolute maximum" the communist side envisaged, given the gravely weakened position of the guerrilla forces.[19] In any case, there was an interval of four years of relative quiet in Indochina.

The first two stages of communist postwar policy posed the central challenges to the Truman administration. It was Truman who conducted the 1947–1951 counteroffensive against Stalin, which blocked the communist offensive at both ends of Eurasia, leaving a western Europe which by 1952 had gathered economic momentum, weathered the war fears of 1950, and built a substantial common military establishment in NATO. In Korea the negotiations for truce went on; but, except in Indochina, the rest of noncommunist Asia, including the Nationalists on Formosa, recovered at least temporary poise while fighting and diplomacy proceeded in the northern peninsula. It was during the Korean War that Japan, reassured by American willingness to fight for Korea, moved from recovery into a phase of astonishingly rapid growth. The communists were thus held around the periphery which had emerged from the Second World War; and in the sense that minimum essential American interests were protected without major war, Truman succeeded where the pre-1914 and interwar statesmen of the West had failed. But he succeeded only at the cost of a split of Germany and Europe. No man can say with confidence that result was avoidable without major war, but it is also clear that Truman's policy —and, in a larger sense, the quasi-isolationist temper of America in the period 1945–1947—did not help to create conditions under which the Cold War might have been avoided.

THE PAUSE: 1951–1956

THERE was much in the early 1950s that foreshadowed problems later in the decade, but until the crisis with Nasser in 1956, it was a relatively quiet time—the only quiet period on the international scene since 1945.

While the Korean War was being fought to a standstill, two forces were present on the scene and gathering momentum—the revolution in military technology and the rise in human and national expectations within the underdeveloped areas. Even before Truman left office and Stalin died, these new forces were moving toward the center of world affairs. Truman began technical and economic assistance to the developing world by launching the Point Four Program in his inaugural address of 1949 and setting up the Gordon Gray Committee whose report of 1950 laid the foundations for later policy in this field. The outlines of a new communist policy to exploit the volatility of the developing world were evident as early as October 1952, at the Nineteenth Party Congress; and they dominated the agenda Truman turned over to Eisenhower in December. Aside from nuclear matters and Korea, the principal issues set before the incoming administration lay to the south: Iran, Southeast Asia, and foreign aid.

But it took time for thermonuclear weapons to emerge and the potentialities of missiles to unfold. Although, for example, India, Pakistan, Burma, and Indonesia emerged from colonialism in the late 1940s, it took time for Moscow to formulate clear policies towards them. Above all, however, in 1953 Moscow and Peking entered a phase where domestic preoccupations were paramount.

Stalin's death plunged the political and bureaucratic life of the Soviet Union into a period of muted power struggle and review and revision of Stalin's policies many felt to be out of date or wrong. From military affairs to agriculture, from the role of the secret police to art and architecture, there was debate and change within the Soviet establishment. And then, in 1956, Khrushchev opened a potential Pandora's box with his denunciation of Stalin's method of rule.

For Mao this was the period when, reconstruction having been accomplished and the Korean War ended, he turned to the first Chinese Communist Five-Year Plan.

Western Europe and Japan were also in a position to concentrate on economic and social problems at home. After the failure of the Berlin blockade and the attempt to conquer South Korea, they were relatively free for more than a generation to move forward in unexampled economic growth rooted in the diffusion of the automobile, durable consumers goods, and the other paraphernalia of high mass-consumption.

Nevertheless, western Europe in particular felt the impact of the nuclear question and the increased volatility of the developing world. The concept of nuclear blackmail was first raised by Khrushchev on a visit to Birmingham in April 1956 and exercised with some vigor during the traumatic Suez crisis later in the year. During that crisis the full meaning of the 1955 Soviet–Egyptian arms deal also became apparent, underlining the possible strategic implications of Moscow's selective military and economic aid policies elsewhere in the developing world. Then in October 1957 came the first Sputnik, posing a new set of problems and triggering a series of crises which are central to this book.

THE DIFFUSION OF POWER, 1948–1957

WHILE Truman and Stalin dueled over the disposition of power across the former battlefields of northern Eurasia and, then, the two nuclear giants began in the 1950s to struggle for the destiny of the developing world, a process was taking place which began to erode the bipolarity of the immediate postwar years. Like many powerful historical forces, it had several different and quite independent roots, although, if a single cause is to be identified, it is the survival and increasing assertiveness of nationalism.

First, the communist world. In 1948 Tito broke with Stalin, and with Western help, he survived. Behind that struggle was Stalin's effort to gain effective control over Tito's political and security apparatus and to throttle the Yugoslav economy by turning off the supply of Czech coke and coking coal on which Belgrade's postwar development program depended. Tito resisted and found through the U.N. Economic Commission for Europe dignified access to Ruhr supplies. He closed the border with Greece and thereby helped bring to an end the communist insurrection there.

In 1953 there was a brief German revolt. In 1956 Gomulka successfully resisted Soviet pressure against the formation of a more nationalist communist regime in Warsaw, and this outcome, in turn, helped trigger the Hungarian revolt. Moscow successfully dealt with these manifestations of rising nationalism in eastern Europe. A decade later Ulbricht still firmly held sway, Polish nationalism was confined within narrow limits, and a government subservient to Moscow ruled in Budapest. But, in Vandenberg's pre-Yalta phrase, the costs to Moscow of "a cordon of unwillingly controlled or partitioned states" gradually emerged. Stalin's eastern European empire ceased to be a secure base for a thrust to the west and became a source of increasing anxiety in Moscow.

Meanwhile, in 1949, Mao won his civil war in China. On assuming power, he said he would "lean to one side"; and he did. Stalin and Mao planned much together on the occasion of Mao's trip to Moscow in January 1950, including the war in Korea. Considerable ties of trade and aid were developed. Nevertheless, Mao was not a satellite. Down to Budapest, he tended to support the forces of nationalism and liberalism in eastern Europe and maintained liaison with Belgrade, undoubtedly to Moscow's discomfiture. On the other hand, he criticized Khrushchev's de-Stalinization policy and generally turned toward a hard policy at home when the Hundred Flowers movement revealed the depth of discontent with Communist China in 1957.[20]

From the beginning, then, Moscow was dealing with a Peking that could not be taken for granted or simply issued orders. Moscow had many cards in its hand, military and economic, but it had to negotiate its relations with the Chinese.

In the West life was also getting more complex, but in a somewhat different way. Truman actively encouraged the movement toward western European unity in the context of the Marshall Plan, and in this he had the explicit support of Congress when the enabling legislation was passed in 1948. Truman set aside the potentialities of a policy of divide-and-rule and accepted the risk that a unified western Europe might in the long run be a rival of the United States. He counted on ultimately shared interests and the ties of history and common culture to yield partnership across the Atlantic.

On the American side the notion of European unity had a long history and great attraction. From an early stage in the nation's history, many Americans looked out on the competing sovereignties of Europe, with their restless and dangerous pushing for power, and concluded that peace could come to Europe only if Europeans were to follow the American example of continental unity. More immediately, it was evident to Americans that the failure of Europe to cope with Hitler had in part stemmed from a lack of unity; and, more than that, there was the experience of de facto unity in the final phases of the war when an American-led SHAEF (Supreme Headquarters Allied Expeditionary Forces) managed briefly to make the Western alliance an organizational reality.

On the European side the experience of the Second World War—of a Europe that had to be rescued from its own failures by the Americans from the west and by the Russians from the east—had convinced many men that the European state system had outlived its usefulness. After the war, quite apart from the immediate threat of communist domination, Europeans began to argue that if continental Europe were to maintain the stature and dignity of even a second-rate power—in a world apparently dominated by Washington and Moscow—European unity would have to be sought. Even more narrowly, some Frenchmen and some Germans saw in the prospect of European unity the only way to end once and for all the mutually destructive enmity of their countries. On both sides of the Atlantic, then, the concept of European unity had a real attraction despite the fact that it also raised grave problems and doubts—most notably in Britain.

In the early days of the Marshall Plan and NATO, the United States was, of course, a dominating presence in the joint efforts of the Atlantic. But the Schumann Plan was launched as early as May 1950, as a major intra-European venture, and the rapid growth of western Europe in the 1950s laid the foundations for increased balance in Atlantic affairs for the long run. In strengthening western Europe, accepting the certainty of a diffusion of power in the Atlantic, and helping create institutions to organize it constructively rather than repress it, Truman set a powerful precedent in American policy.

Meanwhile, colonialism was breaking up, and new moods and ambitions were taking hold in the independent nations of the southern continents, including Latin America. For the United States, as for Moscow and Peking, there were new nations and new men to be reckoned with:

Nehru and Sukarno and Nasser, and the new generation of nationalist leaders in Latin America with increasingly urban constituencies, unwilling to continue the old pattern of simply exporting foodstuffs and raw materials to the industrialized nations of the North Atlantic. And a new Africa of independent states was evidently also emerging. Geography, politics, and history all decreed that the assertive nations of the developing world had to be dealt with by negotiation and a search for areas of overlapping interest, not by a simple binding to Moscow or Washington.

Washington and then Moscow (in prompt imitation) launched programs of economic assistance. Moscow also perceived two other potential levers. First, there were real or believed humiliations from the past, including arbitrary inheritances from colonialism. In the Arab world there was, for example, Israel; in Indonesia, Dutch-held West New Guinea; in the Indian subcontinent, Kashmir. By aligning Soviet policy with such causes, there was political advantage to be gained. A second lever was the possibility of tipping the instinctive neutralism of the new nations toward a systematic anti-Western cast. Here, in fact, Peking felt it had a special advantage, for the Soviet Union, like western Europe and the United States, was a technologically advanced nation and did not quite belong in the club of the poor but aspiring. In the spring of 1955 it moved, at Bandung, with some sophistication, toward leadership among the emerging nations—a posture resumed in New York in 1971. Belgrade also saw in the world of the neutralists a sea in which to swim, strengthening its hand against Moscow without being forced into rigid alignment with Washington and the West.

In its first term, the Eisenhower administration was relatively passive towards these new forces in the world arena. It concentrated on building security arrangements around the periphery of the Soviet Union and Communist China to deter another war like that recently ended in Korea. It was only in the post-Sputnik period and the 1960s that a more systematic and positive American policy towards the developing countries emerged.

While these various economic, political, and organizational forces were moving to dilute the initial postwar concentration of power in the hands of Washington and Moscow, technology was still pulling in the other direction; that is, the emergence of thermonuclear weapons and long-range rocketry. Here, the power to kill massively was piling up disproportionately in the hands of the United States and the Soviet Union. The power was real enough, but its meaning and usefulness were riddled with ambiguity. Such power could clearly be used to deter its rational application by another. But beyond mutual deterrence, it was not immediately evident how it could advance the interests of those who commanded it.

The launching of the first Sputnik opened a period of experiment with that problem, a period as dangerous and eventful as any in modern history.

BOOK ONE

From Sputnik to Kennedy

2

Sputnik and After: The Communist World

Sputnik and Mao

1957 WAS A LIVELY YEAR. IN JUNE KHRUSHCHEV DEFEATED HIS RIVALS, Malenkov, Molotov, Kaganovich, and Shepilov. He achieved a primacy over the Soviet government as well as within the Communist party that did not match Stalin's, but nevertheless ended four years of collective leadership.[1] In August, a successful Soviet test of an ICBM was reported, and the first Sputnik was launched on October 4. On October 15, according to Chinese sources, Moscow promised to increase its support of the Chinese nuclear effort.[2] In November the leaders of the twelve communist parties that had achieved control over nation states gathered in Moscow. The tension between the two great communist parties, rooted in events of the 1920s but colored also by national and ancestral memories reaching back to the thirteenth century, had flared up after Khrushchev's denunciation of Stalin in 1956. But now it seemed to have eased.

Mao arrived in Moscow with a clear and hopeful vision of communist strategy and tactics. In a speech at Moscow University on November 17, he said: "The socialist camp must have a head and this head is the USSR. . . . the Communist and workers' parties of all countries must have a head and that head is the CPSU."[3] Behind this unusual deference to Moscow was Mao's assessment of the balance of forces in the world:

> It is my opinion that the international situation has now reached a new turning point. There are two winds in the world today, the East wind and the West wind. There is a Chinese saying, "Either the East wind prevails over the West wind or the West wind prevails

over the East wind." It is characteristic of the situation today, I believe, that the East wind is prevailing over the West wind. That is to say, the forces of socialism are overwhelmingly superior to the forces of imperialism.[4]

Behind this assessment, in turn, was a vision of how history had evolved since the Second World War. Speaking to his colleagues on November 18, Mao listed ten great postwar events.[5] These included the triumphant emergence of the Soviet Union in 1945; Mao's victory over Chiang Kai-shek; the Chinese Communist role in the Korean War; Ho Chi Minh's victory over the French; the role of Moscow's nuclear threats in Egypt's successful struggle for the Suez Canal; and the withdrawal of the European powers from their colonies. He concluded:

> The superiority of the anti-imperialist forces over the imperialist forces demonstrated by these events has expressed itself in even more concentrated form and reached unprecedented heights with the Soviet Union's launching of the artificial satellites. . . . That is why we say that this is a new turning point in the international situation. . . .[6]

On the basis of this view of the "new turning point" in history, Mao argued that the time was ripe for a unified communist movement to exploit with vigor and confidence its historic opportunities in Asia, Africa, and the Middle East. Clearly, the communist acquisition of nuclear strength and prestige, symbolized by the emergent Soviet ICBM capability and Sputnik, was critical to Mao's assessment. And he wanted that new leverage applied in the developing world in general, and to Asia in particular.

Beneath the surface of unanimity and confidence, however, the debate between Moscow and Peking had already secretly begun, centered on precisely the issues which were later to yield overt conflict and schism.[7] The debate was bilateral, in a Sino–Soviet drafting committee. It was not revealed to the representatives of the other communist parties. Differences were dealt with by compromise language which reflected both points of view.

In retrospect, the most significant issue was the debate on "peaceful" versus "nonpeaceful" roads to communist power ("socialism"); for it bore directly on the doctrinal legitimacy of Ho's revival of war in Indochina. The original Soviet draft presented in the drafting committee apparently omitted the "nonpeaceful" route.

In September 1963 Peking revealed the text of its counterdraft, including these passages:

> It would be more flexible to refer to the two possibilities, peaceful transition and non-peaceful transition, than to just one, and this would place us in a position where we can have the initiative politically at any time. . . . [Communists] must be prepared at all times to re-

pulse counter-revolutionary attacks and, at the critical juncture of the revolution when the working class is seizing state power, to overthrow the bourgeoisie by armed force if it uses armed force to suppress the people's revolution (generally speaking, it is inevitable that the bourgeoisie will do so).[8]

The compromise in the final communique leaned heavily to the Soviet formulation, but Peking (and Hanoi) gained this passage:

> In the event of the ruling classes resorting to violence against the people, the possibility of non-peaceful transition to socialism should be borne in mind. Leninism teaches, and experience confirms, that the ruling classes never relinquish power voluntarily.[9]

There was a parallel contretemps on the question of war and peace, including the possibility of nuclear war. Moscow leaned to "peaceful co-existence." On this matter Peking did not publish its counterdraft; but we have from European communist sources what Mao said to his somewhat chilled colleagues:

> [If] the worst came to the worst and half of mankind died, the other half would remain, while imperialism would be razed to the ground and the whole world would become socialist . . . [we] desire peace. However, *if imperialism insists on fighting a war, we will have no alternative but to make up our minds and fight to the finish. . . .*[10]

Here Peking got less in the communique than it did on the non-peaceful road to socialism; but it got something:

> So long as imperialism exists there will always be soil for aggressive wars. . . . The cause of peace is upheld by the powerful forces of our era. . . . The unity of these powerful forces can prevent the outbreak of war. But should the bellicose imperialist maniacs venture, regardless of anything, to unleash a war, imperialism will doom itself to destruction, for the peoples will not tolerate a system that brings them so much suffering and exacts so many sacrifices.[11]

But Moscow basically carried the day with:

> Were a world war to break out before agreement on prohibition of nuclear weapons is reached, it would inevitably become a nuclear war unprecedented in destructive force.

The broad contrapuntal themes that were more or less successfully harmonized in Moscow in 1957 began to assert themselves with greater clarity in specific contexts.

In February 1958 Chou En-lai pointed in Asia to the situations in South Korea, Vietnam, and Taiwan as elements of the status quo that should not be permitted to continue. In May the Great Leap Forward was undertaken with its extraordinarily ambitious production targets and its equally ambitious ideological pretensions. And in every forum the Chinese argued for a policy of pressing forward with "wars of national liberation" even at the risk of confronting the "imperialists"; and they argued, in a marked shift from the Bandung spirit of 1955, for supporting communists rather than "anti-imperialist" nationalists in the politics of the developing world—or, at least, for preserving their leading role.

Mao's ambitious international vision was underpinned by his belief that if he could use revolutionary political methods to mobilize Chinese manpower for industrial and agricultural development, Chinese growth could be accelerated; and China might, in some fifteen years, become as industrially mature a power as Britain and, in a further generation, catch up and surpass the United States.

One cannot read Mao's pronouncements of this period without sensing that this vision was deeply rooted in his mind and feeling. As one scholar has noted, in the debate with Moscow that evolved, "Some Chinese documents—perhaps those penned by Chairman Mao himself—are masterpieces of crisp invective, and are constructed with impeccable logic, if only one accepts the basic premises."[12]

A number of Mao's premises proved incorrect: the political and economic assumptions underlying the Great Leap Forward; the view of the political development process in Asia, the Middle East, and Africa; the strength and vitality of the United States and western Europe. But his most important error was a double misjudgment of the nuclear question: first, his apparent interpretation of the nuclear balance between the United States and the Soviet Union and what it permitted the communist world to accomplish; second, his assessment of how Moscow would view Peking's aspiration to acquire nuclear weapons on a national basis.

SPUTNIK AND KHRUSHCHEV

KHRUSHCHEV was also in a hopeful mood in November 1957, but the world, as he saw it, and the arithmetic, as he did it, led to conclusions somewhat different from those Mao commended to him and to the communist leadership in general. Khrushchev was prepared to use to the hilt the image of the new Soviet nuclear delivery capacity; but he was under no illusion that this strength had surpassed that of the United States or—a quite distinct matter—had made war with the United States an acceptable risk. Moreover, his chosen arena for the application of Soviet nuclear leverage was Europe rather than Asia. He had real MRBMs and IRBMs targeted on western Europe rather than the fictitious ICBMs allegedly targeted on the United States.

The simple fact is that Moscow decided in 1957 not to produce ICBMs on a large scale, but the Soviet leadership also decided that it would proceed to project to the world, for political and psychological purposes, the image of a rapidly growing, even massive, ICBM capability. As the best historians of this strategy state:

> Beginning in the late summer of 1957, the Soviet leaders, and chiefly Khrushchev, undertook to deceive the West regarding their strategic capabilities. The maneuver is remarkable for its deliberate and systematic character and for the relative consistency with which it was executed over a period of four years.[13]

The ability of Moscow to conceal its military dispositions made this exercise conceivable. The character of the Western press and competitive American politics completed the conditions for making the exercise viable. Khrushchev was, of course, aware of the U-2 flights from 1956; but he did not think the limited U-2 routes would reveal how few ICBMs were, in fact, emplaced.

The first generation of Soviet ICBMs was clumsy. And a massive missile production effort would have interfered with the priority Khrushchev attached to rapid agricultural and industrial growth. Technology and economics argued for a delayed deployment of more efficient ICBMs while secrecy offered the possibility of deception.

The upshot was that by 1961—four years after Sputnik—only a "handful" of Soviet ICBMs had actually been deployed.[14] But the upshot was also that, as of 1960, most of the world's citizens believed that the Soviet Union had outstripped the United States in stragetic nuclear capabilities.

In August 1960 the United States Information Agency concluded:

> While sophisticated political and press opinion tends to regard the current military situation as one of nuclear stalemate in which neither of the two super-powers has any material advantage over the other, the more impressionistic popular opinion has seemingly concluded from Soviet boasts of superiority and American admissions of a temporary "missile gap" that the United States is not only currently militarily inferior to the USSR but will continue to be so for the next decade or two as well.[15]

In early 1960, public opinion polls in five western European countries, showed that the following percentages of people believed the U.S.S.R. to be ahead of the United States in military strength: Great Britain, 59; West Germany, 47; Norway, 45; France, 37; Italy, 32. Only in Italy did a higher percentage believe that the U.S. was ahead.[16] The facts[17] are, however, that American strategic superiority in aircraft was amply maintained down to 1960 and beyond; that except for a very brief interval of marginal Soviet advantage in ICBMs in late 1959 and early 1960 the American buildup of these missiles was much more rapid than the Soviet and from 1960 on our superiority was unquestionable; that the rapid buildup of

Soviet MRBM/IRBM forces supplemented the Soviet ground-force superiority in Europe and, in Khrushchev's phrase, made the western European countries nuclear "hostages" to Moscow.[18] This nuclear pressure on Europe was what Khrushchev mainly counted on in the Berlin crisis of 1961–1962. It was also Khrushchev's medium range missiles which permitted him to reduce the Soviet armed forces from about 5,763,000 in 1955 to 3,000,000 in 1961; although the reduction in ground forces was much more limited (3,200,000 to 2,500,000).

Up to a point, then, Khrushchev's remarkable strategy worked. On its foundation he not only altered the popular image of relative U.S.–Soviet military strength but laid down his ultimatum on Berlin in November 1958. He also proceeded to cut back the Soviet military budget, despite the resistance of the military.

In the end, of course, his strategy suffered a fate conforming to F. M. Cornford's definition of propaganda as "that branch of the art of lying which consists in very nearly deceiving your friends without quite deceiving your enemies."[19]

We do not, in fact, know the extent to which Mao was "deceived." It seems unlikely that Khrushchev shared with him an accurate assessment of relative U.S.–Soviet nuclear capabilities, especially Soviet ICBM production and deployment rates. But in one sense Khrushchev clearly did not deceive Mao. Soviet statements consistently tempered the portrait of rising Russian strength with the underlying judgment that nuclear war would be a disaster to humanity, including the nations and peoples under communist rule. In the whole carefully orchestrated pattern of his claims, Khrushchev avoided at all times the assertion that Moscow was in a position safely to launch a first-strike nuclear war.[20] Mao never asserted the contrary, but he did persist in his assessment that the Soviet nuclear threat should have yielded more for the communist cause than it did under Khrushchev's management. And he permitted himself to peer beyond the outcome of a nuclear war in ways that suggested a casualness about nuclear risks Moscow did not share.

Khrushchev was experimenting with a complex and subtle problem: of what use were all his nuclear bombs and missiles except to deter a nuclear assault that the United States was, in any case, not inclined to undertake? Could a statistical advantage in ICBMs, or a believed advantage, be translated into real estate, political power, or diplomatic influence?

Up to a point both Khrushchev and Mao answered the second question affirmatively. As serious communists, committed to the view that history decrees a progressive expansion of communist power, they both judged that an enterprising policy was called for at the end of 1957. But Moscow was determined not to permit Peking or anyone else to place it in a position where a nuclear war with the United States might occur.

Thus, in military terms Moscow took a more reserved view toward "wars of national liberation" than Peking. Both regarded communist or communist-supported armed insurrection and guerrilla warfare as major tools, notably in the wake of the failure of conventional war in Korea. The Russians argued that civil wars and armed violence in the developing regions, supported across international boundaries with excessive visibility by communists, might lead to hostilities with the West. Mao argued such limited wars would make "the imperialists" more pacific.

Politically, the Russians were prepared to move more slowly than Mao and to align themselves tactically with noncommunist, anti-Western nationalists even at the cost of local communists. The Chinese Communists demurred. They remembered the long Russian relationship with Chiang Kai-shek; the limited assistance they had received from Moscow over their years of struggle; and Stalin's initial assessment that their post-1945 bid for power was historically premature.

Khrushchev believed his new capabilities, and the world's image of them, might protect the Soviet Union from an American first strike; enhance Soviet prestige over a wide front; protect the communist world from decisive riposte if it cautiously exploited opportunities that might open up in the developing regions; exert great pressure on western Europe in general and Berlin in particular; and release Soviet resources for development at home and economic and military assistance abroad. But he did not believe they permitted safe Soviet engagement with the military power of the United States.

Mao's occasional statements suggesting that nuclear war was a thinkable and survivable event, however hedged, made the Soviet leadership and European communists uneasy.

Finally, the Great Leap Forward not only threatened failure in a major communist-controlled nation but also challenged the Soviet view of the correct pace, sequence, and tactics for economic development. It thereby challenged the Soviet claim to leadership in the developing world. Mao evidently hoped to reinforce Chinese leadership in the communist movement and in the developing world by creating a new and successful pattern of accelerated economic and social progress.

These were the issues of substance debated with vigor and theoretical virtuosity within the communist movement as the Sino–Soviet split took shape. For Moscow they added up to a monstrous event: the rise of "factionalism" in the world communist movement, a serious diffusion of political power away from the Soviet Union, and a probably irreversible change in the vision of what world communism was and would become. For other communist leaders—notably, those of Rumania, North Korea, and North Vietnam—the process was a mixed source of anxiety and opportunity, as they played the contending giants off against each other.

3

Four Interwoven Crises in Sino-Soviet Relations, 1958–1960

THEORY AND ACTION

THE ISSUES OF THEORY AND BROAD POLICY THAT EMERGED BETWEEN Moscow and Peking in the post-Sputnik period had meaning for communists, who place great store by theoretical debate. Communist theory and its sacred texts provide an agreed vocabulary. Its terms constitute a dynamic theory of history. These terms permit debate across international boundaries concerning situations in national societies of widely differing cultures and stages of development. Their abstract and apparently theoretical character also permits real issues to be publicly discussed without revealing to the noncommunist world exactly what is in mind or being planned. But among communists, as with the rest of us, general propositions do not settle specific cases. Differences in theory between Mao and Khrushchev came to rest on a good many important specific questions. Among them, four in particular marked the descent from the apparent unity of the Moscow Conference of November 1957 to the barely contained disarray of November–December 1960: Peking's nuclear ambitions; the Lebanon–Jordan crisis; the confrontation in the Taiwan Straits; and Soviet relations with the United States.

THE NUCLEAR QUESTION

THE maintenance of alliances in a nuclear age has proved to be a subtle task. A major nuclear power cannot undertake to protect a nonnuclear power (or a minor nuclear power) unless it can be confident of three things: an underlying harmony of basic objectives; intimate consultation and coordination in foreign policy so that the nuclear power cannot be brought into a major foreign policy crisis, with potentially nuclear implications, against its will; and sufficient control over the actual firing of nuclear weapons so that it can neither be brought into nuclear war without its assent nor lose control of a nuclear engagement, short of a total war. In return, the protected power enjoys such security as massive nuclear deterrence affords, at lower cost, anxiety, and, perhaps, vulnerability than the pursuit of security on a national basis. These are the implicit or explicit terms which have governed the American alliance system, even with respect to France under de Gaulle. They leave ample scope for independence in foreign policy for nonnuclear allies (or lesser nuclear allies) short of critical issues which might lead to war with nuclear implications. But the limits are there.

In the case of the USSR and Communist China, Mao was unwilling to accept the rules which the hideous destructive power of the weapons built into the nature of alliances—a power which transcended ideological fraternity and evoked reactions of brute nationalism on both sides.

Mao's advocacy of "nonpeaceful roads to socialism," his apparent willingness to contemplate nuclear war, and, in this context, his pursuit of a national nuclear capability proved incompatible with a viable Moscow alliance.

The nuclear question has cast so long a shadow that it is worth reviewing the essence of the exchanges of August and September 1963, with their echo of the critical days of 1958–1959. Historians may well regard the passages set out below as reflecting the most significant debate of the third quarter of the twentieth century.

Peking

> In 1958 the leadership of the CPSU put forward unreasonable demands designed to bring China under Soviet military control. These unreasonable demands were rightly and firmly rejected by the Chinese Government. Not long afterwards, in June 1959, the Soviet Government unilaterally tore up the agreement on new technology for national defence concluded between China and the Soviet Union in October 1957, and refused to provide China with a sample of an atomic bomb and technical data concerning its manufacture. . . .

Moscow

> The Chinese leaders are greatly displeased with the Soviet Union for not giving China samples of atomic weapons. It looks as if annoyance with this policy of the Soviet Union and the other socialist states of not spreading nuclear weapons explains the attacks of the Chinese leaders on the USSR's measures in the field of foreign policy—meas-

ures which are aimed at easing international tension and strengthening peace—and especially their attacks on the nuclear test-ban treaty. The Chinese people are experiencing many privations, and that is why such a course in the policy of the Chinese leaders would be more beneficial for the Chinese people, would be more appreciated by them and would be correctly understood throughout the world.

Let us grant that by overstraining its economy the People's Republic of China may finally be able to produce a few atom bombs. Yet how many such bombs would in this case be aimed by the imperialists at the People's Republic of China? Would the Chinese leaders then feel themselves more secure, even though sitting on their own atom bomb? . . .

As history would have it the Soviet Union is the only socialist country that produces nuclear weapons. . . .

It would be naive, to say the least, to assume that it is possible to conduct one policy in the West and another in the East, to fight with one hand against the arming of Western Germany with nuclear weapons, against the spreading of nuclear weapons in the world, and to supply these weapons to China with the other hand. . . .

Peking

The real point is that the Soviet leaders hold that China should not, and must not, manufacture nuclear weapons, and that only the few nuclear powers, and particularly US imperialism, the enemy of the people of the whole world, are entitled to the continued production of nuclear weapons.

The Soviet statement asserts that China can rely on the nuclear weapons of the Soviet Union and need not manufacture them itself; that if it tries to manufacture them it will result in a great strain on China's economy.

Should or should not China itself master the means of resisting US nuclear blackmail?

True, if the Soviet leaders really practised proletarian internationalism, China might consider it unnecessary to manufacture its own nuclear weapons.

But it is equally true that if the Soviet leaders really practised proletarian internationalism, they would have no reason whatever for obstructing China from manufacturing nuclear weapons.

Is not China very poor and backward? Yes it is. The Soviet leaders say, how can the Chinese be qualified to manufacture nuclear weapons when they eat watery soup out of a common bowl and do not even have pants to wear?

The Soviet leaders are perhaps too hasty in deriding China for its backwardness. They may or may not have judged right. But in any case, even if we Chinese people are unable to produce an atom bomb for a hundred years, we will neither crawl to the baton of the Soviet leaders nor kneel before the nuclear blackmail of the US imperialists. . . .

> The moral . . . is that different people have different aspirations, and it is improper to measure the stature of great men by the yardstick of small men. . . .
>
> *Moscow*
>
> The Chinese leaders themselves not so long ago admitted that inasmuch as the Soviet Union had achieved great successes in the production of nuclear weapons, China clearly "need not organize the production of such weapons, especially considering the fact that they are very costly." That was said by none other than Mao Tse-tung in September, 1958.
>
> What has changed since then? Has the nuclear rocket power of the USSR become weaker since that time? On the contrary, the whole world is aware of our country's tremendous successes in this field. If anything has changed, it has been the policy of the government of the People's Republic of China, its attitude towards the Soviet Union, towards the whole socialist community. . . .[1]

But, at the core of the argument was a Soviet position that only gradually emerged: that the avoidance of the diffusion of power in the form of nuclear weapons was a major Russian interest; if it could not be attained, a transcendent objective was to avoid putting Moscow in a position where another power might involve the Soviet Union in a nuclear war; and these state interests overrode considerations of ideological fraternity.

Here, as best we know, is how the conflict arose: from October 1957 down to January 1958 the Chinese Communist military were apparently expecting soon to have available modern Soviet military technology. A new draft training program was issued to the armed forces in January which stated that the Chinese Communist army would incorporate modern military techniques and military science (including atom bombs, chemical warfare, and guided missiles) based on "Soviet advanced experience."[2] By April, however, there had already occurred a complete turnabout: "It is despicable to rely on foreign countries. . . . Men are what count, not weapons. . . . Slavish reliance on the Soviet Union . . . has had a very harmful effect on Chinese military modernization. . . ."[3]

It was probably in this period, between January and April 1958, that Moscow made clear that its nuclear aid was conditional and put forward the "unreasonable demands" which the Chinese rejected.[4] We do not know what those demands were, but John Gittings speculates as follows:

> The crucial issue probably concerned the questions of control and command. As a price for nuclear aid, the Soviet Union may have insisted on one or more of the following: (1) retention of Soviet control of warheads or other weapons supplied, (2) some measures of joint planning and/or command in the Far East, (3) Chinese assurance that independent military initiatives would not be undertaken, e.g. over Taiwan.[5]

It is wholly possible that certain events in the West may have had a significant influence on this issue in Sino–Soviet relations. In the wake of Sputnik, the United States had begun negotiations in November 1957 to install medium-range ballistic missiles in Turkey, Italy, and Britain. These would remain wholly under U.S. control; but firing would require the consent of the host country as well as the United States. The United States also reaffirmed in late October 1957 its special nuclear relation with Great Britain, which led to a formal agreement in August 1958. This agreement permitted Britain to continue the development of a national nuclear capability on the basis of widened access to United States technology.

It may be that what Peking asked of Moscow was, essentially, the kind of quasi-independent nuclear status enjoyed by Britain rather than the more dependent relationship of, say, Turkey and Italy. The Russian arrangements offered to Peking were probably more nearly of the latter type.

On the other hand, despite China's rejection of Soviet weapons under Soviet control on Chinese soil, the Soviets helped implant the nuclear seed in China by assistance at the end of 1957 in construction of a gaseous diffusion plant and in the development of medium-range surface-to-surface missiles.[6]

The beginnings of serious crisis in Sino–Soviet relations over the nuclear matter can be dated, then, in the early months of 1958. This interpretation is strengthened by the fact that on March 31, 1958, the Soviet Union, on its own, ceased testing nuclear weapons and on April 4 sent to Washington and Peking a note including this observation:

> Today only three powers—the U.S.S.R., the U.S.A., and Great Britain—possess nuclear weapons; therefore, agreement on the discontinuance of nuclear weapons tests can be achieved relatively easily. If the tests are not stopped now, within a certain time other countries may have nuclear weapons, and in such a situation it would, of course, be much more difficult to obtain an agreement.[7]

On this view the Great Leap Forward, announced in May 1958, could be taken in part as Mao's response to the prospect that China would have to go it alone in building nuclear weapons. Mao may have judged that accelerated economic development, based on labor-intensive investment, would provide sooner than more conventional economic policies the industrial base for the building of a modern weapons establishment; although, clearly, there were other likely motives for Mao's effort to accelerate the expansion of the mainland economy.

From May to July 1958 a high-level military conference took place in China assessing the implications of the new situation. Probably it was at this time that Mao decided to launch an accelerated program to produce nuclear weapons and planned the military probe in the Formosan Straits.

There is evidence of military opposition to this policy of military independence centering around Defense Minister P'eng Teh-huai. He may have urged Peking to accept Soviet terms for nuclear aid to avoid an interval in which China would face the world without either Soviet support or nuclear weapons of its own. Moscow, aware of the debate within the Chinese leadership, evidently sought to influence its outcome. The nuclear question continued to be discussed between Moscow and Peking down to the final rupture of the October 1957 agreement on June 20, 1959. That rupture occurred only a week after the return from a protracted visit to the Soviet Union and eastern Europe of a Chinese military mission headed by P'eng Teh-huai, who was dismissed from his post at the end of September 1959.[8]

In a manner by no means clear, the nuclear question with China was interwoven with Soviet diplomacy related to a test ban treaty.[9] The Chinese appear to have given the Soviet test ban initiative of 1958 at least nominal support down to June 1959. How does this apparent support square with Peking's evident determination to achieve an independent nuclear capability? Did Peking believe the negotiations would fail? Did Peking bargain for proven Soviet weapons or prototypes as a price for adherence to a test ban treaty when it seemed a realistic possibility in mid-1959? Did Moscow initiate such a bargain?

We do not know. I am inclined to believe that Peking was in fact opposed to the test ban treaty throughout this period; and that it stuck with the view I heard Chinese delegates state at a 1960 Pugwash conference in Moscow—ban all nuclear weapons. No discrimination of the kind inherent in a test ban treaty was acceptable. Given the dim prospects for agreement to ban nuclear weapons totally, this Chinese position clearly signalled a determination to acquire a national nuclear capability.

What we do know is that the experiences since the November 1957 summit in Moscow, against the background of thirty years of awkward relations with Moscow, convinced the Chinese Communists that ideological fraternity would not suffice. Neither in the short run nor the long run could China rely on Russia to advance its interests, despite Sputnik. And a China, with all the grandeur of its long history, with all it had suffered, was not about to accept its current poverty as a reason for committing itself to what it regarded as a tertiary role in a nuclear age. Peking's ultimate statement on nuclear weapons, flowing from an old Chinese fable, was essentially an assertion of national pride rather than of ideological faith: "It is improper to measure the stature of great men by the yardstick of small men."

In retrospect, the Soviet posture towards a Chinese nuclear capability, climaxed by the decision to withdraw nuclear assistance in June 1959, was the critical act in the Sino–Soviet split. It affected, and perhaps dominated, every other dimension of the split.

The debate continued through 1960, punctuated by the start of open polemics with the Chinese publication of "Long Live Leninism" in April, by Khrushchev's personal appearance in June to denounce the Chinese Communists at the meeting of the Rumanian Communist party, and by the tense Hanoi session of the Vietnamese Communist party in September.

In August, Soviet technical assistance and support for several hundred industrial projects was withdrawn, and a rapid decline in Sino–Soviet trade began.[10]

All this came to a head between September and December in Moscow.[11] Before these stormy sessions were over, every issue in contention was fully laid before the party leaders, starting with a 60,000 word letter, dated November 5, bearing Khrushchev's imprint. The Chinese counter-attacked, supported by the Albanians. The other parties took their positions, colored in each case by local preoccupations. The great issue of "factionalism"; the possibility of avoiding war in a nuclear age; peaceful and nonpeaceful routes to "socialism"; the precise language to describe the absent "revisionist" Yugoslavs; policy towards radical noncommunist regimes—all this, plus the dirty linen accumulated between Peking and Moscow over military and economic aid, was fully aired and only cosmetically resolved in the final communique of December 6.

It took many anxious days of negotiation to achieve that document. As one analyst has put it: "The Moscow Declaration constituted, in boxing terms, a victory on points for the Soviet Party";[12] but the Chinese took back to Peking passages in the Declaration that permitted them to live to fight another day.

I was in Moscow at this time attending a Pugwash meeting on arms control with the blessing of the outgoing and incoming administrations. It lasted from November 27 to December 7. Even at our sessions the Russian and Chinese delegates had a number of awkward moments during the formal debate which clearly reflected divergences between the two governments. In human terms the Russians and other communist delegates appeared distinctly more comfortable with their Western than with their Chinese colleagues. Russians talked in private with Americans with evident candor of their anxieties about the Chinese.

At one point a Soviet diplomat attached to the Pugwash meeting asked Jerome Wiesner (later Kennedy's science adviser) and me how we organized our delegation for the positions we took in the arms control discussions. We told him quite truthfully that we had had no delegation meetings in Moscow. Each man expressed his own view. Wiesner said, "We are like a Dixieland band." For an observer, we explained, the end result was a fairly accurate picture of the strands of thought and feeling that entered into the American view of arms control. The Soviet diplomat promptly replied with a wry smile, "We ourselves are now learning something about Dixieland jazz."

When I reported to the President-elect on the conversations in Moscow (long before the terms of the Sino–Soviet split became known) and assessed the possibility that the Soviet interest in arms control might be serious, it was not difficult, on the basis of endless conversation with medium-level Soviet officials and scientists, to put at the head of the list of reasons "The *N*th power problem, centering evidently on China and Germany." Thus, Dixieland jazz was a somewhat understated way to describe the state of affairs in the communist movement as of December 1960.

LEBANON–JORDAN AND QUEMOY–MATSU

ALTHOUGH the nuclear issue, and the visceral nationalism it stirred, lay at the core of Sino–Soviet dissonance, it had been exacerbated over the three previous years by events as distant from each other as the beaches of Lebanon, the Taiwan Straits, and Berlin.

The Lebanon–Jordan and Quemoy–Matsu crises of 1958 ran, respectively, from May to August and from August to October. They were linked in communist thought and controversy because they provided evidence on how the United States would, in fact, behave on the international scene in the wake of Sputnik.

American policy in 1958 belongs with later chapters. So far as the Sino–Soviet debate is concerned, Peking regarded the Soviet response to the American landings in Lebanon as weak. On July 17 the major Peking newspaper said:

> There cannot be the slightest indulgence or tolerance toward American imperialism's act of aggression. . . . If the American aggressors are permitted to do as they wish, then not only will the people of the Middle East be enslaved, but a new world war would be inevitable. . . . Therefore let the people of the whole world take emergency action.[13]

From Khrushchev's point of view the American willingness to move troops to protect its interests in the Middle East in the face of his nuclear posture was an important and unpleasant fact. But Moscow could also note that the Iraqi coup of July 13 was not undone. The Americans and British stabilized Lebanon and Jordan, but did not intervene in Iraq. The Baghdad Pact was now breached. Khrushchev was prepared to accept the costs of the American initiative, settle for the gains as he saw them, and to await patiently another occasion safely to move forward.

Khrushchev's willingness to turn to the United Nations to debate and settle the affair made matters worse with Peking. And his suggestion at one point that India join the Big Four in a heads-of-government conference on the matter must have appeared downright provocative, elevating, as it would have done, a rival of Peking as global spokesman for Asia and the affairs of the developing world generally.

The Middle East crisis contributed one further element to the Sino–Soviet dispute. Kassim, leader of the Iraqi coup, revealed himself as a fairly sturdy nationalist. Tension arose between communists and noncommunists in Baghdad. Then an extreme wing of the Iraqi Communist party involved itself in a tribal uprising in July 1959. The revolt failed. The evidence that Moscow may have counseled caution and that Peking may have supported the communist extremists is only circumstantial,[14] but the incident subsequently became part of the lore of the Sino–Soviet dispute.

Before the denouement of the Lebanon–Jordan crisis and before the formal opening of the crisis in the Taiwan Straits, Khrushchev arrived in Peking for three days on July 31, 1958. Chinese Communist publications, military dispositions, and public rallies during July foreshadowed a move in the Taiwan Straits.[15] Khrushchev and Mao undoubtedly discussed both the Middle East and the impending initiative against Quemoy–Matsu, as well as the more general issues then in contention.[16] Mao apparently hoped to demonstrate to Khrushchev that in the Taiwan Straits, where he had the initiative, major results could be achieved against the United States if one were prepared to accept sufficient risk—and, perhaps, he argued that the risk was not high.

The crisis opened with the shelling of the offshore islands on August 23. It reached an initial diplomatic turning point on September 4 when Dulles suggested the United States might attack the mainland if Quemoy were attacked; Chou En-lai offered on September 6 to renew ambassadorial talks with the United States. It reached a tactical turning point in the third and fourth weeks of the month, when the United States–Nationalist Chinese resupply efforts became effective, and most dramatically on September 24 when ten Chinese Communist MIGs were shot down by Nationalist pilots equipped with air-to-air Sidewinder missiles. On October 6 Peking in effect called off the venture.

Moscow's support of Peking during the crisis was minimal, nervous, and late. High-level Soviet expressions of support for Peking came only after September 6, as the Chinese Communists later pointed out. The basic Sino–Soviet security commitments were reaffirmed in terms which, even then, left some ambiguity as to Soviet behavior if the United States and mainland China should go to war. Moscow was clearly uneasy at involvement in a crisis where its own interests were secondary, where it could not control events, and where the use of nuclear weapons was not wholly ruled out.

Here is Peking's assessment of the Soviet position on the crisis:

> The Soviet leaders expressed their support for China on September 7 and 19 respectively. Although at that time the situation in the Taiwan Straits was tense, there was no possibility that a nuclear war would break out and no need for the Soviet Union to support China with its nuclear weapons. It was only when they were clear

that this was the situation that the Soviet leaders expressed their support for China. . . .[17]

The fact was that Eisenhower proved more redoubtable in facing down Mao's probe than Peking had calculated. Mao did not command the resources to proceed safely; and Moscow was not prepared to throw its military power, or even its full diplomatic weight, behind his effort.

The essentially disappointing outcome of the Quemoy–Matsu crisis undoubtedly reinforced in Peking the view that had emerged in the spring: it would have to acquire a wholly independent nuclear capability and assume that Moscow would not take significant risk in support of Peking's interests in the expansion of its power.

SOVIET RELATIONS WITH THE UNITED STATES

THE year 1958 was also one of initiative for Khrushchev. In that year he decided to apply the leverage of enhanced Soviet nuclear prestige against Berlin, rather than in the Middle East or Asia. On November 10 he declared his intention to sign within six months a peace treaty with East Germany which would terminate Allied rights in West Berlin. Berlin was not a place that greatly interested Mao; and as 1959 unfolded, the sequence of events must have appeared ominous to him. By May 27 Khrushchev's time limit on Berlin slid by without issue. In June, after more than a year of controversy over the nuclear question, Moscow withdrew its support for the Chinese nuclear effort. On August 5 a series of flirtatious Moscow–Washington visits and diplomatic exchanges was climaxed by the announcement that Khrushchev would visit the United States in September and that Eisenhower would subsequently visit the Soviet Union. Khrushchev was evidently hardening in his relations with Peking and pursuing "peaceful coexistence," as he defined it. In Mao's view, Khrushchev and Eisenhower could only come closer at his expense, and Khrushchev promptly confirmed this.

After touring the United States, Khrushchev defended his policy of détente with some vigor in two public statements, as well as in private during his visit to Peking (September 30–October 4, 1959). And in his formal report to the Supreme Soviet on October 31, he marched down the list of Peking's proximate concerns. On Taiwan, he went no further than to assert the legitimacy of Peking's "legal and moral" position. He asserted his "impression" that the United States was seeking no military conflict in Korea. He said the USSR was "against the existence of even the smallest source of war in Laos." And he took an even-handed neutralist position on the Sino–Indian border dispute which had recently flared up.[18]

Khrushchev's polemical style was less lucid than Mao's because of his more complex global constituency. But with a sense of communist righteousness that matched Mao's, he believed in 1959 that the new post-Sputnik image of Soviet military strength could: (1) deter an American first strike; (2) permit the historical forces operating in the developing world to work gradually his way (as in Algeria, Iraq, and Cuba) without accepting the risk of confrontation or war with the United States; (3) permit Russia to support and encourage these "inevitable trends" with economic and military assistance, as well as through local communist parties; (4) remove the bone in his throat, West Berlin; and (5) release Soviet resources to fulfill by 1970 his dream of surpassing the United States in industrial and agricultural production.

Khrushchev's public statements at this time suggest that it was perhaps the fifth possibility which engaged him most of all. This was his central theme in the United States. It was a healing theme in Soviet life where the economy bulked so large and the people hungered for expanded levels of consumption; it was not difficult to view military and foreign policy outlays as diversionary. Speaking at a dinner in Peking on September 30, Khrushchev urged strongly that: "The socialist countries . . . fire the hearts of men by the *force of their example* in building socialism and *thus lead them to follow in their footsteps*."[19] His view of appropriate communist policy in encouraging this sequence was by no means as passive as this exhortation, taken apart, would suggest; but he undoubtedly counted heavily on a continued Soviet surge in production relative to the United States. And this, he felt, was not wholly unrealistic. As of 1959 Khrushchev was enjoying the fruits of the popular illusion that the USSR had outstripped the United States in nuclear delivery capacity. It is not difficult to understand that he would count heavily on the "force of example" that might result from another decade in which Soviet growth rates actually were more than twice those of the United States. Compound interest, if projected on an exponential basis from the 1950s forward, did promise to yield an attractive result.

For Mao, Khrushchev's race of index numbers with the United States was less interesting. What he sought in the Great Leap Forward was the quick creation of an industrial base sufficient to produce both an independent nuclear delivery capability and an economic position among the advanced nations justifying general status as a world power. For Mao, as for many latecomers to industrialization since 1815, economic growth was a derived demand. He was not primarily interested in the expansion of welfare for the Chinese people. He was profoundly interested in rapid industrialization as a route to the dignity and power he felt rightfully belonged to a China long humiliated in the modern world and to the primacy within the communist movement he felt belonged rightfully to the most original and creative revolutionary since, perhaps, Marx and Lenin.

It was not inevitable that these two abiding interests of Mao take the aggressive and radical form they did in the post-Sputnik decade. Peking had earlier exhibited a capacity for more flexible policies at home and abroad. Until the shock of Budapest, Peking was aligned with the liberal communists in eastern Europe. What the launching of the first Sputnik did was to force urgently upon Moscow and Peking an issue which, in any case, would have had to be faced: Peking's nuclear status and the nuclear relationship between Peking and Moscow. And it forced that root issue upon the two capitals in a context where they could agree that a historic phase of communist opportunity had arrived; but they could not agree on the priority, directions, and tactics with which that opportunity should be pursued. Peking decided to go it alone in nuclear matters and to contest Moscow's leadership on a global basis by appealing to the have-nots, within and without the communist world. Both decisions reflected the depth of China's, as well as Mao's, notion of historical grandeur. Blended together, they were to render the Chinese–Russian border a scene of massive and tense military confrontation.

4

Three Crises in the Developing World

Decision in Hanoi

While the Sino–Soviet split was evolving in these terms, and Khrushchev was deciding that the test of nuclear blackmail would come over Berlin, other decisions were taken in communist capitals that yielded major crises in Southeast Asia, the Caribbean, and central Africa. Each in different ways was related to the inherently volatile politics of the developing world. The decision taken in Hanoi cast the longest shadow of all over the 1960s. That decision was to resume an active political and insurrectional effort to take over power in South Vietnam.

Hanoi's long-term objective in Indochina has never been seriously in doubt. At the minimum, it is to control all of Vietnam, Laos, and Cambodia. Its sustained effort to exploit the presence of expatriate Vietnamese in Thailand to build a foundation for guerrilla war suggests ambitions beyond. To achieve these purposes, the North Vietnamese leaders built, in effect, a single Indochinese Communist party, run from Hanoi.[1]

Here is what can be firmly said about the timing of the decision to resume the effort to take over South Vietnam, after the Geneva agreement of 1954.

The period 1954–1956 was taken up with consolidating communist control over North Vietnam at the expense of noncommunist elements within the Viet Minh and the noncommunist institutions which existed in North Vietnam in 1954. During these two years perhaps 1,000,000 North Vietnamese went into South Vietnam as refugees. Also some 100,000 sympathetic South Vietnamese were brought north for political and military training and subsequent reinfiltration. A network of 10,000 communist cadres existed in the South to carry on political opposition to the Diem regime.

Peking had aided Hanoi substantially in the climactic phase of the struggle against the French. It was therefore natural that when victory in the North was achieved, Hanoi would follow closely the bloody method of consolidation used by Mao after 1949 and accept the presence in North Vietnam of a number of Chinese advisers. The period ended in a strong, negative reaction of the peasantry to collectivization.[2]

In October 1956, speaking at the Central Committee meeting of the Lao Dong Party, General Vo-Nguyen Giap made a public statement about excesses over the previous two years.[3] A small peasant revolt was crushed in November 1956 at Nghe An, but it was both a shock and bad international propaganda. In addition, as had occurred in China, there were strong expressions of dissatisfaction with the regime during a brief period of ideological relaxation that parallelled Mao's Hundred Flowers experiment. Truong Chinh, Party Secretary General in this period and leader of the catastrophic collectivization drive, was removed and Le Duan brought back from the South to replace him de facto in late 1956 or early 1957. (Ho formally took over the Secretary-General post. Le Duan's position was regularized in September 1960.) A reorientation of Hanoi's policy towards the Soviet Union occurred in 1957. The Chinese model for collectivization having fallen into some disrepute and industrialization moving towards the center of Hanoi's development planning, Hanoi required the kind of assistance only Moscow could supply.

Returning from the euphoric post-Sputnik Moscow Conference of November 1957, Le Duan told a group of North Vietnamese officials on December 7:

> The Moscow documents have not only confirmed the line and created favorable conditions for North Vietnam to advance toward socialism but have also shown the path of struggle for national liberation and have created favorable conditions for the revolutionary movement in South Vietnam.[4]

From mid-1958 violence in South Vietnam began to increase, mainly in the form of the systematic assassination and kidnapping of GVN (Government of [South] Vietnam) officials rather than armed attacks. It was probably at this time that the infiltration of political and military cadres from the North to the South accelerated from among the South Vietnamese brought north in 1954 and subsequently trained for this mission.

After its May 1959 meeting the Lao Dong Party Central Committee declared: "the time has come to struggle heroically and perseveringly to smash" the GVN; and Giap, shortly thereafter, stated that "the North has become a large rear echelon of our army. The North is the revolutionary base for the whole country."[5] From the second half of 1959 there is no doubt that a purposeful campaign directed by Hanoi was under way to take over South Vietnam; and Hanoi's closely related decision to seize and hold the Laos corridor to South Vietnam can be dated firmly from the May 1959 meeting, although the presence of North Vietnamese forces in the corridor was detected in late 1958 and earlier in 1959.

In the course of 1960 armed attacks by the Viet Cong rapidly increased, including battalion-size attacks on provincial capitals.

In September 1960 the Third Lao Dong Party Congress described the taking over of South Vietnam as "a two-stage affair: first, the elimination of the U.S. imperialists and the Ngo Dinh Diem clique, . . . then the establishment of a national democratic coalition government . . . that would negotiate with the North for reunification."[6] In the tradition of the Viet Minh (and other such communist efforts), it was to be a popular front party.

On December 20, 1960, the formation of the National Liberation Front was announced, built around a group of figures who had worked together, and with the communists, in a Saigon-based Peace Committee since 1954.[7]

The four major factors that entered into this series of decisions were probably these.

First, the failure of French or other diplomacy to force the election by July 1956 envisaged in the Final Declaration of the Geneva Conference of 1954. As Bernard Fall has noted:

> Since the North controlled a population of more than 15 million and the South fewer than 12 million, and since the North could be trusted to "deliver" its electorate in overwhelming numbers, such an election would beyond a doubt have resulted in a peaceful takeover of all of Vietnam by Ho Chi Minh in July, 1956.[8]

Diem was fully aware not only of the arithmetic but also of the swift and bloody consolidation of North Vietnam into a single party police dictatorship. The refugees from the North were a critical component in his political constituency; and he was not prepared for the suicidal course elections represented under these circumstances. As early as January 1955 he posed the question: What would be the good of an impartial counting of the votes if the voting had been preceded in North Vietnam by a campaign of propaganda and terrorism on the part of a police state?[9] He could stand on the 1954 refusal of the South Vietnamese delegates at Geneva to agree at that time to the 1956 election.

In fact, the American commitment to the SEATO Treaty, and its detached posture at Geneva in 1954, must have convinced Hanoi that it would not be handed South Vietnam through a palpably rigged election. The protests from Moscow and Peking at the passage of the 1956 election date were pro forma; and, indeed, on January 24, 1957, the Soviet Union proposed in the Political Committee of the United Nations General Assembly that both North and South Vietnam be admitted to the United Nations, reflecting acquiescence in the emergence of two sovereign states. After July 1956, then, Hanoi had to look to different means if it was to achieve its objective, and it had to acquire support for the effort from Peking or Moscow or both.

Second, there was the pressure being exerted by Diem on the communist apparatus in the South, as part of his broader effort to eliminate opposition and consolidate his rule. It may be that Le Duan's return from the South to Hanoi, in the wake of Truong Chinh's demotion, brought forcefully to the attention of his colleagues the plight of the southern cadres. It is likely that Hanoi's assessment was that continued communist passivity in the South would lead to the full consolidation of Diem's power as the destruction of the communist political structure in the South and the discovery of arms caches proceeded.

Third, Diem's methods in trying to consolidate the fragmented post-colonial political life of South Vietnam created widespread dissidence. He persisted in heavy-handed methods which had served to deal with the sects and other organized minorities in the period 1954–1956. Applied to the population as a whole, these methods narrowed his base among the anti-communist population. On the other hand, his control methods were inefficient, by communist standards. Thus, Hanoi could conclude that Diem was doubly vulnerable to a "war of national liberation."

Fourth, despite Moscow's reticence about "wars of national liberation" that might lead to confrontation with the United States, Ho apparently was able to get Soviet (as well as Chinese) approval for the launching of the new effort.[10] He must have gone deeply into the matter with the Soviet leadership in 1959 and, especially, in the summer of 1960 before the public emergence of the NLF. It may be that his decisive arguments were these: that despite Peking's vigorous espousal of the "nonpeaceful road to socialism" to which Ho attached the highest significance, he would continue his intermediate, conciliatory role in the Sino–Soviet controversy; that he would concentrate on industrialization—on "building socialism"—in the North; and that he could do the job in the South without provoking a confrontation with the United States because his apparatus was already in place and any additional forces would be reinfiltrated Southerners.

One can also surmise that Moscow was uneasy with Hanoi's decision on the basis of contemporary general polemics about "wars of national liberation" and subsequent erratic Soviet policy in Southeast Asia. With the SEATO Treaty in existence, confrontation with the United States could not easily be ruled out; and, as Soviet policy in the Taiwan crisis suggested, Moscow disliked confrontations in regions and under circumstances where it could not control events. Southeast Asia was clearly such an area. But the value of keeping Ho mainly with Moscow in the Sino–Soviet struggle, and the implicit threat Hanoi could deploy of shifting wholeheartedly to Peking's side, may have been decisive. If, as Moscow intended, the Soviet Union was to remain a major power in Asia, inside and outside the communist movement, it was important to avoid a definitive defection of Ho Chi Minh to Peking; for Ho was a figure of real prestige and influence in the world communist movement. Khrushchev's memoir catches vividly both Ho's prestige and the importance attached by Moscow to his position in the dispute with Peking.[11]

The Soviet leadership made its crucial decisions on Vietnam at just the time that the windfall of a communist Cuba had fallen into its lap. It could not rule out the possibility that Ho would succeed. Moscow may have decided, therefore, to back Hanoi in its enterprise so long as it went well, but to do so in ways which would not permit Hanoi to force it into a confrontation with the United States.

On the whole, the Sino–Soviet split probably made it easier for Hanoi to launch its attack on South Vietnam. If Peking had accepted Moscow's offer of modern weapons at the cost of joint planning of military and foreign policy, Hanoi might well have been under greater restraint.[12]

The public emergence of the NLF in 1960 marked the end of a phase of certainly more than two years—and perhaps more than three—of purposeful organizational effort by Hanoi to rebuild, under new circumstances, a political-military organization that would challenge and defeat the government of South Vietnam. This included the activation of the infiltration routes through Laos, evident by the end of 1958. And by the end of 1960 the gathering weight of this effort was already a serious threat to Diem's regime. South Vietnam was clearly Hanoi's primary objective, even though the headlines at the time concerned Laos.

A great deal of postwar history consists of the interplay between the slow-moving process of development in nations at early stages of modernization and the conflicting strategic interests of external powers. Nowhere has this interplay been more palpable, and more tragic for the citizens entrapped, than in Laos. With the possible exceptions of Yemen and the Congo, Laos is the least modernized—the most traditional—of the regions of major strategic conflict. Its population is roughly estimated at 3 million. About half the population is concentrated in the Mekong valley, closely related by race and culture to the Thais. The other half are hill tribesmen, of which the largest group is the Meo, living above 3,500 feet in the sparsely settled interior.

Laos emerged from a fairly permissive French colonialism as a quasi-constitutional kingdom. Effective political leadership lay initially (and still mainly lies) with a few families, French-trained, whose major figures combined ties to the old rural structure of the society with knowledge of the world outside. Negotiations among them, within the agreed structure of monarchy, held together an essentially fragmented regional and social community. The sustained struggle in and over Laos has begun to produce new, more modern men and new relationships transcending family and region; but the old fear of the Vietnamese coming across the Annamite mountains, rather than a new sense of purposeful nationhood, remains the most powerful common tie among the citizens of Laos.

The economy remains primarily agricultural, applying relatively little of modern technology, a long way still from a first sustained phase of industrial expansion.

The torment of Laos arose from two simple strategic facts. First, from both communist and noncommunist perspectives, it is a critical protective buffer for Thailand, whose defense would become exceedingly difficult if a hostile power dominated Laos and commanded the long and easily penetrated line of the Mekong. Second, the best infiltration routes from North to South Vietnam run through the thinly populated jungles of southeastern Laos.

The story of communist policy towards Laos from 1954 to 1961 is immensely complex; but a great deal can be summarized in the following propositions:

1. Hanoi's long-run objective was effective control of Laos through the triumph of the Laotian Communist party, which it dominated.

2. In pursuit of that long-run objective, Hanoi sought to maintain a geographical and political base in Laos.

3. Once Hanoi decided that it would first seek the takeover of South Vietnam, the long-run objective of controlling Laos was subordinated to the immediate objective of gaining and holding control over the Laotian infiltration routes to South Vietnam.[13]

At Geneva in 1954 both the Chinese and the Russians pressed hard for a settlement that would neutralize Laos and forestall an American military presence there. The agreement between the French and the new government in Hanoi provided for Laos as an independent unitary state. It also permitted the communist forces in Laos the right to regroup in the two northern provinces bordering North Vietnam (Sam Neua and Phong Saly), pending, in the case of the North Vietnamese, return to their own country, and in the case of the Pathet Lao (Laotian communists), their integration into the Lao army or demobilization. The International Control Commission was created at Geneva to monitor the withdrawal of North Vietnamese and other foreign forces. The agreement was silent on how the integration of the communist forces was to be accomplished and how the authority of the Royal Government would be reasserted in the two regroupment provinces.

The Laotian communists proceeded with vigor to consolidate the two northern provinces as a political and military base, much as the Viet Cong sought to consolidate positions in the South Vietnamese countryside.[14] The

International Control Commission was not permitted into the region and it was never in a position to verify directly that North Vietnamese "volunteers" had withdrawn, as the Geneva Accords required. Government troops sporadically harassed and were harassed by the Pathet Lao.

But this was a relatively peaceful and political phase in Hanoi's policy toward the rest of Indochina; and the Pathet Lao sought to translate its de facto power in the regroupment provinces into maximum political status in the central government. In 1956–1957 protracted negotiations yielded a coalition government under Souvanna Phouma, with two Pathet Lao ministers. On November 18, 1957, the two provinces under communist control were formally turned over to Royal authority; 1,500 Pathet Lao soldiers were to be integrated into the Royal Lao army. It appeared that the Lao genius for the politics of the extended family had, by patient negotiation, made some sense of the 1954 agreement that Laos should be an independent and truly neutral buffer state.

Throughout these first years the Pathet Lao worked with great industry to expand its organizational structure on a national basis; and their methods clearly reflected Hanoi's tutelage as well as still earlier Chinese Communist methods in rural areas. Propaganda and coercion were judiciously mixed at the village level. Their grass-roots approach was more modern than that of traditional princely politics; and they did relatively well in the elections of May 4, 1958. There was some anxious reaction to this success in Vientiane.

Despite these domestic political uncertainties, Souvanna Phouma took the view that the obligations undertaken at Geneva in 1954 were now fulfilled; and on July 20, 1958, the International Control Commission in Laos adjourned sine die, amid protests by communists who, at this stage, regarded the ICC, on balance, as an instrument to stay the hand of the central government rather than as a restraint on their own operations.

On July 23, Souvanna Phouma was voted out by the National Assembly. He was succeeded by Phoui Sananikone, who had handled Lao diplomacy with some distinction, and who had felt more uneasiness than Souvanna at communist political methods and gains on the domestic scene. He excluded communist ministers from the new government, interpreted neutralism internationally in ways less congenial to the communist world than Souvanna, and sought reforms which would reduce popular discontent with corruption related to the American aid programs.

These Lao domestic events of 1957–1958 coincided with the post-Sputnik decision in Hanoi to reactivate insurrectional operations in South Vietnam. By December 1958 there were clashes between regular North Vietnamese and Lao forces near Tchepone, along the Laos infiltration routes to South Vietnam.[15] Hanoi made clear that it would not permit Vientiane to exercise sovereignty over the infiltration routes unless it was willing to accept complicity in Hanoi's operations against South Vietnam.

This Phoui was not prepared to do. On January 15, 1959, he was granted emergency powers to govern for a year by decree in the face of the crisis caused by the North Vietnamese incursions; and several army officers, including (then) Colonel Phoumi Nosavan, came into the Lao government.

In 1959 Laos moved further toward war. It was in part a civil war, although the Pathet Lao moves were clearly controlled by Hanoi. One of the two Pathet Lao battalions, scheduled for long-delayed integration, decamped from the Plain of Jars on May 19 and moved north where the Pathet Lao were again asserting authority in the old base areas in Sam Neua and Phong Saly.[16] But conflict also began with the North Vietnamese, as Hanoi despatched military cadres to stiffen the Pathet Lao and used regular North Vietnamese units to move men and supplies along the Laos infiltration trails.

In the spring of 1959, as the Sino–Soviet split was widening, the Chinese spoke of its interest in the "civil war" in Laos and hinted, at least, at possible involvement.

The truth of the matter was that, in the face of Hanoi's military and political leverage in Laos and the nation's terrain, the government in Vientiane lacked the power to assert sovereignty over either the infiltration routes to South Vietnam or the two old regroupment provinces. American military aid and training and limited Thai support could not generate that power in the short run; and then, as later, the United States was not prepared to engage its regular forces directly on the ground in Laos. Therefore, authentic Lao nationalists faced, from 1959 forward, a most difficult question: How should they conduct their political and diplomatic life, and military operations, in the face of this inhibited sovereignty illegally imposed by Hanoi? The personal rivalries and ambitions of the limited group of leaders were real enough; but it was over differing views of substance that they maneuvered and clashed.

On December 31, 1959, five military leaders, in the face of communist gains and disarray among the civilian politicians, mounted a coup. But they pulled back when confronted by international and domestic opposition.[17] On January 7, 1960, the King appointed Kou Abhay, an elderly and respected figure, Prime Minister in a provisional government to rule until general elections could take place. General Phoumi, leader of the coup, was made Minister of Defense. The April elections were evidently rigged to keep the Pathet Lao candidates from gaining effective power. A government was set up under Prince Somsanith, with Phoumi its dominant figure. On August 8 a young paratroop battalion commander, Kong Le, conducted a skillful coup d'etat, demanding an end to civil war and a return to neutralist (rather than anticommunist) government. Souvanna Phouma agreed to form a new government. He moved, on the one hand, to bring Phoumi into the government and, on the other, to open negotiations with the Pathet Lao. Phoumi, after appearing to agree, withdrew to his regional base at Savannakhet (south of Vientiane on the Mekong) where he built military strength and gathered support from Thai and American sources, with the clear intention of moving to take control of Vientiane.

At the end of September the Russians asked to open an embassy in Vientiane; their ambassador arrived on October 13. Evidently they wished to throw their weight behind Souvanna Phouma and a neutralist solution. In the short run a neutralist solution would protect Hanoi's major interest in the infiltration route to South Vietnam and reduce the danger of a communist thrust to the Mekong. The latter might well yield a major direct American intervention in Laos, given the depth of the American commitment to Thailand. Anxieties about Peking's policy toward Laos may have also played a part in the Soviet move.

As the Pathet Lao pressed militarily to exploit this disarray (as well as the American election period) and to strengthen their bargaining position for negotiations with Souvanna, Phoumi and Souvanna came closer together, and American aid, briefly suspended, was resumed on October 17, including a direct military aid channel to Phoumi at Savannakhet. This agreement gave Phoumi increased political and military support. Souvanna Phouma received assurances that American aid would not be used against Kong Le's neutralist units; but Souvanna's base was narrowed as he struggled against polarization and civil war.

Negotiations with the Pathet Lao began on October 11. The communists finally agreed to a new coalition government on November 20, but insisted that Phoumi be excluded. A delegation of the National Assembly failed by December 2 to persuade Phoumi to accept this agreement. On December 3 a Soviet airlift from Hanoi to Vientiane in support of Kong Le began with oil shipments. Phoumi's forces began to move towards Vientiane; and on December 9 Souvanna turned power over to the military and left for Phnom Penh. Soviet artillery began arriving by December 11.

After a bloody battle, Phoumi's units provided the necessary margin, and Kong Le was driven from Vientiane by December 16. The King gave temporary powers to Phoumi and Prince Boun Oum. Kong Le moved to the Plain of Jars, with the assistance of the Pathet Lao; and, in effect, this strategic point came under communist control by the end of the month.

On January 4 the United States recognized the Boun Oum government; but on January 7 released a statement that was not inconsistent with a possible return to a more widely based neutralist effort.

From Hanoi's point of view the situation in Laos as of early 1961 was admirable. Militarily, the gravely weakened government in Vientiane was in no position to interfere with the infiltration routes to South Vietnam. The old regroupment provinces were firmly consolidated as base areas along with other areas along the border with North Vietnam. Kong Le's forces had joined with the Pathet Lao in the Plain of Jars, and from that base the communists could press toward the Mekong. Politically, the nationalist forces in Laos were badly fragmented. There was ample scope for communist political activities throughout the country. American policy towards Laos was in open crisis and disarray, with Paris and London in disagreement with Washington. Moscow was interesting itself in the area, complicating affairs to some extent but also reducing the likelihood of Hanoi's being either excessively dependent on Peking or whipsawed by an overt split between Moscow and Peking over policy in Southeast Asia.

As Khrushchev makes clear, Ho Chi Minh used all his influence and prestige in Moscow in December 1960 to bring about the compromises between Peking and Moscow necessary for the Chinese Communists to sign the conference communique—a communique which legitimized, as in 1957, the choice of "a nonpeaceful transition to socialism" Ho had already made.[18]

Decision in the Sierra Maestra

The decision to begin again the effort to take over South Vietnam could be made primarily in Hanoi, although arms from other communist states and minimal political support had to be assured. The crisis over Berlin could be launched by Moscow at a time and under circumstances of its own choice. The crisis over Quemoy–Matsu could, similarly, be initiated by Peking. For the communist world, however, Castro's takeover of Cuba was a windfall. It arose from the political dynamics of a Caribbean island rather than the decision of a communist regime.

The exact relation of Castro to the Communist party, and how it evolved, is a matter of some debate.[19] In his famous five-hour speech of December 1–2, 1961, Castro said: "I am a Marxist–Leninist and I shall be a Marxist–Leninist until the last day of my life." He also stated that his Marxism was an early (but ambiguously dated) development which he concealed in order to attract the widest support he could muster in his insurrection against Batista.

The American government concluded in 1959 that Castro was, to all intents, a communist, a conclusion that was foreshadowed in a report to Eisenhower from Allen Dulles in the final days of 1958.[20] On the other hand, in 1961 Khrushchev told Kennedy in Vienna that "Fidel Castro was not a Communist, but American policy was making him one."[21]

Without entering the rather theological debate on the matter, I would conclude that Castro emerged from a typical background of dissident middle class political thought addressed to the familiar sources of Latin-American discontent: inequitable land-holding; excessive foreign investment; inadequate social services; etc. There is nothing in Castro's early programmatic statements that is either original or particularly communist. Castro's interests, from the time Batista seized power in 1952, were systematically tactical and personal: to overthrow Batista and to be the revolutionary leader who succeeded him. He was evidently obsessed with the role of insurrectional violence and with the concept of personal leadership.

Nothing in communist doctrine particularly affronted Castro. He had no interest in parliamentary democracy or conventional political liberties. His programmatic statements on these themes were patently tactical. Parliamentary democracy was not a congenial medium for his talents and passion for personal leadership. He had no resistance to the idea of government ownership and operation of the economy. He had no clear concept of foreign policy, except a generalized "anti-imperialism." Even on this matter Castro was extremely cautious about anti-Americanism until late in the game.[22] His objective was maximum personal power linked to a vaguely defined revolutionary program whose rubrics were consistent with either communist or noncommunist rule. He was therefore prepared either to work with communists or to resist them if they opposed his unorthodox tactics or challenged his authority.

In 1958, as Batista's strength weakened and Castro's survival in the Sierra Maestra elevated his political stature, the orthodox Cuban communists, hitherto sceptical and even opposed to his enterprise, moved cautiously to support him. On April 9, 1958, they withheld their support for the abortive general strike in Havana called by the July 26th Movement, but by the autumn an agreement was reached to bring the July 26 Movement and the Communist party of Cuba together. This involved, inevitably, a break with the noncommunist members of the July 26 Movement, notably those who had mounted programs of resistance to Batista in Havana, doing much to undermine his regime and enfeeble his thrust against Castro in the hills. That thrust took place in May 1958 when Castro commanded only 300 men. With its failure his band expanded, their central task being psychological rather than guerrilla war.

In 1959, after Castro came to power on a broad political basis, he followed, in a rather erratic and disheveled way, classic communist tactics, at home and abroad. At home he alienated or systematically removed from influence and authority his noncommunist comrades from the July 26 Movement;[23] abroad, he took steps (much like those taken by communists in postwar eastern Europe) which assured the alienation of the United States.

The sequence of events in 1959 and the possible role of American policy in shaping Castro's decisions are considered in a later chapter. From the perspective of the communist world, however, the crucial time was the year of multiple initiatives, 1958. Castro moved then toward a merger with the Cuban Communists, who were in a position to supply to him what he lacked once power was gained: a doctrine and techniques for ruling Cuba as a personal dictator, administrative personnel, and policies for dealing with the external world. There was an alternative. He could have developed from among his noncommunist followers a reformist program and administration and faced down the communists who were, in fact, a minor force in Cuban life.

Possibly, he spoke the simple truth on December 1–2, 1961, that he was for long a communist and simply awaited the proper moment to reveal it. What is clear is that he was not a disciplined member of the regular Cuban Communist party; that a powerful ego and personal desire for power was in him; and even after his commitment to work with the Cuban Communist organization and the communist world had, step by step, been made, these personal qualities and interests remained strong, even paramount. But after his 1958 agreement with the communists, and all that followed from it, Castro's overriding drive for personal leadership had to be exercised within confining limits which he might often resent, or even loosen, but which he could not remove without risking power.

For Moscow, the evolution of affairs in Cuba appears to have been regarded as a vindication of how history was moving in the late 1950s, as well as a strategic development of the first importance. One can assume that when a senior disciplined Communist party member such as Carlos Rafael Rodriguez went to visit Castro in the Sierra Maestra in July 1958 and then returned a few months later to stay with him as an official representative of the Cuban Communist party, he did so with the knowledge and support of Moscow.[24] One can assume that Moscow sought intimately to guide events in Cuba from that time. But the Soviet Union did not create the crisis in Cuban life, and the communist apparatus did not spawn the leader who emerged. Moscow merely exploited that crisis and came to uneasy terms of believed mutual advantage with Cuba's new leader.

The Cuba Castro took over at the beginning of 1959 was dependent on American investments, tourism, and, above all, its place in the United States market through its sugar quota. For serious communists this linkage was critical. Dependence of that kind was judged to be incompatible with the evolution of authentically communist institutions and the exercise of appropriate international discipline by Moscow. Considerations of precisely this kind were decisive, for example, in Stalin's preventing eastern Europe from joining the Marshall Plan. They shaped Chinese Communist determination to shift its trade away from Moscow's control since the withdrawal of Soviet aid in 1960. Even now they play a role in Moscow's uneasy policy toward eastern Europe; for example, its anxiety in 1968 that Czech trade with West Germany might expand to politically dangerous proportions.

The evolution of U.S.–Cuban relations between January 1, 1959, down to the break in diplomatic relations on January 3, 1961, is a tangled tale. But it is clear that Castro at no point sought the economic assistance of the United States, even though it was not ruled out by Washington. Moscow moved strongly in February 1960 to support the Cuban economy, on the occasion of Mikoyan's visit;[25] and Castro sought and received aid in the following months from six other communist regimes. In March Guevara denounced the sugar quota as "slavery." The definitive break in U.S.–Cuban relations came in March, although the Cuban sugar quota was not suspended until July. Parallel to the consolidation of communist influence and power within Cuba, then, these two years saw Cuba linked into vital dependence on the communist world.

The achievement of a strategic foothold for communism in the Western Hemisphere was probably not regarded in 1957 as a realistic, high-priority strategic objective in Moscow. There may even have been some anxiety about so direct a challenge to the United States. But it was a brilliant, even dazzling, acquisition which the Soviet leadership felt an historic duty to accept and make the most of. It was a kind of political Sputnik; and, like Sputnik, it was to prove a two-edged sword. But as of early 1961, the prospects seemed bright.

After the November–December Moscow meeting of the Communist parties, Khrushchev summed up his policy in a long report on January 6, 1961, to a meeting of Soviet Party organizations. He was able to cite Castro's victory in Cuba as the prototype of the kind of "war of national liberation" which could safely be conducted and which deserved unstinted communist support:

> The thunder of the glorious Cuban revolution has reverberated throughout the world. The Cuban revolution is not only repulsing the onslaught of the imperialists; it is spreading, signifying a new and higher stage of the national-liberation struggle, when the people themselves come to power, when the people become the master of their wealth. Solidarity with revolutionary Cuba is the duty not only of Latin American peoples, but also of the socialist countries, the entire international Communist movement and the proletariat all over the world.[26]

For some of the older Soviet leaders, the victory in Cuba evoked, initially, their own youthful excitement at Lenin's triumph. The Russian communists, too, had managed to seize power from a minority position in a broadly based revolutionary situation and eliminated the noncommunists who had shared the initial burden of overthrowing the despised autocrat. The communist victory in Cuba substantially increased their optimism about prospects throughout the developing world.[27]

CONGO: THE FIRST ROUND

THE Congo, however, did something to cool Moscow's ardor. In the Congo Moscow was more openly activist than in Cuba. It looked for but could not find an effective Castro and it lacked a corps of old Communist party members to exploit the opportunities that emerged in 1960 in the wake of independence.

Political underdevelopment was, in fact, the central problem for all sides and factions in the Congo. As the demand for independence accelerated in 1957–1959, Brussels came painfully to the decision that it would acquiesce despite its knowledge of how little it had done to educate and prepare the Congolese for effective self-government. It correctly sensed that the mood of the Congo, like most of colonial Africa, was one of determination to make its own mistakes rather than prolong the time of tutelage. Belgium was not prepared to face the kind of struggle France confronted in Algeria.

Brussels relied on the continuity of the *Force Publique* to preserve minimum law and order as the Congolese took uncertain control of their political life, but that well-trained force of 25,000 contained no native above warrant officer; and it was not prepared to accept continued control by white officers. A revolt broke out on July 5, 1960; and the Congolese crisis was on.

Initially, the two central political figures were the President, Joseph Kasavubu, and the President of the Council (also leader of the major Congolese political party), Patrice Lumumba. They first tried to reinstall the white officers, then to provide native leadership. But the pent-up frustration of the *Force Publique* yielded disorder and violence with a momentum of its own. To protect its nationals Brussels unilaterally despatched on July 8 a force of paratroops; Moise Tshombe declared the independence of Katanga; and Lumumba, feeling deceived by the Belgian government, broke off relations and turned to Moscow for assistance in reestablishing control over Katanga.

On September 2 the first of some fifteen planeloads of Soviet technicians landed in Leopoldville. But in the preceding seven weeks, the possibility of a United Nations route back to Congolese unity had developed. The arrival of the Soviet technicians weakened and isolated Lumumba. The deep impulse of black Africa to keep major powers out of its affairs, which was to assert itself repeatedly in the 1960s, emerged strongly in September.

But the crisis was slow to resolve. Kasavubu sought to replace Lumumba with Joseph Ileo; but Lumumba resisted. The political leadership was in disarray. On September 14 the Army Chief of Staff, Colonel Joseph Mobutu, suspended all three men from their posts and assumed power in the capital, but he lacked the power to unify the country which, by January 1961, was split four ways: Mobutu in control of Leopoldville; Lumumba's lieutenant Antoine Gizenga in Stanleyville; another radical, Anicet Kashamura, in Kivu; and Tshombe in Katanga.

The communist technicians obeyed Mobutu's orders and went home; but Moscow had not lost all hope of gaining leverage in the heart of Africa.

A PERSPECTIVE ON THE POST-SPUTNIK OFFENSIVE

WHAT can be said thus far is that a new, hopeful and energetic phase in communist policy began with Sputnik and Khrushchev's arrival as relatively unambiguous leader of the Soviet government as well as of the Party.

The two central questions within the communist world were: how to exploit the new Soviet nuclear capability and the world's image of it; and how to exploit the accelerating ferment in the developing world, where colonialism was ending and where new men, ideas, and aspirations were emerging also in states long free of colonialism.

Advanced military technology and policy towards nations at very early stages in absorbing modern technology were linked in several ways.

They were linked in the Khrushchev–Mao debate by the question of how much risk of war with the United States could safely be taken to pursue power in the developing continents through the technique of "wars of national liberation."

They were linked by the powerful image in the developing world of a Soviet Union closing fast on, or surpassing, a sluggish United States; and this somehow merged in communist minds with an authentic feeling that the decline of colonialism and the accelerated volatility of the developing world would increasingly throw the United States and western Europe on the defensive while presenting to the communists opportunities which they were inherently equipped to exploit.

There is a revealing passage in Herbert Matthews' *Fidel Castro*:

> Another conviction the Cuban leaders entertained was that the United States had lost ground politically everywhere in the world, would continue to lose more ground, and could not possibly recover what had been lost. They convinced themselves of the reality of American "imperialism" and considered that the United States had an empire in the British and French sense. They felt sure that the American empire would go the way of the other empires and that there would be more revolutions in Latin America.
>
> As Che Guevara put it to me, "Cuba is just a small incident. You will lose everywhere in the world."[28]

Sputnik and its immediate psychological aftermath contributed to this mood. Many communists must have made the linkage that Mao articulated in Moscow on November 18, 1957:

> The superiority of the anti-imperialist forces over the imperialist forces . . . has expressed itself in even more concentrated form and reached unprecedented heights with the Soviet Union's launching of the artificial satellites.

Compared with our knowledge of the Cuban leaders, we have relatively little insight into the minds of those in Hanoi who made the fateful decisions of 1958–1960. But a similar sense that history was on their side and that good communists had the duty to act to make the inevitable happen must have played a part in their decision to restart war in Indochina.[29]

In each of the communist capitals, however, considerations of domestic economic policy interwove with new, ambitious dispositions of foreign policy. These domestic issues were gradually to exert increasing leverage on foreign policy.

The Role of Domestic Policy

By the late 1950s, the economy of the Soviet Union had achieved technological maturity; that is, it had absorbed or had the capacity to absorb all the major modern technologies. It faced grave and chronic problems in collectivized agriculture; consumption was relatively low; but the economy was geared to a high rate of investment, which expanded in the 1950s to about 23 percent of GNP by 1960. GNP increased at an annual rate of over 6 percent in the period 1951–1955; and at a rate only slightly less in the period 1956–1960.

For Khrushchev a major consideration in not putting the first generation of ICBMs into production was his vision of greatly narrowing by 1970 the gap between United States and Soviet overall production levels and achieving primacy in steel and perhaps other major industrial products. He was prepared to enlarge Soviet military and economic assistance abroad in areas where such programs could advance specific major Soviet strategic objectives. But his basic objective was to increase the investment rate even at the cost of a reduced military budget. Sputnik and the ICBM bluff were not the real thing, although he played the game to the hilt; but there is an authentic ring to his vision of overtaking the United States in the production of key industrial products: "This will be a world-historic victory of socialism in peaceful competition with capitalism in the international arena."

This possibility not only tempered his allocations to the military but contributed, in the period 1957–1961, to his relatively cautious and patient stance towards communist techniques and policies of expansion.

In moving toward his vision of communism's (and China's) grand future, Mao presided over an economy that was about a half-century behind that of the Soviet Union. He had substantial assets in the industrial establishment the Japanese left behind in Manchuria; in the light industry complexes which had grown up in the coastal cities during the twentieth century; in the human beings trained for modern tasks in the long troubled period of China's preconditions for take-off; and, above all, in the unity he had achieved on the mainland with the creation of a strong central government in 1949. He confronted a grave and fundamental problem in generating adequate food supplies from a relatively primitive agriculture which engaged three-quarters of the population. But he did begin to move into the first sustained phase of Chinese industrial development in 1953–1958. Mainland China was evidently capable of mounting a take-off if it were prepared to concentrate on development and invest heavily enough in agriculture to overcome the massive, self-inflicted cost of collectivization in damping the peasant's incentives.

But as Mao measured his external ambitions against his economic and technological prospects under conventional policies of growth, he decided he could not wait. In the Great Leap Forward he sought to mobilize what must have appeared his two secret weapons for accelerated growth: the mass of available labor and his capacity for organizing and inspiring the people. This was, moreover, a use of corvée labor with resonance in the long sweep of Chinese history. If the Great Leap Forward worked, it would provide an industrial base for independent production of advanced weapons; a new model for the developing countries in general, as well as an ideological claim for Chinese leadership of the communist parties in these countries; and the resources for a global policy of military and economic assistance at points of strategic interest. And in 1958 he felt all this was possible even though United States GNP was (in 1957 dollars) about $2,500 per capita, the Soviet Union's was about $900, and mainland China's was well under $100.

Ho's domestic problem was, in microcosm, similar to Mao's. But relatively, as well as absolutely, he had a smaller industrial base, despite industrial and mining installations in the North. To move into take-off, he had to relax the pedantic and costly first phase of collectivization, although he could not wholly escape its grave costs, and concentrate on an initial phase of industrial development. Thus, his aid arrangements with Moscow in 1957. In terms of stages of growth, he, like Mao, sought to mount a take-off. Ho needed this kind of progress because, almost certainly to his surprise, the economy of Diem's South Vietnam, supported by American aid, moved forward much more rapidly after 1954 than did that of North Vietnam. And Ho believed he could move down the path of "building socialism" in the North while proceeding with his then relatively inexpensive politico-military adventures in South Vietnam and Laos.

The economy Castro inherited was more advanced than Ho's in technology, average income, and other measures of economic and social progress. But it was heavily dependent on sugar; it contained only limited industrial capacity; and the benefits that flowed from it were distributed inequitably. As Castro's policy evolved in 1959–1960, he sought both social movement toward equality, based on land reform and the rapid extension of the state's welfare services, and an economic surge, based on industrialization and a diversified agriculture less dependent on sugar. This was to be Cuba's strategy for the take-off, for which Castro sought and began to receive substantial economic assistance from the governments of the communist world.

The Failure of Domestic Hopes

In the end, all four of these visions of growth failed. Khrushchev failed because, beneath the surface of the glamorous Soviet growth rates of the 1950s, the leading heavy industry sectors of his mature economy were rapidly decelerating; and, since Khrushchev consciously and explicitly rejected a transition to the stage of the automobile and durable consumers goods, no new, rapidly expanding sectors emerged to counter the inevitable slow-down in the older sectors. He pushed the drive to technological maturity too far and fell off the curve. The Soviet economy slowed down in the 1960s and remained far behind the accelerating American economy.

Mao's Great Leap Forward failed, a failure exacerbated by the withdrawal of Soviet economic aid; and when some revival had been achieved by 1965, Mao plunged the economy into a second major setback, through the Cultural Revolution. He nevertheless pressed on with atomic weapons and missiles to develop a two-level economy with its modern weapons sector moving forward, the rest of industry and agriculture wallowing at levels that on average did not exceed the peak performance of the 1950s until the very end of the 1960s. His hope, and the widespread fear of the noncommunist world, that mainland China would provide in the 1960s a new and attractive pattern for accelerated economic growth did not come to pass. It failed not only because the Great Leap Forward did not work but also because Mao did not give the peasants of China the fertilizers and the minimum incentives necessary to lift the level of agricultural production at a rate compatible with rapid industrial growth and a high rate of population increase.

Ho's hopes in the 1950s for an industrial surge failed because, once launched on the path of taking over South Vietnam, he confronted mounting resistance from the South Vietnamese and their allies. So deep was his commitment to the vision of uniting the former French colonial empire in Asia under Hanoi's aegis that at each critical moment he threw more resources into the effort rather than draw back. And so, in the 1960s, North Vietnam became a tragic funnel for the military supplies required for North Vietnamese manpower to carry on the obsessive effort—supplies granted by Moscow, Peking, and other communist capitals, each for its own reasons. The North Vietnamese economy stagnated and then declined, sustained from abroad with supplies of food, petroleum, and other minimum working capital needed for mere survival. A generation of North Vietnamese were decimated as they created havoc throughout old French Indochina.

Despite massive and sustained net aid at the remarkable level of some $300 million per annum (for a population of only 8 million), Castro could not get Cuba organized to move forward in sustained growth. With this subsidy, he carried out something of his vision of a society providing welfare services (notably medical care and education) to the bulk of the people. But neither industrialization nor diversification of agriculture took hold. A decade after 1960 his great campaign was to produce 10 million tons of sugar. He exhausted the momentum of his revolution in unwise policies, poorly administered, leaving his people exhausted and apathetic. Like Mao in Asia, Castro lost in Latin America of the 1960s the opportunity to produce a powerful example of progress for the developing world. As with the leaders in Hanoi, dreams of expanded regional power diverted energy and talent, thought and resources away from the humane tasks of economic and social progress on which the claim of legitimacy for his revolution ultimately depended.

In different ways, the dispositions made and the balances struck between domestic and foreign objectives in the communist capitals between 1957 and 1961 did not prove viable. But that this would prove the case was by no means clear to the somewhat bedeviled men who bore responsibility in Eisenhower's second term.

5

The Eisenhower Second Term: The Domestic Scene

Introduction

In a poignant passage, Eisenhower notes in his memoirs that he wrote to a friend on November 18, 1957: "Since July 25th of 1956, when Nasser announced the nationalization of the Suez, I cannot remember a day that has not brought its major or minor crisis. . . . Crisis has now become 'normalcy.' "[1] And that was the way it was to be for the next fifteen years for Eisenhower and his successors. The relative calm of the period from Stalin's death to Nasser's takeover of Suez was unique in the quarter-century after the end of the Second World War.

The twin engines of turbulence which Eisenhower had to confront in his second term were precisely those which engaged the communist leaders as they debated and made their several dispositions: the nuclear question; and the accelerated drive towards independence and modernization in the turbulent developing continents.

In addition—like Khrushchev, Mao, Ho, and Castro—Eisenhower faced domestic issues that suffused his actions in military and foreign policy.

In considering here the interplay of domestic and external policy in the last three years of the Eisenhower administration, we shall first apply successively the four analytic tools which shape this book: the problems thrown up by the stage of growth to which the United States had come by the late 1950s; the manner in which the political process mobilized the nation's resources and allocated them among the three abiding tasks of government: security, welfare, and the maintenance of balance in the constitutional order; the major actions taken by the Eisenhower administration in pursuit of the national interest; and Eisenhower's approach to his problems as they reflected facets of the American operating style. The analysis of this period closes with an account of the emergence in the late 1950s of a widespread consensus on the directions American domestic and foreign policy should take in the years ahead and John Kennedy's relation to those views.

"A SPUTTERING ECONOMY"[2]

THE American economy slowed down briefly in 1954, after the Korean war boom, expanded vigorously to 1957, and then moved erratically for the rest of the decade. The result was a marked deceleration in growth and real income, and higher average rates of unemployment. Per-capita disposable income at 1958 prices was $1726 in 1953; $1844 in 1957; only $1883 three years later. Unemployment averaged 4.2 percent for the years 1953–1957; 5.9 percent for 1958–1960.

All this converged with the post-Sputnik international trauma. The USSR was proceeding at an annual growth rate of about 6 percent, more than twice the U.S. rate. The awkward performance of the American economy in these years reinforced Khrushchev's image of an ardent Avis trying harder and closing fast on a bedeviled Hertz.

Looked at more closely, the American economy was feeling the effects of deeply rooted problems. One of the most important was an emerging balance-of-payments problem that would no longer permit a cavalier American approach to inflation.

Since 1945 the United States had pursued policies at home and abroad which allowed its abnormally high postwar gold stock to run down, supplying to others reserves they required as their economies grew stronger. This course was based on the hard-earned lessons of the interwar years, when the United States failed to behave steadily as a surplus nation on whose performance the international monetary system had come to depend. From 1950 a large favorable trade balance was outweighed by military, aid, travel, and net private investment outlays abroad. The Treasury's gold stock fell from its 1949 peak of $24.4 billion to $22.8 billion in 1957. It then fell rapidly to $17.8 billion in 1960. Anxiety about the American balance of payments began to suffuse the international monetary community and enter into domestic policy toward the economy.

American prices had risen sharply in 1956–1957 and, contrary to historical experience, they continued to rise in the recession of 1957–1958. Wage increases in key industries exceeded increases in productivity. The gap was passed along by industry in higher prices, despite idle capacity and slack demand.

Those who argued for a purposeful policy of Keynesian expansion in

1958 had to face this persistent inflationary phenomenon not merely as a domestic problem but also as an international one. Arthur Burns evokes the new shadow cast across American economic policy:

> During 1958, imports rose sharply, exports fell, and our stocks of gold were cut by two billion dollars. More ominous still, foreign financiers, who hitherto appeared to have unbounded faith in American finances, began to whisper serious doubts whether the integrity of the dollar could be counted on in the future.[3]

In this environment the Eisenhower administration acted strongly in monetary and fiscal policy, truncating the business expansion that began in April 1958. It moved from a $12.9 billion federal budget deficit in 1959 to a quarter-billion surplus in 1960. Eisenhower unsuccessfully made the issue of federal spending central to the congressional elections in November. In the rest of his term, he fought pressures to expand security or welfare outlays in the federal budget. His concern was inflation and the related deterioration of the balance of payments.[4]

The constraint on public expenditures, which ran as a paramount theme through the Eisenhower years, became obsessive toward the end of his second term; although, as we shall see, federal as well as state and local budgets expanded in ways which did not quite match the President's rhetoric.

Behind these new immediate pressures a troubled Eisenhower confronted more fundamental forces only dimly understood, just as an ebullient Khrushchev, at the same time, did not fully understand the decelerating forces already at work in the Soviet economy.

The United States had come by the mid-1950s toward the end of a stage of growth which had begun with Henry Ford's Model T and the moving assembly line. Thus far the mass production, sale, and use of the automobile had been the most powerful innovation of the twentieth century—like the nineteenth century railroad—because of its multiple effects. It became a significant, if not dominating, market for steel and engineering products, rubber, glass, oil, and light electronics; it restructured life along suburban lines; it linked rural to urban markets in new, more flexible ways; it created a requirement for large-scale sales and servicing industries; it set up massive social overhead requirements for roads and parking facilities; it played a critical role in a social revolution touching patterns of life from courting to a massive increase in the number of Americans in suburbs. It was accompanied by—and in various indirect ways related to—a boom in the production of various durable consumers goods and processed foods which came to fill homes, as rising incomes and suburban life made personal service expensive and inaccessible: washing and drying machines; vacuum cleaners; the electric refrigerator; the automatic furnace, and then air conditioning; canned and then frozen foods.

The depression and then the war interrupted this pattern, yielding a series of structural reforms (including revolutionary social security legislation) and a return to high levels of employment.[5]

The Employment Act of 1946 confirmed the responsibility of the federal government for the level of employment already registered by the voters of the 1930s; and the lessons learned from the new Keynesian consensus and practical experience, buttressed by the stabilizers built into social security legislation, permitted the stage of high mass-consumption to roll on for another decade after 1945.

Private automobiles in use per million population had increased only from 189,000 in 1929 to 200,000 in 1939, and to 201,000 in 1945. It rose to 323,000 by 1956, at the cyclical peak. The drive to the suburbs was resumed at full throttle after 1945, and the wide range of industries and services linked to the diffusion of the automobile resumed their momentum of the 1920s.

But there was a limit to growth and momentum in the economy: by 1957, 75 percent of American families owned an automobile; of homes with electricity 81 percent had a television set; 96 percent a refrigerator; 78 percent a washing machine; and 67 percent a vacuum cleaner. It became clear that the now enormous automobile and durable consumer goods complex was waning as the basis for American growth in the 1950s.[6] In fact, the growth rates of the late 1950s would have been still lower without the expansion in state and local expenditures to support the expanding suburbs; the roadbuilding to sustain intensified use of the automobile; and the progressive expansion in social security outlays.

The old leading sectors were losing their capacity to drive the American economy forward in Eisenhower's second term. American politics was beginning to reflect what it was Americans would want as per-capita income rose: expanded resources for urban renewal, education, and health, as well as the first awareness of the need to do something about water pollution. These were harbingers of the next stage—the search for quality. They foreshadowed a substantial increase in public outlays in both absolute and relative terms. The leading sectors of the American economy were moving from particular lines of manufacture to certain services in which it was uncertain whether technology would provide the lift in productivity enjoyed in earlier stages of growth.

In the period 1957–1960 the deep roots of the claims for additional public outlays were not widely understood; and the "big spenders" were assaulted by Eisenhower, with vigor and an authentic sense of righteousness.[7] He was the last President to govern in the stage of high mass-consumption. A water pollution bill that would have placed some responsibility in the federal government was vetoed in 1960.

Meanwhile, the movement of the stages of growth elsewhere in the world was having its impact on the American economy. Western Europe and the Japanese moved forward from postwar recovery into the stage of high mass-consumption. America's earlier entrance into this stage had provided a comparative advantage in the industries associated with it, notably automobiles, strip steel, and a wide range of durable consumers goods. By the close of the 1950s Europe and Japan were expanding output rapidly under conditions of efficiency permitted by the mass markets which had emerged with the steady postwar expansion of incomes. International competition increased in fields where the United States had enjoyed a comfortable advantage in the first postwar decade. And the pressure was exacerbated by the aging of the American capital stock relative to newly equipped plants abroad.

The underlying problems of the American economy—and American society—could not be solved merely by a struggle to constrain federal expenditures. But neither could the answer lie in simple Keynesian expansion of public deficits at the cost of a high rate of inflation. Like everyone else's, the American balance-of-payments position had become marginal. The special international economic advantages the United States had enjoyed in the first postwar decade gave way to a more normal competitive position, as the stages of growth moved forward on the world scene as well as in the United States.

Growth and Welfare: Public Resource Allocations in the Second Eisenhower Administration

The following table compares public expenditures (federal, state, and local) for the calendar years 1956 and 1960 as proportions of GNP under five broad headings which reflect the abiding tasks of government.[8]

TABLE 5–1

GOVERNMENT EXPENDITURES AS PROPORTIONS OF GNP, 1956 AND 1960

	1956	1960
National Security	11.1%	10.5%
Interest	1.4	1.5
Law, Order, and Administration	1.9	2.2
Economic and Environmental Services	3.4	4.2
Social Welfare Services	7.0	10.0
TOTAL	25.7	28.5*

* Due to rounding of sub-totals, they fall 0.1 percent short of total. GNP increased in these years from $419 to $504 billion in current prices: in constant (1958) prices from $446 to $488 billion.

Within the volume of real resources, expanding at an average rate not much over 2 percent, state and local expenditures, responding to strongly felt needs in the communities, rose from 8.5 percent to 9.9 percent of GNP; while federal outlays rose from 17.2 percent to 18.6 percent of GNP.

The relative constraint on security outlays in the federal budget was outweighed by the expansion of social security coverage (1954) and the expansion of transport outlays, notably for the national highway network (1956). These movements reflected two major domestic initiatives of the Eisenhower years.[9] The rising proportion of GNP going to these civil purposes reflected also, however, the slow rise of GNP in the latter years of the decade in the face of relatively inflexible increases in outlays flowing from past legislation. Federal expenditures calculated as a percentage of GNP at full employment rose only from 16.9 percent to 17.4 percent between 1956 and 1960.

THE EMERGING RACE PROBLEM

THE critical constitutional issue of the late 1950s was the status of Negroes in the wake of the Supreme Court desegregation decision of 1954 and of more profound changes taking place in the society and in Negro attitudes toward unequal de facto status within it. These constitutional and quasi-constitutional issues of race related, of course, to welfare allocations: for education, urban redevelopment, and social welfare; but that linkage was less clear in the late 1950s than it was to become in the following decade.

The race question was being transformed by the urbanization and northward migration of Negroes and the enlarged opportunities and frustrations that they found. The following table shows the pace of Negro urbanization in the 1950s relative to previous decades.

TABLE 5–2
RURAL VERSUS URBAN NEGRO POPULATION[10]

Year	Urban (millions)	Rural (millions)
1910	2.7	7.1
1920	3.5	6.9
1930	5.2	6.7
1940	6.2	6.6
1950	9.4	5.6
1960	13.8	5.1

Source: Statistical Abstract of the United States, 1930, 1946, 1962.

Between 1940 and 1960 the number of Negroes in the South remained about constant; but the number in the North increased from 2.6 to 7.2 million. The race question in the 1960s was palpably a national, not a regional, issue. The issues confronted by Eisenhower, however, still bore a distinct regional cast.

Eisenhower's major initiative and his major crisis in race relations came in 1957. By the end of 1955 the South became volatile as Negroes in Montgomery, Alabama, began a boycott campaign to end Jim Crow practices on buses; and White Citizens Councils moved toward a dangerous polarization by applying economic pressures against those seeking desegregation in any form. Eisenhower, weighing the whole environment in the South, including the inhibitions on Negro registration and voting, proposed in 1956 a civil rights commission, a civil rights division in the Justice Department, new laws to enforce voting rights, and revision of the law which would permit the federal government to seek in the civil courts preventive relief in civil rights cases.

The legislation was buried in the Senate Judiciary Committee; but, as Eisenhower notes, it was not without its political effects:

> The administration had steered a difficult course between extremist firebrands and extremist diehards. This was due to conviction, not politics. But it is interesting that in the election of 1956, according to a *Congressional Quarterly*, I enlarged the sizable vote I had received four years earlier among Negroes of the North and throughout the South. In the South the Republican national ticket picked up Kentucky, West Virginia, and Louisiana, but lost Missouri. And in thirty-five congressional districts outside the South with a Negro population of 10 percent or more, we increased the Republican vote from an average of 42 per cent in 1952 to 47 percent in 1956.[11]

Eisenhower was no doubt heartened by these results. There is no reason to doubt the sincerity of his conviction that the extension of the Negro vote was both a powerful and widely acceptable lever on racial inequity as a whole. He therefore persisted in 1957 with his civil rights legislation. After a famous battle over the jury-trial provision in the bill, the first civil rights legislation in eighty-two years was passed in the Senate and signed into law on September 8.

Three future presidents were involved in the drama. Vice-President Nixon, presiding over the Senate, proposed that the bill bypass committee and come directly to the Senate floor. This embarrassed the Democrats, including Senator John Kennedy, who supported a proposal that the bill proceed to committee in the normal way, subject to discharge in a week.[12] In a major decision, Kennedy, already on the defensive toward liberals, decided to back the jury-trial proposal. Majority leader Lyndon Johnson, who led the effort in the Senate, believed the jury-trial proposal would bring over enough marginal votes to defeat a filibuster.

This provision required jury trial for local voting officials who defied court orders on the registration of Negroes. It had become a negative symbol to liberals and the last stand of moderate southerners who knew in their hearts that Negro voting could not and should not be obstructed as in the past. Kennedy's decision to support this provision against liberal opposition protected Senator John Pastore's flank in New England and may have made possible ultimate passage of the bill.

But, as Eisenhower acknowledged, it was Johnson's leadership and ingenuity in finding the compromise formula and mobilizing the votes to break Senator Strom Thurmond's filibuster that transformed an initiative that might have been another political but empty gesture (as in 1956), into a limited but substantial movement forward.[13] No major national political figure was pursuing a Southern Strategy in 1957.

Almost immediately on the passage of the civil rights bill, Eisenhower confronted the crisis in Little Rock, beginning on September 3.[14] Governor Orval Faubus of Arkansas revived the doctrine of nullification: he ordered the National Guard to obstruct the ruling of a federal judge, acting on the petition of the Little Rock school board, to integrate the high school. In a byzantine series of maneuvers, Faubus appeared to interpose the Constitution of Arkansas as a barrier to federal law. When that gambit failed, he withdrew the National Guard and opened the way for obstruction of integration by mob action. Eisenhower ordered a thousand paratroopers of the 101st Airborne Division to the scene on September 24th. The crisis gradually subsided; although for local political reasons Faubus continued the battle in various forms down to June 1959.

By later standards both the 1957 legislation and the Arkansas crisis were limited affairs, but the intense feelings aroused illuminated the depth of the problem America confronted. Suddenly Americans observed—and felt—some of the emotions which had almost torn the nation apart exactly a century before. It became clear that the Supreme Court decision of 1954 was not the occasion for self-congratulation on progress achieved but the beginning of difficult times.

This opening of old American wounds had an impact on the world which, in turn, affected the attitudes of some toward foreign policy. The great postwar superpower stood before all as facing major unresolved problems. Eisenhower was sensitive to this, and it may have tipped his policy marginally in a more liberal direction than if he had made his decisions on purely domestic grounds. The strong criticisms abroad of American racism had also a quite different effect: it made some Southern internationalists turn inward, in degree at least, and increased the weight of isolationist and quasi-isolationist sentiments.

These moods converged with anxieties stirred by the recession of 1957–1958. It was mild by pre-1939 standards. Nevertheless, the unemployment rate of 6.8 percent for 1958 was higher than any experienced in the previous decade; complacency was shaken and memories of the depression of the 1930s were revived.

It was against this background of concern at home, where ground believed firm moved and shook, that the Eisenhower administration and the nation confronted the post-Sputnik crises in nuclear affairs and in the developing world.

6

Sputnik, Military Policy, and Space

Soviet and American Approaches to Missiles

The Soviet launching of the first earth satellite in October 1957 had consequences which touched many aspects of American life, from the nation's self-image to its educational system; from the role of scientists in public life to the fate of presidential candidates. Sputnik also posed direct and immediate questions of military and space policy. The big booster required for the first Sputnik (and the even more impressive Soviet orbiting of an 1100-pound vehicle, plus dog, on November 5) confirmed that the Soviet Union had acquired the most fundamental tool necessary for an ICBM capable of directly striking the United States. And quite aside from its military meaning, these and subsequent Soviet performances indicated that Moscow had mounted a more ambitious space program than the United States.

Up to a point, quite rational considerations appear to have governed the differing approaches of Washington and Moscow to missiles. For Washington, the central fact was that the United States had emerged from the Second World War with a first-rate strategic air force; and, in the postwar years, it not only developed new bombers but also acquired forward bases in Europe, Japan, and elsewhere. The United States clearly commanded a powerful deterrent to a major direct Soviet military thrust. The airborne nuclear counter to preponderant communist ground forces in Europe and elsewhere was the foundation for Eisenhower's military and budgetary policies in his first term.[1] The missile was not ignored by the United States. From 1945 research and development went forward on the basis of German experience with the V-2; but the greater accuracy of aircraft made them the preferred delivery vehicle in the short run.

The explosion of U.S. and Soviet thermonuclear devices in 1953 foreshadowed weapons of such destructive range as to compensate for missile inaccuracy; and the 1954 American breakthrough in reducing the size of a thermonuclear warhead made an ICBM clearly feasible. An ICBM development contract for the Atlas missile was issued in January 1955.

Each of the military services moved forward with missile projects; and in 1955 they were in a position to begin to absorb substantial resources. By 1957, the Air Force was developing the Atlas and Titan ICBMs and the Thor IRBM; the Army, the Jupiter IRBM; and the Navy, the revolutionary, solid-fuel Polaris IRBM. Both at the time and in retrospect, Eisenhower could claim that the nation's retaliatory power was assured in the late 1950s by the aircraft in SAC, and that his administration had recognized the coming of the missile age, developed the requisite technology, and asked for and received from Congress the funds to finance production programs.[2] These programs proceeded in a setting of ambiguous priorities, considerable administrative confusion, and imperfect linkage to the scientific world;[3] but they proceeded, goaded on at least as much by interservice rivalry as by concern for what the Russians might be up to.[4]

For the Soviet Union the possibility of delivering nuclear and then thermonuclear warheads with missiles had a different and more urgent meaning than for the United States. Moscow had lived and conducted its policy since 1945 in the shadow of American strategic superiority.[5] Its large ground forces in a sense held western Europe hostage; and Stalin was prepared to consolidate his hold on eastern Europe and blockade Berlin in 1948–1949 despite the American nuclear monopoly. But these and other exercises in the expansion of Soviet power were undoubtedly conducted against a background of some anxiety in the face of the American nuclear delivery capability. And even after nuclear weapons were acquired in 1949—and thermonuclear weapons in 1953—the Soviet nuclear delivery capacity with aircraft could not match SAC. The Second World War had not given the Russian air force experience in long-range mass-flying, targeting, and navigation. Further, the American base structure and the air defense system rapidly building in North America during 1953 seemed to forecast a more or less permanent Soviet disadvantage.[6] The Soviets may thus have felt that if they relied for nuclear weapons delivery on a strategic air command they would remain indefinitely inferior. In relation to SAC they may have felt somewhat as the Germans did about the British Navy in the first half of the century.

On the other hand, Russia had a distinguished history of scientific contributions to rocketry, reaching back to Czarist times, and had used short-range rockets extensively in the Second World War; the fundamental talents in the relevant fields of basic science and engineering were evidently available; and the missile business was, in some of its dimensions, an extension of artillery, in which Russia had traditionally excelled. Moreover, it solved the problem of external bases, since the ICBM could strike America from Russian soil.

Thus, the whole enterprise appeared to provide a way of bypassing an adversary's main strength.

SOVIET AND AMERICAN APPROACHES TO SPACE

AGAINST this background of ardor, it was natural also, in a program under unified military direction, to plan the series of space demonstrations that began with the first Sputnik and ran down to the Gagarin flight of April 12, 1961.

A Soviet technical weakness relative to the United States helped give it a considerable, if transient, psychological and political advantage. Soviet miniaturization of thermonuclear weapons lagged behind that of the United States. Therefore, Moscow went quickly toward very large boosters—larger than those judged necessary in the U.S. to mount a thermonuclear warhead on an ICBM. This proved an initial advantage in space demonstrations. The big boosters could throw heavier pieces of hardware into space.

It is unclear, even now, what military applications for orbiting satellites the Soviet leaders may have had in mind, notably in their swift movement to manned flight. It is clear that they had a firmer grip on the psychological potentialities of the enterprise than their American counterparts. But one can doubt that even the most hopeful and imaginative Soviet advocates of space spectaculars predicted their full initial impact.

The pre-Sputnik American space program was a limited affair, dominated by scientific rather than psychological and political considerations. On July 29, 1955, Eisenhower announced that the United States would undertake to orbit a satellite in connection with the International Geophysical Year—an eighteen month period starting July 1, 1957, in which scientists would collaborate on a worldwide basis to advance knowledge of the earth and its environment.[7]

Eisenhower notes (not quite accurately) that there was no appreciation in the United States government that the launching of the first Sputnik would have a major psychological and political effect; and there was, objectively, no reason for surprise that the Soviet Union might launch the first satellite.[8] The Soviets had made clear as early as April 1955 that they were working on a satellite; at an international meeting in June 1957, their scientists reminded their colleagues of their intention; and as early as November 1956 the American intelligence services estimated that a Soviet satellite could be launched after November 1957. When it was discovered in mid-1956 that the Jupiter booster had the capacity to launch a satellite before the end of the year, the military were divided, but on balance wished to avoid diverting those at work on military missiles. The scientists saw no reason to alter the Vanguard plan or contaminate their enterprise with a sinister military connection. Only a few sensed the emotions that would be stirred in observing for the first time a man-made object, twinkling in orbit beyond the earth's atmosphere.

Post-Sputnik American Military and Space Programs

Immediately after the first Sputnik, Eisenhower ordered an Army Redstone rocket prepared as a backstop for the Navy Vanguard rocket; and, after an initial Vanguard failure in December, the Army successfully launched the first United States satellite on January 31, 1958.

Goaded by the unexpected intensity of public concern and a strong purposeful congressional reaction, led by Lyndon Johnson in the Senate, the Eisenhower administration in the first half of 1958 created the post of Special Assistant to the President for Science and Technology, first filled by James Killian of M.I.T. It also initiated the National Defense Education Act to expand resources for teaching and research in science, mathematics, and languages; and it strengthened central control over missiles in the Pentagon and elevated their effective priority. Finally, the administration reorganized the Department of Defense, reducing the role of the services, thus strengthening the hand of the Secretary of Defense and the Joint Chiefs of Staff as a corporate body, and created the National Aeronautics and Space Administration.

In its first years NASA mounted a purposeful scientific program which surpassed that of the Soviet Union; and it started work on the big boosters and astronaut training which were to make possible the moon flights of the 1960s. The issue of manned flight to the moon was debated within the Eisenhower administration; but the cost of the enterprise led the President to refuse commitment.[9] NASA's budget rose from about a third of a billion dollars in fiscal 1959 to a billion dollars in fiscal 1961.

The military budget presented to the Congress in 1958, however, was in real terms at about the same level as the previous year. Eisenhower successfully resisted pressures from many directions to enlarge military outlays in the post-Sputnik mood.

Eisenhower and the Critics of His Military Policy

Neither the pressures on Eisenhower nor his response was a new phenomenon in Washington. A hard core of concern had been growing for some years among those knowledgeable in military affairs. It took its start from the foreseeable Soviet acquisition of thermonuclear weapons and the achievement of one form or another of an effective delivery system against the United States. These developments were perceived to strike at the foundations of an American policy of primary reliance on the threat of nuclear response to a nonnuclear provocation.

As the Eisenhower administration came to responsibility, it received a report, instigated by Secretary of State Acheson in the final phase of the Truman administration, on the gloomy prospects ahead in the world of thermonuclear weapons. It urged that the nature and dangers of the arms race be fully explained to the American public; that legislation governing atomic secrets be revised to permit collaboration with the nation's allies; and that an effective air defense be developed.[10] In 1953 a serious air defense program was set in motion; but the other two recommendations were, for the time, rejected. The plea for a policy of "candor" was set aside for a complex of reasons, but above all because it was feared it might lead to an irrational expansion of military outlays. The debate on candor was converted into the Atoms for Peace proposal, which yielded the International Atomic Energy Agency, a substantial creative initiative of the Eisenhower years.[11]

As the 1950s wore on, and the intensity of the Soviet drive for missiles wedded to thermonuclear weapons was sensed, along with evidence of Soviet progress in weaponry along a broad front, anxiety increased among those who were knowledgeable. In June 1955, for example, a group was assembled by Nelson Rockefeller at Quantico to prepare proposals for the forthcoming Summit Conference at Geneva.[12]

Assessing the environment of U.S.–Soviet negotiations in June 1955, the group reported a "unanimous belief . . . that the U.S. now enjoys a significant but transitory period of over-all strength vis-à-vis the Soviet bloc." The report argued that

> Because of the technological acceleration of the arms race and the nature of our adversary, we run the risk that he may, at some stage, achieve a technological breakthrough, and that at that time he would be prepared to exploit his advantage by initiating an attack on the United States. Or he might use his superiority for large-scale atomic blackmail, against the United States or other powers.

Because of its timing, the most significant of these public and private commentaries was the Gaither report. In April 1957 a committee was set up under H. Rowan Gaither, Jr., Chairman of the Board of the Ford Foundation, to examine the problem of civil defense. By a process familiar to those who have participated in such committees, it widened its frame of reference to embrace the whole field of strategic policy. Its report was filed in October, in the wake of the first Sputnik; and in November a formal meeting of the National Security Council considered its recommendations. Eisenhower reports its findings as follows:

> The Gaither Report . . . included some sobering observations: (1) that the Soviet Gross National Product, though no more than one-third that of the United States, was increasing at a much faster rate than ours; (2) that the Soviet Union was spending on its armed forces and heavy industry an amount about *equal* to that of the United States; (3) that the Soviet Union had enough fissionable material for at least 1500 nuclear weapons in 4500 long- and short-range jet bombers, 250–300 long-range submarines, and an extensive air defense system; (4) that for more than a year, the Soviet Union had been producing ballistic missiles with a 700-mile range; (5) that the Soviet Union could, by late 1959, possibly launch an attack against the United States with 100 intercontinental ballistic missiles carrying megaton nuclear warheads; and (6) that if such an attack should come, our civilian population would be unprotected, and the planes in our Strategic Air Command (SAC), except for a small fraction of them on "alert status," would be vulnerable.[13]

The generalized anxieties of 1955 (in the Quantico Panel report for example) were now quite specific: Could the Soviet Union develop a missile capability for destroying SAC bases which might make a sudden first-strike rational? Under such circumstances, could the Soviet Union develop a capacity for destroying a sufficient proportion of the American population so that a first strike might be tempting? In the face of expanding Soviet nuclear delivery capabilities, could United States strategic power effectively deter a limited Soviet movement by conventional forces, in Europe or elsewhere, or would expanded United States conventional forces be required to deter such enterprises? In the face of these changes in the strategic balance, including an American vulnerability to direct attack, how could the NATO alliance be kept stable?

Eisenhower responded to the recommendations of the Gaither report by accelerating dispersal of SAC bases and aircraft and by expanding the proportion of aircraft on alert. The American ICBM program was also accelerated, designed to yield in the early 1960s more missiles at sea and in hardened bases not vulnerable to a first strike. An elaborate and expensive system of fallout shelters was rejected; and conventional forces were not expanded.

7

Sputnik and the Atlantic Alliance

The Western European Perspective

At the end of October 1957, Eisenhower took stock of the post-Sputnik situation with British Prime Minister Harold Macmillan in Washington and agreed to make the regular December meeting of NATO in Paris a summit gathering.

The summit meeting of NATO took place against a somber background. The peoples of Europe, as elsewhere, had been impressed by the apparent surge in Soviet power Sputnik symbolized. The November meeting in Moscow of the communist leaders had projected an image of unity, ambition, and confidence. A year after the disarray of Budapest and the failure earlier in 1957 of Mao's Hundred Flowers experiment, the communist world appeared to have fully recovered.

The West had also moved beyond the days of Budapest and Suez. Macmillan, taking over from Anthony Eden, had restored a working accord with Washington, although painful memories were etched in many British minds. In March 1957 treaties signed in Rome created the European Economic Community and the European Atomic Energy Community. They were accelerated by Europe's frustrations in dealing with the postcolonial Middle East on one hand and with Washington on the other. But European security still depended on the United States. And the post-Sputnik blues were deepened not only by American economic recession and the failure of the first Vanguard launching but also by Eisenhower's stroke on November 25, only three weeks before he courageously flew to Paris.

The strictly military meaning of the satellite launchings for western

Europe was somewhat different from its meaning across the Atlantic. The Soviet Sputnik signaled a foreseeable capability to launch a weapon directed against the United States rather than against western Europe. Western Europe had been living for at least the previous year and a half under an explicit threat of Soviet IRBM attack, to which the American SAC, and to a degree the RAF Bomber Command, were the only serious deterrents. The Soviet satellites did not radically alter the European security problem except that to some extent they shook confidence that the United States would maintain sufficient retaliatory power to hold the Soviet Union in check. The Soviets might have an operational ICBM capability some time before the United States. Conceivably, this might lead to an acute vulnerability of American air bases as well as the continental United States, and leave the West without an effective shield.

This possibility led promptly to an American desire to mount IRBM bases in Europe. IRBM bases were vulnerable to a first strike; but perhaps less vulnerable than aircraft sitting on forward bases. In any case, they seemed psychologically and politically more appropriate to mount in the post-Sputnik era than more aircraft on European airfields. Lacking firm knowledge of the pace of Soviet ICBM production, it seemed prudent for the Alliance to concur in principle, although when domestic politics was consulted, only three European nations proved willing to accept the Jupiters or Thors.

In addition, the pace of Soviet military technology led Washington to reconsider its policy of nuclear secrecy towards allies. American spokesmen foreshadowed measures which would not only give Europeans increased access to nuclear weapons but also expand the possibility of European contribution to nuclear research and development. But when the limits of American domestic politics were explored on this point, notably in the Joint Atomic Energy Committee, the permissible increase in European access to U.S. nuclear weapons and technology proved rather narrow.

The most concrete possibility was the offer to interested NATO nations of the technology of the nuclear propulsion system used in submarines. This was put forward at the December 1957 meeting of NATO (and in 1958 to de Gaulle) under the condition that Congress agree. It never did.[1]

For European politicians, the 1957 American proposals to tighten the Alliance in these two respects—IRBM bases and a drawing of Europe closer into the world of nuclear weapons—posed a problem. They came at a time when popular feeling in Europe looked eagerly to alternatives to the nuclear arms race, which hung like a sword of Damocles over Europe's head. There was lively political pressure to explore the possibilities of a high-level arms-control negotiation with the Soviet Union. Moscow, sensing this popular mood in the West, proposed such discussions almost in the form of an ultimatum.

As European leaders confronted this array of problems (while rather enjoying their enhanced importance in the Alliance) they confronted three specific and searching questions.

First, if IRBM bases were granted in order to retain Western retaliatory power over the interval of possible Soviet monopoly in the ICBM, and if the Alliance were tightened for this purpose, where would the Alliance stand when the United States had created its own ICBM capabilities plus a capability to launch IRBMs from nuclear-powered submarines? Was a more intense commitment to the North Atlantic Alliance justified on these relatively short-run grounds?

Second, was it not necessary, in any case, for western Europe to develop its own IRBM capability and thus have a retaliatory power vis-à-vis the Soviet Union, independent of decisions made in Washington or in which Washington had to concur? Would Washington be prepared to risk hideous damage to American society in order to face down a Soviet ultimatum directed at, say, West Berlin, Paris, or London? Was it fair and wise to confront any third nation with this kind of choice?

Third, what in fact were the possibilities for a degree of mutual Soviet and American withdrawal from the heart of Europe? Was there any safe way to experiment with the neutralization of central Europe as proposed in the Rapacki Plan, launched on October 2, 1957, and in George Kennan's Reith Lectures of November–December 1957? These questions would have to be answered before the European peoples would face and accept additional security burdens and risks.

These crosscurrents of thought and feeling in the Atlantic interacted with the twists and turns of Khrushchev's ambivalent policy of the post-Sputnik period; and they did so with uncertainty about the military capabilities Moscow actually commanded.[2]

DEALING WITH NUCLEAR BLACKMAIL

WITH respect to nuclear matters, Sputnik finally led to a tightening of the special nuclear relation between London and Washington in 1958—a move which cast a long and not wholly benign shadow. It led also to the setting up of IRBM bases in Britain, Italy, and Turkey. A NATO stockpile of tactical nuclear weapons was created; but as the consequences of their actual use became clear in war games, NATO doctrine moved in the direction of creating an enlarged conventional capability to deal with possible limited Soviet probes, to enforce "a pause" on Moscow, and thus avoid automatic use of nuclear weapons.

Khrushchev responded to the new IRBM bases with generous and colorful threats, underlining the vulnerability of western Europe to Soviet nuclear attack with medium-range ballistic missiles. As in the Suez crisis of 1956, nuclear blackmail was evoked during the Lebanon–Jordan crisis of August 1958 and the November 1958 Berlin crisis.

Three American Initiatives

Putting aside the limited British nuclear capability, Moscow's nuclear blackmail posed a deep psychological problem for western Europe: it was under explicit nuclear threat but was dependent on the United States to deter or respond credibly to that threat.

In the end, the task of the United States was to prove that, despite the direct threat to America represented by emerging Soviet nuclear delivery capabilities, it could be a reliable ally in facing down threats to European interests, while mitigating the European sense of impotence through participation short of the right to manufacture, own, or fire nuclear weapons. The full test of this posture came in the 1960s, but three important initiatives were launched during the Eisenhower administration.

First, the two-key system. It was agreed that the American IRBMs mounted in Britain, Italy, and Turkey could only be fired with the assent of both the United States and the other nation concerned. This principle was later extended to American nuclear weapons which would, in case of war, be delivered by aircraft or other vehicles owned by allies.

Second, within the framework of the two-key system, tactical nuclear delivery systems were provided to NATO members on a national basis. The precedent raised a problem, however, when the issue arose of providing IRBMs to NATO, in succession to the Thors and Jupiters. Missiles capable of striking the Soviet Union were judged more sensitive politically than tactical delivery systems, posing greater risks in case of accident or loss of control.

Third, partly to solve this problem, Secretary of State Christian Herter floated at the December 1960 meeting of NATO a proposal for a multilateral force of medium-range ballistic missiles. The Paris communique of December 18 observed that "the Council took note of the United States suggestion with great interest and instructed the permanent representatives to study the suggestion and related matters in detail." This was the formal beginning of the story of the MLF, the multinational seaborne missile flotilla that never put to sea.

The Special Problem of de Gaulle

The nuclear issue arose in a quite different form in 1958 when de Gaulle returned to power in Paris. Washington was faced with a genteel version of the problem that bedeviled Moscow in its relations with Peking.

There is a certain historical legitimacy in the parallelism between the French and Chinese responses to the nuclear age. Both France and China had enjoyed positions of self-conscious primacy in the centuries before the industrial revolution took hold. Deeply ingrained in both nations were memories not only of military and political grandeur but also of virtually undisputed cultural hegemony. For France in one part of its being, the emergence of Britain, then Germany, and finally the United States as great powers on the basis of industrial and commercial strength was an affront. French life adjusted rather slowly to the imperatives and opportunities of applied science and technology. It suffered humiliation at the hands of Britain in 1815 and Prussia in 1870–1871. Then came the terrible costs of the First World War, and abject defeat in the Second World War. For China the intrusions of Britain, the United States, and Russia in the nineteenth century and the quick emergence of Japan were similar affronts. China, also, was slow to adjust its values and institutions to the post-Newtonian world.

Against this background the possession of nuclear weapons appealed to both France and China. Such weapons appeared to violate the proportionality between industrial potential and military strength. France could not hope to match the United States or the Soviet Union in total deliverable powers of destruction, but it could still put itself in a position to threaten hideous damage to an enemy. If Moscow could not be totally deterred by a *force de frappe*, a modest nuclear capability could bring it back to equality with Britain and to a kind of primacy over a denuclearized Germany.

For China, with a per-capita GNP of less than $100, the possibility of developing nuclear weapons was also an apparent route to some sort of dignified balance with Moscow and Washington, and a kind of primacy over a denuclearized Japan.

More important, the capacity to produce nuclear weapons appeared to both Paris and Peking as a "ticket to the top table," in Douglas-Home's corrosive electioneering phrase of 1964. If Britain felt independent command over nuclear weapons was a way to keep its status as a global power, when its other bases for power were narrowing, why not France and China, Germany and Italy, India, Japan, and others?

In an environment of strictly bilateral Anglo–American nuclear collaboration, France proceeded with an independent nuclear weapons program in May 1957, confirmed in July by the overt decision to build an isotope-separation plant for the production of U-235.[3] French policy could have found other ways to achieve a nuclear role. Paris could have sought a bilateral nuclear relation with the United States similar to Britain's; bilateral cooperation with Britain; or French leadership in building a European nuclear force.

There were in France, before de Gaulle's return to power, men who thought in terms of such ultimate objectives, once the French bargaining position was established vis-à-vis London and Washington by the decision to go forward with an independent nuclear weapons program. There were, in fact, preliminary discussions at the post-Sputnik NATO meeting in 1957 that might have led down one or another of these paths.[4] The initial framework of the discussion was in rather vague bilateral terms. It suggested storage of United States nuclear weapons on French soil plus French acceptance of Thors and/or Jupiters against American provision to France of information on the Polaris guidance system. Given the nature of American interests (including interests in NATO, British entrance into the Common Market, and control over the right to fire nuclear weapons), the framework of this preliminary discussion was evidently incomplete, just as the almost simultaneous nuclear dialogue between Moscow and Peking proved incomplete. There were also high hurdles ahead in the Joint Atomic Energy Committee, and the redoubtable Admiral Hyman Rickover, if the French track were pursued to a logical end.

And there was more between Paris and Washington to work with in this complex and sensitive terrain than there was between Peking and Moscow. There were no deeply rooted independent ambitions in Paris equivalent to Peking's desire to recover Taiwan, dominate Southeast Asia, and contest Moscow's primacy among the communist parties of Asia and the developing world. There were, in fact, powerful impulses in French political life that looked positively to NATO and a strengthened Europe, including Britain.[5]

But these lines for resolving the French nuclear role were not to be explored for a decade and more. With de Gaulle's return to power on June 1, 1958, the historic strands of affronted French feeling became paramount and were projected in a peculiarly pure form during his period of authority. De Gaulle made the building of an operational nuclear force a first priority. He also put to Eisenhower (in correspondence and via Dulles in 1958, in person in September 1959) the proposition that Britain, the United States, and France constitute themselves a triumvirate to concert political policy, including nuclear policy, in all critical matters around the globe, with each member holding a veto on nuclear issues. He was particularly affronted by the Lebanon–Jordan expedition, where Britain and the United States, without France, moved into an area of old and abiding French interest. But with his acute sense of where power actually lay, he must have known this was an impossible proposition, as he had formulated it.

Eisenhower and Dulles offered de Gaulle all manner of de facto consultation on problems of mutual interest; but Washington was not prepared to elevate France in the manner de Gaulle suggested. Macmillan, with human sympathy and common memories of wartime days in Algeria, probed him, to no avail, for openings to reconciliation, or at least to common paths of action.

On the question of nuclear assistance, Washington recognized that the asymmetry between Britain and France was resented by many in Paris who were not Gaullists. It was also conscious of the problem of nuclear discrimination against Germany. A wide range of proposals was floated, in and out of government circles, to reduce or end the Anglo–French asymmetry. In his final meeting with de Gaulle on February 7, 1959, there is some evidence that Dulles, then mortally ill, suggested that the U.S. might accept a kind of French veto on the use of nuclear weapons in NATO. The question of United States assistance to the French nuclear submarine program was also then not ruled out. But de Gaulle promptly closed off these paths. He announced on March 7, 1959, that the French fleet in the Mediterranean "would no longer be available to NATO in time of war." De Gaulle understood better than some of his sympathizers in Washington that, in the end, propositions of this type would have required an increased degree of French military integration within the Alliance in nuclear matters.[6] In the end, also, they implied movement towards an integrated Europe, including Britain. And de Gaulle had not the slightest intention of going down either road.

The heart of the matter lay in de Gaulle's view of France and its appropriate destiny. He deeply believed that a France submerged in an integrated military and political system would lose its national character. He recognized it might happen—that, in the end, Jean Monnet (who had maneuvered de Gaulle to power in Algeria in 1943), rather than he, would prove more nearly the architect of the French and European future. He respected his adversary and no doubt found it appropriate that two Frenchmen should symbolize and contest which fork in the road history should take. But he was determined not to preside over that historic and definitive change in the nature of French nationalism; and he did all he could do in his time to tip the balance of history the other way.

Furthermore, he was not prepared to build French policy on the assumption that the existing relations among nations were permanent—or sufficiently stable to justify his commitment to the course of Atlantic integration. In November 1959 at a press conference he said:

> Who can say that if in the future, the political background having changed completely . . . that on some awful day Western Europe should be wiped out from Moscow and Central Europe from Washington. And who can even say that the two rivals, after I know not what political and social upheaval, will not unite?[7]

Undoubtedly buried in this portrait of an uncertain future was fear of a revived Germany. To some degree, impossible to establish firmly, the French insistence on a national nuclear capability was affected by a determination that Germany should not again be in a position to attack or dominate France.

There was another dimension to de Gaulle's long vision of the future.

He perceived that China and Russia might clash and Moscow ultimately turn to Europe and the Western tradition of which it was a part; that Latin America might ultimately turn toward Europe; and that sometime, even, a French and European role in Southeast Asia might reemerge. And so by rhetoric, travel, and diplomacy he underlined these essays in geopolitical projection.

But he did not command the power alone to help move the world along these paths. He could have done so with Washington's support by leading Europe toward an integration he could easily have dominated—an integration which would have made Europe a more significant factor in the equation of effective power. He chose a lesser but more congenial role.

De Gaulle once set out the theme which controlled his actions over this range of global policy: "Leaders of men . . . are remembered less for the usefulness of what they achieved than for the sweep of their endeavors. Though sometimes reason may condemn them, feeling clothes them in an aura of glory."[8] De Gaulle's role in history contains important strands of statesmanlike "usefulness" in the highest sense: his coming to London in 1940; his leading the Free French over the next five years; his giving to his nation self-respect (as well as a claim to rank among the victorious powers that Petain and Laval would have denied it); his initial backing of Monnet and the French plan for economic modernization which laid the foundations for recovery and later rapid growth; his solution to the problem of Algeria which, against all odds, was accomplished without another tragic period of Frenchmen killing Frenchmen; his provision to France of a decade's healing stability after 1958; his unyielding rigidity in the face of Khrushchev's essay in nuclear blackmail over Berlin and Cuba.

I am inclined to judge that these passages of what might be called conventional statesmanship outweigh his more sweeping endeavors which, in his time, were marginally costly to the friends of France, comforting to its enemies, and trivial in their impact except to frustrate effective European unity over an important decade. But surely de Gaulle had the right to demand that a balance be struck, as he intended, at a later time, by men enjoying a longer perspective.

In the post-Sputnik years and beyond, the evidence is strong that no arrangement with de Gaulle's France was possible in nuclear matters that would reconcile the interests of the Alliance, as seen from Washington, and the interests of France, as de Gaulle defined them. But it is also true that neither Washington nor London ever put the matter to a test by offering de Gaulle precise alternatives. Indeed, at certain key moments Washington acted to minimize the chance of a reconciliation; for example, the terms of the 1958 revision of the Atomic Energy Act provided for the release of increased information only to those who had made "substantial progress" in matters of nuclear weaponry. It both enlarged the scope of the Anglo–American nuclear relationship and constituted a positive incentive for France to persist in developing an independent nuclear establishment.

Washington and London, then, may not have dealt with de Gaulle in a way best calculated to reconcile the Anglo–American special nuclear relation with the desire to treat Bonn on a nondiscriminatory basis. But the many probings for an opening were deftly deflected by de Gaulle, who often presented propositions he knew were unacceptable. Just as Mao's view of China's destiny in a changing world arena was incompatible with the minimum imperatives of Soviet nuclear collaboration, de Gaulle's view of the French–German relationship—and his broad view of French destiny—precluded nuclear collaboration with Washington. De Gaulle, looking back and looking ahead, in effect agreed with Mao that "It is improper to measure the stature of great men by the yardstick of small men." He believed that intimate collaboration with the United States in nuclear affairs could only reduce France to the stature of a small man. And in his time, when he viewed the will of France as identical with the will of de Gaulle, no full reconciliation with the United States, Britain, Bonn, or Western Europe as a whole was possible.

Berlin and Détente

As the Alliance uneasily debated and adjusted to the post-Sputnik military situation, it also had to deal with the ups and downs of Khrushchev's sporadic application of pressure and pursuit of negotiations on arms control and the German question. In the wake of the second Sputnik, on November 6, 1957, Khrushchev stated publicly that the time had come for a meeting of the heads of the principal governments. His motives were certainly multiple and probably included these elements at least:

(1) to dangle before the peoples of the West the carrot of successful negotiations and thus to damp down a possible buildup of military strength in response to his exaggerated projection of increased Soviet military strength;

(2) to test whether the Western terms on Germany and arms control would be softened in the light of the "new power realities";[9]

(3) to assume a posture of world political leadership corresponding to the military, scientific, and economic prospects which he sought to project;

(4) to explore whether international agreements to limit the spread of nuclear weapons could be reached on Soviet terms.

The most serious negotiations of the post-Sputnik period centered on the possibilities of a nuclear test ban. Khrushchev announced a unilateral cessation of nuclear tests on March 31, 1958. On April 28 Eisenhower proposed a meeting of experts to examine and propose solutions to the technical problems involved in such a ban. Eleven days later, Khrushchev accepted this proposal at a time, we now know, when Peking had rejected, at least initially, Moscow's nuclear offer.

The technical negotiations moved forward. On August 22 Eisenhower proposed that diplomatic negotiations be opened on the basis of the technical findings; and he announced a cessation of American nuclear testing for a year.

But Moscow, in fact, proved unwilling to accept the degree of international monitoring proposed by the experts. There were several phases of further discussion, but the negotiations ran into the ground, leaving to Kennedy the problem of nuclear test resumption.

In November 1960, some two and a half years after they were first suggested, abortive talks were held on methods to minimize the possibility of surprise attack.

The arms control negotiations of these years yielded no concrete results, but they did carry forward an educational process in both the Soviet and American governments, which laid the basis for the real but still extremely limited achievements of the 1960s.

The negotiations on Berlin and Germany were, of course, even less fruitful. Berlin was the point initially chosen by Khrushchev to exercise sustained nuclear blackmail and to establish whether the West was prepared to accept a "new reality." The Berlin crisis, which was to run on for almost four years, began with Khrushchev's statement of November 10, 1958, that he intended to sign a peace treaty with East Germany which would terminate Allied rights in Berlin. It assumed the form of an ultimatum when, on November 27, Moscow allowed an interval of six months for negotiations before proceeding with the East German treaty. Khrushchev counted correctly on the existence of differences among the four Western powers mainly concerned;[10] and he ultimately accepted a foreign ministers meeting on Germany, rather than the summit conference for which he angled so persistently. Macmillan was at this time an equally ardent summiteer, with an electorate particularly disinclined to accept nuclear risk over the question of Berlin.

The foreign ministers meeting opened at Geneva on May 11, 1959. After complex negotiations among the Allies, an agreed package proposal was laid on the table on May 14 covering all the elements for a permanent settlement in central Europe. It reflected a massive and serious body of staff work and interallied negotiation; but, clearly, Khrushchev was not in a mood to settle the German question. Nevertheless, the six-month deadline of November 1957 quietly passed. Khrushchev used the frustrated negotiations in Geneva to parlay his way to the United States and then to the summit meeting, on which he evidently placed great store.

There was a good deal of diplomatic and political theater before Khrushchev got his way, including visits to the United States by Mikoyan and Kozlov and Nixon's debating session in the Soviet Union. Well and truly boxed in, Eisenhower reluctantly announced on August 5, 1959, the exchange of visits between Khrushchev and himself.[11]

At Camp David, Khrushchev took the occasion to assert the continued friendship of the Soviet Union and Communist China and his determination to avoid in Russia the age of the automobile and suburbia. (In perhaps the flattest misstatement of fact by a high Soviet official to an American President—short of Gromyko's talk with Kennedy at the time of the Cuban missile crisis, on October 18, 1962—Khrushchev told Eisenhower that the Soviet poeple "did not care for automobiles, had slight interest in driving around the countryside on a Sunday afternoon. . . ."[12]) But the heart of the business was Khrushchev's posture on Berlin in relation to a summit. Eisenhower succeeded in persuading Khrushchev that if he wanted a summit he would have to withdraw publicly the time limit on his signing a peace treaty with East Germany. This was done, and Eisenhower's visit to the Soviet Union was scheduled to follow a summit meeting in the spring.

THE U-2 AND ITS AFTERMATH

THE U-2 affair and Khrushchev's performance at the Paris summit in May 1960 need little comment here. They left U.S.–Soviet relations in an ugly state of suspension. The atmosphere was exacerbated by the Soviet shooting down of an RB-47 electronic reconnaissance aircraft over international waters on July 1, and by Khrushchev's shoe-banging at the United Nations General Assembly in New York in September.

In 1960 Khrushchev was not about to make either war or peace over the great issues of Germany and arms control. His energies were concentrated on three other fronts. First, he perceived openings in the developing world, notably Laos, the Congo, and Cuba. It was as a leader of radical anticolonialism that he projected himself at the U.N. once summitry had failed. Second, he was absorbed in the Sino–Soviet dispute, as both sides maneuvered in preparation for the Moscow conference of November–December. Third, he was concerned about his internal political position.

In a virtuoso exercise in Kremlinology, Michel Tatu has sought to reconstruct the shifting balance of power and policy in the Kremlin before and after the 1960 Paris summit fiasco.[13] Tatu's thesis is that Khrushchev, despite his apparent political triumphs of 1957–1958, had never consolidated unchallenged primacy in Moscow. His policy toward Peking, his cuts in Soviet armed strength of January 1960, his decentralized approach to the organization of the economy and its planning, and his détente tactics with the West were all under challenge in the presummit period. There is evidence of strain and anxiety in Moscow centered on these questions even before the U-2 incident. And there may well have been some in Moscow who were concerned that Eisenhower's visit to the Soviet Union might stir currents of popular feeling that would be awkward to control.

The shooting down of the U-2 and Eisenhower's final acceptance of direct and personal responsibility for the flight evidently threw Moscow into a phase of turbulent debate. The question of proceeding to Paris and what to do there was undoubtedly argued. Tatu is almost certainly correct that the dramatic breakup of the conference on the spot diluted Khrushchev's power in Moscow and increased the relative leverage of those who took a somewhat harder line in military and foreign policy.[14]

If Khrushchev, as a Russian politician, had the right to complain about Eisenhower's handling of the U-2 incident, Nixon and the Republican Party had cause for at least equal grievance over the timing of the Soviet shoot-down. In a close election no single factor can be isolated as decisive, but a Paris summit which achieved even cosmetic success (like the 1955 Geneva meeting), followed by an Eisenhower tour of the Soviet Union, would have created a quite different setting for the presidential election than the dour, unsettled atmosphere of May to November 1960.[15]

8

Eisenhower's Policy Toward the Developing World

The Approach via The Great Equation

THERE IS SOMETHING EMPTY AND THEATRICAL ABOUT THE HIGH-level visits and conferences, Moscow's hideous threats and pacific proposals tossed into the air in the period October 1957–May 1960, centered on the German problem and arms control.

Elsewhere, however, quite real struggles for power proceeded, not merely fencing. Conforming to Mao's and Khrushchev's 1957 assessments, the critical developments of the immediate post-Sputnik years lay neither in space nor in military hardware, neither in Europe nor in summitry, but in Asia, the Middle East, Africa, and Latin America.

Mao and Khrushchev quarreled over tactics and over who should lead, but each understood the inherent tensions that existed in those politically and socially fragmented societies in painful transition from traditional or colonial to modern modes of organization, crosscut by antagonisms toward the more advanced nations which had been their colonial masters or which had otherwise imposed real or believed humiliations. After all, communism had come to Russia and China in such settings. Both understood the tasks of communism to be the building up of tightly knit and disciplined communist parties for the long pull, accompanied by more overt short-term policies which would move these societies away from Western influence and, if possible, toward the communist world. One of the major changes after Stalin's death was the mounting of a sustained policy toward the developing world, of which expanded Soviet economic and military aid was a major feature.[1]

The initial stance of the Eisenhower administration toward the developing world had been shaped by military and budgetary tactics rather than a theory of history.

The primary objective of American policy in Asia and the Middle East in the period 1953–1956 was to reduce the burden in cost and manpower of holding the line around the periphery of the communist bloc. It was assumed that the primary danger was a recurrence of the type of invasion launched against South Korea. The avoidance of another direct engagement of American ground forces was central to the administration's domestic political strategy as well as to it foreign policy.

The principal method for deterrence was to extend the pattern of bilateral and regional military alliance, created in Europe by the Truman Doctrine and NATO, to those other areas where communist military aggression might occur and which had not been brought within the orbit of direct American alliance in Truman's latter days. In the Middle East a pact of mutual defense between Turkey and Pakistan was signed in May 1954; and the United States became directly linked to Pakistan when SEATO was set up in 1954 in the wake of the Geneva Conference on Indochina. The Baghdad Pact was negotiated with American support but under British leadership early in 1955, linking Iran and Iraq to Turkey and Pakistan. Bilateral security relations between the United States and Japan, provided for in the Japanese Peace Treaty, were consolidated in a Mutual Defense Pact in March 1954; Formosa was linked to the United States by a mutual security pact in 1955. The mantle of more or less explicit American military commitment was thus spread over vast new areas; and these nations were offered American military aid to enlarge and modernize their armed forces.

The Korean War and its unsatisfactory outcome also shaped communist dispositions in these years. The primary communist threat in the developing world after 1953 was not one of overwhelming ground force attack but rather of ideological and economic attraction, of subversion, and guerrilla warfare—what came to be called "wars of national liberation." Neither formal American bilateral pacts nor regional military pacts eliminated the key danger; indeed, they tended to mislead the governments, military establishments, and peoples concerned—including the American people—as to where the danger lay and how it should be headed off or handled.

In these regions American policy in the period 1953–1956 appeared to focus almost exclusively on the new nations' relations to communist military power (and their overt diplomatic position in the Cold War) rather than on their domestic political and economic evolution or on their local and regional ambitions, which generally bulked much larger on the local political scene than the threat of communist invasion.

The somewhat contrary lessons drawn from the Korean War by the two sides yielded a situation that was dramatized by the Twentieth Party

Congress in Moscow in February 1956. The communist world appeared to be concentrating on the extension of power and influence by persuasion while the United States appeared to be trying to hold the balance of power in Eurasia by military means against a military threat that did not then exist. We do not know whether or not adventures of the Korean type might have been undertaken in the absence of the new American pacts. Nevertheless, American policy in these years was not devoted to generating in the underdeveloped countries the kind of attitudes and activities best calculated to frustrate communist policy as it actually took shape after the Korean War.

For instance, in the fiscal year 1955 the bulk of military aid and "defense support" funds went to Indochina, Korea, and Taiwan, with smaller grants to Pakistan, the Philippines, and Thailand. Only about 15 percent of aid was available to countries outside the framework of military pacts, including such major and strategically important nations as Egypt, India, and Indonesia.

Economic aid in the Eisenhower administration, during the years before Sputnik, had one overriding purpose: to assist the nation's Eurasian allies in maintaining deterrent forces on a scale sufficient for the United States to cut down its own ground forces and concentrate on weapons of mass destruction, their means of delivery, and the means of defense against them. In accordance with this view, the American economic aid organization was renamed the Mutual Security Agency; and several forms of economic assistance were placed under military categories on the assumption that Congress would support military but not economic aid.

The Opening of the Great Debate on Development Policy

THE protracted debate on foreign aid for development purposes was, in a quiet way, one of the most dramatic and illuminating strands in the Eisenhower administration. The major actors can be characterized as: a President who wanted to expand foreign aid in this direction but who was deeply concerned with its budgetary consequences; a secretary of state who felt an expansion was needed but who would not throw his weight fully into the scales unless the President made an unambiguous policy decision; a conservative phalanx (George Humphrey, Herbert Hoover, Jr., etc.) that did not believe in development aid; and a liberal cohort (Harold Stassen, C. D. Jackson, Nelson Rockefeller, Allen Dulles, Clarence Randall, etc.) that believed this new dimension of policy was urgently required.

The struggle to associate the United States with the positive and constructive objectives of the underdeveloped areas began in 1953 when Harold Stassen advocated an expansion of assistance to noncommunist nations unwilling to join the United States in military pacts. He made no substantial progress.

The issue was raised in a narrower context by Foster Dulles in the spring of 1954, as the French struggle in Indochina came to a climax. Dulles asked C. D. Jackson, who was retiring from his White House post, to join him for lunch.[2] In a memorandum to Dulles of April 9, Jackson had urged the Administration to launch a "World Economic Plan" in support of the developing nations. Dulles responded positively. He told Jackson with some emotion that he was fighting the struggle against communism with one hand tied behind his back: the economic resources of the United States were not being deployed effectively. He asked Jackson, as a final contribution to the administration, to develop his memorandum and to mobilize the best men and ideas he could around the question of how to make American resources an effective support for policy in Southeast Asia and elsewhere.

Jackson turned to Max Millikan and me at the M.I.T. Center for International Studies. In the early 1950s, a high proportion of our thought and effort had been devoted to the problems of the developing world. We assisted Jackson in organizing a gathering of officials and private citizens at the Princeton Inn on May 15–16, 1954.[3] The problem of stabilizing Southeast Asia in the wake of the Geneva agreements of April was now a pressing one. At Jackson's request we wrote a paper based on the broad consensus at the meeting that a substantial new American initiative was required in the field of development. (The paper was, in effect, a rough first draft of Millikan's and my book, circulated widely in Washington in the spring of 1956 and published in 1957 as *A Proposal: Key to An Effective Foreign Policy*.) Jackson sent the paper to Eisenhower, noting that this was a controversial matter on which the President ought to make a command decision because if he turned the paper over for staffing, he would get back "a box of knives." Eisenhower did not follow Jackson's advice. The paper went from the White House to Dulles, who in turn gave it to his new Undersecretary of State, Herbert Hoover, Jr.

In the meantime, as the Dulles–Jackson initiative was generating, the opponents of this view were hardening their lines. In the course of 1955 they succeeded in making Nelson Rockefeller's position in the government untenable through a campaign against him best described as bureaucratic guerrilla warfare. They felt that his proposals for expanded military and foreign-aid outlays were dangerous. They also succeeded in displacing Harold Stassen with John Hollister, a man initially dedicated to the reduction of foreign aid, although his view softened with responsibility. Herbert Hoover, Jr., was of similar and more durable persuasion. Without clear direction from Eisenhower, Dulles was unprepared to do battle; and Hoover successfully throttled the proposal in the face of considerable support for it in the Department of State.[4]

At a meeting of February 7, 1957, Jackson made a final, gallant effort to relaunch the effort, responding to the rhetoric of Eisenhower's Second Inaugural Address:

> We must use our skills and knowledge and, at times, our substance, to help others rise from misery, however far the scene of suffering may be from our shores. For wherever in the world a people knows desperate want, there must appear at least the spark of hope, the hope of progress—or there will surely rise at last the flames of conflict. . . .
>
> . . . These hopes that we have helped to inspire, we can help to fulfill.[5]

Except for Clarence Randall, Jackson found the opposition, headed by George Humphrey, impenetrable; and, as in 1954, Dulles was not willing to oppose Humphrey under circumstances where Eisenhower had not given prior approval to the policy.

The argument against expanded foreign aid centered on these points:

(1) The expanding pressures for military outlays in the arms race made it essential to cut back on programs of lesser importance to the national interest; and programs of economic aid to nations not militarily allied with the United States belonged in this category.

(2) There was no evidence that economic assistance to such nations brought the United States any benefit in the Cold War. On the contrary, the nations we aided appeared to take pride in asserting their diplomatic independence, often to American embarrassment; and it was, if nothing else, undignified for the United States to appear to be seeking borrowers for its money, notably under circumstances of neutralist behavior.

(3) Since many of the so-called uncommitted nations were socialist, at least verbally, and democracy was unlikely to survive under a regime of state ownership, they were to be written off as ideological as well as military allies.

(4) Few if any of the underdeveloped areas had the administrative and technical talent, the social overhead capital structure, and the political and social will to use more capital effectively. Those that did have these preconditions could get capital from existing international sources; where absorptive capacity did not exist, American grants and loans would be wasted.

These were not trivial arguments. An answer to the first required a willingness to face up to an expansion in the federal budget. An answer to the second required an alternative view of the nature of the American interest in the underdeveloped areas. An answer to the third required an alternative view of the relation between democracy and capitalism and, especially, a more hopeful and dynamic view of the future prospects for private enterprise as the new economies acquired momentum. An answer to the fourth required the offer of substantial long-term American aid as an incentive to mobilize the men and build the institutions required for the effective absorption of capital.

The Opposition Gains Ground

The advocates of enlarged long-term economic aid gradually won ground. The concept was widely aired in 1956 when Millikan's and my paper circulated in Washington, with attendant comment in the press. After a remarkable Senate examination of the foreign aid problem, the Development Loan Fund (DLF) was created on a small scale in 1957. Institutionally, this was a major turn in the road and a substantial achievement by those inside the Eisenhower administration who had quietly been crusading for a new approach to the developing world.[6] In the wake of Sputnik, the crusaders gained ground more rapidly. In 1958, the DLF began to make loans and its funds were modestly expanded. In 1958 some $290 million was raised in Washington to prevent too radical a cutback in the goals of the Indian Second Five-Year Plan; and Senator Mike Monroney proposed a soft-loan window for the World Bank, which came to pass in 1959 as the International Development Association (IDA). An amendment to the Mutual Security Act (sponsored by Senators Kennedy and Cooper) was passed by the Senate in 1958 (in the House of Representatives in 1959), designed to guarantee adequate and sustained support on an international basis for the Indian economic development effort. This laid the foundation for the World Bank India–Pakistan consortium of the 1960s, just as the creation of the Inter-American Development Bank in 1959 provided a critical component for the Alliance for Progress.

Although the public and congressional debate may have been fruitful, notably the Senate examination conducted by the 85th Congress, the heart of the matter lay elsewhere. There was a quiet withdrawal from the Washington scene in 1957 of some who had ardently opposed programs of economic aid over the previous three or four years. They were replaced by men of cautious but different views, who worked in quiet collaboration with like-minded members of the Congress in both parties. This political fact was reinforced in 1958 by the mounting evidence of Soviet reliance on economic policy as an instrument to extend its power and influence in the underdeveloped areas; by the Middle East crisis of the summer of 1958; by a radical deterioration in relations with Latin America centered in part on economic policy; and by the severity of the Indian foreign-exchange problem.

The communist world regarded Sputnik as a powerful symbolic reinforcement for a thrust into the developing world. The shock also helped prepare the way for these changes in the American approach to the developing regions in the period 1958–1960. In fact, at the NATO summit meeting of December 1957, Eisenhower raised the question of improved coordination of development assistance among the Atlantic nations,[7] an initiative which ultimately led to the creation of the Development Assistance Committee of the OECD in 1960.

The change in scale and composition of American foreign aid in these years is reflected in Table 8–1.

TABLE 8–1
THE CHANGING SCALE AND COMPOSITION OF AMERICAN FOREIGN AID, 1957–1960
(in millions of dollars)

	1957[1]	1958[2]	1959[3]	1960[4]
Military Aid	2352	2187	2340	1609
Defense Support	1110	874	881	741
Development Loans and Grants	—	2	66	202
Agriculture (P. L. 480)	187	146	113	107
Technical Assistance and Cooperation	114	140	169	172
Contingency and Other Special Assistance	341	408	407	369
TOTAL Economic Assistance (including P. L. 480 and defense support)	1752	1570	1636	1591
Total Official Flows (DAC definition)[5]	2091	2410	2310	2322
Total Flows (DAC definition, including private investment)[6]	4100	3685	3276	3818

Sources:
1. The Budget of the United States Government for the Fiscal Year ending June 30, 1959, pp. M21 and M23.
2. *Ibid.*, FY 1960, pp. M39 and M41.
3. *Ibid.*, FY 1961, pp. M29 and M30.
4. *Ibid.*, FY 1962, pp. M34 and M35.
5. *1969 Review—Development Assistance: Efforts and Policies of the Members of the Development Assistance Committee* (O.E.C.D.) p. 297.
6. *Ibid.*, p. 296.

Note: DAC figures for official flows of development assistance include Export-Import Bank loans and certain other forms of lending not included in the regular U.S. foreign aid budgets.

These figures exhibit a shift from military aid and military support toward development lending and other economic aid; but they also indicate that the scale of the shift was modest and the decline in private lending over these years yielded a net reduction in total capital flows from the United States to the developing world.

It was inescapable circumstance that validated the new approach towards the developing world and accounts for the changing scale and composition of the aid statistics. The American government operated on Dr. Johnson's old principle: "When a man knows he is to be hanged in a fortnight, it concentrates his mind wonderfully." The gallows took the form of certain major crises of this period, which yielded adjustments in American doctrine, policy, and allocation of resources.

9

Crisis in the Middle East

Lebanon–Jordan

THE AMERICAN LANDING IN LEBANON ON THE MORNING OF JULY 15, 1958, was rooted in the Middle East Resolution signed by Eisenhower on March 9, 1957. After the Suez crisis, Eisenhower concluded that: "The existing vacuum in the Middle East must be filled by the United States before it is filled by Russia."[1] A new basis had to be found to protect "Western rights" and disabuse Moscow and others of the notion that the West was in permanent disarray and the United States neutralized in that area.

The Middle East Resolution authorized American cooperation with and assistance to any nation or group of nations in the Middle East "in the development of economic strength dedicated to the maintenance of national independence." To that end, it authorized upon request programs of military assistance and military aid against armed aggression from any nation "controlled by international Communism."

The problem for the United States in the Middle East during the mid-1950s was the difficulty in defining the phrases "armed aggression" and "controlled by international Communism."

Moscow, Peking, and Washington were operating in a situation with its own churning dynamics that involved a number of elements: the Arab struggle with Israel; the rise of a new generation of Arab radical leaders; Nasser's effort to encourage the rise of such leaders (notably, in Syria, Saudi Arabia, Iraq, and Jordan) and the nationalist resistance to Nasser's domination; the Bedouin–Palestinian schism in Jordan; the Moslem–

Christian schism in Lebanon; and the tensions between the Arabs and non-Arab Moslems in Turkey and Iran.

Moscow and Washington were, in this turbulent modernizing region, dealing with situations where their control over events was dilute, and where national and regional objectives were, in the end, paramount.

The Middle East crisis of 1958 climaxed a series of lesser crises which took place over the previous year and a half. Arab radicals, inspired if not wholly controlled from Cairo and Damascus, pressed ardently against the moderate governments in Beirut and Amman, as well as against the Saudis and the pro-Western government in Baghdad.

In May 1958 Lebanon went before the United Nations Security Council to accuse Egypt and Syria of arming the rebels and instigating revolt on the issue of a second term for President Camille Chamoun. The question of sending American armed forces to Lebanon was raised at this time. By early July the situation had eased somewhat, but the amphibious forces of the United States Sixth Fleet, which had been ordered to the eastern Mediterranean at this time, remained close by.

On July 14, 1958, however, both the new Arab Union of Jordan and Iraq and the Baghdad Pact were broken. The Hashemite monarch of Iraq was overthrown and murdered, along with the Crown Prince and the Prime Minister, Neuri es-Said. The revolution was led by young military officers, Nasserite and anti-Western; but there was no firm evidence of Cairo's hand in the enterprise, let alone Moscow's. The acute anxieties of Jordan and Lebanon led Hussein and Chamoun to request British and American armed intervention to protect their independence under the Middle East Resolution of 1957. United States seaborne forces, already close by, began to move unopposed across the Lebanese beaches the day after the coup in Iraq. On July 17 British paratroopers moved into Jordan, where a plot against Hussein had failed.

It is the cumulative buildup of tension and trouble in the Middle East which explains Eisenhower's instant response to the Iraqi coup of July 14th: "That morning I gathered in my office a group of advisers to make sure that no facet of the situation was overlooked. Because of my long study of the problem, this was one meeting in which my mind was practically made up regarding the general line of action we should take, even before we met."[2]

Eisenhower's decision to move on July 15, before the meaning of the Iraqi coup could be fully assessed, was based on an instinctive judgment that the Middle East was getting out of hand, rather than on precise evidence that "armed aggression" from a nation "controlled by international Communism" had occurred or was about to occur.

Robert Murphy was promptly launched into the Middle East along with the Marines. His mission was to comfort a harassed and ill Chamoun; to commit him to the early election of a successor; and to explain to the new leader in Baghdad, Abdul Kassim, and to Nasser the limited objectives of the American initiative.

The operation stabilized the Middle East for some time. There was no move against the new government of Iraq, as Moscow and Peking feared. American influence was not used to keep Chamoun in power, as he may have hoped. Nevertheless, the Anglo–American landings strengthened Jordanian, Lebanese, and Saudi confidence in their ability to survive against radical nationalists, backed by Moscow and Cairo. The military operations provided a demonstration that, in the face of nuclear blackmail, the United States was prepared to move military forces in defense of its interests. That demonstration increased the degree of independence even radical Arab nationalists felt they could assert against Moscow.

With Peking pressing its flank, Moscow had to react. It did so by demanding a high-level meeting of heads of state. It hoped to bring Britain and the United States to the bar as opponents of nationalism. As during the Suez crisis, the threat of missiles and "volunteers" was also invoked, but in ways which did not commit Moscow to move. Moscow resisted Peking's pressure for what it regarded as excessive reaction. A series of exchanges between Eisenhower and Khrushchev on the forum in which the matter should be debated led finally to the convening of the United Nations General Assembly, which Eisenhower addressed on August 13. By this time the Middle East was relatively calm, the Presidential election in Lebanon having taken place at the end of July.

EISENHOWER'S SPEECH OF AUGUST 13, 1958: A PERSONAL NOTE

DULLES initially urged a narrow focusing on the question of indirect aggression. He left Washington for a conference in Latin America, to return on Friday, August 8, but before leaving town he had asked C. D. Jackson and me to come to Washington to develop materials for Eisenhower's speech before the United Nations. Our inclination was to put the question of indirect aggression in a larger context of the rise of radical Arab nationalism and to focus on the possibility of regional development in the Middle East. In addition, we wanted to counteract the image in the Middle East and elsewhere evoked by Moscow's use of nuclear threat during the Suez crisis.

On Friday, August 8, we were installed in a large State Department office normally used by ambassadors on leave in Washington. We assembled our thoughts and drew ideas from many parts of the bureaucracy, including Lewis Strauss and his AEC's water-desalting crusaders and the State Department Policy Planning Staff. We talked at length with Vice-President Nixon, who appeared to agree with the line we were about to take. We worked together most of the night, aided in the frenetic effort by Henry Owen of the Policy Planning Staff—later my deputy and successor in that institution. Jackson was able to hand a draft to Dulles during breakfast at Dulles' home early on August 9. With a nod of approval in principle, the draft was then given to those bearing operational responsibility in the government. At the Treasury, Robert Anderson made sure that resources, including a diversion of oil revenues, would be available for Middle East development if the Arab world responded. The document moved forward, after the usual redrafting, to Eisenhower, its essential structure unchanged.

In the delivered speech before the United Nations, Eisenhower reaffirmed and extended American commitment to the Baghdad Pact in the wake of Iraq's probable defection. He thus isolated the problems of the Arab world from those of the non-Arab Moslems to the north and foreclosed a possible Soviet move to neutralize the whole of the Middle East. Second, he sought United Nations support for continued Lebanese independence under the less Western-oriented but presumably stable government that emerged from the 1958 crisis. Third, he suggested a United Nations standby force that would represent an alternative to the direct application of British and American power in the region. Fourth, he proposed that Israel and the Arab states agree on a moratorium in arms purchases that might reduce mutual fears and, conceivably, set the stage for a definitive settlement. Fifth, he offered substantial economic assistance to the Arab world, including a diversion of Western oil revenues for regional economic development. The whole program was framed by the demonstration that the United States and Britain were not prepared to abandon the World War II truce lines in the face of Soviet missile and "volunteer" threats.

The broad objective of the speech was not merely to reaffirm American opposition to direct and indirect aggression but also to hold up a vision of American support for a constructive expression of Arab nationalism —and the nationalism of others in the developing world.

In the preface to Book III of his memoir, Eisenhower quotes this passage from his August 13 speech:

> The world that is being remade on our planet is to be a world of many mature nations. As one after another of these new nations moves through the difficult transition to modernization and learns the methods of growth, from this travail new levels of prosperity and productivity will emerge.
>
> This world of individual nations is not going to be controlled by any one power or group of powers. This world is not going to be committed to any one ideology.
>
> Please believe me when I say that the dream of world domination by one power or of world conformity is an impossible dream.[3]

So far as doctrine was concerned, the need to deal with Arab radicalism accelerated the shift in Eisenhower's initial stance towards the developing world. His August 13 speech acknowledged that what the

United States was prepared to do for radical Arabs in their most disruptive mood, the United States must be prepared to do in Latin American, Asia, and Africa as well. The criterion that economic aid should be an instrument of support only for those joined with the United States in military alliance against the Communist bloc was altered. The objective of economic assistance as a means for supporting the emergence of independent states, focusing their ardent nationalism increasingly on the modernization of their societies, had been enunciated under circumstances likely to commit the United States over a long future. In the context of American economic foreign policy since 1953, this was a radical departure.

Tactically, Eisenhower's speech provided a graceful backdrop for the August 21 General Assembly resolution pledging noninterference among the Arab states in each other's affairs and instructing the Secretary General to facilitate the withdrawal of British and American troops from the area. On October 25th the United States forces were out of Lebanon, and Chamoun's successor, General Fuad Chehab, was installed.

Eisenhower was good enough to drop me a note on August 18 thanking me for my work on his speech at the United Nations. I took the occasion to urge a vigorous follow-through in American policy to make the most of his initiative, the interval of relative calm in the area, and the possibility of encouraging Arab nationalism to turn to economic development. I would not judge the subsequent Middle East policy of the Eisenhower administration as vigorous. On the other hand, in retrospect I would judge the political raw materials of the area more intractable and the margin of American influence more limited than I believed—or at least hoped—in August 1958.

10

Crisis in Latin America

EVENTS AND ADVOCACY WERE SHIFTING EISENHOWER'S APPROACH to Latin America in much the same way as they shifted his approach to the Middle East. Down to 1958, despite prescient lobbying by Milton Eisenhower, the administration's approach to Latin American development had been primarily through encouragement of private investment. Export-Import Bank loans had expanded, and in 1956 the International Finance Corporation was created within the World Bank, in effect to subsidize private ventures in the developing world. In the post-Sputnik period, however, a new sense of urgency and initiative began to emerge. The riots in Lima and Caracas which greeted Nixon's visits in May 1958 "brought home to all of us the clear truth that, as the Vice-President reported at the end of his trip, 'the threat of Communism in Latin America is greater than ever before.' "[1] In a letter to Eisenhower of May 25, President Juscelino Kubitschek of Brazil used the occasion of the anti-Nixon demonstrations to propose Operation Pan-America, a sustained, cooperative effort in economic and social development on the scale of the Marshall Plan at least. The gathering consensus north and south of the Rio Grande yielded action that fell short of Kubitschek's vision but still created the Inter-American Development Bank, for which American support was announced in July 1958, and support in principle for Latin American economic integration and for commodity stabilization agreements.

In 1959 the emergence of Castro as at least a de facto communist underlined this general assessment of the volatility of Latin America.[2]

The administration moved slowly with respect to Cuba, in part hoping for the best, in part heeding Ambassador Philip W. Bonsal's counsel to avoid actions which would permit Castro to blame his transition to communism and the Soviet orbit on American actions, and in part, conscious that the Cuban revolution was regarded with hope by many in Latin America while American intervention in the hemisphere was unpopular, even among Castro's enemies.

There is a widespread view that the United States, by its diplomatic and political performance in the period 1958–1960, converted Castro, a humane Latin American radical, into a communist and working member of the communist world. Except for Khrushchev's charge to Kennedy at Vienna in 1961, it is a view hard to support with facts. Even Herbert Matthews exonerates Washington of the charge and describes American policy as "forbearing and patient" during the critical months of 1959–1960 "under great provocations."[3]

How, then, does one explain the transition in Eisenhower's policy from the arms embargo against Batista of March 14, 1958, which greatly strengthened Castro, to the decision two years later to organize and train Cuban refugees to overthrow Castro? The answer lies in the interaction between two underlying factors: the inner political compulsions that moved Castro into progressively deeper reliance on the communists and then on Moscow, and the underlying nature of American policy in the Western Hemisphere.[4] At every critical fork in the road, Castro judged that he could move closer to his abiding vision of personal, revolutionary rule in Cuba—and leadership in Latin America—by going where Raúl Castro and Che Guevara wanted him to go than by aligning himself with the non-communist moderates of the July 26th Movement and the benign good will of Ambassador Bonsal. A rational Cuban economic relation to the United States required continuity in the sugar quota and, probably, other forms of economic assistance from Washington, if there was to be rapid economic and social progress in Cuba. Decent working ties with the United States did not preclude nationalization of some industries or radical experiments in social and economic policy, as Mexico, Bolivia, Venezuela, and other Latin American nations had demonstrated. But such ties did have a price. They required that Cubans and Americans sit down and talk seriously and regularly about their mutual problems with a view to settling them rather than generating confrontation.

But as Castro subsequently made clear, his grasp on the problems of Cuban economic and social life in 1959–1960 was infirm. He was, and remains, a classic revolutionary romantic. He saw the issues before him in terms of broad political imagery—above all the self-image of an emerging successful revolutionary leader. In a quite straightforward way, it was to the public projection of this image in Cuba and elsewhere in the hemisphere that Castro devoted himself as a virtually full-time job in the months after his takeover of January 1, 1959. On this basis, with endless appearances on Cuban television, Castro consolidated his popular support and put himself in a position to move in any direction he chose, including the removal of key figures in the liberal noncommunist government he initially set up. By the end of March it was clear that the Cuban moderates were losing ground, although they were still active, notably in economic affairs.

A part of Castro's problem of imagery was to settle his relation to the United States. Should he find a dignified way to work with Washington? Or, should he strike a revolutionary's anti-American posture, reaching back to strands of resentment deep in Latin American memory and feeling?

It is in this context that his curious trip to the United States in mid-April 1959 is to be understood. It was curious because Washington had indicated it was prepared to discuss economic issues, including assistance to Cuba; the Cuban economic ministers accompanying Castro were prepared in detail to make proposals; on April 2, 1959, Castro told a Cuban television audience that he would seek credits in the United States; he then instructed his advisers not to raise economic matters.[5] On the other hand, in the United States and Canada, and then in Argentina, Uruguay, and Brazil, Castro took pains to project the democratic intentions of the Cuban revolution and to align himself, in the spirit of Kubitschek, with a large-scale American aid program to Latin America. There is evidence that this made the communists in Cuba uneasy.

Castro's posture as he returned to Havana on May 7 was ambivalent: he had decided not to use the occasion of his visit to the United States to regularize his relations with Washington, or, as Raúl saw it, "to surrender"; but he had not foreclosed the option of working within the hemispheric system.

Meanwhile, ambivalence within the American government towards Castro also persisted. There were those long convinced that he was, in effect, taking Cuba into communism; that the hemisphere was thereby endangered; and that action against him was required. But policy followed Bonsal's patient and more hopeful lead from Havana; and Castro did not put the divergent views to the test by posing the question of economic assistance.

The triggering event in Washington's relations with Castro proved to be domestic rather than international. In a move evidently long planned, Castro took up on his return from abroad an agrarian reform law which was promulgated on May 17 in a dramatic ceremony in the Sierra Maestra. So far as American policy was concerned, the promulgation of the land reform law had two effects. First, it led to a mild, almost routine United States statement of concern of June 11 that "prompt, adequate and effective compensation" be made to Americans whose property was confiscated. The formula used was long familiar. It had been generated by the Mexican oil nationalization of 1938. The American note not only recognized the

Cuban right to nationalize but spoke benignly of the role of land reform in social progress. Second, and decisively, it generated bloody conflict within Cuba and brought to a head the struggle between Cuban communists and moderates, leading Castro, to throw in his lot wholeheartedly with the former. He at last became fully aligned with Raúl and Che; and the more conventional old-line communists became his key agents in every part of the political structure. A good deal of the conflict was a product of the crude, ill-planned way Castro went about the complex business of land reform. The slide to dictatorship and reliance on the communists was accelerated by the illegal and sometimes brutal way in which Castro reacted to the opposition his program generated—a reaction that broke definitively his ties to many of his noncommunist colleagues in the July 26th Movement. As he found himself increasingly beleaguered, he moved from the euphoric, ambivalent mood of early 1959 to a harsh defiance, and then to the consolidation of a rather pedestrian communist regime.

Starting in mid-1959 Castro eliminated or accepted the resignations of his principal noncommunist supporters; moved communists into all commanding positions in his regime; shifted his economic and military ties from the United States and the Western world to Moscow; and made Havana a center for both communist and anti-American propaganda as well as insurrectional enterprise.[6] Perhaps Castro had long planned to move down this road. More likely it was the net product of conflicting attitudes whose relative strength was only revealed when difficult choices were placed before him.

It was this process that pushed Washington from anxious ambivalence to alarm; and without imputing any higher morality or wisdom to the American government, it is hard to see, even with hindsight, what it could have done to prevent events from taking the course they did, given the personality of Castro and the lack of effective unity among the noncommunist elements in Cuban political life; although former Ambassador Bonsal can still argue, as he did at the time, that American policy in 1960 should have eschewed the suspension of the Cuban sugar quota and other hostile acts, leaving open at least the possibility that Havana's ties to Moscow would have been looser and more reversible and that the play of political forces within Cuba might in time have permitted Cuba to escape on its own the dictatorship clearly emerging in 1959–1960.[7]

Eisenhower, sensing the gathering dangers in the hemisphere as Castro began to rely on communists at home and abroad, toured Latin America in February–March 1960, underlining his commitment to democracy, nonintervention, progress for the people, reform, receptivity to private capital, and a common front against communist imperialism.

On March 17, 1960, shortly after his return, Eisenhower directed the CIA to organize a wide political grouping of Cuban exiles (excluding communists and supporters of Batista) and recruit and train a force capable of guerrilla action inside Cuba. Aware of the possible contradiction between passive acceptance of Trujillo's regime in the Dominican Republic and activism against Castro, Eisenhower supported the OAS investigation of the Dominican Republic, which found Trujillo's regime guilty of "flagrant and widespread violations" of human rights.

Similarly, Eisenhower sensed the link between economic sanctions against Cuba and expanded assistance to the rest of Latin America. He notes: "On the day I signed the proclamation reducing imports of Cuban sugar [July 6, 1960], I met with foreign policy advisers to discuss a new aid policy for Latin America."[8] Under Gerard Smith, the Policy Planning Staff had been designing such a new approach in response to ideas germinating within Latin America. Douglas Dillon, with strong support from Herter, Milton Eisenhower, and others, threw his weight behind Smith's concept of cooperative programs, social as well as economic. These were incorporated in September in the OAS Act of Bogotá, a clear precursor of the Alliance for Progress.

In concept, North American and Latin American notions of what was required in the hemisphere had come closer together.

11

The Crisis in Indian Economic Development

A QUITE DIFFERENT KIND OF COMMUNIST PRESSURE MOVED THE question of India and Indian economic development toward the center of policy-making. Starting in 1952–1953, both India and Communist China launched their first Five-Year Plans. Colonial history in India and the interplay of China with the external world (including the Japanese occupation of Manchuria from 1931) had yielded both nations a rather similar initial industrial base by the late 1940s, when India achieved independence, and the communists consolidated control over a unified mainland.[1] The major difference was the higher initial productivity of agriculture in China, where the early development of double-cropping made possible the support at minimum levels of a much larger Chinese population (approximately 580 million to India's 360 million in 1952).

It became widely felt in the 1950s that the relative progress of the two nations' development—the one under communism, the other under democratic rule—would constitute a kind of pure ideological test of great significance. Leaders in emerging nations were more interested in the political organization and ideology that would produce rapid economic and social progress than in the abstract virtues of democracy. Some Western analysts agreed with the communist assessment that a strong centralized dictatorship would be more effective than a democratic government in mobilizing the investment resources necessary for rapid growth. And down to the failure of Mao's Great Leap Forward in 1959–1960, it seemed possible Peking might vindicate that judgment. It did achieve initially a higher investment rate than India, despite large military outlays. What undid Mao and the optimistic analyses of Communist China's prospects was agricultural policy. The peasants were caught up in a sequence of collective structures and were denied both adequate incentives and adequate fertilizers, pesticides, and other resources for increasing agricultural productivity. But that was not generally apparent in 1958.

India, like most of the nations of the Middle East, was a neutral. It was a big and articulate neutral. Therefore, aid to India posed starkly the distinction between aid for development purposes and aid to support a military ally.

The issue of policy for the United States became acute in the early stage of the Indian Second Five-Year Plan, beginning in 1956–1957. This plan aimed for rapid expansion of the metallurgical, engineering, and chemical industries, and the creation of a heavy-industry base for further development. The industrial targets required larger direct foreign exchange resources than had been estimated; and the momentum of private investment combined with two bad harvests compounded the foreign exchange crisis.[2]

Thus, at just the time when Communist China appeared to be surging ahead in the Great Leap Forward, India had to cut back its Second Plan targets. Foreign aid was insufficient; and India's own foreign exchange reserves were being drawn down at a dangerous rate. The Indian leadership, and the friends of Indian democracy abroad, were plunged into pessimism and concern that was heightened by substantial Soviet economic aid which began to flow to India in 1955.

The United States (and other countries) responded to the Indian foreign exchange crisis of 1958 on an ad hoc basis. Total external assistance to India was approximately as follows:

1956–1957	$240,000,000
1957–1958	$560,000,000
1958–1959	$715,000,000
1959–1960	$620,000,000
1960–1961	$825,000,000

American aid to India had begun early in the 1950s on the basis of Truman's Point Four program, with the exuberant support of Ambassador Chester Bowles.[3] The Korean War cut across the whole program of assistance to developing nations. Nevertheless, a series of able U.S. ambassadors to New Delhi (George V. Allen, John Sherman Cooper, and Ellsworth Bunker) kept the technical assistance program alive and expanding; and they lobbied doggedly for expanded flows of long-term capital on soft terms. Substantial amounts of agricultural produce moved during the decade, notably to relieve famine in 1955 and 1956. Only in 1958–1959 did a regular source of soft loans emerge from the Development Loan Fund.

But the scale of the effort did not match the scale of the problem; and uncertainties about the flow of external aid from year to year made planning difficult and inefficient. The flavor of the debate over aid to India is reflected in this extract from an exchange between Senator Kennedy and me before the Senate Foreign Relations Committee on February 27, 1958.[5] It obviously has something of the character of a put-up job, designed to build materials in the record he could, and did, later use.

> *Kennedy:* On the question of India, do you think that the proposed economic assistance which the administration has decided to give to India is sufficient to meet the minimum requirements for successful Indian development and American policy in that area?
> *Rostow:* I believe the present aid program, which amounts to about $290 million this year, is grossly inadequate. It is enough to keep them from cutting back their 5-year plan too far . . . but it is by no means enough . . . to give the Indians confidence to go ahead boldly to fulfill their plan.
> *Kennedy:* . . . Isn't there some sort of a competition—certainly an indirect one, if not a direct one—between China and India in solving problems which are quite similar in many cases?
> *Rostow:* There is a great competition. . . . The Chinese Communists are investing a somewhat higher proportion of their gross national product in their total development program than the Indians, but they are putting a much, much higher proportion into industry. . . . They are counting on the ability of a totalitarian control system to squeeze from a relatively static output in agriculture increasing amounts of food . . . for population increase . . . increased urbanization; and . . . foreign exchange. . . .
>
> . . . I do not believe that the Chinese Communist are going to get through the coming decade without a fairly radical revision in their agricultural policy.
>
> On the other hand, if the Indians cave in . . . then a really quite mediocre Chinese performance is going to look like the wave of the future throughout the world of underdeveloped countries.
> *Kennedy:* What would you consider a minimum figure of aid that the United States ought to extend to India?
> *Rostow:* . . . Max Millikan and I . . . calculate that the Indians ought to be confident of a flow of foreign exchange from the United States over the next 4 years of about half a billion dollars, as compared to the present 290. Of the half billion, perhaps 25 percent . . . might take the form of surplus American foodstuffs and fibers. . . . In addition to that, I think India should get increased help from Japan. I believe the Japanese are ready to enter into coordinate arrangements with us, and so would Germany and the rest of Western Europe. . . . Under those circumstances, countries like Canada, Switzerland, and Sweden, which can only make small contributions . . . would add to the international effort. And you would get a real barn raising.

It was in these post-Sputnik days that the concept of stable, long-term support for Indian and Pakistani economic development emerged, with many voices in support—from Barbara Ward Jackson and Chester Bowles to the cables flowing from New Delhi to the State Department. From his speech of March 15, 1958, it was led from the Senate by John Kennedy.

Because of its acceptance of military ties to the United States, Pakistan was already receiving substantial assistance. After 1958, it used that assistance effectively, although inequitably proportioned between the East and West wings. Nevertheless, it was judged wise to propose that the international community deal with both nations of the Indian subcontinent on the same terms. The Kennedy–Cooper Resolution passed in the House of Representatives at the close of 1959. It recommended that the administration "invite other friendly and democratic nations to join in a mission to consult with India on . . . joint action to assure fulfillment of India's Second Five Year Plan and the effective design of its Third Five Year Plan." The World Bank soon despatched to the subcontinent its three wise men: Oliver Franks, Herman Abs, and Robert Sproul. Their report laid the basis for the consortium which began to operate in May–June 1961.

As the new decade began, aid to India and Pakistan found an increasing place in Eisenhower's policy. The Development Loan Fund was used primarily for this purpose; a large four-year program of aid in surplus agricultural products was announced on May 4, 1960. In September Ayub and Nehru had agreed how to divide the waters of the Indus and its tributaries, allowing the massive support organized by the World Bank from the international community (announced February 29, 1960) to be made effective in developing these resources for both nations.

By the close of 1960 the Indian planners could make their dispositions with some hope that a regular and reliable flow of economic assistance might be available for the Third Five-Year Plan.

As in Latin America and the Middle East, the nationalist and modernizing revolutions on the Indian subcontinent, and communist efforts to exploit them, substantially shifted Eisenhower's policy in his second term.

12

Crisis in Southeast Asia

GIVEN THE ROLE OF TROUBLE IN VIETNAM AND LAOS IN THE 1960S and the character of the problems confronted there by Eisenhower's successors, his observations in *Waging Peace* are revealing.

With respect to Vietnam, there are two kinds of references.

First, South Vietnam is listed among the nations where United States defense support provided soldiers around the periphery of the Communist bloc at much less cost than if the United States military stood guard.[1] This perspective, linked to memories of the Korean War, correctly reflects the manner in which United States military aid was principally used in the 1950s; that is, to build conventional forces to deal with a possible overt direct assault across the demilitarized zone at the 17th parallel. Although insurrectional violence and then guerrilla warfare began in South Vietnam, starting in the second half of 1958, American military advisers were exceedingly sluggish in adapting their strategy, tactics, and training to the politico–military guerrilla offensive already well under way by the end of 1960. Only in 1960 did American military thought in Saigon begin to shift seriously toward the problems of counterinsurgency.

Second, there are several references to the effect on South Vietnam of a failure to deal successfully with other problems in the area; e.g., Quemoy–Matsu in 1959,[2] and Laos in 1960.[3] The latter evoked Eisenhower's articulation of the domino theory:

> We were determined to preserve the independence of Laos against a takeover backed by its neighbors to the north—Communist China

> and North Vietnam. For the fall of Laos to Communism could mean the subsequent fall—like a tumbling row of dominoes—of its still-free neighbors, Cambodia and South Vietnam and, in all probability, Thailand and Burma. Such a chain of events would open the way to Communist seizure of all Southeast Asia.[4]

There is no perception here that Hanoi's primary initial objective might be South Vietnam and that control over the Laos corridor to South Vietnam was what Hanoi sought above all to consolidate in 1959–1960.

With respect to Laos, Eisenhower describes in a straightforward way his opposition to Souvanna Phouma's neutralist effort, his support for Phoumi and Boun Oum, and the emergence of communist control over the Plain of Jars as Kong Le moved there from Vientiane.[5] There is no recognition in his analysis that the Laotian government lacked the military power to exercise effective control either in the northern provinces or in the southern corridor to South Vietnam. Eisenhower quotes his statement at a meeting on January 2, 1961: "It's my conviction that if we ever have to resort to force, there's just one thing to do: clear up the problem completely."[6] How precisely American forces could be effectively applied to the interior of Laos was a problem Eisenhower did not have to confront as he left, with deep regret, "a legacy of strife and confusion" to his successor.[7]

The deterioration of Diem's political position among noncommunist groups, leading to an attempted military coup on November 11, 1960, is not mentioned by Eisenhower, although the American Ambassador, Elbridge Durbrow, had filled the cable lines with anxious analyses of Diem's deficiencies and used up his capital with Diem in pressure and advice to mend his ways.

The thought and policy in the American government on Laos and Vietnam was undoubtedly more subtle than Eisenhower's memoirs would suggest. Indeed, his own account almost certainly does not reflect fully the complexities he himself perceived at the time.

Eisenhower's problem with South Vietnam was basically the same as that of his predecessor and his three successors: How could military action be combined with the creation of a political base capable of frustrating the thrust of Hanoi to take over an area judged critical to the balance of power in Asia? Truman had faced the decline of French colonialism. Eisenhower, in the wake of the Geneva Accords of 1954, faced the question of whether Diem could create a viable political base. There were those in Washington in 1954 who were profoundly sceptical of the possibility; and the sceptics included Ambassador Lawton Collins in Saigon. At that time Diem's problem was to assert his effective authority over various armed sects. Diem was on the brink of losing American support when on April 28, 1955, he succeeded in defeating the Binh Xuyen units, organized by the gangster group which in practice dominated the life of Saigon.

From that time Diem moved forward with considerable success, including progress in weeding out the communist structure left behind in 1954. But as Hanoi revived insurrection in 1958, his weaknesses as the ruler of a lively, modernizing, postcolonial society became increasingly clear: he could not mobilize or energize the full talents of the military and civil bureaucracy, and this led to a decreasing ability to protect the people in the countryside; and he dealt with the citizens of the country with a lack of confidence which generated apathy and resentment. A setting of insecurity, apathy, and resentment created a situation which Hanoi and the Viet Cong could exploit with increasing effect.

But guerrilla operations move slowly. The situation in South Vietnam was eroding, but there was no crisis as palpable as that in Laos, as the Eisenhower administration came to its end.

Nevertheless, Eisenhower's memoir is significant. The lack of attention given to Hanoi's gathering, quiet, but mortally dangerous, offensive against South Vietnam; Eisenhower's silence on the dilemma posed by Diem's peculiar mixture of strengths and weaknesses; the inherent incapacity of the Laos authorities to assert sovereignty over their territory bordering Vietnam, especially the infiltration trails to the south; the limits and dilemmas of a massive application of American force in Laos itself; Eisenhower's failure to face the implications for the American military force structure of simultaneous crises in Berlin and Laos—all this is a true portrait of Kennedy's inheritance in Southeast Asia.

13

From Eisenhower to Kennedy

THE CHARACTER OF THE TRANSITION

THE TRANSITION FROM EISENHOWER TO KENNEDY PROVIDED MORE drama than most passages of power in a democracy: from a soldier-statesman of seventy to a pragmatic idealist of forty-three; from a Protestant rooted in the rural American heartland of pre-1914 days, impressed by the progress he had seen in his lifetime and by the opportunities he had personally been granted, to an upper-class Irish Catholic from the urbane Northeast, shaped by a vivid sense of the weaknesses of the West that had produced the Second World War and by the exhilaration and tragedy of that war he had seen as a junior officer; from a man with a visceral faith that the old verities of American life would suffice to one who sensed that America, as well as the world, required perhaps more change than it was capable of managing if it was to survive. The latter difference was fundamental; for, above all, the succession of Kennedy to Eisenhower was a transition from a President who innovated as little as his responsibilities required to one who aimed to set the affairs of America and the world on new paths that reached far beyond the eight years to which he looked forward on January 20, 1961.

The inescapable problems of a changing America and a volatile world set limits on Eisenhower's underlying conservatism; the inescapable realities of American politics and an intractable world set limits on Kennedy's impulse to innovate. Eisenhower was more of an innovator than he would have chosen to be, Kennedy, less.

EISENHOWER, THE RELUCTANT INNOVATOR

EISENHOWER did not, then, seek in the Presidency great new domestic or foreign goals, except to move the world toward stable peace. He believed, perhaps more profoundly than Taft,[1] that the role of the federal government should, in fact, be diminished: "I was determined, if humanly possible, to carry on the fight to conduct a revolution which would reverse the trend of the budgets of the past twenty years."[2] Eisenhower was prepared to accept budget deficits at times of high unemployment. But this was not a matter of Keynesian doctrine: there was no realistic alternative available as federal revenues declined in times of recession in the face of a federal budget that was only marginally under the President's control. His advisers offered no way to escape the cost-push inflation of the latter fifties except to cut back the rate of growth. He lacked a clear conception of the link between a high and steady rate of growth and the availability of public revenues. He was whipsawed, therefore, by conflict between a sense of what he ought to do and a sense of duty to budgetary rectitude as the principal instrument for fighting inflation.

For example, Eisenhower came to understand the extraordinary value of foreign aid resources in the conduct of foreign policy. In 1958 he encouraged a massive effort by a citizens committee, headed by Eric Johnston, to rally public support for the program he had put before the Congress. I served on Johnston's committee. In February we had a remarkable gathering in Washington, addressed by, among others, Eisenhower and Nixon, Truman and Acheson, Stevenson and Allen Dulles, Fulton J. Sheen and James Killian. Eisenhower received his ardent lobbyists in his office on April 8, 1958. Expecting a statement of encouragement and an injunction to carry on the good fight, most of us were shaken to hear a troubled and wistful monologue about the overriding need to balance the budget, closing with the rhetorical question: "Where are we going to get the money from?"

In military policy it is somewhat harder to assess the extent to which Eisenhower's conservatism in domestic matters colored his budgetary dispositions. Certainly Operation Candor, the project to dramatize the meaning of thermonuclear weapons, was rejected in 1953 in substantial part because it might lead to pressures for exaggerated military outlays which would endanger the budget. Certainly budgetary considerations played a part in the restrained reaction of Eisenhower to the pressures for expanded military programs which Rockefeller and others urged upon him from 1955 forward and to the vastly stronger political pressures that followed the launching of the first Sputnik. Some things he said and wrote suggest this: for example, he said that we must "devise and maintain indefinitely a military posture of such effectiveness that the Communists will abandon any thought of all-out military attack against us or our allies, and to support this military capacity so prudently as to avoid undermining our economic soundness. We need an adequate defense, but every arms dollar we spend above adequacy has a long-term weakening effect upon the nation and its security."[3] In part, Eisenhower may have believed that existing military dispositions were basically adequate.

But the question he and his successor confronted was not an all-out military attack against the United States or its allies. They faced oblique pressures in Berlin, the Caribbean, the Congo, and in Southeast Asia, any or all of which could lead to claims on United States conventional military forces, as Eisenhower fully recognized in the case of Laos.

The conservative bias in Eisenhower was strengthened by the easy success of his first term. Accidents of history had yielded a transient phase of relative tranquility abroad and effortless prosperity at home. By later standards, the race issue was quiet. Stalin's death set the stage not only for a period of domestic preoccupation in the Soviet Union but also for a settlement of the war in Korea. Mao turned to his first Five-Year Plan and the Geneva Accords of 1954 provided an interval of four peaceful years in Indochina. From his first major foreign policy statement as President on April 16, 1953, Eisenhower emerged, with evident deep conviction, as a man seeking to move the world toward peace.

American strategic superiority, combined with the new pacts around the periphery of the communist world, promised to deter further aggression of the kind confronted in Korea. Western Europe and Japan moved from reconstruction into sustained and vigorous growth; and foreign aid could easily shift to the military and economic support of allies in the developing world who manned the defense perimeter from South Korea to Turkey. In typical American style, the United States appeared to have converted the challenging crisis of Stalin and the Cold War into an ongoing, institutionalized process. With all quiet from Berlin to Seoul, there was a strong impulse in America to turn inward and relax. This impulse was strengthened by the presence in the White House of a deeply trusted, temperate, experienced soldier, whose low-key style encouraged a sense that things were manageable, and being managed.

It seemed for a little while as if America, after the turmoil of protracted innovation in domestic affairs and on the world scene, had again been granted a phase where government could operate successfully by relatively familiar process. The American operating style had always been marked by successive phases of creative innovation, usually in the context of urgent crisis, followed by reduction of the innovation to ongoing process. Eisenhower came to power in an America where the New Deal innovations had long since been reduced to ongoing process. Truman's duel with Stalin had yielded NATO and a viable western Europe at one end of Eurasia, a successfully defended South Korea and a prosperous Japan at the other.

The structure of the American economy after the Korean War yielded a surge of expansion, rooted in the familiar processes of the automobile age. Even the troubling phenomenon of Joe McCarthy could be viewed as a relic of a troubled past which the normal workings of American political life would and did reject, although not without damage and danger.

But Eisenhower's first term was illusory. Beneath the surface calm the H-bomb and missilery were transforming the problem of the strategic balance. The locus of trouble and struggle was shifting southward, as communists exploited the increased volatility of the developing world. The Egyptian arms deal in 1955 and the political and economic programs that followed in its wake had demonstrated how the pacts built to prevent a second Korean-type war could be outflanked.

Eisenhower recognized that a new phase in foreign policy had begun, initiated by Nasser's nationalization of the Suez Canal in July 1956 and rendered melodramatic by the launching of the first Sputnik some fifteen months later. Equally, a new phase in domestic life began with the recession of 1957–1958, the emergence of acute balance-of-payments difficulties, the growing demand for increased public services, and heightened racial tensions.

Eisenhower was not insensitive to the new array of problems. He was not a rigid dogmatist. His innovations were real, but late and somewhat reluctant. Moreover, he was inhibited by a deeply rooted conviction that public problems should be posed in ways that minimized emotional divisions. This conviction, which has a great deal to be said for it in a democratic society, nevertheless set limits on the pace of innovation he was prepared to contemplate in a rapidly changing environment.

In terms of national style, he was a gifted and healing politician for a time of relative stability, consolidation, and slow rate of change. When he did choose to move, he found himself further limited by a lack of public resources which, in part at least, flowed from his own economic policies.

There is something moving and gallant, as well as something sterile, about Eisenhower's extensive foreign travels of 1959–1960 as he sought to bring to bear the last substantial asset he had, his personality and what it symbolized, to stabilize a world moving beyond the reach of the policies he was prepared to launch.

Eisenhower's concept of the national interest conformed to that which emerged from the cumulative American experience in the twentieth century, becoming increasingly explicit after 1945. He aimed to hold the balance of power out of potentially hostile hands in Europe and Asia (as well as in the Middle East and Africa); to resist the military intrusion of extra-continental powers into the Western Hemisphere; and, on this basis, he sought movement toward stable peace. He left his successor with a threat to the European balance in the form of Khrushchev's unresolved ultimatum on Berlin; a threat to the Asian balance in the form of the Laos situation;

and a threat to the Western Hemisphere in the form of Castro in Cuba. The Congo crisis was unresolved, although Eisenhower had thrown his weight behind the United Nations effort to salvage Congolese unity and frustrate a potentially dangerous Soviet intrusion. On the other hand, his Lebanon–Jordan initiative with the British had temporarily stabilized the Middle East, a quite substantial achievement. He moved in his second term toward a more promising policy in the developing world than his initial stance because it was more clearly aligned with the pervasive objectives of economic and social development and unencumbered independence. But his new aid policy was not conducted on a scale appropriate to the magnitude of the problem.

In the world as it has been since 1945, no American President can expect to turn over to his successor an international agenda clear of dangerous unresolved problems. That received by Kennedy from Eisenhower was peculiarly difficult, marked as it was by post-Sputnik communist initiatives that had not run their course.

In terms of stages of growth, Eisenhower, to the end, viewed the American economy (and national economic policy) primarily in terms of the criteria of high mass-consumption; that is, in terms of what the private sector might provide in goods and services.[4] He resisted an expanded federal role in the society that was emerging as families began to reach beyond the age of the automobile and suburbia to enlarged outlays for education and health and to deal with the accumulated forces of degeneration that had rendered the cities distressed areas. As the evolution of the stages of growth in Europe and Japan generated pressure on the American balance of payments, he reacted defensively with policies that dampened the American rate of growth.

In terms of the mobilization and allocation of public resources, the slow rate of growth of the economy in his second term resulted in a shortage of revenues, only partially compensated by the high FY 1959 federal deficit ($13 billion). He could correctly claim at the time (and in retrospect) that his allocations for nuclear deterrence were adequate; but in circumstances where a crisis was latent in Berlin, and acute in Southeast Asia, his dispositions with respect to the scale and mobility of conventional forces were inadequate. The bulk of existing American conventional forces in continental reserve were earmarked for NATO; and he commended to his successor the sending of U.S. forces to protect Southeast Asia if necessary.

Eisenhower's responses in his second term to new problems emerging at home and abroad were more substantial than is often appreciated. His second term was quite different from his first in terms of men, ideas, and courses of action, notably in foreign policy. But it came widely to be sensed, even within his administration, that his dispositions did not match the nation's problems. In the spring of 1960 Nixon and Arthur Burns proposed a more expansionist domestic policy, as Burns' calculations indicated a trough just before the election,[5] but their proposals were turned down. In the wake of the summit failure in Paris, Christian Herter, stimulated by the Policy Planning Staff and backed by Douglas Dillon and Livingston Merchant, pressed for a substantial expansion in the military budget; but the initiative failed.

After the election of 1960, Eisenhower made a systematic effort to mount an orderly transition and to prepare the new President for his responsibilities. Kennedy was briefed regularly on the world scene by Allen Dulles. On November 17, 1960, he was informed for the first time of the training of refugees in Guatemala for infiltration into Cuba; on November 29, of the shift from an infiltration-guerrilla plan to a straightforward invasion.

Between the election and January 20, 1961, he saw Eisenhower twice: on December 6, 1960, and then on the day before the Inauguration.

We have Eisenhower's memorandum for the record of the first meeting[6]; and there are at least three sets of notes on the second.

The nagging balance-of-payments problem was discussed at both sessions, with Eisenhower recommending the withdrawal of some U.S. forces from Europe "unless other arrangements could, at the very least, stop the drain on our gold."[7]

But it was Laos that occupied the bulk of the more substantive session on January 19. Eisenhower and Herter underlined the critical importance of Laos, urged that it be handled, if possible, by invoking the Manila Treaty and SEATO, and pointed to the reservations in Paris and London about military action. Eisenhower concluded, however, that Laos was so vital an area that unilateral American military action should be undertaken, if necessary to save the situation. So far as the records show, and in Kennedy's memory, the word Vietnam was not uttered.

At some point in this period, as Kennedy told me, Eisenhower promised to support him fully in foreign policy except under one circumstance: if he permitted Communist China to enter the United Nations. In that case, Eisenhower said he would take after him in public.

The Bipartisan Consensus of the Late 1950s

In fact, the agenda passed by Eisenhower to Kennedy was vastly more complex than the conversations between the two men suggest. For some time, Republicans as well as Democrats had been addressing themselves to that agenda on the common assumption that, irrespective of party, the administration coming to responsibility on January 20, 1961, would have to strike out in new directions. That bipartisan consensus had a profound effect on Kennedy's thought and policy. It defined most of the initial directions in which he sought to innovate, although its inadequacies concealed issues that posed for Kennedy some of his most searching and difficult challenges.

The new consensus on domestic, military, and foreign policy which emerged in the late 1950s is reflected in the Rockefeller Panel reports[8] and the report of a Commission on National Goals, appointed by Eisenhower, which delivered its findings after the election of 1960.[9]

The Rockefeller Panel reports were generated by Nelson Rockefeller's failure to persuade Eisenhower to enlarge military and foreign aid expenditures at the end of 1955. The panels began to meet in 1956, and the reports were published individually over the period January 1958 to September 1960.

The panels included about one hundred citizens with links in all regions of the country to business, labor, banking, education, religion, philanthropy, journalism—in fact, virtually all fields. The members drew on another hundred specialized consultants. Taken all together, those who participated constituted as much of an elite as American democracy yields. They probed critical questions of military policy, economic foreign policy, domestic economic and social policies, education, and the future of the democratic process in America.

Goals for Americans, the report of the Commission on National Goals, was assembled and written by similar groups (with some overlaps) and emerged with similar conclusions.

Broadly speaking, this was the consensus:

> Substantially enlarged military outlays were required to build a secure second-strike nuclear force and to increase the size and mobility of conventional forces.
>
> In this effort NATO should be re-invigorated and its doctrines and force structures modernized to overcome a rigid reliance on nuclear weapons; and the Atlantic Community should work increasingly as partners in matters of trade, money, and aid.
>
> More purposeful efforts were required to move toward arms control arrangements with the Soviet Union and to explore the possibilities of enlarged contacts with eastern Europe.
>
> Increased outlays were required from ourselves and others to accelerate growth in the developing regions; and, within this effort, special consideration should be given to accelerated economic and social development in Latin America and the newly emerging independent states of Africa.
>
> Radically increased public expenditures were required at home: to rehabilitate urban areas; to enlarge outlays for health and social security; to enlarge and improve the quality of the educational system.
>
> To finance these enlarged public outlays the real rate of growth must be sharply increased and steadily held at 4 percent or higher.

This was, essentially, the broad framework of ideas and policies that Kennedy accepted in the late 1950s. He was not, of course, a passive or uncritical recipient of this consensus. He was in the middle of it, getting to know its strengths and weaknesses, talking directly and at length with many of those who were architects of its various elements, later assembling many of them for support in his campaign, to write postelection task force reports, and to participate in his government.

When, for example, Kennedy delivered a major address in the Senate on June 14, 1960, less than a month before the Democratic Convention, aside from some ad hoc remarks on easing tensions over Berlin and the Middle East, his ten points closely followed this consensus, which can be seen in his own detailed formulations in *The Strategy of Peace*.[10] This congruence arose simply because these were the ideas in the air as thoughtful men weighed the scale and character of the nation's current and foreseeable problems against the pattern of Eisenhower's second-term policies.

FOUR MAJOR INADEQUACIES OF THE BIPARTISAN CONSENSUS

THE consensus of the late 1950s proved insufficient or incomplete on four points: race, inflation, guerrilla warfare, and the reaction of the affluent young against the values and institutions that had evolved as America moved through the stage of high mass-consumption. All were to constitute major problems in the 1960s, three of them in Kennedy's time.

The Negro's drive for full citizenship is referred to in both reports, including an eloquent passage by Henry Wriston in *Goals for Americans*,[11] but the scale and latent emotional violence of the race issue were universally underestimated. The problem of inflation was recognized in both reports,[12] but there was relatively little thought developed on how to reconcile price stability with the accelerated rate of growth universally recommended and little also on the related question of the American balance of payments. In military policy the emphasis on the buildup of conventional forces and their mobility did not fully take into account the special nature of guerrilla warfare, its deterrence and frustration.

With respect to the race question, Kennedy's own experiences with Negro leaders in politics probably did more to educate him in the late 1950s than any of his formal advisers, although in Harris Wofford he had working with him an ardent and sensitive civil rights advocate. As the election of 1960 revealed, Kennedy had earned, at least relatively, the confidence of the Negro community. Typical of the period, however, the two passages in *The Strategy of Peace* touching on race relate to expanded economic and educational opportunities for Negroes.[13] There was in 1960 no clear foreshadowing of the drive for full racial equality and the passionate search for a new kind of dignity and identity that was to emerge with the coming of age in the 1960s of the next generation of Negro leaders.

With respect to guerrilla warfare, I was probably more focused on the problem than most of Kennedy's advisers before he came to the Presidency. The special problems of guerrilla warfare were borne in on me by three experiences of the 1950s: an examination of the prospects for Communist China and of American policy in Asia, which required study not only of Mao's strategy in the takeover of China but also of communist operations in Indochina, the Philippines, Malaya, and Indonesia; a growing interest in the problems of underdevelopment in general, which led naturally to a concern for the inherent vulnerability to guerrilla warfare of societies in transition from traditional to modern forms of organization; and work by James E. Cross and Lucian Pye at M.I.T., whose insights I was privileged to share. Cross was studying the lessons to be drawn from past and contemporary experiences in guerrilla warfare; Pye had studied and written with distinction about the guerrilla campaign in Malaya, and, especially, about the human beings caught up in the communist insurrectional effort. In *The United States in the World Arena* I drew more sharply than was then conventional the distinction between limited and guerrilla warfare, noting that a repetition of what had happened in Indochina up to 1954 "clearly represented a pattern which, if repeated on a sufficient scale, could lose the balance of power in Asia, the Middle East, and Africa."[14] There were, of course, Americans like Edward Lansdale who had had recent major practical experience with the curious mixture of politics and violence involved; and within the Kennedy administration there were to be others with earlier operational experience, notably Dean Rusk.

But in 1958–1960 these matters were not discussed in the Kennedy camp as major issues. Up to January 20, 1961, and beyond, it was certainly Kennedy's own knowledge of Indochina, including a formative visit in 1951, that most strongly shaped his approach to guerrilla warfare—notably his conviction that the interest and will of the people involved must be engaged.[15] And as early as August 1958 he saw the danger of Soviet nuclear strength as going beyond the temptation of launching a direct assault: "Their missile power will be the shield from behind which they will slowly, but surely, advance—through Sputnik diplomacy, limited brush-fire wars, indirect non-overt aggression, intimidation and subversion, internal revolution, increased prestige or influence, and the vicious blackmail of our allies."[16] This was a fairly accurate portrait of what he was to confront as President two and a half years later.

The emergence of the dissident white affluent youth, entranced by old anarchist doctrines in the guise of a New Left and experimenting defiantly with unconventional patterns of life and behavior, was the least anticipated development of the 1960s. On the other hand, the issues that concerned the volatile young were not new. For example, the question of man and bureaucracy was the obsessive theme of retrospective novels about the Second World War as well as a good many postwar novels (e.g., *The Man in the Gray Flannel Suit*). Anyone teaching in the late 1950s knew the depth of the concern among students about the survival of civilization in a nuclear age and the yearning to do something about the bulk of humanity in the developing world rather than to just accept the bureaucratic escalator and the life of suburbia. There were a good many harbingers of the Peace Corps.

Moreover, as the fruits of high mass-consumption became more widely diffused, the inadequacies of that way of life were explored in Galbraith's *The Affluent Society*, my own *The Stages of Economic Growth*, and other works of the period. In fact, the original context of the phrase "the New Frontier" was the following: ". . . what to do when the increase in real income itself loses its charm? Babies, boredom, three-day weekends, the moon, or the creation of new inner, human frontiers in substitution for the imperatives of scarcity?"[17]

But still, I know of no clear foreshadowing in the 1950s of the goings on which began in Berkeley in the autumn of 1964. The phenomenon was evidently rooted in the volatile minority of a new generation, born during or after the Second World War, which, in a pattern familiar since Plato, took for granted what had been cumulatively achieved in the past and articulated a new set of dissatisfactions and objectives. The international character of student dissidence suggests the inevitability of the problem. Kennedy's election, in fact, may have postponed its emergence in the United States; for he appeared to leapfrog a generation of political leadership and symbolized, for a time, a victory for the young. Aside from the trauma of his assassination, and the dark shadow it cast on the whole society, Johnson's succession appeared to represent a return to generational normalcy in American politics, making easier a stance of revolt by the young. In any case, I know of no task force reports to Kennedy on how to deal with youthful dissidence.

With respect to the reconciliation of rapid growth and price stability, there was some anticipation among Kennedy's advisers and in the elite consensus as a whole, but price stability was not then a major concern of the reigning Democratic economists. Just as the military experts generally rang the changes on a second-strike capability, conventional forces, mobility, a reorganized NATO strategy, and arms control, the conventional economic experts focused, in rather orthodox Keynesian terms, on fiscal and monetary policies that would increase the rate of growth, if necessary, by means of substantial deficits in the federal budget.

For example, in Kennedy's task force report on "economic conditions in the United States" (written by Paul Samuelson), the fundamental observation on inflation is that fear of it should not inhibit an expansionary policy. The possibility of a cost-push inflation emerging before full employment was reached is clearly recognized. But, in its key passage, the report commends waiting until it emerged before grappling with it:

> . . . the goal of high employment and effective real growth cannot be abandoned because of the problematical fear that reattaining of prosperity in America may bring with it some difficulties; if recovery means a reopening of the cost-push problem, then we have no choice but to move closer to the day when that problem has to be successfully grappled with.[18]

Kennedy himself was acutely aware of the problem. In a letter to me of February 1, 1960, he wrote that he intended during the campaign "to discuss a great deal . . . the entire matter of economic growth and how we are to bring about such growth without dissipating our gains in inflation." He was not only aware of the economic problem but of his potential vulnerability to the Republican charge of being fiscally irresponsible and a "big spender." This was no trivial matter since in the same letter he said he intended to deal also with the excessive allocation of "our national wealth to private welfare, while failing to meet the needs of society—housing, education, etc.—which can only be met through governmental allocation of national resources."

A political campaign was not an easy setting for dealing with this sensitive and complex reconciliation; and, to the best of my knowledge, only two of Kennedy's advisers at the time were pressing the issue hard in his camp: Kenneth Galbraith[19] and myself. Our view differed from the task force report on the economy in urging that cost-push inflation be faced promptly, at the bottom of the recession, before recovery set in motion a vicious circle of demand-pull and cost-push price increases, extremely difficult to manage once under way.

Since the early 1950s, before the American balance-of-payments problem had emerged, I had written about the implications for inflation in democratic societies where "unemployment is no longer to be regarded as an act of God."[20] I urged that Keynesian policies were not enough and that labor, business, and government would have to come to agreement on a wage and price policy that would reconcile a high and steady rate of growth with price stability, or even decline. As an economic historian and economist, I came to a conclusion I still hold: the optimum setting for growth and stability is a regime of constant money wages and falling prices. I believed a reconciliation of growth and price stability (or decline) would require changes in outlook and in economic analysis "no less profound than those wrought by the Keynesian revolution."[21]

The experience of the American economy in the late 1950s, with its corrosive cost-push inflation at a time of substantial unemployment, in an environment of balance-of-payments pressure, heightened my concern. In addition, I pressed for measures to modernize the American capital stock, since western Europe and Japan had substantially re-equipped their industry with new plant in the 1950s. The American productivity advantage, fundamental to our long-run balance-of-payments position, was endangered. I was sure that the domestic and foreign policy objectives of the next administration, if it was Democratic, would depend for their fulfillment on reconciling a higher rate of growth with a new wage and price discipline and measures to modernize American industrial capital rapidly.

In June 1960 I argued fully the case in public at a meeting at the Harvard Business School. During the campaign, as Nixon pressed Kennedy on "fiscal irresponsibility," I suggested that Kennedy and George Meany might exchange letters looking toward a commitment to hold the wage and price line under a full employment policy. In a letter of September 5, 1960, Archibald Cox reported the marked, but understandable, lack of enthusiasm in Kennedy's Washington headquarters for the idea:

> I talked with Arthur Goldberg at some length about your proposal for an exchange of letters between the Senator and George Meany looking toward a commitment to hold the wage and price line under a full employment policy. Arthur felt that there was no chance whatsoever of securing any such commitment from the labor unions.
>
> Their judgment, with which I concur, is based more upon the impossibility of finding anyone in the labor movement who can give such a commitment, in the face of internal union politics, than on a fundamental disagreement with your suggestion. Certainly there is a good deal of support among the larger unions for the view that the current wage-price situation is a hopeless treadmill.

After the election I bore down on this point more than on any other with Kennedy. In November he asked me to suggest a list of task forces and task force leaders to convert military and foreign policy ideas into operational policies covering fifteen subjects. After fulfilling his injunction in a lengthy memorandum, I took the occasion to add:

> I cannot emphasize too strongly that the capacity of the new Administration to do what it wants to do at home and abroad will depend on promptly breaking the institutional basis for creeping inflation, notably in the key steel[22] and automobile industries; and on driving hard to earn more foreign exchange and to increase domestic productivity over a wide front. Without determined action in these areas it will be extremely difficult to bring the domestic economy back to reasonably full employment without inflation; and this means that we shall not have the federal revenues to give extra needed thrust in military and foreign policy. If we do not evoke American effort and sacrifice for communal goals at home, we run the danger of being forced by the balance of payments position and inflation into substituting rhetoric for action abroad.

I introduced these domestic matters into the foreign policy agenda because I did not believe his economic advisers had sufficiently explored the institutional and negotiating problems of creating a noninflationary expansion in output and employment.

My most important communication with Kennedy on this matter was at breakfast in Boston on January 9, 1961. He went to attend his last meeting as a member of the Harvard Board of Overseers, to talk with some of the men he wished to recruit for the administration, and to say his farewell to Massachusetts before assuming the Presidency. He had flown up the night before because my role in the administration was unsettled and he wished to discuss it with me at breakfast.

I arrived at 122 Bowden Street to find the hallway outside his apartment in excited disarray. A large number of Boston political friends and well-wishers milled around to say good-by to their boy, observed by a somewhat distracted Secret Service team. I was admitted to find Kennedy alone, emerging from his bath; and we settled down in the kitchenette.

It was, I knew, the last time I would talk to him in the old way. I asked if we could first put aside the question of my possible job and consider a matter of substance. I told him that all our hopes and policies, domestic and foreign, hinged on reconciling higher growth with price stability and maintaining a sturdy balance-of-payments surplus. This was true of military policy and foreign aid. I recalled how Britain's role in the world was attenuated by a failure to solve this problem during the interwar years, but there would be no America behind us if we failed. I then underlined that his domestic program required more public revenues which only growth could provide, since a tax increase was not politically realistic. In fact, a tax decrease might be required to achieve steady growth, given the manner in which the existing tax structure tended to frustrate expansion. Therefore, to make a high rate of growth viable, he had to move promptly to gear wage increases to increase in productivity, to increase productivity, and to assure that industry would not exploit labor's self-discipline to raise prices and expand inequitably the share of profits. A wage freeze and price cuts would be even better. All this required a new kind of collective bargaining procedure in our society which he would have to construct and lead. The heart of the matter lay in the steel and automobile industries; but there would be many difficulties, especially in the construction industry. But we had to begin, and begin soon and learn along the way.

I concluded that this was, certainly, the most important piece of advice I could give him as he took up his new responsibilities.

He said he understood and would come back to it, which he later did. Then he turned to the primary business he had in mind.

After a final brief discussion of Laos, he dressed and we went down in a bulging elevator to the then crowded lobby, as he headed for Cambridge. His farewell: "See you a week from Friday," which was January 20.[23]

Looked at in the sweep of American political history, Kennedy's was a rather peculiar agenda. Except for Washington's two terms (when the installation of the controversial Hamiltonian program at home was interwoven with intense debate over the stance of the new nation toward the

Anglo-French struggle), the United States was generally privileged to concentrate on the major problems of either domestic or foreign policy but not both. In this century Wilson could launch the New Freedom before confronting the realities of the First World War. Roosevelt launched the New Deal in an America locked into isolationism, and that program had run its course well before the outbreak of the Second World War. Truman could face the Cold War crisis of 1945–1952 from a base which did not generate acute political pressures for domestic innovation.

In the late 1950s, however, pressures and problems at home gathered momentum, while the situation in Southeast Asia, the Caribbean, Berlin, and the Congo shadowed the international scene and the American nuclear posture was in question.

The agenda that Kennedy inherited from Eisenhower stretched, then, across the whole front of domestic and foreign policy.

His problem was peculiar in another sense. Major innovations in American policy at home and abroad usually occurred in a setting of acute crisis. There was widespread concern but no clear, single, overt crisis in 1960. (There is little doubt that Eisenhower would have been overwhelmingly re-elected if he could have run again in 1960.) The task for an activist President was not easy. Perhaps the nearest equivalent was Theodore Roosevelt's problem of getting the country moving upon succeeding McKinley in 1901, although Roosevelt's problems were trivial compared to the Kennedy agenda of 1961.

Kennedy's campaign theme arose from his appreciation of this state of things. In the autumn of 1959 and the early months of 1960, I accepted a series of speaking invitations in various parts of the country. As I met and talked with people, I found widespread concern. Some were worried about missiles, others about the state of American education; many were worried about our slow rate of growth, others about our balance of payments; some knowledgeable men were troubled about relations across the Atlantic, others about the increasing possibilities of serious trouble in Latin America and other developing regions; and still others were concerned about decay in the cities, which was vastly more swift than emerging plans for urban rehabilitation.

In the spring I was invited, along with others working with Kennedy, to a party in a Beacon Hill apartment. The Senator arrived late. As we talked in the crowded room, I told him I knew what the first sentence of his acceptance speech should be: "This country is ready to get moving again and I'm prepared to lead it." I then explained why I judged the phrase a reasonably accurate summation of the nation's diffuse uneasiness. We talked at length about the theme a few weeks later, flying in the *Caroline* from Washington to Boston. In May he sent word back from the preconvention primary in Oregon that he'd been trying the phrase out and rather liked it.

Whatever the virtues or demerits of the campaign theme, it reflected accurately Kennedy's appreciation that the nation confronted a wide range of difficult problems of which it was not fully aware; that these had not yet reached the point of crisis; that vigorous anticipatory initiatives in many fields would be required to bring American society and the international scene back to a better balance without major crises; but that major crises were more likely rather than less in the time ahead when, hopefully, he would bear the responsibilities of the Presidency.

JFK: An Innovator on the Eve of Responsibility

John Kennedy, the man and the shock of his death, evoked a memorable set of statements from those who knew him. Much of this *témoinage* was written in the wake of his assassination, with openheartedness and sensibility as well as grief. These statements were shaped not only by depth of feeling but also by a consciousness of how sharply Kennedy himself distinguished sentiment from sentimentality. That literature, taken altogether, constitutes a rare portrait of a remarkable and engaging human being.

My purpose here is more narrow and mundane. It is to sketch briefly, from my knowledge of Kennedy in the period 1958–1960, certain qualities as they then appeared which colored his approach to the Presidency, its management, its problems, and the innovations he hoped to set in motion.

I first talked seriously with Kennedy in February 1958. Toward the end of 1957 he had asked for my help on the question of enlarged assistance to India. Our dialogue expanded out over the whole field of foreign and military policy and to the domestic scene. He requested my regular support as he sought the Democratic nomination and the Presidency.

I saw him from time to time over the next three years and remained steadily in touch on issues of substance while I continued my work as a teacher. I was neither an old friend from school or war nor, in those days, a day-to-day working colleague. I was, simply, an early member of what was to become in 1959–1960 a large group of academics interested in problems of public policy who were purposefully recruited by Kennedy. We were about the same age. Our outlook on affairs was similar: we were too young to have been rooted deeply in the adventures of the New Deal; we had seen America in trouble and then in triumph as junior officers during the Second World War; we were greatly concerned with the dangers to both America and the wider cause of stable peace on the world scene; we sensed that the domestic agenda was shifting beyond the then familiar categories of conventional liberalism. We communicated tersely and easily. Ties of confidence and mutual regard developed. I concluded in early 1958 that he could be a first-rate President.[24]

To seek and gain the Presidency against long odds was a major enterprise. It evidently absorbed a high proportion of his time, energy, and resourcefulness. It took immense attention to detail to tip each of the marginal factors in the right direction against the quiet but heavy weight of anti-Catholic sentiment. I glimpsed occasionally the process of winning re-election in Massachusetts massively, and subsequently building a national organization, battling through the primaries, carrying the convention at Los Angeles, and winning narrowly in November. On a few occasions he initiated talk with me about some of the problems and choices he faced along the way. But I was not a working part of that political enterprise, which Sorensen describes as well as it is ever likely to be described.[25] I merely supplied ideas, position papers, and drafts for speeches and articles from the rear.

I did, however, get to know deeply Kennedy's mind on matters of military and foreign policy and on some critical questions of domestic policy as well. I could observe how he dealt with men and ideas—and, sometimes, with women and children and the roar of life surrounding a young senator on his way up.

Kennedy, like all serious politicians, was interested in ideas. Politicians understand better than most men that ideas are an essential raw material for effective action. This was true even of Eisenhower, who was not by instinct or conviction an activist President. Nevertheless, from the beginning he consciously accepted the strain with Foster Dulles of having C. D. Jackson and then Nelson Rockefeller in the White House. Thereafter, within the limits of his budgetary and balance-of-payments constraints, he was receptive to ideas generated, for example, by Milton Eisenhower and Douglas Dillon, as well as Robert Bowie and Gerard Smith in the Policy Planning Staff, backstopped by the fertile brain and indomitable spirit of Henry Owen.

Kennedy's instinctive view of the Presidency was activist, and he viewed the time ahead as one requiring new initiatives. His run for the Presidency took place at a period of great intellectual ferment related to public policy. He was a living part of that ferment and, finally, its leader in action.

But he was not an intellectual in the usual sense. He did not enjoy the elegant elaboration of ideas for its own sake. Ideas were tools. He picked them up easily like statistics or the names of local politicians. He was a resourceful political innovator, not an inventor or scientist. He wanted to know how ideas could be put to work. His most typical response to an idea was: "What do you want me to do about it today?" His disciplined courtesy and good manners were strained by the extensive exposition of ideas with which he was already familiar. He would tap his teeth and fuss with his tie. His personal intellectual interest was in history and, especially, in the history of politics and politicians in the Anglo-American world. He saw the politician as hero, often frustrated, sometimes confronted with choices that tested and strained the fabric of his character and spirit, but striving to do great things.

He sought out experts, but he was also systematically suspicious of them. He was conscious that his course of action, even as a senator, required him to orchestrate a great many different ideas and considerations that no single adviser or expert could take fully into account. He made this point in the only conversation I ever had with him that began with an abstract observation. It was in March 1960, between the two halves of the Wisconsin primary. He was briefly in Washington, and we spent a good part of a long, relaxed morning going over many matters.

He observed that experts were essential but one had to be alert to the factors they left out of account which might be crucial. He illustrated the proposition with reference to the question of whether or not he should enter the forthcoming West Virginia primary—an issue on which he had made no public announcement at that time. He said the experts were against it on three solid grounds: Hubert Humphrey was to the left of him and this gave Humphrey an initial advantage in a state where many Democrats were poor, unemployed, and deeply attached to the New Deal; the people were 95 percent Protestant; and if he lost he was out of the race for the nomination. But, Kennedy said, the experts left out one simple, overriding point: he had no right to go before the convention and claim to be a candidate if he could only win primaries in states with 25 percent or more Catholics. So, he said, "I am going in."

On the Presidency itself, he once, after a review of the difficult issues lying ahead, posed the question of how a man could conceive of seeking the job when the problems were obviously bigger than mortal men should have to handle. He then observed that one of five mortal men would, in fact, be the Democratic candidate: Adlai Stevenson, Hubert Humphrey, Stuart Symington, Lyndon Johnson, or himself. Stevenson, he felt, had had two chances, which was all the party owed him. Humphrey, whom he liked and respected, he honestly felt would not be a better President than himself. Symington was charming but somewhat lazy. Johnson had the best claim on the nomination in terms of experience and performance; and he "wants the same things for the country that I do." But Kennedy doubted that anyone from Johnson's part of the country could get the nomination. Therefore, he felt he could go forward in good conscience.

Behind his drive for the Presidency was, clearly, an intent to achieve greatness, in the sense that American historians use the term in assessing incumbents of the past. This thrust for "greatness" was, in part, a matter of temperament, of political party, and of the tasks ahead as he saw them. It fitted the Greek definition of happiness which he often cited: the maximum exercise of a man's capacities against standards of excellence.

Without any evidence from Kennedy himself, I also concluded that he wanted not only to prove that a Catholic could be President, but also that the first Catholic President would stand before history as a "great" President. I judged then and later that this element contributed a special dimension—a kind of overdrive—to his efforts.

In England in early 1959 I was once asked by a distinguished British observer of affairs why Kennedy, who was obviously working hard for the nomination, was spending so much time on the Indian aid program. It did not seem to this man a vote-getting issue. I replied that, while marginally, it might help Kennedy alter his image favorably among the Democratic liberals who were giving him some considerable trouble, it was basically because the question of aid to India was something important and creative that he could influence from where he was. Politics was his chosen medium; he was a senator, and this was something a senator could do that might not otherwise get done.

In talking of his profession, Kennedy was always both respectful and humorous. He believed politics provided a maximum opportunity to do good and useful things for others and to leave a constructive imprint on one's times, but that it was also full of struggle and human frailty, of surprises and occasions for resourceful improvisation. As President his image of maximum confusion was: "This is the wildest thing I've seen since the West Virginia primary."

Kennedy evidently enjoyed the details of his craft and respected their importance. He never pretended they were in any way beneath him or second-order business. But he was also amused by its problems: whether it was to get a strong enough opponent in 1958 to bring out the full Democratic vote or to find a formula for not offending New England textile protectionist pressures while holding to a liberal stance on foreign trade.

An understanding of the realities of political life does not allow many illusions about the human condition; but Kennedy was one of the least cynical men I have known. Humor was his reconciling solvent.

Kennedy's administrative style was distinctive. It did not fit the hierarchical pyramids to be found in textbooks on administration: it was like the spokes of a wheel. When he formed a bond, it remained firm. His enormous energy permitted him to deal with a great many people on a bilateral basis, weaving their efforts into his tasks as he saw them. His method was that of the extended family. He was part of a big family. It was the nucleus of his political organization. He put each member to work in ways that could help, according to his talents. And, as he mobilized others to come aboard, the method persisted.

It was rooted in an assessment of human beings that was both affectionate and hard-minded. He actively enjoyed the variety of talents and personalities that assembled around him as the drive for the Presidency gathered momentum. He respected each man for what he was. There was reliability in his acceptance of men to work with him. There was also a firm assessment of where each might be useful and where not.

Behind it all was a quality that he concealed in his determination to maintain a private life but that ultimately projected and helped account for the power his image and memory were to attain: a direct and spontaneous reaction to human situations.

Talking privately of the Wisconsin primary, he held out his hand and said: "I have a big hand, but I've been talking to fellows with hands twice as big as mine from milking cows. They get up at five in the morning, and because the milk price is too low, they work these hours and live this life for damned little."

He once kept his wife and sister, Mrs. Stephen Smith, both pregnant, waiting at the North Terminal of the Washington airport where the *Caroline* was kept. Two of Abe Chayes' children were running about the place, as we all awaited a ride to Boston. It was a hot and sticky day. Kennedy arrived with one more phone call to make. He then took charge: put the women into the bunks; strapped in the children with a flash of conversation that lit up their faces; settled down to fish chowder, a haircut, and talk.

Despite the increasing complexity of his life, his dealings with people remained immediate and comfortable.

The closeness of his election was no surprise. Several times as senator —and several times as President—he noted that, with the special exception of Roosevelt, all the post-Civil War Democratic Presidents had been elected by a minority of the voters: Cleveland, Wilson, and Truman. He concluded that the balance of feeling in the electorate lay with a "moderate, decent, conservative margin," which a Democratic candidate had to reach. It was, therefore, impossible to build a victorious base on the left wing of the Democratic party.

Kennedy came to the Presidency with no illusion that the agenda before him would yield easily to his leadership. He was not borne down; for he had come out on the right side of close things, from injury in the war to the 1960 election. He had seen enough of life and read enough of history to know that the possibility of failure—or even tragedy—was also real. But this was where his life had brought him, where he had sought to be. It gave him the chance for the maximum exercise of his capacities against standards of excellence in his chosen field. He came to the job with zest and a sense of adventure, as well as the caution of a politician used to counting votes in situations too close for comfort and of a man who knew that in a nuclear age tragedy might not only be personal but cosmic.

BOOK TWO

The Kennedy Administration

14

Introduction to Book Two

KENNEDY'S TASK AS PRESIDENT, AND THE COURSES OF ACTION HE set in motion, conformed closely to the image of what would be required which grew in his mind as the 1950s came to an end and he moved to responsibility. A little to his surprise, he faced just as much trouble and need for innovation, over just as wide a front, as he had said he would confront if elected; and trouble came not in a tidy sequence like task-force reports, but with all the awkwardness and confusion of history unfolding, day by day, step by step.

First, there was the domestic scene where resumed growth had to be reconciled with price and balance-of-payments stability and, on that basis, new social programs launched, and the Negro moved forward toward full, unencumbered citizenship. The high level of unemployment in 1958–1960 (averaging 5.9 percent) had damped the high rate of increase in prices which marked 1955–1958; but the balance-of-payments deficit continued to run high (averaging $3.7 billion annually in 1958–1960), with gold draining off at an annual rate of $1.7 billion. This trap had to be broken if the nation was to enjoy again a high level of employment and the public revenues necessary to meet the growing demands for public services reflected in the rise of state and local government outlays in the late 1950s.

Second, the Berlin crisis was unresolved. Relations with Moscow were tense. It was still to be seen how Khrushchev would make his dispositions with respect to his new adversary; but latent Allied differences over Berlin, notably between Bonn and London, made it likely that pressure would be revived.

Third, beyond the palpable crises centered on Cuba, Southeast Asia, and the Congo, the whole developing world was in a ferment. Eisenhower's moves in Lebanon and in the Quemoy–Matsu crisis had helped, as had his new dispositions with respect to Latin America and the Indian subcontinent; but from Indonesia to Iran to the Caribbean, pressures were gathering, exacerbated by the policies of Moscow and Peking, which threatened major disruptions in the balance of power. And in the northwest Pacific, South Korea was volatile, and Japan tense and uncertain about its future, in the wake of the riots which had prevented Eisenhower's visit in 1960.[1]

Fourth, although the post-Sputnik anxiety about a Soviet missile advantage sufficient to tempt Moscow to a first strike was easing, there was widespread anxiety about the scale and mobility of American conventional forces, in case of multiple crises, and about an apparent excessive reliance on highly vulnerable aircraft as the delivery vehicles for the nuclear deterrent. There was a new military policy to be defined as well as space goals to be set.

Finally, there were the longer-run initiatives to be set in motion on the world scene: in aid, trade, and monetary affairs; in relations with NATO, Japan, Latin America, the Middle East, Africa; and, above all, if possible, with the Soviet Union in the field of arms control.

With greater or lesser success, Kennedy dealt with these problems and possibilities. The result was a turnaround in the directions of domestic policy and in the balance of forces on the world scene.

The initialing of the test ban treaty on July 25, 1963, symbolized the hard road traveled in foreign policy over the previous thirty months, with the Cuba missile crisis a pivotal turning point.

If there was an equivalent on the domestic scene, it also came in 1963 with the gathering support of the business community for a tax cut not linked to a reduction in federal expenditures. The reception accorded Kennedy's December 1962 speech to the Economic Club of New York and the campaign of advocacy that followed permitted Kenneth O'Donnell to conclude by May 1963 that Walter Heller should: "Stop worrying about the tax cut. It will pass—and pass big. Worry about something else."[2]

These exertions interacted with the politics of the Soviet Union and the communist world to yield by 1963 not merely an end to the post-Sputnik offensive but also an exacerbation of the Sino-Soviet conflict whose terms were brought into the open in virulent polemics.

Writing in 1963 the Foreword to the volume of his *Public Papers* of the previous year, Kennedy could say with some confidence: "Future historians, looking back at 1962, may well mark this year as the time when the tide of international politics began at last to flow strongly toward the world of diversity and freedom."[3]

But in 1963 there were, as O'Donnell suggested, other things to worry about. In the course of that year the race issue asserted itself with accelerated momentum and in somewhat new and explosive terms. And South Vietnam, inadequately sealed off in the aftermath of the Laos Accords of 1962, riven by a domestic conflict which began in May and came to a tragic climax with the assassination of Diem in November, moved from precarious but real progress toward military as well as political disintegration.

Kennedy's hope of seeing the great issues of the 1960s dealt with step by step without domestic convulsion or war, was thus shadowed before his death. He left to his successor both a foundation for further progress and a painful convergence of foreign and domestic crises.

15

Growth, Price Stability, and the Balance of Payments

THE COMPLEXITIES OF KEYNESIANISM IN THE REAL WORLD

NEXT TO THE HAUNTING FEAR THAT HE MIGHT PROVE TO BE the human being who took the world into nuclear war, Kennedy's most recurrent and acute anxiety centered on the balance-of-payments position of the United States. In part, this anxiety was political. The nation's banking and financial community was not, by and large, made up of Democrats. To whatever natural suspicions they harbored of a big-spending Democratic President might be added a certain degree of satisfaction at his political discomfiture. The role of "fiscal responsibility" as an issue in the campaign of 1960 did not diminish this concern, underlined as it was by a run on gold late in October and in the pre-Inaugural period, and by the transitional briefings by Eisenhower and his secretary of the treasury.

More important, Kennedy had a firm grasp of both the economics and the economic symbolism at work. He knew that the American balance-of-payments position was related to the course of American productivity and of American prices relative to the other major trading nations of the world. He also knew that whatever the underlying realities, the state of balance or imbalance in the federal budget was taken in the international community as a conventional symbol of responsibility or irresponsibility with respect to balance-of-payments policy.[1]

But if getting the country moving again meant anything, it meant increasing the rate of growth, cutting the level of unemployment, and ending the stop-and-go policies of the late 1950s. If a 2 to 3 percent rate of growth were to persist, neither federal, state, nor local governments would command the revenues required for the welfare goals he had articulated, for the expanded infrastructure the cities required, or for the national security goals he had set.

Despite his amiable, self-deprecatory stance as only a moderately good student of undergraduate economics at Harvard, Kennedy had long understood the pure Keynesian case for lifting the level of employment and the rate of growth by unbalancing the federal budget, grossly if necessary. But he knew his task was more subtle and complex than pure Keynesian doctrine allowed: to lift productivity for the long pull; to cushion pressures on the balance of payments by shorter-run devices; to achieve wage-price understandings that would permit expansion without inflation; and, on these foundations, to persuade the business and financial communities that a large, purposeful deficit—a tax decrease without an expenditure cut—was sound economic policy.

In human and institutional terms, the execution of this policy required the orchestration of Walter Heller and the Council of Economic Advisers; Kermit Gordon of the Budget Bureau; Douglas Dillon at the Treasury; Arthur Goldberg at Labor; Luther Hodges at Commerce; and in the end, it was critically important that William McChesney Martin at the Federal Reserve Board also be aboard. Under Kennedy's leadership this team came to an effective working consensus with the passage of time.

In political terms Kennedy's policy meant bringing along the leaders of business, labor, and the financial community, as well as the public and the Congress—Wilbur Mills, above all. It was, inevitably, a complex and fitful process[2]; and with the tax bill still pending, it was still incomplete on November 22, 1963.

The six major steps taken were these:

The acceptance of substantial federal budget deficits in fiscal years 1961–1964.

Stimulus to business investment through administrative reform of depreciation guidelines, the investment tax credit enacted in 1962, and efforts to increase the application of modern science and technology to sectors of the economy where productivity increases were sluggish.

Short-run measures to reduce the current account balance-of-payments deficit by reducing dollar expenditures abroad; expanding exports (including, notably, increased sales of military equipment to Germany to offset dollar outlays there); reducing the attractiveness of holding private funds abroad, including a widened spread between short- and long-term interest rates; and efforts to induce foreigners to hold their assets increasingly in dollars rather than to draw gold from American reserves, including a network of medium-term lending (the Roosa bonds) which bought some time in the balance-of-payments statistics.

Measures to expand the effective supply of labor by manpower training and to move toward more liberal trade policies, thus putting increased competitive pressure on both wages and prices.

The bringing in of wage-price guideposts, for which a potential institutional forum was created with the setting up of the Labor-Management Council as early as February 16, 1961.

Launching and carrying forward the campaign for a tax reduction and tax reform.

Of these, the wage-price guideposts were the most significant innovation, since their initial success helped create an economic, political, and psychological setting in which the tax cut gradually became politically acceptable to initially resistant groups.

THE FIRST SOCIAL CONTRACT

IN the historical and analytic literature on wage-price guideposts, the story usually begins with Kennedy's letters of September 6 and 14, 1961, to the steel industry and the steel union urging, respectively, price and wage restraint as the agreement of January 1960 came to an end and negotiations for a new contract had to be undertaken.[3] These exercises in jawboning were then followed by the formal enunciation of wage-price guideposts in the *Economic Report of the President* of January 1962, and, notably, the *Annual Report of the Council of Economic Advisers* dispatched with it to the Congress.[4] By January 1962 Kennedy was so deeply committed to affecting the outcome of the steel negotiations that he and the Council of Economic Advisers felt it wise to articulate the principles emerging in more general terms.

Interwoven with the formulation and public projection of the guideposts, however, was a rough-and-ready understanding which laid the foundations and provided legitimacy for the jawboning about steel wages and prices, which reached its climax in the Kennedy-Blough confrontation of April 10–13, 1962. This crude social contract was the forerunner of what ultimately will be required if high and steady rates of growth are to be reconciled with relative price stability. And the hinge on which the enterprise turned was automobiles rather than steel.

On the basis of my conversation with Kennedy of January 9, 1961 (see p. 123), he urged me to talk with Arthur Goldberg about the possibilities of inducing labor wage restraint geared to productivity increases and appropriate price restraint by industry. Guideposts along these lines were evidently required if the Labor-Management Council, already envisaged, was to have substance. We had lunch together on February 1, 1961, the day after a vigorous but inconclusive discussion in the Cabinet Room on wage-price policy.

I put the case to Goldberg in much the same strong terms I had done to the President-elect three weeks earlier in Boston. Goldberg, of course, understood the concept fully. Out of hard-won experience he also understood vividly a dimension of the problem to which the economists were initially less sensitive: the human and institutional difficulties involved in bringing a fragmented labor movement, with lively competition among its leaders, negotiating their contracts at different times under different economic circumstances, to effective agreement on wage-price guideposts. He was skeptical the job could be done without legislation. He did not believe an immediate voluntary price-wage agreement was possible. But since the stakes for domestic and foreign policy were high and legislation was beyond the range of practical politics, he agreed we would have to try with the tools of Presidential leadership and executive branch persuasion. We frankly considered the difficulties. In particular, we agreed the construction unions would constitute a major obstacle, and this would prove peculiarly important in a decade when a high rate of growth required enlarged outlays on housing and urban redevelopment.

Having reported this exchange to Kennedy, I returned to the crisis-filled world of foreign policy. On April 5 I came back to Kennedy on the wage-price issue, focusing, in particular, on the critical role of the coming automobile negotiations:

> The negotiation of the wage contract in the automobile industry will be a crucial event for both our domestic and foreign policies. The Big Three contract expires on August 31; and the Union will have a major strategy meeting on April 27. . . .
>
> We should, I believe, use every device at our command to persuade the two parties to go for a wage freeze and price cut. . . .
>
> Although we cannot be sure that the auto contract will set a voluntary national pattern, we can be sure that the national pattern will go against us if the auto settlement is inflationary. . . .
>
> A good auto settlement would only be the beginning, of course. The pattern would have to be worked out by industries—construction, steel, textiles, etc. But it is the proper place to begin. And if we don't begin here, we may not begin at all.

Even without a wage freeze, an automobile price cut was possible. Productivity increases there were sufficient to permit both a wage increase equal to the average national increase in productivity (say, 2½ percent) and a price cut, without reducing profits.

I raised the issue again briefly at the close of a memorandum of April 28 on foreign policy strategy:

> We shall need more money for these purposes, among others: increased military aid; increased assistance in the struggle against subversion; some enlargement in the American military establishment; probably some increased assistance to NATO; and acceleration of the

space effort. These expenditures, if they are not to be wholly matched by an increase in tax revenues, require policies which assure the country that inflation will not promptly result, bringing with it a deterioration in our balance of payments. We must, therefore, proceed with urgency—starting with the auto negotiation—to get voluntary price and wage control.

On June 5–6 I was asked to chair sessions of the annual Advertising Council briefings by administration officials.

The senior speaker at these sessions was Vice President Johnson who, in the wake of his trip to Asia, made a powerful and moving appeal in support of Kennedy's foreign aid proposals. With Kennedy's approval, I took the occasion to outline the case for wage and price restraint as fundamental to the national effort abroad as well as at home. These remarks were reported to Walter Reuther who called Kennedy and expressed his objections in strong terms.[5]

Kennedy, quite typically, was prepared to encourage his aides to explore a new line of policy, but wished to feel firmer ground under his feet before he became fully committed. He therefore told me to call on Reuther and see if I could persuade him. On June 20 I went around to his rather dramatic office in the steel and glass U.A.W. building near the Washington railroad station, noting that the labor movement had come a long way since my parents met in a pre-1914 socialist Sunday school.

Stanley Ruttenberg was also present. Reuther took the offensive. In lively language he suggested that it was inappropriate, as the first initiative of the new administration, for "White House professors" to throw their weight against a labor movement whose efforts had elected the first Democratic President in eight years. He expressed at some length and with a certain vividness the view that my proposition, as reported to him, was naive as well as inequitable.

I responded that by upbringing and political persuasion I was rooted in the social democratic tradition and did not require instruction in the rights and virtues of labor. There was nothing in that tradition that required labor leadership to contribute to inflation, which always worked against the interests of labor as a whole; to force stop-and-go policies and low rates of growth; to deny public authorities the tax resources required for expanding welfare outlays; and to attenuate the nation's capacity to meet its military and foreign aid obligations in a dangerous world.

I then explained, with less color and more technical detail, why I believed it was in labor's interest, as well as in the national interest, to settle for a wage increase of 2½ percent in the forthcoming negotiations with the automobile industry.

Reuther took all this well. There was the beginning of a twinkle in his eye as he turned to the business at hand.

Conscious that his negotiations preceded those in the steel industry, he asked if he were damn fool enough to agree, could Kennedy assure that McDonald wouldn't do better?

I said this was a reasonable condition.

He then asked that if they were both damn fools enough to agree, could Kennedy assure that their restraint wouldn't be exploited by a rise in steel prices?

I said my proposition assumed no exploitation of labor restraint with respect to both auto and steel prices. There was no intention to shift the distribution of income in favor of profits. He said we shouldn't worry about auto prices. He could look after them. The steel price, however, was crucial. He expressed some doubt that "White House professors" could deal effectively with the leaders of the steel industry.

I feared he would raise the question of construction wage rates, for which I had no credible answer. But he did not.

I then summarized what seemed to emerge: auto and steel wage negotiations geared to the average increase in productivity with no exploitation by the steel industry of labor restraint through price increases. I asked if I could inform the President that he agreed to this position. He said he did not agree; but I could tell the President that Reuther would consider it.

I reported back. Kennedy chuckled and said I was a pretty good negotiator for a professor. And, except for some proposals that emerged after a lunch with Dillon, before I went off to Vietnam in October, I withdrew from domestic crusading, leaving matters in the hands of thoroughly capable colleagues.

This story is told because Kennedy, in fact, acted in terms of the proposition which emerged from the June 20 talk with Reuther. What subsequently transpired between them I do not know; although Kennedy saw Reuther on August 4 and August 16, on the latter occasion alone and off the record.

The key actor for Kennedy in this phase was Arthur Goldberg. He monitored the automobile negotiations during the spring and summer and entered even more deeply into the steel negotiations.

Negotiating habits and traditions differed in the two industries. The automobile union and industry leaders had hammered out, over the years, rather sophisticated and civilized criteria for negotiation, centered on the course of productivity in the industry. Government intervention in these negotiations was rare. Goldberg was, however, in occasional touch with Reuther.[6] His past close connections with Reuther and current responsibilities as secretary of labor permitted and required a somewhat elliptical and diplomatic approach. In language less blunt than my exchange with Reuther of June 20 (of which Goldberg was not then aware), Goldberg, with Kennedy's support, communicated the rationale for the administration's policy of linking wage increases to the average level of increase in productivity; and he assured Reuther that he could assume that the steel settlement would match the restraint Goldberg was urging upon him. Goldberg acknowledged the difficulties in the construction industry but said Reuther's problem as a labor leader lay in the manufacturing sector —a political fact true for the 1960s, less true for Reuther's successor in the more service-oriented world of the 1970s.

Kennedy also discussed the automobile negotiations several times with McNamara; but they proceeded to the final phase without deep government intervention, although Goldberg assisted in finding a formula for certain narrow but sticky issues at the very end.

In steel, the tradition was one of strikes leading to one form or another of government involvement—or even dictation of settlement—under crisis conditions. Kennedy and Goldberg were, therefore, sensitive to three major considerations: the possible consequences for the whole economy of the shock of a major strike; their implicit commitment to Reuther concerning the steel wage settlement; and the critical importance of the wage-price outcome in steel for the President's economic policy as a whole. Goldberg was, for all these reasons, more deeply involved in the steel negotiations from beginning to end.

Over the summer of 1961 the Bureau of the Budget, the Council of Economic Advisers, and a group of Democrats in the Senate also took a hand. Kermit Gordon called to Heller's attention rumors in the business and financial press that a price increase was contemplated in the steel industry. Acutely aware of the substantive and symbolic role of steel prices in the economy, they called the possibility of an increase to Kennedy's attention. A group of somewhat frustrated liberal senators was enlisted to apply some heat to the steel industry. Led by Senator Albert Gore, they had themselves quite a day on August 22, 1961, urging the President to use the full powers of his office to prevent a rise in steel prices.[7] Roger Blough was to regard the Senate onslaught as the beginning of the steel-price war of 1961–1962.[8]

The Public Record

On September 5, as Reuther's negotiations with General Motors moved toward a climax, Kennedy sent telegrams urging a settlement fair to both parties "which preserves price stability in the industry."[9]

On September 6, as the outlines of a restrained auto settlement emerged (about 2½ percent hourly wage increase, including fringe benefits), Kennedy addressed himself immediately to the leaders of the steel industry. He cited the satisfactory state of profits in the industry and asked them to absorb the wage increases (scheduled under the 1960 agreement to go into effect October 1) without raising prices. Looking forward, he said:

> If the industry were now to forego a price increase, it would enter collective bargaining negotiations next spring with a record of three and a half years of price stability. It would clearly then be the turn of the labor representatives to limit wage demands to a level consistent with continued price stability. The moral position of the steel industry next spring—and its claim to the support of public opinion—will be strengthened by the exercise of price restraint now.[10]

On September 8 McDonald, knowing where Reuther was coming out and with the President's appeal to the steel industry leaders on the public record, pledged to Kennedy his cooperation in assuring that the public interest would be recognized in the 1962 steel negotiations. On September 14 Kennedy responded to McDonald that the public interest in price stability "implies a labor settlement within the limits of advances in productivity. . . . The whole nation has benefited from the price stability in steel for the last three years. We count on all concerned to maintain this stability."[11]

As the President moved toward deep personal commitment in the steel wage and price settlement, the Council of Economic Advisers addressed themselves to the complex principles involved in applying wage-price guideposts to the economy as a whole, to achieve "non-inflationary wage and price behavior."[12] In a full exposition, the Council was admirably candid about the intellectual complexities and practical difficulties their policy entailed.

As the narrow community of those interested in technical economic matters was absorbing and debating the guidepost formulation, Kennedy's operational scenario, managed vigorously by Goldberg, unfolded in good order down to March 31, 1962. He was then able to telephone messages to the industry and labor leaders in steel, congratulating them on a settlement that was "obviously non-inflationary."[13] Wage rates remained constant, but fringe benefits yielded the same kind of 2½ percent hourly increase Reuther had negotiated in September 1961. It was also the first steel settlement negotiated without a strike since 1954.

Then came the fateful request of Roger Blough to see the President at 4:40 P.M. on April 10. Blough read the announcement scheduled for public release at 7:00 P.M. of an across-the-board rise in steel prices of $6 per ton: a 3½ percent price increase. The government felt that productivity and profit prospects in steel justified no increase in prices, given the recent settlement.

The seventy-two hours that followed have been documented about as exhaustively as the Cuba missile crisis.[14] Blough was quite clear that Kennedy had persuaded McDonald to accept a settlement in accordance with the wage-price guideposts on the assumption of no price increase in steel[15]; but he was not legally bound to the semi-explicit social contract that had unfolded in the wake of the automobile settlement—a contract without a clear constitutional precedent.

To some extent Blough's action in raising steel prices was an effort to defeat what he regarded as a dangerous constitutional precedent. Looking back on the Senate debate of August 22, 1961, he later said: "To my knowledge this is the first time any President has been publicly called upon to exercise control without authority of law—over the price of an entire industry—and initiate or participate in a whole series of administrative and legislative actions of a punitive nature if that control were not accepted."[16] And so he let Kennedy move to hold down the steel wage increase and link it publicly and privately to steel price restraint, without formally committing himself to price stability or otherwise showing his hand. Then he challenged the whole enterprise with his fait accompli.

Kennedy had found and then seized on a remarkably fortunate moment. The economy was in recession. The depressed economic environment since 1958 left a legacy of muted expectations with respect to wage increases as well as anxiety within labor about the level of employment. The accidental sequence of the automobile and steel negotiations provided a unique opportunity to nail down the pattern of a wage-price policy Kennedy needed, aided by two labor leaders who combined a lively competitive sense with considerable statesmanship, by a secretary of labor who had earned over the years the confidence of both, and by an ardent team of first-rate economists.

There was also the fact that neither market conditions nor equity required an increase in steel prices; and that the structure of the steel industry was not only imperfectly competitive but imperfectly monopolistic, as the critical defection of Inland Steel demonstrated.

The fate of the guideposts, defined in general terms early in 1962, obviously hinged on the de facto success of the automobile and steel negotiations and on the effort to hold the steel price. The emergence of Kennedy's rough-and-ready social contract demanded that Blough and the steel industry rescind the price increase of April 10. The President would have been in an impossible situation with respect to Reuther and McDonald in particular, the labor movement in general, if it had stayed on the books: the recently proclaimed wage-price guideposts would have been an empty box.

Kennedy's massive offensive against Blough and the price increase was, therefore, an essential act of policy, as well as the reaction of a man who felt that the President of the United States had been double-crossed.

On the other hand, lacking a formal legal or constitutional base for forcing rescission, the President had to improvise a series of ad hoc pressures on United States Steel which alarmed some critics who thought it an excessive use of the executive power. Kennedy's battle with Blough was imperfectly understood, in part because the underlying linkage of steel-price stability to the prior auto (as well as steel) wage negotiations was not widely appreciated, even within the government.

The Upshot

With respect to steel prices, the outcome was salutary. John Sheahan concludes:

> Either the emotional costs of the 1962 conflict with the steel industry were so great, or the lesson so firmly driven home, that no further conflicts over price increases occurred during the next two years. The steel firms did not hesitate to raise some prices in 1963 and subsequently, but they no longer tried to repeat the practice of across-the-board increases on all products by all firms. Instead, some products went up and others down, with different patterns among companies, suggesting careful study of differential costs and competitive conditions rather than a mechanical upward march.
>
> The net result of these more discrete price changes in the steel industry was not to accomplish quietly what had been blocked publicly. The wholesale index of iron and steel prices at the end of 1963 was exactly where it had been at the end of 1961.[17]

The outcome in the automobile industry was less satisfactory. Given the higher productivity increase in the automobile than in the steel industry, the correct guidepost outcome for prices, given the 1961 wage settlement, should have been a decline. In the course of the early 1960s this price reduction was not, in fact, brought about. There was, therefore, a disproportionate rise of profits in the automobile industry; and this contributed, along with other factors, to the later breakdown of wage-price guidelines.[18]

In the fragmented construction industry, as expected, the low productivity increase was combined in subsequent years with disproportionately high wage increases: above 4 percent per hour.[19] The bringing of the construction industry into the social contract remains a major unresolved problem of American society.

But, overall, the price performance of the American economy under Kennedy was remarkable by previous standards and roughly met the objectives he had set, as the following table suggests.[20]

TABLE 15–1

SOME ECONOMIC INDICATORS FOR THE UNITED STATES, 1957–1965

Year	Consumer Price Index	Av.	Wholesale Price Index	Av.	Implicit Price Index GNP	Av.	Industrial Production	Av.	GNP in Constant Prices	Av.	Per Capita GNP in Constant Prices	Av.	GNP per Person Employed in Constant Prices	Av.	Hourly Earnings	Av.	Unemployment Rate	Av.
	Annual percent change from preceding year																Annual average	
1957	3.5		3.6		3.7		0.9		2.1		0.6		2.0		5.8		4.3	
1958	2.7	2.1	2.3	1.6	2.5	2.4	–7.0	2.4	–1.6	3.0	–3.2	0.9	0.0	1.8	2.2	3.9	6.8	5.5
1959	0.8		–0.2		1.7		12.6		6.6		4.6		4.0		4.3		5.5	
1960	1.5		0.8		1.6		3.0		2.7		1.4		1.0		3.1		5.6	
1961	1.1		0.0		1.3		0.9		1.6		–0.2		1.4		3.0		6.7	
1962	1.1		0.3		1.0		7.8		6.1		4.8		4.5		2.9		5.6	
1963	1.3	1.3	–0.3	0.4	1.4	1.4	5.1	5.7	3.8	4.5	2.5	3.0	2.3	2.8	2.8	3.0	5.7	5.6
1964	1.4		0.4		1.6		6.4		5.6		3.5		2.7		2.8		5.2	
1965	1.6		1.8		1.9		8.3		5.5		4.5		2.9		3.6		4.6	

These figures exhibit:

—a marked acceleration in GNP;

—the maintenance down to 1965 of a low level of price increases;

—a high level of productivity increase (roughly measured by GNP per person employed, in constant prices);

—increases in hourly earnings, for the years 1961–1965, which approximated, on the average, increases in productivity (both about 3 percent);

—a relatively modest rate of decline in unemployment until 1964–1965, when the tax cut took hold, in an environment where the advantages of depreciation guidelines and investment credits had, at last, come to be understood and acted on in the American business community.

The whole effort yielded lower rates of price increase than in most of the other major trading nations[21]: the average annual American consumer price increase for the period 1961–1965 was 1.3 percent as opposed to 3.6 percent for the United Kingdom, 3.6 percent for the Netherlands, 3.7 percent for Sweden, 3.8 percent for France, 2.8 percent for Germany, 1.6 percent for Canada. These relative price movements—a kind of internal U.S. devaluation—strengthened the underlying American balance-of-payments position and the international monetary system, with its continued dependence on dollars as a reserve supplement to inadequate flows of gold to the central banks.

In the shorter run, the events of September 5, 1961–April 13, 1962, provided the foundation for Kennedy's later uninhibited advocacy of a tax reduction. With a framework of relative wage-price stability more or less assured, and the economy showing signs of faltering in its expansion, Kennedy committed himself in the summer of 1962 to seek in 1963 a permanent tax cut.[22] But Keynes' *General Theory* contained little guidance as to how one got from where Kennedy was on January 20, 1961, to, say, his confident stance before the New York Economic Club on December 14, 1962.

16

The Allocation of Public Resources

THE FOLLOWING TABLE INDICATES THE BROAD MOVEMENT IN scale and allocation of public resources during the Kennedy administration.

TABLE 16–1

GOVERNMENT EXPENDITURES AS PROPORTIONS (%) OF GNP, 1960–1964

	1960	1961	1962	1963	1964
National Security	10.5	11.0	11.1	10.9	10.0
Interest	1.5	1.4	1.4	1.5	1.4
Law, Order, and Administration	2.2	2.4	2.4	2.5	2.2
Economic and Environmental Services	4.2	4.6	4.4	4.4	4.5
Social Welfare	10.0	11.0	10.8	10.9	11.2
TOTAL	28.5*	30.3*	30.1	30.1*	29.4*

* Due to rounding, total differs slightly from sum of components.

At a time when GNP was averaging an annual increase of about 4 percent, there was during the Kennedy administration an increase in the proportion of GNP allocated by the federal government of about 1 percent;

about ½ percent in state and local expenditures. Federal grants-in-aid to state and local governments moved up rather sharply from $6.9 billion in 1961 to $8.4 billion in 1963 and $9.8 billion in 1964.

The bulk of the increase in federal outlays was in military and space expenditures: the former responding to specific budgetary changes made by Kennedy, notably in the context of the Berlin crisis of 1961; the latter (rising from $744 million in fiscal 1961 to $4.170 billion in fiscal 1964) reflecting the May 1961 decision to proceed to manned moon flight. There was a significant expansion in the level of foreign aid but not on a scale comparable to military and space outlays.

The increase in civil outlays reflects Kennedy's initiatives in accelerating public works expenditures and certain modest legislative successes in the fields of education, housing and redevelopment, public health, labor and manpower training, and in enlarging the flows of income to agriculture. Some of these yielded small increases in outlays, but were germinal; they represented limited beachheads later expanded. But, by and large, these figures demonstrate Kennedy's failure to achieve in his time the legislative breakthroughs in education, medical services, and the war on poverty which he sought or envisaged.

Kennedy's legislative record is substantial, notably so if one includes measures put by him to the Congress, but not passed until after his death.[1] Theodore Sorensen can argue, on the basis of testimony from Democratic and Republican congressional leaders, that the measures put to the Congress, but not acted upon before his death (including the Civil Rights and tax bills), would, in any case have passed in the second session of the 88th Congress.[2] But historians may well debate whether Kennedy could have wrung more legislation from the Congress if he had devoted more energy to the task, commanded more experience of the legislative process, and set aside possible inhibitions arising from his transition to the White House from a relatively junior role in the Senate.

It is clear that the massive legislative revolution of the 1960s took place during Lyndon Johnson's Presidency.

It was my impression at the time, and still is in retrospect, that Kennedy was content to move relatively slowly in bringing about the major domestic reforms to which he was committed. He was acutely conscious of the conservative shift in the structure of the Congress as the result of the election of 1960, as compared to 1958. Aided by the outcome of the Cuba missile crisis, he did relatively well in the congressional elections of 1962 for an off-year effort; but, still, the Congress he confronted in January 1963 was conservative in terms of his objectives. I believe he intended to carry forward public education and advocacy, hoping that a substantial victory in 1964 would bring with it a more amenable Congress. Something like this longer-run train of thought, as well as Kennedy's hopes for the second session of the 88th Congress, was embedded in his reference from the poet Arthur Clough in this exchange during his final press conference of November 14, 1963.[3]

> "Mr. President, I think a few minutes ago you said it would be unfortunate if the tax bill and the civil rights bill don't get through. You just said also it is the worst attack on the foreign aid bill since its inception. Several appropriations bills are still hung up in Congress, the first time in history this late. What has happened on Capitol Hill?"
>
> "My judgment is that by the time this Congress goes home . . . in the fields of education, mental health, taxes, civil rights, this is going to be a record that is going to be—however dark it looks now, I think that 'westward, look, the land is bright,' and I think that by next summer it may be."

Kennedy's perspective on domestic legislation was, in a sense, precisely the opposite of his successor's. Johnson knew that history, the decision of the Republican Convention of 1964, and his own efforts had granted him in January 1965 a Congress that would, for a little while, do his bidding. He decided to use this opportunity to the hilt; and he did so with voracious energy, dedication, and skill.

Kennedy viewed the pursuit of his domestic objectives as a slow, incremental, uphill climb.[4] In this respect Kennedy's Presidency falls somewhere between Franklin Roosevelt's and Johnson's on the one hand, and Truman's on the other. The former two pressed their transient but ample congressional opportunities to the limit. Truman concentrated on foreign policy, putting before the Congress a set of legislative proposals he knew were substantially doomed to frustration in his time, but which, nevertheless, built a political record for him and the Democratic party and carried forward a long-term educational process. Kennedy's domestic effort was more hopeful and substantial, less cosmetic, than Truman's; but it was built around what he felt might be accomplished over an eight-year span.

On the domestic side, he knew his most urgent objective had to be a resumed high rate of growth reconciled with relative price stability and an improved balance-of-payments position. To that task he devoted the same kind of personal attention and compulsive concern for detail that he did to his major foreign policy crises. On other major domestic fronts he built his case and his political strength while moving forward in small steps.

But there was a major exception—civil rights, as the issue emerged in the course of 1963.

17

The Race Crisis of 1963

The Underlying Problem

In his confident and cautiously optimistic State of the Union message of January 11, 1963, Kennedy devoted only a short passage to civil rights, focused on the vote. Exactly five months later he delivered the strongest statement ever delivered up to that time by an American President in support of full equality for the Negro as citizen; and he outlined sweeping new legislation to accomplish this goal.

In those five months the chemistry of the nation's life had yielded a sudden upsurge of Negro feeling and action—and white reaction—that threatened to tear the society apart. The underlying basis for the explosion was, of course, the deeply rooted inequality of the Negro's status which Kennedy caught in vivid statistical terms:

> The Negro baby born in America today, regardless of the section of the Nation in which he is born, has about one-half as much chance of completing high school as a white baby born in the same place on the same day, one-third as much chance of completing college, one-third as much chance of becoming a professional man, twice as much chance of becoming unemployed, about one-seventh as much chance of earning $10,000 a year, a life expectancy which is seven years shorter, and the prospects of earning only half as much.[1]

By and large, these gaps in opportunity and status were narrowing, not widening, in 1963. They illuminate an important part of the race problem, but they do not explain the storm which gathered in 1963; gained momentum down to, say, the aftermath of Martin Luther King's assassination in 1968[2]; subsided uneasily, and perhaps temporarily, in the time that followed, leaving the race problem transformed but not resolved.

Constitutional crises of the kind experienced by the United States in the period of 1963–1968 derive usually from the convergence of two kinds of forces: accumulating discontent with existing political or social reality; and catalytic circumstances or events. The onset of the American and French revolutions, the British Reform Bill crisis of 1832, the continental revolutions of 1848, and the Russian Revolution of 1905 can all be usefully viewed in these terms. And so can the crises in our time in the social and political life of Canada, Northern Ireland, and Belgium.

The backdrop for the American race crisis of the 1960s is familiar:

1. The massive movement since the 1930s of the Negro from rural to urban areas, particularly in the northern central cities from which whites were moving to suburbia.

2. The stirring of Negro hopes by the 1954 Supreme Court decision on desegregation and the dashing of those hopes by the subsequent slow implementation and evidently limited capacity of school desegregation to deal with the full range of Negro inequities.

3. The wars in Korea and Vietnam, requiring full Negro participation in the ultimate responsibilities of citizenship, stirring a demand for full rights to citizenship.

4. The emergence in the course of the 1960s of a new, assertive Negro generation.

5. The impact on American Negroes of the entrance of the new African nations into world politics, with sovereign rights.

6. The pervasiveness of television, dramatizing inescapably, day after day, the gap between suburban and ghetto life.

In 1961–1962 Kennedy had used a wide range of executive powers to move the Negro toward equal status: from positive support for the Supreme Court's integration decision to the appointment of Negroes to high posts in his administration. Existing law and administrative authority were vigorously exercised over a wide front in voting rights, housing, employment, and education. And in 1962 Kennedy quietly issued the executive order against racial discrimination in federal housing.

In 1962 Kennedy also laid before the Congress proposals to prevent discriminatory literacy tests in qualification for voting; and he proposed a constitutional amendment to abolish poll taxes. The former failed in the Senate; the latter ultimately became the Twenty-fourth Amendment to the Constitution. On February 28, 1963, Kennedy came back to the Congress on the voting issue; proposed technical and financial assistance to accelerate school desegregation; and urged the renewal of the Civil Rights Commission. It was a distinctly limited, low-key package.

Kennedy was inhibited from going further by the situation in Congress. The resistant coalition of southern Democrats and Republicans demonstrated its capacity to frustrate civil rights legislation after the limited breakthrough of 1957. Moreover, Kennedy was reluctant to force this divisive issue in Congress as he sought to round up Democratic votes in support of other domestic legislation, notably the tax bill.

THE CATALYTIC EVENTS

ALTHOUGH the race problem had clearly become a national rather than a regional problem by the 1960s, the events which transformed the scene came in the heart of the South: in Oxford, Mississippi, then in Birmingham, Alabama.

The first case arose toward the end of September 1962. The Fifth Circuit Court of Appeals directed the federal government to enforce the Court's order that James Meredith be admitted to the University of Mississippi, in the face of the defiant obstruction of the state's governor and lieutenant governor. Like Orville Faubus of Arkansas in 1957, Governor Ross Barnett sought a kind of nullification, a formula which would formally comply with the Court's order but, by unleashing mob violence, would create circumstances that would lead to Meredith's de facto withdrawal. With Barnett's connivance, Meredith was registered quietly at the university; but Barnett failed to use fully the state police to quell the mob which converged on Oxford. The force of 550 federal marshals mobilized could not cope; the arrival of Mississippi National Guard units had only enflamed the mob. In the end, some 20,000 Army troops were brought in to pacify the town. The racial tension was so intense that it was judged necessary to segregate briefly certain Army units to avoid further casualties.[3]

The need to use federal troops to install a qualified Negro student in a state university stirred the majority of white Americans, as it affronted the Negro community.

But it was Birmingham's police commissioner, T. Eugene Connor, who did more than any single individual to set in motion a new phase in the struggle for civil rights. Martin Luther King, under urgent pressure from his constituency to move forward boldly, decided to mount a campaign of nonviolent resistance to segregation in all its forms in Birmingham. The locale and timing of his effort guaranteed maximum tension, since Birmingham was perhaps the most old-fashioned city in the nation in terms of segregation; and the police were under the control of a determined enemy of change, Connor.

The result was the sight of men, women, and children demonstrating peacefully for elemental rights most Americans felt were rightfully theirs, set upon by police dogs, knocked down the streets by powerful fire hoses, and thrown into jail en masse. The events in Birmingham of April–May

1963 were a challenge to the conscience of most white Americans and a challenge to the courage, and the sense of racial fraternity, of every Negro. The challenge was hurled into every home by television.

Kennedy had no legal authority in Birmingham equivalent to the orders of the Fifth Circuit Court of Appeals. He could only use the powers of the attorney general to try to bring reconciliation to the torn Birmingham community. Frustration mounted among whites as well as Negroes. Rioting broke out in many cities. The underlying political conditions in the nation had changed: new legislation was now both needed and more possible.

THE NEW PROPOSED CIVIL RIGHTS LEGISLATION

KENNEDY decided on May 31 that he would propose new legislation; and urgent staff work began in the government. But he carefully chose his moment to move. A lawsuit similar to that which had desegregated the University of Mississippi was making its way through the courts of Alabama, whose university was the last stand of segregation among the state institutions. On June 11, 1963, the issue came to a climax with Governor George C. Wallace posturing at the doorway of the university registration building, performing his constitutional ritual dance with Nicholas Katzenbach of the Justice Department, and then acceding to the entrance of the two new students.

Kennedy's proposals, delivered from his office by radio and television that evening, foreshadowed major legislative proposals with respect to open public facilities, and federal action to accelerate school desegregation. Eight days later he sent his special message to the Congress on civil rights and job opportunities.

Embracing but going beyond his proposals of February 28, Kennedy proposed federal legislation "to guarantee all citizens equal access to the services and facilities of hotels, restaurants, places of amusement and retail establishments"; explicit authority for the attorney general to initiate in the Federal District Courts action to force the pace of school desegregation; and additional resources to accelerate manpower training to bring Negroes (and others) effectively into the working force. He also announced his intent to create by executive order an independent Community Relations Service to help bring local communities to consensus on measures to implement the law and to maintain racial peace.

Beyond the terms of the new legislation, Kennedy threw the full weight of the Presidency into the moral crisis which America faced "as a country and as a people. It cannot be met by repressive police action. It cannot be left to increased demonstrations in the streets. It cannot be quieted by token moves or talk. It is time to act in the Congress, in your State and local legislative body, and, above all, in all of our daily lives."

He understood the depth of feeling that had emerged in 1963; he knew that legislation could only go a limited way to solve the Negro's problem and then only over a considerable period of time; but what could be done by law, he felt, should be done. And for a time, at least, it might keep the passions at work within the normal political process.

Although the Congress did not act over the summer on the proposals in Kennedy's June 19 message, the summer of 1963 was on the whole quieter in the cities than had been expected. Nevertheless, voices of white backlash and Negro extremism emerged strongly. To hold his constituency, Martin Luther King felt a massive, peaceful demonstration in support of full civil rights was required, in support of Kennedy's legislation—and more.

By dint of careful organization, engaging Negroes and whites, government and private groups, the gathering of 230,000 on August 28 came off well—in Kennedy's phrase, as a legitimate call for a "redress of grievances." The nation heaved a sigh of relief, as it saw a grave threat to public order brought within the familiar frame of the nation's political life.

The forces at work, however, did not permit a once-and-for-all resolution of the crisis that had emerged. Kennedy's successor found himself almost immediately again riding a tiger.

THE UNDERLYING DYNAMIC DISEQUILIBRIUM

THE nature of Kennedy's and then Johnson's problem can be illuminated by going back to Gunnar Myrdal's temperately optimistic analysis in *An American Dilemma*,[4] published in 1944. Myrdal's analysis was based on three central propositions.

First, he took the de facto cultural, social, economic, and educational gap between Negroes and whites in America as both the cause of Negro discontent and a principal cause of discriminatory white attitudes toward the Negro.

Second, he viewed society as an interacting process, not as a structure determined by economic, social, political, or any other single set of forces. Legal action, for example, did not have to await changes in "underlying attitudes"; these attitudes could be altered, in degree, by legal action. A rise in the Negro's economic status did not have to await, for example, strictly economic changes, but could be brought about by improvements in Negro education.

Third, he judged the forces at work in American society would produce, on long term, a benign rather than a vicious circle. Ultimately, because of America's commitment to the principles of the Enlightenment incorporated in the nation's birth, Myrdal believed Americans would gradually move to narrow the gap.

At first, Myrdal's hopeful prediction seemed to be correct. And it would still apply to the prospects for, say, 75 percent of the Negro population who are more or less successfully geared to the classic American escalator of educational, economic, social, and political progress. But, as a theory, it did not embrace several factors at work in the generation after his book was first published, which yielded the rather sudden crisis in 1963.[5] These discontinuities set limits on the pace at which the critical gap could be reduced and, simultaneously, raised Negro expectations of favorable change. Taken together, these discontinuities decreed that racial progress in America in the third quarter of the twentieth century would be a cyclical process at best: a source of revolution or counterrevolution at worst.

The cause of frustration, above any other, was the expansion of the northern ghettos within which a substantial proportion of the Negro community became entrapped. Family structure and motivation in the ghetto produced a young population not equipped to enter the working force at levels that matched their expectations; unskilled labor opportunities were either diminishing, barred by union restrictions, or less attractive than illegal commerce or survival on welfare payments.[6] The upshot was that a substantial proportion of the Negro population moved beyond the reach of the basic socializing institutions of American society: family and school, church and welfare institutions, the police and the courts, and the economy itself. Efforts to bring this group of, perhaps, four or five million human beings within the effective grasp of these institutions were increasingly undertaken in the course of the 1960s. But the process was slower and more frustrating than, say, the flow of Negroes from southern farms to northern and southern factories in earlier decades.

Against this background of slow progress, if not degeneration, in Negro ghetto life, with all its built-in intractability, there emerged a new, impatient Negro generation which adopted a stance and style well evoked by Richard Young:

> Whether or not white acceptance of the concept of racial equality during the 1940's was hypocritical, it seems clear that this significant change in white attitudes had a deep effect on how Negro Americans viewed themselves. No longer caricatured in the mass media and told that they were inferior to whites in their schools, Negroes grew up in the post-war period—particularly in the North—with a pride that was to inaugurate a new chapter in American race relations. No longer passive, second-class citizens in a culture which defined them as inferior, they acted with the impatience of white Americans in seeking quick solutions to their problems. Turning first to mass demonstrations in the late 1950's, then to civil disobedience, and finally to urban riots, large numbers of blacks, mostly young, expressed their frustrations over the fact that they were denied socio-economic equality to whites.

> The young Afro-American of the 1960's—if I might suggest an ideal type—is unlike the Negro of the past. He is assertive, defiant, courageous, and impatient. He wants solutions to complex socio-economic problems "*now*."[7]

Harking back to doctrines of Marcus Garvey earlier in the century, some Negro groups revived a search for "nationhood" and "self-determination."[8] The Black Muslims, expanding from a movement which began in 1913, agitated for territory either within the United States or elsewhere, while conducting a battle within the ghettos against social degeneration on behalf of Negro pride and the homey virtues. The Black Panthers, founded by Huey Newton and Bobby Seale, who were born just before or during the Second World War, looked to violent revolutionary struggle, shifting from simple black nationalism to some kind of association with extreme radicalism on the world scene. Stokely Carmichael, also of that generation, founded in 1960 the Student Nonviolent Coordinating Committee (SNCC) which was to popularize the phrase "Black Power" and give it substance with the notion of Negro control of the ghettos, viewed as a kind of inner colony requiring liberation.

By 1963, then, various groups of Negroes had begun to search for dignity by routes other than progress through the classic absorption of a minority in an expanding American society. The full impact of their efforts, often articulated in violent terms, with much borrowed Marxist and communist rhetoric, was to come later in the 1960s. But their presence in the Negro movement was both a goad to action by Negro and white moderates and a factor heightening the element of white backlash which emerged strongly in 1963.

The third factor not fully encompassed in the Myrdal equation is the pace of change American society could manage without raising the most classic of constitutional dilemmas: the balancing of justice and order. Progress in racial matters—as in most other matters—is inherently unsettling. It stirred one kind of resistance if it was focused on peaceful efforts to open state universities, public facilities, and the polling booths to Negroes. It stirred much wider anxiety and resistance when Negro methods became violent, rhetoric became revolutionary, and security of life and property seemed threatened.[9]

A kind of rough dynamic equilibrium existed, then, in the thirty years before 1963: the rate of improvement in the Negro position in American society did not sufficiently depart from either Negro or white expectations to produce a major sustained political crisis. There were ample frictions and occasional riots. There were millions of lives lived in quiet rage and concealed humiliation, shortened in length, diminished in quality; there were enormous economic and cultural losses to the nation and the world; but the balance between justice and order, still grossly inequitable, proved consistent with the continuity of a slowly changing constitutional and social system.

THE KENNEDY DILEMMA

THIS dynamic equilibrium was struck by two forces, related to each other, but distinct: the new generation of Negroes whose expectations had altered and to whom the old pace of change was unacceptable; a set of ghetto problems, not new but rapidly expanding, increasingly intractable, with wide repercussions on the viability of city life as a whole. Changing Negro expectations required a more rapid closing of the gap, if dynamic equilibrium were to be maintained: the expanding northern ghettos slowed down the rate at which the white-Negro gap could, in fact, technically be closed. Those—Negro and white—who were committed to seeking a solution within the American political process were splayed across a widening chasm, notably in the North.

Although Kennedy, on balance, kept these anxieties and resistances within tolerable limits in 1963, their existence was manifest.

The maximum progress he could accomplish was not enough to satisfy the new generation of Negro leaders. In May, for example, Robert Kennedy went to New York to discuss the race issue with a group of young Negro intellectuals and activists. In the course of what proved to be a frustrating and ill-tempered three-hour session, a young Negro, Jerome Smith, told him he felt like vomiting to have to plead before the attorney general for the rights he was inherently entitled to as an American.

Robert Kennedy evidently found the occasion upsetting; but as Kenneth Clark (who was present) suggests, its shock, along with other evidence of the explosive state of the race problem, may have had its effect:

> We left convinced that we had made no dent or impact on Bobby. In fact, my personal judgment was that we had widened the gap. Whatever rapport had existed before was disrupted; it may very well have been that Bobby Kennedy was more antagonistic to our aspirations and goals than he was before, because the clash was so violent.
>
> But then at the end of May, Vice-President Johnson gave that Gettysburg talk and in June, Jack Kennedy gave that famous civil-rights speech of his, which contained many of the same ideas. So our conclusion that we had made no dent at all was wrong.[10]

Kennedy and his administration were also bedeviled by Negro leaders who in private expressed understanding of the limits within which he had to act and of the political risks he had taken, but felt impelled in public to press him beyond the possible and to do so in terms which alarmed the swing voter—in Kennedy's phrase, the "marginal, decent, conservative opinion" that he and his successor ultimately had to carry.[11]

As Sorensen notes: "Polls showed a majority in white America in favor of the Kennedy [civil rights] bill, but they also showed a majority feeling that Kennedy was pushing too fast."[12] Among the states where Kennedy's popularity fell was one critical for the 1964 election, Texas[13]: from 76 percent in February 1962 to 62 percent in September, at the time of trouble in Oxford, Mississippi. With the Cuba missile crisis, those approving Kennedy's performance rose in December to 71 percent; but after the grinding racial crisis of 1963, the figure stood at 50 percent in September 1963. For the South as a whole the approval rate was 44 percent.

18

The Organization of National Security Affairs, 1961

THE ORGANIZATION OF WORK ON MILITARY AND FOREIGN POLICY in the government is a subject which engages a small group of experts and students of certain branches of political science. There is only one truly important thing to be said on the subject: the work should be organized in ways congenial to the incumbent President.

When a man becomes President his working style has already been set, even if he is, by Presidential standards, young. His character and experience have already taught him how best to absorb information, hear conflicting opinions, deal with subordinates, array the alternatives, assess the impact of one course in one area on all the other areas where he bears responsibility, weigh the timing for action in one field against things proceeding in others—and, finally, to reach a decision with whose heavy consequences he will have to live, and, along with him, the nation and all mankind. Men do these things in quite distinctive ways. What matters is what they decide, not how they reach a decision which, in its essence, will always involve values and perceptions, memories and dreams they can never wholly articulate.

Under the American Constitution only one man is commander-in-chief; and he is also charged with the conduct of foreign affairs. In complex ways those powers are shared with the Congress; but within the executive branch only the President (and Vice President) have been elected. All others are appointed by the President, or are responsible to appointed officials. They are there to serve the President.

It follows that the task of the executive branch is to respond to the

President's working style as well as to his policy. Having seen and done some work in Washington under six successive Presidents, I still find it remarkable how that massive bureaucracy shifts its style, tone, and manner as Presidents come and go, while maintaining, in each of its departments, a stubborn continuity of its own.

There will always be those who believe they know better than the President what ought to be done, who believe if he were only better informed, he would agree with them. And they may postpone, deflect, dilute, even defy orders—or take their case to the press. There will always be abiding bureaucratic vested interests and habits. For example, Kennedy once, in his early days as President, wanted a sign removed which he thought inappropriate. He asked, casually, that a subordinate take care of the matter. He was told a few days later by the attorney general that it was still there. He tried again. The effort failed. He finally determined the obscure unit of bureaucracy which had responsibility, the exact point within it where power over signs lay, and personally gave the order. He concluded: "I understand now. A President must say something three times to be obeyed." And most Presidents will find something like this true, from time to time, in far graver matters.

But when all this inevitable personal proprietorship over the national interest and bureaucratic inertia is taken into account, the responsiveness of the executive branch to the single individual who leads it is a kind of minor recurrent miracle.

It took some time, but the military and foreign policy complex was reshaped by Kennedy. The heart of it lay in two men: his secretary of defense and his secretary of state.

In Robert S. McNamara he found a man to whom he was prepared to entrust extraordinary and rarely diluted authority in the Pentagon. McNamara chose his own team of civilian subordinates. And, with Maxwell Taylor's movement to the post of chairman of the Joint Chiefs of Staff on October 1, 1962, Kennedy had a military team with which he was comfortable.

Despite his undisputed primacy in the Pentagon, McNamara disciplined himself to a perception which greatly eased the task of both Kennedy and Johnson, as well as Rusk. He understood that military power was the servant of larger political purposes. He knew that military action, indeed, the routine day-to-day operation of a military establishment as large as America's, had profound political and diplomatic significance. The intermingling of military and political policy and action is so deep that clean lines can only rarely be drawn. He consciously and systematically deferred, therefore, to the secretary of state when Rusk took a firm position. And his formal advice to the Presidents he served was routinely in the form of draft memoranda, symbolizing his total acceptance of the decision at which the President would arrive after weighing all the considerations bearing on the problem. In McNamara's time the Pentagon generated, of course, an ample range of differences with the State Department at working levels. These were usually quietly resolved by the two secretaries. The intimacy, ease, and mutual loyalty with which McNamara and Rusk worked was only matched in the post-1945 years, perhaps, by the Acheson-Lovett team in the Truman administration.

Dean Rusk was at least as self-disciplined as McNamara, but in a different way. He had a deep understanding of military problems, based on long and varied experience. His basic view, however, was that diplomacy had failed—he had failed—whenever resort to force was regarded as necessary. He knew also that, in the world as it was in the 1960s, force was an inescapable element in the equation of diplomacy. For example, his first request of me, between Kennedy's election and the Inaugural, was to set down the best answer I could to the thought most on his mind: How do we deal with the world while avoiding nuclear war? He often referred to "the trade union" of foreign ministers. He felt it to be a club of men whose duty it was to see if the human race could come through a terrible passage of history without destroying civilization. His evident sincerity on this point was recognized by his colleagues and often evoked an answering response.

Administratively, Rusk's problem was vastly more complex than McNamara's because Kennedy was determined to deal intimately with foreign affairs and to reshape foreign policy, piece by piece. McNamara's reorganization of the Pentagon and of the American force structure was, perhaps, even more radical than Kennedy's innovations in foreign policy; but Kennedy did not monitor that reorganization in the way he engaged in foreign policy.

For a strong President the difference was inevitable. The President is, inescapably, a major day-to-day actor in foreign affairs, as well as the architect of foreign policy. He meets and negotiates directly with an endless flow of chiefs of government and foreign ministers. On small occasions and large, he is expected to articulate foreign policy in detail not expected of him in military affairs. Therefore, many more hands were at work, in the White House and elsewhere, in foreign than in military affairs during Kennedy's time.

In this setting, Rusk drew a sharp line between his two roles: administrator of the State Department and personal adviser to the President. He deeply respected the post of secretary of state. He never forgot he was in a line stretching back to Jefferson. But modeling himself on George Marshall, Rusk kept his ego under extraordinarily tight rein. He was, I think, the least self-indulgent man I ever worked with. He was the senior adviser to the President, rendering advice on questions he believed men "should approach on their knees." He systematically avoided debate in large meetings. It was, in his view, inappropriate to his office and of no service to the President. He generally rendered his net judgment to the President directly and privately, at the President's request or when he judged the time was right. The primacy Rusk accorded his relations with the President had its cost. He could not fully brief his subordinates on all that transpired between himself and the President. The risk of leaks was always real; and a President needs and deserves private counsel, with free give and take, not promptly spread throughout the bureaucracy. But that meant Rusks's subordinates in the State Department from time to time were flying blind—a situation Rusk felt they should accept with the same equanimity as officers who execute orders without knowing all the considerations which led the commanding general to issue them. On the other hand, within the State Department Rusk encouraged at planning meetings of senior aides wide-ranging discussions, including the advancing of "unthinkable thoughts." In the more or less regular sessions we had together, usually over the weekend, when I was State Department planner, he was speculative, reflective, and candid. But advising the President was his ultimate duty, as he saw it, along with executing the President's decisions. The only show of emotion I ever saw Rusk allow himself was in a disheartened and disheveled meeting immediately after the Bay of Pigs debacle. It took place in the Cabinet Room. The President had stepped out. He pounded the arm of the President's chair and said: "It is this man we must think about."

Unlike McNamara, Rusk did not choose all or even many of his initial subordinates. He lived and worked with an array of men Kennedy wished to see engaged on one aspect or another of foreign affairs. This Rusk accepted, dealing with all in an even-handed, reserved way which did not exclude moments of sensibility and humor, as well as shrewd assessment. Like a high-ranking general in the field, he accepted the flow of subordinates that came his way as decreed by distant higher authority; although, also like a high-ranking general, he used his influence occasionally to get the key men he wanted most. The degree to which he would share his thoughts inevitably varied among his subordinates; but there were no "Rusk men" in his State Department, only fellow soldiers of the line.

The post of secretary of state in the 1960s was certainly the most exacting post in the government. It was loaded with inescapable overhead commitments: protracted ordeals before congressional committees; overseas trips to international conferences; an endless flow of meetings with ambassadors; White House and diplomatic dinners; state visits, with the need for fine-grained exchanges with foreign ministers; an intense series of bilateral exchanges at the annual gathering of the foreign ministers in September for the United Nations General Assembly—all this plus the need to administer a large department; to be fully informed on the state of a fissionable world; to be responsible for the daily flow of cables to every corner of the globe, of which a half-dozen were liable to carry heavy freight and require that every word be weighed; and then, the need to be prepared to render advice to the President at any hour of the day or night.

The ultimate burden of a President is, of course, greater. But he does his business in his home or some other congenial place; he has greater control over his schedule and over whom he sees; he is debarred from appearing before congressional committees; and his staff is small.

Both the President and his advisers were caught up in the 1960s in a little noticed but quite revolutionary change in the scale and intensity of foreign affairs which had occurred in the period between, say, 1945 and 1961. The change in scale arose from the coming to statehood of a great many former colonial nations. Membership in the United Nations, for example, was 59 in 1949, and 112 in 1963. Even more important, however, was the growing intensity of the problems in the southern continents, as the drive for modernization accelerated and the focus of the Cold War struggle came to rest upon them.

It is only a partial exaggeration to say that the secretary of state from 1945 to 1952 was a super-assistant secretary of state for Europe. America faced difficult problems in postwar China; the Japanese occupation and the Treaty; the troubled birth of Israel; and war in Korea. But Latin America was quiet. The ferment in Africa, the Middle East, South and Southeast Asia was primarily a headache for the European colonial powers. Acheson's life as secretary of state was overwhelmingly taken up with problems along the axis from London to Moscow. His most important act in Latin American policy was, perhaps, to order George Kennan's explosive report of March 1950 to be sequestered—"locked away and hidden from innocent eyes."[1] Acheson's advice to Truman that the United States face up to the attack in Korea in June 1950 was determined rather more by his concern for the balance of power in Europe than in Asia: he viewed the attack as a direct challenge by Moscow to Washington that had to be met if nascent NATO were to emerge as viable.

Kennedy and Johnson, Rusk and McNamara dealt with a quite different world. The planet had become a single, sensitively interacting global community. From the point of view of American policy, as well as Russian and Chinese, history had destroyed the shield of colonialism; and Latin America was in a new state of ferment. In the 1960s the intensity of communications between Latin America and Washington, and the gravity of the issues, almost matched those of Europe in the immediate postwar years. Africa, the Middle East, and Asia proved capable of generating, at any moment, crises of the first order of magnitude; and this meant they required endless attention and monitoring, even in apparently quiet times. In short, the traditional orientation of American foreign policy across the North Atlantic had demonstrably ended.

It is this revolution in the world's political structure that explains more than anything else the rise in importance of the post of special assistant to the President for national security affairs.

This new dimension in the organization of national security affairs began to take shape in the 1950s, as experience unfolded with operating the structure created by the National Security Act of 1947 and the advisory council it set in motion.

From the beginning, the heart of the matter lay in two quite distinct problems: first, how the President chose to receive advice on national security matters; second, how coordinated staff work should be generated among all the arms of national security policy at a time when diplomacy itself, in the old-fashioned sense, no longer sufficed. Intelligence, foreign aid, information projected overseas, stockpiling at home, and, above all, military policy had to be woven together with conventional diplomacy.

On the first issue, Truman, like his successors (including Eisenhower), did not use extensively the full formal structure of the National Security Council (NSC) in actually arriving at critical operational decisions. He sought the advice of the men he wanted to hear when he wanted to hear them on specific matters as they arose—notably, George Marshall and Dean Acheson, Robert A. Lovett and Averell Harriman.

With respect to the second problem, coordinated staff work was generated, based on older wartime and immediate postwar precedents, bringing State and Defense closer together; for example, the re-examination of military policy after the first Soviet nuclear explosion in 1949, called NSC 68.

When the Soviet Union acquired nuclear weapons, and the possibilities of a standoff in major weapons became more real, the psychological element in the struggle also rose in priority. After a protracted examination, the problem of psychological warfare came to be conceived primarily as the task of making and executing a policy that would dramatize the areas of overlap between the purposes of the United States and those of other nations.

The Eisenhower administration recognized and accepted this conclusion when in 1953 it converted the Psychological Strategy Board into the Operations Coordinating Board, whose function was to assure coordinated execution of policy decisions already arrived at by the President.

Eisenhower also elevated the formal status of the NSC and the NSC Planning Board. And there emerged, as well, a most useful Thursday lunch at the under secretary level, chaired by the under secretary of state.

As an occasional consultant to the Eisenhower administration, I was able to observe the evolution of its formalized NSC structure. I came to share a judgment arrived at also by some of the men most centrally involved. We concluded that both the NSC Planning Board and the Operations Coordination Board (OCB) had become instruments for generating papers that did not, in fact, come to grips with the heart of the problems they addressed. At formal NSC meetings the President was forced to sit through the elaborate exposition of problems that told him little he did not already know and which did not clearly pose the questions which he had to decide. One man charged with making a part of this apparatus work, late in the Eisenhower administration, concluded: "If we make Ike sit through many more of these pointless meetings, we'll literally kill him."

The reason for this atrophy was quite simple. A strong secretary of state does not wish to place critical and sensitive issues into interdepartmental committees, especially when they expand out to include representatives of departments only marginally involved. Foster Dulles was quite capable of translating this wish into action. A strong secretary of defense may wish to lay his hands on some of the key issues of diplomacy, but does not wish his critical pieces of business spread about for general debate and advice. So, also, with a strong secretary of the treasury; and most national security problems have price tags attached to them. Thus, extremely able men were busy, day after day, drafting papers on problems where the key components were missing.

After citing the many departments and agencies involved in foreign affairs, Eisenhower's own conclusion was this:

> Policy decisions affecting these far-flung operations were my responsibility, but for daily coordination, I early organized the Operations Coordinating Board (OCB). Its membership included important officials of agencies which were directly in charge of specific foreign operations. It functioned fairly well. However, I came finally to believe that this work could have been better done by a highly competent and trusted official with a small staff of his own, rather than by a committee whose members had to handle the task on a part-time basis.[2]

Indeed, for this very reason, a key figure in the Eisenhower administration, Andrew Goodpaster, functioned as a personal aide. Foreshadowing tasks McGeorge Bundy and his successors would undertake, Goodpaster dealt with all manner of national security problems requiring the President's participation, on occasions when the secretary of state or defense, the director of Central Intelligence, the chairman of the AEC, etc., did not choose to take up the matter directly with the President.

All this was quite well known to Kennedy when he asked Bundy and me to go to work in the White House on national security affairs—a perspective underlined for him by a special report of Senator Henry Jackson's Subcommittee on National Policy Machinery, published shortly after the 1960 election. We knew Kennedy would wish our advice on how to reorganize or dispose of the machinery and staff we had inherited. We briefly discussed the problem in Cambridge before going to Washington; agreed we would probably recommend a simpler plan, but agreed, also, that we should study the situation on the spot rather than recommend action on the basis of our existing information and prejudice.

In coming to a responsible judgment in Washington, I read a sampling of perhaps a hundred planning and OCB papers; talked with staff members who had helped operate the machinery; and probed hard at the question of whether a reform of the existing machinery could render it vital.

I concluded that the problem of getting full cooperation from the Department of State was insurmountable, because a strong secretary of state could, would, and, perhaps, should keep out of large interdepartmental committees critical elements in the diplomatic equation. I agreed, in effect, with a dictum of C. D. Jackson's addressed to precisely this problem: "Since you can't lick 'em, join 'em." I therefore proposed that the task of interdepartmental coordination be passed on to the secretary of state; and a much smaller staff be built around Bundy to serve narrowly Presidential purposes. Interdepartmental coordination of the kind reflected in the papers I had read was an essential part of government; and such working-level papers should be available to the President. They represented raw materials which the President's senior advisers should have available; but they were not—and could not be—focused with sufficient precision on the issues the President would have to decide at a particular moment. Bundy had arrived at a similar conclusion.

We took our plan to Kennedy, who approved. But he noted that we were somewhat odd bureaucrats: here we were, handed a substantial empire—slots, budgets, and all—and our first recommendation was to liquidate a good part of it.

The essential decision was to separate two parts of the abiding NSC problem: assistance to the President in preparing for and executing his decisions; and the task of interdepartmental staff work. The latter we would monitor with our small staff, but not try to manage from day to day. The OCB was formally abolished on February 19, 1961.

In *Present at the Creation*, Acheson said: "I saw my duty as gathering all the wisdom available and communicating it amid considerable competition. The alternative we have seen in doubtful operations in the Roosevelt, Kennedy and Johnson administrations, when the President has used the White House staff as the agency for collection and evaluation of wisdom."[3] Acheson, I believe, misjudged the matter. If he had served as secretary of state in the 1960s, he would, I suspect, have recognized the need for, and welcomed, the Bundy staff. The flow of business that only the President could, in the end, decide had become so massive and the preoccupations of the secretary of state so wide-ranging that an extra man, and staff, was required:

1. to keep the President fully informed;
2. to watch over the linkages between State, Defense, AID, the Treasury, Agriculture, and other departments increasingly involved in foreign affairs;
3. to follow closely the development of issues within the bureaucracy so that the President would know what lay behind recommenda-

tions coming forward—notably the options rejected or washed out by bureaucratic compromise and the precise reasons why others were proposed;

4. to assist the President in his expanded personal role in diplomacy: speeches, visitors, and foreign correspondence; press contacts and trips abroad; briefings for meetings with his advisers;
5. to make sure the President's decisions were executed.

A man charged with this kind of responsibility ought to be one whose judgment the President would wish to hear, among others, before he made a decision. Kennedy and Johnson did solicit the views of their special assistants for national security affairs. But the existence of the post emerged from brute necessity, not as an effort to dilute the powers of the secretaries of state and defense.

Kennedy was, from the first, lucid about the mission of his special assistant for national security affairs. He explained it in identical terms to Rusk, McNamara, Bundy, and me. He did not wish us to substitute for the secretaries of state and defense. He was conscious of Franklin Roosevelt's technique of creating overlapping authorities and profiting from the friction, and he wanted no part of it. No decision in their fields would be taken without hearing the two secretaries and giving their advice heavy weight. On the other hand, he wanted to make sure that he had available all the possible options before making a decision. He was determined not to be imprisoned by the options the bureaucracies might generate and lay before him. It was the duty of the special assistant for national security affairs to assure that independent statement of the options.

Many other functions emerged, but those were our instructions in January 1961.

Kennedy had initially thought I might take the post of State Department planner. For good and sufficient reasons Rusk preferred an old friend and colleague, George McGhee. For ten months I functioned as deputy special assistant to the President for national security affairs.

There was plenty for both Bundy and me to do. We first split up the crises. He took Cuba, the Congo, and Berlin, although I joined in the latter from time to time. I took Laos, Vietnam, Indonesia—and the developing world, generally, except Latin America, where Goodwin and Schlesinger operated. I also was assigned the organization of policy planning from the White House end.

It was not an ideal bureaucratic arrangement, especially for Bundy. But the urgency of the tasks, old friendship, mutual respect, and devotion to a common boss made it viable; and there was more than enough for both of us to do. I moved to the planning job at State when McGhee was elevated to the post of deputy under secretary of state, in a massive reorganization of November 1961.

Given the responsibilities borne by the United States in the 1960s, I would guess something much like Bundy's post would have had to be invented later if it had not been created in January 1961. I am inclined to think Rusk and McNamara would agree.

Bundy's mission, as it emerged, is to be understood primarily as a substantial expansion of Goodpaster's role under Eisenhower. He became a major source of advice, as well as organizer of advice, for the President. But Bundy executed his mission with extraordinary sensitivity to the prerogatives of the secretaries of state and defense. He was constantly aware of the need to bring and hold close together the three critical actors: the President, Rusk, and McNamara. What the bureaucracy saw was the vital new figure, and his lively staff, probing, questioning, voraciously gathering intelligence and cables, making sure the President's interests, outlook, and decisions were effectively communicated to the bureaucracy. What the bureaucracy did not see was Bundy's awareness of the problems confronted by Rusk and McNamara, and his quiet actions to try to lighten their burdens as well as the President's.

A word about planning. As Kennedy came to grips with the inescapable crises on the national agenda, he interested himself personally in the design of a planning program. The planners themselves met weekly for lunch at State: with Paul Nitze and Henry Rowen from Defense; Richard Bissell and Robert Amory from CIA; George McGhee and one or more of his colleagues at State (depending on the subject matter); Bundy and myself from the White House.

By February 24, 1961, Kennedy had gone over carefully and approved a list of nineteen tasks arrayed under five headings, the fourth of which was Kennedy's own innovation:

1. Problems of military force and policy; e.g., the deterrence of guerrilla warfare.
2. Certain urgent situations; e.g., Berlin, Vietnam.
3. Foreseeable problems on which planning and action should begin now in order to exploit the presently available but narrowing range of choice; e.g., reappraisal of our relations with Nasser.
4. Potential points of strength where purposeful action might be effective in consolidating or improving our position; e.g., Turkey.
5. Areas relating to possible future negotiation with the Soviet Union; e.g., scientific cooperation.

Assignments were made to named individuals, in an effort to avoid the anonymity and dilution of committee products; and target dates set for each report. The lists were revised with the flow of events, special task forces emerging, for example, on Berlin (under Acheson) and South Korea. By the end of May the list had been expanded to some fifty items, with eleven subjects selected as high priority which might call for NSC treatment or some other form of Presidential decision within two or three months.

The general image of Kennedy's first days as President is sometimes projected as one of light-hearted improvisation until the sobering experience of the Bay of Pigs. For those engaged intimately with him in foreign affairs, it was a sober—even somber—time from the beginning, although confronted with a certain visceral good cheer. He once greeted Bundy and me as we came into his office: "What's gone against us today?"

But it was also a time of planning, of looking ahead to better days. Some of the planning exercises launched then ran into the sand; others laid the foundations for major lines of action.

I recall in those early days running into a party of four late one cold night, between the White House and the Executive Office Building. The two lead characters plodding through the snow could be identified by the glow of cigars at markedly different levels. They turned out to be the President and his shorter companion, Charles Bartlett, accompanied by a pair of men from the Secret Service. Kennedy, evidently in a cheerful mood, asked why I was working so late. I told him I had a tough boss. Briefly serious, he said he wanted to make sure we in the White House got on top of planning and stayed there. Kennedy, in fact, did enter into the planning business more deeply in those early days than any other postwar President.

19

Military, Arms Control, and Space Policy

Budgets and Doctrines

MILITARY AND SPACE EXPENDITURES LIFTED SHARPLY IN KENnedy's first year (fiscal 1962); and they continued to rise —slowly in the former case, rapidly in the latter.

	National Defense	Space Research and Technology
	(in billions of dollars)	
FY 1961	47.4	.7
FY 1962	51.1	1.3
FY 1963	52.3	2.6
FY 1964	53.6	4.2

Kennedy's first move on the defense budget came on March 28, 1961, when he sent a special message to the Congress proposing changes for FY 1962 outlays. These reflected the bipartisan consensus of the late 1950s (which McNamara's initial study of the military establishment confirmed) as well as his vigorous new civilian management of the Pentagon.[1]

The proposed net increase of $650 million reflected somewhat over a billion dollars in new outlays and proposed savings for the coming year of about $400 million.

McNamara moved swiftly to bring the military budget towards greater rationality by using two devices: the program packages; and cost-benefit analysis applied to each major component of expenditure within the packages.

The program packages cut across the three service budgets and grouped defense expenditures by military tasks. The major increases were in the two categories Kennedy had long forshadowed: "strengthening and protecting our strategic deterrent and defenses" and "strengthening our ability to deter and confine limited wars."

The first involved increased outlays to accelerate the production of second-strike Polaris and Minuteman delivery systems as well as to increase the effective delivery capacity of aircraft (via Skybolt) and to decrease the vulnerability of SAC to a first strike by expanding its airborne alert capacity, increasing ground alert, and improving the early-warning system.

In the second category Kennedy requested additional funds for research on non-nuclear weapons; to expand sea- and airlift; to increase the non-nuclear capacities of fighter aircraft; and to expand personnel trained for guerrilla operations.

McNamara's application of cost-benefit analysis to various projects in the research and development stage yielded substantial reductions in supplementary nuclear weapons delivery systems. His initial survey of the defense establishment as a whole launched a process of closing down redundant military bases.

The special message reflected innovations in doctrine as well as in the balance of forces. By the end of March 1961 Kennedy and his administration were already acutely aware of the distinction between conventional and guerrilla war; and this was natural for men who had, over the two previous months, learned more than they ever wanted to know about Laos and Vietnam, the Congo, Castro's dreams and machinations in the Caribbean area, and Khrushchev's doctrine of Wars of National Liberation. Guerrilla warfare problems emerge sharply in national defense policy as a distinct category for the first time in this budget presentation.

The document is also of interest for what lay behind a modest request ($16 million) for increased outlays to assure an invulnerable command and control system governing the firing of nuclear weapons. Official doctrine in the 1950s assumed that a nuclear engagement with the Soviet Union would lead, more or less automatically, to full-scale attack on the Soviet Union, mainland China, and eastern Europe, as well as full release of Soviet weapons against western Europe and the United States. Among the issues raised in developing the bipartisan consensus of the 1950s was the question of a less convulsive response by the United States should Soviet nuclear weapons be fired by accident or design, short of a total salvo.

Against that background, Kennedy was briefed early in his administration on nuclear war plans by a Joint Chiefs of Staff team. The briefing was conducted with special secrecy in the oval Yellow Room in the Mansion, somehow an incongruous setting for a discussion of nuclear war. The responses of the briefing team to Kennedy's sharp questioning, as he probed at the President's capacity to exercise his authority over the use of nuclear weapons, were imprecise.

Kennedy emerged thoroughly persuaded that there was insufficient capability for the President to exercise discrimination and control should nuclear conflict come. This assessment lay behind the basic policy enunciated in the March 28 message: to create a nuclear capacity "more flexible, more selective, more deliberate, better protected, and under ultimate civilian authority at all times."

Kennedy's determination to expand conventional and counter-guerrilla capabilities was carried forward in his State of the Union message of May 25, 1961. It requested additional resources (including helicopters) for the Army, and provided for accelerated capacity to mobilize Army reserve divisions and an expansion of Marine Corps strength.

In terms of resources, however, the Berlin crisis provided the threat and the occasion for Kennedy's major lift in the military budget. In his talk to the nation of July 25, he said some three and a quarter billion dollars would be asked of the Congress to expand available conventional forces sharply. The new appropriation bill moved swiftly into law on August 17.

The evolution of military expenditures under Kennedy emerges clearly from the following table, set out in terms of McNamara's program packages:

TABLE 19–1

DEPARTMENT OF DEFENSE EXPENDITURES, FY 1961–1964[2]
(in billions of dollars)

	FY 1961	FY 1962, original	FY 1962, final	FY 1963	FY 1964
Strategic retaliatory forces	—	$7.6	$9.1	$8.4	$7.3
Continental air and missile defense forces	—	2.2	2.1	1.9	1.9
General purpose forces	—	14.5	17.5	17.8	18.1
Airlift and sealift forces	—	.9	1.2	1.4	1.3
Reserve and Guard forces	—	1.7	1.8	1.8	2.0
Research and development	—	3.9	4.2	5.1	5.4
General support	—	11.4	11.8	13.2	13.9
Civil defense	—	—	.3	.1	.1
Retired pay	—	.9	.9	1.0	1.2
Military assistance	—	1.8	1.8	1.6	1.1
Proposed legislation for military compensation, etc.	—	—	—	—	—
Total obligational authority	$46.1	44.9	51.0	52.2	52.5
Less financing adjustments	3.0	1.3	1.5	1.1	1.5
New obligational authority	43.1	43.6	48.5	51.1	51.0
Adjustment to expenditures	+ 1.6	+ 1.0	− 1.2	− 1.1	− 1.3
Total expenditures	44.7	44.6	47.3	50.0	52.3

The expenditures reflect the surge and then the decline in outlays for missiles, as Polaris and Minuteman programs expanded and ran their course. They indicate also the scale and timing of Kennedy's action to expand conventional forces and their mobility.

Starting in January 1962, McNamara's annual budget presentation became the occasion for an authoritative statement of the administration's security policy. The document was developed in both classified and unclassified versions. Its details were hammered out first in the Pentagon, then with the Bureau of the Budget and the participation of other White House aides. It was cleared with the President, the secretary of state, and a few other high officials. But it was an annual event—and tour de force—of McNamara and his staff. Doctrine, hardware, and dollars were brought together in an impressive way. Current budgets were worked out in the context of a five-year forward-planning period. McNamara's first such presentation included the case for a buildup of NATO conventional strength. It responded to the experience of the Berlin crisis and Kennedy's doctrine that a choice was needed between "inglorious retreat or unlimited retaliation." There was also a substantive passage on "the problem of sublimited wars."[3]

A year later McNamara's presentation, in the wake of the Cuba missile crisis and Nassau, reflected the debate on nuclear problems within the alliance and the search for a beginning to nuclear arms control.[4]

This presentation (February 6, 1963) also touched on a military issue which helped make impossible the writing of an agreed Basic National Security Policy paper (BNSP) in the Kennedy administration; namely, the puzzling question of when, if at all, tactical nuclear weapons might be used. Here is McNamara's lucid statement of an unresolved dilemma:

> . . . we may well be faced with situations in Europe where it would not be to the advantage of ourselves or our allies to use even tactical nuclear weapons initially—provided we had the capability to deal with them through nonnuclear means. Nuclear weapons, even in the lower kiloton ranges, are extremely destructive devices and hardly the preferred weapons to defend such heavily populated areas as Europe. Furthermore, while it does not necessarily follow that the use of tactical weapons must inevitably escalate into global nuclear war, it does present a very definite threshold beyond which we enter a vast unknown.
>
> This does not mean that the NATO forces can or should do without tactical nuclear weapons. On the contrary, we must continue to strengthen and modernize our tactical nuclear capabilities to deal with an attack where the opponent employs such weapons first, or any attack by conventional forces which puts Europe in danger of being overrun. We mean to defend Europe with every kind of weapon needed.[5]

It is a dilemma not confined to the effective defense of western Europe.

The problem arose also in a wider context. On the books when Kennedy came to responsibility was the BNSP of the Eisenhower administration. It was a short document. It contained a passage, consonant with the Eisenhower administration's public stance, which almost, but not quite, identified any military engagement with the Soviet Union as tantamount to the initiation of general nuclear war. Negotiated language had softened the sharpness of the problem; but it was both obscure and, despite revision as late as 1959, essentially a product of the atmosphere of the early 1950s, before thermonuclear weapons had fully emerged, as well as the rockets on both sides to deliver them. Nuclear war plans reflected the convulsive character of the doctrine. As the plans were being modified, it was initially judged wise to change, as well, the existing statement of Presidential policy.

Therefore, one of the first planning tasks assigned by Kennedy in 1961 was a revision of the BNSP. George McGhee, then chairman of the State Department's Policy Planning Council, led a civil-military group. Work moved forward slowly, as befitted the solemnity of the business; and a rough draft was in existence when I took over the planning job in State in December. We carried it forward on the principle that we should be lucid and, even at the cost of length, expose problems rather than find agreed bureaucratic language which would obscure them. Unlike its predecessor, the draft covered a wide range of civil problems bearing on American security, notably in the developing world. Kennedy, Rusk, and McNamara followed the drafts. Talking to my wife from Hyannis Port, Kennedy once told her he was "spending the weekend reading Walt's latest book." It was no one's book, but an earnest communal effort to set out an administration's view of the national interest and national policy in a highly charged nuclear and revolutionary world.

The role of tactical nuclear weapons proved, however, a tough nut to crack. There were differences of view in the Pentagon which McNamara finally chose to deal with by gradual mutual education rather than by fiat, even Presidential fiat.

The draft BNSP was left with an agreed statement of the dilemma posed by the tactical nuclear question; that is, tactical nuclear weapons were extremely important as a deterrent against massive conventional attack, in Europe as elsewhere, but their actual use could produce civil and human destruction on a vast scale, in some cases (depending on locale) tantamount to the strategic use of nuclear weapons.

There were other problems, as well. The most significant was the extent to which a President's hands might be tied by his approval and distribution of such broad guidelines. It was quite possibly this consideration rather than any unresolved issue of substance that determined the outcome. Kennedy finally decided that we would regard the draft BNSP as a useful working paper but not circulate it as Presidentially approved doctrine. There was no significant loss to national policy; although there was a felt need for some such document at working levels in the military and civil bureaucracy concerned with national security affairs.[6]

The exercise did, however, yield two clear, positive results: it led to a fresh definition of a substantial group of new planning tasks and to more systematic efforts at contingency planning throughout the government.

ARMS CONTROL

As Kennedy moved, step by step, to revise military policy, the American force structure, and its management, he acted equally on his commitment to intensify the search for arms control. The Arms Control and Disarmament Agency was formally created on September 26, 1961, and the appointment of William Foster as its first director announced.

From the earliest days of the Kennedy administration an extraordinary amount of human energy and intellectual talent were poured into designing and discussing with Soviet delegates large and narrow schemes of arms control. It was heartening, moving—and somewhat odd—that the struggle was carried forward with such fervor in an atmosphere of multiple crises down to the Cuba missile confrontation. Intense meetings on arms control theory and policy were conducted to a counterpoint of enlarging arms budgets, Soviet nuclear threats, tanks jockeying dangerously at the Berlin checkpoints, and a Southeast Asia evidently capable of exploding into substantial war. The only hard event in the field of arms control over those twenty-one months was the resumption of atmospheric testing of nuclear weapons by the Soviet Union (August 30, 1961), and then by the United States (April 25, 1962). American underground tests were resumed promptly in the wake of the Soviet test of August 30, responding to Kennedy's order of September 5, 1961.

Early in the new administration, John McCloy had gone to work with Valerian Zorin on what Washington called "total and universal disarmament," and Moscow "general and complete disarmament." The critical elements of rationality in American policy designed to articulate this great utopian vision were: that the process should unfold by stages; that effective controls should accompany each stage; and that international peacekeeping institutions of increasing strength should be developed as the stages were implemented. In September, on the eve of Kennedy's address to the United Nations General Assembly, a statement of principles governing an approach to total disarmament was agreed upon. Its major gap was Soviet insistence that only the arms being destroyed would be subject to international inspection, not the arms retained in the various stages—a piece of theology which had greatly engaged the Pugwash session in Moscow of the previous winter, which Kennedy would not accept.

But staff work had also proceeded on a more pragmatic level. The accumulated experience of government work on arms control in the 1950s was combined with concepts developed outside and, especially, with the enthusiasm of the new men who at last could test the viability of their conviction that arms control must and could be moved forward. As a result, Kennedy could lay out the following concrete proposals when he spoke before the United Nations Assembly on September 25, 1961, in the shadow of the resumed Soviet atmospheric tests:

> —First, signing the test-ban treaty by all nations. This can be done now. Test ban negotiations need not and should not await general disarmament.
>
> —Second, stopping the production of fissionable materials for use in weapons, and preventing their transfer to any nation now lacking in nuclear weapons.
>
> —Third, prohibiting the transfer of control over nuclear weapons to states that do not own them.
>
> —Fourth, keeping nuclear weapons from seeding new battlegrounds in outer space.
>
> —Fifth, gradually destroying existing nuclear weapons and converting their materials to peaceful uses; and
>
> —Finally, halting the unlimited testing and production of strategic nuclear delivery vehicles, and gradually destroying them as well.[7]

This list proved to be a fairly accurate statement of the negotiating agenda of the 1960s and beyond.

Until the Soviet resumption of atmospheric tests at the end of August, Arthur Dean carried forward the negotiation of the test ban treaty in Geneva; and with stubborn persistence, contact was maintained with the Russians on both the test ban and more general disarmament proposals, down through the "endless spring and summer" which preceded the Cuba missile crisis.[8]

The notion that the Cuba missile crisis might open the way to progress on arms control arose in many minds. In my case, it emerged from my responsibility as chairman of a special Planning Subcommittee of the NSC, created during the crisis. At its first formal session on October 24, 1962, one of the major tasks assigned was "the shape of a political settlement," on which my deputy, Henry Owen, was to work with disarmament experts. (The other tasks were less benign, including the design of rules of engagement for a protracted war at sea and of measures for increased pressure on Cuba, including alternative means for taking out missiles and installations.)

On October 25 I forwarded, at his request, a paper to McGeorge Bundy on a possible summit meeting, with this observation:

> Khrushchev had in recent months given us a number of reasons to believe that he might be at a crossroads in policy. The Cuba

> MRBM deployment represents his attempt to explore the "hard" fork in the road. If he is rebuffed in this attempt, and if interesting opportunities—if only of an atmospheric level—for useful East-West negotiation are simultaneously opened up to him in other areas, he may conceivably be tempted to explore the alternative option.

Immediately after the worst of the crisis had passed, on October 29, this further comment was made in the fifth report of the Planning Subcommittee:

> Two observations emerged on the subject of negotiation with the Soviet Union. Historically, the instinctive reaction of the USSR to an international setback is to regroup, to consolidate, and to avoid, for a time, fresh initiatives. If that is their reaction on the present occasion, they may not press for a summit; or if a summit takes place, they may use it merely as an occasion to hold to firm previous positions. In that case, there may be no significant movement forward. On the other hand, it is conceivable that Khrushchev himself may wish to move forward towards a détente on Berlin and to leave behind him some achievement in the field of arms control and disarmament. In this case, some forward movement at a summit is conceivable. There is as yet no basis for a judgment as to the course Moscow will, in fact, follow. In the light of these alternatives, we should be prepared, should a summit take place, with an array of proposals, ranging from a mere reaffirmation of the *status quo* through limited, to quite radical steps forward; and use the occasion of such negotiations as a means of assessing the policy and intentions of the Soviet Union.

Almost immediately I learned that some Soviet minds were working along similar paths. On October 30 academician E. K. Federov, a distinguished Soviet scientist who worked on arms control problems, at whose apartment I had dined in Moscow in December 1960, called on me at his request. He had been at a conference at Andover, Massachusetts, during the crisis week. He observed it was an "unpleasant" week for a Soviet citizen to be in the United States, but he was moved by the fact that his American contacts had been even more hospitable than they would have been under normal circumstances. After going over a good many matters, he turned to the question of arms control. We talked, in particular, about the size of the reduction of forces in the first phase of a general disarmament scheme. He concluded that the recent crisis might not be in vain if it led to heightened efforts to produce a disarmament agreement.

That same evening I had dinner at the Finnish Embassy—the first social event I had attended for some time. Anatoliy F. Dobrynin was there, performing with a strained but rather gallant heartiness. In the presence of the Swedish ambassador, he suddenly asked if I thought we could now make progress on disarmament. I said this was our hope; but there was one thing that the Soviet Union would have to bear in mind.

Every nation has its own deep memories which color its foreign policy, rationally or otherwise. For the Soviet Union there are the memories of recurrent invasion from the west, notably from Germany. For the United States there is the memory of Pearl Harbor occurring while diplomatic talks were still taking place with the Japanese. The reassurances of Soviet Foreign Minister Andrei Gromyko to the President about offensive weapons in Cuba, coming at a time when they were in fact being installed, touched a deep nerve among Americans. Moscow would have to count on a very powerful insistence from the United States on effective inspection in any arms control and disarmament arrangement.

Dobrynin then asked if I really meant there were fears here of another Pearl Harbor. I said that, in the sense I had just indicated, there were. He then turned to the Swedish ambassador, Gunnar Jarring, and said that he had known him for ten years and asked if what I had said was true. The Swedish ambassador said that he could confirm exactly what I had told him. Dobrynin said this was important and then went on immediately to ask what I thought of a test ban monitored by stations emplaced within the Soviet Union and elsewhere without international personnel. I said that I was in no position to make a judgment about the adequacy of methods for inspecting underground tests; but I was confident that, if we agreed to a test ban, including underground tests, the President would have to be assured that the risks of violation were very low.

In a lighter vein I told him that Federov that very afternoon had said that our 30 percent arms cut for the first step of a general disarmament scheme was an inadequate beginning; that he (Dobrynin) was much more conservative than his scientific colleague. He replied that we had to begin to turn down the arms race urgently at some point and perhaps the more modest step of a test ban, including underground tests, was the place to begin.

I am sure there were other contacts of a similar kind in those days. I cite these experiences of a State Department planner because they illustrate how early the concept emerged on both sides that it was time to move in another direction after the Cuba confrontation and that a test ban treaty was the most possible initial step.

On December 19, 1962, Khrushchev wrote Kennedy that the "time has come now to put an end once and for all to nuclear tests, to draw a line through such tests."[9]

The key issue proved to be precisely that which Dobrynin and I had discussed; that is, whether American opinion would accept, in the wake of the Cuba missile crisis, the maximum degree of verification Khrushchev was prepared to offer with respect to underground tests. What he offered were two or three annual inspections limited to earthquake areas—the point being that it was theoretically impossible to distinguish by external monitoring earthquakes from underground nuclear explosions. On the

American side, judgments of the minimum requisite number of inspections ranged from five to eight. Kennedy, pressed by the Joint Chiefs of Staff and the Senate, stuck with eight. He wanted the test ban treaty badly; but he believed its ratification by the Senate would not be easy. He could not afford a convincing case by the opposition that it might endanger American security; and, in all conscience, he had no basis for trusting the Russians. Moreover, there was something fundamentally wrong with Khrushchev's approach: in nuclear matters it is in the interest of both sides that each side feel secure that an agreement is being kept. A serious arms control agreement should be generous, not niggling, with respect to verification—a point Soviet scientists would acknowledge in private conversation.

In this setting, the old notion of a test ban treaty limited to environments which could be monitored from outside the Soviet Union naturally re-emerged, in the Congress and the executive branch, as a simple, limited but clean step forward. On May 27 in the Senate, Thomas Dodd joined Hubert Humphrey, an indefatigable crusader for arms control, in proposing that the President offer once again a limited test ban treaty.

Khrushchev's exchanges with Kennedy, between December and June, were grumpy. They probably reflected both Khrushchev's struggle to regain stature after the Cuba missile debacle and relations with Peking.[10] But they led finally to an explicit acceptance of a negotiation in Moscow. Khrushchev's message arrived two days before Kennedy's American University speech of June 10, 1963. Coming on the eve of negotiations, that speech—its rhetoric, its evident reaching out for a new path in American–Soviet relations—had substance. For Khrushchev, set back in Cuba, and as a result, embroiled with Peking worse than ever, it was an easement. Kennedy still left open the possibility of a comprehensive test ban with "vital and responsible safeguards." He also announced that the United States would not conduct atmospheric tests if other nations also refrained, but asserted this policy was no substitute for a treaty.

On July 2 Khrushchev publicly disposed of the inspection issue by advocating a limited test ban outlawing tests in the atmosphere, in outer space, and underwater. At Vienna, two years earlier, he had flatly rejected Kennedy's plea to decouple the test ban from the negotiation of a general disarmament scheme: now he was ready to go, as he had indicated to visiting Harold Wilson as early as June 10.

Having crossed the Rubicon on this sensitive matter with Peking and cut the Gordian knot with Washington on inspection, he was ready to receive the American and British delegations, with Averell Harriman the central figure. There were problems of devising agreed language on a few points. And there was a typically Russian effort to gain a little extra by linking the test ban to a nonaggression treaty between NATO and the Warsaw Pact states and getting a bit of de facto recognition for East Germany. But there was no weight behind this gambit. A little American stubbornness dealt with it. Khrushchev was not in a mood to let Harriman go home without settling the matter: he needed the treaty at least as much as Kennedy wanted it.

The Soviet Union had not firmly decided that its only rational course was to abandon dreams of expansion and to set about using its influence to shape a world safe for the Russian peoples and others. With the outcome of the Cuba missile crisis, peace had not come to the world. But the post-Sputnik offensive was over. Castro was sulking. The Berlin ultimatum had come to its end in the Caribbean. For a time, at least, a dangerous fever in Moscow had peaked and subsided. The split with Peking now became wholly overt, with the mutual publication of documents bearing on its nature and origins. Moreover, as the American economy accelerated, the Soviet economy was palpably slowing down and its old agricultural problems were worse than ever. Moscow needed—and got—help in the form of sales of American wheat. With so much of its ideological dream in disarray, it was good for Khrushchev and the Soviet Union to emerge as a leader and great national power behaving with responsibility, moving at least a small step toward the control of nuclear weapons, setting in motion the Moscow–Washington hot line, accepting quietly mutual inspection by satellite photography, joining in a United Nations resolution against the orbiting of weapons of mass destruction in outer space.

When Johnson came to responsibility, he faced a quite different Soviet Union than had Kennedy. He understood this and acted from the first days on his perception that progress beyond the atmospheric test ban treaty ought to be possible.

SPACE: "HOCKING THE FAMILY JEWELS"

IN December 1960 Eisenhower received a report on long-run plans for manned space flight, prepared by a panel headed by Donald Hornig. Hornig's group estimated manned lunar flight would cost between $26 and $38 billion. Eisenhower is reported to have asked why such an enterprise should be undertaken.[11] He was told it was a great adventure in discovery like Columbus' voyage to America. His alleged reply: "I'm not about to hock my jewels."

The future of manned flight in space was left to the Kennedy administration. Out of post-Sputnik politics and the rhetoric of the 1960 campaign Kennedy was broadly committed to a more active space program than Eisenhower; but his administration also contained scientists skeptical of manned flight, especially the moon enterprise. And it contained men gravely concerned with the resources which would have to be allocated.

Kennedy's first major decision was to assign Johnson a central role in space policy. He sought legislation which would make the Vice President, instead of the President, chairman of the National Aeronautics and Space Council. Congress acted on this request on April 20, 1961. Johnson had for long led the Senate and, in a sense, the country toward a policy of wholehearted exploration of space; and Kennedy was concerned about the need for his extraordinarily vigorous and experienced Vice President to find maximum scope for his energies and talents within the inherently narrow confines of the office.

Meanwhile, Johnson had been assigned the task of finding the man to head NASA. James Webb was suggested; Kennedy agreed; and Webb was sworn in by February 14.

As is often the case within government, Kennedy's basic decision on where to go in space was forced toward resolution by a budgetary problem. On March 17 Webb asked approval for an addition of $308 million to the Eisenhower budget of $1.1 billion requested for NASA in FY 1962. Webb said the increase was necessary if the United States–Soviet gap in space capabilities was to be closed in a decade. In his view, the last Eisenhower budget had underfunded the program in terms of stated space objectives. On March 23 Kennedy made an interim decision to add enough to the budget to cover critical launch vehicles and propulsion units ($142 million); but he was clearly groping at that meeting for a sharper focus than a ten-year program to close a generalized space gap.

On April 12, 1961, the Soviet Union climaxed a series of impressive space exercises with Yuri Gagarin's one-orbit flight, including his challenge, in a telephone conversation with Khrushchev: "Let the capitalist countries catch up with our country." On April 17 the Bay of Pigs operation was launched. On April 20 Kennedy asked Johnson to establish in what space programs the United States might surpass the Soviet Union and what it would cost. Eight days later the Vice President reported ad interim that neither the Soviet Union nor the United States then commanded a capability for a manned flight to the moon; the Soviet Union had an initial advantage in boosters: "However, with a strong effort, the United States could conceivably be first in those accomplishments by 1966 or 1967."

Both technical analysts and those drawn in to consult with them had been coming for some time to the conclusion that manned flight to the moon was the most likely answer. The successful American suborbital flight of May 5 helped clear away some medical doubts about man in space. Over the weekend of May 6–7 Webb and McNamara formulated a detailed plan for Johnson which he forwarded to Kennedy before leaving on a trip to Southeast Asia. And on May 25 Kennedy set the target in his State of the Union message of landing a man on the moon and returning him safely to earth before the decade was out. The Congress promptly acquiesced.

At lunch in Vienna on June 4 Khrushchev told Kennedy that he was placing certain restraints on projects for a flight to the moon. (In retrospect, it appears he had probably decided to rule out manned flight but to proceed with an unmanned landing.) Khrushchev went on to explain that the project was so expensive it would interfere with military defense outlays. He was, therefore, resisting pressure from Soviet scientists: the United States was rich and should go first; the Soviet Union would follow.

The day before his assassination Kennedy spoke of the commitment to space in these terms:

> Frank O'Connor, the Irish writer, tells in one of his books how, as a boy, he and his friends would make their way across the countryside, and when they came to an orchard wall that seemed too high and too doubtful to try and too difficult to permit their voyage to continue, they took off their hats and tossed them over the wall—and then they had no choice but to follow them.
>
> This Nation has tossed its cap over the wall of space, and we have no choice but to follow it. Whatever the difficulties, they will be overcome. Whatever the hazards, they must be guarded against.[12]

There were rational arguments for the enterprise: to deal finally with the post-Sputnik space trauma, underlined by Gagarin's exuberant challenge; to prevent a Soviet space superiority sufficient to tempt Moscow with military applications; to generate and apply the scientific and technological spinoffs that might emerge.

And there were rational arguments against it: the cost; the possibility of acquiring much of the scientific data by an unmanned trip to the moon; the possibility of failure.

Kennedy only raised the issue with me once; and my response was limited to the extremely narrow basis for judgment I commanded.[13] I would guess that his decisive considerations were to foreclose a Soviet military advantage in space, open an area for harmless competition and, perhaps, United States–Soviet collaboration, and make sure the first man on the moon was an American—a tossing of the cap over the wall.

It has been suggested that the Bay of Pigs debacle might have tipped the balance of Kennedy's judgment in favor of the dramatic new enterprise. April–May 1961 were, indeed, difficult months; and Kennedy worked hard to right the ship. I worked particularly closely with the President in that period. He made a number of decisions in those days that cast long shadows. I do not believe any were made that would not, in any case, have been made. Kennedy's grasp on where he wanted to go in the long run remained firm.

Kennedy's decision on the moon flight was the most important space decision of his administration. But other matters came up before him: the decision on the best method for getting to the moon, in which the long-shot concept of a vehicle descending from moon orbit won out; the effect of U.S. and Soviet nuclear explosions in space on radiation; the fear that

Soviet docking experiments might foreshadow a military use of space; the question of U. S. space objectives beyond the moon.

In a sense, the most serious long-run problem for the American space effort in Kennedy's time was the successful outcome of the Cuba missile crisis. Instinctively, fear of the Soviet Union in the United States diminished. Dimensions of the competition between Moscow and Washington that had come into focus and gathered intensity after Sputnik began to appear less urgent, space among them. Critics emerged or re-emerged. On July 29, 1963, in explicit response to the critics, Kennedy asked Johnson for supporting evidence on the military value of the space program. Two days later Johnson replied, with the unanimous support of the Space Council, concluding: "The space program is expensive, but it can be justified as a solid investment which will give ample returns in security, prestige, knowledge and material benefits." But when Kennedy suggested on September 20, 1963, that a joint manned lunar program might be worked out with the Soviet Union, the Congress barred any such agreement without its approval and forbade expenditure of NASA funds for such a purpose without congressional assent. Apollo stayed on course. But the political forces making for a reduction or stretch-out in the space program slowly gathered strength from the Cuba missile crisis forward.

Like foreign aid and the nuclear problem in NATO, diminished support for the space program reflected a sense that Soviet power had been reduced; the world was no longer being shaped by a nose-to-nose competition between Moscow and Washington but by more diffuse influences and more oblique contests. The Cold War was not ended by the Cuba missile crisis; but it was rendered, for a time at least, less acute and direct.

20

Kennedy's Policy toward the Developing World in General

American Interests and Moral Responsibility

Kennedy took the developing world seriously. His education might easily have led him to what might be called an Atlantic view; that is, that what mainly mattered to the United States was relations with western Europe and that other problems should be subordinated to America's interests in the developed world. But it did not. He understood in his bones the meaning of the ending of colonialism and the rising ferment in Latin America as well as Africa, the Middle East, and Asia.

There were three clear, converging strands in his perspective.

First, that in the long run, Cold War or not, the evolution of these areas would matter greatly to the kind of environment in which Americans would live. He believed "widespread poverty and chaos [could] lead to a collapse of existing political and social structures which would inevitably invite the advance of totalitarianism into every weak and unstable area. Thus our own security would be endangered and our prosperity imperilled. . . . the fundamental task of our foreign aid program in the 1960's is not negatively to fight Communism: its fundamental task is to help make a historical demonstration that in the twentieth century, as in the nineteenth—in the southern half of the globe as in the north—economic growth and political democracy can develop hand in hand."[1]

Second, he was acutely conscious that as of the early 1960s the developing areas were the focus for communist strategy: ". . . in our time these new nations need help for a special reason. Without exception they are under Communist pressure. In many cases, that pressure is direct and military. In others, it takes the form of intense subversive activity designed to break down and supersede the new—and often frail—modern institutions they have thus far built."[2] Kennedy believed that the balance of power could be shifted against the noncommunist world by such communist strategies and tactics.

Third, he felt there was an inescapable moral duty for the more advanced nations to help the less advanced—the rich to help the poor. As Kennedy said in his Inaugural Address, it was to be done, in part, "because it is right."

Thus, he launched the 1960s as the United Nations Decade of Development "on which will depend substantially the kind of world in which we and our children shall live".[3]

Although partly reflecting the bipartisan consensus of the late 1950s and the influence of some of his advisers, the President's views on national interest and the developing world were deeply rooted in personal experience and private assessments of his pre-Presidential years: his personal observation of Vietnam in 1951 and his subsequent assessments of 1954 and 1956[4]; the study which lay behind his controversial statements on Algeria in 1957[5]; his work in the Senate as chairman of the Subcommittee on Africa of the Foreign Relations Committee[6]; his reflections on the meaning for Latin American policy as a whole of the emergence of Castro[7]; his engagement in the problems of India and the meaning of the ideological competition between India and China.[8]

THE 1961 AID MESSAGE AND THE EVOLUTION OF KENNEDY'S PROGRAM

AGAINST this broad background Kennedy's Special Message to the Congress on Foreign Aid of March 22, 1961,[9] sought to shift the existing program in the following directions:

—a unification of technical assistance, lending, Public Law 480, and other scattered activities;

—a concentration on national development plans as opposed to specific projects; with priority for nations making serious and coherent self-help efforts "to reach the stage of self-sustaining growth";

—a multilateral approach, designed to draw other industrialized nations systematically into the effort on a larger scale;

—authority from the Congress for long-term (five-year) authorization and borrowing authority to make dollar-repayable loans.

Eisenhower's final aid request of the Congress was high: some $800 million more than the sum actually voted in the previous year. For the first

TABLE 20-1
THE CHANGING SCALE AND COMPOSITION OF AMERICAN FOREIGN AID, FY 1960–1964
(in millions of dollars)

	1960	1961	1962	1963	1964
Military Aid	1609	1449	1390	1721	1485
Defense Support	741	1013	618	494	371
Development Loans and Grants	202	427	619	1005	768
Agriculture (P.L. 480)	107	199	242	216	1704
Technical Assistance and Cooperation	172	*	*	*	226
Contingency and other Special and Development Assistance	369	449	792	718	816
Total Economic Assistance (including P.L. 480 and defense support)	1591	2188	2271	2433	3885

* Included in development grants, 1961–1963.

	1960	1961	1962	1963	1964
Total Official Flows (DAC definition)	2702	2943	3272	3627	3611
Total Flows (DAC definition, including private investment)	3818	4549	4355	4579	4770

Sources: Derived from annual budgets of the U.S. government and from *1969 Review: Efforts and Policies of the Members of the Development Assistance Committee.*

year Kennedy, therefore, stayed with Eisenhower's request for a $4 billion economic and military authorization, but proposed to shift allocations toward development loans, repayable in dollars over long periods.

Even this aid increase appeared difficult to get from a rather conservative Congress. Sorensen's low-key first draft of the aid message was geared to the rather gloomy prospects on the Hill. Kennedy evidently wished to aim somewhat higher. He had Sorensen send the draft to me for revision. And, when Kennedy approved the new directions suggested by me (and, perhaps, by others), Sorensen, quite typically, carried forward in a more heroic direction with verve and elegance.

In 1961 Kennedy moved the foreign aid program some distance toward the goals he had formulated in the late 1950s; although its momentum was damped by initial administrative problems and then, in 1963, by increased congressional resistance, in the post-Cuba missile crisis letdown of anxiety about the Cold War.

Nevertheless, Kennedy achieved a good deal. He got from Congress the authority to make long-term commitments; although he did not get the borrowing authority for aid lending he sought. The latter would have been a bold innovation, relieving development lending (not grants) from the annual appropriations cycle. It might have sustained the level of American capital flows to the developing world in the latter 1960s. But it was rejected as "back-door financing" and a dilution of congressional power over the purse strings. Completing an initiative he undertook as a senator, Kennedy launched the India and Pakistan consortia arrangements in the World Bank with a strong U.S. contribution, inducing proportionate contributions from others. This not only strengthened development programs affecting the lives of some 40 percent of the people in the developing world, but also set a pattern for multilateralism which was rapidly extended in the 1960s. He launched the Alliance for Progress as well as the Peace Corps. When the American contribution to development is measured as a whole (including the World Bank, IDA, the Inter-American Bank, etc.), the lift in resources made available in the early 1960s is quite impressive: an increase of one-third.

The figures reflect the new programs for South Asia and Latin America, as well as a somewhat enlarged effort in Africa. There is a significant decline in defense support as development lending expands. And there is a major element not reflected in the table which reaches beyond Kennedy's time. His strong advocacy of international support for serious development efforts helped induce other nations to expand their contributions, a trend which continued as the 1960s wore on. In 1960 the United States supplied 57 percent of official development assistance. Kennedy's lift in the American effort was not promptly matched, and by 1963 the figure was 60 percent. In 1968 the expanding contributions of others (notably, Canada, Germany, Italy, Japan, the Netherlands, and Sweden), combined with growing congressional resistance, had brought the American proportion of an enlarged total down to 52 percent.

21

Some Crises in the Developing World

Politics and People

There was, of course, more to Kennedy's policy toward the developing world than aid programs. More of Kennedy's time was taken up by the raucous vicissitudes of political development than by the somewhat more antiseptic world of economic development.

He was dealing with nations at different stages of growth from, say, primitive Mali to sophisticated but self-frustrated Argentina. They all had political problems at home. Many had ambitions or strongly felt frustrations abroad. Kennedy's support for development as an objective independent of whether nations were allied with the United States was an easement in America's relations with the developing world. And there was a basis for Kennedy's faith that if the developing nations would concentrate their energies on the tasks of domestic economic and social development, their independence would be less endangered and the world would be somewhat less volatile. It was some such perception which, ultimately, led the American public to associate foreign aid with peace and permitted the foreign aid program to make its way through a barely acquiescent Congress year after year. But these were forces that took time to work themselves out. Meanwhile, Kennedy had to deal with the men who bore responsibility for their nations from day to day in an untidy, contentious world, whose inherent volatility was heightened though not created by the Cold War. It was one thing to take a relaxed posture toward neutralism in principle, a quite different matter to deal with Tshombe, Sukarno, Nasser, and Nkrumah, as well as the bedeviling tension between India and Pakistan.

CONGO, ROUND TWO

KENNEDY inherited a Congo still split, its government unable to rule; and a United Nations military presence, evoked in 1960 to help the new nation achieve minimum conditions for statehood (see pp. 52–53).

The Congo question ran like a tragi-comic thread through the Kennedy administration from its earliest days down to January 16, 1963, when the defeat of Moise Tshombe by a United Nations force ended, for a time, at least, Katanga's secession.[1] American policy was carried forward through the awkward but essential medium of United Nations committees, the Secretariat, and a multinational force in the field; by diplomacy across the Atlantic; by ambassadors and special missions to the Congo; by domestic politics; and, finally, by a special military mission.

The Soviet threat, initially set back, remained latent, if the United Nations could not deliver on the promise of unity. The rest of Africa watched the outcome closely. Tshombe, ruling rich Katanga, symbolized a perpetuation of colonialism in a critical area. In his thrust for Katanga's independence, he had significant support from Brussels, Paris, and London, as well as sympathy from a minority in American political life. Understanding well the schism in the West on this matter, Tshombe mounted a hard-driving, well-heeled lobby in Washington and elsewhere to press the case for Katangan independence.

Kennedy had two concerns in the Congo, both of which led him to support the nation's unity. First, he wished to avoid the emergence of a communist base in the heart of Africa. He judged this outcome unlikely if Congolese unity was assured. Second, given the African view of Katangan independence as a neo-colonial venture, he concluded that without an effective American stand in support of Congolese unity, all his benign interest in Africa, and the new aid programs, would be without meaning to Africans, or to the American interest in Africa. Without a Congo policy there could, in effect, be no African policy. Therefore, in the end Kennedy felt the central government would have to be backed in its drive for unity, if possible by the United Nations, if necessary by the United States. Like everyone else who worked on this slippery, multifaceted problem, he stared from time to time at the attractions of withdrawing United States interest, concern, and support for the United Nations effort. But, in the end, he stayed with the venture.

On the other hand, with the need for maximum unity in the West in the face of pressure on Berlin, he had to minimize the corrosiveness of differences across the Atlantic about Congo policy. With ample potential claims on American military resources, he also had to minimize the likelihood of direct American engagement. With vigorous opposition to his policy in the Senate and, to a degree, within his administration, he encouraged the United Nations to carry forward the effort, by diplomacy and negotiation to the maximum degree possible, although the possibility of using military power to force the issue was there from the early days of 1961.

The critical issue was foreshadowed in the meeting of the United Nations Security Council which took place in the inflamed atmosphere which followed the announcement of Patrice Lumumba's death on February 13, 1961. The resolution of February 21 provided for the withdrawal of Belgian and mercenary forces in support of Tshombe; the convening of the Congolese parliament; the reorganization of the Congolese army; and a role for the United Nations forces in avoiding civil war which included "the use of force if necessary in the last resort." Events finally determined that the use of force would be not merely to avoid civil war but also to achieve Congolese unity by reinforcing the government's hand in civil war.

Before a solution was achieved, however, diplomacy and politics had to prove their impotence.

First, an effort was made to exploit the natural gifts of Africans for intertribal diplomacy. Protracted talks yielded a new government in August 1961, headed by Cyrille Adoula in Leopoldville, and an end to the Gizenga secession; but Tshombe held aloof.

Second, in September the United Nations force was frustrated in acting to effect the withdrawal of Belgian and mercenary forces, in part by a single jet trainer in the hands of Tshombe—an aircraft which obliquely contributed to Hammarskjold's tragic accidental death. But increased United Nations military pressure, assisted by American transport aircraft, brought about an agreement on December 21 in which Tshombe appeared to accept the full authority of Adoula's central government.

Third, there followed a period in which Tshombe stalled. An effort was made to press on him a concrete United Nations Plan for Reconciliation which came to grips with the critical issues: sharing in the mining revenues and tax payments generated by the Katanga copper mines; the integration of the Congolese Army; a general amnesty; and a political organization that would, while recognizing the central government, give Katanga a fair sense of representation.

Finally, as it became clear that Tshombe was not negotiating in good faith, the whole lumbering machinery at work on the Congo moved to a showdown: the United Nations; the United States government; the shaky Congolese government (with some of its members beginning again to look to Moscow); and, to a degree, even the Europeans. Tshombe threatened a scorched-earth policy. The United States dispatched a small military mission and offered increased military supplies. On January 16, 1963, an enterprising Indian brigadier of the United Nations Force, Reginald S. Noronha, produced a small-scale version of Patton's 1945 crossing of the

Rhine contrary to orders—at the Lufira River before Jadotville. And with much nervousness in many capitals, the job was done.

Tshombe's procrastination had used up a good deal of his capital abroad; and, with the Cuba missile crisis and the Berlin threat behind him, Kennedy was prepared for somewhat greater risk than earlier to solve the problem.

The Congo story of the 1960s was by no means at an end; but the United Nations had produced and used a fighting force to grant unified statehood to a nation whose primitive stage of development did not permit a government capable of consolidating sovereignty on its own.

THREE REVOLUTIONARY ROMANTICS

A GREAT deal of history in the first postwar generation centers on what I have called the aggressive Revolutionary Romantics.[2] On coming to power out of anticolonial struggle or other revolutionary circumstances, in nations at an early state of economic and political development, they chose to allocate a high proportion of their scarce resources, talent, and governmental energies to the redress of real or believed past grievances. They built their domestic policies, in varying degrees, around continued "anticolonialism" as a hopefully unifying theme in inherently fragmented societies. They established, essentially, one-man rule. And they engaged in more or less bloody exercises in the expansion of power in their regions. The roster of leaders that fall into this category includes: Mao, Ho, Castro, Sukarno, Nasser, and Nkrumah.

Kennedy's problems with the first three are dealt with elsewhere. Here we consider briefly how he dealt with Indonesia, Egypt, and Ghana when led by Sukarno, Nasser, and Nkrumah.

SUKARNO

KENNEDY actively disliked few men. He understood that people were complicated, imperfect, and unique. He understood that problems might well look different from where they stood than from where he stood. He entered with compassion and authentic interest into the extraordinary burdens borne by those leading new nations. But he came to dislike Sukarno strongly.

His attitude toward Sukarno had nothing to do with Indonesia's policy toward the United States. Kennedy simply felt that Sukarno was inexcusably callous and self-indulgent in managing the fate of more than a hundred million human beings who deserved a better life. Moreover, Sukarno's egocentrism, a trait not unusual in politicians, was peculiarly blatant and sometimes offensive. For example, when he and Keita of Mali were instructed to present in Washington the resolutions of the Belgrade neutralist conference of September 1961, Sukarno ignored his colleague and ruthlessly dominated the initial interview with Kennedy. Keita, tall in his tribal robes, maintained a dignified silence until the private interview Kennedy arranged with him.

Acheson said of Truman that he was "free of the greatest vice in a leader, his ego never came between him and his job. . . ."[3] Of the leaders in recent history, Sukarno belongs at the other end of the spectrum.

Kennedy's feelings toward Sukarno in no way interfered with his conduct of policy toward Indonesia, where serious issues were involved. He sought to turn Sukarno's interests to economic and social development and away from his absorption in external adventure and rather empty posturing on the world scene.

When Kennedy came to deal with Indonesia, Sukarno had built a personal regime over the three previous years. He used his army to balance the large Indonesian Communist party; entered into a massive Soviet arms deal; fabricated a gim-crack ideology with native, Marxist, and Western strands (*Pantja Sila*); and was campaigning obsessively for the turning over of Dutch-held West New Guinea (West Irian) to Indonesia. In the course of all this he had let his inherently feeble economy run down, despite the rich natural resources within it. Sukarno was responding in his own way to real problems, built into the fabric of postcolonial life. It was the dilettante, fragile, and dangerous character of his solutions that caused anxiety.

Kennedy raised the issue of development directly with Sukarno on his visit in April 1961. There was occasion to do so. Indonesia had produced a grandiose eight-year development plan. For its execution, however, it required not only the kind of serious stabilization program recommended by the International Monetary Fund, but expanded foreign exchange earnings as well. That meant stable relations with foreign oil firms, among others. Even more, it demanded a concentration of resources and political energies on development rather than on military supplies and external military adventures. On this point, Sukarno responded to Kennedy with some candor. He said politics had to come first. Economic development was too slow. The people had to be unified. The civil politicians were self-seeking and corrupt. That was why he had to take over fully in 1958 and provide in *Pantja Sila* an indigenous unifying ideology. Only his personal rule and the regaining of West Irian could hold his people together. They were unified on West Irian: "Give it to me, Mr. President," he said. "Please give it to me."

On Indonesian feelings about West Irian, Sukarno was correct. All articulate factions in Indonesian politics pressed hard on this issue. Their legal ground was that Indonesian sovereignty over the area was implicit in the 1949 agreement with The Hague which ended colonial rule.[4]

Whatever the international legal niceties, Kennedy had to face certain facts. First, the Dutch, as a matter of pride, did not wish to surrender West New Guinea to Sukarno's new imperialism, as they saw it; but they were not willing to fight to defend it. Kennedy was not about to take on an additional war in Southeast Asia where no vital American interest was involved. Moreover, Kennedy knew that important elements in Dutch political life, in fact, wished to remove all barriers to a revival of commercial and trading ties with Indonesia, including the issue of West New Guinea. Second, on this matter the Indonesian Army was with Sukarno, and the links between the United States and the Indonesian military (the training of officers in the United States and an imaginative civic action program in the villages) would be attenuated if the United States backed the Netherlands.[5] Third, it was clear that if Indonesian political life was ever to turn to the laborious tasks of modernization and of finding regional harmony in Southeast Asia, the issue of West Irian would have to be removed from its agenda.

The turning point in American policy came in the wake of the United Nations rejection of the Dutch plan for a U.N. trusteeship after a debate in which the United States tried still to keep out of the quarrel. On November 30, 1961, Sukarno, speaking to the Indonesian Army Staff College at Bandung, committed himself to "liberate" West Irian and said "the present moment is the proper time."

On December 19 Sukarno proclaimed national mobilization.

Pressures mounted on the United States to force a direct Dutch–Indonesian negotiation. And after a good deal of preliminary jockeying (including a trip to Indonesia by Robert Kennedy), this result was achieved.

Ellsworth Bunker, loaned to the United Nations, quietly conducted talks in the Virginia countryside between the Dutch and Indonesians. The negotiation yielded a transfer of West Irian to the United Nations and, then, after a face-saving seven months, to Indonesia. The issue of West Irian was settled, for a time at least, in May 1963.

Kennedy quite consciously accepted the blame in Dutch political life for the settlement. He knew that, in fact, many Dutch politicians as well as citizens were relieved that the problem had been lifted from them; that some Dutch business interests were looking forward to the settlement to resume old ties in Indonesia; and, in any case, America's shoulders were broad enough to carry the burden.

Kennedy's position on West Irian was taken on the merits, in terms of American interests. It would have required American military action to prevent the Indonesians from acquiring West Irian; such action would have put the United States athwart Indonesian nationalism and played into the hands of Moscow, Peking, and the Indonesian Communist party; the fate of the people in West Irian might well have been easier under a United Nations trusteeship than under Indonesia, but the legal and moral case for the Dutch position was shadowed by events in 1949 and thereafter; the issue was not, in itself, a matter of vital American interest.

There was also some hope for the future if West Irian were out of the way: that Sukarno might turn to concentrate his energies on economic and social development (or permit other Indonesians to do so); that the military might enjoy more political freedom of action in their dealings with Sukarno.

Kennedy did what he could to encourage the first possibility, including a successful effort to arrange a settlement between the Indonesian government and the American oil companies operating there. But the whole enterprise became embroiled in a second contentious regional issue, the expansion of Malaya to Malaysia and the drawing within it of the British Crown colonies of Sarawak, Brunei, and British North Borneo. This process proceeded parallel to the negotiation to settle West Irian. There were evident sensitivities in Manila as well as in Djakarta about the transfer of the Crown colonies to Kuala Lumpur. Those of us working on Indonesia took Sukarno's capacity to avoid conflict and violence over the formation of Malaysia as a measure of his willingness to turn his back on external adventure (as he had quite explicitly promised) once he had West Irian.

The simple fact is that Sukarno could not bring himself to settle down to the modernization of Indonesia and let the matter of Malaysia be dealt with peacefully. On January 8, 1963, he denounced the whole notion of the expansion of Malaya and two weeks later the "confrontation" was on, backed by Indonesian military and guerrilla operations to upset the transfer of the Crown colonies.

Nevertheless, diplomacy continued to work. Under Australian inspiration, representatives of the Philippines, Malaya, and Indonesia met in June 1963 and came to agreement that the formation of Malaysia should proceed if the Secretary General of the United Nations or his representative should ascertain this was the will of the majority of the peoples involved. This was to be done not by a fresh plebiscite but by an ex post study of whether the last election in the Borneo territories in fact reflected a popular decision to join Malaya.

On September 14, 1963, U Thant published his report concluding that the majority in North Borneo and Sarawak did, indeed, wish to join the enlarged Federation.

The next day Djakarta announced that Malaysia was illegal and would not be recognized. The formal establishment of Malaysia on September 15 provoked anti-British riots. Indonesia cut off trade with Malaya. The United States suspended shipments of arms and ammunition to Indonesia.

This brief summary does not do justice to some of the complexities involved, including actions by London, Washington, and Kuala Lumpur, which made Indonesian acceptance of U Thant's findings somewhat more difficult than they might otherwise have been.[6] But the critical fact was that Sukarno could not resist using the issue of Malaysia as the basis for his domestic politics. He could not bring himself to turn to the mundane tasks of Indonesian economic and social development.

The Cold War did not create the issues of West Irian and Malaysia. They arose from early postcolonial history. But struggles to expand or resist the expansion of communist power suffused them, as well as the efforts to encourage or divert Sukarno from the path of confrontation.

I do not regret the American effort to channel Sukarno onto another path. And in Kennedy's time, from the earliest days in his administration, I did all I could to encourage that policy. But my observation of Sukarno in his talks with Kennedy, and extensive conversations with his entourage, did not encourage optimism. The test was clearly Sukarno's ability to resist confrontation with Malaysia, once West Irian was settled. I was inclined to regard his commitment to confrontation in January 1963 as evidence that the American effort with Sukarno had failed.

NASSER

JUST as Kennedy's efforts to channel Sukarno's nationalism toward domestic development came unstuck with the Malaysian confrontation, his parallel enterprise with Nasser ran into the ground over Cairo's inability to resist involvement in Yemen when civil war followed the death of the Imam in September 1962.

As of January 1961 relations between the United States and Egypt seemed more promising than in the case of Indonesia. Despite continued Soviet work on the Aswan Dam and the continued flow of Soviet arms, Cairo's ties with Moscow had become somewhat strained since the Lebanon–Jordan crisis of 1958. Khrushchev openly denounced Nasser's repression of Egyptian communists in January 1959 and, in March, *Pravda* threw its weight against further efforts at uniting the Arab countries under Nasser's leadership. The withdrawal of Syria from the United Arab Republic in late September 1961 further enhanced Cairo's sense of nationalist isolation. Arab–Israeli tension subsided. With the situation in his region somewhat unpromising, Nasser was in a phase where economic and social development at home seriously engaged him.

Unlike Sukarno, Nasser had generated quite sophisticated development programs and commanded a first-rate group of planners capable of moving them forward. Egypt, despite its poverty and the acute pressure of population on limited arable land, was a more advanced country than Indonesia: the latter was still developing the preconditions for industrialization; Egypt was already in its first phase of industrialization and was capable of sustaining it, if it concentrated on the task. Nasser had more to work with than Sukarno and could look forward to quicker results.

Kennedy moved, step by step, to exploit these circumstances. The first move was through correspondence rather than economic policy. The initiative was Nasser's. He responded in a lively and evidently personal letter to a routine Presidential message to the Arab chiefs of state. Kennedy answered promptly. The minister of culture in Cairo then invited Mrs. Kennedy to attend the debut of *son et lumière* at the pyramids. Although she could not go, Henry Cabot Lodge, independently invited to Cairo, arrived with a letter from Kennedy to Nasser. The Bay of Pigs yielded a second round of correspondence, including a candid statement of the American position from Kennedy and a remarkably understanding response from Nasser. By May 1961 the tone of the Egyptian press was distinctly less anti-American. The new ambassador, John Badeau, an Arabist, arrived at mid-year under mildly propitious circumstances.

Meanwhile, in Washington the Egyptian ambassador, Mostafa Kamel, was earnestly at work to consolidate the new tone emerging between the two chiefs of state. At his request I had lunch with him on November 22, 1961. He argued that the United States must not take the neutralists too seriously or let their position on world issues annoy us. It was a major asset of the Kennedy administration that we were prepared to help the neutralists maintain their independence, despite disagreements on some world issues; and this asset should not be lost.

He then turned to the Middle East and noted that Arab–Israeli relations were quiet. They should be left alone for a time. The possibilities of a more basic settlement would gradually emerge as domestic progress was made by all parties. There was no inclination on the part of Cairo to exacerbate the situation. In effect, he said that Cairo was willing to leave the issue of Israel on the back burner.

He thought the United States should try to bring the Arab states together on a constructive basis and concert our Middle East policies with our major western European allies.

He believed it crucial to the future stability of Egypt and to United States–Egyptian relations to expand systematically our economic cooperation with three items in particular: long-term P.L. 480 assistance; development loans for grain storage and distribution; a loan of short-staple cotton to cover the major gap in the current cotton harvest, so that Egyptian long-staple cotton could be exported.

We then talked about the possibility of moving toward a consortium arrangement through the World Bank, which would organize Western assistance behind the Egyptian five-year plan. Citing Indian, Pakistan, and Nigerian experience, I emphasized that the crucial element in any consortium arrangement was the organization of a domestic program that was persuasive to the major lending countries and to the international development institutions. Understanding the personal nature of our exchange, he said he would try to elicit a response from Cairo on his own authority.

On the afternoon of December 6 he solemnly delivered a second message. He had been instructed at the highest level to accept American economic advisers within the Egyptian planning effort. He underlined that only first-class men would be useful: "We have enough second raters of our own."

He had also been instructed to accept the notion of a consortium arrangement which would, on an open basis, mobilize Western assistance for the Egyptian economic development effort.

In explaining these two matters, he made it clear that we were to understand this as a major political move by Egypt with respect to the United States and the West. Forces were moving very rapidly in Egypt, and, if we wished to keep Egypt out of dangerous hands, we should respond as promptly as possible.

Within existing appropriations and policy, aid to Egypt had already been expanding, notably P.L. 480 loans and grants of food. In 1961 the figure was about $144 million as opposed to $107 million for the previous year.

A long-term P.L. 480 commitment was extremely important for Nasser. His cities were now heavily dependent on the flow of American grain. But before moving forward, Kennedy wished the best assessment possible of Egypt's economic prospects; and he was struck by Nasser's request for "first-class" advice. He therefore asked Edward S. Mason of Harvard, a man of wide international experience, extraordinary integrity, and the acknowledged dean among American economists working on development problems, to go to Egypt.

Mason was first in Egypt March 1–18, 1962. He was treated with openness by officials on all levels in the Egyptian government and reported his conclusions both to Nasser and Kennedy. He found that Egypt's development plans were intelligent but overambitious in seeking an 8 percent rate of growth in real national income, a rate its level of investment and commitments to social welfare could not sustain. Moreover, the Egyptian foreign exchange position was weak and required a cutback in imported raw materials and a slackening in industrial production. A partial crop failure had brought overall growth to a temporary standstill, as opposed to a 6 percent increase in the previous year. Nevertheless, Mason concluded, with adequate assistance from abroad and a sustained effort at home, an average increase of about 5 percent might be achieved in the years ahead. The United States could help substantially with a multiyear program of aid in agricultural products under P.L. 480.

Kennedy decided to go ahead. He signed a three-year P.L. 480 agreement with Egypt on June 30, 1962; and the aid program for FY 1963 provided for an expansion in other forms of assistance as well. Egyptian signature to an investment guarantee agreement was mildly reassuring that Cairo's intention was to stay with its domestic knitting and maintain businesslike relations with the West.

Nasser's decision to intervene in Yemen, in response to the request of Abdulah Sallal, after his coup of September 1962, gradually undermined this fragile effort to isolate a limited but stable area of overlapping interest between Cairo and Washington.[7] From Nasser's point of view, the appeal of the Republican forces in Yemen for military assistance was hard to resist. Here was what appeared to be an Arab "modernizer" of Nasser's stamp, recognizing his leadership in the struggle to overthrow the old feudal forces which had permitted the humiliation and subservience of the Middle East. Nasser's image of himself and what he stood for in the Arab world was at stake. And besides, he believed the 30,000 troops he initially invested in the enterprise would quickly install his ideological brother.

But Yemen was not Egypt. It was vastly more primitive. The tribes were still powerful and quickly acquired support from Saudi Arabia, which did not want Nasser on its border. Nasser's army, equipped with Soviet weapons appropriate to conventional warfare, became bogged down. Down to 1967 the presence of some 70,000 Egyptian troops was required to keep Sallal's government in power, with dilute control over the country.

From the American point of view, Nasser's decision was a setback in both the short run and the long run. Immediately, it raised the question of pressure on Saudi Arabia. Ellsworth Bunker, with his remarkable gifts for dealing with political life in the developing world, was enlisted to try to negotiate the withdrawal of the Egyptian forces. But Sallal's military weakness made this impossible, except on a symbolic scale, attractive as it was to many in Cairo as well as in Washington and Riyadh.

More fundamentally, it was fairly definitive evidence, like Sukarno's commitment to the Malaysian confrontation, that Nasser's view of his interests, his mission and his destiny was not compatible with keeping his military forces at home and concentrating on the modernization of Egyptian society.

There is an important distinction to be drawn in American dealings with the Romantic Revolutionaries: a distinction between their anti-American rhetoric and their inability to focus their efforts on economic and social development. The former was irritating and especially troublesome to the Congress. The latter opened up the possibility of dangerous crisis and conflict. Kennedy was aware that, at best, the United States would have to live with a good deal of unpleasantness in its dealings with them. In his final press conference of November 14, 1963, speaking of Indonesia, Egypt, and others, he said: "These countries are poor. . . . They are nationalist, they are proud, they are in many cases radical."[8] He did not believe that actions by the Congress denying them assistance would be helpful: "I don't think threats from Capitol Hill bring the results which are frequently hoped." He recalled the unsatisfactory outcome of the American decision on the Aswan Dam. He expressed some hope that the Malaysian confrontation might end and the limited withdrawals from Yemen might accelerate. But he also said "quiet work" might not succeed. What he wanted was a chance to do that quiet work; that is, by diplomacy and the offer of assistance to move them toward a concentration of effort in economic and social development.

He concluded:

> I think it is a very dangerous, untidy world. But we are going to have to live with it. I think one of the ways to live with it is to permit us to function. If we don't function, the voters will throw us out. But don't make it impossible for us to function by legislative restraints or inadequate appropriations.

He was by no means sure that his policy of nursing Sukarno and Nasser toward a channeling of their nationalism into domestic modernization would work. As of November 1963 the grounds for hope were limited; but he still wanted the freedom to continue to try and the time to permit the balance sheet to be drawn up in a rational way.

NKRUMAH

KENNEDY'S problems with Nkrumah were not as difficult as those with Sukarno and Nasser, but they were difficult enough. They provided an occasion to test and explore the complexities of the doctrine that long-run rather than short-run American political interests should guide aid allocations. At the core was Kennedy's decision, finally made in November 1961, to support with American funds the construction in Ghana of a large dam which would, among other things, ultimately permit local supplies of bauxite to be reduced to aluminum with cheap power. Kaiser Industries and Reynolds Metals were involved. The project had been generated in the late 1950s by Robert Jackson, an adviser to Ghana. Out of his wartime work in the Middle East, Jackson, an Australian, became one of the pioneers in assisting the developing nations. He was also the husband of Barbara Ward Jackson, a friend of Kennedy's and of some of his advisers.

By 1961 Nkrumah's performance in Ghana and on the world scene had cast a pall over the enterprise which hung in the balance. Unlike Sukarno and Nasser, Nkrumah had no clear territorial ambitions around which to rally his nation. His external adventures were, essentially, rhetorical and political, not military. He had come to power in a former colony long nurtured toward independence—in fact, the first colony in black Africa to be granted independence (1957). Its economic resources were promising. Its literacy rate (25 percent) was the highest in black Africa. In cocoa it had a major export crop; and it commanded, initially, handsome foreign exchange reserves. It was well endowed, relative to other new African nations, with trained men, including bureaucrats and politicians who had acquired considerable practical parliamentary experience in the latter days of colonialism.

On the other hand, Nkrumah confronted the three classic problems of government in a setting of underdevelopment, once he came to power as leader of the Convention People's Party (CPP):

1. how to achieve effective national unity, and effective centralized government, in a nation where tribal authority and tribal loyalty were still quite powerful;

2. how to mount a foreign policy that would grant a sense of dignity and independence to a nation coming, new and weak, onto a crowded world scene;

3. how to move forward in economic and social development from a base that was promising but inherently unbalanced and regionally uneven.

Nkrumah's solution to the first problem was to move toward a highly personal dictatorship. Starting in 1957 he systematically threatened and weakened all major elements of potential opposition by legal and extra-legal devices: the leaders of tribal and religious parties; his major political opponents; the courts; the press; the regular army. He organized gangs of bully boys within the CPP; a secret police; a personal guard trained by eastern Europeans; and a special unit of the army under his personal command.

In foreign policy Nkrumah was limited by his dependence on the Western cocoa market and Western economic assistance. But he struck a radical stance in two directions: by a strong rhetorical appeal for African unity; and by developing strong ties to communist states. Like a good many others of his generation, he carried anticolonialism over into a bloody-shirt policy of "anti-imperialism," without wholly breaking his ties to the West.

In economic policy he was erratic and profligate, running through his accumulated foreign exchange reserves, building (like Sukarno) expensive, sterile public monuments, refusing to heed his own sober development economists and friendly foreign advisers.

On the pedestal of the statue (now removed) which Nkrumah erected of himself in front of the Parliament House in Accra he had these words inscribed: "Seek ye first the political kingdom, and all other things shall be added unto it." There is a sense in which the building of a national political life in a new postcolonial state is inescapably the priority task, to which dispositions in economic and foreign policy must be closely related if they are to be viable. But Nkrumah's inscription was a highly personal injunction which drove him to isolation and failure, not to the unification of Ghana in a new sense of nationhood.

But in 1961 he was a lively figure, with some charismatic appeal to his own people, making quite an impression on the international scene as a radical neutralist leader.

> For a time President Nkrumah's intimidatory steps appeared to consolidate his rule. Chiefs no longer made demands on behalf of local autonomy or tribal interests. The voices of the intellectuals and professional men of the early opposition were stilled, at least at home. The resounding declarations and mobilizationist talk were no longer challenged. The crowds still turned out to cheer Osagyefo [victorious

leader]. The civil servants quietly went about their development tasks; the army appeared to stay loyal.[9]

At the time, Nkrumah was not regarded (by, say, Edgar Kaiser, his peripatetic colleague Chad Calhoun, or Barbara Ward Jackson) as beyond saving. Robert Kennedy, on the other hand, after an African trip, emphasized that some of Nkrumah's contemporaries among the new African leaders already regarded him as a bad lot—using his nation as a base for the satisfactions of a personal leadership which did not, in fact, promise to advance the cause of African unity, security, or development.

Kennedy's meeting with Nkrumah on March 8, 1961, went well; and there is reason to believe that Nkrumah spoke before the press with sincerity in the Fish Room that evening: ". . . meeting you has been a wonderful experience for me, and I really mean that."[10] But he was promptly off on other wonderful experiences in Peking and elsewhere.

Kennedy's decision to proceed with the Volta Dam was not made, then, with any naiveté about Nkrumah; nor was it made hastily. On June 29, 1961, Kennedy wrote Nkrumah telling him that the "major issues involved in negotiations for the United States Government's share of the financing of the dam and smelter have now been resolved"; but he reminded Nhrumah that he had to bring his dealings with the World Bank to a successful conclusion.

On September 13 I forwarded to Kennedy a report that Nkrumah, in the Soviet Union, had agreed to the training of some four hundred officer cadets there for an "African High Command"; but I also sent along evidence of both opposition by the Ghana Army Defense Staff and skepticism that any such number of qualified candidates could be generated.[11]

On October 2 I lined up for Kennedy the case for and against canceling the arrangements on the dam, concluding that the weight of the argument was for going ahead after some further probing and unless things turned radically for the worse in Ghana.[12]

On October 20 Kennedy dispatched Clarence Randall to make a final review on the spot of the wisdom of American participation in the project. And at an NSC meeting on December 5 Kennedy announced his decision to go ahead with the financing of the dam.

NSC meetings are rarely, if ever, occasions for a President to make up his mind. And this was no exception. Kennedy had, after balancing all the considerations and risks, decided to go ahead. It was, nevertheless, a meeting of some interest and substance.

John McCone, recently appointed director of the CIA, began by drawing a portrait of Nkrumah's rule, concluding that while he had, indeed, become rather deeply enmeshed with assorted communists, he was, in the end, a nationalist. Rusk at one point suggested that before proceeding the President might consult with the congressional leadership. Kennedy said: "No. This is one where we'll have to take the risks ourselves." Robert Kennedy, who attended NSC meetings regularly after the Bay of Pigs incident, was sitting just behind the President. The President noting amiably his brother's well-known opposition to the loan, said: "The attorney general has not yet spoken but I can feel the cold wind of his disapproval on the back of my neck."[13]

Nevertheless, he approved the loan.

The balance of considerations in Kennedy's mind was, I believe, that the United States government was so deeply involved with the interested private firms that they might have a legal case if the financing were withdrawn; and that Harold Macmillan, anxious to keep a member of the Commonwealth from straying totally out of the fold, had strongly urged the United States to proceed. Also many African leaders would have read Kennedy's withdrawal as placing Cold War considerations above the long-run interests of the African peoples: the experience of Aswan, six years earlier, was in everyone's mind. And there was hope that Ghana, if not Nkrumah, would recover its equilibrium by the time the dam was completed.

On the other hand, Kennedy knew that in the short run he was strengthening Nkrumah's hand within his country and weakening the hand of his democratic opposition; and that he was assuming serious risks in the Congress with his aid program as a whole, if Nkrumah were to stray too far from the fold.

The essential gamble of the United States in the developing world of the 1960s was on the ultimate strength of the determination of nations to maintain their independence. A world of truly independent nations would not accept the hegemony of a major single power in Europe, Asia, or the Middle East; in Latin America independent nations would balance their concern about the possible intrusion of the Colossus of the North with a will to keep extra-continental powers out of the Western Hemisphere; and in black Africa independence meant trying to limit and control the role of all non-African states in shaping the continent's destiny. Minimum American interests could thus be satisfied by authentic independence, although such independent nations would not necessarily be either pro-American or replicas of American political structure. The strength of American policy in the developing world relative to Moscow and Peking rested on this proposition. Whatever their tactical maneuvering, and short-period alignment with particular national interests of developing nations, communist interests could not, in the end, comfortably settle for true independence. And this distinction between the ultimate interests of Washington on the one hand, and Moscow and Peking on the other, gradually had its effect.

India–Pakistan

A gambling faith in a nation's ultimate determination to assert its independence could see Kennedy through his decision on the Volta Dam; but it offered no clear guidelines for dealing with the deeply embedded hostility of India and Pakistan. Here were two evidently independent nations whose domestic politics, economic development, and foreign policy were shadowed and distorted by an obsessive conflict rooted far in the past but exacerbated by an accident at birth; namely, the unforeseen acquisition of Kashmir by India.

Kennedy, from the beginning, was conscious of how limited the American margin of influence was in this as in other such quarrels. He made this clear to President Ayub Khan of Pakistan in their meetings of July 11–13, 1961. Ayub made a strong case for the desirability of a settlement between India and Pakistan, on military as well as economic grounds. He complained of Nehru's failure in the past to exploit Ayub's willingness to take political risks in Pakistan to end the quarrel. He then spread a map of the Kashmir region before Kennedy and with a certain purposeful vagueness indicated that he was prepared to make some concessions to achieve a resolution, although it was clear that his initial negotiating position included Pakistani acquisition of the critical Vale of Kashmir.

Kennedy would not be drawn. He said the American interest was certainly that the quarrel be settled. He could promise to urge Nehru to enter seriously into negotiations on the occasion of his visit to Washington. He could not promise to use economic assistance to India as a lever to force New Delhi to make a settlement agreeable to Karachi. He observed that men were inclined to think the other fellow could be pressured by economic considerations, but of course they were too proud to yield to such pressure on a vital interest. He then told Ayub that one of the things he had learned in six months of responsibility was how little capacity the United States commanded to resolve matters of this kind. He cited several examples, among them the quarrel of Austria and Italy over the Tyrol. Here were two nations which owed their independence and prosperity substantially to the United States; but he could not bring them together. In the subcontinent the problem of Kashmir could only be resolved by Ayub and Nehru.

Some fifteen months later the Chinese attack on India, roughly timed to the Cuba missile crisis, provided an occasion for greater American activism and, in degree, greater leverage. In the wake of the Chinese attack, the United States and Britain entered negotiations to expand military assistance to India. This raised in Washington the specter of American arms used by both sides in a regional conflict, since Pakistan had been receiving American military aid for some years. The American case in New Delhi for an Indian negotiating initiative was somewhat strengthened. The prompt American response to the Indian crisis in contrast to Moscow's ambiguous deportment elevated American prestige and popularity, for the time being at least. More important, the stark threat of Chinese attack and the dissipation of illusion about Peking's intentions toward India made an effort to settle the fratricidal quarrel somewhat more viable in Indian political life; although some Indians argued that Pakistan missed a great opportunity to generate good will in India by not rallying to India's side at the critical moment. Karachi did not, of course, intervene against India but there was some evident satisfaction at New Delhi's discomfiture. The Indian mood was not softened when the Pakistanis sat down with the Chinese to settle certain border ambiguities. Peking was evidently interested in maximizing differences between India and Pakistan; although Pakistan's decision to seize the occasion to settle its border with China was understandable and sensible.

Out of this setting, a ponderous India–Pakistan negotiation was launched at the end of 1962. It took the form of a series of meetings, taking place alternately in each country and conducted virtually in public, with British and American officials eagerly aspiring to midwifery. As the fourth round failed to yield results in mid-March 1963, Kennedy and Rusk asked me to go out to make an independent assessment of the prospects for an accommodation; and to put to the leaders in the two countries the strongest possible case for moving forward toward a settlement of the Kashmir problem. I was accompanied by Robert Komer of the NSC staff, an old friend and colleague.

I was in the subcontinent April 1–7. As agreed in advance in Washington, I argued in New Delhi that India could not successfully conduct a "three-front war": the struggle for economic and social development; defense against China; and conflict with Pakistan. I argued in Karachi and Dacca that for a short period there might be Indian interest in a settlement and some Anglo–American leverage. Pakistan should make the most of this opportunity.

In both countries I found men wholly conscious of what was at stake. In neither did I find a driving determination to settle the quarrel. The most interesting convergence of thought was on the basic military problem of the Indian subcontinent. Indian military and civil leaders underlined to me that India's major vulnerability was not across the Himalayas but from a Chinese attack through Burma. They freely acknowledged that the American position in Southeast Asia was a major contribution to India's defense, keeping, as it did, the Chinese from Burma; and that the right defense solution for India was joint planning with Pakistan to defend the northeast frontier. Ayub took precisely this view when I met with him in Dacca. But clearly good sense was not about to prevail.

There were three powerful inhibitions against a settlement. First, of course, were old Muslim–Hindu tensions reaching back over the centuries, exacerbated by vividly remembered mass violence as the two nations were born out of colonialism in 1947. Second, there was short-run politics: neither Nehru nor Ayub could measure the explosive forces that might be released in multiracial India and a geographically split Pakistan where hostility to India was an important unifying bond. Third, there was Nehru's conviction that India's size and military weight did not require a politically painful adjustment in the status quo; and this was balanced by the conviction, among some Pakistanis at least, that Indian unity was transient and Hindu military capacity trivial.

Despite the depth and reality of these problems, I believe Nehru, as leader of the larger state, had the responsibility actively to seek a settlement; that Ayub was prepared for a good deal less than Pakistani acquisition of Kashmir; and that Nehru's prestige and authority were such that he could have weathered the political consequences of a compromise solution.

On the return flight I wrote as gloomy an assessment as I ever filed on a major issue of foreign policy, trying to make clear the interdependence of domestic politics in the two countries, and the inhibition of politicians on both sides in taking the steps in the dark required to move toward a resolution of their potentially mortal dilemmas.[14]

Kennedy read my report and asked me to come over to talk about it on April 8. His final question was this: Is their quarrel more intractable than ours with the Russians or the Arabs' with the Israelis? I told him I thought it was fundamentally more difficult than our relations with the Russians, because less rational, perhaps less difficult than the Arab–Israeli tension, where there was no equivalent to common life under British rule, including shared educational, military, and civil service experience, and the human ties and memories that went with them.

I recalled this experience when, in April 1965, President Chung Hee Park of South Korea asked me to convey this message to Washington: "I have not been in politics long. But I have already learned one lesson: it is easier to keep a quarrel alive than to settle it. Nevertheless, tell President Johnson that I shall settle our differences with Japan." Despite riots in the streets of Seoul, he did.

Park was a rare postwar statesman. I believe the failure of Nehru to exploit his prestige and Ayub's genuine willingness to find a solution to the Kashmir problem is one of the truly tragic failures of the postwar world. We have still not seen the end of its painful ramifications.

SOME OTHER CASES

KENNEDY was the first American President to engage deeply and personally in the problems of political life in the developing world. He did so because they bore directly on American interests; but he entered into them with fascination and human sympathy. He did not deflect Sukarno from the Malaysian confrontation nor Nasser from Yemen. He did not lead Nkrumah from the cul-de-sac into which he drove himself. Nor did he jockey Nehru and Ayub into coming to grips with Kashmir. But he did convey to the leaders of the developing world, in general, his respect for the burdens they bore; and he somehow projected to their peoples a compassionate concern that the lives of their children be better than their own. The Peace Corps was a legitimate symbol of his projection which, his death revealed, reached into peasant homes from the Nile Valley to the Andes mountains.

In his private meetings with chiefs of government, Kennedy had a particular style. They approached him with curiosity, but often with a certain reserve of dignity. They represented poor but proud nations. Here they were dealing with a man who commanded stockpiles of bombs and gold beyond their calculation, whose actions, one way or another, bore directly on their destinies. Kennedy would usually begin by outlining with candor his problems at home and abroad. And he would do so in language not markedly different from the terms he would use with his staff. There was no condescension in it. He emerged rather suddenly as a recognizable fellow politician doing the best he could within limitations that were, in their essence, not unfamiliar. More often than not this would evoke an equally candid response.

Kennedy found some of his problems in the developing world more yielding than others. South Korea, for example, after mounting a young officers' coup in 1961, proceeded in reasonable order toward an election in 1963 and a remarkable acceleration in growth. Iran, for which Khrushchev had had such high revolutionary hopes, weathered some difficult days and under the Shah's leadership began to move forward in a remarkable way. Latin America as a whole surmounted the tremors set in motion by Castro and moved forward with increasing steadiness in the second half of the 1960s, although, notably in Argentina and Brazil, at the cost of military government. A good start was made on the basis of the new aid legislation with economic assistance to Nigeria and Tanganyika. Kennedy weathered the crisis that followed the assassination of Trujillo and launched Bosch as President of the Dominican Republic with as ample a dowry of good will and economic assistance as he could manage.

But, of course, the problems faced in the developing world were long-term in character. In the early 1960s the nations of the south were entering new phases in their own histories. There were lessons they alone could learn, mistakes they had to make. What America could do for them was limited; and even that margin depended for its efficacy on what they could do for themselves.

What Kennedy did was to break cleanly from the mold of the first Eisenhower administration, the mold already under transformation in the post-Sputnik years. He articulated the vision of a world expanded now to embrace the southern continents, a world of nations modernizing but true to their own cultures and visions of the future, a world of diverse nations to whose independence and progress the United States was prepared to contribute. And this rhetorical vision, backed by his own personality and the new development programs, shifted the cast of America's relations to the developing world in a useful direction.

22

The Bay of Pigs and Latin American Policy

Castro: A Romantic Revolutionary Close to Home

KENNEDY'S PROBLEMS WITH THE AGGRESSIVE REVOLUTIONARY Romantics in Djakarta, Cairo, and Accra were important; and they involved strategically significant parts of the world. The unyielding internecine tension on the Indian subcontinent was also a serious matter, diverting, as it did, significant talents and resources from essential tasks of development on behalf of more than a half-billion human beings, distorting the political life of two major nations, and rendering each, in different ways, increasingly vulnerable to external influence and manipulation. But for a working American politician these problems were relatively peripheral compared to the presence of Castro in Cuba.

By January 1961 Castro was an acknowledged part of the communist world, handsomely backed by the Soviet Union and other communist states. He was actively engaged in subversive action in Latin America and was holding up to the continent a revolutionary solution for its many economic and social ills. The communist base ninety miles from Florida was a direct and inescapable challenge to a vital American interest long incorporated in the Monroe Doctrine and a living part of the American political debate. And, as the result of Eisenhower's order of March 1960, Cuban opponents of Castro, assembled in Guatemala, were undergoing the final phase of military training for an invasion of Cuba, under the leadership and instruction of officers of the United States government.

The Bay of Pigs: One Man's Experience

AT 7 A.M. on the morning of Tuesday, April 18, 1961, I attended my first meeting on Cuba.[1] The Bay of Pigs operation had begun the day before. As I came to work early I met Ted Clifton, the President's military aide, in the White House Situation Room and asked him how it was going. He said badly. Later McGeorge Bundy asked me to come along to a meeting in the Cabinet Room.

At the far end of the table were the three senior officers of the CIA: Allen Dulles, Pearré Cabell, and Richard Bissell. The President, Bundy, Clifton, and I were the only others present.

Dulles reported the operation was failing: the men were trapped on the beaches and Castro's forces were moving systematically against them.

I had old and close ties to the three men reporting the incipient debacle. Dulles I had known a little from wartime OSS days, but well and warmly since 1951. With Cabell I had shared wartime years as a planner for the American air forces in Europe. Bissell was a friend of some thirty years, to whom I owed my start as an economist and much more. Here they were telling our President their plan had failed and, three months into his administration, he was about to confront unmitigated disaster.

They were wholly professional, Kennedy completely calm. But all were evidently shaken.

After the meeting I asked Bundy if I could help in the mop-up. I did not know how my friends had gotten into this situation. I had no sense of higher wisdom or virtue. But I thought a fresh man might be useful. Bundy —and then Kennedy—agreed. I went over to the CIA operational headquarters, located in a temporary building along the Potomac, to monitor the situation.

The reports coming in chronicled the closing in of Castro's forces on the beachhead. The morale of the Washington team engaged in the operation progressively disintegrated. This was not the first tactical defeat Americans had ever suffered, nor even the worst that I had observed; but it was painful to see their composure break up. Bissell, however, remained collected as the men around him begged that he ask the President once more to throw American military power into the balance. As the situation on the beaches moved to final disaster during the night, he asked that I call the President, who was at a congressional reception, and arrange a meeting. Its purpose was to inform Kennedy and permit him to exercise such options as were available. I did so.

It was a session in the Oval Office no one present is likely to forget: the President, Rusk, and McNamara in white tie; General Lyman Lemnitzer and Admiral Arleigh Burke in full uniform with medals; the stark human tragedy of the men on the beaches and the reports of the Revolutionary Council in almost suicidal disarray; Bissell coolly laying out the options.

The limits and dilemmas of power—the relationship of power to the fate of human beings—was never more clear or poignant.

Kennedy was deeply and personally concerned with the fate of the men on the beaches, but he was not about to throw the full strength of the carrier-based aircraft into the battle and reverse his fundamental position that this was a conflict between Cubans, not a war between the United States and Cuba. The possibility of the men moving off the beaches into the hills was raised. It became starkly clear (to me, for the first time) that the option of moving from an invasion to a guerrilla operation was precluded by geography and the choice of the invasion beach. Kennedy decided to permit a limited number of fighter sorties to protect the handful of old bombers operating in support of the operation. The purpose was to buy time in the hope that at least some of the men might be withdrawn. He ordered American naval craft to go in close for the same purpose. Rusk pointed out that we would thereby be more deeply committed. Kennedy raised his hand just below his nose and said: "We're already in it up to here."

Bissell was instructed to inform the entrapped men to disengage as best they could, either to boats or into the countryside. As Bissell left the room, Kennedy told him to keep his chin up.

Adolf Berle and Arthur Schlesinger were then dispatched from the meeting to the hardest mission of all: to meet with the Revolutionary Council in Florida and inform its members of the limits within which Kennedy was prepared to act.[2]

Somehow, it was difficult to go home that night. Some of us stayed around until almost four in the morning.

Hour by hour, day by day, the full measure of the failure, with its repercussions at home and abroad, pounded in on Kennedy and his advisers. Every detail hurt. There was an initial numbness, except for Kennedy who moved to accept full personal responsibility and pull the nation and his administration together. I saw only one reflection of his inner feeling: sitting in the rocking chair in his office, he was looking at the Washington *News*, whose headlines shouted the final capture of the expedition. Then he let the paper crumple onto the floor without a word.

On April 19 Kennedy met with his advisers at length in the afternoon, an afternoon climaxed by the five o'clock arrival of the leaders of the Revolutionary Council. It was a meeting at once painful, dignified, and necessary.

At one point, in mid-afternoon, the President left the room for a few minutes and Robert Kennedy spoke in anguish. He said we would have to act or be judged paper tigers by Moscow. We just could not sit and take it. All the famous talent assembled around the Cabinet table ought to be able to think of something to do. There was no response, as we awaited the President's return.

I had not known Robert Kennedy before his brother's inauguration and had never before spoken seriously to him. I asked if we could step out of the Cabinet Room for a moment. On the portico near the Rose Garden I told him that if you're in a fight and get knocked off your feet, the most dangerous thing to do was to come out swinging. Then you could really get hurt. Now was a time to dance around until our heads cleared. We would have ample opportunity to prove we were not paper tigers in Berlin, Southeast Asia, and elsewhere. This was a time to pause and think. He looked up expressionless. He finally said: "That's constructive."

The next day he came back to me and posed the question: If we shouldn't act now, what should we do about Cuba? He said I had a duty to come up with a plan. I promised to collect and set down my thoughts.

On April 20 Kennedy delivered his defiant speech to the American Society of Newspaper Editors and the nation knew it had a leader who could absorb a severe blow and maintain command. It was the speech of a fighting Irishman.

As I worked through those long days with my colleagues, I was troubled, however, that the obsession with Cuba would divert thought and energy from the paths of action on which Kennedy had begun. I therefore wrote a long memorandum to him on April 21 and circulated it to Rusk, McNamara, and Bundy. It began in much the spirit of my talk with Robert Kennedy:

> Right now the greatest problem we face is not to have the whole of our foreign policy thrown off balance by what we feel and what we do about Cuba itself. We have suffered a serious setback; but that setback will be trivial compared to the consequences of not very soon regaining momentum along the lines which we have begun in the past three months.[3]

Over the weekend Cuba was temporarily pushed off the front pages. De Gaulle was at the peak of his troubles in Algeria. There was a threat that dissident French paratroopers would descend on Paris. De Gaulle appealed to the French people to block a *coup d'état*. On Sunday, April 23, Kennedy called from Glen Ora and asked me to come into the White House quietly to monitor what was happening in France and to keep him informed. I settled down in the White House shelter, where there was both communication equipment and a bunk. The only news available, in fact, came from David Schoenbrun's CBS broadcasts from Paris. It gradually became apparent that the descent on Paris would not take place; and I used the time to try my hand at a new approach to the problem posed by Cuba, as Robert Kennedy had suggested.

It had begun to be clear to me from Tuesday morning to Sunday night how the Bay of Pigs had come about. As Cuba emerged under communist control, a visceral reaction developed in the government that this was an outcome with which the United States could not live. Eisenhower shared this feeling, as his memoirs make clear, although his sentiments about Castro cannot be translated into a prediction of what he would have done about the Bay of Pigs plan if he had come to the moment of decision. The fears were in part military, in part ideological, in part an ancestral sense that the Monroe Doctrine had been unacceptably violated. On the other hand, there was no basis in American foreign policy, OAS doctrine, or in international law that justified the United States going to war because a Latin American nation had gone communist. It had clearly happened because of the internal dynamics of Cuba, not because communist arms and men had moved illegally across international frontiers.

Simultaneously, however, a way of escaping the dilemma appeared to emerge. Out of Castro's quite real betrayal of his comrades in the July 26 Movement and of the humane democratic society they sought, there had come to the United States not Batista reactionaries, not mercenaries, but men prepared to give their lives to undo the perversion of Cuban history Castro had brought about.

The appeal of supporting these men on a clandestine basis was, under the circumstances, irresistible—an appeal strengthened, perhaps, by the successful CIA-backed overthrow of President Jacobo Arbenz in Guatemala some seven years earlier.

The Cuban operation, as it evolved, acquired, of course, a momentum of its own; and it proved, of its nature, incapable of being handled on a clandestine basis. It therefore lacked strategic surprise and was technically inadequate in many respects, some of which are summarized below. But the fatal flaw, as I saw it that Sunday night, lay in the failure to distinguish the kinds of circumstances in which an American President could or could not bring American force overtly to bear. In the *United States in the World Arena* I had argued:

> It appears to be a characteristic of American history that this nation cannot be effective in its military and foreign policy unless it believes that both its security interests and its commitment to certain moral principles require the nation to act. . . . When idealism alone seemed to be the basis for positions taken the nation did not back its play. . . . Equally, the nation has not been effective when confronted by situations where its power interests might be involved but where a persuasive moral basis for American action was not present.[4]

A covert operation, by definition, cut across the "moral basis" for the engagement of American forces. And, before the event, Kennedy had drawn a sharp line between supporting Cuban dissidents and sending American forces into battle. Nevertheless, as I observed the denouement of the operation on Tuesday, I could not help feeling that some of the men involved had come to believe that in the last analysis Kennedy would be unable to hold to the policy he had expressed repeatedly, in public and private, before the event; namely, that this was a conflict among Cubans and regular United States forces would not be available for it. Somewhere within them, one felt, was the perhaps unconscious judgment that Kennedy simply could not afford to let it fail. It was not only the men on the beaches who, until the end, had "an unshakable conviction that they would not be let down. It was inconceivable that they would be stranded."[5]

But Kennedy did hold to his policy. The operation had failed. And Castro had to be dealt with in other terms.

Sitting in the White House shelter, I began by listing on a yellow pad the specific dangers to the American interest that might arise from Castro's Cuba: the training and infiltrating of subversive agents and guerrillas; the invasion of neighboring states with Soviet arms; Soviet missiles aimed against the United States; an attack on Guantanamo or the Panama Canal; communist radio propaganda; and an example of economic and social development that would prove attractive in Latin America.

For each I suggested lines of action legally and morally open to the United States and, especially, to the hemisphere acting in concert on the principle of collective self-defense.

I called Robert Kennedy from the shelter and told him I would be ready to respond to his question by morning. The next day I went to Hickory Hill for an early breakfast. As we walked around the grounds I outlined this functional, overt, legal approach to dealing with Castro.

He seemed relieved that a coherent approach to Cuban policy had been formulated and he urged me to circulate it in the government. This I did through the committee, headed by Paul Nitze, charged with coordinating policy toward Cuba and the fate of the Cuban refugees in the United States.[6]

The Bay of Pigs: A Retrospective Evaluation

There have been a good many retrospective evaluations of the Bay of Pigs operation, public and private.[7] Evidently, it was flawed in terms of political and military intelligence. It could not be kept secret before the event and there was no strategic surprise; no coordination with dissidents in Cuba; an underestimation of the cohesiveness and strength of Castro's ground and air forces and of his ability to round up and neutralize his opposition. It was flawed tactically by the failure to provide sufficient air power and to protect the supply ship with its critically important ammunition supply. (Technically, the operation ended with an ammunition shortage.) And the option Kennedy believed the men would have—of going to the hills if the invasion failed—was, in fact, foreclosed by the choice of the landing site.

The basic strategic flaw was, of course, political. If some fifteen hundred men were to serve as a catalyst in the overthrow of Castro, the burden of the effort would have to be borne by those already inside Cuba who were prepared to struggle for this result. And that meant organization, leadership, planning, and close coordination. Such possibilities may have existed, but they were not built into the enterprise.

All in all, it appears to have been an effort beyond the capacities of the CIA to mount successfully. And in such a covert enterprise, it was impossible to bring to bear all the talents and resources of the American government that would have been relevant.

That the plan was inherited from a previous administration by new men also played a role. Allen Dulles and his people were respected professionals and so were Lemnitzer and the Joint Chiefs. It was hard for the new men to pit their judgment with confidence against their predecessors'; although the President finally drew the hard line on his own by refusing to engage regular American forces to salvage the enterprise, if the initial plan failed.

And there was a brute political fact. Cuba was part of American politics. Kennedy had taken an activist position during the campaign. The dissolution of the brigade in Guatemala would have brought the men back to Miami. The story would out. Kennedy would be charged with having lacked the courage to back an enterprise that Eisenhower had prepared to eliminate communism from Cuba by the action of brave Cubans.

Sorensen flatly states that Kennedy regretted not having called off the operation[8]; and, although I worked closely with the President in the post-Bay of Pigs days, I have no evidence to challenge that assessment. Clearly, the short-run consequences of revoking the plan could hardly have been as painful as the debacle. In a larger sense, however, there may be some insight in a judgment of the event from a rather unlikely source. Gunnar Myrdal, for whom I had worked as a special assistant in the Economic Commission for Europe in 1947–1949, came to Washington later in the spring. He greeted me cheerfully by announcing we had a great President. I said I thought so, but we hadn't yet done much to prove it. I asked him what led to his assessment. Myrdal said: the Bay of Pigs—if Kennedy had called it off, he would have been ruined politically at home. He never would have freed himself of the charge that Castro's continued existence in Cuba was due to his failure to back Eisenhower's plan. But if he had engaged American forces to salvage a failing covert operation, he would have been ruined abroad. Now, suggested Myrdal, Kennedy could go on.

And Kennedy was determined to go on. Talking about my memorandum of April 21, he said the United States could simply not afford to brood or sulk or engage in protracted debate or passive introspection. Britain had gone through such a phase over Suez, France over Algeria. And freedom could survive because each represented only 6 or 7 percent of the free world's power. But the United States was 70 percent of that power. If we did not keep our perspective, if we did not continue to act effectively, the whole delicate and dangerous equilibrium of power in the world would come unstuck.

By his example, Kennedy brought his team back onto its feet. There was, however, much personal introspection and fresh thought about the organization of the executive branch. We—Kennedy and his men—were clearly responsible for the debacle, not abstract bureaucratic entities. There was no one else and would not be until the next election. We'd better get on top of our business. Bundy wrote a reflective memorandum to Kennedy which was as fine a piece of paper as I had ever read in government. In his own way, each of the others engaged in military and foreign policy asked: What went wrong, what must we now do to avoid further error? Kennedy brought in Maxwell Taylor to conduct a formal inquest. He also told Bundy and me to build up the flow of information to the Situation Room; and Bundy was asked to shift from a comfortable, high-ceilinged room in the Executive Office Building to a small office in the White House west basement close by the flow of traffic. (Remembering those days, I resisted all efforts to have that office redone in White House modern when I occupied it in 1966–1969. I felt it should remain as spare as a city editor's office.)

In getting back on our feet we had an asset. We had all seen, in one context or another, what tactical defeat looked like during the Second World War. (In my case, it was the dangerous and frustrating days of 1942–1943 when it appeared quite likely that daylight bombers, in which America had invested vast resources, would fail to penetrate German antiaircraft and fighter defenses without unacceptable losses.) We had known what it was to take stock, make new dispositions, and get on with the job. My wife caught this mood one night. I came home at three in the morning. She was sitting up in bed and said: "I've not seen you for years more cheerful or effective. You're an odd lot. You're not politicians or intellectuals. You're the junior officers of the Second World War come to responsibility." It remains a not bad characterization of the Kennedy administration.

The Two Punta del Estes

Kennedy's post-Bay of Pigs policy toward Latin America emerged in two meetings at Punta del Este in August 1961 and January 1962. They dealt with the ideological and security challenges posed by Castro.

The first was formally a conference of the Inter-American Economic and Social Council. It was the climax to the series of initiatives that had begun when, in 1958, President Juscelino Kubitschek of Brazil had proposed Operation Panamerica as a kind of equivalent to the Marshall Plan for Latin America. Proximately, its purpose was to give substance to Kennedy's speech of March 13 formally launching the Alliance for Progress as a common effort to move Latin America into sustained economic and social progress.

The goals defined and agreed on at Punta del Este touched the whole spectrum of Latin America's endemic problems: housing, land reform, education, health, tax reform, domestic price stability, export prices, economic integration.

Fundamentally, however, the Charter of Punta del Este was a commitment of the Latin American governments to their peoples that economic and social progress, in all their dimensions, would move to the center of political life. Certainly the most important technical commitment of the Charter of

Punta del Este was agreement that "each of the countries of Latin America will formulate a comprehensive and well-conceived national program for the development of its own economy." The heart of the commitment for the United States was to supply, from public and private sources, some $20 billion for investment in Latin America of the $100 billion estimated as necessary to achieve an average annual 5 percent growth in GNP.

Kennedy's rhetoric—the rhetoric of democratic revolution—aimed to break through the crust of Latin American politics to strengthen and hearten those in Latin America dedicated to these purposes. The offer of enlarged American assistance was to provide not merely resources and increased American diplomatic leverage, but also a means of increasing the domestic political authority of those who, by generating serious measures of self-help, would permit their nations to qualify for increased loans from public resources.

Kennedy was not naive about the length of time this effort would require. He knew how deep-seated the problems of Latin America were and how slow-yielding to solution they were likely to be. But he knew also that he was not shouting down a rain barrel: there was a Latin American generation emerging, competent and dedicated, oriented to action rather than rhetoric. And with these men and women he sought to make common cause.

There was both danger and unreality in the initial focusing of the Alliance for Progress around Kennedy and what Washington could and would provide. It was dangerous because it encouraged the illusion that the resolution of Latin America's problems could come from outside the area, by some kind of North American magic and money. It was unreal because, at most, only 20 percent of the material resources required could come from the United States, and a much smaller proportion of the political, institutional, and human effort that was even more important.

It became apparent, therefore, that the machinery of the Alliance for Progress should be altered so that, in image and in fact, it would be more an enterprise of Latin American cooperation and less an aid program run from Washington. As early as April 1962 Rusk underlined the abiding truth that the United States could be only a "junior partner" in the Alliance for Progress.[9] This insight, shared among thoughtful Latin Americans, led to the creation of the Inter-American Committee on the Alliance for Progress in November 1963, a development Kennedy greeted with some enthusiasm in his last major statement on Latin America, in Miami, on November 18.

An evaluation of the Alliance for Progress belongs later in this book (see below, pp. 424–425, 429–430). In Kennedy's time it was plagued by inevitable weaknesses. As the Inter-American Committee on the Alliance for Progress (CIAP) said in a report of November 1964:

> The Alliance for Progress is now completing its third year. Given its essential character, it was inevitable that progress be relatively

> slow in the initial stage. Past patterns of economic and social policy cannot be suddenly halted and sharply reversed. It takes time to develop national plans and programs which are not merely statements of aspiration and priority but which are effectively linked, in both concept and execution, to specific projects and tasks in the sectors of the economy. It takes time to formulate, legislate, and execute programs of fiscal and agrarian reform, and to gather the fruits of expanded educational, health, housing, and community development programs. It takes time to prepare projects and negotiate loans for their financing; but it takes even more time to execute projects and thus to put to effective use the requisite funds. It takes time to assemble the men and to build the institutions necessary to implement the economic and social objectives of the Punta del Este Charter. It takes time to convince men and women throughout the Hemisphere that the Alliance for Progress is a serious, sustained venture worth the commitment of their minds and hearts, and worthy of their confidence.
>
> Moreover, the years 1961–1962 were marked by a continuing deterioration in the terms of trade for Latin America which reduced import capacity and damped the rate of growth in Latin America as a whole.
>
> For all these reasons the over-all figures for Latin American growth did not achieve in 1962–1963 the target set at Punta del Este; although they approximated the Punta del Este targets, if abstracted from the specific situation in two major countries.[10]

The two major countries were Argentina and Brazil, caught in a stop stage of the stop-and-go policies that marked the inflationary pattern of their economies.

In addition, as with AID as a whole, Kennedy took more time than he should have in getting the administration of the Alliance for Progress into effective order at the Washington end. In one of the oddest sessions with a President I can recall, Kennedy once found himself enmeshed with the problem of recruiting secretaries and mobilizing typewriters when he assembled around the Cabinet table the working-level officials and tried to get to the bottom of the initial bureaucratic confusion in the Latin American AID office. The result was that American resources, even those committed as loans, were not flowing out to Latin America at the promised rate in the first two years.

Nevertheless, from 1961 Latin America, out of the interplay of its own dynamics and Kennedy's leadership, was off on a new course.

Cuba was part of it. And Che Guevara undoubtedly enjoyed his role at Punta del Este in August. He could credit Castro with generating the Alliance for Progress (a half-truth) and explain why it was bound to fail and give way to the model of the communist revolution in Cuba. Kennedy was deeply concerned with the possibilities of Cuba as a showcase. He did not see how, with some $300 million in net annual Soviet aid, Cuba could fail to become a showcase of economic and social progress. He once said to me: "Khrushchev only has 7 million Cubans; I've got to be concerned with the future of 200 million Latin Americans. He's bound to do better." None of us in the early 1960s could have believed that Castro would accomplish so little with his indigenous resources and lavish external assistance over the decade.

If Cuba was a peripheral goad at the first Punta del Este conference, it was central at the second, in January 1962. This was a foreign ministers meeting called at the insistence of Venezuela, Colombia, and the Central American states to deal with the problem of indirect aggression across the Caribbean from Havana in the form of propaganda, the training of guerrillas, and their subsequent infiltration and supply with money and arms.

The question was: What diplomatic and economic sanctions, if any, could and would the OAS take in concert?

The diplomatic problem confronted at Punta del Este was a variant of a situation that had become familiar. Washington, in its period as a global power, had discovered a kind of natural law: governments were philosophical and passive about problems in direct relation to their distance from the scene of crisis. On Berlin, for example, western Europe was quite alert, but Asia prepared to accept whatever formulae that would appear to make the problem go away. On, say, Indochina the obverse was true.

At Punta del Este the countries bordering the Caribbean were determined to act against Cuba. Those at a distance were less activist. President Arturo Frondizi of Argentina and Jorge Alessandri in Chile wanted no more trouble with the left than they already had. Something of the same was true in Mexico. Brazil was, in effect, without government, with President Janio da Silva Quadros literally on a slow boat from China, its delegation led by an able, cynical foreign minister, Santiago Dantas, with an admirable excuse for inaction.

The American delegation was under quite unambiguous instruction from Kennedy to effect the removal of Cuba from the OAS. And the congressional members of the delegation made it clear to Rusk that hard, concerted action against Cuba was required to maintain congressional support for the Alliance for Progress. Most of those from the executive branch believed such action was necessary for the stability of Latin America itself. A few were more concerned with what excessive American zeal about Cuba might do to the internal life of Argentina, Brazil, and other countries distant from the Caribbean arena.

There is a certain looseness in Latin American political life, a certain play, that imparts to an OAS gathering more political vitality than, say, a conference of Atlantic nations. Instructions are less precise, communications to the capitals less efficient, the number of actors greater. What takes place on the spot is living politics rather than merely the day-to-day negotiation of sharply defined positions coming over the cable lines.

The second Punta del Este meeting was like that. It was somewhere between an American political convention and a formal diplomatic conference. It was spiced by the presence of a Cuban delegation, headed by Osvaldo Dorticós, president of Cuba, and included the bearded, long-time orthodox communist Carlos Rodriguez. It earned part of its per diem by selling Cuban cigars in the lobby of the hotel where meetings took place. At one point we found a Cuban bodyguard sitting in the midst of the American delegation behind Dean Rusk. One of his security officers returned the courtesy and the nonsense stopped. Dorticós hammered away at American policy; but he was dull and overplayed his hand with endless sneering references to the Bay of Pigs. He was easier to cope with than Guevara at the earlier Punta del Este meeting.

There were two central problems: to exclude Cuba from the OAS and to generate an agreed doctrine (and an OAS institution) to deal with Cuban subversive activities.

Mexico, despite its desire not to become overtly embroiled with Castro, supplied the doctrinal key. In a speech that went beyond anything an American secretary of state could say, the Mexican foreign minister produced the concept of "incompatibility." He recalled that Bolivar had affirmed that the hemisphere was committed to the pursuit of democracy and that absolute monarchy was incompatible with its political life. He acknowledged that Latin America had not achieved the Bolivarian goal; but democracy remained a shared hemispheric aspiration. Now democracy was challenged in the hemisphere by the contemporary equivalent of absolute monarchy: communist totalitarianism. This was equally incompatible with the life of the region.

With this ideological underpinning, endless patience, and round-the-clock shirt-sleeves sessions with his colleagues, Rusk sought with every resource of diplomatic experience and language a unanimous resolution. In the end, he was able to round up only the necessary two-thirds majority of fourteen. This had to be done without the votes of Argentina, Brazil, Chile, and Mexico. The last, having contributed the decisive formula, abstained on the vote to expel Cuba on the grounds that a further complex legal procedure was required to implement "incompatibility" by expulsion. There was an understanding all around that the grounds for these reserved positions were, simply, a desire to avoid unpleasant domestic political strain in the four countries.

Uruguay, reacting instinctively to pressure from its two great neighbors, overcame legalistic scruple, reached out, as often in the past, to a larger, Atlantic connection, and went with the majority. The fourteenth vote was Haiti's, made easier by the promise of resumed American support for enlargement of an airfield—support which, for other reasons, never came to pass.

Behind all this lively politicking was an earnest and seriously meant threat. The Caribbean nations, whatever their domestic politics, democratic or otherwise, were determined not to be left alone with the weight of Castro's operations against them. They said they would be prepared to form with the United States a special grouping outside the OAS to deal with Castro. This neither the United States nor the larger nations of Latin America wanted. That inhibition, supported by a call from President Kennedy to President Lleras Camargo of Colombia, yielded the bare two-thirds vote to exclude Cuba from the OAS plus a resolution adopted unanimously (excepting Cuba) proclaiming the doctrine of incompatibility and excluding Cuba from the Inter-American Defense Board.

It was on these two resolutions that Rusk and the foreign ministers concentrated amidst the apparently shapeless swirl of a hemispheric diplomatic gathering.

Meanwhile, in a committee room inhabited by lesser officials, further resolutions of some consequence were hammered out to deal more directly with the threat posed by Cuba. These included the creation of a Special Consultative Committee of Experts on Security Matters to monitor and suggest measures to combat Cuban subversion; to suspend arms traffic to Cuba; and to study the possible extension of a trade embargo against Cuba. This was my primary arena of activity. Following upon the work I had done in the wake of the Bay of Pigs, I sought consensus on a set of propositions which would supply a legal hemispheric framework to deal not only with further Cuban subversive activity but also with the danger of Soviet (or even Chinese communist) use of Cuba as a military base. The list of functional dangers set out in my memorandum of April 21, 1961, and in my exchanges with Robert Kennedy were explicitly in mind.

The language we negotiated with our colleagues in the basic security resolution included the following:

> To urge the member states to take those steps that they may consider appropriate for their individual and collective self-defense, and to cooperate, as may be necessary or desirable, to strengthen their capacity to counteract threats or acts of aggression, subversion, or other dangers to peace and security resulting from the continued intervention in this hemisphere of Sino–Soviet powers, in accordance with the obligations established in treaties and agreements such as the Charter of the Organization of American States and the Inter-American Treaty of Reciprocal Assistance.

Aside from enunciating a general hemispheric doctrine, that resolution provided also that nations could work individually or in collective groups smaller than the OAS to defend themselves against communist security threats. The Caribbean nations thus had what they wanted; and OAS nations less directly concerned would not be automatically committed to action which would be politically painful or inconvenient. This resolution was later invoked usefully in the Cuba missile crisis and was the backdrop to the American, and then OAS, intervention in the Dominican Republic.

Everyone went home reasonably well satisfied. What made the exercise work was the reality, beneath the surface of many tensions and differences, of an ultimate loyalty to the Inter-American system. No one could dictate the outcome, which, indeed, had to be created on the spot. On the other hand, there was also a sense that all the various attitudes in play had to be reconciled, in one way or another.

Rusk was the first American secretary of state who entered with depth, sensibility, and respect into the human emotions and politics that shaped Latin American diplomacy. He treated his Latin American colleagues precisely as he did his European colleagues: as mature men, working out of difficult domestic settings, trying to make some order, trying to build islands of security and progress in a dangerous world. In his dealings with Latin Americans or those from other developing regions, he wholly lacked the implicit condescension of the Atlanticist view. He took them all as fellow members of the trade union of foreign ministers; and this was a great strength at Punta del Este.

Kennedy was pleased with the result, which reconciled his objective of getting effective collective action without either splitting the OAS or putting the United States at crosspurposes with the Latin American countries which found anti-Castro measures an additional burden on their domestic political life. He did ask, somewhat wistfully, why we had not generated a better press: reporting of the conference had generally portrayed the effort as essentially an American arm-twisting exercise rather than as an effort to reconcile the interests of Caribbean and non-Caribbean states within the OAS.

Kennedy was determined to avoid in his time "another Cuba" in the hemisphere. And he quietly set in motion contingency thought on how the United States might move, if possible with others, to prevent it. The second Punta del Este meeting provided a political and legal basis for such a course; although it did not determine what could and would be done in particular circumstances.

It was the outcome of the Cuba missile crisis which lifted, for a time, the weight of communist pressure on Latin America; but that crisis arose not out of the political dynamics of a developing region but from the other dimension of the post-Sputnik offensive: nuclear blackmail and the point at which Khrushchev had chosen to test its efficacy—Berlin.

23

The Nuclear Question: Vienna, Berlin, and the Atlantic Community

The Revival of the Berlin Crisis

KHRUSHCHEV PUT THE QUESTION OF BERLIN ON ICE AFTER THE Camp David meeting with Eisenhower in 1959; and he left it latent after the breakup of the Paris summit meeting of May 1960. Shortly before Kennedy's inauguration he revived it in these words:

> The international positions of the GDR—the outpost of socialism in Western Europe—have become stronger. The positions of the United States, Great Britain, and France have turned out to be particularly vulnerable in West Berlin. These powers are still trying to cling to the old statutes. They cannot fail to understand that sooner or later an end will come to the occupational regime in this city. It is essential to continue, step by step, to bring the aggressive imperialist circles to their senses, to compel them to take the actual position into account. If they are stubborn, we will adopt decisive measures. We will conclude a peace treaty with the GDR because we are fully determined to insure the conclusion of a peace treaty with Germany at last, to do away with the occupational regime in West Berlin, and thus to eradicate this splinter from the heart of Europe.

And he laid this proposition before Kennedy at Vienna virtually as an ultimatum.

He did so out of a convergence of pressures from within the communist world and a sense of opportunity as he examined the military, diplomatic, and political dispositions of the West.

The pressures, in part, arose directly from Walter Ulbricht. East Germany was feeling strongly the attractive power of West German freedom and prosperity. West Berlin not only projected the contrast into the heart of East Germany, but it also provided an osmotic channel for escape to the West. In his brief account of the Berlin crises of 1958–1959 and 1961–1962 in his memoir, Khrushchev is something less than candid. But there is an authentic ring to his passage on the dilemma of East Germany at the time.[1] Ulbricht obviously had a vital interest in insulating East Germany from the attractions of the West, if possible by eliminating West Berlin.

This narrow interest was heightened by the pressure of those who, since Sputnik, had argued systematically that Soviet nuclear strength was capable of yielding substantial gains for the communist world, if wielded with sufficient boldness. Tatu, for example, reports a Warsaw Pact meeting in Moscow in the summer of 1961 in which the Albanians, obviously speaking for the Chinese, demanded the signing of the unilateral German peace treaty.[2]

Khrushchev's inclination to probe further at the West was almost certainly reinforced by his political situation at home, notably weakened since the U-2 incident and the breakup of the Paris summit meeting. He badly needed a success in foreign policy to strengthen his hand within the Presidium.

The situation in 1961 was, of course, somewhat different from that in 1958 when the sliding Berlin ultimatum had first been laid down. The image of Soviet ICBM strength relative to the United States had been considerably deflated by new intelligence. Kennedy was already launched on an expansion of the American military establishment. But Khrushchev faced a fact and a question.

The fact was that, however small his ICBM capacity, he had western Europe well targeted with missiles of shorter range. And this threat could be linked to the palpable reluctance of Bonn, Paris, and London to risk nuclear war to save the Western position in Berlin.

The question was Kennedy. Could Kennedy, a young, inexperienced, wealthy bourgeois, as Khrushchev saw him, face down a Bolshevik, hardened over forty-three years of revolution and the mafia-like political struggles of Soviet political life, in a nuclear test of will? And could Kennedy do so while holding together a somewhat uncertain alliance?

Kennedy's actions in the Bay of Pigs gave Khrushchev grounds for hope —or, at least, raised doubts as to how Kennedy might behave in a tough confrontation. His actions in Laos and in military policy generally were less reassuring. But, clearly, Khrushchev came to Vienna on June 3 determined to conduct the test.

Vienna: The Background

Berlin had been, of course, from the first days of the Kennedy administration the subject of urgent thought and planning. The planning list Kennedy approved on February 23 included, among others, these two items: "The Political and Military Aspects of the Berlin Crisis" and "A Position on Germany for Possible Four-Power Negotiations." The latter posed, by way of example, these questions: What alternative approaches to the Berlin and German problems should be explored? Would it be desirable to shift the emphasis from Berlin to German unification? Is there any basis upon which the United States could accept a confederal approach to unification? Is a deal on a Berlin corridor versus acceptance of the Oder–Neisse line possible and in our interest? Acheson was enlisted in early February to work with all elements in the government, and Henry Kissinger as a consultant to Bundy. Macmillan's visit in early April was the occasion for preliminary talks on Berlin which revealed the strength of the British desire to avoid a confrontation.

But once the meeting with Khrushchev was agreed on, it was clear Kennedy would have to wait and see what kind of a problem he really faced.

He found he had quite a problem. Khrushchev had evidently gone to Vienna to put the issue of Berlin to Kennedy in stark terms, including a formal, carefully prepared memorandum. I know of no more direct challenge made at a meeting of chiefs of government than Khrushchev's to Kennedy at Vienna on Berlin.

But there was more to Vienna than Berlin; and the positions taken on Berlin are best seen in the context of the dialogue as a whole.

Kennedy had focused on Soviet policy from the beginning. On the weekend after the Inaugural he called a meeting of Soviet experts to explore Khrushchev's intentions: literally my first memorandum for Kennedy as President (January 21) was to set down seventeen questions in preparation for the meeting. He decided in subsequent weeks that a face-to-face meeting with Khrushchev would be useful; and on March 9, in response to a letter from Kennedy, Khrushchev agreed. As the time approached, Kennedy solicited ideas widely.[3] He studied Khrushchev's life and pattern of action, including a biography by Lazar Pistrak (*The Grand Tactician*) available in galley proofs.

In a decision which has been widely questioned, Kennedy decided to take the initiative and pose the question of United States–Soviet relations in general terms.[4] The general position taken by Kennedy and Khrushchev's general response suffuse not only what might be called the ideological debate of June 3 but also the three substantive items examined in detail on June 4: Laos, arms control, and Berlin.

VIENNA: THE DEBATE ON POWER AND IDEOLOGY

THE central theme of the debate between the two leaders was the relation between power and ideology. The problem, as Kennedy put it before lunch on June 3, was: how the two countries could avoid actions which would endanger the peace under circumstances where they were engaged in ideological competition or allied with other countries.

So far as power was concerned, Kennedy took the position that the United States and the Soviet Union were evenly balanced; and the power position in the world as a whole was in precarious balance. Therefore, each side should avoid actions which would shift the power balance against the other. Neither, Kennedy argued, could accept such a shift imposed by the other.

With respect to ideology, Kennedy said the competition would inevitably proceed; the two nations took different views of the probable outcome; the United States could accept diverse outcomes in particular countries if peoples decided for themselves without external intervention; but danger would arise if ideological changes became associated with strategic changes in the United States–Soviet balance.

The United States desired that peoples make their choices freely through elections as Americans understand them. But Kennedy recognized this was not possible in many parts of the world—for example, not in Cuba, Spain, or Poland. Accepting this fact, the common task was to deal with the world in ways that avoided a shift in the strategic balance, to which Moscow or Washington would have to react by using force.

Illustrating his proposition, Kennedy said Yugoslavia, India, and Burma were extremely satisfactory situations so far as the United States was concerned. None was wholly aligned with the United States in either ideology or power. A problem would arise if the communist cause were to win in certain areas and if those areas were to associate themselves closely with the Soviet Union. That would pose precisely the kind of strategic problem for the United States that would arise for the Soviet Union if, for example, a government were created in Poland that associated itself closely with the United States. The United States had serious strategic interests in the world. These were incorporated in alliance commitments. Paraphrasing Churchill, Kennedy said he did not come to his present responsibilities to undo those commitments. The prestige of the United States and the balance of power in the world depended on his honoring them. He would.

Khrushchev could not, of course, accept this view. It sharply distinguished ideology from power and called for a separation of the strategic status quo from the ideological patterns history might peacefully yield. It thus ran counter to the fundamentals of communist doctrine. Talking as a chief of government, rather than as leader of a major Communist party, Khrushchev had some difficulty replying with total candor. Nonetheless, he entered into the debate with verve.

With respect to ideology, he asserted the United States wished to build a dam against the spread of ideas and the will of the people. The people in each country would decide the outcome, eventually on the basis of whether their economic aspirations were being achieved. He pointed to unrest in Iran, Turkey, Pakistan, South Korea, and Taiwan. The United States was supporting, for strategic reasons, unpopular regimes. They were not yielding a satisfactory standard of living for the peoples concerned. They would inevitably be overthrown. The United States should not blame the Soviet Union for this outcome.

There were other places where the Soviet Union would be active. The Soviet Union supported anticolonial struggles such as those in Angola and Algeria; and it lent its sympathy and support to "wars of national liberation." But it did not interfere directly. It would not impose ideas by war. (Here, Khrushchev evidently could not expose his debate with Mao on the appropriate degree of communist external involvement and the appropriate degree of risk to be accepted in supporting "wars of national liberation.")

Khrushchev did not address himself directly to the strategic point Kennedy had underlined; namely, the possible disturbing effects of an expansion of Soviet power by linkage to new communist regimes that might emerge. He chose to take head-on the American view of its strategic position in the world. When Kennedy stated that the balance of power was delicate, he meant, of course, that the existing position, including the structure of American alliances and forward positions, was acceptable if it were not significantly altered. Here Khrushchev plunged in.

In Asia, he challenged bluntly the legitimacy of the American strategic interest in Taiwan and Southeast Asia and the pacts which reflected it. He said that if the Soviet Union were in China's place it would probably have attacked Taiwan long ago. In Europe, he challenged the legitimacy of NATO. He recalled that at Yalta Roosevelt had said U.S. forces would not remain much over two years; Khrushchev seemed to imply that by staying in Europe the United States had deceived the Soviet Union. He attacked the American base structure surrounding the Soviet Union. He said that when Kennedy stated the United States had commitments, it made a bad impression in the Soviet Union. The United States had no right to interfere in the various areas of the world. Asking pardon for his bluntness, he said American commitments around the world stemmed from megalomania, from delusions of grandeur. The Soviet Union could not reconcile itself to their legitimacy. He contrasted this situation with a Soviet policy of encouraging national independence.

At the polemical height of the debate Khrushchev denied flatly the American interest in the balance of power in Europe or in Asia.

Perhaps feeling that he had gone too far in this somewhat explosive passage, Khrushchev concluded on the note Kennedy had earlier struck: a great deal of restraint was required because of the prestige and national interests involved; the Soviet Union and the United States should not step on each other's toes and should not infringe upon the rights of other nations, big or small. Kennedy quickly picked up the theme, and a sustained discussion of Laos followed.

Before considering how this rather extraordinary exchange was linked by both men to concrete issues, I would make some observations.

First, both Kennedy and Khrushchev were markedly uneasy with the problems of politics in the developing world. Kennedy acknowledged candidly the gap between the American desire for representative democracy and the political facts of life in many parts of the noncommunist world. He acknowledged that governments would change if they did not increasingly satisfy the desires of their peoples. He expressed no cheap confidence in the early and universal emergence of democracy as Americans understood it, but fell back on his basic strategic proposition and a plea for noninterference in the historical outcome.

Khrushchev stuck with a rather simple economic theory of political stability and freedom which he later articulated:

> In order to feel moral constraint, moral oppression, or moral bondage a man must have a highly developed and highly refined conception of what human freedom is all about. Most people still measure their own freedom or lack of freedom in terms of how much meat, how many potatoes, or what kind of boots they can get for one ruble.[5]

At Vienna, in choosing the cases to needle Kennedy with (Spain, Turkey, Iran, South Korea, and Taiwan), Khrushchev was obviously thinking in terms of meat, potatoes, and boots; but, with hindsight, he chose badly. All these nations subsequently made remarkable material progress in the 1960s. He also referred to Nasser's and Nehru's anticommunism, but did not regale Kennedy with communist doctrine about the transitory historical role of such anti-imperialist nationalists.

Politics in the developing nations was a continuing puzzlement to both Moscow and Washington. Neither had developed adequate theories or operational concepts of political development, whose vagaries are the backdrop to a good deal of the strategic struggle of the decade, as well as to the debate at Vienna.

Was Kennedy's approach at Vienna useful or counterproductive? Should he have gone directly into the working agenda?

Lacking firm knowledge of how Khrushchev (and his colleagues) reacted to the debate, no one can be dogmatic; and, evidently, what Kennedy said did not deter Khrushchev from seeing whether Kennedy would back his play. I am inclined to think the general discussion was useful for three reasons. First, Kennedy proved himself capable of articulating, without benefit of advisers, a clear and coherent point of view. As Khrushchev later said: "He had a precisely formulated opinion on every subject."[6] Communists respect those who hold a lucid ideological position different from their own. Second, as the confrontations in Berlin, Cuba, and Southeast Asia unfolded, Moscow had a map of Kennedy's mind which proved wholly consistent with his later actions. Thus, the exchanges at Vienna may have contributed credibility to Kennedy's policies at critical moments, a credibility already beginning to emerge in Khrushchev's somewhat anxious probing at Vienna on the question of the possible dispatch of American Marines (in May 1961) to Laos. Third, Kennedy could subsequently feel that he had said all he could to minimize the possibility of miscalculation. He faced what he had to face after Vienna in good conscience.

THE SPECIFIC ISSUES

ON Laos there was, up to a point, a convergence of view between Kennedy and Khrushchev on both ideological and balance-of-power grounds. Washington and Moscow agreed that a neutralist government headed by Souvanna Phouma and a militarily neutralized Laos would meet their respective interests. In response to Kennedy's position, Khrushchev denied that Viet Minh forces were involved in Laos; he wished to circumscribe the powers of the International Control Commission in establishing the presence of foreign forces so as to avoid supra-national behavior; and he urged that negotiations of substance should not be made contingent on a cease-fire.

There was enough agreement, however, to provide a framework for subsequent diplomacy at Geneva.

Kennedy did not raise the crucial issue: North Vietnamese movement through Laos against South Vietnam. He left it for negotiation by Harriman.

The issue of the potential supra-nationality of the ICC was then carried over into the discussion of arms control. Khrushchev said events in the Congo had taught the Soviet Union a lesson: it would not permit a single chairman of a commission on arms control to act with the independence Hammarskjold had displayed in the Congo. There had to be a three-man body, implying a veto for each. He would only drop his troika proposal if the test ban were linked to a plan for general and complete disarmament.[7]

Here ideology and power were linked in a different way. Khrushchev took the view that the United States commanded a political and ideological majority in the United Nations. It might well prove transient. But he was not about to risk international espionage in the Soviet Union at the indirect behest of the United States, by permitting a single, allegedly neutral director of a control commission to monitor a test ban treaty.

When Kennedy underlined the urgency of the test ban treaty as a way of heading off nuclear proliferation, Khrushchev replied with an implicitly Chinese argument: while Britain, the United States, and the Soviet Union are negotiating in Geneva, France goes on testing; if there is no link between a nuclear test ban and disarmament, other countries may say that they are in an unequal position and might act like France.

There was, in the end, no progress.

Then Berlin. Khrushchev regarded all of Berlin as territory of East Germany. He said he would sign a German peace treaty by December. He would like to do so in agreement with the United States. The treaty would permit what the West calls West Berlin's freedom. And neutral troops could be stationed there. If the United States did not wish to sign a treaty, he would do so with East Germany. The United States would then have to negotiate its position in Berlin with East Germany: the treaty would end wartime agreements and block American access to Berlin. If there was to be war over the issue, the United States would have to initiate that war by challenging East German control over the access routes.

Khrushchev ruled out the negotiation of German unity. He said Adenauer in fact did not wish the unification of Germany. Therefore, it was time to make peace on the basis of the realities. The Soviet Union would sign a peace treaty; the sovereignty of East Germany would be observed; any violation of that sovereignty would be regarded by the Soviet Union as an act of open aggression.

To salvage American prestige, an interim agreement of perhaps six months might be envisaged. This would turn responsibility for the Berlin problem over to the two Germanies; but the result must be the same. Access to West Berlin would be under control of East Germany. Western wartime rights in Berlin must end by the close of 1961.

Kennedy said American rights in Berlin arose from the Second World War. Neither the American military presence nor access to West Berlin could be unilaterally ended by the Soviet Union or East Germany. A United States which accepted Khrushchev's proposal would not be regarded as a serious nation. It would lose its allies in western Europe. Kennedy did not propose to act in a way that would deprive the Soviet Union of its ties in eastern Europe; but he did not assume office to accept arrangements totally inimicable to American interests.

Kennedy probed to make sure he fully understood the sharp edges of Khrushchev's proposition. A final private conversation on the afternoon of June 4 confirmed that Khrushchev would sign the peace treaty in December if the United States refused an interim agreement; and the two days ended with Kennedy's celebrated prediction of a cold winter.

The Berlin Crisis

It proved to be a hot summer. The crisis was curiously stylized. Khrushchev had put a verbal challenge to Kennedy, backed by a diplomatic aide-memoire. He then awaited Kennedy's move. But no troops were marching in the days after Vienna, no shots were being fired. It was a time of feverish bureaucratic debate and of intense diplomacy within the Western Alliance.

In Washington it was agreed that an improvement in the American military posture in Europe was required not merely for symbolic reasons but also to meet certain possible specific contingencies that might arise along the access routes to Berlin. The issues Kennedy had to decide were: the scale of the military buildup; whether it should be dramatized by a proclamation of national emergency; whether the expansion in the military budget should be accompanied by a call for increased taxes; and what negotiating posture the West should assume as it hardened its military position.

Kennedy's critical problem, as Khrushchev knew, was in Bonn and London, not Washington. Adenauer did not want war over Berlin; and London did not even want confrontation, although Macmillan was personally sturdy. Drew Middleton's appraisal in *The New York Times* of July 17 that the problem of holding the British public firm was "the toughest leadership problem the Conservatives have faced in ten years of office" was quite accurate, putting aside Macmillan's problem of overcoming the disarray after Suez.

De Gaulle's bland intransigence kept French anxieties from coming to the diplomatic surface. De Gaulle took the formal view that there was, simply, nothing to negotiate about.[8]

At every opportunity, however, Soviet officials, from Khrushchev down, took the opportunity over the summer of 1961 to heighten and underline the schisms in the West over Berlin. For example, at a two-hour lunch on July 17, the Soviet ambassador, Mihail Menshikov, sought to drive the lesson home to me, knowing that the American position on Berlin was rapidly crystallizing. He said we could not count on our allies. If the crisis intensified, the West Germans would leave West Germany as fast as the East Germans were leaving East Germany. We should not count on the French, despite de Gaulle; nor on the British. I called his attention to Hitler's underestimate of the will of the British: it was easy to underestimate how citizens in a democracy would behave at a time of crisis. He said now there were nuclear weapons. I agreed but pointed out that, backed against the wall, men generally behaved bravely, even if irrationally, and that, in the end, men often took the view they would die only once.[9]

Reflecting on that somewhat ghoulish conversation, and on other evidence of Moscow's systematic campaign of nuclear blackmail against Europe, I sent Kennedy a memorandum on July 22, in which I argued that the somewhat hesitant moods of our allies, while understandable, did not justify a weakening in the American position. I recalled that Washington, not London or Bonn, had its finger on the atomic trigger. It was one matter to face the possibility of atomic war if your political leaders have their finger on the trigger: it is a quite different matter if someone else's leaders are in that position. I noted also that each nation has just so much stomach in it for facing war. The capacity of the Europeans for this kind of thing is—and should be—somewhat lower than ours, given the history of the last half-century.

I concluded by noting that the allies might stay together to the end or that the crisis might abort at a relatively early stage; but in any case, that we ought to be prepared in our minds for the possibility of a relatively lonely stage; and, recalling *High Noon*, we ought to accept it without throwing our sheriff's badge in the dust when the crisis subsided.

In fact, the crisis did abort at a relatively early stage. As tension mounted in July, the flow of East Germans to Berlin and the West increased rapidly. Kennedy's speech of July 25 contributed to the flow by bringing the crisis into sharp focus. He asked for over $3 billion to expand the military budget; for authority to increase the size of the armed forces by some 217,000 men; for doubled draft calls; and he ordered up some reserves. Essentially on economic grounds, Kennedy did not ask for a tax increase and he rejected the proclamation of a state of emergency as excessively inflammatory. While recognizing the legitimacy of Soviet interests in central and eastern Europe and offering to negotiate in general terms, it was unmistakably a tough speech. Congress acted on it promptly; and there was evidence of solid support in every part of the country.

The flow of East German refugees to the West accelerated. The figure for July was over 30,000. The East Germans began to inhibit travel to West Berlin by August 11. To the fear of war was added fear that the time for getting to the West might be growing short. Khrushchev's unyielding response to Kennedy's speech, on August 7, exacerbated the tension—and the flow of refugees.

Meanwhile, Rusk met in Paris with his British and French colleagues to concert a diplomatic position. As they gathered, Moscow suggested its desire to talk, but did not withdraw its threat of a unilateral treaty. There was agreement on the posture of the Alliance toward the crisis; but the French insisted successfully that no new grand diplomatic initiatives should be immediately taken. It was agreed that negotiations on Germany were acceptable only if they were well prepared and entered into without preconditions. The North Atlantic Council supported this posture in a session of August 8.

As the days in August ticked off, the bleeding white of East Germany, rather than diplomacy, became the central fact in the crisis. More than 10,000 East Germans left for the West in the first week of the month. Kennedy was conscious that vital interests of the Soviet Union were now at stake. Walking along the colonnade, between the Mansion and his White House office, he said to me one day early in August: "Khrushchev is losing East Germany. He cannot let that happen. If East Germany goes, so will Poland and all of eastern Europe. He will have to do something to stop the flow of refugees—perhaps a wall. And we won't be able to prevent it. I can hold the Alliance together to defend West Berlin but I cannot act to keep East Berlin open." The building of the Berlin Wall began on August 13.[10]

The Wall

THERE was some initial concern about Khrushchev's intentions: Was the closing off of East Berlin a cut-rate end to the crisis or the creation of a firmer base for harassing the lines of access to Berlin? In either case, there was painful and reluctant agreement—in Bonn and Berlin, as well as London, Paris, and Washington—that the Wall should not be challenged by military force. There was also anxiety about the morale of the West Berliners. They were cut off not only from friends and family (and a part of the work force), but also from the mission of demonstration which the relative openness of Berlin had permitted.

To assert his determination to keep the access routes open and to cheer the West Berliners, Kennedy asked Johnson to go to Berlin; and some fifteen hundred American troops moved down the highway to reinforce the Berlin garrison, to be greeted by the Vice President. General Lucius Clay, who had seen West Berlin through the blockade of 1948–1949, went along.

As the expedition was hastily prepared on August 19, McGeorge Bundy (who was working on a draft letter to West Berlin Mayor Willy Brandt) asked me to prepare a draft speech for the Vice President. I did so briskly; and the draft survived pretty well the line-by-line scrutiny of Kennedy, Johnson, and Rusk at a meeting in the Yellow Room in the Mansion. I wrote in the phrase from the Declaration of Independence—committing "our lives, fortunes, and sacred honor"—for two reasons: to underline Kennedy's position at Vienna that he would not accept an unfavorable shift in the balance of power; and to reinforce in Moscow's mind that, whatever wobbliness Soviet diplomats might detect and report from other capitals, the American commitment to Berlin was unambiguous.

More significant, perhaps, was the commitment not only to "the survival" but to the "creative future" of West Berlin. Having followed German affairs since August 1945, I was troubled from the beginning by the problem of West Berlin's viability in the face of the Wall. That remarkable community of people had been sustained over the years by a sense of their mission to the East. It would not be difficult to maintain their standard of living; but could West Berlin, walled off, remain a city worthy of a young man's investing his life?

I raised this matter with Clay, who had accepted again serving in Berlin. And, in part at his suggestion, various economic measures of support were promptly undertaken by the Germans. On coming to the State Department in December 1961 my first initiative, fully supported by my colleagues in the European Division, was to send William Jorden of the Planning Council to Bonn and Berlin to explore with all concerned a wider-ranging program that would link Germany constructively to the outside world. The program that emerged had many elements, including special training in engineering and electronics, in which West Berlin excelled, for students from developing nations. A young economist, Karl Schiller, came from Hamburg to take over the Berlin Viability program. It proved a quite useful launching pad to the higher reaches of Social Democratic politics. But it was the people of West Berlin who defeated, in the decade that followed, Khrushchev's frequent prediction in the latter months of 1961 that the city would wither and die in the face of the Wall.

From Berlin to Cuba

Khrushchev was not content, however, to rely on that prediction. Diplomacy continued in exchanges of letters between Khrushchev and Kennedy but, especially, in endless sessions between Rusk and Gromyko. With an endurance and a repetitiveness worthy of Molotov in his prime, Rusk reiterated the three essential U.S. conditions for a Berlin settlement: political freedom for the West Berliners; the presence of American forces; the right of civil and military access to West Berlin. Meanwhile, all manner of larger proposals for a German settlement were canvassed; but Khrushchev was interested in gaining control over all of Berlin and consolidating a communist East Germany within his Warsaw Pact system. He was not interested in ending the division of Germany and Europe.

Early in 1962 Khrushchev launched a potentially quite dangerous probe against the air corridors to Berlin. He undoubtedly hoped this pressure might heighten differences among the allies and perhaps lead to a favorable negotiation on Berlin. It made few headlines because it was Allied policy to deal with the incipient crisis in low-key; and there was relatively little diplomatic debate because a contingency plan had been formulated to deal with such harassment and given sufficient governmental approval to provide NATO Commander, General Lauris Norstad, a free hand. It was one of the few occasions I can recall when a contingency plan was precisely relevant. An able four-power group had worked steadily through the autumn of 1961, including German as well as British, French, and American representatives. Foy Kohler and Paul Nitze were leaders on the American side.

The Soviet enterprise began on February 7. The Soviet controller in the four-power Berlin Air Safety Center (BASC) told his three Western colleagues that all altitudes in the Berlin–Frankfurt corridor up to seven thousand feet would have to be reserved for Russian military transport planes for three hours on the morning of February 8. The Western controllers reminded the Soviet representative that he would have to file flight plans and that Western military and commercial flights would proceed as usual. On five further occasions in the period February 11–18 the exercise was repeated.

On February 14–15 Soviet fighter aircraft buzzed Allied aircraft dangerously. The three Western powers protested in identical notes that Soviet harassment was "running grave risks"; that the Soviet Union would be held responsible for the consequences of any incidents; and that "certain military contingency plans" had been put into effect. The latter involved the assembly of Allied fighter aircraft for quick reaction and escort duty if necessary.

After a relatively quiet period, buzzing resumed in the second week of

March, as well as the dropping of metallic chaff to interfere with Allied radar reception and traffic control. This second action Kennedy characterized, in a press conference of March 14, as "a particularly dangerous kind of action." He urged Moscow "to avoid incidents that are liable to lead to actions and counteractions which can only intensify the danger."

The crisis eased at the end of March, although unscheduled Soviet aircraft intruded from time to time over the subsequent month. In May the Soviet controller in BASC, who had over the previous three months performed in an erratic and occasionally threatening way, returned to his usual professional working style.

By late April Khrushchev had shifted to another more dangerous plan to acquire leverage over West Berlin. But before considering the Cuba missile crisis, it is worth examining the evolution of Atlantic diplomacy in the face of Khrushchev's pressures of 1961–1962.

KENNEDY'S ATLANTIC POLICY

THE spring of 1962 was a period when a good deal of thought was being given in Washington to questions of European policy. Berlin was relatively quiet except for the buzzing incidents just recounted, but the threat of further pressure from Moscow was still in the air. The memory of the previous summer's crisis was fresh. The issue of Europe's long-term role in nuclear matters was heightened by this vivid experience of nuclear blackmail.

Britain was seeking entrance into the Common Market; and de Gaulle had not showed his hand. This hopeful possibility automatically brought the nuclear question to the center of the stage by posing the question of how the British national nuclear capability would be absorbed into a politically enlarged Europe. London obviously regarded its nuclear capacity as a bargaining asset in the negotiations at Brussels.

Meanwhile, the American economy was not moving forward with the élan necessary to reduce the unemployment rate substantially; the balance-of-payments problem was a source of continued constraint and anxiety; and the situation in the developing nations required enlarged flows of aid and other actions to cushion the decline in their earning power from falling export prices to which Europe had to make a greater contribution if international action were to be effective.

On January 25, 1962, Kennedy had made a major move in Atlantic policy. He sent a special message to Congress on foreign trade policy that asked for revolutionary authority to negotiate with the Common Market as a unit, but this was clearly not enough. Some kind of equivalent coordination in monetary affairs and aid to the developing world was necessary.

When I went to work at the State Department Kennedy kept open a channel of direct communication, with the understanding that everything I sent to him would go simultaneously to Rusk. In June I sent several memoranda on European policy to Kennedy. And, upon his return from a trip to Mexico, I talked at some length with him about these memoranda late in the morning of July 2. We discussed the whole complex of ties across the Atlantic.

He observed that in the 1950s the United States had spent its time collecting nuclear bombs, while Europe had been rounding up gold. What was needed now was some way in which Europe could assume increased responsibility for the state of the world economy, thus reducing the burden carried by the United States; and the United States would have to find ways of sharing with the Europeans the responsibilities of decision in nuclear matters. The heart of it, he thought, was this: If there was a single political authority in Europe, he could work out an arrangement for joint control over nuclear matters. But Europe was split: "I'm the President of the United States, but who's the President of Europe?" We talked about the proposal for a multilateral nuclear force within NATO; and he probed at why Bonn might be interested when, clearly, he could not surrender to Bonn the right to fire American weapons.

We canvassed, as well, the problems in aid, trade, and money.

One of the memoranda he had read suggested that the concept of an across-the-board partnership between the United States and Europe might be the subject of a major address by the President or secretary of state.

Kennedy concluded by saying he had to make a speech on July 4 at Philadelphia; he would like to make it on this international theme rather than in a more conventional patriotic style: would I send a draft over to Sorensen as soon as possible. That afternoon my deputy Henry Owen and I put our heads together and fulfilled his instruction.

The key passage in Kennedy's speech was this:

> We believe that a united Europe will be capable of playing a greater role in the common defense, of responding more generously to the needs of poorer nations, of joining with the United States and others in lowering trade barriers, resolving problems of commerce, commodities, and currency, and developing coordinated policies in all economic, political, and diplomatic areas. We see in such a Europe a partner with whom we can deal on a basis of full equality in all the great and burdensome tasks of building and defending a community of free nations.
>
> It would be premature at this time to do more than indicate the high regard with which we view the formation of this partnership. The first order of business is for our European friends to go forward in forming the more perfect union which will someday make this partnership possible.
>
> A great new edifice is not built overnight. It was eleven years from the Declaration of Independence to the writing of the Constitution. The construction of workable federal institutions required still

another generation. The greatest works of our Nation's founders lay not in documents and in declarations, but in creative, determined action. The building of the new house of Europe has followed the same practical, purposeful course. Building the Atlantic partnership now will not be easily or cheaply finished.[11]

The final caution was seriously meant. As with the Alliance for Progress and arms control, for example, Kennedy knew the road to European unity and the Altantic partnership would be long and rough, stretching far beyond his time. He was not in the least naive about the obstacles in the way; no President in the early 1960s could be. Not only the reality of de Gaulle but the stubborn persistence of old European rivalries and suspicions pounded in daily with the flow of cables. But he wanted to define a path that ran with the grain of both history and the long-run American interest; and, indeed, a decade later, as this is written, it is still too soon to say that his Grand Design, often prematurely buried on editorial pages, will not come to pass.

But as President he had, above all, to act from day to day in the face of things as they were, not as they might become. This meant small steps in the right direction, as well as the buffeting of events which either frustrated action or pushed it off course. Only in the field of trade could he find the political base for a clean breakthrough, with the signing of the Trade Expansion Act of 1962, on October 11—launching a negotiation which Johnson saw skillfully through to completion five years later.

There was, however, some forward movement on other fronts. First and most urgently, the balance-of-payments burden imposed by the presence of American forces in Germany was offset by enlarged German military purchases in the United States. On the occasion of Foreign Minister Heinrich von Brentano's visit in February 1961, Kennedy considered and tentatively supported a multilateral approach in the Alliance to the offset problem. But Douglas Dillon at the Treasury and the Pentagon argued successfully (against me, among others) for a quick, pragmatic, bilateral solution through increased German outlays for American military hardware. This solution was made possible, essentially, by Khrushchev. His pressure on Berlin induced a rapid expansion in the German military budget.

Second, under Kennedy's leadership, the German, Italian, and Japanese contributions to economic development were expanded and the basis laid for a more general increase in non-American development contributions later in the decade.

Third, the President threw his weight strongly behind the OECD and invested the time and talent of first-rate men, like Walter Heller, Robert Roosa, James Tobin, and David Bell, in expanding its agenda in aid, monetary affairs, and the coordination of economic policy in general.

Fourth, Kennedy encouraged a variety of initiatives that would enlarge the area of political consultation within NATO on problems transcending NATO's borders, including the creation of a planners' club, the Atlantic

Policy Advisory Group (APAG), of which I was the first American member.

Fifth, the President took special pains to build a new relationship with Japan, and this aspect of his policy belongs, in part, with his policy across the Atlantic. The broad rhetorical (and operational) concept on which Kennedy and his administration worked was to bind up in partnership the richer nations of the north and, from that strengthened base, to assist and protect the independence of the less developed nations of the south. There were, of course, special problems with Japan, particularly after the bruising Japanese political battle of 1960 to carry forward the defense agreement—a battle that had resulted in the cancellation of Eisenhower's visit. Edwin Reischauer was sent as ambassador to establish ties that might reach deeper into Japanese society than the Foreign Office. Regular bilateral Cabinet-level meetings were arranged on the occasion of Premier Hayato Ikeda's visit of June 21–22, 1961. A serious mission was sent to review the American administration of Okinawa where Japan retained ultimate sovereignty and over which a major problem was emerging in Japanese politics. The review resulted in substantial changes in American policy on Okinawa, instituted by executive order on March 19, 1962. And Kennedy, not without debate within his administration, decided, on the occasion of Ikeda's visit, to throw his support behind full membership for Japan in the OECD, bringing the Japanese fully into the club of the more advanced nations of the north.[12]

THE MULTILATERAL FORCE (MLF) TO OCTOBER 22, 1962

CLEARLY, however, the nuclear question was the central issue in European policy with which Kennedy had to grapple. It arose proximately from Khrushchev's post-Sputnik posture and, especially, from his decision to use his nuclear threat against western Europe in an effort to force a change in the status of West Berlin. More fundamentally, however, it arose from the curious but powerful way that nuclear weapons—which it was in no one's interest to fire—suffused and sharpened the relations among nations, communist and noncommunist alike.

When Kennedy came to responsibility, these were the essential facts about the nuclear position within the Alliance:

1. a British nuclear capability, linked to bombing aircraft (the V-bomber force), was in being;
2. a French nuclear capability was building, also linked to bombing aircraft (the Mirage), rooted in French technology;
3. a two-key system controlled rapidly obsolescing American Jupiter and Thor missiles in the United Kingdom, Italy, and Turkey;
4. German ground and air forces were being equipped to deliver American tactical nuclear weapons, under two-key controls;

5. the overwhelming responsibility for deterring Soviet nuclear weapons targeted against Europe as well as the United States rested with the American nuclear establishment as a whole, including the Strategic Air Command, Polaris submarines at sea, and the emerging force of Minutemen in hardened sites in the United States.

Looking to the future in the late 1950s, the technical question had arisen: What should replace the obsolescing British aircraft, as well as the Thors and Jupiters? Simultaneously, the political question had arisen: Should not there be under NATO command, in Europe, MRBM's (medium-range ballistic missiles) to deter the Soviet MRBM's target against Europe? Under the weight of Soviet nuclear blackmail, and spurred by the revival of their economic and political strength, Europeans sought a less passive role in their own defense.

To meet these pressures, the United States had offered in the spring of 1960 to sell, or help Europeans make, Polaris missiles to be equipped with U.S. nuclear warheads. These would be land-based and under a two-key system. This proposal, associated with Secretary of Defense Thomas Gates, was rejected for essentially the same reasons that a number of European nations had rejected Eisenhower's proposal at the December 1957 NATO meeting for the location on their soil of Thors or Jupiters: the missiles would generate popular anxiety and political opposition. Psychologically, at least, they would heighten the sense that the nations which accepted them had become prime Soviet targets. On the American side, also, there were doubts, mainly centering on the security of control arrangements over such sensitive strategic weapons.

A review of the problem was then undertaken by Robert Bowie, former head of the Policy Planning Staff. His report of August 1960 suggested that a NATO multilateral force should be moved to sea, with missiles mounted in submarines manned by mixed crews, including Americans, under the command of SACEUR (Supreme Allied Commander Europe). It would be financed and owned collectively by the participants. It envisaged that American warheads might be transferred to the custody of this force, requiring change in American law. This was the proposition put by Secretary of State Christian Herter to the NATO ministerial meeting on December 16, 1960, after prior soundings in the latter part of November (see above, p. 77).

On April 25, 1961, Kennedy reaffirmed within the government a policy of holding out to the Europeans this offer of a multilaterally owned and controlled NATO seaborne missile force. On May 17, speaking to the Canadian Parliament in Ottawa, he said the United States looked "to the possibility of eventually establishing a NATO sea-borne force, which would be truly multilateral in ownership and control, if this should be desired and found feasible by our Allies, once NATO's non-nuclear goals have been achieved."[13]

As Americans and others stared at this proposition, a whole set of questions emerged of which these were basic: First, would European outlays for such a force interfere with the buildup of conventional forces in NATO? Second, in such a multilateral force would an excessive number of fingers on the safety catch detract from its military efficiency or even make it an unreliable element in the total Western deterrent system? Third, assuming these and other problems could be solved, and a militarily reputable force be developed, as reliably controlled and credible as the rest of the Western nuclear establishment, would the Joint Atomic Energy Committee of the Congress—and the Congress as a whole—change the law to permit the sale of warheads to this collective NATO institution? Finally, could the NATO multilateral force (MLF) be squared with the American desire to discourage nuclear proliferation?

The exigencies of the Berlin crisis of 1961 postponed systematic examination of these problems. But it also brought home to the Europeans the painful realities of nuclear confrontation, in which they were Moscow's primary political and psychological target but almost totally dependent on the United States to manage their destiny. The issue was, therefore, quite alive as the December 1961 NATO ministerial meeting approached.

On December 14, in Paris, Rusk told his colleagues that the declaration of President Kennedy at Ottawa stood: if there were NATO members who believed there were advantages in moving ahead, the United States would be glad to discuss this point with them. The United States considered a multilateral force (MLF) the means of deploying MRBM's most consistent with NATO cohesion. To make explicit that the door to a bilateral solution was closed, McNamara added that the United States would not be prepared to facilitate procurement of MRBM's for a NATO force that was not truly multilateral in ownership and control.

On March 1, 1962, U. Alexis Johnson, speaking for the secretary of state, told the Joint Congressional Committee on Atomic Energy that the NATO allies were interested in such a proposition and that the United States would be discussing it with them in the near future. On April 18 Kennedy formally approved as executive branch policy the American offer to join its allies, if they wished, in developing a modest-sized (on the order of two hundred missiles), fully multilateral NATO sea-based MRBM force. On the issue of control, the United States would wish to know the views of its allies. In the American view, however, such a force would probably require advance authority to respond to a large-scale nuclear attack and a voting system requiring American approval for firing in all other cases. At the Athens meeting of NATO in May 1962 (dominated by McNamara's famous attack on small national nuclear forces) the offer was reaffirmed in greater detail.

Meanwhile, Kennedy came to perceive the depth of the problem of submarine security, real and political. Admiral Hyman Rickover, a man of long-demonstrated influence with Congress, was determined that the United

States should not transfer modern submarine technology to other nations. Therefore, Kennedy set a group in the Navy to study whether a surface MLF was feasible. A report of June 25, 1962, concluded that surface ships were indeed a secure and viable platform for missiles. On September 18, 1962, the Belgium permanent representative to the North Atlantic Council proposed that a collective study be undertaken on the creation of the MLF. The German representative announced his government's willingness to participate in and contribute funds and personnel if NATO decided to constitute an MLF. On October 22, the day Kennedy delivered his speech on the Soviet missiles in Cuba, an American team (Gerard Smith and Rear Admiral John M. Lee) presented the findings of the American study of the MLF to the North Atlantic Council as a basis for its work.

There were, of course, differences within the American government on the proposal, as it had evolved down to October 22. From a narrow American military point of view, the two hundred additional missiles were not significant; in the end, the United States could not permit the MLF an independent right to fire the missiles. On the whole, the American view of an appropriate NATO strategy would have placed a higher priority on increased European outlays for conventional forces than on their sharing ownership in the surface fleet. Moreover, it was still to be demonstrated that mixed manning could be militarily efficient.

Politically, there were also unresolved problems. The Congress would have to be carried; and there was about the proposal an implication of widened German participation in nuclear matters that stirred visceral fears in segments of American public opinion as well as in Britain and elsewhere. Technically, the MLF provided no more access—probably less—to nuclear weapons than existing two-key arrangements for the delivery of tactical nuclear weapons by German aircraft and surface-to-surface nuclear artillery. But the psychological and political problem was there—in Europe as well as in the United States.

Finally, there were these further problems: winning British participation, which was critical; overcoming the schisms on nuclear matters in Italian and Belgian politics; determining the ultimate reaction of de Gaulle (who, up to this point, had taken the view that he "understood" the German interest in the proposition although France would not participate); and squaring the MLF with a nonproliferation treaty.

As of October 22, 1962, advocates of the MLF had developed answers or potential answers to all of these questions; but it was not difficult to understand that elements in the United States government, with differing responsibilities, would take positions of skepticism, reserve, or opposition to the MLF.

The real question was: What was it that generated dedication to the enterprise among some and led Kennedy, Rusk, and McNamara to put forward and support the proposal?

First, in the short term, the concept of the MLF offered America the real possibility of managing the nuclear deterrence of the Soviet Union through effective participation of the European allies. This was important because the heart of Khrushchev's pressure on Berlin arose from his MRBM threat against Europe rather than his ICBM threat against the United States. The MLF offered America's allies a share in their own defense rather than total reliance on the actions of a distant American President.

Second, there was the question of Germany and Italy. Britain and France had national nuclear capabilities of a sort, and in different ways they flaunted that fact as a means of maintaining their great-power posture in a time of collapsing empires. Germany, on NATO's front line and contributing an increasing proportion of NATO's ground forces, was left out of a strategic role in dealing with Khrushchev's pressure. The essence of Atlantic policy toward Germany and Italy since the Marshall Plan had been to bring them into multilateral arrangements where they could be treated as equals: but in nuclear matters they were, in effect, still being dealt with as third-class citizens of the Alliance. The MLF would, to a degree, restore the balance among America's European partners.

Third was a technical fact. Solid-fuel missiles of the Polaris type would increasingly be substituted for aircraft and the obsolescing Thors and Jupiters. If there was not some form of collective instrument like MLF, the alternatives for America were: to sell missiles or make available their technology on a national basis to European nations; or to carry a higher proportion of the nuclear load at precisely the period when European power and responsibility were naturally rising relative to that of the United States.

In the longer run, the advocates of the MLF saw the institution not merely as a way of dealing with certain inescapable short-run problems within NATO, but also as a device for bringing the European nations politically closer to each other and to the United States.

Because the United States–European nuclear relationship remains a live issue today, with Britain entering the Common Market, it is worth recalling how it looked in 1962. If de Gaulle would accede to British entrance into the Common Market (and there was temperate optimism in the spring and summer of 1962), it was judged important to the American interest that British and French nuclear capabilities be brought together in such a way as to avoid a break in coordination and control between European and American nuclear weapons. Having faced the reality of nuclear confrontation, it was borne in on Kennedy, Rusk, and McNamara that nothing would be less acceptable to the United States than an alliance within which others claimed the right to fire nuclear weapons (or otherwise put the United States at nuclear risk) without the assent of the American President. I have never seen harder faces than those of high American officials reading intelligence reports of Frenchmen peddling the doctrine that the *force de frappe* was a cheap finger on the American nuclear trigger. I do not believe that was de Gaulle's view; but there was in Europe the latent possibility of building what was called a "loose European nuclear force" that might have that characteristic. There were Germans who saw in such a loose nuclear arrangement—a kind of nuclear club of *patries*—a route into the strategic nuclear business. Someday, if, in Kennedy's phrase, there was a "President of Europe," the United States might be able to work out a tight and reliable coordination of nuclear forces and ways of moving together in dangerous crises; but a loose European force was judged a direct danger to the American interest and a development which would weaken and perhaps disintegrate NATO.

If de Gaulle did not accede to British entrance into the European community, there was the problem of holding the line to await a better day. The key to a solution was judged to be a closer association between Britain on the one hand, and Germany and Italy on the other. In 1962 the MLF offered a way of achieving that kind of interim association on a critical issue which bypassed the possible Common Market veto in Paris.

When Macmillan had come to Washington to talk with Kennedy in early April 1961, Kennedy had puzzled with his advisers before the event as to what posture he should adopt with respect to Britain's entry into the Common Market. He decided that he should not take the initiative in pressing Macmillan, although he recognized fully the American political interest in the outcome. But at the very opening of the formal talks in the Cabinet Room, Macmillan removed the problem from the agenda. In a vivid statement, he said that his generation had seen two bloody wars arise out of the tensions in central Europe. The elements of danger and instability were still there. Europe and Western civilization could not survive a third such war. Therefore, it was Britain's duty, on political and security grounds, to go into Europe and to work side by side with the continental Europeans to keep the peace. He intended to do so. Unfortunately, Macmillan did not make this insight the political basis in Britain for the Common Market negotiations of 1962. He felt politically safer in basing his public case on economic grounds. Nevertheless, Macmillan was not alone in understanding within Britain that a close tie between London and Bonn was essential for the stability of Europe and the West. And there were supporters in both British parties for the MLF and for a shift of the attenuated British national nuclear capability to a collective Atlantic organization.

There was, of course, also opposition to the MLF in British political life. The Navy scorned mixed manning—an attitude which ignored the long history of mixed manning in the British maritime operations, including Admiral Nelson's crew of a dozen nationalities aboard the *Victory* at Trafalgar.[14] There was still a good deal of the British self-image as a world power, distinct from Europe, and this attitude had tragically inhibited Britain from taking the leadership in Europe offered to it in 1947 and still available to it without effort in the early 1950's. There was also anti-German sentiment, understandable but sterile. There was, among some professional diplomats, a desire to keep the national nuclear capability as a bargaining counter in the Common

Market negotiations. Nevertheless, as of 1962, the balance of political thought in London did not rule out a British decision to join the MLF if, say, the United States, Germany, Italy, and the Netherlands were ready to move ahead.

Thus, although the enterprise was uncertain, the policy of the United States, as of October 22, 1962, was one of laying the proposition before the Europeans, having taken responsibility for intensive and creative staff work to find solutions for the many difficult problems involved. American policy also ruled out a solution to the MRBM problem by sale or transfer of missile technology on a bilateral basis.

The Winter Crisis of 1962–1963

THEN three things happened which, taken together, tossed the MLF—and much more—around like a cork at sea.

First, there was the Cuba missile crisis in late October and its outcome. Instinctively, men (starting with the citizens of West Berlin) knew that the game of nuclear blackmail that Khrushchev had launched after Sputnik had, for a time at least, run its course.

Second, de Gaulle (perhaps aided by the tensions of the Cuba crisis) won, on October 28, 1962, unexpectedly solid support of 62 percent in a national referendum. The issue was Presidential election by popular vote, but the referendum was regarded as a personal test. And only a few weeks later he acquired a clear parliamentary majority for his party, the first single-party majority in modern French history. His political future earlier in 1962 had been viewed as somewhat uncertain, uncertain enough for the National Assembly to challenge him directly on October 5; but by the end of November he had firm ground under his feet for years ahead; and he felt Moscow had been removed as a serious threat to western Europe.

Third, there was Skybolt. Skybolt had been conceived in the 1950s as a device to prolong the effective life of American strategic bombers in the period when Soviet antiaircraft capabilities were rapidly improving. It was a complex two-stage missile carried under the wing of a bomber that could be released a thousand miles from its target. Although there were serious doubts about the feasibility of this device, an agreement was reached in March 1960 between Britain and the United States that the United States would bear the research and development costs of carrying forward Skybolt; the British, in parallel, agreed to make available the Holy Loch base in Scotland for United States nuclear submarines and to abandon its effort to develop its own medium-range ballistic missile; the United States would sell a hundred Skybolt missiles for the British V-bomber force at a price which would not include research and development.

Under such a scheme the British national nuclear capability would become wholly and explicitly dependent on American technology; and, even then, it would consist of a bomber force whose viability could not be envisaged with confidence beyond, say, 1970. Nevertheless, in the short run, important elements in the British diplomatic posture (particularly the domestic posture of the Conservative government) rested on this uncertain base.

Skybolt did not prosper. Its early tests failed and development costs mounted. On January 29, 1962, in hearings before the House of Representatives Subcommittee on Department of Defense Appropriations, McNamara had frankly described how the research and development estimates for Skybolt had risen from $170 million to almost $500 million over the previous eighteen months. Ominously, he evoked an analogy with the ill-fated B-70 bomber.

Early in November 1962 McNamara decided that the cost of the enterprise and its prospects no longer justified going on with it. On November 8 and 9 McNamara warned the British ambassador and Minister of Defense Peter Thorneycroft that he was leaning toward cancellation. In a classic exercise in absentmindedness and human frailty, for a month no one took hold of the problem posed by this impending decision for Anglo–American relations and the relations of both countries to Europe. Kennedy thought Macmillan was at work on the problem. Macmillan thought it was Kennedy's responsibility to come up with an alternative offer; and, in any case, he was puzzled as to how to proceed under circumstances where he did not wish to rock the boat with de Gaulle and faced a severe Navy–Air Force split in his government.[15] McNamara was conscious of the explosive potential of a leak; but postponed visiting London to deal with the matter, under the press of other business.

McNamara's intent to cancel Skybolt leaked to *The New York Times* on December 7; and the issue came instantly to the center of British domestic politics. McNamara went to discuss the matter with Thorneycroft on Monday, the 10th, on the eve of the December NATO meetings (December 13–15).

The situation in London could hardly have been more difficult, exacerbated by Acheson's just but painful remark on December 5 in a speech at West Point that "Great Britain has lost an empire and not yet found a role." To some in Britain it looked as if the cancellation of Skybolt was a purposeful device for forcing the end of the British independent nuclear deterrent role. Without final commitment, the issue of substituting Polaris missiles in British nuclear submarines for Skybolt was raised by Thorneycroft and viewed not unsympathetically by McNamara. To deal with the problem, a Kennedy–Macmillan meeting was arranged in the Bahamas for December 18–21. Before going to Nassau, Macmillan called on de Gaulle on December 15.

De Gaulle, now confident that the Russians were gravely set back by the Cuba missile crisis, and greatly strengthened by the French referendum, made it clear to Macmillan, as best we know, that he was not prepared for British entry into the Common Market.[16] At Nassau, Macmillan, doubly weakened by Skybolt and de Gaulle's intransigence, rejected various propositions Kennedy put to him and made a passionate plea for Polaris submarines as an alternative to Skybolt; and this Kennedy finally granted.

The Polaris alternative had, of course, been in the wind since early December. It was intensively discussed among the Americans who attended the NATO ministerial meeting in Paris. Rusk listened at length to the arguments against it from all his assembled senior diplomatic advisers at Charles E. Bohlen's residence. McNamara and I tramped the streets of Paris one night arguing through the problem.

Among those working on European policy, it appeared to have these disadvantages: by perpetuating a British nuclear capacity, it would make more difficult a collective solution to the European nuclear role. Moreover, it would violate the prior American policy of not making available IRBM's or MRBM's on a bilateral basis and would strengthen de Gaulle's argument that Britain still looked to its bilateral ties across the Atlantic rather than to Europe for its future. Finally it would underline the third-class nuclear status of Germany and Italy, weaken their support for British entry into Europe, and upset the effort of previous years to encourage Europe to move toward collective rather than national solutions to its security and other problems.

Kennedy and his advisers at Nassau were, of course, not insensitive to these considerations. But they were burdened by a sense of obligation arising from the intensified nuclear entanglement with Britain in the wake of Sputnik. And they felt the power of older Anglo–American ties, as the full meaning of the 1960 deal for Holy Loch, as the British saw it, was pressed upon them. Moreover, Britain was a real ally in a complex world. In the Bahamas, Europe, with a strong de Gaulle and a fading Adenauer, must have seemed something of an abstraction.

Kennedy did the best he could, backed against the wall by a political crisis allowed to get out of hand, deriving from a recalcitrant piece of military hardware. He acceded to Macmillan's eloquent and passionate claim for the Polaris missiles as a condition for maintaining continued British confidence in the tie to Washington. But, recognizing the larger impact of the deal on Bonn and Rome, the President sought and achieved agreement that the United States and Great Britain would use their best endeavors to develop a multilateral NATO nuclear force in the closest consultation with other NATO allies. The British also threw into the pot their notion of a multinational force (without mixed manning) in which the United States and the United Kingdom would place under NATO command some part of nuclear forces already in being. In addition, the French were to be jointly approached and offered, in effect, all that would be required to make the British and French positions symmetrical. (It appears that Macmillan did not tell Kennedy how negative de Gaulle had been at Rambouillet.)

It was a moment of maximum leverage for de Gaulle if he chose to move within the framework of the Atlantic Alliance. He received the Anglo–

Saxon ambassadors in Paris enigmatically and kept his counsel—even from his close advisers. On the afternoon of January 14, 1963, de Gaulle, confirming his Rambouillet position, delivered his flat veto of Britain's entry into Europe, exploiting the Nassau meeting to good debating effect. Simultaneously, the Franco–German treaty, in preparation for some time, came to the center of the stage. De Gaulle decided this was the moment for a maximum effort to bring to life his abiding version of a European continent led by France.

De Gaulle imposed in his press conference a painful choice on Bonn. There was a great deal in Adenauer to which de Gaulle could appeal, with his vision of a continental Europe, led by Paris, freed increasingly from Anglo–Saxon influence. Adenauer had old personal scores to settle with the British reaching back to early days in the occupation of Germany. More than that, he was a West German Catholic whose political roots lay in the failure of the Frankfurt Parliament of 1848 and its aftermath. He regarded Prussian dominance of German unification as tragic. A part of him, as Khrushchev correctly perceived, never wanted German reunification, with Prussian Berlin again the capital. Although de Gaulle regarded Adenauer as a provincial, and West Germany as a non-nation, Adenauer found much deeply congenial in de Gaulle and his vision.

But Adenauer was also head of the German government. When George Ball laid before him, on January 14, 1963, the same day as de Gaulle's press conference, a flat American offer to proceed with the MLF, he found it attractive. More important, Washington asked of Bonn, with brutal directness: In what ways will the Franco–German pact affect Germany's commitments in NATO? In Europe, Germany's partners in the Common Market (EEC) wanted to know if Bonn was looking to Franco–German hegemony on the Continent. Whatever Adenauer's personal vision, the balance of power in German politics lay with the Common Market and the Atlantic tie. Thus, when the Franco–German treaty came before the Parliament in Bonn, the Bundestag wrote a preamble that stated that the agreement would not affect Germany's rights and obligations derived from its other treaties, referring explicitly to NATO and the EEC. So far as de Gaulle was concerned, this undid the Franco–German treaty. He recognized clearly that, while he had frustrated British entrance into the Common Market and upset the Americans no end, he had failed in making the rich and provincial Germans (as he viewed them) his satellites. He comforted himself with philosophic observations on how short lived treaties, like roses and the beauty of young girls, sometimes were.

THE MLF AGAIN: A TRANSIENT SECOND-STAGE BOOSTER

THE meaning of these interlacing events for the MLF was, in the short run, to elevate its apparent role in American policy. A letter from Kennedy to Adenauer on January 18, backing George Ball's visit to Bonn, told him that the United States intended to press forward "with utmost vigor." On January 30 Kennedy approved, in principle, negotiations to establish the MLF so long as the American veto in the control arrangements was maintained and the negotiations were conducted in such a way as to avoid damage to American prestige.

Livingston Merchant, a senior ambassador, was added to the earlier team of Gerard Smith and Admiral John Lee, appointed to explore actively the possibilities of support for the MLF, which they did from February 22 to March 17 in Paris. At the end of March Kennedy suggested that he and the other heads of government interested might sign a preliminary MLF agreement during Kennedy's visit to Europe in June. Macmillan's reserve prevented the interim agreement on Kennedy's European trip. But beginning in July, eight nations, without final commitment, began technical discussions in Washington. By October a military subgroup continued in Washington while the nonmilitary aspects of the agreement were carried forward by a working group in Paris. On July 13 Kennedy asked McNamara to see if an experiment might be conducted in mixed manning on an American vessel; and on October 25 the idea was approved in principle. The United Kingdom, the Netherlands, Germany, Italy, Greece, and Turkey joined in the experiment.

In Kennedy's time, then, in the wake of the tumultuous events from October 1962 to January 1963, the MLF appeared to be going forward with more explicit and higher-level American support than in the past and with increased administrative energy. The urgency of finding an alternative to the Common Market for serious British association with the Continent gave the MLF real political weight. Moreover, it fitted Kennedy's findings after a total review of European policy which he conducted in the wake of de Gaulle's January press conference. Ambassador David Bruce was brought back from London to examine afresh whether the American posture toward Europe—support for European unity and the Atlantic partnership—was still a viable framework in the face of de Gaulle's January performance. The upshot was a reaffirmation of the old-time religion, incorporated in Kennedy's speech in the Paulskirche in Frankfurt on June 25, 1963. It firmly and in greater detail reasserted the doctrine of the Grand Design stated in Philadelphia a year earlier. It included this passage on the MLF:

> Nevertheless, it is natural that America's nuclear position has raised questions within the alliance. I believe we must confront these questions—not by turning the clock backward to separate nuclear deterrents—but by developing a more closely unified Atlantic deterrent, with genuine European participation.
>
> How this can best be done, and it is not easy—in some ways more difficult to split the atom politically than it was physically, but how this can best be done is now under discussion with those who may wish to join in this effort. The proposal before us is for a new Atlantic force. Such a force would bring strength instead of weakness,

cohesion instead of division. It would belong to all members, not one, with all participating on a basis of full equality. And as Europe moves towards unity, its role and responsibility, here as elsewhere, would and must increase accordingly.[17]

But, as 1963 moved to its tragic end, there were major unsolved problems, and the road to the MLF looked to Kennedy longer and less urgent than it did immediately post-Nassau:

—Although the British participated fully in the staff work, there was no firm commitment in London to go forward to the end of the line.

—The Italians and Belgians had unsolved political difficulties despite high-level appreciation of the importance of the enterprise in linking Europe and the Atlantic on a critical matter over a period made difficult by de Gaulle's posture.

—The problems that might arise in American politics and the Congress had not yet been confronted.

But while Kennedy intended to keep the MLF in play, as his strong personal interest in the mixed-manned experiment indicated, the environment was changing. Above all, the outcome of the Cuba missile crisis and the movement forward to the nuclear test ban began subtly to alter the setting of the problem. It was one thing to mount a proposition of this kind and to carry it forward in the face of Khrushchev's day-by-day underlining of Europe's vulnerability to nuclear pressure and attack. The urgency would obviously be less and the difficulties to be overcome greater in quieter times. It was in Johnson's administration that these undercurrents of 1963 were strongly to assert themselves.

THE MLF: A PERSONAL VIEW

MY net judgment of Kennedy's approach to the MLF is not dogmatic, as will emerge. Nevertheless, on balance, I believe he was wrong not to decide in 1961–1962 that American leadership should be used quietly but firmly to see the project through to the end.[18] The issue of nuclear arrangements in the Atlantic was a fundamental strategic issue with far-ranging political implications. It was a major interest of the United States that a loose European nuclear arrangement be foreclosed and the nuclear defense of the West be firmly anchored in an Atlantic structure. It was not good enough for Kennedy to say this was a matter on which the United States was prepared to proceed if others wished to do so.

I make this judgment in full awareness of all the difficulties never overcome; and with a lively respect for their reality. And I do so in the knowledge that the nuclear question in the Atlantic subsided gradually in the course of the 1960s, covered by intensive nuclear consultation (launched with great seriousness by McNamara) and by other arrangements. I hold this view for two reasons. First, because the failure of the MLF left Europe politically dead in the water for the rest of the 1960s. The European idea lost momentum with the youth as well as in the foreign offices. (I once heard German Defense Minister Von Hassel say he could recruit better young men for the multilateral force than for the German Navy.) The most active leaders in the European movement and the most active supporters of the Atlantic connection were disheartened by the ultimate outcome of the MLF. Europe settled back to a comfortable interval of relative isolation, fragmentation, and disengagement from responsibility. The burdens of the United States on the world scene were relatively increased by the character of European moods and policies in the 1960s. And to some extent this was a result of the failure of the MLF.

In short, the organization of Europe and its relation to the United States has been and remains a vital American interest. Even in earlier postwar years the United States could not shape Europe to its purposes; but it has had a major stake in the outcome; and Washington's influence was great whether used actively, passively, or negatively.

In particular, American deference to British views in 1962 and thereafter was, I believe, almost as costly to the British (as well as the American) interest as American acquiescence in 1947, at British insistence, in a "weak" secretariat for the Marshall Plan organization in Paris. Britain thereby denied itself the opportunity for continental leadership, already in its hands in the person of Oliver Franks, who was shifted to Washington as ambassador at a critical time. British failure to join Europe through the MLF permitted virtually a decade of sterility or worse in Britain's relations with the Continent to pass.

As a public servant in the 1960s, I was conscious of the tragedy Europe had brought on itself so often over the centuries by its internecine quarrels and, in particular, of the tragic story of Europe since 1914. I was conscious, too, that if Europe was to overcome this heritage, alive in the memories and politics of every European nation, it was unlikely to do so without American leadership and the Atlantic tie; for with all the complex crosscurrents it sets in motion, the American presence in councils with Europeans has been, over the past generation, a factor tending to reduce and heal old divisions among Europeans and, thereby, to strengthen the foundations of a Western civilization sore beset. To that unifying and healing process I believed the MLF would contribute in a vital and sensitive area. If that view earns me a place in the footnotes of history as one of the "theologians" who fought and lost the battle for the MLF, I shall be pleased to be there.

Second, the nuclear problem remains latent and unresolved. With the passage of time, it is quite likely to arise again—as Britain again moves toward Europe, and as the American role in Europe relatively diminishes. The danger of a loose European nuclear arrangement could easily re-emerge. A linking of nuclear forces across the Atlantic satisfactory to all parties under such circumstances is not impossible to envisage; but I think it quite possible that an American administration in the 1970s will regret the MLF Atlantic framework was not put in place at an earlier time.

On the other hand, I recognize that, if we are all lucky, the issue at stake may wither. The world could, conceivably, turn to progressive measures of arms control. The tensions down the center of Europe may abate; the Atlantic nations may never again have to live through and manage a nuclear crisis; the question of Europe's nuclear role and the asymmetry between the British–French and German–Italian positions may never again arise, nor the threat of a loose European nuclear arrangement.

It could, under these circumstances, be judged that Kennedy's (and then Johnson's) policy of two and a half cheers for the MLF was quite sound.

As a historian, I would conclude that in the short run it was the successful outcome of the Cuba missile crisis which, by ending also the rolling Berlin crisis of 1958–1962, fatally undermined the MLF (given Kennedy's cautious stance), despite the artificial second-stage booster generated by the tangle at Nassau. The short-run costs of pressing the MLF appeared to outweigh the short-run benefits, as the urgency of the problem diminished. And the long-run benefits (notably, the avoidance of the possible future dangers of a loose European nuclear arrangement) did not appear sufficiently real to shift the calculus. The importance of that failure cannot yet be assessed. I should be delighted if history proves the MLF unnecessary; and if the problems that gave rise to its formulation quickly and permanently subside. But we cannot yet perceive the end of the road in either nuclear arms control or in the Atlantic relationship, or judge whether the Cuba missile crisis will, in fact, prove to be a nonrecurrent event—a kind of Gettysburg of the Cold War.

24

The Cuba Missile Crisis: "Khrushchev at Bay"

Two Hypotheses

THE CUBA MISSILE CRISIS IS CLEARLY ONE OF THE BENCH MARKS IN modern history. All its consequences cannot, even now, be assessed; for example, the subsequent gross expansion of Soviet nuclear and naval capabilities. It is also a crisis about which, at the American end, a great deal is known.[1] The purpose here is not to rehearse the details but to try to put the crisis into perspective as Khrushchev's climactic effort in the post-Sputnik offensive and to lay a basis for analyzing its subsequent wide-ranging effects within both the communist and noncommunist worlds.

While the literature on the missile crisis itself is ample, there is still ambiguity, debate, and unavoidable ignorance about why, when, and how Khrushchev and his colleagues decided to risk putting the missiles into Cuba.

Elie Abel, a competent and vivid chronicler of the crisis, explains its origins essentially on the grounds that Kennedy's performance down to October 22, 1962, had persuaded Khrushchev that he lacked the fiber to force the removal of the missiles once they were secretly installed.[2] He points to the Bay of Pigs, Kennedy's failure to knock down the Berlin Wall, and Khrushchev's alleged assessment of Kennedy in Vienna. Something like Abel's view is the conventional judgment.

Before the event, as well as during and after, I took a somewhat different view. I judged that Khrushchev, in the spring of 1962, was under extremely powerful pressures to retrieve a waning situation. On August 20, 1962, I gave a speech at the National War College entitled "Khrushchev at Bay"[3]; and it was in similar terms that I initiated discussion of the situation during the following week in meetings with my fellow planners throughout Washington and my colleagues in the State Department, including Dean Rusk.

Why was Khrushchev at bay? He was at bay because by the spring of 1962 his initial post-Sputnik hopes and dispositions had grossly failed: he had greatly committed himself on Berlin but had been unable to shift the Western position; he had failed to achieve a foothold in the Congo; Castro was isolated and neutralized by the OAS, and the Alliance for Progress dimmed longer-run prospects for communist expansion in Latin America; prospects in Southeast Asia were reduced by the July 1962 Geneva Accords on Laos and Kennedy's commitment to Vietnam after the Taylor mission.

On the strategic level, the image of the missile gap had been reversed and the Berlin crisis had triggered a substantial expansion of American arms. This, in turn, increased pressure on Khrushchev for expanded Soviet military outlays to which he had to accede at some cost to economic growth.[4] Aside from increased military outlays, the Soviet economy was slowing down (and there was acute difficulty in agriculture) at a time when American growth was accelerating. Finally, the Moscow meeting at the end of 1960 had failed either to unify the communist movement or to isolate Peking.

All this translated into real political pressures on Khrushchev as the Soviet leader.

Those pressures were evident at the Twenty-Second Party Congress, which opened on October 17, 1961. Out of the Congress emerged a situation where Khrushchev, continuing to use de-Stalinization as a political weapon, failed to eliminate some of his opponents; and he found his power further hedged about by the new constitution of the Presidium, as it had been since the aftermath of the U-2 incident.[5] He was also denied by the decisions of the Congress the resources he wished to invest in agriculture and the expansion of civil consumption.[6] The military had clearly found allies at the Congress and successfully asserted their interests. A whole range of constraints on civil consumption was put into effect in the spring of 1962, including a rise of 20–30 percent in the price of meat and butter.

Khrushchev was under unrelenting ideological pressure from Peking (and Albania) to move forward more decisively against "the imperialists," and Ulbricht had not been fully satisfied by the Wall.

Thus, in the spring of 1962, Khrushchev was looking for a quick success which would enhance his political prestige and power in Soviet politics; enhance his authority in the international communist movement and reduce the pressures on him from Ulbricht as well as the Chinese; redress the military balance cheaply in terms of resources, and thereby permit more Russian resources to flow into civil investment and consumption; and provide leverage for the resolution of the Berlin problem he had sought without success since 1958.

Khrushchev's rationale after the missile crisis was couched in terms of an alleged Cuban request for the missiles to fend off an alleged impending invasion by the United States: a view Castro promptly denied and then elaborated at length in a speech of March 13, 1965, reprinted in *Pravda*.[7] Khrushchev's memoir, nevertheless, tries to perpetuate his initial rationale. But he also acknowledges that he sought, with MRBM's already available, to equalize the nuclear balance of power.

> In addition to protecting Cuba, our missiles would have equalized what the West likes to call "the balance of power." The Americans had surrounded our country with military bases and threatened us with nuclear weapons, and now they would learn just what it feels like to have enemy missiles pointing at you; we'd be doing nothing more than giving them a little of their own medicine. And it was high time America learned what it feels like to have her own land and her own people threatened. We Russians have suffered three wars over the last half century: World War I, the Civil War, and World War II. America has never had to fight a war on her own soil, at least not in the past fifty years. She's sent troops abroad to fight in the two World Wars—and made a fortune as a result. America has shed a few drops of her own blood while making billions by bleeding the rest of the world dry.[8]

Khrushchev's Plan and Its Rationale

Khrushchev dates the time when the idea seized him—when "all these thoughts kept churning in my head"—to his visit to Bulgaria, completed on May 21. He then describes how he came back to Moscow and persuaded his colleagues to launch the plan, making clear it was collectively approved.

Khrushchev may or may not be precise about timing. His dating of events in his memoir is notably fuzzy. He evidently did not have his files with him in his dacha after retirement. In any case, a good deal was happening in the spring of 1962 in Moscow.[9] In late April two Soviet marshals, associated with the missile command, were relieved of their posts, to be restored only in November. Possibly they opposed the Cuban venture, which may have been discussed at a Presidium meeting at the time of the Supreme Soviet, April 22–25. The tone of Soviet statements about Berlin began to harden, after a quiet interval, on May 3 when *Pravda* carried a major article on Berlin warning the West that "whoever sows the wind will reap the whirlwind." The Soviet–Bulgarian communique of May 21 revived the threat of a separate peace treaty. The June Warsaw Pact communique promised the West "a bitter awakening."

On April 28, in the week when the hardening on Berlin could be noted, Cuban Minister of Public Works Osmani Cienfuegos was seen by Khrushchev, who also saw the Cuban ambassador on May 5. At the beginning of June, Khrushchev spoke of a new flow of arms to Cuba which might have a salutary "effect on the minds of those who are thinking of starting a new war." At just this period Washington was receiving reports from Moscow[10] that Chinese diplomats were going about town saying they were quite pleased with the Russians who had found a "new way" to solve the Berlin problem.[11] Raul Castro arrived in Moscow on July 2, and enlarged flows of military equipment moved to Cuba during that month, continuing through August. With the scale of the operation impossible to conceal, increased arms deliveries to Cuba were formally announced September 3, on the occasion of Che Guevara's stay in Moscow.[12] Khrushchev then undertook his campaign to deceive Kennedy on the character of the shipments and to "reassure" him on Berlin.

On September 12 *Pravda* carried the following statement:

> The Soviet Government has authorized Tass to declare that the Soviet Union does not need to ship to any country, to Cuba for instance, any actual equipment in order to repel aggression and deal a retaliatory blow. The explosive force of our nuclear capabilities is so powerful and the Soviet Union has such a large number of powerful rockets for the delivery of these atomic warheads that there is no need to seek any site for their installation outside the borders of the Soviet Union.

Six days earlier Dobrynin had sought out Sorensen and dictated the following personal message from Khrushchev to Kennedy:

> Nothing will be undertaken before the American Congressional elections that could complicate the international situation or aggravate the tension in the relations between our two countries . . . provided there are no actions taken on the other side which would change the situation. This includes a German peace settlement and West Berlin. . . .[13]

To the flow of visitors through Moscow that summer, Khrushchev reaffirmed that the question of Berlin and a German peace settlement would be quiet until after the American election in November; but if the West did not accept his position, there would be serious trouble thereafter. He linked such talk to the possibilities that might open for negotiation upon the occasion of his visit to New York.[14]

Khrushchev's objectives were, then, quite clear: to present Kennedy with the installation of the missiles as a fait accompli under the cover of an enlarged flow of conventional arms; and to come to New York after the congressional elections in November and bargain on Berlin, bases, and other matters from a position of strength cheaply achieved: MRBM's under the American radar screen targeted at the major American cities. As he had underlined at Vienna (in talking about his treaty with East Germany), the situation Khrushchev planned to create in Cuba was one where Kennedy would have to start the war.

At the time, my own crystal ball was by no means that clear; but it was not wholly opaque. The minutes summarizing my presentation to

Rusk and my colleagues on August 28 include this passage, following on a description of the frustration of the post-Sputnik offensive and the hopeful prospects it might open up:

> . . . before things get better they may get worse. We must view the present and immediate future as a time of special danger. Khrushchev may seek to break out of his frustrations. Three areas appear to merit special watchfulness:
>
> —*The arms race*: Khrushchev may stake heavily on an important breakthrough that would furnish a hard military base for a renewed offensive.
>
> —*Berlin*: Khrushchev may feel under strong compulsion to achieve at least one success to which he can point, and may be prepared to step up the risk rate over Berlin.
>
> —*Cuba*: Khrushchev may be unwilling to accept as final the failure of Cuba to produce automatic gains in Latin America and may decide to increase substantially Soviet outlays and risks to secure a payoff from Cuba.

Why did Khrushchev believe the Cuba missile plan might work? Why, if Berlin was a major objective, did he not take greater risks there? Tatu responds to these questions as follows:

> The lengthy negotiations conducted with the West for years had convinced him [Khrushchev] that the Atlantic camp would regard any violation of freedom of access to West Berlin as a *casus belli*. By placing his rockets in Cuba, on the other hand, Khrushchev was doing nothing illegal and was on the contrary forcing his opponent to act illegally if he wished to react at all. . . . In 1961 Kennedy had in fact appeared much firmer on Berlin—where he held out against the very violent pressure of that summer by taking military measures, and so forth—than on Cuba, where he had not dared push his Bay of Pigs operation to its logical conclusion. As seen by the resolute gambler in Moscow, Cuba was the weak spot.[15]

I rather doubt Tatu's observation on the Bay of Pigs. Soviet missiles in Cuba were a different matter than a Cuban refugee operation against Castro. Kennedy at Vienna could not have been more explicit about how he would react to an effort to shift the balance of power; and this, in the most literal sense, is what Khrushchev set out to do.

But I agree with Tatu that it must have seemed attractive to Khrushchev to be acting legally while putting Kennedy in the position of having to initiate military action with no legal basis except some OAS resolutions Khrushchev had probably never read. Looked at from Moscow, the installation of missiles in Cuba must have seemed, in one sense, as legal as the placing of American missiles in Turkey. Khrushchev knew, of course, what

Kennedy had said at Vienna about shifting the balance of power. He knew of the Monroe Doctrine and the OAS posture generalized from it, which would deny the legitimacy of extra-continental military intrusion in the hemisphere. What he did not assess correctly is the depth of feeling and determination his act would evoke from Kennedy (or, in my judgment, from any other American President) and the unanimity of the hemispheric response.

KENNEDY REACTS

As rumors of offensive missiles in Cuba spread, Kennedy set about trying to disabuse Khrushchev of the notion that he would remain passive if offensive missiles turned up. On September 4 he said "the gravest issues" would arise if their presence was established; and on September 13 he volunteered this carefully drafted statement:

> If at any time the Communist buildup in Cuba were to endanger or interfere with our security in any way, including our base at Guantanamo, our passage to the Panama Canal, our missile and space activities at Cape Canaveral, or the lives of American citizens in this country, or if Cuba should ever attempt to export its aggressive purposes by force or the threat of force against any nation in this hemisphere, or become an offensive military base of significant capacity for the Soviet Union, then this country will do whatever must be done to protect its own security and that of its allies.[16]

It was a quite complete formulation of the functional approach to Cuba which had emerged since the Bay of Pigs.

As September unfolded, Khrushchev may have had doubts; for example, he never committed himself publicly to go to the U.N. General Assembly. But the operation was rolling, and he was going to see what would happen.

I remember recalling in September 1962 the biography of Khrushchev we had read in galley proofs before Vienna. In a vivid chapter it described the substantial engineering risks Khrushchev took in building the Moscow subway to meet his tight deadline.[17] He was a gambler. If, in fact, he felt at bay, I thought he would go out with a bang rather than a whimper. With the missiles moving across the Atlantic in September, he was embarked on the greatest gamble of his career. I suspect he relished those days. There is even a flavor of pleasurable excitement as he recalls in his memoir the days of most acute crisis: "[I] slept on my couch in the office—and I kept my clothes on. I didn't want to be like that Western minister [Guy Mollet] who was caught literally with his pants down by the Suez events of 1956 and who had to run around in his shorts until the emergency was over."[18]

But I believe the Soviet plan was written in such a way as to exclude war with the United States. Khrushchev's statement on this point carries conviction: "I want to make one thing absolutely clear: when we put our ballistic missiles in Cuba, we had no desire to start a war."[19] At no stage during the crisis did the Soviet armed forces go on an alert equivalent to that which governed American forces. The Presidium had acquiesced in Khrushchev's plan; but it had also decided that the gamble would involve Khrushchev's political career, not all the Soviets had achieved since 1917.

The high-level Washington scene from Monday, October 15, to Sunday, October 28, has been about as fully described as any time and place in modern history. In essence, there were these distinct moments of decision: Khrushchev's decision not to force the blockade on October 24; Khrushchev's decision to cease erecting the missiles and to withdraw them on October 28; Castro's decision to reject inspection (circa October 30); Khrushchev's decision to withdraw the IL-14 bombers on November 20.

Once it was decided in Moscow that the blockade would not be forced, Khrushchev had to see what might be salvaged. Kennedy had to see that nothing of substance was salvaged while minimizing Khrushchev's humiliation. The quiet but real buildup of conventional military power in Florida and elsewhere was decisive. I took part in the discussions of October 27 on the appropriate scale of the air strike (which probably would have occurred on Tuesday, October 30) and supported McNamara's case for a limited attack rather than a total assault embracing all the Cuban air bases and antiaircraft installations. Khrushchev smelled the seriousness of all this, and, essentially, his letter of the next day ended the matter, although weeks of tangled diplomacy followed.

A Planner's Observations

I have little to add to knowledge of the mechanics of these events, among other reasons because of my limited part in the day-to-day unfolding of the crisis. I was in Europe during most of the week of deliberations preceding Kennedy's speech of October 22, attending a meeting of the Atlantic Policy Advisory Group, the NATO planners' club created to expand the area of political consultation. I also went to Berlin to see how the viability program was coming along in the face of the Wall. Landing in New York on Friday the 19th, I was told to return promptly to Washington rather than to a Camp David session that had been arranged previously. My first official contact with the crisis was a session in the White House Situation Room on Sunday night, October 21, to go over the draft of Kennedy's speech of the next day. Subsequently, I managed a planning group set up in support of the ExCom (Executive Committee of the NSC). Our contributions were in the form of written reports and the various enterprises we spawned in the form of military plans and diplomatic initiatives. I attended only a few of the ExCom sessions, but I was there on the memorable occasion (October 24) when news arrived that Soviet ships had stopped outside the quarantine area and Rusk made his famous remark on eyeballs and the first blink. As a planner at the time, and in historical retrospect, I would make only a few observations.

First, the genius of Kennedy's blockade—"selective quarantine," as it was termed—was, in part, that it required Khrushchev to initiate military action. It was the obverse of the dilemma posed for the United States by Soviet interference with Allied traffic to Berlin. Khrushchev had to start the war if his merchant ships were to go through.[20] One had the feeling that Soviet contingency planners had never done the kind of laborious work Western planners carried out on the questions of harassment of the Berlin routes. It is even possible that Moscow never anticipated a quarantine or blockade as one of Kennedy's options.

Second, the rallying of the Latin Americans during the missile crisis carried elements of conviction and credibility that were not wholly anticipated. The unanimity of the OAS was an impressive political fact in Moscow, at the United Nations, and elsewhere; and the evoking of the Punta del Este Resolution II of January 1962 gave Kennedy a solid legal basis for his action, urging, as it did, "member states to take those steps they may consider appropriate for their individual or collective self-defense, and to cooperate, as may be necessary or desirable, to strengthen their capacity to counteract threats or acts of aggression, subversion, or other dangers to peace and security resulting from the continued intervention in this hemisphere of Sino-Soviet powers. . . ."

Third, there were real differences of view in the administration as to how dangerous the situation really was; that is, on whether Khrushchev was conducting a hair-raising, precarious probe or whether the Soviet Union had decided to put real muscle behind the endeavor. From any perspective, it was an exceedingly dangerous interval; but one's judgment of Soviet motivation and intent mattered a good deal in assessing how near we all actually were to nuclear war. It was one thing to view Khrushchev's initiative as a full-fledged, deeply meant Russian strategic challenge in the Caribbean; another, to regard it as an incredibly risky gamble by a man at bay, who would back down if he met resolute force. These differences, intensely felt, came to rest on the question of whether Kennedy should negotiate out the Turkish missiles to achieve a settlement. Kennedy carried a liability he had earlier tried to liquidate[21]; but he preserved the integrity of NATO by not bargaining a European asset against a direct American interest. In so doing, I suspect his assessment of the risks was somewhat higher than that of those who had concluded that Khrushchev's gamble was a desperate effort to retrieve a waning situation but not a determined Soviet strategic thrust to shift the balance of power.

Fourth, the Washington bureaucracy was remarkably light on its feet, more generally responsive, alert, and effective than I had seen it in the twenty years or so over which I had observed or participated in its workings. It operated less like a governmental machine than like a regimental command post in combat, despite the extraordinarily complex military and diplomatic enterprise under way. There was, throughout, a sense of direct and personal command by the President.

The planning group over which I presided, representing some of the best minds in the second level of government, was quite like-minded in interpreting the crisis, its origins, and the implications for the future. We had been meeting without fail every week on one concrete problem after another, followed by a lunch in which we would exchange wider perspectives. We had the advantage of time to reflect at length on the meaning of the sharpening Soviet position on Berlin since the spring. In the wake of my War College talk, "Khrushchev at Bay," we had canvassed the possibilities of a convulsive effort by Khrushchev to retrieve his waning position. We thought his three major options were: Berlin, an orbiting weapon in space, Cuba. As I recall, Ray Cline of the CIA was the most perceptive among us. I closed the meeting on August 21 by observing we might be about to see the greatest act of risk-taking since the war. Cline said: "Maybe we're seeing it right now in Cuba." But none of us thought Moscow was about to risk nuclear war. Therefore, our individual and collective advice, from the beginning to the end of the crisis, was to keep the pressure on Moscow until the missiles and bombers were out. The only thing we thought had to be bargained away was the quarantine imposed on October 22.[22]

The planners met for some weeks after the peak of the crisis had passed to probe at its implications.

We all were conscious that the tactical situation in the Caribbean had peculiar advantages for the United States, given the preponderance of naval, conventional air, and ground strength that could be brought to bear relative to that which Moscow could mount. We did not believe the outcome of the crisis justified an exuberant or casual application of American military power to resolve other issues in dispute.

One recommendation was to see if Khrushchev was prepared to move along the other fork in the nuclear road: toward a nuclear test ban.

In the longer run we judged that Moscow would conduct a fundamental review of its military strategy. The upshot might be: a revision in military doctrine which would not rule out limited clashes of United States and Soviet military power, accompanied by a buildup in Soviet conventional military strength; a radical long-term expansion in Soviet ICBM capabilities to achieve a solid balance in United States–Soviet nuclear power; a second effort to achieve an economical shift in the nuclear balance (e.g., weapons orbiting in space); a serious Soviet move toward arms control.

In fact, the Soviet Union did move in the post-Cuba missile crisis years toward a radical buildup in strategic nuclear strength; and it eased cautiously toward the negotiation of a missile agreement as its nuclear strength came into balance with the United States. It also appears to have drawn Mahanist conclusions from its experience with American naval power in the Caribbean. The Cuba missile crisis, in effect, rendered anachronistic current Soviet military doctrine. The great post-Stalin review of Soviet military strategy organized by Marshal V. A. Sokolovsky (published May 1962) had shifted doctrine, to a degree, toward missiles, leaving a diminished though still large role for conventional ground forces.[23] No naval officer contributed to Sokolovsky's volume.[24] The debate Sokolovsky straddled was between "radicals" (like Khrushchev) who believed nuclear missiles permitted a sharp reduction in conventional ground force and naval strength, and "conservatives" who thought in terms of protracted war in Europe, on the ground, in continuity with the sweep of Russian history. On the eve of the Cuba missile crisis, the Sokolovsky volume tended to favor the position of the "radicals," but its moderation tempered the more sweeping pronouncements of Khrushchev, leaving ample place for conventional forces and military claims on the Soviet budget.

But the Sokolovsky doctrine did not fit the case of Cuba. More generally, it did not match a Soviet policy of seeking power and influence in the developing regions, across seas over which Russian military power had never sought to project itself, except in the disastrous Russo–Japanese War. The setback of the Cuba missile crisis dramatized that gap between Soviet policy and its military force structure. It undoubtedly led to the buildup of Soviet naval (as well as strategic nuclear) strength in the 1960s; and, by demonstrating the advantages of logistical proximity, the Cuba missile crisis may well have induced Moscow to concentrate its expansionist zeal for a time in the Middle East.

POLITICAL CONSEQUENCES: MOSCOW AND PEKING

POLITICALLY, the outcome of the crisis had two major effects in the communist world: it undercut Khrushchev's already eroded power base in Moscow; and it led to a new phase of violent and open polemic between Moscow and Peking.

Tatu cites impressive evidence that Khrushchev began to lose power and status within the collective leadership from as early as October 23, the day after Kennedy announced his response to the challenge.[25] The signs were both symbolic and substantive. They included the renaming on October 25 of the town of Khrushchev to Kremges; oblique attacks on Khrushchev's use of de-Stalinization as a political instrument against his opponents; a shift away from economic liberalism in November; and increased pressure on Soviet intellectuals and artists. A low point came in February–March 1963 when Khrushchev appeared somewhat helpless and disheartened. On February 28 he referred to the fact that he would soon be sixty-nine years old and *Pravda* published his concluding remark: "Thank you for having gathered here to cheer me up, as it were."[26] This was also a time when Moscow made a serious effort to play down the quarrel with Peking, which had accused Khrushchev of first taking excessive risk in launching the Cuba missile crisis and then failing to back his play.

At this point, it appeared that Kozlov, backed by the anti-Khrushchev group in the Presidium, would soon emerge as his successor. But about April 10 Kozlov suffered a severe heart attack; and by the end of the month Khrushchev was engaged in a limited but vigorous comeback. On April 20, 1963, he was confident enough to tell an Italian newspaper director: ". . . there are times when the rule of one far-seeing man is better than that of several who cannot see."[27]

On this basis he moved to the test ban treaty and revived his campaign against Stalinism. But, while he had gained a transient tactical victory in Kremlin politics, his post-Sputnik strategy was in a shambles. As 1963 drew to a close, nuclear blackmail as a means of pressure on western Europe was, for the time, a discredited device; nowhere in the developing world did he have effective leverage; the Soviet economy was in evident disarray, with a bad harvest requiring large grain imports; and relations with Peking had never been worse.

Peking's Parallel Adventure

We do not know, of course, exactly what went on in Peking—and between Peking and Moscow—in the months after the Chinese got wind of the Cuba missile plan in the spring of 1962. The best guess at the time ran about as follows: when Peking learned of the Cuba plan in the spring of 1962, it decided it would prepare for a simultaneous exercise in the expansion of power, despite the deep economic crisis on the mainland. It may have reasoned that if Moscow succeeded quickly in the Caribbean, China ought to be able to stand before the world communist movement as at least equally activist in moving forward against "the imperialists." If Moscow became embroiled for a protracted period with Washington, Peking could envisage a reasonably free hand along the Indian frontier. But it was cautious. It chose a locale where American air and naval power could not easily be brought to bear against the Chinese forces engaged. It chose an issue where American commitments were minimal and there was little or no danger that their probe might lead to American attack on the Chinese mainland.

The move from Tibet against India obviously required considerable preparation, given the logistical problems involved and the need to accumulate stockpiles as well as combat-ready forces. The protracted Indian–Chinese debate about the ambiguous border provided an occasion.[28]

What actually happened over the Cuban missiles may have been the one outcome Peking had not anticipated; that is, a quick withdrawal. But the Chinese were already committed by the time Kennedy made his speech announcing the quarantine. The shift from border skirmishing to Chinese assault can be dated from about October 20. Special groups in the American government were set up to monitor the affair. Ambassador John Kenneth Galbraith's understandably urgent cables from New Delhi began to be answered by October 27. By Monday morning, October 29, Washington was in a position to devote quite a lot of attention to the Chinese–Indian problem.

By October 26 Nehru, rejecting mediation, had asked for selective American military assistance. Aid was granted, including special equipment in short supply and an airlift of supplies to Indian forces operating at high altitudes. On November 20 Kennedy announced he would unleash Averell Harriman the next day to "assess Indian needs"; and on November 21 the Chinese announced that they would stop shooting and withdraw by December 1 from Indian territory, as they defined it. Harriman spent perhaps more time in India discussing Kashmir than arms shipments.[29]

Although the Chinese clearly outmatched the poorly prepared and awkwardly positioned Indian forces, they created an enemy: they incurred some of the costs of the Franco–Prussian War of 1870 without gaining an equivalent of Alsace–Lorraine.

The Russians offended New Delhi by not coming promptly to its assistance and offended Peking by refusing to side with China and by not cutting off its existing military aid agreements with India. The Russians in New Delhi were in the position of expressing the wistful hope that, while they understood the need for American assistance, a formal United States–Indian pact would not emerge.

FROM SCHISM TO SPLIT

AGAINST the background of events in the Caribbean and the Himalayas, the Moscow–Peking debate moved from theoretical polemic to fishwifery. The Chinese attacked Khrushchev's Caribbean performance as both "adventurism" and "capitulationism." Khrushchev reminded Mao that he had done nothing about Hong Kong and Macao. The Chinese began to recall the origins of the Sino–Soviet border in czarist imperialist expansion, and thus to question its legitimacy.

These unseemly exchanges gave way to more formal ideological polemics, rooted in appropriate Leninist texts, on the occasion of Tito's visit to Moscow in December 1962. Peking took the view that Khrushchev was violating the agreed Moscow statement of December 1960. The upshot was a tendency for the communist movement to veer toward a sharper split in the early months of 1963: the European parties, except in Albania, grouping around Moscow; the Asian parties moving closer to Peking. In fact, however, the groupings were loose. The net effect of the intensified conflict between Moscow and Peking was to provide greater freedom of action and expression throughout the communist movement as a whole and, indeed, to breed or heighten splits within national communist parties.

In short, both the outcome of Khrushchev's Cuban venture and his subsequent movement toward détente with the United States served to accelerate the diffusion of power within the communist and noncommunist worlds.

Among the consequences of this process was Hanoi's movement away from a middle position between the two communist giants toward an alignment with Peking closer than any since 1957. It was against this background, out of its own tragic dynamics, that the fragile postcolonial political structure of South Vietnam fell apart.

25

Southeast Asia

Reading the Lansdale Report, February 2, 1961

In his first few weeks in office Kennedy set aside a half-hour late on Thursday afternoons for us to take stock. These sessions were soon overwhelmed by the intensive flow of regular business. Before the second of these meetings, Andrew Goodpaster, who had stayed on for a transitional period from the Eisenhower administration, handed me a report, urged me to read it and to consider calling it to Kennedy's attention. It was a twelve-page account of Vietnam, viewed on the spot as of early January 1961, by Brigadier General Edward Lansdale whose experience there went back six years. He had earlier worked closely with Magsaysay in dealing with the Huk rebellion in the Philippines. He knew more about guerrilla warfare on the Asian scene than any other American. He had an extraordinary sensitivity and respect for the political problems of postcolonial nations and for the human beings caught up in them. No one had a better right to form an assessment of the situation in Vietnam and to have that assessment taken seriously.

When I went in to see the President at 3:40 P.M. on February 2, I told him I had a paper I thought he ought to read. He said time was tight and he was committed to another appointment in a half-hour: should he read it all? I said yes.

Lansdale's report described the rapid progress the communists had made during 1960 in extending their influence and control in the Vietnamese countryside. Their forces were expanding both by large-scale infiltration from the north through Laos and by increased Viet Cong mobilization in the south. He found the communists much nearer a takeover than he had realized from reports read in Washington. He judged that 1961 would prove a fateful year. He described Prime Minister Ngo Dinh Diem, his strengths and weaknesses, and the opposition to Diem, which he had canvassed extensively. He felt that another coup would, in time, be attempted despite the failure of November 11, 1960; and the communists would be more alert to exploit it next time.

Lansdale urged that the United States continue to support Diem and work with him. He noted that he and Diem were friends; but also that Diem had put other friends of his in jail or exiled them—his friendship was not blind. But he also felt it urgent to encourage the opposition to organize itself constructively. At the moment, it was wholly negative, without plans or ideas. If an opposition party developed, Diem would have to group his supporters into a larger political organization that might temper his operating style. A kind of two-party system could emerge that might, at some stage, permit an orderly transfer of power, if Diem did not learn how to exercise his leadership in a less personal and disruptive way.

On the American side he urged specific changes in personnel, attitude, and practice.

On balance, he thought Vietnam could be saved if the United States used its full influence to encourage the Vietnamese to organize and operate in new ways. But his account of the situation clearly reflected the possibility, or even likelihood, of major crisis in Vietnam in the coming year. It was a somber but constructive report—concrete, lucid, and well written.

As Kennedy looked up, he said with curiosity: "This is the worst one we've got, isn't it? You know, Eisenhower never mentioned it. He talked at length about Laos, but never uttered the word Vietnam."[1] We talked for a while about the links between the problems in Laos and Vietnam and about the painful difficulties guerrilla warfare could impose on a young, troubled nation. He instructed me to go deeply into the problem of Vietnam and get him some materials to read about guerrilla warfare in general. He soon had the works of Mao and Guevara around the Mansion as well as Khrushchev's passages on "Wars of National Liberation" from his speech of January 6, 1961.

Kennedy had followed Vietnam for many years, at least since his visit in 1951. He had twice spoken about it in the Senate, including a speech in praise of Diem. He did not have to be told how grave a matter it was if Lansdale's portrait was correct and Diem's grasp over the political life of South Vietnam was disintegrating under the mixture of increased communist pressure and noncommunist dissidence.

LAOS

WHILE the President took stock of the slow-moving degeneration under way in South Vietnam, Laos was in roaring crisis and could not wait.

On March 9, 1961, Kennedy asked me to set down what we had done about Laos since January 20. My response contained the following points:

> We decided to seek a diplomatic solution in Laos based on a neutral commission. As a means of maximizing our bargaining position, an offensive was to be launched by General Phoumi against the Plaine des Jarres, which called for its capture, on our estimate, in the period of February 6–27.
>
> . . . In line with our diplomatic proposal, the King of Laos made his declaration of policy on February 19; but the neutral proposal had evidently failed by the end of February. Neither Burma nor Cambodia would play.
>
> By February 27 it was also clear that General Phoumi was incapable of coping with the armed resistance of the opposition. . . . On March 6–7 a probing operation by the Pathet Lao forces pushed General Phoumi's forces out of the Phou Khoun road junction, the area from which he had hoped to launch his offensive. Although General Phoumi has stated his intention of regaining the road junction, the capabilities and morale of his forces are in question.
>
> On the diplomatic front, pressures are growing for an ICC conference. Diplomatically the British support for our position has been somewhat ambiguous; and the French have been, on the whole, openly dissident with respect to both Phoumi and ourselves.
>
> In short, our initial dispositions with respect to Laos, both diplomatically and militarily, have not succeeded; and we enter a new phase.

The summary did not do justice to the extent of the military and political disarray in that harassed kingdom; but Kennedy did not need to be reminded of the colorful details.

The fact was that the Pathet Lao (plus some North Vietnamese forces) were well on the way to military victory and a takeover of Laos, backed by Soviet arms shipments and the airlift. American power alone could prevent that outcome.

Kennedy was not about to see Laos fall to the communists; but every experience of the situation in his first weeks of responsibility drove him to the conclusion that American forces should not engage there, if there was any way to avoid it: Laotians had little sense of national cohesion and limited military ability; the supply lines from Thai ports were long; the geography of the country decreed an extremely long front along the Mekong; the terrain, beyond the Mekong valley, was forbidding; Laos bordered on Communist China and American engagement there threatened to draw in Chinese forces, as had the movement toward the Yalu in Korea in 1950.

But Kennedy's task, as he saw it, was to convince the communists that he would, in fact, fight if necessary to avoid a communist takeover while seeking a political settlement.

In a press conference of March 23 Kennedy moved on both fronts. He dramatized memorably the importance he attached to the emergence of a neutral, independent Laos, and the extent to which exterior forces were engaged and responsible for the expansion of communist control over parts of the country. And he threw his weight behind a British proposal for "a prompt end of hostilities and prompt negotiation."

For the long pull, this was the occasion when Kennedy first impressed on the American people and the world his unambiguous commitment to the defense of Southeast Asia as a whole, as well as of Laos:

> No one should doubt our resolutions on this point. We are faced with a clear and one-sided threat of a change in the internationally agreed position of Laos. This threat runs counter to the will of the Laotian people, who wish only to be independent and neutral. It is posed rather by the military operations of internal dissident elements directed from outside the country. This is what must end if peace is to be achieved in Southeast Asia. . . .
>
> My fellow Americans, Laos is far away from America, but the world is small. Its two million people live in a country three times the size of Austria. The security of all Southeast Asia will be endangered if Laos loses its neutral independence. Its own safety runs with the safety of us all—in real neutrality observed by all.[2]

In the short run, the problem was to orchestrate persuasively American military moves, which would make Kennedy's ultimate commitment credible, with the diplomatic process he wished to set in motion. In the first weeks of the Kennedy administration the government had vacillated between pure diplomacy and the raw use of power in dealing with Laos. In a memorandum of March 10, 1961, I made the case to Kennedy for a more effective orchestration of the political and military instruments available to him.[3]

Given communist policy, the problem was not abstract and philosophical. Moscow and Hanoi evidently had in mind Dien Bien Phu and the Geneva Conference of 1954. They wanted an international conference without a cease-fire, so that military advances in the field could steadily improve their position at the negotiating table. Kennedy, quite conscious of the 1954 analogy, wanted a cease-fire before the conference. Between March 23 and the opening of the Geneva Conference on May 16, Kennedy had to make a whole series of moves to convince the communists that he would use force in Laos if they did not stop their creeping movement toward the Mekong. I reported to Kennedy, for example, on April 17 that communist forces were probing toward the Mekong town of Takhek and that some military action might be required if "we do not wish to enter the conference with Laos split." General Lyman Lemnitzer and Averell Harriman, then in Southeast Asia, told him that the American bargaining position at the conference would be strengthened if some U.S. forces were stationed across the Mekong in Thailand. Kennedy's most significant action in this direction came early in May when he loaded Marines stationed at Okinawa, against a background of congressional consultations in which, with the exception of Senator Styles Bridges, he had no support for putting forces into the area. His action (much on Khrushchev's mind at Vienna) convinced Moscow that a cease-fire would have to be accepted; the Marines remained on Okinawa and the way was open for the fifteen months of diplomacy that yielded the Laos Accords of 1962.

Hanoi was prepared to have Laos fall into its lap with a modest effort; but it did not wish to induce the engagement of American forces in Southeast Asia. Its primary target was South Vietnam. All it needed for that exercise were the infiltration trails through Laos.

Laos by no means disappeared from Kennedy's agenda with the opening of the Geneva Conference in May. A three-ring circus proceeded, requiring many Presidential decisions: the rehabilitation of Souvanna (begun by Harriman in March) and American support for him as the central figure in Lao politics; the terms of the settlement itself; and a series of communist cease-fire violations climaxed by substantial attacks in May 1962 at Nam Tha and elsewhere that subsided only after Kennedy sent some 5,000 American troops to Thailand and dispatched units of the Seventh Fleet to the Gulf of Thailand.

VIETNAM: FIRST MOVES

WITH the opening of the conference at Geneva and a wobbly cease-fire, Kennedy was free to turn to the problem of Vietnam, strengthened by the appointment early in June of Maxwell Taylor as a personal military adviser to the President.

Kennedy had decided, out of these first four months of experience, that if he had to engage American forces in Southeast Asia, he would do so in Vietnam rather than Laos. He wished, of course, to avoid any fighting, there or elsewhere; but he had arrived at some basic conclusions which ran counter to the thrust of the military contingency plan for the area he had inherited, SEATO Plan Five.

That plan had elements of flexibility but was geared, essentially, to holding the long line of the Mekong in Laos and thus defending Thailand and the rest of Southeast Asia. Every aspect of Laos convinced Kennedy it was the wrong place to do battle. Vietnam appeared to have relative advantages, which Kennedy once tersely ticked off to me in these terms: relatively speaking, it was a more unified nation; its armed forces were larger and better trained; it had direct access to the sea; its geography permitted American air and naval power to be more easily brought to bear; there was the cushion of North Vietnam between South Vietnam and the Chinese border.

It was not easy for the Joint Chiefs to shift their perspective, although an extraordinarily disheveled NSC meeting of April 27, 1961, revealed palpable reservations among some of the military about actually engaging American forces along the Mekong.[4] From that time forward, and, especially, after the Geneva Conference opened, a different approach to Southeast Asia had to be evolved. Given Hanoi's priorities and the gathering weight of communist pressure, its focus came to be Vietnam.

Kennedy's formal actions on Vietnam in 1961 can be summarized as follows:

January 28: approved negotiation with Diem on new counterinsurgency plan to train and expand South Vietnamese forces, which involved $42 million of U.S. assistance against a series of military and civil reforms on the part of Saigon.

April 29: approved slight increase in Military Advisory Group to support 20,000 expansion in Vietnamese armed forces.

May 9: sent Vice President Johnson on a six-day trip to Southeast Asia.

June 9: received Diem's letter proposing 100,000 increase in Vietnamese armed forces and requesting United States economic and training support for the expansion.

August 11: approved support for 30,000 increase in Vietnamese military forces if United States and Vietnamese agreed on a plan to use those forces.

September 27: received report of communist temporary seizure of provincial capital, Phuoc Vinh, heightening sense of crisis in Washington and Saigon.

October 18: sent Taylor mission to Southeast Asia.

November 22: approved all but two major recommendations of Taylor report: dispatch of 6000 to 8000 United States operational force and Diem's request for Lansdale as a personal adviser.

The Key Issues

The first issue was strategic: Should the United States decide to prevent the fall of Southeast Asia to the lively communist offensive under way in Vietnam, Laos, and, at a lower but potentially dangerous level, in northeast Thailand? Vice President Johnson, who had been sent to Vietnam in the first half of May, made a report that contained the following observations: that Kennedy's willingness to negotiate with the communists over Laos had shaken the confidence of Asians in the American commitment; that the communist offensive was real and aimed at the whole of Southeast Asia; that the struggle was far from lost, but only American leadership and commitment could tip the balance; that the Asian leaders did not want

American fighting forces under present circumstances; that Vietnam was critical; we had to help or throw in the towel in the whole area; Diem was complex, sore beset, remote from his people, and surrounded by persons less admirable and capable than himself; that the enemy was not only communism, but hunger, ignorance, poverty, and disease.

Kennedy turned over the fundamental questions posed by Vietnam during the spring and summer, buying time with limited commitments of additional American resources.

In a joint memorandum of July 27, this is how Taylor and I (who were then working as a team on Southeast Asia) stated for him the choices he confronted:

> to disengage from the area as gracefully as possible;
>
> to find as soon as possible a convenient political pretext and attack with American military force the regional source of aggression in Hanoi; or
>
> to build as much indigenous military, political and economic strength as we can in the area, in order to contain the thrust from Hanoi while preparing to intervene with U.S. military force if the Chinese Communists come in or the situation otherwise gets out of hand.

Before deciding American power and influence had to be used to save Southeast Asia, Kennedy asked himself, and put sharply to others, the question: What would happen if we let Southeast Asia go? Kennedy's working style was to probe and question a great many people while keeping his own counsel and making the specific decisions the day required. Only this one time do I recall his articulating the ultimate reasoning behind the positions at which he arrived. It was after the Taylor mission, shortly before I left the White House for the State Department.

He began with domestic political life. He said if we walked away from Southeast Asia, the communist takeover would produce a debate in the United States more acute than that over the loss of China. Unlike Truman with China or Eisenhower in 1954, he would be violating a treaty commitment to the area. The upshot would be a rise and convergence of left- and right-wing isolationism that would affect commitments in Europe as well as in Asia. Loss of confidence in the United States would be worldwide. Under these circumstances, Khrushchev and Mao could not refrain from acting to exploit the apparent shift in the balance of power. If Burma fell, Chinese power would be on the Indian frontier: the stability of all of Asia, not merely Southeast Asia, was involved. When the communist leaders had moved—after they were committed—the United States would then react. We would come plunging back to retrieve the situation. And a much more dangerous crisis would result, quite possibly a nuclear crisis.[5]

Having decided that the costs of failing to hold Southeast Asia outweighed the burden of meeting the challenge, Kennedy then had to choose between the broad tactical options Taylor and I had put to him: to go directly to the source of the aggression or to strengthen the hand of those under attack.

In another joint memorandum (of August 4), this is how Taylor and I stated our understanding of Kennedy's position at that time:

> As we understand your position: you would wish to see every avenue of diplomacy exhausted before we accept the necessity for either positioning U.S. forces on the Southeast Asian mainland or fighting there; you would wish to see the possibilities of economic assistance fully exploited to strengthen the Southeast Asian position; you would wish to see indigenous forces used to the maximum if fighting should occur; and that, should we have to fight, we should use air and sea power to the maximum and engage minimum U.S. forces on the Southeast Asian mainland.

Then Kennedy had to decide if a strategy of minimum United States engagement was militarily and politically viable. It was not self-evident that the task was possible; for example, here is how I set out the balance sheet to Kennedy on July 21, as seen in Washington:

> The battle in Viet-Nam evidently hangs in balance. Positive and negative forces are at work. . . .
>
> *Positive Forces.*
>
> These are the positive forces as they can be perceived at this distance.
>
> —A degree of tactical success achieved by the GVN armed forces; e.g., in suppressing the Viet Cong election offensive; in conducting the delta sweep; in the ambush of July 16; in generally moving over to a more offensive posture.
>
> —The reassurance of Diem and his government of continued U.S. support, despite events in Laos.
>
> —The slow beginning of decentralized order in the army and in intelligence collection.
>
> —The increased international awareness of the aggression being conducted against Diem from Hanoi.
>
> Taken together, these forces have held the line—but not more—in recent months.
>
> *Negative Forces.*
>
> —The almost certain build-up of Viet Cong forces in recent months, looking towards an expanded offensive.
>
> —The build-up of the Viet Cong base in Southern Laos, evidently designed to increase the military pressure on Viet-Nam in the months ahead.

—The continued insecurity of the population and their unwillingness to take the risks of denying food and intelligence to the Viet Cong, and of supplying it to the Viet-Nam cities and Diem's government, respectively.

—The threat of rice shortage in the Viet-Nam cities.

—The persistence of pockets of serious disaffection in the officer corps of Diem's army and the apathy and fatigue of many of his soldiers.

—Diem's inability to link himself and his government with popular aspirations, including the weakness of his programs of village development and civic action.

—The lack of a program of positive national goals and purposes: the negative, anti-Communist stance of Diem's political appeal.

Finally, there was the question: If Kennedy's strategy had some chance of viability, what, precisely, should the United States do to maximize the chance of its success by its military, political, and economic actions in Vietnam?

In the crisis atmosphere which developed after the Phuoc Vinh incident late in September, Kennedy sent Taylor to Southeast Asia essentially to answer these latter questions: Was his general concept of strategy viable; if so, what tactical actions should be taken?

DID THE SOUTH WANT AN INDEPENDENT, NONCOMMUNIST DESTINY?

THE most fundamental question on Kennedy's mind was this: Did the people of South Vietnam want an independent noncommunist future or would they, in fact, prefer to go with Ho Chi Minh and Hanoi? In a private conversation, Kennedy instructed me, as second man in the Taylor mission which went to Vietnam on October 18, to try to answer this question above any other. He recalled the situation under the French, as he had seen it in 1951 and studied it down to 1954. He had seen a quarter of a million military men rendered impotent because the people didn't want French rule. He said all our help, including combat troops, would be useless unless there was an underlying desire of the leaders and people to have an independent destiny in the South. He distinguished this question sharply from the question of Diem—his strengths, weaknesses, and viability. That question, already famous in Washington, was central to the formal agenda of the Taylor mission.

As part of General Taylor's mission (see pp. 274–278) in Vietnam, I undertook to probe Kennedy's question about the political aspirations of the South Vietnamese people in as many different ways as I could. Through political officers in the Embassy with extensive anti-Diem contacts, I met a good many opposition figures. I listened to their complaints, with which

Saigon was full. I then would ask: Do you wish a unified Vietnam under Hanoi? The prompt and universal answer was negative. I then probed at why they held this negative view. They were often surprised that I put the question with evident seriousness. The tone of the conversation then changed from colorful efforts to lobby an American official on Diem's deficiencies to quiet reflection. They described in detail what had happened in the north between 1954 and 1956; the changed view of Ho Chi Minh as the refugees came and reported their experiences. Some had family ties in the north and managed still, somehow, to communicate. Some were southerners who did not like the important role assumed by the northerners since that time; but they did not wish what happened in North Vietnam to happen in the South. This was true of anti-Diem teachers and lawyers, labor leaders and politicians, soldiers and bureaucrats.

Then I probed at attitudes in the hamlets, villages, and small towns. There, of course, the concerns were primarily local. As in almost all developing nations, central government was regarded as a distant instrument taking away sons and money. The Army was as much an intruder as a protector, making off with chickens and rice. They wished to be left alone to raise their food in peace and enjoy the round of family and village life. The communists were feared. They, too, laid claim on sons and rice—plus intelligence on the movement of government forces. It was also clear in the rural areas that communist propaganda and operations had changed since 1954. There was a pro forma effort to identify Diem and the Americans with French puppets and colonial times. But, in fact, the Viet Cong operation was based on proving the government could not rule and that the Viet Cong were the wave of the future to whom the farmer would have to accommodate himself. The technique was terror: the systematic assassination or kidnapping of local officials, including health, education, and agricultural officers.

What the villagers wanted most of the government was security; then, education for the children, medical services, and economic assistance, in about that order. There was a land reform problem in some areas, but it generally appeared farther down the list.

I also interviewed communist prisoners, candidly guided by a Vietnamese officer who, with some sophistication, distinguished those who were likely to tell me what they thought I would like to hear from those who, to a degree at least, would speak their minds. Some had gone north in 1954 and had been infiltrated to the south after 1958. Others were local recruits. Their attachment to communism was, in some cases, real; but they had read nothing by Marx or Lenin, Mao or even Ho. They thought of communism as "equality for the people." When asked if he had found equality in the north, one responded: "Oh, no. I was with the military. I had officers." They struck me, in general (like the Malayan guerrillas Lucian Pye had questioned[6]), as young men in a developing region who had been caught up for the first time—and found various degrees of satisfaction and disappointment—in a modern organizational structure reaching beyond family, hamlet, and village. Despite the great attention given political matters by the Viet Cong, it struck me then more as a sophisticated bureaucratic operation than a political movement with great resonance.

I concluded from my personal contacts and all the other evidence I could quietly gather that the problems of South Vietnam were ample but that they did not include a massive popular desire (or a substantial desire among the educated elite) for either communism or unification under Hanoi. In subsequent years I have seen no evidence to alter that assessment and much to reinforce it.

I reported my findings to Kennedy by detailing precisely the character and limits of my probing, as well as my net conclusion. I am sure that, as always, he formed his assessment on wider evidence and testimony than mine.

The communists, however, were not counting on winning a popular majority in a free election. And it was clear to all of us on the Taylor mission that South Vietnam could be lost unless there were substantial changes.

THE TAYLOR MISSION

THE Taylor mission was organized in a particular way. Its military and civil members were instructed to regard themselves as individuals rather than representatives of departments or agencies. Immediately after takeoff from Andrews Air Force Base, Taylor and I talked at length with each member of the mission. The questions each was responsible for answering were discussed and then formally set down. It was a little like two professors going over the outlines for a series of student term papers.

Taylor said that upon arrival in Saigon they were to fan out and go wherever they had to go to get the best answers they could to these questions. They were to keep social occasions to the minimum and use the mission's credentials to see anyone they thought necessary at any level. They would write individual reports, and these would be included without change as appendixes to the submission to Kennedy.

In Vietnam Taylor and I generally stayed together; although I wandered off, with his knowledge, to pursue the particular question Kennedy had put to me: Did the South Vietnamese really want to be independent and noncommunist?

After our visit in Vietnam, we went briefly to Thailand where we sought to induce the Thai military to concentrate more on their incipient guerrilla problem in the northeast rather than on the acquisition of sophisticated and largely irrelevant military hardware for their regular armed forces. The apparently hawk-like character of the Taylor mission prevented a visit to Laos, whose affairs were already under negotiation in Geneva.

But, at Kennedy's insistence, we overflew two Mekong airfields to assess their operational condition. In all the discussions about putting troops into Laos, Kennedy could never get from the military a satisfactory answer to the question of whether those airfields could be used effectively to bring in American forces. Taylor decided they were in reasonable operational shape. We also examined from the air the terrain of the Ho Chi Minh trail.

After a day in Hong Kong, where we were briefed on the deplorable state of the Chinese mainland economy, Taylor took us to Baguio in the Philippines. He believed a report of this kind should be written with full concentration, in a quiet place, at relative leisure. We worked for several days in that cool hill station, at last bringing together what each of us had learned and what we had severally concluded.

We agreed that South Vietnam was caught up in a double crisis of confidence: doubt that the United States was determined to save Southeast Asia and doubt that Diem's methods could frustrate and defeat communist purposes and methods. Related to these was a vicious circle of bad military tactics and bad administrative arrangements in South Vietnam. These yielded a defensive, reactive military posture which was permitting the Viet Cong to create conditions of frustration and terror, certain to lead to a political crisis if a positive turning point was not soon achieved.

The report described at some length Diem's administrative style and its consequences. He sought to maintain all the strings of power in his own hands while fragmenting power beneath him. Poor military intelligence resulted directly from this method, as well as the uncertainty and lack of initiative of his generals. Beyond the military, Diem's operating style led him to mistrust excessively intellectuals, administrators, and a promising younger generation who were badly needed to give his administration vitality and contact with the people. Placed on the sidelines or otherwise frustrated, they spent their time and energy in complaints against the regime while their country moved toward a communist takeover they did not want.

The assets of South Vietnam were also described: the armed forces, substantial but capable of improvement; Diem's stubborn courage; the willingness of the military and civil administration to work with Diem if given half a chance; a new generation of younger men in their thirties, military and civil, with energy and a willingness to get on with the job; the resilience of the Vietnamese economy; the lack of widespread positive communist appeal.

The report concluded, in general, that the war in its present stage could not be won by direct American action. It had to be won by the Vietnamese. On the other hand, Americans, working with the Vietnamese, from Diem's palace out to the villages, could induce a much better, aggressive, more confident performance from the Vietnamese military and civil establishment.

The report noted that Diem had requested Lansdale as a personal adviser and we might wish to envisage a limited number of Americans, acceptable to Diem as well as Washington, in key ministries. An advisory structure over the whole field of military operations was then outlined. The introduction of helicopters on a large scale was recommended, as well as the buildup of air support for Vietnamese military operations. It was concluded that to execute this program of limited partnership, a change in the charter, the spirit, and the organization of the Americans in South Vietnam would have to be envisaged.

To enhance the leverage of military advisers, helicopters should not be used in support of Vietnamese operations without clearance of the American advisers.

Taylor also recommended that an American military task force with engineering capabilities be put into Vietnam: to symbolize the seriousness of the American commitment to Southeast Asia and to strengthen morale; to conduct logistical operations, notably road building and flood relief; to constitute a reserve military force in case of a crisis situation; and to constitute an advanced party if contingency plans for the area were invoked. One reason for the recommendation was anxiety about the buildup of communist forces in the Vietnamese plateau, which might quickly move to the coast and cut the country in half—a situation which in fact developed in 1965. The presence of an American force in the country might help deal with such a sudden surge of communist effort there or, conceivably, a move out of the communist base in Zone D against Saigon. The great flood in the delta would give such an American force an immediate useful engineering task.

THE QUESTION OF DIEM

THE Taylor report discussed bluntly the question of Diem as an administrator and politician. The report recommended a strong U.S. effort to achieve a series of de facto administrative changes in the Diem government by persuasion, negotiation, and a network of American advisers at every level, rather than Diem's removal in favor of either a new civilian government or a military dictatorship. It was judged too dangerous to engineer a coup under the existing tense circumstances since it was by no means certain that the United States could control its consequences and potentialities for communist exploitation. It was also not clear that there were better executives ready to take over if Diem should go. It struck Taylor and me that even among those military men who might lead such a coup there was still substantial respect for Diem and, at that time, an evident unwillingness to assume all the responsibilities that would go with such an action.

On the day before the Taylor mission completed its work in Vietnam, I spent three hours, at Diem's request, with his brother, Ngo Dinh Nhu. Nhu's office in the palace was piled high with books and government papers. It somehow reflected his training as a librarian. Nhu talked with candor about his brother who, he felt, had virtue and courage but whose methods were not modern. He was too soft. Nhu described the kind of elaborate, highly centralized political and administrative structure that he believed was needed to hold the country together, reaching from Saigon down to the villages. It was clear that he felt he was the man to organize that kind of more modern system to supersede Diem's benign but inefficient mandarin rule.

Nhu talked with the lucidity of a French-trained intellectual: his categories clear, but his touch inhuman. He was proud of how he had gone immediately to the province of Phuoc Vinh after the province chief had been beheaded publicly in September, conducted an inquest on the affair, and reorganized things on the spot. But Nhu seemed to have little feel for the kinds of men, military and civil, emerging in this postcolonial society and how they might be organized in a less egocentric fashion than he evidently envisaged. He was not, essentially, a politician, as I briefly saw him, but rather an intellectual, eager to impress the pattern of his mind on reality, close to power and looking to the exercise of more.

At the final session between Diem and the Taylor mission, Diem suddenly turned to me. He said he had heard that I had talked at length with his brother. He wanted to know what, as a student of developing nations, I thought of South Vietnam. I told him I felt he had done a remarkable job in pulling together the country after 1954. Now, under grave challenge, he had the asset of a new generation of military and civil officials dedicated to the independence of their country. His place in history would depend on whether he could manage a transition from the present system of rule, which had been initially necessary, to an administrative system which gave wider scope to the energies and talents I had observed all over the country. I cited examples, both military and civil.

"These men you have met talk well," he said, "but they cannot do the job." He picked up the telephone next to him and waved it as he said, "The job can only be done with this."

I tried again. I said that in my experience you never knew how much responsibility a man could handle until you gave him a chance. I would hope that he would give his various subordinates increasing degrees of responsibility and thereby establish those who could actually perform and those who could not. Diem turned back to Taylor.

I left pessimistic about the possibilities of change in Diem. But I hoped Lansdale, working side by side with him over a period of time, might gradually bring about a conversion.

The Question Beyond

Taylor's letter of transmittal to Kennedy also included this much-quoted passage:

While we feel that the program recommended represents those measures which should be taken in our present knowledge of the situation in Southeast Asia, I would not suggest that it is the final word. Future needs beyond this program will depend upon the kind of settlement we obtain in Laos and the manner in which Hanoi decides to adjust its conduct to that settlement. If the Hanoi decision is to continue the irregular war declared on South Vietnam in 1959 with continued infiltration and covert support of guerrilla bands in the territory of our ally, we will then have to decide whether to accept as legitimate the continued guidance, training, and support of a guerrilla war across an international boundary, while the attacked react only inside their borders. Can we admit the establishment of the common law that the party attacked and his friends are denied the right to strike the source of aggression, after the fact of external aggression is clearly established? It is our view that our government should undertake with the Vietnamese the measures outlined herein, but should then consider and face the broader question beyond.

KENNEDY'S DECISIONS

THE Taylor report was delivered, on arrival, to Kennedy. There were extensive discussions and debates about it. Kennedy ruled against putting forces into South Vietnam at the time. The contingency we feared was covered by providing for a Marine unit close by in the China Sea, which might be put ashore quickly should a decisive communist move be attempted. The advisory structure the Taylor mission outlined was, essentially, approved; the number of American advisers in Vietnam expanded radically; and the support for the South Vietnamese in military hardware and other resources was substantially increased. As Kennedy rose from the Cabinet table, having indicated the elements in the Taylor report he finally approved, he remarked: "If this doesn't work perhaps we'll have to try Walt's Plan Six"; that is, direct attack on North Vietnam. He acted, in short, in precisely the spirit of Taylor's and my paraphrase of his view as of August 4 (see above, p. 271): he took the minimum steps he judged necessary to stabilize the situation, leaving its resolution for the longer future, but quite conscious that harder decisions might lie ahead.

A White Paper—the Jorden report—detailing the nature of Hanoi's operations against South Vietnam, was published as background to the formal exchange of letters between Kennedy and Diem, released on December 15.

The experiment in limited partnership between the United States and South Vietnam was thus set in motion, with one notable exception. Diem's request for Edward Lansdale as a personal adviser was not accepted. The reasons lay deep in the American military and the civil bureaucracy. The

American ambassador and the ranking general in Saigon—and the departments backstopping them in Washington—did not want another American that close to Diem.

In my last memorandum, dated December 6, 1961, to Kennedy on Vietnam before going to the State Department as a planner, I had noted that all the choppers and other gadgetry supplied South Vietnam would not help without first-class military leadership; and "it is equally crucial that we free Ed Lansdale from his present assignment and get him out to the field in an appropriate position. He is a unique national asset in the Saigon setting; and I cannot believe that anything he may be able to do in his present assignment could match his value in Southeast Asia."

Kennedy did not overrule the bureaucracy in this matter. It is by no means certain Lansdale could have altered the tragic course on which Diem was launched; but he represented a kind of last chance.

But for the next seventeen months, down to the political crisis that began on May 8, 1963, the limited partnership did not work too badly.

LIMITED PROGRESS: DECEMBER 1961–MAY 1963

IN the kind of war fought in South Vietman in 1962–1963 success by one side draws to it rice and recruits, intelligence and improved morale. These factors reinforce the initial direction in which the advantage is flowing. The rate of movement is slow, however, because guerrilla warfare usually involves sporadic engagement and low rates of attrition. The guerrilla force cannot engage massively because of its size and vulnerability in open combat, while the defending forces cannot impose a high rate of attrition because a guerrilla force is scattered and strives as a condition for survival to evade sustained combat.

With no fixed front, the war moved unevenly: in Vietnam it was almost as if there were forty different wars, one in each province. To measure the direction and pace of a guerrilla war is, therefore, not easy. One must rely on experienced observers, who, knowing a province well, can determine from day to day whether the area controlled or influenced by the guerrillas is expanding or contracting from a dozen small indicators: the attitudes of the villagers; the morale of the government officials; the flow of intelligence and rice; the offensive or defensive mentality of the local military forces, the number and kind of incidents of violence.

In addition, properly used, statistics can help. The statistics on Vietnam gradually improved over the years of conflict there, notably as the American advisory groups expanded and could verify and report directly. Given the often obscure circumstances of combat, statistics could never be wholly accurate. Nevertheless, they could serve as indexes.

These were the rules I applied in using the statistical data on Vietnam:

use data from as many different independent sources as possible; draw no conclusions unless other data, independently collected, point in the same direction; draw no conclusions unless the movement of the data is substantial; draw no conclusions unless the data have exhibited in the past evidence of deterioration as well as progress; draw no conclusions unless the broad direction of movement exhibited in the statistics is confirmed by non-statistical evidence from reliable observers on the spot.

When these rules were applied, it proved quite possible to use statistics to provide a partial substitute for the lack of a fixed front, and its movement, in assessing the course of the war in Vietnam.

In 1961 all the indexes reflected deterioration. From January 1962 down to the early months of 1963, they reflected modest improvement. Starting in May 1963—but notably after July—there was clearly marked deterioration in the government's military position.

For example, in early 1962 GVN losses exceeded those of the Viet Cong; by the end of 1962 the ratio had turned favorable; by the summer of 1963 the ratio was, again, unfavorable for the GVN, at about the level of a year earlier.[7]

The favorable trend in 1962 was reflected, also, in the scale and number of Viet Cong attacks: total incidents (including assassinations, kidnappings, etc.) decreased by 18 percent in the second half of 1962 as compared to the first half; total armed attacks by 19 percent; company and larger-sized attacks by 40 percent. From about July 1963 Viet Cong attacks sharply increased.

Although Viet Cong casualty figures at that time might well have been inflated, relative Viet Cong and GVN casualties told a similar tale of improvement and, then, deterioration. Taken with other evidence, they were significant: Viet Cong casualties rose by 26 percent in the second half of 1962 as compared with the first half; GVN casualties rose by only 13 percent. By the end of the first half of 1963, Viet Cong casualties were down and GVN casualties were rising more rapidly than earlier. Increased Viet Cong efforts in the third quarter of 1963 resulted in a 46 percent rise in casualties; but GVN casualties rose even more rapidly (52 percent).

Behind the story of a year and a quarter's real but limited, uneven, and fragile progress lay an infusion of material resources, confidence, and advisers to South Vietnam. There were some 11,000 American advisers and supporting personnel in South Vietnam by the close of 1962. One of the most effective advisers was R. G. K. Thompson, a British officer with extensive experience in Malaya. Diem received his proposals of November 11, 1961, for the gradual expansion of the secure area in the Delta. His ideas generally conformed with those of the Taylor mission: Taylor and Thompson had talked at length together in Saigon. And, although there were some differences in detail between Thompson's views and those of the American military on the spot, there was agreement that he was pushing in the right direction. Thompson's emphasis on the buildup of the Vietnamese regional and popular forces, and the police, was salutary. In a move of great consequence, Diem put the pacification program in the hands of his brother Nhu. From Diem's point of view, the move was understandable. If the program were in the hands of the military, then political control over the bulk of the Vietnamese population would pass from his hands. The elevation of Nhu, however, was one key to the political crisis of 1963.

Nevertheless, Nhu pushed the strategic hamlet program forward in 1962–1963 with real vigor. Nhu's concept was, in part, to relocate peasants from insecure areas to new hamlets. This raised many problems, including the unwillingness of peasants to move. Nevertheless, after a rocky start, by August 1962 a national plan was in effect, based on clear priorities. By the end of September the Vietnamese could claim that of 11,316 hamlets planned, 3,225 were completed, containing over 4 million people, or a third of the total population. Approximately 6,000 strategic hamlets were completed by May 1963.

TABLE 25–1

CONTROL OVER RURAL POPULATION IN SOUTH VIETNAM
(excluding 1,600,000 in major cities)

	GVN effective control %	GVN ascendency %	No effective control %	Viet Cong ascendency %	Viet Cong effective control %
July 1, 1962	47	29	1	14	9
October 1, 1962	49	27	6	10	8
December 1, 1962	51	27	5	9	8
April 1, 1963	54	27	5	7	7
July 1962–April 1963	+7	−2	+4	−7	−2

The effort was subject to much criticism: the relocation of peasants was resisted in some cases; security provisions were uneven; some of the strategic hamlets were rather more paper than real creations; the resources for improving education, health, and agricultural productivity in the hamlets were insufficient; Nhu was obviously using the hamlet system to build a personally controlled political system in the countryside. But, on balance, there is no doubt that the GVN slowly extended the proportion of the rural population under its control. The Vietnamese figures on which Table 25–1 is based were subject to considerable suspicion; although they later reflected the downward turn in affairs and, in retrospect, probably suggest pretty well the order of magnitude of the limited progress achieved from July 1962 to April 1963.

What happened in 1962 was that the deterioration of 1960–1961 was halted by the new American equipment (notably, helicopters), which permitted the Vietnamese military to act more aggressively; by pacification programs, although their results were uneven; by the relations between the American advisers and the Vietnamese military, which varied from man to man and place to place, but on the whole were reasonably good. The problem of effective national leadership and organization of the South Vietnamese effort, however, was not solved. Diem continued to hold all the strings in his hands, except for those he passed to Nhu, who was rising in importance. Diem, haunted by the possibility of a military coup, kept a close rein on his military, who easily lapsed back into passivity.

The result was that the inherently painstaking work of building up the local strength to expand the area of security in the countryside went slowly; and the attack on the communist main force units, which had to be kept away from the villages if pacification was to succeed, was pursued with less vigor and effectiveness than it should have been by the regular South Vietnamese forces (ARVN).

Most observers at the time, and historians, are likely to agree with the assessment made by Michael Forrestal and Roger Hilsman as of January 1963:

> Our overall judgment, in sum, is that we are probably winning, but certainly more slowly than we had hoped. At the rate it is now going, the war will probably last longer than we would like, cost more in terms of both lives and money than we anticipated, and prolong the period in which a sudden and dramatic event could upset the gains already made.[8]

Reflecting the fragile progress of 1962, Kennedy, in his State of the Union message of January 14, 1963, said: "The spearpoint of aggression has been blunted in Viet-Nam. . . . But complacency or self-congratulation can imperil our security as much as the weapons of tyranny. A moment of pause is not a promise of peace."

VIETNAM, 1961–62—A PERSONAL VIEW

IT may be well for the reader to know the presuppositions and judgments on Asia I brought to my role as a public servant and the views at which I arrived under the impact of circumstances as they unfolded after January 20, 1961. A writer's perspective, consciously or unconsciously, colors how a story is told.

I had worked intensively on Asian problems in the 1950s, notably in the period 1953–1955. I directed a project at M.I.T. on Communist China—its probable future course, its relations with the Soviet Union and the rest of Asia, and its implications for the United States. The project resulted in the publication of *The Prospects for Communist China* (1954) and *An American Policy in Asia* (1955), as well as a substantial number of books, monographs, and essays by others with whom I was associated.

An American Policy in Asia explored at length the complex of American military and nonmilitary interests in Asia and possible threats which might arise to them. The underlying judgment at which I had arrived was this: ". . . it is a persistent interest of the United States that no single power or power grouping militarily dominate either western or eastern Eurasia. . . . In Asia the threat [of this] would become virtually a reality should either Japan or Southeast Asia be lost to the Free World."[9]

I regarded (and regard) Southeast Asia as a critical area for these four reasons: it contains some 200–300 million people (about the size of Africa or Latin America) with all that implies in potential military resources; it dominates the sea approaches of the Southwest Pacific; it dominates also the sea approaches of the eastern sector of the Indian Ocean; it is a critical buffer area between China and the Indian subcontinent, with Burma the potential Ardennes.

My recommendations included proposals for an expanded regional effort in economic development, as well as a substantial passage on what was called "The Soft War":

> What we face in Asia—and we face it now—is the possibility that new territories will fall to the enemy by a combination of subversion and guerrilla warfare. Such operations do not require masses of troops or modern equipment. They do not demand that Soviet or Chinese Communist troops cross borders and create, politically as well as militarily, targets for major American military strength. In Vietnam, Laos, Cambodia, Thailand, and possibly in Indonesia as well, the enemy is now conducting this targetless warfare in which he is a professional and we are amateurs.
>
> Such aggression confronts the Free World and the United States with a major challenge. It is clear that we cannot act alone to stem Vietminh activities in Southern Vietnam. We can only be effective if the Vietnamese themselves and their government are prepared to resist; but, if they are prepared to resist, then the United States can contribute a significant margin of help. It should be recalled that Communism has several times been set back by the Free World in this kind of muted warfare: in the Philippines, where a few years back the situation was almost as precarious as in South Vietnam; in Burma, where on its own the newly independent government made an almost magical recovery from initial chaos; in Greece, where a substantial civil war had to be fought.
>
> Success in resisting the combination of subversion and guerrilla operations depends directly on the political, economic, and social health of the area attacked. A substantial part of American and Free World

> policy must be devoted to eliminating or preventing those circumstances under which subversion can succeed. . . . It should be a major aim of American policy to prevent situations in Asia from degenerating to the point where guerrilla and other limited operations can take effective hold; but we must be prepared to meet them now and in the future.[10]

These were the views—the prejudices, if you like—to which I had come in studying Asia in the early 1950s. They were not necessarily relevant or correct, but they had not been arrived at casually. On the other hand, I had not followed closely in the late 1950s the evolution of affairs in Laos and Vietnam. When Kennedy had asked me about Laos on January 9, 1961, in Boston, I told him I simply didn't know enough about the situation to give him a judgment. He seemed relieved at my candor.

On being assigned Southeast Asia on the White House staff, I started, therefore, afresh. I found that Hanoi was guiding intimately the guerrilla operations that threatened to take over both Laos and South Vietnam. I studied with care the interweaving of local elements of dissidence with Hanoi's direct role: as de facto controller of both Lao and South Vietnamese communists; director of military operations; source of training and infiltration of (mainly) southern-born military and political cadres brought north from South Vietnam in 1954; supplier of limited regular North Vietnamese military units for critical supporting roles in Laos and in assuring the security of the Ho Chi Minh trail through Laos; negotiator of support for the operation in Peking and Moscow; etc.

I studied also, of course, the indigenous postcolonial political situation in Laos and South Vietnam. What they faced were particular versions of the quite familiar process of political, social, and economic modernization, Laos at a much earlier stage than Vietnam. It was quite clear that if Hanoi were to leave Laos and South Vietnam alone, they would face great problems. There would certainly be turbulence. There might well be some armed dissidence. But there was not the slightest reason to believe that the inherent strength of communism in either Laos or South Vietnam would lead to a communist takeover without the critical marginal role of Hanoi.

When, on June 28, 1961, I spoke on "Guerrilla Warfare in the Underdeveloped Areas," a speech delivered at Fort Bragg, personally cleared by Kennedy, I put the problem squarely in the context of the inherently turbulent setting of modernization, concluding:

> . . . it is important that the whole international community begin to accept its responsibility for dealing with this form of aggression. It is important that the world become clear in mind, for example, that the operation run from Hanoi against Viet-Nam is as clear a form of aggression as the violation of the 38th parallel by the North Korean armies in June 1950. In my conversations with representatives of foreign governments, I am sometimes lectured that this or that government within the Free World is not popular; they tell me that guerrilla warfare cannot be

won unless the peoples are dissatisfied. These are, at best, half truths. The truth is that guerrilla warfare, mounted from external bases—with rights of sanctuary—is a terrible burden to carry for any government in a society making its way towards modernization. As you know, it takes somewhere between ten and twenty soldiers to control one guerrilla in an organized operation. Moreover, the guerrilla force has this advantage: its task is merely to destroy; while the government must build and protect what it is building. A guerrilla war mounted from outside a transitional nation is a crude act of international vandalism. There will be no peace in the world if the international community accepts the outcome of a guerrilla war, mounted from outside a nation, as tantamount to a free election.

The sending of men and arms across international boundaries and the direction of guerrilla war from outside a sovereign nation is aggression; and this is a fact which the whole international community must confront and whose consequent responsibilities it must accept. Without such international action those against whom aggression is mounted will be driven inevitably to seek out and engage the ultimate source of the aggression they confront.

I suspect that, in the end, the real meaning of the conference on Laos at Geneva will hinge on this question: it will depend on whether or not the international community is prepared to mount an International Control Commission which has the will and the capacity to control the borders it was designed to control.

Operationally, two judgments flowed from this analysis. First, I placed an exceedingly high priority on closing off the infiltration trails from North Vietnam to South Vietnam, notably the trails through Laos. The western end of the Demilitarized Zone (DMZ) along the 17th parallel is difficult mountainous terrain and capable of use for infiltration of men and supplies; but it is more capable of blockage than the spacious network of trails that was created in southeastern Laos, with multiple exits from North Vietnam over the mountain passes and multiple entrances into South Vietnam from Laos and Cambodia.

At the time of the Taylor mission, at the end of 1961, the monthly infiltration rate from the north was estimated at 500–700 highly trained military and political cadres—mostly southerners, but some North Vietnamese regulars were already in evidence. To gauge the weight these men imposed on the life of the South, one had to multiply their numbers by at least ten, since the terrible arithmetic of guerrilla warfare decreed that it took ten to twenty soldiers on the government side to frustrate one guerrilla. This was the kind of ratio that operated in Greece and the Philippines, Malaya and the Indian guerrilla problem in Assam.

I did not doubt that the South Vietnamese could, in time, build, equip, and organize a military and civil operation to deal with the communists if the flow from the north could be halted. While I was also sure that the job inside South Vietnam deserved exceedingly high priority in all its dimensions, and while I had great sympathy for Robert Thompson's ideas and for later American efforts to press forward pacification and village development, I was skeptical that Vietnam could be saved, except at prohibitive cost, if the Vietnamese frontier remained open to infiltration. In a memorandum to Kennedy of November 24, 1961, I noted, for example: ". . . none of the recent guerrilla wars has been won with an open frontier; the Greek war was won when the Stalin–Tito fight closed the Yugoslav frontier and fractured the Greek Communist Party; there was no Communist frontier in Malaya or in the Philippines." I felt it was most unwise to permit Hanoi the right to counter whatever improvement the South Vietnamese might achieve in their performance at an exchange rate of ten or twenty to one, by continued infiltration. I believe I understood the weaknesses of Diem and the inherent social and political fragmentation of South Vietnamese society as well as anyone working at the task. I knew these were typical characteristics of a transitional postcolonial society, and would take time and the emergence of new generations to correct and yield a solid sense of nationhood backed by efficient central administration. But I did not feel those weaknesses justified acceptance of an open frontier, where limited increases in infiltration could balance painfully achieved progress in military, administrative, and political performance.

But how could the frontier be closed?

The first hope was diplomacy and the conference on Laos, to which I referred in my Fort Bragg talk. From beginning to end I regarded the closing of the Laos trails as the primary American interest in the Laos conference.

A second method was by various attempts to interfere with the infiltration routes by air attack, ground harassment, and guarding the South Vietnamese frontiers. The nature of the terrain, the length of the frontiers, and the low density of traffic made such methods costly, although I canvassed them with my colleagues. One of the most imaginative of the ideas generated was that an American engineering force, with appropriate protection, build a large highway across Laos to the Thai border, linking to Route 9 in South Vietnam, just south of the DMZ. The Asian highway envisaged for the future explicitly includes such a road.

The third method was by direct attack on North Vietnam sufficiently costly to induce Hanoi to end its war against South Vietnam. I had in mind not only the possibility of air action but, after a suitable program of diplomatic warning, moving forces into North Vietnam itself—not in the area around Hanoi, but north of the DMZ, perhaps as far as Vinh. I first raised this possibility with Kennedy in a memorandum of June 30, 1961.

The holding of a portion of North Vietnam would permit certain of the supply routes to South Vietnam to be cut directly from within. More important, it would constitute a serious hostage for North Vietnamese actions in Laos and South Vietnam. I did not believe (nor did the intelligence community) that Peking would intervene unless American forces moved into the Red River delta; and I did not believe the Soviet Union would intervene in Southeast Asia in any case, given the peripheral and ambiguous nature of its interests in the area and the logistical problems it would confront. Moscow was prepared to support Ho to avoid losing his support in the world communist movement, and it came to enjoy American discomfiture in Southeast Asia. But it did not want the Chinese to take over in Southeast Asia upon American withdrawal, and it did not want a military confrontation with the United States in an area where its strategic interests were secondary and its capacity to bring power to bear limited.

On balance, therefore, I deeply feared the consequences of a strategy which permitted continued infiltration and which dealt only with its disruptive consequences. I felt it would tempt Hanoi to persist; the struggle would be protracted; and, at some time, if the situation disintegrated, the United States would intervene convulsively, as it had done late in the other great military crises of the twentieth century.

This is how I evoked my frame of mind during the Kennedy years in an oral history interview with Richard Neustadt, April 11, 1964, well before the massive American intervention of the next year. Recalling earlier periods of public service, I said:

> Until 1961 I had never taken home a problem of public policy and worried about it, in the sense that it was on my mind when sleep got light. But I did worry about Vietnam—where it was hard to get people to understand how tough a well-advanced guerrilla war, with an open frontier, is. My nightmare was—and it remains—that we wouldn't deal with it early enough. Things would go very bad. Then we would have to deal with it convulsively, in a war. We would let the thing sag away from us into a mess where nothing short of a substantial war with Communist China would redress the balance. I had a sense that unless I could get people to understand it and face it early this might be the outcome. I wasn't afraid that we wouldn't fight to save Southeast Asia. I was sure we would and I am sure we will. But I was afraid that we would do so under certain circumstances that were too damned dangerous in a nuclear age and too costly.

But in 1961–1962, at Geneva, some grounds for hope emerged. In dealing with the Soviet delegate, Georgiy Pushkin, Harriman found and sought to consolidate an apparently solid meeting of minds. In many exchanges, embracing a thick cable file, Pushkin said the Soviet Union wanted a truly neutral Laos—like Finland. Moscow would undertake responsibility for overseeing the agreement as co-chairman of the conference. When pressed hard by Harriman on the Laos infiltration routes to South Vietnam, he said Moscow was in a position to guarantee the compliance of both Hanoi and the Pathet Lao. Pushkin was not prepared to accept International

Control Commission (ICC) teams operating in fixed bases along the infiltration routes; but the understanding between Washington and Moscow about the latter's responsibility to end the infiltration of South Vietnam via Laos was as explicit as a diplomatic understanding could be, short of a formal treaty.

During 1962 I had no operational role on Southeast Asian problems. From my post as planner at State, as I worked on other matters, I watched with some hope the gradual improvement of affairs in Vietnam and the emergence of the Laos Accords.

The Laos Accords were signed on July 23, 1962. They were to go into effect seventy-five days later, at the end of the first week in October, the delay providing time for the withdrawal of all non-Lao military forces. The agreement provided, inter alia, that the signatories, including Hanoi, "will not introduce into the Kingdom of Laos foreign troops or military personnel in any form whatsoever, nor will they in any way facilitate or connive at the introduction of any foreign troops or military personnel . . . they will not use the territory of the Kingdom of Laos for interference in the internal affairs of other countries. . . ." The ICC was empowered to go anywhere in Laos to investigate violations, on agreement with the government and the vote of a majority. There could be no Polish veto, as in the case of the 1954 Geneva agreement on the functioning of the ICC.

By early October it was clear Hanoi did not intend to withdraw its forces from Laos or to cease using the infiltration trails in violation of the Accords. Against the background of the slow but fragile progress of 1962 and the unresolved problem of Diem, I regarded the continued use of the infiltration trails as a firebell in the night. I felt the United States should move promptly and decisively to force a confrontation on the violation of the recently signed Geneva Accords, backed as they were by the unambiguous understandings achieved by Harriman with Pushkin in Geneva.

For the first time in almost a year I addressed myself formally to the problem of Southeast Asia in a memorandum to Rusk sent also to Kennedy on November 28, 1962. The occasion was Mikoyan's trip to Washington after his woebegone experience with Castro in the wake of the Cuba missile crisis. Its title was "Mikoyan, the Laos Agreement, and Continued Infiltration Into South Vietnam":

> The President's and your conversations with Mikoyan offer an opportunity to raise the question of continued Communist infiltration into South Viet Nam via Laos. . . .
>
> You will recall that in the course of the Geneva conference Pushkin agreed with Governor Harriman that the Soviet Union would take responsibility for ending infiltration into Viet Nam via Laos. There is no question but that such infiltration continues. The order of magnitude is debatable; but the most responsible estimate runs at something like the rate of 500 per month.

This is a very significant figure for three reasons.

First, one must multiply by 15 or 20 to measure the burden of each guerrilla on the Viet Nam establishment. Roughly and conservatively speaking, a rate of infiltration of this magnitude sets up a requirement on the Vietnamese side of an extra 7500 soldiers a month, or the equivalent in improved efficiency. Casualties imposed on the Viet Cong can limit this burden, but it should not be regarded as trivial.

Second, the infiltrators are well trained cadres who form the bone structure of the Viet Cong effort, the bulk of whose membership (perhaps 70 percent) are recruited in South Viet Nam itself. The infiltrators are, therefore, disproportionately valuable to the Viet Cong.

Third, this continued flow, symbolizing the continued North Vietnamese responsibility and backing for the Viet Cong effort, is an exceedingly important morale factor within the Viet Cong movement.

On the whole, the position in South Viet Nam has been slowly improving; but there is no sign of an early end of the war so long as this illegal burden is accepted.

As many of us have emphasized, more had to be done and has to be done by the South Vietnamese and by ourselves in political, economic, as well as in military terms, in order to liquidate the Viet Cong operation which embraces about 20,000 troops; but the continued acceptance of the infiltration burden is capable of prolonging the war for a very long time. It is, in fact, very likely that this is Ho Chi Minh's objective. A recent interview with the men in Hanoi (by Bernard Fall) underlines their faith that the U.S. will wear out in its support of South Viet Nam in time.

Before he left for India Governor Harriman urged us to keep the Viet Minh issue—and continued Viet Cong infiltration—at the top of the post-Cuba negotiating agenda with the Russians. . . .

The essence of the matter appears to me to be this:

The Soviets are not assuming their responsibilities under the Geneva agreement, after the passage of enough time for us to be clear that this is either a willful act or a lack of capacity to impose their position on Ho Chi Minh;

We are continuing to accept on our side of the truce lines of the cold war a serious illegal act at a place where U.S. prestige and interests are heavily committed. . . .

The whole lesson of the cold war, including the recent Cuban crisis, is that the Communists do not escalate in response to our actions taken to preserve our position on our side of the truce lines of the cold war.

It is much better to put pressure on now, against the background of recent Vietnamese progress, than in a waning situation.

Kennedy did not accept this advice; and it is not difficult to understand why. As of November 1962 it appeared the problem of Vietnam had been reduced to an ongoing process, with limited elements of hope. Vietnam was no longer in imminent danger; Laos was in vastly better shape than it was when he came to responsibility. He had just successfully come through a terrifying confrontation with Moscow. To initiate a major crisis over a limited flow of men down obscure jungle trails was not an attractive prospect. Moreover, if the crisis was initiated, he had to be prepared to back his play with the application of American force against North Vietnam and, if necessary, American ground forces in South Vietnam at least. He had managed Southeast Asia for almost two years without committing American combat forces. Why, in an apparently quiet time, should he now assume that risk?

Behind his decision was a more general characteristic of American policy, deeply rooted in the habits and attitudes of the nation. The basic strategic interests of the United States on the world scene are negative: that the balance of power not be shifted in Europe or Asia to the point where either of those regions might come under the control of a single potentially hostile power, and that no major power install itself in the Western Hemisphere. This negative stance had decreed since 1916–1917 that the United States act with military power only in extremis; that is, when the balance of power was actually endangered, as with unrestricted German submarine warfare in the Atlantic (1917), the fall of France (1940), the attack on South Korea (1950).

With hindsight, however, I would judge Kennedy's failure to move promptly and decisively to deal with the violation of the Laos Accords the greatest single error in American policy of the 1960s[11]; for before too long he and his successor were confronted with "the waning situation" a good many of us had feared might emerge in Vietnam.

THE POLITICAL CRISIS OF 1963

THE crisis that began with a Buddhist protest in Hue on May 8, 1963, is a major event in American, as well as Vietnamese, history: it reversed the course of the war; it led to the coup of November 1 against Diem; it persuaded Hanoi to exploit fully the subsequent political and military disarray by introducing regular North Vietnamese units into South Vietnam in 1964; owing to further military disintegration, it led to the large-scale introduction of American forces in the summer of 1965 and all that followed.

The chronology of the 1963 crisis can be set out as follows:

May 8: Government troops fire on Buddhist protest demonstration, killing nine, wounding fourteen. Nationwide Buddhist protest began.

May 18: U.S. Ambassador Frederick Nolting urges Diem to take steps to meet Buddhist grievances, including compensation for victims and reaffirmation of religious equality. To this end, the Vice President of South Vietnam meets, inconclusively, with the Buddhist leaders. The demonstrations continued and on June 11 the first Buddhist suicide by burning occurs.

June 8 and 12: United States warns Diem that the United States may have to disassociate itself from his Buddhist policy.

June 16: Joint GVN–Buddhist communique outlines elements of a settlement; but Buddhist protests intensify in late June and July as radical Buddhists move to leadership over moderates.

June 27: Kennedy announces Henry Cabot Lodge as new ambassador.

July 14: Ambassador Nolting, taking leave, urges Diem to moderate Buddhist policy and repudiate recurrent inflammatory statements of Madame Ngo Dinh Nhu, then in Europe.

August 21: Under cover of martial law urged by generals, Nhu uses his own security forces to attack pagodas and arrest some 1400 Buddhist monks. Protest extends to students; military gravely disturbed.

August 22: Lodge arrives in Saigon.

August 24: Washington sends Lodge a cable saying the United States can no longer tolerate Nhu's position of authority in the wake of his attack on the pagodas; if Diem is unable or unwilling to remove him, the generals are to be told that the United States will be prepared to discontinue economic and military support and provide assistance to them in a period of interim breakdown of the GVN. This is the signal that Washington is prepared to contemplate a military coup and support a subsequent government.

August 25: Lodge approves August 24 cable, but tells Washington that an ultimatum to Diem would be fruitless.

August 31: Generals call off coup planning, lacking unanimity and wishing to avoid bloodshed.

September 2: Kennedy, in TV interview, expresses disappointment with Diem's handling of Buddhist crisis, suggests "change in policy and perhaps personnel. . . ."

September 10: General Victor Krulak (military) and Joseph Mendenhall (State) instructed to make whirlwind tour of Vietnam. They report back optimistically and pessimistically, respectively, on state of war and politics.

September 14: After several weeks of debate, American commercial import aid program for South Vietnam is held up.

September 23–October 2: McNamara–Taylor mission is sent to assess situation. They propose announcement of withdrawal of 1000 American troops by end of year to put pressure on Diem.

October 2: Evidence from Colonel Conein (CIA liaison with military) that coup-plotting has resumed.

October 8: United Nations General Assembly votes to send fact-finding team to Saigon to investigate charges of Buddhist repression.

October 10: General Minh informed that the United States does not wish "to stimulate" a coup, but would not "thwart a change in government."

October 17: GVN informed that the United States aid for special forces used by Nhu in pagoda raids has been cut off.

Late October: Washington receives evidence that coup-plotting is actively under way; also that Diem might be prepared to accede to Washington demands.

November 1: Coup begins. Diem and Nhu killed evening of November 2.

November 5: New government announced, with Minh as president; former Vice President Tho as premier; Don as minister of defense.

November 8: United States recognizes Minh government. Viet Cong activity surges in wake of coup.

November 20: Rusk, McNamara, and others from Washington review military, political, economic situation in Honolulu with officials from Saigon.

Stripped of its strategic significance and seen in terms of Vietnamese politics, the story of Diem's overthrow is in no way remarkable. Military coups are endemic in the developing world. Like Syngman Rhee of South Korea, Diem was a stubborn, dedicated man from the first generation, as it were, of anticolonial politics. His initial strength in Vietnam was that he had taken his distance from the French (as had Rhee from the Japanese). He had kept the faith and then established his legitimacy by producing the beginnings of a nation out of the post-1954 disarray in the South.

In the manner of rulers in traditional societies, he trusted, almost literally, only his family. To work through quasi-modern bureaucratic and administrative chains of command was wholly alien to his experience. The modernizing students, technicians, and soldiers emerging in the society were, in human terms, alien to him. It was, in a sense, natural and inevitable that his day would pass as Vietnam moved forward.

To this background of inherent transience was added, however, Buddhist opposition, heightened by Diem's Catholicism, and the determined activism of Nhu and his wife.

The Buddhists who organized and protested against Diem were, and are, a limited, complex political group in Vietnamese society. Although Buddhism is widespread in Vietnam, the organized Buddhists are not a dominant, or even unified, political force. They are made up of a number of vying factions. In the manner made familiar around the world later in the 1960s by radical student leaders, it was Diem's harsh reaction to their protests, rather than the substance of their demands, that gained them a widening circle of sympathy. And this the radical Buddhists well understood. They manipulated the American press corps in Vietnam in a sophisticated way, arranging their demonstrations and immolations for television cameras. They generated through the media powerful support in the United States, where they appeared the authentic spokesmen for a Buddhist majority against a hard-handed alien and Catholic ruler. The truth was, as the United Nations investigating group established, that Buddhists were not disadvantaged in South Vietnamese society. And the organized Buddhist groups did not, in fact, speak politically for the Buddhist population of South Vietnam. Nevertheless, in confronting Diem and provoking Nhu, they touched a sensitive nerve, both in South Vietnam and in Washington; for they brought to a head the long-gathering discontent and frustration with Diem's regime and the rise within it of Nhu. If there was one event more than any other that tipped the balance against Diem within the American government, it was Nhu's raid on the pagodas of August 21, conducted without Army approval, on the eve of Lodge's arrival, in the certain knowledge that it ran counter to American advice and opinion as well as to understandings reached with Diem that he would pursue toward the Buddhists a course of moderation.

But to run a war put great burdens on Diem; and it necessarily expanded the role of the one group which, evidently, most threatened him—the military. They were the best-organized, most competent institution in Vietnamese society. He needed the military but feared them and spent a good deal of time trying to neutralize them politically. But he could not run the country alone, despite great energy and intelligence. He needed Nhu. The American pressure to get rid of Nhu must have seemed to him tantamount to stripping him of a good part of his power.

But, as Nhu moved forward, the opposition to Diem hardened. By and large, the military and others were prepared to work with Diem, despite his curious style. He was respected. But they were not prepared to see Nhu take over. Even then, it took the convergence of three urgent facts to lead the military to act against Diem: the widening of dissidence, beyond the circle of organized Buddhists, to students and other groups; the deterioration in the military situation during the second half of 1963; the United States guarantee of continued support if the coup were successfully carried out.

The military had seen real progress in 1962 and the early months of 1963. They felt that with the United States, the war could someday be won. Despite all their prior grumbling, it was only when they came to believe the war would be lost if Diem and Nhu stayed that they were ready to move together.

For Kennedy, and those working with him in 1963, this crisis in post-colonial political development was an agony. A few had long urged that the United States go about overthrowing Diem. In conventional terms of national policy, there were two deterrents: a coup might not succeed, or it might succeed but lead to chaos which the communists could effectively exploit.

Even after Nhu's attacks on the pagodas and the dispatch of the famous cable of August 24, there was much doubt on both these points. And there were other dimensions of anxiety as well. The United States was trying to help the South Vietnamese consolidate their independence as a nation. In fact, of course, South Vietnam depended on American support; but, equally, the war could not be won unless the South Vietnamese increasingly took their own destiny in their hands. For the United States to detonate a coup was to intrude profoundly in the politics of another nation, to weaken its gathering sense of independence, and to deepen the American commitment. There is no more searching problem in American diplomacy than how and when to use American leverage in a dependent nation when the basic objective of policy is to help that nation learn to stand on its own feet.

Finally, there was a human element. With all his patent inadequacies, Diem had been for some nine years a kind of partner with the United States in the task of holding a critical part of the world from communist grasp and trying to build an independent nation. Only the egregious performance of Nhu made it possible for American officials to act in ways which encouraged Diem's removal. And, to the end, Lodge made it clear that the United States, if called upon, would act to assure his safety.

Kennedy was hit hard by Diem's assassination, which finally came on November 2. He felt that, wrong-headed as Diem may have been, his dogged and, by his lights, wholly honorable struggle for the independence of his nation should not have ended by assassination in the back of an American-built personnel carrier. But in dealing with the problem, as a matter of policy, Kennedy drew a sharp line between the rule of Diem and Nhu and the underlying support for the American effort in Vietnam and Asia, just as he had drawn a sharp line between the assessment of Diem and the underlying desire of the South Vietnamese for an independent destiny, at the time of the Taylor mission. As the Buddhist crisis unfolded, crystallizing many wider elements of the opposition to Diem, stirring sentiment in the United States and elsewhere in the world, he took his distance from Diem in public as well as in private.

On September 2, in a television interview with Walter Cronkite, Kennedy said:

> The repressions against the Buddhists, we felt, were very unwise. Now all we can do is to make it very clear that we don't think this is the way to win. It is my hope that this will become increasingly obvious to the government, that they will take steps to try to bring back popular support for this very essential struggle. . . .
>
> Our best judgment is that he [Diem] can't be successful on this basis. We hope that he comes to see that, but in the final analysis it is the people and the government itself who have to win or lose this struggle. All we can do is help, and we are making it very clear, but I don't agree with those who say we should withdraw. That would be a great mistake. I know people don't like Americans to be engaged in this kind of an effort. Forty-seven Americans have been killed in combat with the enemy, but this is a very important struggle even though it is far away.
>
> We took all this—made this effort to defend Europe. Now Europe

> is quite secure. We also have to participate—we may not like it—in the defense of Asia.[12]

On September 9, in a similar interview on the *Huntley–Brinkley Report*, Kennedy again described candidly his dilemma in dealing with Saigon, but flatly reasserted his view of the fundamental strategic importance of Southeast Asia:

> *Mr. Brinkley:* Mr. President, have you had any reason to doubt this so-called "domino theory," that if South Vietnam falls, the rest of Southeast Asia will go behind it?
>
> *The President:* No, I believe it. I believe it. I think that the struggle is close enough. China is so large, looms so high just beyond the frontiers, that if South Viet-Nam went, it would not only give them an improved geographic position for a guerrilla assault on Malaya, but would also give the impression that the wave of the future in Southeast Asia was China and the communists. So I believe it.

And down to his final words, spoken and prepared for delivery in Texas, Kennedy never shifted from his 1961 position, painfully arrived at, that the burdens of holding Southeast Asia outweighed the costs, and that America had to participate in the defense of Asia as it had in the defense of Europe.

I believe Theodore Sorensen's summation is just: ". . . if asked why he [Kennedy] had increased this nation's commitment, he might have summed up his stand with the words used by William Pitt when asked in the House of Commons in 1805 what was gained by the war against France: 'We have gained everything that we would have lost if we had not fought this war.' In the case of Vietnam, that was a lot."[13]

26

Kennedy as President

A General Perspective

THE DIFFERENCE BETWEEN THE KENNEDY AND EISENHOWER ADMINistrations in military and foreign policy is not one of 180 degrees. In its latter years the Eisenhower administration was moving away from its first-term posture as it reacted to a sequence of crises: in missiles and space; in the organization of the Pentagon; in its approach to NATO; in its doctrinal view of the meaning to the United States of the developing world and in aid policy toward Latin America, the Middle East, and India. Dean Rusk had his forerunner in Christian Herter; Robert McNamara in Thomas Gates; James Webb in Keith Glennan; George Ball in Douglas Dillon; Fowler Hamilton and David Bell in James Riddleberger.

The difference was in a shift from defensive reaction to initiative: in the articulation of policy in lucid long-run terms; the gearing of administration to a longer horizon of effort; and in the enlarged scale of resources mobilized. It was also the case that Kennedy came to responsibility with a series of major post-Sputnik crises unresolved; and the first charge on his time, energy, and political capital was to deal with them—from Berlin to Laos, from the Caribbean to central Africa.

In addition to threats to the national interest, Kennedy faced the need to adjust radically the thrust of economic and social policy as America moved into a new stage of growth; and he faced a critical constitutional problem in balancing the imperatives of justice and order, centered on the Negro's place in American society. He dealt simultaneously with these problems of security, welfare and growth, and the constitutional order; and he sought to do so while avoiding the usual pattern of the national style—convulsive innovation in the context of acute crisis.

On balance, he succeeded over a wide front. But, with the possible exception of nuclear blackmail, the problems with which he was dealing had, as he well knew, a life that extended beyond the 1960s. And he left two of these—Vietnam and the race issue—at an acute stage for his successor.

Kennedy's character—the counterpoint within him of vital energy and sophistication, commitment and objectivity, inner confidence and self-deprecatory humor, candor and blarney, reticence and human concern—left an enduring imprint on those close to him and on many beyond. And his impact was more than cosmetic: it helped link in his time a new generation to older commitments and to abiding principles in American society. It made somewhat easier the acceptance of the innovations he launched abroad and at home. But he will be assessed, as he would have wished, on what he did and failed to do about the matters of substance that concerned him.

The National Interest

Kennedy ended, for a time at least, the technique of nuclear blackmail. The missile gap may have been a creature of Khrushchev's duplicity, combined with inadequate American intelligence and competitive party politics; but the IRBM threat to Europe was real. And Kennedy held the balance of power in Europe against the threat to Berlin and to the viability of NATO rooted in that threat.

The missiles in Cuba were also real; and Kennedy sustained the OAS principle that no extra-continental power shall establish in the Western Hemisphere a military base.

With the passage of time, if the world is lucky, it may become increasingly difficult to recapture what it was like to face a nuclear threat, to reckon nuclear war as a serious possibility. Perhaps only those who sat around the Cabinet table at critical moments in 1961–1962 will really know the pain of staring out across the White House lawn to the bustle of Washington life through the iron gates, thinking of the hundreds of millions of men, women, and children who were in jeopardy, and yet, judging that the threat had to be resisted, though the risk was real. For Khrushchev, that complex, humane gambler-bandit, did not stop until he felt the knife on his skin. There was in those crises a mysterious process of communication, transcending all the conventional and unconventional signaling of diplomacy. Until Kennedy actually decided where he would stand, even at nuclear risk, Khrushchev kept moving. Once he decided, Khrushchev somehow knew and drew back.

Kennedy was not a morbid man. But those close to him knew he was haunted by the fear that he might be the man whose decisions led to nuclear war. It was a good deal to ask of a human being—to protect the possibility of civilization by putting it at risk. Eisenhower and Johnson also carried this burden, as does Nixon.[1] But thus far the burden was most harsh and explicit in Kennedy's time, when the crises in Berlin and Cuba brought U.S. and Soviet arms into direct confrontation.

Kennedy also met the challenge to the balance of power in central Africa and in Southeast Asia; although it was clear in 1963 that the road ahead in Vietnam would be long and dangerous.

Kennedy knew that his task in the developing world transcended its military defense. He launched doctrines and policies focused on the right to independence outside the structure of military pacts and on economic and social development. These not only blunted communist efforts but ran with the feelings and ambitions of the more than billion human beings involved.

Finally, Kennedy, from beginning to end, pressed across the din of confrontation toward reconciliation with Moscow on the nuclear question. And he began with the atmospheric test ban treaty. If one accepts Kennedy's view of the kind of world he confronted and the American interest within it, he succeeded in his time. Two and a half years after Vienna, what he told Khrushchev rang true. With the benefit of hindsight, it may emerge that he presided over the most acute stage of the Cold War and achieved a favorable turning point.

The New Stage of American Growth

At home Kennedy perceived that the United States had moved as a society beyond the stage when the diffusion of the automobile, durable consumer goods, and the life of suburbia would suffice. He also understood that, as western Europe and Japan moved forward into high mass-consumption, the balance-of-payments position of the United States had become marginal, like everyone else's. But American responsibilities were disproportionate.

The great nuclear strength of the United States alone made credible its alliances and its resistance to communist expansion by lesser means in many parts of the world; and the United States wished to discourage others from amassing that kind of strength. Kennedy accepted the inescapable American responsibilities that flow from a policy of nuclear nonproliferation. He also understood that an inflationary America would put into jeopardy its balance of payments and, thereby, its capacity to bear those responsibilities. Therefore, he pioneered a new kind of national self-discipline in the form of wage-price guideposts.

He understood that the stage into which America was entering required increased public outlays at home which politically could not be generated by higher tax rates. Therefore, he needed a high and steady rate of growth to generate additional public funds.

And so he nursed the economy forward while constraining prices; mobilized the increased resources he felt he needed to protect the national interest; and pointed the way toward the tasks in education and health, the cities and the elimination of poverty that were central to the search for quality that lay ahead on the American public agenda.

His legislative achievements were not trivial—they were clearly outmatched among his predecessors only by Franklin Roosevelt, with Woodrow Wilson's record an arguable case. But they certainly did not fulfill his rhetorical goals and hopes for American society. Thoughtful observers could feel he did not drive hard enough in the Congress. Certainly, it was Lyndon Johnson who changed the legislative framework of American society decisively. But Kennedy's perspective in this terrain was two terms as President, given the conservative structure of the Congress in his time and the urgency of his international tasks.

The Constitutional Balance: Justice and Order

In a sense, the installation of wage-price guideposts was a constitutional act conducted in a pragmatic way: an ad hoc understanding among men of the same community, rather than a strictly defined social contract. There was no precedent in law or custom for the kind of implicit deal worked out with Walter Reuther and David J. McDonald for the pattern-setting 2½ percent wage settlements in automobiles and steel in 1961–1962; and there was no formal basis for insisting in 1962 that the steel price increase be rescinded. There was only an understanding among men who had to understand each other if the public good was to be protected. Roger Blough was right in sensing that the precedents would cast a long shadow. And before American democracy learns how to reconcile high and steady growth with reasonable price stability, understandings of these kinds will have to be reached in more explicit and, probably, contractual forms.

But the constitutional issue above all which Kennedy confronted and, finally, grappled with was the accelerated demands and expectations of the Negro for full citizenship in American society. As the racial crisis of 1963 mounted, he used the powers of the Presidency fully to keep the struggle within the bounds of American law and politics. He forced the issue of public accommodations before the Congress as a matter of federal law and national conscience, accepting the political cost. On this issue, he was probably on his way to success. But, as with Vietnam, his death left to his successor the responsibility and burden of dealing with an unresolved crisis of great momentum.

THE NATIONAL STYLE

IT was these two matters—Vietnam and the race issue—that defeated one of the largest of Kennedy's hopes.

Kennedy was conscious that in domestic and in foreign policy Americans had normally introduced innovations in a setting of acute crisis. In foreign policy, he feared convulsive and excessively energetic American actions in a nuclear age. It was this fear that led him at Vienna to expose to Khrushchev his fundamental views on the balance of power, so that miscalculation could be avoided. And, with Mikoyan, in November 1962 after the Cuba missile crisis, the danger of miscalculation, and convulsive military response, was the theme to which he returned.

At home, an essentially conservative Congress set technical limits, as Kennedy saw it, on the pace at which he could innovate; but by temperament, I believe, he preferred to move gradually, through education, persuasion, and small steps that would permit him to carry along the moderate conservative center of American political life where, he deeply believed, the balance of national power ultimately lay.

I had talked with Kennedy in general terms about the American way with innovation in the late 1950s. It was a central theme in the book I was finishing, *The United States in the World Arena.* I returned to the theme in June 1963.

The occasion was the publication of several articles (most notably by Sidney Hyman and Louis Halle[2]) criticizing Kennedy for not having achieved more than he had in liberal domestic legislation. On June 19 I wrote a memorandum in response to these views which were then endemic in the liberal community.

I sent it to the President's secretary, Mrs. Evelyn Lincoln. Kennedy, as he passed through her office, would quickly flip through the pile of paper on her desk to see if there was anything to which he should promptly respond. In this case, Kennedy was on the phone at length discussing the memorandum within an hour or so after I had dispatched it from my office in the State Department.[3]

The memorandum was entitled: "The European Trip and 'Greatness' in the 1960s." Its principal points follow:

> None of the commentaries on our Administration has, in my view, captured the central problem we face in achieving "great" results.
>
> Commentators generally measure our performance against Wilson, Roosevelt, and Truman. They find a lack of grand movement forward.
>
> What they forget is that these great affairs of the past were crisis reactions to past national failures: the protracted frustration of the Progressive movement in both parties in the decade before 1912; the attempt to retrieve the nation's isolationism in 1917; the great depres-

sion; the effort to retrieve the nation's isolationism of the 1930's; the attempt to retrieve in 1947 the hasty demobilization after World War II and the initial misconceptions about Stalin's intentions; and the attempt in Korea to retrieve the consequences of a weak conventional military establishment in the Far East and of low postwar military budgets in general.

> Our problem is different. Without the advantage of major crises (and consensus that major crises bring), both abroad and at home, our task is to bring about major change towards larger objectives by small increments.
>
> Because of events between 1957 and 1961, we have had to shift the unfavorable balance in the cold war we found ourselves confronted with in January 1961: in military affairs, space, Southeast Asia, Africa, Latin America, Cuba, and Berlin. We have had to engineer the movement from European dependence to partnership. We have had to shift the approach to the underdeveloped areas over from "alliance vs. neutralism" to a policy rooted in the objectives of their independence and development.
>
> At home we have had to change the approach to wage and price policy, budgetary policy, education, health, and race problems.
>
> Both at home and abroad, as I say, we have had to move by a succession of small increments. This has required clarity about our objectives amid much inertia, opposition, and confusion; stubborn pressure; and the steady application of great energy over sustained periods of time to achieve a sequence of small movements forward, rather than grand breakthroughs in the form of a flood of revolutionary legislation or war.
>
> We are now in mid-passage. Both abroad and at home we have made much more progress than is generally realized; but we still have some distance to go before we can lay claim to "greatness."

The balance of the memorandum applied the concept in greater detail to foreign policy in general, Europe and the President's forthcoming trip in particular.

After reading this memorandum on June 19, Kennedy said that this was precisely the perspective he held on what he had been trying to do; he instructed me to write and publish an article on the theme. He returned doggedly to it in subsequent weeks. While a President's perspective is always more complex than he can fully articulate, and certainly more complex than he is prepared to articulate to any one adviser, I believe his response to this memorandum illuminates a good deal about the way Kennedy looked at things in 1963.

But in 1963 forces beyond his control in American society and in Southeast Asia destroyed the viability of this vision. The problems of race at home and Vietnam abroad were to confront Johnson with the task of innovating in a more classic American style, that is, in a setting of acute crisis. And it was to confront him with the virtually unique problem of innovating radically in both sectors at the same time; for the domestic crisis permitted Johnson to engineer "a flood of revolutionary legislation" while he also faced war.

In discussing de Gaulle (see above, p. 81) I recalled his dictum: "Leaders of men . . . are remembered less for the usefulness of what they achieved than for the sweep of their endeavors. Though sometimes reason may condemn them, feeling clothes them in an aura of glory." In the years immediately after his death, there was a tendency to apply something like this criterion to Kennedy. There is, and there may remain, an extra dimension attached to the memory of Kennedy compounded of his personality and his tragic death. He touched those close to him and far away, making his death a family affair—the loss of one of great promise, unfulfilled. This has thrown across his administration a sense of incompletion true only in part. For there was content to the sweep of his endeavors. He turned an America which had about fulfilled Henry Ford's vision of how the assembly line could enrich the lives of average citizens to a new agenda. Kennedy's New Frontier was the search, in many directions, for an American life of higher quality. He set the nation on a long, essential questing path. Abroad, the America he led could not play God in a world of increasingly diffused power; but his rhetoric was not empty. It was backed by the strength of a nation that could and did, under his guidance, leave an imprint of substance on every continent. Whether in converting nuclear confrontation to the test ban treaty or giving new expression to abiding strands of American idealism in the Peace Corps or replying to de Gaulle's veto of Britain's entry into Europe by his June 1963 reaffirmation of the Grand Design, Kennedy's impact ran with the grain of those forces making for a world of stable peace and human decency—long as the road may prove to be beyond November 22, 1963. And if America does not destroy a generation's effort to keep a dangerous world in balance, by an excessive withdrawal from responsibility, history may record that Kennedy presided over the virtually bloodless Gettysburg of the Cold War in the Caribbean in October 1962; although the Battle of the Wilderness was still to be faced in Southeast Asia.

These words from his Inaugural Address may seem excessively rhetorical in safer, more ambivalent times; but they rang true in his day, as Kennedy acted upon them: "Let every nation know, whether it wishes us well or ill, that we shall pay any price, bear any burden, meet any hardship, support any friend, oppose any foe to assure the survival and success of liberty."

They were the creed, as well, of Kennedy's successor, whose fidelity to them was even more sternly tested.

27

Johnson Before the Presidency and at the Beginning: A Personal Impression

THE FIRST TIME LYNDON JOHNSON CAME TO MY ATTENTION AS more than a public figure whose doings were recorded in the press was in the early spring of 1957, at the home of Arthur Schlesinger, Jr. Schlesinger was just back from Washington where, on March 30, he had called on the Senate majority leader.[1] Like Kennedy, Johnson had acute problems with the liberals in the Democratic party. He explained to Schlesinger what was involved in putting through a piece of liberal legislation. He described each member of the Senate, man by man: his constituency and problems; his biases and possibilities; how he might be moved on one issue and remain unmovable on others. The building of a Senate majority around a specific piece of legislation emerged as an intensely human task of persuasion. He said his health and region ruled out Presidential ambitions. He asked for liberal support in doing his job. What Schlesinger described was a sensitive, professional, virtuoso performance. From it emerged the portrait of an authentic, deeply-rooted liberal, measuring progress by what could actually be accomplished rather than by doctrine or rhetoric; formidably energetic; extraordinarily sensitive to people; a master of the legislative process; weighed down by the problem of gaining understanding and support from eastern liberals; inhibited in his possible pursuit of the Presidency by the memory of his 1955 heart attack and by the heritage of Appomattox and all that preceded and followed it.

The Presidency was to bring into play other qualities in Johnson; for example, a redoubtable inner strength which permitted him to pursue a steady, complex course amidst powerful, conflicting pressures, with a declining political base. But the qualities evident in Schlesinger's 1957 interview are a fair, quick portrait of Johnson in the 1950s.

Friends and critics have tried to probe beneath—to explain the man.[2] As with Kennedy, I would not pretend competence in such a task, recalling this observation in James Gould Cozzens' *By Love Possessed*:

> A man's temperament might, perhaps, be defined as the mode or modes of a man's feeling, the struck balance of his ruling desires, the worked-out sum of his habitual predispositions. In themselves, these elements were inscrutable. There were usually too many of them; they were often of irreducible complexity; you could observe only results. . . . The to-be-observed result was a total way of life.[3]

Certainly, the Texas hill country was fundamental to Johnson's way of life: marginal land and relative exemption from slavery contrasting with the rich cotton-growing soil of East Texas. Certainly, a family embedded in politics. Certainly, a visceral revolt against the irretrievable wastages of poverty, hunger, and disease he could observe in the life around him, notably in the Mexican-American community. Certainly, out of his early years, rules of conduct which he believed should govern one man's relations with another—an acceptance of legitimate differences and fierce loyalty when a pact is made. And there was, of course, the National Youth Administration and the precocious ties to Franklin Roosevelt. But the Boston Irish produced only one John Kennedy and the Texas hill country only one Lyndon Johnson. As always, we are dealing with a unique human being.

Aside from Kennedy's comment on Johnson as a possible Presidential candidate, my knowledge of Johnson, beyond the Schlesinger portrait, began when he was Vice President. Two things were clear in 1961. First, like Dean Rusk, Johnson appeared reluctant to express a view in large meetings. As Kennedy solicited opinions around the table, Johnson would often nod, either in assent or to let pass the opportunity to speak. I was present at many—by no means all—sessions where the Vice President took part; but I recall only three occasions in 1961 when he expressed opinions of substance in a large meeting: to urge a man-by-man canvass of the civil and military leaders of the Pentagon on the question of military intervention in Laos; to support a tax increase in connection with the Berlin buildup; to suggest that the aid organization ought to recruit better administrative talent, perhaps from the business community. Knowing something of his history in the Senate, and his famous energy, one was evidently observing a man under sustained self-discipline and restraint.

Second, it was clear that Kennedy took extraordinary pains to keep the Vice President informed. For example, Kennedy rescheduled a major item on the agenda in a foreign policy meeting because Johnson's plane was late, circling in bad weather over Washington. He also saw a good deal of Johnson alone. In a relationship inherently awkward, no modern President dealt with his Vice President in as serious and substantive way as Kennedy with Johnson.

I had little opportunity to get to know Johnson in those years beyond formal meetings. In June 1961 I watched him deliver to the Advertising Council the most effective speech in support of foreign aid I had ever heard, and I had heard many. I saw him briefed for his mission to Berlin in August 1961. In October 1962, at the International Conference on Middle Level Manpower in San Juan, Puerto Rico, I worked with his staff on a Johnson speech that helped internationalize the Peace Corps concept and stimulate coordination among various national efforts.

My first full impression of Johnson came a month into his Presidency. He called a meeting in the Cabinet Room on December 23 to discuss themes for his first State of the Union message. Three geological layers, as it were, of Johnson's advisers were there: friends from the longer past, Clark Clifford, Abe Fortas, and James Rowe; Kennedy men, including McGeorge Bundy and Theodore Sorensen; and his emerging new staff, including Walter Jenkins, Bill Moyers, Horace Busby, and Jack Valenti.

With only a small card of notes before him, he spoke and led a discussion of several hours, conveying the thoughts and feelings he wanted the message to incorporate. After noting that he spoke more slowly than Kennedy, he said he desired a shorter draft.

Then he turned to the military balance. He felt the American military position was stronger than in January 1961: ready forces were greater, and the split between Moscow and Peking had weakened the other side. He wanted American strength secure, but that was not enough. Recalling the Cuba missile crisis, he said the task was to meet our commitments in ways that preserved civilization. We had to remember that other men were like us. They also believed that what they were doing was right. We had to understand how things looked from where they stood if we were to improve East–West relations. We had to try. It would take great patience. The United States would honor its commitments from South Vietnam to Berlin, but we had to find some way to act, rather than react. A solution in Vietnam had to be found.

On foreign aid, he talked of accelerating the Alliance for Progress, with the new appointment of Tom Mann as senior official for both political and economic affairs in Latin America; and speculated on how to get greater support in Congress.

In domestic affairs, civil rights was at the top of the list. Then the tax bill. He would move ahead with the poverty program, but he wanted it to be a positive effort to fulfill human needs and widen opportunity. Poverty was too negative a concept. (General discussion yielded no satisfactory alternative phrase.) We had to fulfill Kennedy's program and move beyond. He wanted to see military resources shifted to education, human needs, and manpower development. Education was discussed at length. It was agreed that Johnson had a chance to break through the religious barrier which had frustrated Kennedy. He was evidently prepared to try.

It was a confident, heartening, and unifying performance. I returned to my office in the State Department glad I had decided earlier in the month to stay in government.

BOOK THREE

The Johnson Administration

28

Introduction to Book Three

THE DOMESTIC AND FOREIGN ENVIRONMENT JOHNSON CONFRONTED as President was more complex than that Kennedy had faced in 1961. Abroad, the two great issues of the post-Sputnik world remained central: the nuclear question and the unfolding drama of modernization in the developing regions. But there were crosscurrents within each which required a diversified policy built around increased possibilities for constructive action as well as increased danger.

In the wake of the Cuba missile crisis, there was a decent hope, at least, that Moscow might continue down the road begun with the limited test ban agreement of 1963. Simultaneously, Moscow had to deal with the bid for leadership in the communist world and in the developing regions of Peking, which was moving rapidly toward an independent nuclear capability and beginning to recover from the disastrous Great Leap Forward. The split hardened and military forces built up on both sides of the Sino–Soviet frontier from 1965. At home and in eastern Europe, Moscow faced the dour consequences of the failure of Khrushchev's ebullient hopes and dreams. All this contributed, in different ways, to Soviet willingness to normalize relations with the United States over a considerable range. But Moscow persisted with a high-risk expansionist policy in the Middle East, the Mediterranean, and the Indian Ocean, while rapidly increasing its nuclear and naval forces.

The environment in the developing regions was changing in three major respects. First, there was less fear of the Soviet Union after the Cuba missile crisis and a greater readiness to assert policies independent of Washington, notably on local and regional issues. Second, practical experience in economic development had increased and the length and difficulty of the process of growth became more clear. Issues of food production and population increase, in particular, became more urgent. Third, the aggressive Romantic Revolutionaries began to confront the conflict between their expansionist enterprises (including the resistances they generated abroad) and the imperatives of neglected welfare at home. Each moved toward crisis rooted in this conflict; but the timing was uneven and the resolution of the crisis, in some cases, protracted.

In four cases—Sukarno, Ben Bella, Nkrumah, and Mao—the military moved to restore balance to policies distorted by dreams that could not be fulfilled in the face of the realities of power and economics. This happened also in Brazil, although João Goulart's ambitions were primarily domestic. With Indonesia, Brazil, and Ghana, the resolution of the crises permitted Johnson to throw his support behind successor governments as they turned to tasks of domestic economic and social progress. In China and Algeria, the resolution of the crisis extended beyond Johnson's Presidency.

Ho's bid to take over South Vietnam by introducing regular North Vietnamese forces, in the wake of the political crisis in Saigon of 1963, faced Johnson with his greatest single problem.

In Europe, de Gaulle, who had failed to achieve hegemony in western Europe by binding Bonn to Paris, was able, nevertheless, to obstruct western European unity and to complicate the tasks of NATO and the Atlantic partnership in several directions, including monetary affairs.

At home, Johnson confronted a nation shocked by Kennedy's assassination; less worried about Moscow's challenge after the Cuba missile crisis than it had been in the previous five years; eager, once again, to turn away from foreign affairs and somewhat more ready than before to face domestic issues arising from past neglect and the emerging problems of the search for quality. The search for quality was to include experiments with confrontation and violence by a volatile minority of affluent white youth reacting against the values, institutions, and policies they associated with the stage of high mass-consumption as well as with the war in Vietnam. But, above all, Johnson faced the urgent Negro demand for full citizenship under circumstances where law and public policy could only begin the transformation of the ghettos and the deeply rooted subculture that had built up within them. The clash between the desired and the possible produced the ghetto riots of 1965–1967.

Johnson moved to deal actively with all dimensions of this agenda, its opportunities and dangers. His Presidency breaks naturally into three rough phases:

November 1963–July 1965: A shift toward domestic priorities, including a surge of economic expansion and the passage of revolutionary legislation in civil rights, education, and medical services, financed in part by a decline in military outlays.

July 1965–June 1968: A period of multiple, interacting crises dominated by the war in Vietnam and explosive violence in the cities; but, also, a period of continued forward movement in domestic legislation, in negotiations with Moscow, the evolution of regionalism in the developing world, and in Atlantic military and economic affairs. The strains of the period yielded a break in the wage-price guideposts in 1966, subsequent price increases, and severe balance-of-payments pressures. They also produced a deep schism in the Democratic party centered on Vietnam.

June 1968–January 1969: With the failure of Hanoi's Tet and May offensives, and the remarkable military and political response of the South Vietnamese, a decisive corner was turned in Vietnam. Tensions over the war, heightened by the Tet offensive, eased somewhat with the opening of the Paris talks, although the Tet trauma left abiding marks on American public opinion. After the violence that followed Martin Luther King's assassination, passion in the ghettos abated and the summer of 1968 was relatively quiet. Passage of the tax bill in June, combined with other measures, stabilized the balance-of-payments position and the international monetary system. The signing of the nonproliferation treaty opened the way for agreement to start the SALT talks. The May riots in France reduced de Gaulle's leverage in Europe and the Atlantic, opening the way for more normal relations between France and its allies.

Johnson, by immense exertion and a steady balance, transited this period when the abiding dimensions of political life were all in active and simultaneous crisis: contention over the legitimacy of the war and the nature of the American security interest in Asia; contention over the appropriate balance among the objectives of growth, price stability, and welfare, endangering the dollar and the world's monetary system; and contention over the appropriate balance between justice and order, notably with respect to the Negro but also to the antiwar movement. By the summer of 1968 the fevers at home and abroad had begun to subside, despite the violence during the Democratic Convention in Chicago in August. That subsidence was rooted both in changes in the nation's domestic and international situation and in changing attitudes toward them. The war, in fact, had peaked with the Tet offensive and its failure, opening real prospects for reduced hostilities if not peace. Violence in the ghettos had peaked in the convulsion after Martin Luther King's assassination, if not during the previous summer. Johnson's March 31 withdrawal from the election of 1968 contributed to a more temperate mood and freed his hands, in his final ten months as President, to help achieve a better balance.

In dealing with a convergence of war and acute domestic crisis unique in modern American history, Johnson used up much of his political capital; and he did so consciously. But he maintained his policy toward Asia; moved the nation's social and race policies massively in the directions he believed right; brought the international control of nuclear weapons closer to reality; and shifted relations between the United States and the rest of the world in ways that promised to lighten the relative burden borne by the United States while enlarging the capacity of others to shape their own destiny. The years 1965–1968 were a wracking, crisis-ridden, exhausting, but also creative period in American history. Johnson left to his successor an ample agenda of problems, but an agenda potentially more manageable than that he or his predecessor had confronted.

29

Growth, Price Stability, and the Balance of Payments

The Overall Performance

TABLE 29–1 SUGGESTS THE CRITICAL ELEMENTS IN THE ECONOMIC expansion of 1963–1968, including, also, evidence of the accelerated inflation which emerged after 1965.

The main features are these:

—a 28 percent expansion of GNP in real terms, over the five years;

—a decline of unemployment below the 4 percent "minimum";

—acceleration from an annual rate of price increase less than 2 percent to over 4 percent;

—an increase in the federal budget by two-thirds, reflecting a radical expansion in both social welfare and military expenditures: the budget was marked by modest deficits, excepting the large deficit of FY 1968 and the surplus of FY 1969;

—a serious decline in the nation's net export surplus of goods and services, due to the disproportionately high level of imports that accompanies high levels of employment and to a rise in U.S. export prices. Severe balance-of-payments pressure emerged in 1967.

In physical terms, the American economy and the American political process generated the inputs required to meet Johnson's commitments to both foreign and domestic policy; and with Vietnam expenditures leveling off after the Tet offensive (in FY 1969), and the tax increase and balance-of-payments measures of 1968, Johnson was able to turn over to Nixon both a budget and a balance-of-payments surplus.

He also turned over an economy with considerable inflationary momentum. Given the continuing and central importance of the struggle to

TABLE 29–1

THE AMERICAN ECONOMY, 1963–1968
(in billions of dollars)

	GNP (in current prices)	GNP (in 1958 prices)	Net Exports of Goods and Services (in current prices)	Balance of Payments (official reserves transaction basis)	Federal Government Outlays (FY)	Federal Surplus or Deficit (–) (FY)	Prices (GNP deflator 1958 = 100)	Output per Man-Hour: Total Private Sector (1967 = 100)	Unemployment Rate (%)
1963	591	551	5.9	–2.0	111	– 4.8	107	88	5.7
1964	632	581	8.5	–1.6	119	– 5.9	109	91	5.2
1965	685	618	6.9	–1.3	118	– 1.6	111	93	4.5
1966	750	658	5.3	+0.3	134	– 3.8	114	98	3.8
1967	794	675	5.2	–3.4	158	– 8.7	118	100	3.8
1968	865	707	2.5	+1.6	178	–25.2	122	103	3.6
FY 1969	—	—	—	—	184	3.2	—	—	—

reconcile steady growth and relative price stability, this aspect of the story deserves to be looked at in some detail.[1]

The Coming of Inflation

The relation between price increases and growth rates during the Johnson administration is reflected in the Chart 29–1 for phases of the period running from the first quarter of 1963 to the third quarter of 1969.[2]

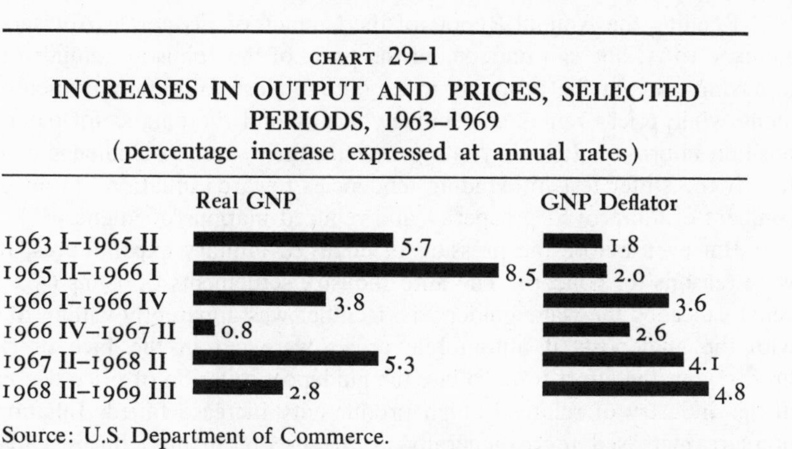

CHART 29–1
INCREASES IN OUTPUT AND PRICES, SELECTED PERIODS, 1963–1969
(percentage increase expressed at annual rates)

It shows the remarkable reconciliation of a high growth rate and price stability down to mid-1965. Then comes a powerful surge in output, at an annual rate of 8.5 percent. This followed enlarged military expenditures for Vietnam in the third quarter of 1965 against a background of acceleration in both the private economy and in public outlays for nonmilitary purposes. In 1966 prices moved up. Deceleration followed in both output and prices down through the first half of 1967, brought about by monetary restriction, a consequent decline in housing construction, and elements of fiscal restraint. Finally, there was a second powerful surge in both output and prices through the first half of 1968, with output decelerating and prices accelerating in the following fifteen months—the latter, in part, a charge on the Nixon administration (see below, pp. 537–540).

The Nature of the Challenge

Johnson struggled through these years with three interwoven problems. First, there was a pioneering experiment to see if price stability could be reconciled with an American economy growing at its maximum normal rate (say, 4 percent) when unemployment was also close to or below its desirable minimum (say, 4 percent). Under any circumstances, this would have been a delicate experimental operation.

Then, there was a surge in military outlays starting in the second half of 1965, the scale of which was underestimated, notably for FY 1967.

Finally, there was an increase in public outlays for civil purposes, stemming from old and new social welfare legislation, which not only expanded effective demand (given the budget deficits of the period), but also pushed the price of certain services, notably medical services, upward.

Reading the Annual Report of the Council of Economic Advisers for January 1965, one can understand the pride of the Johnson administration in having brought the economy to a point so close to minimum unemployment, while prices remained relatively steady and the balance-of-payments position improved. It is easy, also, to share their sense of challenge as they faced "the stiffer test in avoiding tendencies towards inflation" in an environment of "improved prosperity and reduced margins of idleness."[3]

But even before the pressure of enlarged military expenditures, there were reasons for concern. The auto industry settlements of 1964 (5.2 percent) exceeded the wage guideposts. Reuther was apparently willing to stay with the guideposts if automobile prices were cut in the face of rising profits[4]; but the effort to negotiate the guidepost criterion of price decreases in this industry of relatively high productivity increase failed. Inflationary pressure increased more generally as the use of manufacturing capacity reached 90 percent in the first half of 1965, signaling bottlenecks in some sectors and the probability of price increases. At the same time, the rate of productivity increase slowed somewhat as full employment was approached.

But, by and large, the performance of the economy in the first half of 1965 justified continuing an expansionary policy beneficial in many directions, among them a narrowing of the gap between white and nonwhite unemployment rates and incomes.

THE DELAYED REACTION, 1965–1966

IN the second half of 1965 the economy accelerated under pressure from new military orders, increased military spending, and the expectations set in motion by this demand added to an economy already approaching the full-employment margin. The economists in the Johnson administration were somewhat slow to recognize the power of the upsurge.[5] But by January 1966 they realized they had a bear by the tail, a fact highlighted by evidence of accelerated plans for business investment plus the actual acceleration of GNP (and rapid decline of unemployment) in the second half of 1965.

In an ideal world the tools available to government would then have been firmly orchestrated to damp the rate of growth, keep unemployment at a "safe" level, and maximize the chance that the wage-price guideposts would be held. That would have meant: first, a mix of fiscal restraint (including a prompt and substantial tax increase); second, monetary limitation (including higher interest rates) designed to keep unemployment at about 4 percent; third, intensive consultations with union and industrial leaders, notably in industries whose contracts came up for negotiation in 1966–1967, designed to gear the wage-price guideposts to, say, a 3.2 percent average productivity increase.

What actually happened was a unilateral shift to high interest rates by the Federal Reserve Board early in December 1965. This cut quickly into housing construction but also weakened the case for a tax increase. Coordination between the executive branch and the Federal Reserve Board was quickly re-established, but the effort to launch a balanced fiscal-monetary program to damp inflation was compromised. Limited fiscal measures damped the rate of increase in effective demand, notably in the first half of 1966,[6] but did not prevent continued excessive demand for labor. Ad hoc governmental efforts to limit wage and price increases in particular cases were continued.[7] Their effects were substantial but not sufficient to overcome the inflationary pressures at work.

Johnson's fundamental problem in 1966, as he and his advisers saw it, was the lack of any substantial support for an adequate tax increase in Congress or among business leaders. Speaking to the Business Council in December 1968, he recalled: "We knew we needed action on taxes in 1966. Many of you in this room will remember what happened when, in the month of March 1966, I asked how much support you would give me. Not a hand went up. And I was told that I could get but four votes in the Tax Committee of the Congress out of twenty-five." As Arthur Okun, then in the Council of Economic Advisers, later wrote:

> . . . to the untrained eye, the economy seemed to be doing remarkably well. Anybody who wanted to slow things down was a killjoy. All the favorable consequences of the boom were clear: Profits were soaring; consumer living standards were improving dramatically; poverty was declining sharply; and the promised land of 4 percent unemployment was finally being reached. On the other hand, there was no compelling evidence of acceleration in prices and wages, deterioration of the balance of payments, skyrocketing of interest rates, or acute pressures in financial markets. All these unfavorable consequences of the boom were still forecasts rather than facts.[8]

In 1966, then, Johnson had to rely primarily on monetary policy, with its distorting effects on housing and the capital markets generally. He did induce Congress to accept certain limited fiscal measures. These—a reversal of automobile and telephone excise tax reductions, a speedup in corporate tax payments, and the introduction of graduated income tax withholding—plus a cutback in government nonmilitary outlays promptly reduced the inflationary impact of the federal budget. Indeed, the national income and product accounts (reflecting the actual impact of the federal budget on effective demand) show a surplus for the first half of 1966 as shown in Table 29–2[9]:

TABLE 29–2

FEDERAL SURPLUS OR DEFICIT (—), 1966–1967
(billions of dollars, by quarters)

Year	Quarter	Amount
1966	I	2.0
	II	3.7
	III	– 0.3
	IV	– 2.8
1967	I	–11.2
	II	–13.3
	III	–12.9
	IV	–12.2

THE 1966 BREAKDOWN OF THE WAGE-PRICE GUIDEPOSTS

THE deficits starting in the second half of 1966 reflect a deceleration in tax revenues which resulted from a successful cooling of the boom plus continued high government expenditures.[10] High interest rates were joined with a suspension of the income tax credit in September 1966. As Chart 29–1 shows, output and price increases slowed down in the first half of 1967. But negotiated wage-rate increases did not: they rose (over the life of the contracts) from 3.3 percent in 1965 to 3.9 percent in 1966, to 5.0 percent in 1967, to 5.2 percent in 1968. This is where inflation took hold.

In January 1967 Johnson asked for a 6 percent tax surcharge to permit the economy to move forward with less monetary stringency. Congress failed to act, however, until June 1968.[11] By that time the administration's request was for 10 percent, and monetary policy had been excessively eased. The upshot was a surge in output and prices from mid-1967 to mid-1968; output damped but prices were still rising when the Nixon administration took over in 1969.

A CLOSER LOOK AT 1966–1968

AN opportunity to head off the inflationary surge of 1966 emerged from the deceleration of the economy from, roughly, the fourth quarter of 1966 to the summer of 1967. Inventories rose and private capital investment declined. The seasonally adjusted unemployment rate, which had fallen as low as 3.5 percent in November 1966, rose irregularly to 4.3 percent in October 1967.

This rather remarkable 1966–1967 deceleration in an economy supporting a substantial war had its impact on the labor market and is reflected in the following Table 29–3 of hourly earnings, as opposed to negotiated wage increases.[12]

TABLE 29–3

INCREASES IN AVERAGE GROSS HOURLY EARNINGS OF PRIVATE NONAGRICULTURAL PRODUCTION OR NONSUPERVISORY WORKERS, 1960–1968

	Percentage change per year				
Industry	1960 to 1964	1964 to 1965	1965 to 1966	1966 to 1967	1967 to 1968
Total private*	3.1	3.8	4.5	4.7	6.3
Mining	1.9	3.9	4.5	4.6	5.0
Contract construction	3.6	4.2	5.1	5.7	7.1
Manufacturing	2.9	3.2	4.2	4.0	6.4
Durable goods	2.8	3.0	3.9	3.4	6.3
Nondurable goods	2.8	3.1	3.8	4.9	6.6
Wholesale and retail trade	3.5	3.6	4.9	5.2	7.1
Wholesale trade	3.0	3.6	4.6	5.5	5.9
Retail trade	3.6	4.0	4.9	5.2	7.5
Finance, insurance, and real estate	3.3	3.9	3.3	4.5	6.6

*Includes transportation and public utilities and services, not shown separately in this table.

NOTE: Data relate to production workers in mining and manufacturing, to construction workers in contract construction, and, generally, to nonsupervisory workers in all other industries.

Source: Department of Labor.

The components moved irregularly, but the overall shift from 4.5 percent to 4.7 percent in hourly earnings between 1966 and 1967 was modest: there was, in fact, a decrease in manufacturing, slightly outweighed by increases in construction and services. But in 1967 wage rate and benefit increases surged up.

Tables 29–3 and 29–4 exhibit another important shift between 1966 and 1967. In 1966 wage and benefit increases in nonunion establish-

TABLE 29–4

WAGE AND BENEFIT DECISIONS, 1965–1968[13]

Measure	Median annual rate of increase in decisions reached in—			
	1965	1966	1967	1968
Major collective bargaining situations*:				
Wage and benefit changes (packages):				
Equal timing†	3.3	4.0	5.2	6.0
Time weighted (actual timing)‡	§	4.7	5.5	6.6
Negotiated wage-rate increases averaged over life of contract:				
All industries	3.3‖	3.9	5.0	5.2
Manufacturing	§	3.8	5.1	4.9
Nonmanufacturing	§	3.9	5.0	5.9
Negotiated first-year wage-rate increases:				
All industries	3.9	4.8	5.7	7.2
Manufacturing	4.1	4.2	6.4	6.9
Nonmanufacturing	3.7	5.0	5.0	7.5
Wage increases in manfuacturing:				
All establishments	3.7	4.2	5.3	6.0
Union establishments	3.6	4.1	5.5	6.5
Nonunion establishments	4.0	4.4	5.0	5.0

* Except for packages, data are for contracts affecting 1000 workers or more. Package cost estimates are limited to settlements affecting 5000 workers or more (10,000 in 1965). The package cost of a few settlements affecting relatively few workers has not been determined.
† Based on estimated increases in hourly costs at end of contract period and assumes equal spacing of wage and benefit changes over life of contract.
‡ Takes account of actual effective dates of wage and benefit changes.
§ Not available.
‖ Based on settlements affecting 10,000 workers or more.
NOTE: Possible increases in wages resulting from cost-of-living escalator adjustments (except those guaranteed in the contracts) were omitted.
Source: Department of Labor.

ments were greater than in union establishments (4.4 percent versus 4.1 percent): in 1967 the reverse was true (5.0 percent versus 5.5 percent). In 1966 nonmanufacturing wage and benefit increases were greater than in manufacturing (5.0 percent versus 4.2 percent): in 1967 the reverse was true (5.0 percent versus 6.4 percent). These figures reflect competitive tension in the demand for labor in 1966 and its easing in 1967.

In 1966 labor leaders were under great pressure to do as well as the nonunionized sectors of the labor market. They became exceedingly restive with the wage guideposts. The figures for 1967 reflect the determination of organized labor to redress the inequities in the 1966 situation.

The inequities were dual, as seen by union leaders in the key manufacturing sectors. First, there was the disproportionate rise in nonunion and service wage rates. Given the softened labor market of 1967, this might have been surmounted if a second inequity had not emerged and been dramatized—the break in the wage guideposts in the airline machinists' strike and negotiation of July–August 1966.

In 1965–1966 the Johnson administration worked hard to hold down wage settlements and avoid surges in prices of basic materials through private consultation, public exhortation, and the release of surplus stocks. The steel settlement of September 1965 was modest, about 3 percent, after strong Presidential pressure. With pressure from the Maritime Commission (and its control over shipping subsidies), a seaman's strike at about the same time was also settled on terms that met the guideposts. The government, after a determined struggle, set a good example in 1966 by persuading Congress that government salary increases should lag a bit at a time of potential inflationary pressure. But the strike of airline machinists broke the guideposts in the summer of 1966, with a 4.9 percent settlement, under circumstances where the prestige of the administration was laid on the line and failed. There were other guidepost violations in 1966, notably the New York Transit settlement (6.3 percent) and a West Coast lumber settlement (5.8 percent). But, because of the dramatic setting, including the possibility of special emergency legislation, the outcome of the airline negotiation was critical.

As in the automobile case of 1964, productivity and profits were high in the airlines industry. Airline fares should have come down, by guidepost criteria, just as automobile prices should have been brought down in 1964. The government had the Civil Aeronautics Board, which might have played a role similar to that of the Maritime Commission a year earlier; that is, it could have cut airline fares in view of current profits. Unfortunately, this tool was not employed, except to make clear that no increase in fares would be permitted as a result of the strike. The issue moved toward a confrontation, which raised the question of strike-breaking legislation. Johnson faced two problems in the Congress: doubt that an airlines strike would have effects justifying definition as a "national emergency"; and a secretary of labor, Willard Wirtz, whose testimony before Congress left an equivocal impression about the administration's attitude toward strike-breaking legislation. It became increasingly doubtful that Congress would vote for such legislation.

Against this uncertain background, a 4.3 percent increase was negotiated with the union leaders at the end of July. This broke the guideposts principle but could (like the 1964 automobile settlement) be justified ad hoc because the industry's high productivity and profits permitted absorption of the wage settlement without an increase in airline fares. The Johnson administration gave a somewhat nervous blessing to this provisional settlement. But the 4.3 percent wage increase was rejected by the union membership, and the strike was finally settled at 4.9 percent. The government was in disarray. A historian of the crisis concludes:

> The Secretary of Labor commented that the attempt to enforce the guideposts had prolonged the strike. The president of the machinists' union stated that the agreement "completely shatters" the guidepost concept. The President, and his Labor-Management Advisory Committee, meeting shortly thereafter, concluded that some new approach to wage restraint had become necessary.[14]

The failure of the Johnson administration in the airline machinists' strike was, I would guess, not inevitable, despite the inflationary pressures of the previous year. A cut in airline fares, plus greater unity and determination in the administration, might well have seen a less disruptive settlement. It can be argued that the Johnson administration chose poor ground for a major battle. Few workers were involved and an out-of-line settlement might not have had great influence if arrived at quietly. Once the administration drew a line in the dust, however, the battle had to be won if the guideposts were to be held in the face of the pressures in the economy during most of 1966 and the many significant labor negotiations scheduled for 1967.

Because of this failure to make the airline machinists' settlement conform to the guideposts, the country was denied the possible benefits of lower wage and price increases during the general slowdown of 1967. Writing about policy for the upsurge which began in mid-1967, Arthur M. Okun, in *The Political Economy of Prosperity*, heads this section "The Second Chance."[15] There was a second chance to get a better-balanced mixture of fiscal and monetary policy, if Congress was willing to act promptly on Johnson's recommendation for a tax increase. But after the airline machinists' settlement, the third leg of the stool, wage guideposts, was gravely weakened.

Part of the problem lay in the organization and intellectual climate of the executive branch. The federal government is reasonably comfortable in coordinating fiscal and monetary policy. Strains may arise, from time to time, between, say, the Treasury and the Federal Reserve Board, but in recent years the need for close working relations is widely understood and generally honored. Moreover, despite occasional theological debate, theory and experience have led to a wide consensus among economists on the need to use both monetary and fiscal instruments and on how, in general, they are best deployed in relation to each other.

There is no equivalent intellectual consensus or body of common experience with respect to either wage settlement or price setting. Especially with respect to wages, there is a distinct club made up of labor economists, arbitrators, and industrial and union experts on labor negotiations. To them, the kind of wage-price guideposts enunciated by the Council of Economic Advisers in early 1962 looks bare, abstract, and overrestrictive.

The labor expert is trained to focus on a particular negotiation, between a union and an employer, taking place at a particular time in a particular complex setting. There is nothing built into his craft to suggest how a negotiation should be conducted among labor leaders, and there are no clear and agreed criteria to suggest the quid pro quo in price policy for labor self-restraint.

Neither the Kennedy nor Johnson administrations organized the executive branch to bring together in a coordinated and effective way those concerned with fiscal and monetary policy on the one hand, and wage negotiations and price policy on the other. Johnson himself, aided by Joseph Califano, Robert McNamara, and the Council of Economic Advisers, had to try to orchestrate the disparate instruments the government commanded and the perspectives it contained.

After the battle over the airline machinists' strike was fought and lost, labor negotiations were largely left to go their way, as Wirtz wished; although a rearguard struggle continued through 1967 and 1968 to monitor and avoid excessive price increases in individual cases. The results were significant, as all were to learn when Nixon abandoned the effort in early 1969, but inflation continued.

Farewell Advice

In 1968 Johnson organized a Cabinet Committee on Price Stability which reported toward the close of his administration. Among his final observations in his Economic Report to the Congress in January 1969 were these:

> It is understandable that, with living costs rising sharply, labor cannot now accept wage agreements limited to the rise in productivity. It is also understandable that, with production costs increasing, business cannot now hold prices entirely stable.
>
> But the process of deceleration must take hold for both prices and wages. . . . A decisive step toward price stability in 1969 requires labor and business to accept some mutual sacrifices in the short run to preserve their enormous long-term interest in prosperity and a stable value to the dollar. . . .
>
> The Nation should never again be subjected to the threat of fiscal stalemate.[16]

On the eve of their departure from Washington, the members of the Council of Economic Advisers, their wound stripes well earned, offered their successors even more specific advice on guideposts that would decelerate inflation. With the tax increase in June 1968—and a better grip on the international monetary situation after March—inflationary expectations somewhat abated. A dialogue about the mutual responsibilities of government, industry, and labor had, perhaps, a better chance of being resumed productively.

They concluded:

> New wage agreements would move halfway back to the ultimate productivity standard next year if labor accepted wage settlements that would bring the average increase in money wage rates a little below 5 percent. Business would display comparable restraint in pricing if it intensified its efforts to offset rising costs through greater efficiency and if it absorbed a share of unavoidable increases in costs through acceptance of lower profit margins.
>
> This could be translated into a general rule that business agree to absorb increases of up to 1 percent in unit costs and accept as a guide in price decisions a profit target no higher than the average achieved in the years 1967–1968.[17]

A Conclusion

THERE were a good many lessons to be learned from the first protracted national experience with wage-price guideposts.

One could conclude that the guideposts were impossible to sustain if fiscal and monetary policy did not hold unemployment above the level where nonunion labor received higher wage increases than union labor loyal to the guideposts; that it was necessary to act with great promptness, strength, and policy coordination before the wage-price spiral took hold, as it did in 1965–1966; that it was necessary to look ahead to future wage settlements and assure that current wage settlements were consistent with a demand for later acceptance of the guideposts; that it was necessary to assure price decreases in situations where high productivity would yield abnormal profits if labor accepted the guideposts standard; that it was necessary to educate better the Congress and the public (as well as industry and labor) on how fiscal, monetary, and wage-price guideposts related to each other and to national policy; that it was necessary to organize the executive branch more effectively to keep this three-legged stool stable.

Nevertheless, with all the imperfections and difficulties of 1965–1968, the regime of wage-price guideposts provided the nation with lower levels of price increase, at given levels of unemployment, than had earlier experience (see Chart 29–2).[18]

The figures for the Kennedy–Johnson years lie, virtually without exception, to the left or below those of the Eisenhower years, indicating a lower unemployment rate for a given rate of price increase or a lower price increase with a given level of unemployment; the economy's aberrant performance in 1969 and, especially, 1970–1971 comes through vividly.

CHART 29–2

U.S. UNEMPLOYMENT RATE AND PERCENTAGE CHANGE IN PRICES, 1954–1971*

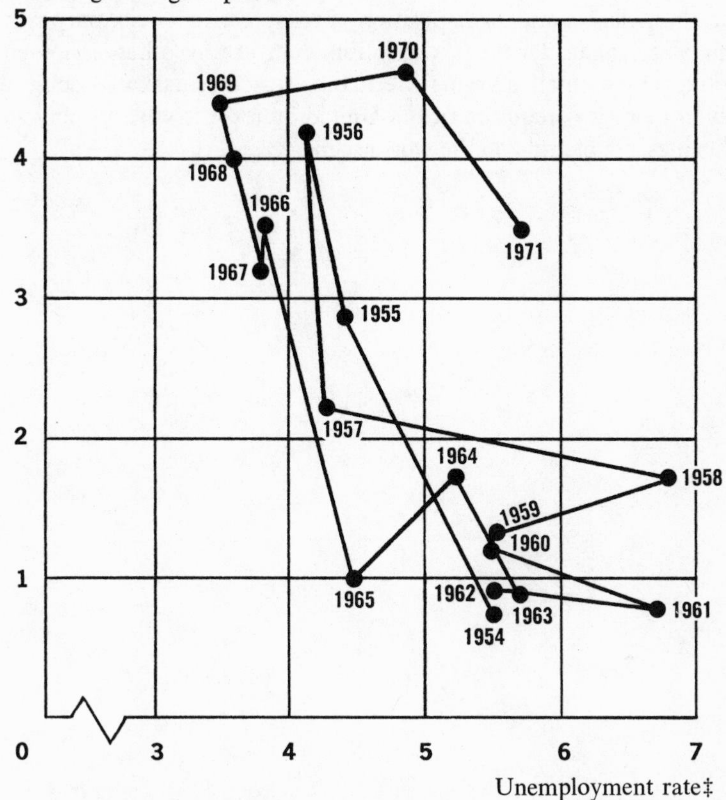

* Price change for 1970, partly estimated; for 1971, both price change and unemployment rate are the author's [Gardner Ackley] forecasts.
† Prices are represented by private nonfarm deflator; change is measured from first quarter of the year shown to first quarter of the following year.
‡ Average for year.

In a capital error, the Nixon administration, rejecting the counsel of Johnson and his advisers, concluded that wage-price guideposts were too difficult to manage and that it should fall back on fiscal and monetary policy alone.

The Johnson administration conducted under extraordinarily difficult circumstances the first test of whether price stability could be reconciled with a sustained level of unemployment around 4 percent. There was not only a war, but a war whose scale and impact proved difficult to measure, arriving at a moment when the balance in the economy between inflationary and noninflationary growth was delicate and relatively small additional pressures could have large inflationary consequences. And it was a war conducted in a society simultaneously undergoing revolutionary change in both its social legislation and its disposition of resources for social purposes. That all this was managed with less inflation than in any other major country, excepting (by a small margin) Germany, was a remarkable achievement. But even more was required of the United States if it were to play successfully its inescapable role on the world scene.

30

The Allocation of Public Resources

A War and a Social Revolution: The Numbers

Table 30–1 measures the broad movements in the scale and allocation of public resources during the Johnson administration. These figures, covering a period of rapid growth in GNP, are marked by the 1963–1965 decline in the proportion of outlays for security purposes, the 1965–1967 rise of 1.5 percent, and the subsequent post-Tet subsidence; the slow 1963–1965 increase in the social welfare proportions and the

TABLE 30–1
GOVERNMENT EXPENDITURES AS PROPORTIONS OF GNP, 1963–1969

	1963	1964	1965	1966	1967	1968	1969
National security	10.9	10.0	9.5	10.1	11.0	10.7	10.1
Interest	1.5	1.4	1.3	1.3	1.3	1.4	1.4
Law, order, and administration	2.5	2.2	2.3	2.2	2.4	2.5	2.7
Economic and environmental services	4.4	4.5	4.4	4.3	4.4	4.6	4.4
Social welfare	10.9	11.2	11.5	12.3	13.6	14.2	14.6
TOTAL	30.1*	29.4*	28.8*	30.2	32.6*	33.4	33.3*

* Due to rounding, totals differ from sum of components.

more rapid increase of 1965–1968; and the approximate stability of proportionate allocations to other governmental functions, which rose with GNP.

The net outcome during the Johnson administration was a remarkable rise of 3.26 percent in GNP devoted to social purposes, covered almost precisely by an increase of the proportion of GNP mobilized and disbursed by federal, state, and local governments.

Of this increase, 40 percent represents an expansion in federal outlays; 60 percent, state and local. But the federal role was larger than these proportions suggest. There was a doubling in federal grants-in-aid to state and local governments: from $9.1 billion in 1963 to $18.3 billion in 1968. These played an important catalytic role in lifting state and local outlays, which, in turn, were made possible by a high rate of economic growth and expansion in tax revenues.

Net federal security expenditures (including space, foreign aid, etc.) increased by some $30 billion in the period 1963–1969; social welfare expenditures by $72 billion: cumulative total expenditures in the two categories increased by $97 billion and $182 billion, respectively, over the same period.

In rough and ready terms, then, Johnson generated about twice as much additional federal funding for the social revolution of the 1960s as for national security, including the war in Southeast Asia.

THE CONTENT OF THE SOCIAL REVOLUTION

TABLE 30–2 reveals the directions in which resources were allocated, on a federal level, among the major social programs.[1]

In the FY 1970 Budget Message, Johnson summarized as follows the role in the 1960s of federal aid to state and local governments:

> To help cope with the relentless rise in public service requirements facing the Nation, the Federal Government has provided large-scale financial aid to the 50 States and their 80,000 local governments. Budget outlays for Federal aid will more than triple in the course of only a decade, rising from $7 billion in 1960 to about $25 billion in 1970. The increase from 1964 alone represents a doubling in amount. Between 1964 and 1970, Federal aids will have added a cumulative total of over $110 billion to State and local funds.
>
> Federal grants to State and local governments now make up more than one-fifth of total Federal spending for civilian domestic programs, and represent about 18 percent of State and local revenues.[2]

THE LEGISLATION

BEHIND all this was a massive flood of domestic legislation. Historians will compare and debate Roosevelt's New Deal versus Johnson's Great Society.

TABLE 30-2
CHANGING STRUCTURE OF FEDERAL OUTLAYS: MAJOR SOCIAL PROGRAMS, FY 1964–1969*
(in billions of dollars)

Program	1964 (actual)	1968 (actual)	1969 (estimate)	1970 (estimate)	Change 1964–1970
Major social programs:					
Social insurance trust funds (excluding Medicare)	22.7	30.2	33.3	37.2	+14.4
Welfare payments and services	3.4	4.6	5.3	6.1	+ 2.6
Education and manpower training	1.6	6.4	6.5	7.2	+ 5.6
Health (including Medicare)	1.8	9.7	11.4	13.0	+11.2
Low- and moderate-income housing	†	0.9	0.9	1.1	+ 1.1
Community and regional development	0.8	1.8	2.4	3.3	+ 2.4
Total	30.4	53.7	59.8	67.8	+37.4

* Figures have been rounded to nearest $100 million.
† Less than $50 million.

Both shifted the allocation of public resources substantially to social (and, in the case of the New Deal, to economic) services.[3] In terms of the relative resources re-allocated, the Great Society was a more massive affair than the New Deal. In neither case, however, can the meaning of the new laws and policies be assessed simply by quantitative standards. The actions and policies of each period must be set against the problems the nation confronted. And we clearly require a longer perspective to put the Great Society programs in a firm historical context. In scope as well as scale, however, it is clearly a monumental affair.

Toward the close of his administration, Johnson's Cabinet presented to him a scroll listing by short title and year of passage some two hundred substantial pieces of foreign policy and domestic legislation of his Presidency. The bulk of the domestic legislation is listed in Table 30-3 under functional headings.

An array of this kind is, of course, an imperfect way to assess the content, significance, and impact of a legislative program. Some of the legislative acts are landmarks in American history, others are of minor importance. In some cases, the direction of legislative action was significant, but the resources made available did not match the scale of the problem. In some cases, the administrative approach taken to a problem proved or may prove inappropriate. But this listing does suggest clearly the scale and directions of Johnson's effort. It also indicates that despite his waning political capital, he was able to maintain forward momentum down through 1968, including the Better Housing and Fair Housing and Fair Federal Juries legislation. Taken all in all, there is nothing quite like it in American history.

TABLE 30–3

MAJOR LEGISLATION BY FUNCTION: JOHNSON ADMINISTRATION

Education

General

College Facilities (1963)
Library Services (1964)
Aid to Education (1965)
Aid to Higher Education (1965)
Arts and Humanities Foundation (1965)
International Education (1966)
Scientific Knowledge Exchange (1966)
Cultural Materials Exchange (1966)
Education Professions (1967)
Education Act (1967)
Public Broadcasting (1967)
College Work Study (1967)

To Expand Opportunity for the Disadvantaged

Vocational Education (1963)
Indian Vocational Training (1963)
Manpower Training (1963)
Older Americans (1965)
Vocational Rehabilitation (1965)
Manpower Training (1965)
Teachers Corps (1966)
New G.I. Bill (1966)
Summer Youth Programs (1967)
Guaranteed Student Loans (1968)
Aid to Handicapped Children (1968)
Vocational Education (1968)

Medicine

Nurses Training (1964)
Medicare (1965)
Heart, Cancer, Stroke Programs (1965)
Mental Health Facilities (1965)
Health Professions (1965)
Medical Libraries (1965)
Child Health (1965)
Community Health Services (1965)
Military Medicare (1966)
Deaf-Blind Center (1967)
Health Manpower (1968)
Heart, Cancer, Stroke Programs (1968)

Improved Infrastructure

Federal Airport Aid (1964)
Urban Mass Transit (1964)
Federal Highway (1964)
Water Resources Research (1964)
High-Speed Transit (1965)
Water Desalting (1965)
Traffic Safety (1966)
Highway Safety (1966)
Tire Safety (1966)
Water Research (1966)
Urban Mass Transit (1966)
Federal Highway Aid (1966)
Gas Pipeline Safety (1968)
Fire Safety (1968)

Hazardous Radiation Detection (1968)
National Water Commission (1968)

To Retrieve Past Neglect of the Environment

Clean Air (1963)
Pesticide Controls (1964)
Clean Air (1965)
Water Pollution Control (1965)
Clean Rivers (1966)
Air Pollution Control (1967)
Aircraft Noise Abatement (1968)

To Preserve and Enhance the Environment

Campobello International Park (1964)
Medicine Bow National Park (1964)
Ozark Scenic Riverway (1964)
Fort Bowie Historic Site (1964)
Wilderness Areas (1964)
Revenues for Recreation (1964)
Fire Island National Seashore (1964)
Highway Beauty (1965)
Assateague National Seashore (1965)
Whiskeytown National Recreation Area (1965)
Delaware Water Gap Recreation Area (1965)
Cape Lookout Seashore (1966)
Guadaloupe National Park (1966)
Fish-Wildlife Preservation (1966)
Oil Revenues for Recreation (1968)
San Rafael Wilderness (1968)
San Gabriel Wilderness (1968)
Redwoods Park (1968)
Flaming Gorge Recreation Area (1968)
Biscayne Park (1968)
Scenic Rivers (1968)
Scenic Trails (1968)
North Cascades Park (1968)
Colorado River Reclamation (1968)

Racial Equality

Civil Rights Act of 1964
Voting Rights (1965)
Fair Housing (1968)
Fair Federal Juries (1968)

Expanded Social Welfare for the Disadvantaged

War on Poverty (1964)
Food Stamp (1964)
Social Security Increase (1965)
Anti-Poverty Program (1965)
Aid to Appalachia (1965)
Child Nutrition (1966)
Child Safety (1966)
Mine Safety (1966)
Food Stamp (1967)
Indian Bill of Rights (1968)
School Breakfasts (1968)

Law and Order

Criminal Justice (1964)
Law Enforcement Assistance (1965)
National Crime Commission (1965)
Drug Controls (1965)
Juvenile Delinquency Control (1965)
Narcotics Rehabilitation (1966)
Bail Reform (1966)
Anti-Racketeering (1967)
Safe Streets (1968)
New Narcotics Bureau (1968)
Juvenile Delinquency Prevention (1968)
Gun Controls (1968)
Federal Magistrates (1968)
Dangerous Drugs Control (1968)
Military Justice Code (1968)

Consumer Protection

Truth-in-Securities (1964)
Truth-in-Packaging (1966)
Protection for Savings (1966)
Wholesome Meat (1967)
Flammable Fabrics (1967)
Product Safety Commission (1967)
Wholesome Poultry (1968)
U.S. Grain Standards (1968)
Truth-in-Lending (1968)

Urban Renewal	Rent Supplements (1966)
Housing Act (1964)	Urban Research (1967)
Housing Act (1965)	Urban Fellowships (1967)
Model Cities (1966)	Better Housing (1968)

THE UNFOLDING OF JOHNSON'S PROGRAM

JOHNSON began by achieving passage in 1964 of legislation placed before the Congress by Kennedy—notably, the tax and the civil rights bills. He also translated into a working plan and legislation the poverty program on which Kennedy had started staff work within the government.[4]

Behind this pre-election effort in 1964 were three powerful, converging forces. First, the nation was in a mood to turn to domestic tasks. The outcome of the Cuba missile crisis and the test ban treaty seemed to promise the coming of quieter times on the international scene. The test ban had proved a popular theme as Kennedy moved about the country in the summer and early autumn of 1963. Meanwhile, the mounting pressure of the civil rights movement dramatized not only the inequities of the South, but also the denial to the Negro of educational and economic opportunity in the North. This shift in the nation's mood did not, in itself, guarantee forward movement in a still conservative Congress, but it provided a different setting than that which had persisted since October 1957.

Second, there was Kennedy's assassination and Johnson's approach to the task of uniting the nation. There was an impulse in America to fulfill the plans of a President prematurely taken from the scene. Johnson perceived this; and he recognized, as well, that a deeply shaken but energetic people would find some easement in acting together to do things they knew in their hearts ought to be done. In the traditional American counterpoint between high ideals and conventional special interests, the strength of idealism rose, for a time, in the wake of the assassination. And, in the best sense, Johnson exploited this fact.

Third, there was Johnson himself and what he wanted to do with his time as President. Johnson had moved toward a national rather than state or regional view of politics, at least from the time of his emergence as majority leader in the Senate. Since 1961 he had operated fully as a national official. But as Vice President, his scope for initiative was exceedingly narrow. Now he was granted the real but limited powers of the Presidency to chart a national course to which the political life of the nation had to react. He was, therefore, at last free to throw his weight fully behind policies in which he had come to believe deeply: policies which would bring the Negro to full citizenship, lift the burdens of poverty from the disadvantaged, widen the range of opportunity for all, and in every sense make the nation a more decent place in which to live.

These three forces converged in 1964 with a security situation that permitted McNamara to cut his outlays from $53.7 billion in FY 1964 to $49.6 billion in FY 1965. The first phase of Johnson's social program was, in a sense, financed by the Pentagon.

Then came the Presidential campaign, which created the setting for the legislation of Johnson's second term. Barry Goldwater was a kind of junior partner in the creation of the Great Society just as Bull Connor helped create Kennedy's civil rights proposals of 1963.

Goldwater's nomination in 1964 reflected many forces at work within the Republican party, including accidents of personality and adventitious circumstances.[5] Among them was a strong minority reaction to the racial and social policies that Kennedy had launched and that Johnson was evidently determined to carry through and expand. If international pressures were easing, clearly there was a choice for the nation. It could reallocate resources to the private sector and diminish the role of the federal government, including its role in pressing the Negro's case. Or, it could turn with enlarged resources and energy to the emerging domestic agenda. In selecting Barry Goldwater the Republican party dramatized that choice, which was just what the candidate set out to do.

The 1964 election was cross-cut by the gathering storm in Southeast Asia and a brief but intense period of domestic urban riots, notably in New York in July and Philadelphia in August. There was much in 1964 that foreshadowed the critical issues of the next four years, including George Wallace's strong showing in some northern Democratic primaries and the explosion at Berkeley in the autumn. But in the 1964 campaign the issues were general, almost ideological, rather than focused by acute crisis; and the domestic posture of the two candidates was probably fundamental—in effect, a test of the legitimacy of all that had transpired since the election of 1932. The electorate, sensing instinctively Goldwater's strong pull away from the central positions of American life, gave Johnson not only an extraordinary Presidential mandate but also a Congress which, for the first time since 1932, was prepared to respond wholeheartedly to a President's liberal leadership.

Johnson approached this opportunity with a lively sense of American political history in general and vivid memories of Franklin Roosevelt's second term. Without ever having read, perhaps, Arthur Schlesinger, Sr.'s, analysis of the liberal–conservative rhythm in American politics, he felt in his bones that the time available to get great things done was limited. And this instinctive knowledge was reinforced by a personal memory. He was first elected to Congress in 1937 in a special by-election. He redoubtably supported Roosevelt, including the court-packing plan then under intense national debate. But he came to a Washington where Franklin Roosevelt had, in fact, lost his capacity to move his program through the Congress.

Johnson decided, in effect, to exhaust his domestic mandate in his time.

This was not only because he wanted to be the best President he could be —both as an individual and as the first southern President since the Civil War (with the ambiguous exception of Wilson). And it was not only because he believed the time for legislative action would be short. It was also because, in his judgment, even a maximum effort would not match the scale of the nation's problems and his dream of what the nation should become.

Like a great vacuum cleaner, he sucked into the White House every constructive idea he could draw, from both private life and the bureaucracies. One major device for this purpose was the task force report. The flow of reports, drawn up by outside groups as well as interagency committees, continued unabated down through 1968. These formed an important part of the basis for Johnson's legislative revolution.

Like all profound changes, the social programs of the 1960s created new problems as they solved old ones.

Johnson achieved an irreversible breakthrough in the role of the federal government in education. But the radical expansion of higher education brought students into colleges with uncertain intellectual interests and motivation; expanded undergraduate classes, diluting the human ties between teacher and student; in some cases, lowered the quality of undergraduate teaching, as faculties simultaneously struggled to upgrade their graduate schools while undergraduate classes were expanding inexorably; and projected a sense that college was a form of mass technical training rather than the education of a limited elite of intellectual excellence.

Johnson finally succeeded in getting medicare legislation through Congress, and, along with it, brought about an irreversible breakthrough in the role of the federal government in providing medical services. But the radical expansion of publicly financed medical services (combined with a high private income elasticity of demand for such services) created grave bottlenecks and an abnormal rise in medical costs. And clearly, despite these great breakthroughs of the Johnson years, education and medical services remain high on the national agenda of the 1970s.

So, also, the new dimensions of conservation. Major moves were initiated in the 1960s to reduce air and water pollution and to improve the physical environment. But the resources mobilized in no way matched the scale of the tasks.

The Johnson years saw also the greatest movement forward on civil rights since Emancipation. A good many thoughtful Negroes regard Johnson as more profoundly their friend than Lincoln, to whom the great issue was national unity rather than racial equality. Embedded within the race question, however, was the most baffling problem Johnson addressed at home—the Negro ghetto. He focused the nation's attention upon it; mobilized a substantial flow of resources to it; and experimented with a wide variety of tools to try to set in motion a benign, self-reinforcing process within it. A good deal of Johnson's educational, medical, social, urban, and law-and-order legislation was, in fact, addressed to ghetto problems, which were to prove in their own way as intractable and slow-yielding as those of Southeast Asia.

31

Problems of Race, 1963–1969

Some Background Observations

WHATEVER HIS PERSONAL RACIAL ATTITUDES, A MODERN American President tends to become color-blind in office. In pursuit of national political power, the Negro vote is an important variable. A Presidential aspirant comes to deal with Negro leaders in exactly the same way he deals with others who speak, or are believed to speak, for groups of voters. In a thoroughly dispassionate way, he examines the polls reflecting Negro opinion, the size of political crowds in Negro districts, their enthusiasm or passivity. And as he comes closer to or attains Presidential responsibility, the magnitude of the race question in contemporary American life is borne in on him. It becomes a highly professional concern, in all its complexities and potentialities for good or ill in determining the nation's fate, and his own.

In foreign policy it is quickly borne in on a President that less than a quarter of the globe's nations are predominantly white. As a President peers into the face of a fellow chief of government, foreign minister, or ambassador, he is usually talking to a man from Asia, the Middle East, or Africa. As often as not, the face of a representative from Latin America will reflect the complex racial history of that part of the world. A President's mind is not on the color of that face but on the problems he is grappling with; the quality and integrity of the man before him; the problems that man or his government is trying to solve; and, above all, on finding a way to persuade him to do or get done the things the President believes most urgently need doing.

Previous reactions to race and color, whatever they may have been, recede, atrophy, or actively change.

Theodore Sorensen has evoked well the transition of John Kennedy between 1953 and 1963 from mild and quiet support of civil rights to fervent leadership.[1] I would guess that Kennedy had thought little about the race problem in America before he entered politics after the Second World War; it did not figure significantly in his six years as a congressman. Perhaps only as a senator from 1953, and especially after 1956, when the Presidency became a realistic possibility, was the issue set before him inescapably. Massachusetts was a place that did not accurately reflect the scale and specific gravity of the race problem in America.

Texas, of course, was different. The issue was alive every day, as well as in the strongly remembered past. There were few Negroes, it is true, in the Hill Country, where, in an almost technical, geological sense, the South ends and the Southwest begins. Many German-born settlers there had opposed Texas' withdrawal from the Union. Its founding President, Sam Houston, in fact, had taken that view. But, still, Texas was part of the Confederacy, and this circumstance cast a long shadow. In 1930, as Johnson turned toward politics, the Negro population of Texas was about 15 percent and the population of Mexican origin about 12 percent, of whom almost 40 percent were Mexican born. The realities of discrimination could not be easily evaded.

Johnson has never set down a full account of how his thinking and feeling evolved in this matter. We do know he felt outrage at the wasted human possibilities he saw among his Mexican-American pupils in Cotulla.[2] He ran strongly in Mexican-American and Negro districts in his Senate races. But until he managed the Civil Rights Act of 1957 through the Senate, his voting record on civil rights was conventionally southern. On the other hand, he refused in 1956 to sign the Southern Manifesto criticizing the Supreme Court's decisions on school desegregation; and at about the same time, he broke loose from the southern opposition to the admittance of Hawaii as a state of the Union.[3] As President, he did more to bring the American Negro to full citizenship than any of his predecessors, with the exception of Abraham Lincoln.

Only Johnson himself could tell the inner story of this evolution. But probably two things were simultaneously true of the years between, say, his going to Washington as Congressman Richard Kleberg's assistant in December 1931 and the emergence of the race issue in national politics during the 1950s. First, as a human being of sensibility, he regarded the discrimination around him as both a troubling, unjust fact of life and a weakness of his state and his region. Like Dean Rusk and other southerners of his generation, Johnson had thought and felt the issue of race much more deeply than most northerners, to whom the question appeared primarily as the unresolved moral problem of a region in which they did not live. Second, as a striving politician, the race issue was not central to the agenda on which he had to take positions in the 1930s and 1940s. The struggles in the Washington of these years did not force a bringing together of private values and public positions on this issue.

In the late 1950s, however, the two strands within him began to converge. He moved onto the national stage at about the time the Supreme Court both reflected and strengthened the gathering pressures for movement forward on civil rights. The two strands began to unite in the late 1950s as Senator Johnson took the civil rights bill of 1957 in hand and worked for Hawaiian statehood. They came closer together when, as Vice President, Johnson served as chairman of the President's Committee on Equal Employment Opportunity. Johnson shared the 1963 race crisis with Kennedy; and his eloquent Gettysburg speech on May 30, 1963, foreshadowed Kennedy's address a few weeks later.[4]

Johnson's private values and public position became fiercely interlocked when he moved to the Presidency. He was viewed by most American Negroes as a southern politician. He took over from an assassinated President who, within the year, had become something of a true hero to the Negro. Five months before his death Kennedy had thrown his full weight behind the civil rights movement and placed before the Congress a civil rights measure cutting across still deeply embedded southern customs—but a measure still to be passed when Johnson took office. As President, Johnson wished to do what he regarded as right and necessary for the country. He also wished to free the South from the obsessive grip of the race question.[5] No one privileged to observe Johnson in the White House can doubt that what he did as President about the race problem conformed to the deepest private values a man can hold.[6]

THE CIVIL RIGHTS ACT OF 1964

DEATH and violence were the catalysts for the three great civil rights acts of the 1960s: Birmingham and Kennedy's assassination for the Act of 1964; the march from Selma to Montgomery and the murder of James Reeb for the Voting Rights Act of 1965; the assassination of Martin Luther King, Jr., for the Open Housing Act of 1968.

Kennedy used to remark often that two Chinese characters were used to define the word crisis: one meaning "danger," the other, "opportunity." It was on this insight, independently perceived, that Johnson carried forward the civil rights struggle in the context of national turmoil and pain.

His strategy in 1964 was to nail his flag to the mast and fight for an undiluted bill. The battle was fought on the issue of cloture—the necessity to rally at least sixty-seven votes in the Senate to end the filibuster. The principal antagonists were the President and one of his oldest friends, Senator Richard Russell. The field commander in the Senate was Hubert Humphrey. The decisive element was in the mind and heart of Everett Dirksen.

Within Dirksen was an instinct and desire to throw his weight behind the great measures that shaped American policy—at home and abroad—when he felt the time was ripe and the stage was set to perform as the reconciling patriot. He had done so, for example, in 1948 in the debate on the Marshall Plan with his injunction: "Do it. Do it now. Do it right." In 1964 he played a similar role: "The time has come for equality of opportunity in sharing in government, in education, and in employment. It will not be stayed or denied. It is here . . . America grows. America changes. And on the civil rights issue we must rise with the occasion. That calls for cloture and the enactment of a civil rights bill."

The vote was 71 to 29. Essentially, Jim Crow, for some time under erosion, was dead. With few exceptions, the action of Congress met surprising and heartening voluntary compliance.

The Civil Rights Act of 1965

Of all the limitations on Negro citizenship, the hardest to justify were those which, de facto, denied him the vote. Viewing the complexities of life as it had evolved in the South since 1865, many observers sympathetic to the Negro's plight came to believe that a long-run solution lay in a full mobilization and expression of Negro interests through the ballot. And, in their hearts, some southern politicians looked to an expansion of the Negro electorate as the most promising route to lift from them the incubus of racism.

The Civil Rights Acts of 1957, 1960, and 1964 had moved against the discriminatory use of vote tests by providing for challenge through federally instigated litigation. This was a slow counterpunching procedure that permitted evasion and delay. Johnson's proposal of March 15, 1965—and his message delivered personally before a joint session of the Congress—proposed a more direct route. It asked for legislation which would:

> Strike down restrictions to voting in all elections—Federal, State, and local—which have been used to deny Negroes the right to vote.
>
> Establish in all States and counties where the right to vote has been denied on account of race a simple standard of voter registration which will make it impossible to thwart the Fifteenth Amendment.
>
> Prohibit the use of new tests and devices wherever they may be used for discriminatory purposes.
>
> Provide adequate power to insure, if necessary, that Federal officials can perform functions essential to the right to vote whenever State officials deny that right.

Eliminate the opportunity to delay the right to vote by resort to tedious and unnecessary lawsuits.

Provide authority to insure that properly registered individuals will not be prohibited from voting.[7]

Four months later Johnson signed the bill in the Rotunda of the Capitol.

Between 1964 and 1968 an extra million Negroes registered in the South, an increase of almost 50 percent. The proportion of Negroes registering to the Negro population of voting age moved up from under 30 percent in the 1950s to about 60 percent by 1968. There was still a gap to close, for the proportion among whites was over 80 percent; but black power, in one of its most critical dimensions, was on the march.

THE GHETTOS AND THEIR GRIEVANCES

A mood of optimism suffused the civil rights leadership and its friends as the new civil rights bill was signed on August 6, 1965. It appeared, as Johnson said, that "today we strike away the last shackle of those fierce and ancient bonds. Today the Negro and the American story fuse and blend." And, indeed, history is likely to record that the emergence of the Negro voter in the South, after the legislation of 1965, was decisive to that region's transformation.

As a critical turning point was achieved in the South, the race problems of the North promptly and forcefully asserted themselves. On August 11, 1965, five days after the signing at the Capitol, rioting broke out in Watts: thirty-four persons were killed; hundreds were injured; almost four thousand arrested; and property damage ran to some $35 million. The mounting succession of hot summers peaked in 1967, but there was an explosion of rage and despair in April 1968 upon the assassination of Martin Luther King, Jr. Relatively speaking, the summer of 1968 was quiet: there were nineteen deaths in urban riots in June, July, and August as opposed to sixty-eight in the previous year.

As the ghettos proclaimed their pathology in these four years of chronic violence, the Johnson administration carried forward a phase of vigorous experiment which has not yet run its course. The issue was what to do about the Negro ghettos. It is certainly one of the most complex questions ever faced by both social science and political policy in American history.

Although remedy is still the subject of controversy, the nature of the problem is familiar (see above, pp. 151–152). In a protracted process, stretching over decades, the Negro moved north to the central cities as the whites flowed to the suburbs. The progressive social and economic elevation normally associated with movement to the cities did not occur for a substantial proportion of the new urban dwellers. Jobs, moving with the whites to the suburbs, were not there to absorb and upgrade unskilled labor; the demand for unskilled labor was, in any case, declining within the American economy; housing and schools deteriorated; the welfare system, while often something of a magnet as compared to rural poverty, provided inadequate resources for a decent urban life and set up incentives that tended to divide inherently unstable families; the political structure and, in particular, the hard-pressed police were viewed as unresponsive or actively hostile to the citizens of the Negro districts spreading out in the heart of the nation's major cities; escape to the suburbs for those who could afford it was blocked or inhibited by de facto housing segregation; a subculture—and a sub-economy—rooted in drugs and violence, emerged, corroding large areas and populations, with no built-in capacity to lift the economic and social level of its members. By 1968 the twelve largest central cities contained over two-thirds of the Negro population outside the South and almost one-third of the Negro population in the United States. Of these, some 2.5 million Negroes lived "in squalor and deprivation in ghetto neighborhoods."[8] And the buildup was still in motion. All projections of the 1960s forecast a further concentration of Negroes in the central cities. To hold central-city ghettos to their size as of 1968, the Kerner Commission estimated, would require the annual movement of 450,000 Negroes to the predominantly white suburbs—nearly ten times the then current rate of Negro out-migration. The ghettos were a problem in themselves and represented a structural change in the cities as a whole, tending to burden intolerably their capacity to pay their way and solve their problems.

The Kerner Commission gave the following ranking to the grievances generated among ghetto citizens who had, in many cases, come north in search of greater freedom and opportunity: the first level of intensity included police practices, unemployment and underemployment, and inadequate housing. The second level of intensity included inadequate education, poor recreation facilities and programs, and ineffectiveness of the political structure and grievance mechanisms. The third level of intensity included disrespectful white attitudes, discriminatory administration of justice, inadequacy of federal programs, inadequacy of municipal services, discriminatory consumer and civil practices, and inadequate welfare programs.[9]

Three Lines of Approach

Aside from neglect, which the nation had practiced for decades, there were, in effect, three possible approaches to the ghetto problem; and the Johnson administration experimented with all three.

First, there was the functional approach. It led to new, sharply focused federal programs to get at specific aspects of ghetto life: Operation Head Start, for example, to give the children early motivation and training to maximize the chance that they would seize and exploit more conventional educational opportunities at a later time; vocational training programs to prepare unskilled workers for job openings that might be available; slum clearance projects to provide better housing; special private enterprise programs, induced or aided by the federal government, to recruit and train the hard-core unemployed.

The second approach was one of development. It accepted the fact that ghettos were, to some degree, analogous to underdeveloped countries. The remedy was to be found, therefore, in analogy with policy toward developing nations. This meant two things: first, establishing a local political authority that would assume responsibility for formulating and executing a long-range development plan, including self-help measures, and that could negotiate "foreign aid" with federal, state, and other institutions; second, a perspective on the ghetto as a total economic and social complex whose regeneration required a "total" plan. Something like this approach was incorporated in the Model Cities legislation.

The third approach rejected the notion that the ghettos should be treated as underdeveloped enclaves within American society and relied primarily on a high overall rate of growth in the economy to draw the Negro ghetto dweller into the mainstreams of American life, as his Irish, Italian, and Jewish predecessors had been drawn in the past.

THE FUNCTIONAL APPROACH

THE functional approach arose from the War on Poverty: conceived in the Kennedy administration; launched into a brief heroic period in 1964; hardened and consolidated in December 1967, after successfully running the gauntlet of congressional criticism.[10]

The scale of the total effort—and its major components—is suggested by Table 31–1 listing outlays for FY 1969.

These programs engaged not only the Office of Economic Opportunity, but also the Departments of Labor, Agriculture, Housing and Urban Development, and Health, Education, and Welfare. They tried simultaneously to get at some of the roots of the problem (e.g., low levels of education and working skill) and at some of the symptoms (e.g., poor housing); to stimulate new attitudes of confidence and responsibility by encouraging community action; and, through income maintenance, Medicare, and Medicaid, to keep people fed, clothed, housed, and provided with medical services.

Meanwhile, the business community was brought into the effort by the National Alliance of Businessmen. In January 1968, under Johnson's personal leadership, this group undertook to train and find jobs for men and women from the ghettos. The program (called Job Opportunities in the Business Sector [JOBS]) was based either on pledges which could be ful-

TABLE 31–1[11]

FEDERAL ANTIPOVERTY EFFORT, FY 1969
(millions of dollars)

Manpower		2,114
Individual improvement		10,005
Education	2,301	
Health	7,002	
Nutrition	702	
Community betterment		1,503
Housing	405	
Economic development	293	
"Catalytic" programs	805	
Income maintenance		12,190
Social insurance	8,631	
Public assistance	3,459	
	Total	25,812
	OEO Programs	1,960
	Other	23,853

Source: Office of Economic Opportunity.

filled by private recruitment or by training hard-core unemployed, in which case government reimbursement was provided. VISTA, a kind of domestic peace corps, engaged a different constituency in ghetto problems.

The functional programs generated in the 1960s are extremely difficult to evaluate. They aimed to achieve widely differing results; some operated over periods too short for evaluation; data are hard to come by and ambiguous; it is almost impossible to separate the effects of these programs from all the other factors operating on urban life, notably the powerful economic boom of the 1960s. The Johnson administration concluded quite early that the functional approach, while necessary, would not suffice.

The Development Approach

STIMULATED by the urban riots of 1965, plus some thoughtful observations by Walter Reuther, the Johnson administration turned to a somewhat different approach, which became the Model Cities program—laid before the Congress on January 26, 1966, and signed into law on November 3, 1966. Model Cities was a lively example of the interplay between an abstract concept and the slow-yielding realities of political and bureaucratic life. The abstract concept was a total transformation of the rotting central cities through a systematic, concentrated, and massive application of resources. One of its architects set out the concept as follows:

> A slum is a group of decayed and rotting buildings. It is also poverty. It is hunger. It is inadequate education. It is denial of job opportunity. It is discrimination. It is the infection of rat bites. It is despair and frustration.
>
> Once we recognize that a slum is all these things, it becomes clear that health workers, transportation experts, educators, psychiatrists, vocational training, and tax experts—all these and more are needed and they are needed at the right time and in the right place. From the very beginning, the approach must be inter-disciplinary and total.
>
> Under this program local communities are asked to assemble all their resources—public and private—together with all available Federal programs and submit a comprehensive plan not only to build apartments, transportation systems, sewers, or hospitals, but to give people in the area the opportunity for self-development at the same time. The Federal government will pay a substantial bonus to help get the job done.[12]

The "substantial bonus" was the offer of the federal government to meet 80 percent of the local costs of executing the "comprehensive plan." When such a plan was approved, the funds would come in a "block grant," rather than in piecemeal support of particular programs. The aim was to demonstrate that a systematic approach, amply funded, could break the back of the urban problem. Fifteen cities were envisaged as the initial recipients. In original concept there was to be an on-the-spot "metropolitan expediter" who would have in his hands all the federal resources allocated. A $3.2 billion program was envisaged over five years, building from the first year (when only planning grants would be made) to annual outlays of $1 billion in federal resources in the final two years.

In fact, political pressures forced the number of recipient cities from 15 to 75, and then to 150. Then the powers envisaged for the metropolitan expediter were judged to be too great relative to those of local mayors, and his role was reduced in power and visibility.

Meanwhile, the bureaucracies in Washington resisted the new program. They did not wish to surrender to Model Cities funds granted to them by the Congress for functional programs. And it proved impossible to generate additional supplementary funds for Model Cities on a requisite scale. Finally, the community representatives generated in Model Cities areas—"to give people in the area the opportunity for self-development"—had to be fitted into conventional political life. In some cases, the inevitable initial frictions yielded constructive results. In others, the outcome was less salutary.

The funds authorized and expended in the Model Cities program are given in Table 31–2.

TABLE 31–2

FY	New Obligational Authority	Expenditure
1967	11.0	0.7
1968	212.0	4.2
1969	312.5	15.4
1970	575.0	85.8
1971 (est.)	575.0	380.0
1972* (est.)	—	450.0

* The Nixon administration proposes to incorporate Model Cities in the new Urban Communities Development complex.

Although funds expended built up to a reputable total by FY 1972, their scale, combined with the diffsuion of effort, in no way matched the concept. The simple fact is that Model Cities, as initially envisaged, has never been tried.

Nevertheless, this effort, compromised and diluted by the political process, greatly stimulated local urban planning and participation in planning. In the "block grant" it provided an attractive form of federal assistance that gave local authorities greater responsibility and flexibility in the allocation of resources, just as development loans were generally more attractive to developing nations than project lending. Some six hundred cities, of all sizes and in all parts of the country, expressed interest in participating before the Act of 1966 was passed or shortly thereafter.

By the autumn of 1968, 150 cities had qualified for designation as Model Cities and received one-year planning grants to develop coherent programs; and by December 22, 1968, Atlanta and Seattle were notified that their comprehensive plans had been approved and first-year implementation grants were made.

Local pride and vested interests assumed new forms. Just as the bulk of the community action agencies generated by urban poverty programs as a whole survived the inevitable tensions with City Hall, it proved difficult to submerge or destroy the Model Cities concept. Nevertheless, initial evaluations of Model Cities revealed that its programs were uneven in design, structure, and impact; that the coherence and coordination of planning and execution were often more apparent than real.[13] Model Cities, as the American political process brought it to life, did not yet constitute a method for lifting ghetto life into a benign cumulative process of growth.

Overall Growth and its Limitations

Beyond the choice and tension between the functional and the development approaches was a larger issue, put most strikingly by Andrew Brimmer. Setting aside social, cultural, and political criteria, Brimmer argues: ". . . the only promising path to genuine economic progress of the Negro in America is an accelerated widening of opportunities in an integrated economy." The economic development approach to the ghetto, in his view, represents an inefficient use of national resources, as well as the Negro's talents and resources.[14] Employment in the ghetto can, at best, only absorb a small proportion of the Negro working force; and Negro executive ability can be more productive and better rewarded outside than within ghetto firms. To Brimmer's technical argument can be added the wider concern that public policy, by "gilding the ghetto," might perpetuate the forces of segregation.

A legal bridge between the development approach and the vision of a fully integrated American society was the Open Housing Act of 1968. In the wake of Martin Luther King's assassination, Johnson achieved passage of legislation, which might, in the long run, break down the discrimination in housing that had helped create the ghettos and, worse, had blocked the Negro's path to suburbia. Raising, as it did, fundamental fears about the value of the white man's property and the environment of his neighborhood, this piece of legislation was perhaps the most politically sensitive of the civil rights acts of the 1960s.

The Open Housing Act of 1968 embodied the concept that the ghettos of America are not underdeveloped nations but are linked to the larger life of the nation. The fate of the ghetto and the fate of the Negro in America in the 1960s were tied not merely to the functional and development efforts in the cities, but to the larger dynamics of the society as a whole—its growth, the changing makeup of the working force, and the demand for labor.

The upshot of all three approaches was an overall narrowing of the gap between whites and nonwhites in two critical respects: income and education. For example, the proportion of Negro men in the age group twenty-five to twenty-nine with four years of high school or more rose from 36 percent in 1960 to 60 percent in 1969, the corresponding increase for white men was from 63 percent to 78 percent. From 1959 to 1967 family incomes of nonwhites relative to whites rose from 54 percent to 62 percent, although the larger average size of nonwhite families lifted the proportion of per capita family income only from 45 percent to 51 percent.

The "Deepening Schism" within the Negro Community

Looked at more closely, however, the 1960s saw what Brimmer has called a "deepening schism" within the Negro community[15]: a tendency for long-term unemployment to increase among nonwhites, as a proportion of the total; an abnormally high rate of unemployment among nonwhite teenagers; and a sharp rise in nonwhite families headed by females below the poverty level, notably those with family members under eighteen.

Table 31-3 shows clearly the latter phenomenon.[16]

TABLE 31–3
PERSONS BELOW POVERTY LEVEL IN 1959 AND 1968, BY FAMILY STATUS, SEX, AND RACE OF HEAD
(numbers in thousands)

	1959	1968	Percentage Change
White, Total	28,484	17,395	−38.9
In Families with Male Head, Total	20,211	9,995	−50.5
Head	4,952	2,595	−47.6
Family Members under 18	8,966	4,298	−52.1
Other Family Members	6,293	3,102	−50.7
In Families with Female Head, Total	4,232	3,551	−16.1
Head	1,233	1,021	−17.2
Family members under 18	2,420	2,075	−14.3
Other Family Members	579	455	−21.4
Unrelated Individuals	4,041	3,849	− 4.8
Negro and Other Races, Total	11,006	7,994	−27.4
In Families with Male Head, Total	7,337	3,710	−49.4
Head	1,452	697	−52.0
Family Members under 18	4,097	2,032	−50.4
Other Family Members	1,788	981	−45.1
In Families with Female Head, Total	2,782	3,439	+23.6
Head	683	734	+ 7.5
Family Members under 18	1,725	2,334	+35.3
Other Family Members	374	371	− 0.8
Unrelated Individuals	887	845	− 4.7

Source: U.S. Department of Commerce, Bureau of the Census, *Poverty in the United States 1959 to 1968*, Series P-60, No. 68, December 31, 1969.

These divergences in the evolution of the Negro community clearly relate to the pathology of ghetto life and are likely to emerge as the hard core of the race problem in the coming generation.

THE BANFIELD COUNTERATTACK

IT is to the nature of what is normal and what is pathological about contemporary urban life that Edward C. Banfield addressed himself in his book *The Unheavenly City*.

Given the complexities of the problem, it was inevitable and wholesome that some should draw back from the efforts of the Johnson administration and pose the question: Is all this activism about the concentration of the Negro in the central cities really necessary? Is the process under way in the cities all that different from the absorption of immigrants in the past? Are the programs being mounted helpful or unhelpful?

Banfield begins by explaining the dynamics of the modern cities in terms of three variables: population growth, transport technology, and the distribution of income among the urban population. Taken together, these decree the pace at which population will spread to the suburbs, leaving the poor in the urban center. It was the operation of these variables that, in the past, both produced the earlier urban ghettos—in response to successive waves of immigration—and then dissipated them out to the suburbs, as education and rising incomes in an urban setting worked their socializing magic. Banfield links this economic concept of urban dynamics to a notion of four social classes, psychologically defined as follows: an upper class, governing its actions to a long horizon, with confidence that its members can shape the future to its purposes over a considerable range, prepared in a spirit of *noblesse oblige* to act on behalf of the community; a middle class, capable of gearing its actions to the future, but a future defined in terms of getting ahead in its own time and terms rather than in terms of public causes; a working class, whose members strive but with less hopeful prospects and a greater sense of being at the mercy of uncontrollable forces; and a lower class, living from moment to moment, its households usually female-based, with no sense of confidence among its members that they can shape their destiny. While passive and fatalistic about their prospects in society, they are prone to violence and to various forms of impulsive behavior yielding short-term satisfaction.

On this basis he concludes that the heart of the ghetto problem lies in that portion of the Negro community that has acquired a lower-class mentality; and it is not, therefore, primarily a problem of race. Furthermore, a long period of time will have to pass before the dynamics of American society can improve that critical portion of the problem. Finally, the rhetoric generated about the ghetto problem has been dangerously misleading, and a good many of the measures undertaken by the federal government and other public bodies have been counterproductive.

He argues, for example, that the heavy expenditures on road networks into the central cities have made it easier for those in the suburbs to commute to the cities but have not made it easier for those in the ghettos to gain easy access to jobs in the suburbs. He argues that larger expenditures on new public housing have reduced the supply of cheap housing in the ghettos but have not upgraded existing housing—a policy which would have made better economic and social sense. He argues that minimum wage laws have diminished the access of unskilled ghetto labor to jobs. With respect to vocational training, he takes the view that the job performance of those who have had such training is only slightly better than those who have not, the critical variable being not skill but the psychological capacity to work regularly; and a fetish has been made of completing high school—an achievement substantially irrelevant to many of the unskilled jobs that might be available.

Banfield concludes with a dozen recommendations,[17] none of which he regards as likely to be feasible. The two principal items among them are that we cool our rhetoric and run the economy at less than 3 percent unemployment.

My conclusions on policy toward this range of issues are set out at a later stage. So far as the 1960s are concerned, Banfield's analysis (originally published in 1968) reflects well the inherent complexities of the urban problem as it emerged as a public issue from, say, Watts in 1965 to the Kerner Commission report in 1968. Banfield is quite correct in saying that many fundamental aspects of the urban problem of the 1960s and beyond are a version of earlier American experience; and they will, in the end, be resolved by a version of dynamic economic and social processes familiar from the past, operating over a substantial period of time. But, despite his psychological theory of class, in the end he recognizes: "The most conspicuous fact of life in the city is racial division. . . . The misfortune, amounting to a tragedy, is not that Negroes got to the city but that they got there so late and then in such great numbers in so short a time."[18] The tragic facts of racial discrimination and a late wave of immigration are not easily exorcised by looking nostalgically at successes of the past. The passive neglect of the 1950s and earlier cannot return, even if that were desirable. What happened in the cities in the 1960s, and in men's minds as they contemplated the cities, is irreversible. It is no wonder that some Negro leaders, taking stock of where their people were, how they were trapped, what the time horizon for escape might be, saw the problem as the emergence of colonies, which had to struggle and negotiate for their independence and integrity. And some of the best results of the programs of the 1960s consist in giving to the urban Negro communities institutions that permit them to formulate their views and press them more effectively on local political and bureaucratic life. In a disheveled way, public policy helped create in the 1960s a new version of the older Irish, Italian, and Jewish urban political machines. Indeed, in some cases community action groups have proved the training ground for men who later entered the electoral arena. But, when the camera is pulled back, as it were, to view the urban areas as a whole, with all their inescapable links to the national society, the ghetto must be seen as part of the cities, and the cities as part of the nation. And there is, of course, an urban problem to be dealt with: a problem of generating the resources to maintain, from a waning tax base, the facilities not only to provide for the poor but also to maintain a decent and orderly life for those who do not flee to the suburbs.

What we can observe after 1965, then, is a typical exercise in the national style: the recognition of a problem long neglected which had reached crisis proportions; vigorous experimental grappling with the problem from many directions; a phase of ardent debate. By 1972, however, a consensus had not yet been reached and the problem had not yet found a solution by an ongoing process. But only a few years of experiment had been expended on a deeply rooted set of problems that would, evidently, only yield in response to a sustained effort. As a matter of social science, it was much too soon to conclude that no answers could be found.

A Conclusion

UNDER Johnson's leadership, the nation turned to face the race question as at no previous period since Reconstruction. The Civil Rights Acts of 1964 and 1965 radically reduced grave social and political injustices in the South. And a flow of legislation and executive action opened a phase of experimental action on many fronts to end the corrosion of the cities. The Housing Act of 1968 widened the path of escape from the ghetto.

As noted earlier, the clash between the urgent demand for full Negro citizenship and the inherently long-run character of the problem of the ghettos produced a dangerous crisis. Southern hotels and restaurants could almost instantly be desegregated; southern electoral rolls could be expanded rapidly; but the northern cities could, at best, only be transformed gradually.

There was shock on all sides as the character, complexity, and depth of the problem were suddenly recognized. The ghetto riots were one manifestation. They were triggered, in the usual case, by the assertion of police authority; but they spread out to embrace attacks on stores owned by whites and to a general release of pent-up frustration as order disintegrated. The damage done was primarily to Negroes. And, in the end, this was sobering. There was a racial component in these riots; but there was also a substantial element of the violence latent within man as a social animal, when the restraints upon him are lifted.[19]

The recognition that the ghetto problem was long term, and integrated cities a distant prospect, struck hard at the older Negro leaders. Many of them had focused on the problems of the South and lived, implicitly at least, with the old image of escape to the North as a road to liberty. New Negro leaders, rooted in the problems of the ghetto, emerged. A great deal hung in the balance of American life as they took stock of what could or could not be done and on what path they should lead.

As in the developing world, the temptation was strong for new leaders to turn to the language of revolution and the methods of violence. And some did. The alternative—the struggle toward equality via education and jobs and collaboration with a predominantly white community—was slow and full of frustration. But in the 1960s the balance slowly tipped toward development rather than violence. Johnson's leadership—the resources and talents he assigned to the ghettos, the paths of constructive action he opened for ghetto leaders—made a great difference and bought precious time.

32

The White Affluent Radicals

JUSTICE AND ORDER: THE DOUBLE CRISIS

FINDING THE APPROPRIATE BALANCE BETWEEN JUSTICE AND ORDER is as fundamental a problem as any faced by society. In the period 1965–1968 the United States experienced a double version of this problem: the race question, as it emerged in the period 1963–1965 in the South, 1964–1968 in the North; and the performance of the white affluent radicals starting at the Berkeley campus of the University of California in the autumn of 1964 and running down to the Cambodia–Kent State University demonstrations in the late spring of 1970. The issues shifted from civil rights and university governance to fasten, in large part, on Vietnam; but the issues, including Vietnam, were merely themes in a root-and-branch attack on American society and its institutions, an attack underpinned by the doctrines of the New Left.

Negro and white dissidence and violence were linked at a few points; but they are essentially distinct, and even somewhat contrary. The links were the experience of many white youths with civil rights protests; the real (but minor) role of various kinds of revolutionaries in both black and white movements; the efforts of Negro students in some colleges to press for Black Study programs, increased autonomy, and lowered admission and graduation requirements; and the effort by certain black and white leaders to link Vietnam to the race question. But operationally, blacks as a whole refused to be diverted by Vietnam.[1]

Vietnam was certainly an intensifying factor in the United States. But the protest of affluent radical youth was an almost universal phenomenon in the richer nations of the world in the 1960s. Vietnam was not a significant issue at Berkeley in 1964. A fundamental explanation must look beyond the war.

The Negro and white dissident movements of the 1960s were contrary in this sense: with minor exceptions, the Negro was demanding the full benefits, real or believed, of the present stage of high mass-consumption; many white dissidents were in active revolt against the real or believed values of that stage of development. In a sense, black radicals sought entrance to contemporary American society just when white affluent radicals sought exit or the society's radical transformation.

The Four Critical Factors

Like the race question, the problems posed by the dissident and radical youths of the 1960s quickly generated a vast literature. Explanations of the phenomenon vary, of course. And as with many large-scale events, we have more potentially relevant factors than we need: there are, for example, Vietnam and Spockian child care; the mega-university and affluence; drugs and purposeful communists; a new life style and the deadly sprawl of bureaucracy.

In my view, four factors are necessary and sufficient to explain the student unrest of the 1960s in the richer noncommunist nations, including the United States.

First, some of the young, born of well-to-do and generally left-tilted families, reacted in a classic way against the values and structure of their society, as a previous generation had reacted against Babbitry and materialism.[2] In the 1960s a vast majority in North America, western Europe, and Japan still had much to ask of the age of automobiles, consumer durables, and suburbia; but they were fewer than in the 1920s. And one could observe the drive for things beyond gadgetry and what it could offer: mass education and public medicine, travel and recreation. It was an understandable time for the volatile affluent margin of a new generation to strike off in search of new objectives while simultaneously taking for granted, or rejecting, the old.

Second, the educational revolution of the post-1945 years posed major problems in college life for some students. As demands increased from public and private institutions for specialized professionals, men in some fields, which appeared less relevant and functional, felt left behind, rejected by what they came to believe was a heartless bureaucratic–technocratic society; and they became dissidents. A very high proportion of the affluent radicals, from Berkeley to Nanterre to Tokyo, came from sociology, philosophy, political science, and literature—fields that have "a restricted and ambiguous place in contemporary society."[3] The radical expansion of undergraduate colleges, sometimes accompanied by inadequate expansion of physical facilities, but in almost all cases by a dilution in the quality of teaching, heightened the inevitable sense of loneliness among a good many undergraduates and reduced the sense of loyalty to their educational institutions. The expansion of the university population also diluted the old sense that higher education was a relatively sure road to elite status; and, by rendering higher education a more mundane middle-class requirement, it brought to the universities many with little genuine intellectual interest and increased the number of those who looked beyond the university with a sense of insecurity.

Taken together, this background of anxieties and concerns helps explain where many of the radicals were recruited; where certain explosive issues for confrontation were found by the radical leaders; and, above all, why the student majority was generally passive when radical scenarios were set in motion and sometimes supportive when they came to the stage when students were being hit on the head by police. As François Crouzet said of Nanterre:

> . . . the Nanterre *enragés* numbered 150 on March 22, and 300 at the utmost a few weeks later; they could attract to their meetings 1,000 to 1,500 students, while total enrollment at Nanterre was 12,000. But a large majority of students remained passive; they neither supported the *enragés* nor resisted them, they did not appear seriously shocked by their excesses and observed a neutrality which not infrequently was rather benevolent (and in fact, many sided with the extremists after May 3). It would be foolish to deny that there was widespread malaise in the French student world, which made things easy for the extremists. This malaise can be explained by the very large numbers of students in places like Nanterre and the Sorbonne, by the low intellectual level of many of them, and by the widespread anxiety about employment prospects for graduates.[4]

Third, there was the catalytic role of various communist (or anarchist) doctrines and leaders. Given the history of McCarthyism in the 1950s, there is an understandable reluctance of analysts to place much emphasis on this factor, when, clearly, many other factors were in play and when the radical leaders themselves represented an often contending spectrum rather than a monolithic unity. Nevertheless, the student demonstrations and campus riots of the 1960s cannot be fully understood without accepting the fact that a certain number of hard-working and quite professional radicals were steadily at work, usually implementing the strategy well articulated by Rudi Dutschke in Berlin: "We only need to break their domesticated rules of the game, which make any protest ineffective—and nightsticks are used. That means: we have the possibility, through provocation, of exposing the concealed authoritarian, pre-fascist structure of this city and this state." Through provocation and confrontation, some of the radical professionals sought to polarize Western societies on the classic theory that led German communists of the 1930s to fight the Social Democrats and open the way for Hitler's coming to power.

Fourth, in the face of campus violence there was profound uncertainty as well as deep schisms among those responsible for university life. There was nothing in the prior experience of most administrators to suggest how the technique of purposeful confrontation should be dealt with in a university. Faculties were split among those who, up to a point, sided with the students, including (or despite) their methods; those who opposed; and those who, frightened or dismayed by the unexpected phenomenon, fled the scene in fact or in spirit. It took time for administrators chosen for other gifts to feel their way toward the most effective methods for isolating the radicals who sought violence; time for faculties, which had come to take universities as automatically assured institutions, to resurrect and animate the principles on which the viability of a university depends; time for students to assess the net consequences of purposeful confrontation and violence.

Student violence in the 1960s forced on all concerned a re-examination of the meaning of university life; and it forced on a new as well as older generation re-examination of the role of violence in the democratic political process.

I believe these factors, taken together, explain the international phenomenon of student unrest and violence in the 1960s: the shift from high mass-consumption to the search for quality; the educational revolution; the purposeful, professional agitators; and uncertain, split responses from administrators and faculty. There is a possible fifth factor of which I am less sure: the internationalization of student life, not merely by television but also by travel. The mobility and freemasonry among the students of the world is a remarkable fact; and it may have contributed something essential to the parallelisms in doctrine and behavior from California to Paris, Cambridge to Berlin, New York City to Tokyo.

Political Consequences

The student problems of the 1960s were essentially international in their critical elements; but, clearly, in the United States they were connected with Vietnam in a special way. Aside from their interplay with foreign policy, however, they had a considerable impact on national life.

First, they helped, along with racial violence (and violent racial rhetoric), to produce the profound law-and-order reaction which dominated the Presidential election of 1968. There are few more dramatic reversals of fortune than that between Goldwater's 38.5 percent of the popular vote in 1964 and the 56.9 percent of Nixon and Wallace combined four years later;

and it should be put that way, given the issues paramount in the voter's mind in 1968.[5]

Second, as part of this reaction the electorate exhibited a new reserve toward higher education. A phase of skeptical stock-taking was bound to come as the federal and state governments moved to complete under Johnson the postwar revolution which had seen the population of students in higher education grow from 1.5 million in 1940 to some 7 million in 1968. But the pause and drawing back came at a bad time for private and public institutions alike, given their financial problems.

Third, it forced dissident youth to reappraise violence as a political tool, a process parallel to that which occurred in the Negro community, leaving the Weathermen and the Black Panthers, respectively, somewhat isolated.

Fourth, there was a polarization of Democratic party politics as the left wing shifted in sympathy with and under pressure from the radical youth.

Fifth, despite the powerful negative impact of student radicalism on the American electorate, there emerged considerable willingness to pay attention to issues the young considered important. Confronted by a wave of student protests and demonstrations not new in theme or spirit but new in scale, American society did not accept the proposition that the ardent, articulate, affluent, radical youth possessed special wisdom which ought to be taken as revealed truth; nor did it blindly react to provocation with counterviolence, although there were occasions when the police or National Guard did precisely that. While insisting that law and order be maintained and the institutions of the society preserved, it listened with troubled attention to what was being said and weighed it. It is still too soon to measure confidently the net impact of this phase of ardent advocacy and violence, of defensive reaction and attentive listening.

There is a certain irony that Johnson, who did more than any predecessor to widen opportunity for students and Negroes, should have had to preside over a period of acute student and Negro dissidence and even violence. He was conscious of that irony and spoke of it, for example, in his final talk with Robert Kennedy on April 3, 1968.[6] But the irony is only superficial: Johnson acted to widen opportunity for some 22 million Negroes and some 50 million students. Racial and student violence were substantial enough problems; but they involved relatively small numbers and, in the case of students, they involved issues that only obliquely related to educational opportunity. There is no necessary contradiction between a period of constructive progress on a broad front concurrent with considerable unrest and violence.

For Johnson, student unrest, linked as it became to the war in Vietnam, added an extra dimension of strain to the inherent burdens of the Presidency—one of the dimensions of strain he hoped his decision not to run again, disclosed in his televised speech of March 31, 1968, would ease. There is a special quality in a society's reaction to student unrest: awareness of student inexperience and a capacity for mercurial unwisdom is balanced by a sense that the students are a part of the future and, after all, our children. But Johnson knew well that the demonstrating students were a small minority; he was not prepared to revise the American Constitution and substitute their judgment for his.

As their principal political target, Johnson listened, tried to understand, and went about his business. That included doing about all the political process could possibly do in five years to move American society toward canons of decency and quality, and moving a rather unyielding international society in the direction of stable peace, as he understood that objective.

33

The Organization of National Security Affairs

JOHNSON'S ADVISORY SYSTEM FOR NATIONAL SECURITY POLICY WAS built initially around Rusk, McNamara, and Bundy. As a colleague, he had seen these men at work for almost three years. He admired each of them. As a matter of principle, he sought continuity with Kennedy's administration. And he knew from many Washington years, during six administrations, that, taken collectively, they were a rare combination of talent, experience, mutual loyalty, and dedication to the Presidency. In general, Johnson respected Kennedy's ability to attract and select talent. And, I would guess, this was nowhere more true than at the apex of national security policy. There were two major changes in the five subsequent years, but down to the end Johnson organized the flow of advice to him around the men holding these three posts, with Rusk, *primus inter pares*.

It was, of course, more complicated than that. There was, for example, the Tuesday lunch. It began early in 1964 and met irregularly down to March 1965, when the crisis in Vietnam deepened and the sessions became quite regular. It became a kind of regular National Security Council (NSC) meeting, with an agenda reaching far beyond Vietnam. Its membership widened in 1966 to include regularly the chairman of the Joint Chiefs of Staff and the director of the Central Intelligence Agency. Virtually from the beginning, the President's press secretary—Bill Moyers and, then, George Christian—was there and sometimes others of his staff. The Vice President came occasionally, as did others; for example, Arthur Goldberg, Ellsworth Bunker, and General Westmoreland, depending on the agenda and their presence in Washington. If the secretary of state or the secretary of defense was out of town, his deputy would come.

The Tuesday lunch was a curious blend of formality and informality. The agenda was prepared and the President's decisions transmitted with full formality. I would check on Monday with Rusk and McNamara (later Clark Clifford) to see what issues they wished to raise. If I had suggestions for the agenda, I would discuss them with one or the other, or both, depending on the issue. I would also arrange that any necessary documents be assembled; e.g., a draft cable, a negotiating proposal, a factual background paper. I usually sent the agenda and attached annexes to the President on Monday night, although occasionally an annex—or the agenda itself—might not be ready until early Tuesday morning. The agenda always contained an item "Other" to permit anyone around the table to raise a matter newly arisen on Tuesday morning. I recorded the decisions taken by the President.

Records of the discussions themselves were kept erratically until late 1966, when Tom Johnson, deputy press secretary, was assigned the task on a regular basis. This was done for historical rather than operational purposes, since the give and take of the sessions was not reported back to the departments, only the decisions. The secretary of defense transmitted all military instructions; although these were also recorded in my office and I informed my liaison officer with the Joint Chiefs of Staff. Rusk preferred that I immediately inform the head of his secretariat, unless the action required was so delicate that he wished to handle its execution personally. I transmitted State's instructions in a telephone conversation immediately after the meeting, the substance of which my secretary recorded and of which Bromley Smith, executive secretary of the NSC, was promptly informed. Bundy had operated in a similar way.

This rather conventional and orderly bureaucratic procedure was conducted in a deceptively informal setting. Perhaps more remarkable for Washington life, the atmosphere was leisurely. The pressures seemed to lift a bit, and those taking part—eating the President's food in his home—reacted and performed in a way hard to do around the Cabinet table. Those attending the lunch would arrive in the White House sitting room, at the west end of the Mansion, promptly at one. Tomato juice, sherry, or whatever would be served. There was usually an interval before the President arrived, after his last morning appointment. This might be taken up with preliminary discussions of agenda items, gossip, or the brief appearance of Mrs. Johnson or some other member of the family.

Johnson would arrive, soon or late, depending on his schedule, and join in the conversation, drinking his inevitable low-calorie Dr. Pepper. He would discuss whatever happened to be on his mind: the last appointment, a problem in the Congress, a newspaper column, an item in the morning's intelligence that intrigued him. Unless some matter was extraordinarily urgent, the conversation would flow with the President's interest to the table.

At a moment of his choice, he would pull the agenda and attached papers toward him and the formal business of the meeting would proceed, as we ate. Once we started work on the agenda, it was rarely interrupted until its items were fully dealt with; although Johnson would occasionally skip an item if he wished to deal with it at another time, in another setting. If Rusk had a sensitive matter (notably, new appointments), he or I would indicate that to Johnson before the meeting; and Rusk would see Johnson alone after lunch. McNamara would also occasionally use that interval for a private conversation.

The meeting usually closed about 3 o'clock; but it sometimes continued later into the afternoon, to the understandable anxiety of those who had to deal with men arriving for appointments with the secretary of state or the secretary of defense.

The Tuesday lunch was only one of many ways Johnson received advice before making decisions in military and foreign policy. But it was important for a number of reasons. The only men present were those whose advice the President wanted most to hear. Also, the group was small, which minimized the possibility of leaks (I can recall none).

Then, the atmosphere set by Johnson, and the strong collegial sense among those regularly attending, encouraged extraordinary candor. Clashing, exploratory, or even frivolous views could be expressed with little bureaucratic caution and with confidence no scars would remain. It was a deadly serious but somehow intensely human occasion.

The meeting was regular. There were many other occasions when the President could and did communicate with each of those regularly at the Tuesday lunch. But there was some virtue in assuring a stock-taking session among these men. It provided a common base for the week's actions, a common vision of the President's current frame of mind. It was a particularly valuable device when a war was being fought and there was, quite literally, an unbroken flow of diplomatic contacts looking toward peace.[1]

Although the heart of the many-sided NSC process was the Tuesday lunch, some formal NSC meetings were held in the Johnson administration. As in all administrations, they served a variety of purposes: to ratify a decision already arrived at by the President, after a final round of discussion; to hear a report from a returning ambassador or special emissary; to debate an issue on which the President evidently would soon have to decide; etc. The major difference between an NSC meeting and a Tuesday lunch was that more people were automatically invited, including especially the secretary of the treasury, the director of the USIA, and the ambassador to the United Nations. It also meant that invaluable public servant, Bromley Smith, who served as a special assistant to both Bundy and myself, participated in his formal capacity as executive secretary of the NSC and took full notes.

In the last three years of the Johnson administration, the NSC was used in a somewhat more systematic way than earlier in the 1960s. After returning to the White House in 1966, I took stock of the historical use of the NSC. I concluded that there were two kinds of NSC meetings to be avoided. First, a meeting on an important matter at which the President would be under pressure to make a major decision. The NSC was, generally speaking, an extremely poor place for the President to make up his mind finally on a specific issue. A President usually decides a major matter after hearing argument over a protracted period of time; after a great deal of reading; and after developing as clear a picture as possible of the consequences of alternative courses of action. More often than not he will make up his mind while alone—after one final rereading of a document, or one last telephone call. A formal session in the Cabinet Room with some dozen men around the table and another dozen or more behind them along the walls is not a good setting for a final decision.

There was another kind of NSC meeting that lowered the value of the instrument for Presidents. This was a session dealing with problems that might be interesting and important but on which the President was not likely to have to act soon, if ever. Kennedy and Johnson were greatly interested in a variety of subjects on which no decision was likely to be required in the foreseeable future. They were prepared to read extensively about them. For example, from 1966 through 1969 there was on my staff a first-rate scholar and foreign service officer, Alfred Jenkins, who kept in touch with the whole community of governmental and nongovernmental students of China. All major matters affecting the internal conditions of mainland China were regularly reported to the President. Johnson followed closely the ups and downs of the Cultural Revolution, the movement of forces on the Sino–Soviet frontier, etc. On the other hand, a President generally dislikes using his scarce working time, and that of his senior advisers, for formal meetings that have no operational content.

In the light of those judgments, I suggested to Johnson that the NSC be used primarily for generating and exposing a series of major problems on which decisions would be required of the President, not at the moment but in some foreseeable time period. Johnson agreed. Some twenty NSC meetings of this anticipatory type were held between April 1966 and January 1969.[2] They proved useful in forcing the departments to present a coherent picture of a problem and of the alternatives confronting the President as seen in the bureaucracy. Even more important was the chance to hear the President's initial reactions and to reshape staff work, if necessary, with a perspective on the problem that might have been neglected initially.

Typical NSC meetings of this type were, for example: a review of developments in Indonesia over the previous year in anticipation of the annual meeting at The Hague of countries assisting economic development in Indonesia; a review of the food–population balance in the world over a ten-year period—a review which, in fact, once led to a decision on the spot to expand United States wheat acreage; a review in the late summer of major issues likely to arise for Presidential decision during the autumn meeting of the United Nations General Assembly. This kind of modest but purposeful formal NSC session was, I believe, useful.

In addition to the Tuesday lunch and formal NSC meetings, a great many other sessions were organized to consider specific problems at particular moments. Johnson personally decided whom he wished to attend. There was, for example, a whole series of sessions on the Middle East; on India's food problem in the period 1965–1967; on the Kennedy Round trade negotiations; on the monetary crises and innovations of the period; on arms control negotiations. For each, papers and an agenda were prepared by the President's staff; and, more often than not, a paper had been formulated by one or more departments. To all intents and purposes, these were NSC meetings.

In addition, Johnson kept open and used many other channels of communication and advice. He talked personally more often than anyone knew to old colleagues in the Senate. He consulted Dean Acheson and other members of the old foreign affairs establishment. He regularly sought the views of old friends like Abe Fortas and Arthur Krim, and occasionally Ed Weisl, James Rowe, and Tommy Corcoran. He saw members of the press singly or in small groups in the time between his nap and dinner, often in the small office off the President's Oval office. Whenever they were in town, he met with Jean Monnet and Barbara Ward Jackson.

Then, of course, there was the normal flow of papers generated by interdepartmental staff work. This flow had been reshaped in a particular way by Kennedy and carried forward by Johnson. Kennedy wanted the State Department to lead the inevitable and necessary task of interdepartmental coordination in foreign affairs. In abolishing the Operations Coordinating Board, he decided, in effect, that the White House role in this process would be secondary rather than primary. State Department leadership did gradually evolve in the course of the 1960s: a Cabinet-level arms control group (the Committee of Principals) chaired by Rusk; a senior interdepartmental group (SIG) chaired by the under secretary of state; a special Vietnam committee also chaired by the under secretary of state; interdepartmental regional groups (IRG's) chaired by the assistant secretaries of state responsible for Europe, Latin America, Africa, the Near East and South Asia, and the Far East.[3] It took considerable persuasion to induce the hard-pressed under secretary of state, Nick Katzenbach, to bring SIG to life. Once set in motion, Katzenbach ran the group with skill and, I believe, made it a useful instrument of government.

This interdepartmental staff work was meant primarily to prepare the President's senior advisers to advise him. The President, of course, received the major papers developed in the bureaucracy. They were essential background for discussion with his senior advisers. But, inevitably, they did not contain all the elements that had to enter the President's decision.

The NSC staff closely followed the development of these papers. They understood them intimately and could tell the President what lay behind the recommendations that ultimately came to him. While members of the NSC staff regularly took part in the work of these committees, they clearly could not speak for the President until he had decided. Therefore, they drew a sharp line between personal judgments expressed to working colleagues and Presidential decisions or attitudes which they were in a position to convey.

Like Kennedy, Johnson was a voracious reader, capable of absorbing and retaining a vast amount of information and of spotting in a long document the critical assumptions, facts, and recommendations. Virtually every day ended for Johnson at one or two in the morning, or later—with his night reading. From all over the government, those who had access to the President—Cabinet members, agency directors, members of his personal staff—submitted memoranda for this ritual. After the day ended, even after major official social occasions at the White House, Johnson would for several hours read this mass of material with the greatest care. And the next morning there would flow out into the bureaucracy an array of decisions, instructions, or broad reactions. It was an exercise much like Kennedy's weekend reading but a more massive and purposeful process. It was also a great burden. (It often crossed my mind after March 31, 1968, that if Johnson had no other reason for not running again, ridding himself of the burden of night reading would suffice.) But it permitted Johnson a rare intimacy of command over what was happening and what was thought in every corner of the government.

In May 1964 Johnson asked me to undertake, in addition to planning in State, the post of United States member of the Inter-American Committee on the Alliance for Progress (CIAP).[4] The CIAP job gave me a rare opportunity both to get to know Latin America and to see more of Johnson at work.

At the Honolulu meeting on Vietnam in February of 1966, Johnson indicated he wanted me to come over to the White House in the wake of Bundy's departure, but it was not until a few moments before the announcement of my appointment on March 31, 1966, that the matter was firm. I returned to work at the White House about 7 o'clock the next day, after more than four years at State.

The job of special assistant for national security affairs was, as redesigned in 1961, already five years old when I moved into it on April 1, 1966. Over the two previous years, I had come to know Johnson reasonably well; but, as State Department planner, I was in no sense among his inner circle of advisers in that period. On the other hand, Johnson had set up a direct channel through which I could forward ideas, speech drafts, planning papers, etc. The channel was opened in June 1964 to set down my views on

Vietnam. But it was not until the spring of 1965 that, with White House encouragement, the flow became fairly regular.

I found Johnson's working style and habits more like Kennedy's than I had supposed. Both understood that a central part of their task was to receive a wider range of alternatives than the bureaucracy was likely to lay before them. Therefore, they reached far outside the executive branch for ideas and insights. But they were also determined that the essential structure of the bureaucracy be managed in an orderly way—Johnson perhaps a little more than Kennedy, although the portrait of Kennedy as a casual and haphazard administrator is grossly overdone. Both tried to stimulate the bureaucracy to produce new proposals: for example, Johnson, probably triggered by a column of Walter Lippmann's written from Lima, Peru, set me to work in the State Department on a study of the inner frontiers of South America and their possibilities for development.

Kennedy and Johnson both absorbed a vast flow of intelligence data. In my period at the White House under Johnson, I made sure he received a regular daily flow of intelligence from the military, State, and CIA. I took some pains with my colleagues to try to get this flow into as readable form as possible. The result was that Johnson received directly the morning CIA and military intelligence summaries as well as a cable summary from State. In the late afternoon State would forward summaries of major cables received or sent during the day. In addition, State provided each evening a summary of its major activities that day; e.g., hearings on the Hill, regional meetings around the country, major conversations with ambassadors in Washington, etc.

I also sent the President cables and intelligence items I thought would be of interest. When a major problem came on the horizon—e.g., the increasing tension in the Middle East in the spring of 1967, the 1967–1968 Tet offensive, or the Soviet move into Czechoslovakia—I kept a wide range of intelligence flowing to Johnson so he could develop an independent feel for the situation. There is a difference between a summarized report or cable and a full text.

The special assistant for national security affairs has four major tasks. First, he must be in a position to lay before the President the widest possible range of options. Here the quality needed, above all, is terse, lucid, dispassionate analysis. There is a whole school of contemporary political science that views decision-making as a competitive struggle within the bureaucracy. There is an element of truth in this view; but it is second-order truth. The departments and agencies of the bureaucracy represent, in effect, pieces of the President's responsibility. When they clash, it is essentially because the President's various responsibilities compete for scarce resources, including that scarcest of all—political capital. In the end, the process of deciding is not a battle among bureaucracies, it is the weighing in one man's mind of conflicting interests and imperatives; the setting of priorities; the allocation of scarce resources. That is the way the American Constitution is written; and that is the way it happens.

Thus, the primary role of a special assistant is to help generate the material that will permit the President the widest range of options within which to make a decision.

The second major task is to help assure that a President's decision is executed. This is straightforward enough if the decision consists in the dispatch of a cable or the granting of a development loan. It may be a lot more difficult and take much longer to project successfully a broad Presidential attitude or policy; for example, to persuade the State Department that the President is much less interested in country A's problem X (which it has been pressing on Washington) than in having country A do something about America's problem Y, which may be rather embarrassing in A's domestic politics. It is an endless problem in a world where the diplomat is trying to keep good relations between two countries under circumstances where he is more likely to be sensitive to the other fellow's political problem than that of the American President. The ambassador who does not develop a local parochialism (Charles Bohlen, for example, was superbly well-balanced about de Gaulle) is a rare character. In any case, a not always pleasant task of a Presidential assistant is to assure the sharp edges of a Presidential decision are not dulled in execution.

A third task is to help the President in what might be called in-house foreign policy business. For example, Rose Garden speeches that do not justify full consultation with the secretaries involved; informal meetings with the press (formal press conferences with Kennedy and Johnson involved careful preparation in the major bureaucracies and consultation with the secretaries of state and defense); the planning of visits by foreign dignitaries to the White House and of Presidential trips abroad; the drafting of letters to congressmen and others; etc. I underlined to my successor, Henry Kissinger, the amount of time he would have to budget in working directly with the President on these and other in-house functions. He found it improbable and, no doubt, thought it an aberration of the Johnson administration which the new broom would sweep clean. He quickly acknowledged that he had found many more inescapable Presidential tasks than he would have guessed.

The fourth task is one of advice. A special assistant handling the materials and functions indicated above ought to be someone whose advice the President would like to hear. But he must separate clearly his own view from his exposition of a problem and of alternative possible actions in response to it. He must be able to present another man's case as well as the man himself could. A special assistant for NSC affairs who could not do this comfortably—who used his post for explicit or implicit lobbying—would not last in his post for more than a few weeks, at least under Kennedy or Johnson. There is no matter over which a President is (and must be) more sensitive than the inevitable biases of his advisers as they lay alternatives before him and execute the decisions he makes. I would rate the role of adviser as the least important among the NSC special assistant's functions.

After I came from the State Department's Policy Planning Council, where my business for more than four years had been the generation of new initiatives in foreign policy, Rusk and Johnson considered how to handle my role as an "idea man." The agreement reached was quite simple: I was free—indeed, encouraged—to give the President any suggestions for new initiatives in foreign policy, but I was simultaneously to inform Rusk so that he could formulate a judgment of his own should Johnson raise the matter with him. This procedure worked quite smoothly. In fact, many suggestions for changes in policy I passed initially not to the President but back to colleagues in the working bureaucracy.

I found some generalizations about Johnson to be false or misleading when I began to work with him from day to day. One was the notion that while he was knowledgeable in domestic affairs, he had little depth or instinct in dealing with foreign affairs. This caricature was based both on factual error and a misjudgmment of the nature of modern international politics.

By the time Johnson came to the Presidency, he had already acquired wide practical experience of the world. He had traveled on every continent. Perhaps more important, as Democratic majority and minority leader of the Senate, he had consulted with Eisenhower at critical moments during the 1950s and had seen at close range the shape of foreign policy problems as they emerged in the White House. Given the cross-purposes between Eisenhower and the Republican Senate leader, William Knowland, Johnson's assistance in the Senate was peculiarly important to Eisenhower's Presidency—an assessment I once heard Eisenhower volunteer. As Vice President, Johnson was briefed regularly and, at Kennedy's insistence, shared day by day for three years the flow of Presidential decisions in foreign policy as a close observer free to comment and undoubtedly asking himself: What would I do in his shoes?

In the three years I worked with Johnson, he performed as a thorough professional in foreign policy, with a factual knowledge of particular issues and how they had evolved often reaching back over twenty years and more.

The second common misapprehension is that domestic politics and international affairs are essentially different worlds. "Domestic politics" evokes an image of problems settled by grubby compromises in back rooms. The image of diplomacy is of a formal, elegant, and vastly more sophisticated form of negotiation.

There is, of course, a difference between domestic and foreign politics. It lies in the fact that national sovereignty exists, and latent within it, the possible use of force. Moreover, two chiefs of government cannot resolve their differences by appealing to the same electorate. They must lay their achievements and deficiencies in foreign policy before different electorates or other constituencies (e.g., the Central Committees of Communist parties). When two chiefs of government meet in relative privacy they often give each other a picture of their domestic political situations, usually with candor—sometimes with extraordinary candor. In that framework they explore what they can do together. They identify the areas where they must, inevitably, disagree. And they find the best means they can to live with those differences, without inflaming them. On the many occasions when I observed Kennedy and Johnson dealing with fellow chiefs of government, they were dealing in the end with wholly recognizable political situations. The experience and ability to judge men that Johnson had acquired in thirty years of American political life were highly relevant to the conduct of foreign policy, as was his direct knowledge of the issues.

Occasionally Johnson's alleged lack of sophistication in foreign affairs is illustrated by the quotation of earthy language and analogies he is reported to have used in relation to some diplomatic problem. There is a reason for Presidents—and others—engaged in foreign affairs to emerge on occasion with rather vivid and relatively simple final summations. After all the complexities of a problem have been examined—the historical setting, the statistical data, prior agreements and their fine print, formal diplomatic exchanges, the array of (sometimes conflicting) American interests involved—in the end, whether a man takes one fork in the road rather than the other turns on questions of priority and character which are, essentially, simple. Both Kennedy and Johnson had a tendency, after absorbing the most sophisticated documentation and briefings Washington could supply, to pose the ultimate issue rather starkly. The most extended discussion I ever had with Kennedy about French foreign policy began when he asked me one day in his office: "Why is de Gaulle trying to screw us?" I adduced all the elements I could evoke from the French past, the General's personality, and his vision of the world, of France, and of himself. We discussed all this, and concluded that since de Gaulle couldn't make much of a dent on the enemies of France, he asserted himself against its friends. Kennedy's final comment was: "That's cheap."

With Johnson no more than with Kennedy can the occasional impulse to articulate complex foreign policy issues in simple terms be taken as a lack of understanding or sophistication. If Presidents do not always talk like professors of international relations it is because they are in the business of making decisions rather than orderly exposition. They are different lines of work.

Johnson's reputation in Washington was that of a hard taskmaster. Johnson did work hard and long, bringing all he had to the task. He expected the same of his staff. Occasionally he could speak explosively, more often than not when there was a press leak. In this he was much like Kennedy, although their style in profanity reflected a generational difference. Presidents assume that their task is not easy and that a good deal of frustration is to be expected from the American political process and an intractable and volatile world. But leaks to the press from their own subordinates, usually inaccurate but complicating inherently difficult business, appear one more burden than their oath of office really required. Contrary to Washington mythology, Johnson—in my experience—tried to minimize telephone calls at home and other intrusions on family life. He forbade my secretary to get me off the tennis court when an early-morning call found me there. I called him at night much more often than he called me. He found time to concern himself with the well-being of the families linked to him. The loyalty he had the right to expect as President was reciprocated in deeply human terms. When a special effort was made and came off well, he would indicate his satisfaction. When an error was made, it was noted but quickly buried, with, perhaps, some teasing.

After I had gone to work with him, I was often asked how I found it. My reply was: I have never worked for a more considerate man. This may have been taken to be excessive loyalty. But it was quite true.

34

Military Policy and Arms Control

The Setting

The Cuba missile crisis—the dangers of nuclear instability it revealed and its outcome—increased both the urgency and the possibilities of moving forward with the Soviet Union on a nonproliferation treaty (NPT) and a bilateral nuclear arms agreement. The urgency of an NPT was heightened by the explosion of the first Chinese nuclear weapon in 1964, increasing, as it did, the pressure on others to follow the de Gaulle–Mao route, notably Japan and India. The urgency of a U.S.–Soviet bilateral strategic understanding was heightened by an accelerated Soviet military effort which included an antiballistic missile capability. The Soviet ABM's promised to set off another massive round of competition in the strategic arms race unless agreement was reached on both offensive and defensive missiles. The possibilities of progress were increased by the failure of nuclear blackmail over Berlin and Cuba; the willingness of a western Europe less frightened of Moscow and more confident of Washington to acquiesce in the long-run implications of the NPT; the expansion toward equality with the United States of Soviet strategic capabilities; and the depth of the split between Moscow and Peking.

Nevertheless, it was a long and rocky road from the test ban treaty of August 1963 to the signing of the NPT and the agreement in principle to hold strategic arms limitation talks (SALT), announced on July 1, 1968.

THE COMMUNIST WORLD 1963–1969

A major step along the way was Khrushchev's removal from power on October 14, 1964. It is clear that Khrushchev was in contention with some of his colleagues well before his removal on a number of matters: how to deal with China; the priority of heavy versus light industry and agriculture; the size of the military budget; the proper approach to agriculture; policy toward West Germany; the appropriate length of the planning period in the Soviet economy.[1] The triggering issue may, as Tatu argues,[2] have been a matter of power rather than of policy: a reorganization plan of Khrushchev's for agriculture which, in fact, would have reduced the authority of his Presidium colleagues. If those who plotted the coup against Khrushchev were reacting to such a specific threat to their authority, they were also reflecting the decline of Khrushchev's authority since the Cuba missile crisis—a decline broken only briefly by Kozlov's illness and the celebration of Khrushchev's seventieth birthday in April 1964. Khrushchev continued to talk like the boss and felt confident enough to be away from Moscow more than half the time, a good deal of it abroad, during the first eight months of 1964. But, as seen from Washington in 1963–1964, he projected the image of a man whose words did not necessarily have consequence.

The team of Brezhnev–Kosygin–Podgorny did not immediately launch any new, clear lines of policy. There was a brief cessation of Sino–Soviet polemics in the aftermath of Khrushchev's removal; but in 1965 Soviet policy began to reflect the event that occurred the day after the coup against Khrushchev—the explosion of a Chinese nuclear weapon. The Soviet response, no doubt strengthened by the further hardening of relations with Peking (from about March 1965), was a slow but steady expansion of its military strength in key areas along the 6800-mile Chinese border. The number of Soviet divisions in the area rose over the next six years from about fourteen in 1965 to well over forty, with the increased force much more nearly at combat readiness. A parallel expansion in air strength was undertaken. These Soviet forces carried with them an ample nuclear capability. This effort was matched by a large increase in Chinese forces near the Soviet frontiers and a shifting of Chinese strategic reserves to points accessible to those frontiers. From 1965, then, both sides came to regard the frontier as potentially hostile, a fact reflected from time to time in border skirmishes.

In addition, Moscow re-engaged in Southeast Asia. In Khrushchev's latter days, as the communists gained ground in Vietnam in the latter half of 1963 and the first three quarters of 1964, Hanoi seemed firmly fixed in Peking's camp.[3] Hanoi did not respond to a Soviet suggestion in July 1964 for a Geneva Conference on Laos[4] or to Soviet support for the American proposal of August 1964 to bring the Tonkin Gulf incident to the United

Nations. By February 1965, however, Kosygin was in Hanoi, accompanied by military aid officials; and at the Soviet Twenty-third Party Congress in Moscow (March–April 1966) Le Duan was warmly praising the Soviet Union, despite Peking's highly articulate boycott of the occasion.[5] Moscow, pressured by London (in turn, encouraged by Washington), was willing at this time to contemplate a reconvening of the Geneva Conference to include Vietnam as well as Laos; but when Hanoi refused to engage in negotiations, Moscow settled for the half-loaf it had enjoyed from 1957 to 1963, in the form of a Vietnamese communist position midway between Moscow and Peking.[6] It adopted within the communist world the attractive posture of calling on Peking for cooperation in support of Hanoi, cooperation that Peking appeared systematically to deny.

The year 1965 was a bad one for Communist China. It began well enough with Indonesia's withdrawal from the U.N. and overt alignment with Peking, as North Vietnam appeared to be moving to victory in the South.

But in June the Algiers conference failed. Peking and Djakarta had been planning a "Second Bandung" since April 1961. More than sixty Asian and African nations were to attend. It was to open in Algiers on June 29, 1965, preceded five days earlier by a foreign ministers meeting. Its purpose was to bring the full political weight of the Afro–Asian world to bear against "American imperialism." There were a good many difficulties: the preparatory meeting at Djakarta in April 1964 had agreed to send invitations to South Korea and South Vietnam, but Algeria did not wish to see them invited; New Delhi wanted the Soviet Union and Malaysia invited, Peking did not. As these conflicts increased in intensity, ten African nations, some affronted by crude Chinese Communist efforts at political penetration, announced they would not attend.

The critical issue was Soviet participation. Khrushchev had indicated in August 1964 that he did not wish to participate: his successors let it be known they did. Much embarrassment was saved by Boumedienne's ouster of Ben Bella on June 19 which provided an excuse for a postponement of the conference that proved to be a cancellation. Clearly, however, Peking's posture as leader of the Afro–Asian world, noncommunist as well as communist, was damaged.

In July President Johnson acted with force to prevent Hanoi's takeover of South Vietnam: Peking neither wished to engage American forces nor did it command the kind of sophisticated antiaircraft equipment Hanoi most required to mitigate the regular U.S. bombing of the North that had begun in March. Moscow gained ground, relatively, in Hanoi and within the communist world.

Peking's position was further weakened by its rather ineffectual posturing during the India–Pakistani war of September 1965. And Peking's hope for consolidating its link with Indonesia was frustrated in October by the failure of the communist coup against the Indonesian army leadership.

In ways we do not yet wholly understand, this series of major setbacks abroad—perhaps, especially, the communist debacle in Indonesia—helped trigger the Cultural Revolution in China.[7] It began in November 1965 and, with many stop-and-go phases, dominated life on the mainland over the next three years. At its core was Mao's insistence that the political, social, and cultural life of mainland China not settle down to the more or less orderly routines of a poor nation seeking modernity. Like Mao's method of guerrilla warfare, of agricultural collectivization in the early 1950s, and the Great Leap Forward, the roots of the Cultural Revolution are to be found in his March 1927 analysis of the energy and violence that could be released by revolutionary organization and manipulation of frustrated masses of people.[8] This time it was not the peasants that interested him, but the youth. He mobilized the youth to destroy the Communist party and government bureaucracy he himself had built, and to discredit Liu Shao-chi and his allegedly "revisionist" colleagues.[9] In effect, Mao, as a kind of grandfather, tried to create a coalition between himself and his grandchildren against his own sons. In the end, the sons prevailed.

Mao launched the Cultural Revolution just as the Chinese economy had recovered from the failure of the Great Leap Forward. Production again declined. The struggle also produced a partial disintegration of the party and governmental control apparatus, leaving the military in a predominant administrative and political position as the paroxysm ran its course. The schools were closed. The youth—temporarily elevated and encouraged to conduct a new revolution against their elders—were, in the end, turned off and sent in large numbers to rural areas.

For a time, mainland China almost ceased to have a foreign policy; but certain important strands in domestic policy persisted. While military production in general declined in 1966–1968, work on nuclear weapons and missiles continued. And there was a quiet shift, in the midst of the turmoil Mao had created, toward a more rational agricultural policy, with increased manufacture and import of chemical fertilizers and some concessions to peasants' incentives in a countryside where the Cultural Revolution had loosened the party's grip on the villages.

While Johnson followed, as closely as intelligence reports permitted, this extraordinary passage in Chinese history, there was little he could do about Peking during the Cultural Revolution except project the hope that, in time, the great talents and energies within mainland China would be harnessed to constructive purposes and linked in more benign ways to Asia and the rest of the world.[10]

Moscow Moves to Strategic Parity

WHILE forces in Asia were moving in ways Moscow could only marginally influence or control, Brezhnev, Kosygin, and Podgorny moved strongly in an area they could control: the Soviet military establishment. They decided to seek naval as well as strategic nuclear parity—or even, superiority—with the United States. The Soviet decision to accelerate military outlays probably reflected the departure of Khrushchev; the sense of military inferiority felt during the Cuba missile crisis; expanded military requirements on the Chinese border; and the prospect of serious arms talks with the United States. If, as Johnson pressed so hard upon them, an effort had to be made to level off the strategic arms race by negotiation, the Soviet leaders must have concluded (as the charts on pp. 374–376 suggest) that parity, at least, was the only acceptable basis for entry into the SALT talks.

Johnson's Policy Toward the Soviet Union

It was in this dynamic, complex, strategic setting—and with a substantial war in Southeast Asia from mid-1965—that Johnson sought with stubborn determination to widen and consolidate the areas of common interest between the United States and the Soviet Union.

The principal areas where progress was made or negotiations completed in Johnson's time were these:

the nonproliferation treaty
strategic arms negotiations
mutual cutback in production of fissionable materials
treaty on returning astronauts
Outer Space Treaty
demilitarization of seabeds
Civil Air Agreement
Consular Convention
renewal of biennial Cultural Exchange Agreement
renewal of Atomic Energy Exchange Agreement
law-of-the-sea discussions
agreement on cooperation in field of water desalting
agreement to discuss peaceful uses of atomic energy
improved weather exchanges

Even the most modest of these agreements—for example, the renewals of the two-year cultural exchange agreement—usually required laborious and protracted negotiation. Taken together, these agreements clearly represented the most substantial progress toward the normalization of United States–Soviet relations since 1945. To the list should be added the significant role of the United States–Soviet dialogue in ending the India–Pakistani war of 1965 and in assuring the Arab–Israeli war of 1967 would not escalate into a direct United States–Soviet confrontation.

CHART 34-1–5
TRENDS IN U.S. AND SOVIET STRATEGIC AND NAVAL FORCES, MID-1962–1971

CHART 34-1
U.S. AND SOVIET OPERATIONAL ICBM LAUNCHERS

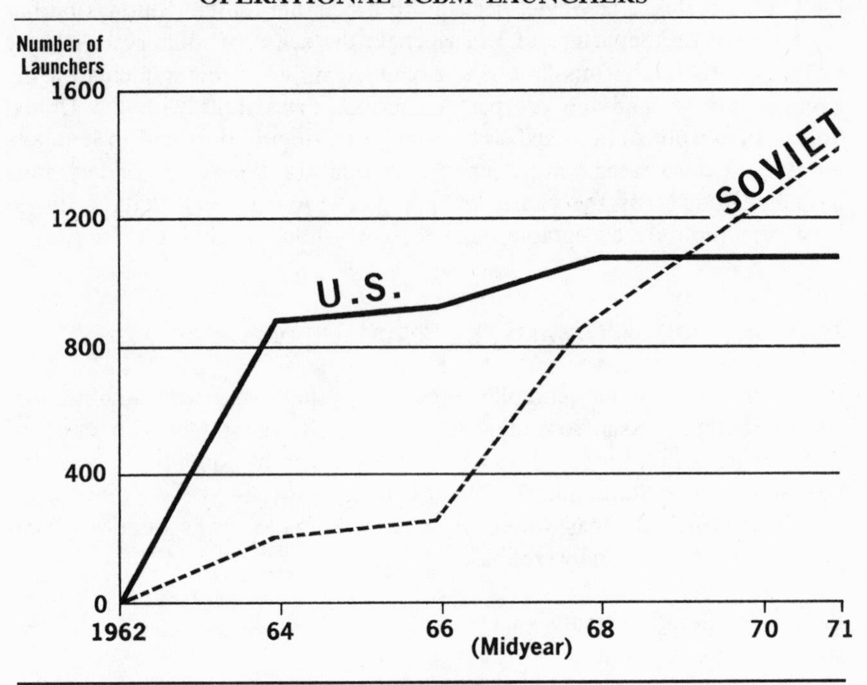

CHART 34-2
U.S. AND SOVIET OPERATIONAL SLBM LAUNCHERS

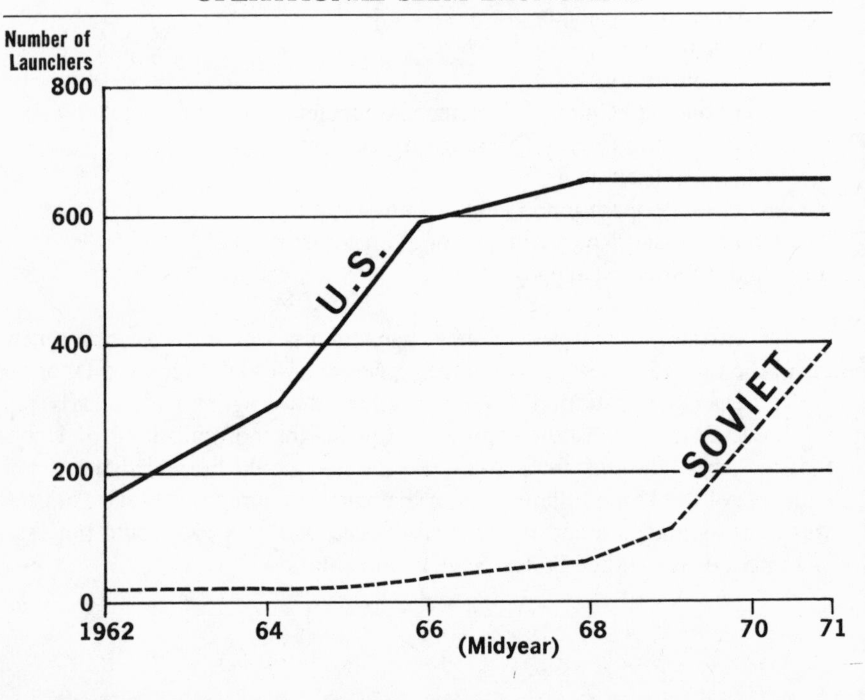

CHART 34-3
TOTAL U.S. AND SOVIET
INTERCONTINENTAL DELIVERY VEHICLES
(ICBM LAUNCHERS, SLBM TUBES AND STRATEGIC BOMBERS)

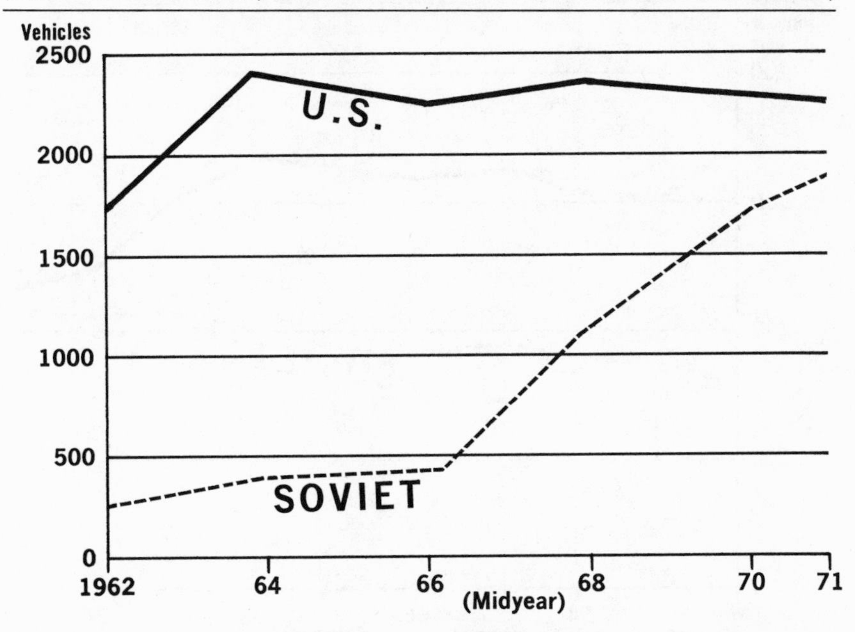

CHART 34-4
U.S. AND SOVIET
ACTIVE-DUTY STRENGTHS—LAND FORCES

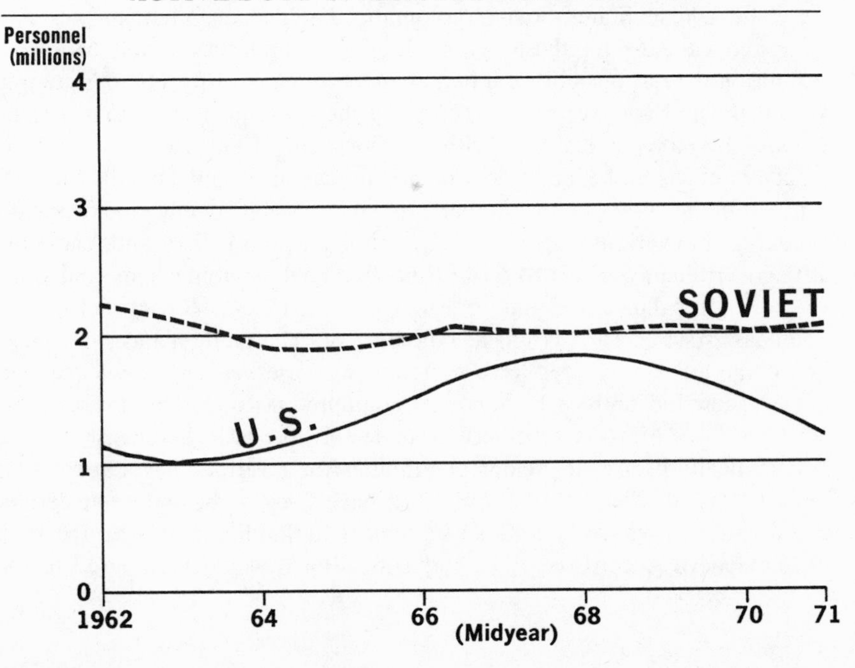

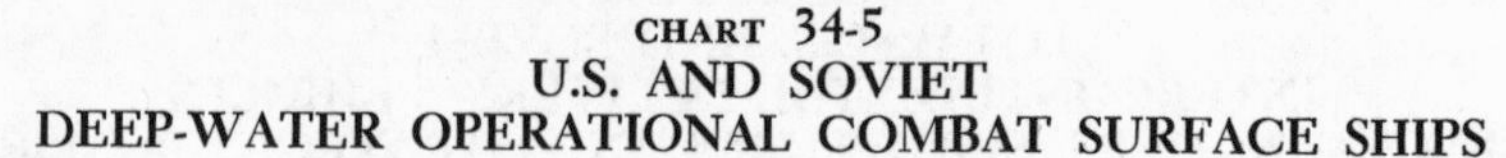

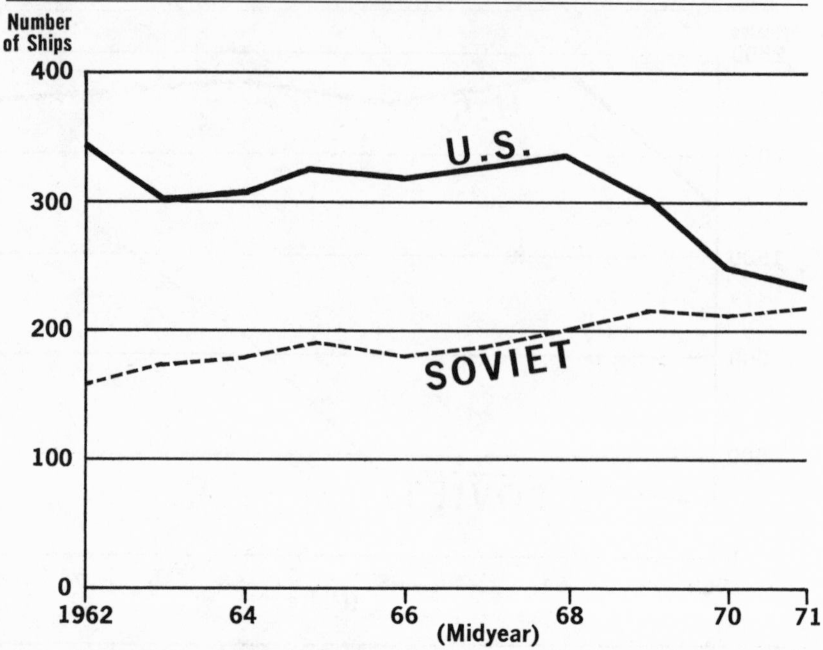

Source: Statement by Admiral Thomas H. Moorer, U.S. Navy, chairman, Joint Chiefs of Staff, before the House Armed Services Committee, March 9, 1971.

The United States–Soviet diplomatic dialogue on Vietnam was intimate and candid over these years. Both sides understood well Moscow's default on the responsibilities it had assumed in Geneva for Hanoi's compliance with the Laos Accords of 1962 and the consequences of that default. It was, therefore, a dialogue with no moralizing from the Soviet side in official contacts and a good deal of private candor about Hanoi's intransigence. On the other hand, Soviet diplomats systematically and cynically encouraged in various ways American politicians, journalists, and, occasionally, government officials to wishful hopes about bombing halts and other gestures. On balance, I would not rate the United States–Soviet dialogue on Southeast Asia of 1963–1969 as constructive. The maintenance of contact and communications does have a certain intrinsic value in a nuclear age; but Moscow did nothing to honor its commitments under the Geneva Accords on Laos of 1962 or otherwise to restore peace in Southeast Asia. It systematically projected greater possibilities for a serious negotiation than, in fact, existed. Clearly, Moscow could have lived with, and even derived certain advantages from, a stable settlement in Southeast Asia on the basis of the Geneva Accords of 1954 and 1962. But it was not prepared to pay the price for such an outcome. It gave other Soviet interests a higher priority, notably Hanoi's place in the Sino–Soviet split and the discomfiture of the United States.

But contrary to a widely held view, the intensification of the war in Southeast Asia from 1965 in no way obstructed serious exchanges of view or important agreements between Moscow and Washington. Moscow did exhibit sensitivity to cultural exchanges of a highly public kind at intense moments in the Vietnamese war; for example, a visit of the musical production *Hello Dolly* was canceled as well as the visit of an American basketball team. But, in general, the Soviet leadership was not in a mood to let Vietnam get in the way of other serious business it judged to be, on balance, to Soviet advantage.

The Nonproliferation Treaty and SALT

The two most significant enterprises undertaken between Moscow and Washington in Johnson's years were the nonproliferation treaty and the agreement to hold the SALT talks. These two ideas were not new, of course. Both were listed, among other negotiating possibilities, as early as Johnson's letter to Khrushchev of January 18, 1964.[11]

They did not begin seriously to move forward, however, until the Rusk–Gromyko exchanges at the meeting of the United Nations General Assembly in September 1966, although the proximate origins of the effort, on both sides, lie two years earlier in the Chinese explosion of a nuclear weapon.

The negotiations on NPT and SALT, while technically independent, were closely related not only in substance but in time. They began almost simultaneously in December and January 1966–1967 and carried on until the nonproliferation treaty was signed and the agreement to hold SALT talks simultaneously announced on July 1, 1968. The Soviet invasion of Czechoslovakia and the coming in of a new American administration postponed the latter from early October 1968 to November 17, 1969.

Behind these long negotiations lay the interim resolution, at least, of a major array of issues in Washington and Moscow—and, so far as the NPT was concerned, in many other capitals as well.

The first issue was the role of nuclear weapons in NATO. The initial Soviet formula would have denied states that did not now possess nuclear weapons "the right to participate in the ownership, control, or use of nuclear weapons." This was unacceptable to Washington and to NATO as a whole. It would have put in question existing two-key nuclear arrangements (which involved the "use" of nuclear weapons) and even the kind of intensive nuclear consultation and planning being developed under McNamara's leadership among the NATO defense ministers (which, after a fashion, involved the "control" of nuclear weapons). In the course of 1966 it became increasingly clear that Moscow was prepared to abandon language that would weaken NATO so long as an MLF or any other alliance arrangement involving the transfer of American weapons to joint ownership would be excluded. It was Gromyko's willingness, expressed to Rusk on September 24, 1966, to proceed on a much narrower formula—prohibiting "the transfer" of nuclear weapons—that set the NPT seriously into motion, although it was not until December 5 that agreed language was actually established. There was a certain irony in this resolution of the problem. The language Moscow agreed to involved critically the question of transferring a share in the ownership of nuclear weapons, as under the MLF formula. This rather capitalist question was elevated by the Russians over the more fundamental questions of access to and the right to fire nuclear weapons.

Now something big seemed possible. It was to take stock of how to proceed in the wake of the Rusk–Gromyko talks in New York that Johnson assembled his senior advisers at Camp David on October 1.[12] Out of it came an instruction to proceed patiently in ways which authentically met the interests of the non-nuclear nations rather than by pressure. Consultation with these nations was shifted substantially from the Arms Control and Disarmament Agency (ACDA) to State Department channels. This was the major operational result of Rusk's October 3 summary of Johnson's conclusions reached after the Camp David discussions:

> We are opposed to the proliferation of nuclear weapons. We are not going to turn our weapons over to any other nation. To stop the spread of nuclear weapons is urgent. The responsibility for firing U.S. nuclear weapons rests with the President of the U.S. This is true as a matter of law, policy and intent. We see no prospect that it will or can be changed. But we cannot undertake a treaty obligation which commits us to act as if there were no alliance. The United States has committed itself to collective security, beginning with the UN Charter. We cannot say to our allies that these matters are none of their business.
>
> There is no great thrust at present that we move quickly to alliance nuclear arrangements. But we should not preclude treaty arrangements in the future—not involving proliferation—which might be necessary to restrain allies and preserve the alliance.

This was not a matter of bureaucratic in-fighting or the victory of one group in government over another. It reflected the nature of the NPT, if it were ever to be taken seriously.

The NPT was, fundamentally, a quite different kind of measure than, say, the test ban treaty or the kind of agreement sought in the SALT talks. These required self-denying actions by the Soviet Union and the United States, just as the Consular Convention, the Cultural Conventions, and the air agreement required positive actions by the two great powers.

The NPT required that Moscow and Washington forego nothing that they actively wished to do. As of 1966, neither the Soviet Union nor the United States was about to pass out nuclear weapons or additional nuclear weapons technology to their allies. Each had breached the principle of nonproliferation in the past, but as of 1966, Moscow and Washington were concerned that the number of powers controlling the right to fire nuclear weapons not be expanded beyond the five who then possessed them—the United States, the Soviet Union, France, Great Britain, and Communist China. And their concern lay in the noncommunist rather than in the communist world. It centered notably on Germany, Japan, India, and Israel. Moscow's control over eastern Europe (except Yugoslavia and Albania) was sufficient to assure nonproliferation. Yugoslavia did not aspire to nuclear weapons, Albania lacked the technological capacity to make them. Communist China was unlikely to pass out weapons or weapons technology lightheartedly, once it came to understand their meaning, even to its loyal friends in Tirana; but, if Peking chose to do so, there was little Washington or Moscow could do to prevent it, except to try to persuade potential recipients (e.g., Albania, North Korea, or North Vietnam) to sign the NPT.

Despite such marginal and remote contingencies within the communist world, the NPT was, essentially, a constitutional arrangement for the organization of the noncommunist world. It had to be justified within the nations mainly concerned—before their parliaments and their peoples—on grounds of national interest, not as a benign exercise in détente between Washington and Moscow. And within Washington, it also had to be similarly justified.

Because it apparently asked so little of the United States, the full significance of the NPT was not, in fact, profoundly understood within the executive branch, within the Congress, or throughout the nation.

A part of the rationale was, of course, clear. The NPT, if implemented, would restrict the number of independent fingers on nuclear triggers. A kind of simple mathematical case could be made that the fewer the independent fingers, the lower the statistical chances that a nuclear weapon might be fired by accident or design. This was an argument on behalf of humanity rather than anyone's national interest.

But there was a narrower American interest, rarely articulated; namely, that the emergence of additional nuclear-weapons powers could weaken the structure of collective security in the noncommunist world at critical points.

The United States was allied with certain nations whose fate or possible re-alignment would gravely affect the balance of power in Europe and Asia: for example, Germany, Italy, and Japan. Out of a somewhat erratic series of diplomatic statements and events, the United States had also acquired significant responsibilities toward Israel, as well as toward certain

Arab and Moslem states in the Middle East. But that was not all. In the wake of the first Chinese Communist explosion of a nuclear weapon, Johnson had made the following carefully designed statement on October 16, 1964: "Even if Communist China should eventually develop an effective nuclear capability, that capability would have no effect upon the readiness of the United States to respond to requests from Asian nations for help in dealing with Communist Chinese aggression." Then, on October 18, Johnson, in advocating an NPT, added this: ". . . the nations that do not seek national nuclear weapons can be sure that if they need our strong support against some threat of nuclear blackmail, then they will have it." These statements threw a mantle of nuclear protection—of a kind—across India and certain other Asian states not formally aligned with the United States. The statements reinforced in India the implicit assumption that America would respond if China attacked India—an assumption built up out of American support for India in the face of the Chinese attacks during the autumn of 1962.

But if any state to which the United States was committed produced nuclear weapons and asserted an independent right to fire them, the United States would confront a grave dilemma: to avoid the possibility of another nation—by its own initiative—drawing the United States into nuclear war, the United States would have to dilute or withdraw its security commitment in parts of the word judged vital to the American interest.

That dilemma did not arise in the case of Britain for geographic and policy reasons: geographically, Britain did not have physical contact with the Soviet Union nor did it lie close to the line down central Europe where the balance of power was drawn; in terms of policy, Britain was committed to the closest nuclear consultation with the United States and (excepting Suez) pursued a policy which did not raise the nuclear specter.

In the case of France, the geographical arguments were similar; and, despite de Gaulle's apparent posture, French policy (again, except for Suez) generally avoided posing nuclear problems for the United States. For example, de Gaulle refused the proposal of a loose German association with the *force de frappe* in trying to draw Adenauer into close association with Paris in 1963.[13] Nevertheless, some cold thoughts were thought —and, at least once, cold words said by Washington to Paris when the notion was raised by irresponsible Frenchmen that the *force de frappe* was a device to guarantee, if necessary against American will, that United States nuclear weapons would be used in defense of Europe.

It was Suez more than any other event in the noncommunist world that underlined the nature and limits of an alliance system in a nuclear age. The United States took its distance from Britain and France in that affair for a number of reasons, not least because the Anglo-French action, not agreed to in Washington, had evoked from Moscow gestures of nuclear blackmail. Memories of Suez undoubtedly played a role in subsequent

British and French persistence with national nuclear capabilities. By 1966 the Sino–Soviet split had demonstrated even more clearly to all observers what could happen to allies who manufactured nuclear weapons when they fell out over the substance of policy.

Finally, only those who followed intimately the calculations made in Bonn and Jerusalem, Tokyo and New Delhi, understood how closely the NPT and its future viability hinged on the reliability of the United States as an ally. Inherently there was a simple but profound nationalist difficulty with the NPT. Nations were being asked consciously to deny themselves weapons they could easily produce. And they were being asked to do so at a time when London, Paris, and Peking appeared to attach great political and prestige value to those weapons. Nevertheless, there was a rational case for signing the NPT even in narrow nationalist terms. It was that the deterrent power of the American military establishment—nuclear and non-nuclear, taken together—was vastly greater than any nuclear and non-nuclear military deterrent that could soon be developed in, say, Germany, India, or Japan. And if the decision were to be made to produce nuclear weapons, the nations concerned would face an extremely awkward and even dangerous interval—an interval when ties with the United States would be weakened, before an alternative deterrent force could be built. For Germany and Japan there would, in addition, be extremely heavy diplomatic pressure from abroad; and for India, the danger that Pakistan might invite Chinese Communist nuclear power into the subcontinent.

The argument for nonproliferation in the noncommunist world thus depended in a fundamental way on the reliability of American commitments. Primarily to cover the possibility of American unreliability, the following language was written into the NPT:

> Each Party shall in exercising its national sovereignty have the right to withdraw from the Treaty if it decides that extraordinary events, related to the subject matter of this Treaty, have jeopardized the supreme interests of its country. It shall give notice of such withdrawal to all other Parties to the Treaty and to the United Nations Security Council three months in advance. Such notice shall include a statement of the extraordinary events it regards as having jeopardized its supreme interests.

In the case of Germany, for example, Chancellor Kurt Kiesinger made clear to Johnson in August 1967 that the continuity of the American commitment to NATO was what would be required if the "supreme national interest" clause of the NPT was not to be raised.

While the leaders of each nation weighed these basic—even mortal—issues, the debate and negotiations on the NPT focused initially on important but lesser matters: the assurance that nations that signed the NPT would not be denied any benefits from the peaceful uses of atomic energy;

and the precise manner in which the International Atomic Energy Agency (IAEA) (of which the Soviet Union was a member) would inspect the nuclear facilities of the European Atomic Energy Agency (EURATOM).

In the end, these issues were resolved. Moscow accepted essentially Western formulae; and it should have done so. It gained by the NPT, but, essentially, contributed nothing to it. The strains that had to be weathered lay primarily within the noncommunist world, not among the communist regimes. Moscow's nuclear crisis with Peking had come, at the latest, in 1963 over the test ban treaty, although it had taken shape some five years earlier.

The essential nature of the NPT could be perceived more clearly as it moved toward its climax. Moscow and Washington came under strong pressure from the potential signatories on two points: to offer some kind of protection to the signatories against the threat of nuclear attack; to commit themselves to try to end the nuclear arms race and to bring about effective measures of arms control.

For the United States the first issue raised potentially the question of extending the nation's security commitments at a time when neither Johnson, the Senate, nor the public was in a mood to do so. The commitment made on June 17, 1968, in the U.N. Security Council was the following:

> The United States affirms its intention as a permanent member of the United Nations Security Council to seek immediate Security Council action to provide assistance in accordance with the Charter to any non-nuclear weapon state party to the treaty on the nonproliferation of nuclear weapons that is a victim of active aggression or an object of a threat of aggression in which nuclear weapons are used.[14]

The Soviet Union and the United Kingdom made virtually identical statements at the same time. Johnson reiterated the commitment—potentially of great consequence—on July 1, as the NPT was signed.

On the question of arms control, Johnson renewed pressure on Moscow soon after the Soviet Union and the United States jointly tabled the NPT on January 18, 1968. Four days later, as he expressed to Kosygin satisfaction over the progress of the treaty, he urged that the SALT talks be undertaken promptly. Formally, the NPT and the SALT talks were not linked except in the treaty's preamble where the signatories declare "their intention to achieve at the earliest possible date the cessation of the nuclear arms race and to undertake effective measures in the direction of nuclear disarmament." In a larger sense, however, both Washington and Moscow understood that, over a period of time, the NPT was unlikely to survive if the two nuclear superpowers conducted an uninhibited arms race.

Kosygin, in effect, accepted this common-law linkage. After further prodding by Johnson on May 2 and June 22, he agreed to a joint U.S.–

Soviet announcement, on the occasion of the July 1 signing of the NPT, that SALT talks could take place "in the nearest future."

It is by no means certain that, in the end, the NPT will in fact limit the number of nuclear-weapons powers to the present five. And it is by no means certain the SALT talks will succeed, by explicit or implicit agreement, in fully containing the strategic arms race.

Of their nature, however, bringing the NPT to life and agreeing to enter and then engaging in the SALT talks had significant consequences for the substance and texture of U.S.–Soviet relations.

Nothing could better dramatize the reality of the diffusion of power away from Washington and Moscow than the NPT negotiations. They happened because the most dangerous kind of diffusion of power was taking place; and even further nuclear diffusion was probable. The Chinese nuclear explosion of October 1964 and the MLF were, in fact, the immediate goad to get on with the NPT. Against all manner of ideological resistances, the strands of anxiety detectable in Moscow in December 1960 (see above, pp. 34–35)—centered on China and Germany—moved to the center of Soviet policy.

But before an NPT could be agreed on, Moscow had to sit side by side with the United States and stare, with a common understanding, at the problems confronted by EURATOM and NATO, and India, Japan, and many other nations, if the NPT was going to be accepted. Those problems, of national and regional pride and power, were peculiarly independent of ideology. One could glimpse during the NPT negotiations a little of what the world might be like if Moscow decided that its maximum attainable objective was a reasonably orderly and safe environment for the Soviet Union, achieved by close collaboration with the United States.

The SALT talks were, of course, bilateral, given the enormous gap between the nuclear capabilities of the United States and the Soviet Union on the one hand, and the other three nuclear-weapons states on the other. And in both Washington and Moscow narrowly national economic and military arguments could be adduced for launching the negotiations. But there was also an element of recognition that if the world was to be bound by the NPT, the two superpowers would have to try, at least, to behave with greater responsibility in the arms race. The pressures generated in a world of diffusing power thus helped bring the SALT talks to life.

Once the dialogue was launched—even on an exploratory basis, as it was during the Johnson administration—it was clear that it would have the powerful effect of forcing each government to get, as it were, inside the other's skin in nuclear matters. Before there was any chance of an agreement, an extraordinary degree of mutual understanding in highly sensitive matters would have to be developed.

This slow transmutation in attitude may emerge in historical perspective as more important than the formal negotiations launched or completed with Moscow in these years. But the outcome hinges not merely on what transpires between United States and Soviet negotiators, but also on the Soviet assessment of American strength and will.

THE ABM AND THE SALT TALKS: KEY ISSUES

As Washington came to know the actual state of the United States–Soviet strategic balance in 1961, as opposed to Khrushchev's projected image, it proceeded with plans to create an assured second-strike capability in the form of Minuteman and Polaris missiles; but, from the peak in FY 1962, outlays for strategic offensive and defensive forces declined.[15] They resumed a gradual rise from FY 1967 in response to developments in the Soviet Union.[16]

The buildup of Soviet missiles after the Cuba missile crisis was closely observed, including the development and deployment around Moscow of an ABM system. The emergence of Soviet ABM's lay at the heart of the resumed expansion in U.S. outlays for strategic purposes. In testimony as early as March 2, 1965, before Soviet ABM's were deployed, McNamara made clear that most new developments in the U.S. strategic forces were geared to "the possibility that an opponent may deploy a relatively effective antimissile defense system around his urban industrial areas."[17] The American anticipatory response included penetration aids, especially multiple, independently targetable, re-entry vehicles (MIRV's); research and development on U.S. ABM's; the development of the larger Poseidon missile capable of mounting MIRV's; etc.

Behind these technological developments and the outlays required to give them substance was an evolution of thought in Washington—and, then, in Moscow—which gradually brought potential elements of rationality into the inherently fantastic and ironic world of nuclear weapons.[18] Exchanges between U.S. and Soviet scientists and, more important, McNamara's bold public expositions of the grotesque arithmetic of mutual deterrence, gradually forced U.S. and Soviet political leaders to begin, at least, to look at the problem in similar terms. Although I do not believe a quantitative approach to the problem of taming nuclear weapons is sufficient, it is an initially necessary condition. And I am inclined to believe that McNamara's role in forcing America, its allies, and the Soviet Union to view the nuclear problem in, roughly, similar terms may well be judged his greatest contribution as a public servant in the 1960s.

The heart of the matter lay in two concepts, capable of at least rough measurement: an "assured destruction" capability and a "damage-limiting" capability.[19] Any American weapon capable of striking a Soviet target in the wake of a Soviet first strike or intercepting a Soviet weapon aimed at American strategic forces contributed to an "assured destruction" capabil-

TABLE 34–1
JOHNSON ADMINISTRATION
SUMMARY OF THE DEPARTMENT OF DEFENSE PROGRAM BUDGETS*
(fiscal years: in billions of dollars)

Major Military Programs	1962	1963	1964	1965	1966	1967	1968	1969 (est.§)	1970 (est.§)
Strategic Forces†	11.2	10.4	9.4	6.9	6.8	6.9	7.6	9.1	9.6
General Purpose Forces	17.7	17.9	17.7	19.0	29.5	32.7	32.4	33.2	33.1
Guard and Reserve Forces	1.7	1.8	2.0	2.1	2.3	2.7	3.2	2.7	2.9
Airlift and Sealift	1.0	1.4	1.3	1.5	1.7	1.9	1.9	1.6	2.1
Research and Development	4.2	5.1	5.3	4.9	5.3	4.8	4.4	4.7	5.6
Military Assistance (Department of Defense)	.1	1.6	—	—	—	1.6	1.8	2.7	2.5
General Support—Total	13.5	13.1	13.6	14.5	19.8	22.4	25.2	26.6	27.3
intelligence and communications	3.2	—	—	—	4.7	5.3	5.7	6.0	6.2
logistics	4.2	—	—	—	5.3	7.1	8.2	8.8	9.0
personnel	5.1	—	—	—	7.2	8.5	10.0	10.3	10.7
administration	1.0	—	—	—	2.6	1.5	1.3	1.5	1.4
Sub-Total	49.4‡	51.2	49.4	48.7	65.4	72.9	76.2	80.7	82.1

* From Annual Budget presentations to the Congress. Some categories among Major Military Programs altered for purposes of uniformity.
† From FY 1968 presentation continental air and missile defense forces grouped with strategic forces to underline inappropriateness of old "offense–defense" distinction when concepts of "assured destruction" and "damage-limiting" concepts adopted. I have also included civil defense in this category.
‡ Actual obligational authority granted includes "adjustment for retired pay accrual," not included here.
§ Estimates as given in final budget presentation to the Congress for the Johnson administration. See below, pp. 548–549, for actual figures under the Nixon administration.

ity.[20] Any American weapon (or civil defense measure) capable of reducing civilian casualties or industrial damage in a Soviet first strike contributed to a "damage-limiting" capability. These clarifications in thought and measurement crystallized in the Department of Defense toward the end of 1966 and formed a part of McNamara's presentation to the Congress in March 1967.[21]

He proposed that a deployment of the Nike X (ABM) system should not be undertaken by the United States in order to defend American cities. The essence of his argument was simple[22]: a full U.S. ABM system would cut U.S. fatalities to a level (20 to 30 million) so low that the Soviet Union could not be confident that the United States would not undertake a first strike. Therefore, the Soviet Union would have to react with a radically enlarged program of missiles and penetration aids to negate the U.S. ABM system; and it could do so at much less cost than the U.S. ABM system, given the estimated economies of offense over defense at that time. The outcome would be much as it was under current approved programs, after vast new expenditures on both sides, and a period of international instability.

Thus, McNamara argued for an "assured destruction" capability as the heart of deterrence, setting aside a "damage-limiting" capability versus the Soviet Union as essentially chimerical. McNamara's case against full deployment of ABM's to protect American cities was formally challenged by the Joint Chiefs of Staff in private, before the President. The critical meeting took place December 6, 1966, on the ninth floor of the Federal Building at Austin, Texas, as Johnson was arriving at final decisions on the FY 1968 budget. The arguments on the ABM were publicly aired before the Congress on March 6, 1967. General Earle Wheeler expressed the heart of the Joint Chiefs of Staff case in these terms:

> The Joint Chiefs of Staff don't know whether the Soviet overall objective is strategic nuclear parity, or superiority. In either case, we believe that their probable aims are one or more of the following.
>
> First, to reduce the United States assured destruction capability—that is, our ability to destroy their industry and their people.
>
> Second, to complicate the targeting problem which we have in directing our strategic forces against the Soviet Union.
>
> Third, to reduce U.S. confidence in our ability to penetrate Soviet defenses, thereby reducing the possibility that the United States would undertake a preemptive first strike against the Soviet Union, even under extreme provocation.
>
> Fourth, to achieve an exploitable capability, permitting them freedom to pursue their national aims at conflict levels less than general nuclear war. . . .
>
> In regard to this last point . . . at the time of Cuba, the strategic nuclear balance was such that the Soviets did not have an exploitable

> capability, because of our vastly superior nuclear strength. . . . regardless of anyone's feelings about the situation in Vietnam, we think it quite clear that we would have had even more hesitation in deploying our forces there, had the strategic nuclear balance not been in our favor.[23]

Confronted with this difference in perspective between McNamara and the Joint Chiefs, Johnson had canvassed in December the perspective of others in the executive branch; e.g., Nicholas Katzenbach (in Rusk's absence at NATO), Llewellyn Thompson, Foy Kohler, Donald Hornig. His central question: How would the Soviet Union react to U.S. deployment of an ABM system designed to protect American cities? The response was universally in support of McNamara's prediction that the Soviet Union would have to respond by enlarging its offensive capabilities on an appropriate scale.

The upshot was a compromise. Johnson decided to ask Congress for a limited ABM system that would provide defense against a comparatively small Chinese ICBM attack in the 1970s; defense against an accidental missile firing by the Soviet Union or anyone else; limited protection for the Minuteman ICBM force. In addition (via a letter to Kosygin, delivered in January 1967), Johnson increased his pressure on Moscow for SALT talks, whose desirability was agreed on by all hands, including the Joint Chiefs of Staff. In June Johnson tried—and failed—at Glassboro to extract from Kosygin a firm time and place for the SALT talks to begin.

Against that background McNamara announced the decision to seek a limited ABM system on September 18, 1967, in a speech at San Francisco, using the occasion to underline the case against a general ABM system. The limited ABM program went forward while Johnson continued to pursue Kosygin doggedly for a time-and-place decision on the SALT talks, achieving his breakthrough by mid-1968.

After the July 1, 1969, Soviet agreement to SALT talks, staff work in the American government on a negotiating position—which had been going forward at working levels for years—went into high gear, under Rusk's chairmanship of the Committee of Principals. Given the inherent complexities of the problem, there was a general expectation that Johnson would, in the end, have to arbitrate civil–military differences before a negotiating position was achieved. But in the following weeks a full consensus was reached. Johnson was in a strong position to open the talks in 1968, if the Soviet invasion of Czechoslovakia had not intervened. A highly placed Soviet diplomat, long interested in the SALT talks, told me during the summer of 1968 that, after long travail, the Soviet government had also arrived at an initial position that he, as a serious man, would be pleased to take into negotiation.

Johnson's compromise ABM solution left open the possibility of moving forward with a full ABM program to protect the cities if three conditions were satisfied: the SALT talks did not yield satisfactory results; the Soviet ICBM and ABM effort justified a further expansion of U.S. strategic forces; and the relative costs of U.S. ABM's and ICBM's made an ABM effort economical. His compromise also provided a hedge in case Wheeler might be correct and McNamara (and the intelligence community) incorrect in assessing the second Soviet defense constellation as an ABM and not an antiaircraft system.

SOME UNRESOLVED ISSUES POSED BY WHEELER

ALTHOUGH Johnson—and Nixon—could move forward on the basis of the 1967 compromise, there were some fundamental issues embedded in the McNamara–Wheeler debate that the compromise did not settle. Wheeler implied that Kennedy's behavior in the Cuba missile crisis and Johnson's decision to go into Vietnam in 1965 were significantly affected by the fact that in a total nuclear exchange with the Soviet Union, American society would, in some meaningful sense, better survive than Soviet society. Conversely, he implied that a Soviet Union confronting an America with an "assured-destruction" but not a "damage-limiting" capability would be prepared to take greater risks in non-nuclear aggression.[24]

We live in a world where the answers cannot be found in numbers alone; and, surely, Wheeler was correct when he asserted that: "Deterrence is a combination of forces in being, and state of mind." But I am not sure he was correct when he linked the state of mind fairly rigidly to a "damage-limiting" (or "society survival") capability.

Stalin undertook the Berlin blockade and the attack on South Korea when he had, in the one case, no nuclear-weapons capability; in the other, a highly limited one. As Khrushchev makes clear, Stalin was worried about excessively overt Soviet involvement in the attack on South Korea and pulled back his advisers at the last minute.[25] But Stalin, Kim, and Mao nevertheless went ahead with their adventure. Some twelve years later, lack of a Soviet "damage-limiting" capability did not prevent Khrushchev from putting his missiles into Cuba.

In 1962 Kennedy did not regard the nuclear balance at a time of crisis primarily in quantitative terms. He regarded nuclear war as a horror beyond which he could not peer, including (as it would in 1962) the almost certain incineration of western Europe as well as a good part of the Soviet Union and a substantial but lesser part of the United States. He proceeded to do what he felt he had to do because he judged the acceptance of a gross U.S. strategic setback outweighed the limited but real risk of nuclear war.

In 1965 and subsequently Johnson took great pains to move in Southeast Asia in ways that would minimize the risk of a confrontation with

Moscow or Peking which might lead to nuclear war; but, like Kennedy (and Eisenhower at the time of the Lebanon–Jordan crisis of 1957), Johnson was not deterred from essential defensive actions by the fear they might yield nuclear war.

It is my best judgment that the relatively favorable nuclear arithmetic of 1961, 1962, and 1965 gave Kennedy and Johnson some comfort—but only extremely limited comfort—in making their critical decisions. Much more important was reasonable confidence that rationality would prevail in Moscow; and that Moscow would not take a legitimate U.S. defensive reaction against a communist thrust as an occasion for escalation that might risk nuclear war.

On the other hand, the assessment of American will, unity, and determination can, evidently, affect substantially the decisions of others to undertake adventures, irrespective of American military potential (vide, Hitler and the Japanese military in the 1930s), or American military hardware, including a nuclear-weapons monopoly (vide, Stalin, 1945–1949).

McNamara's Underlying Position

Just as a formal arithmetic approach to strategic deterrence is insufficient, so also is a formal diplomatic assessment of the meaning of the SALT talks. Precise and explicit agreements are likely to be hard to come by; and if and when they are reached, they are likely to leave substantial elements of continuing technological competition.

Neither Johnson, Rusk, nor McNamara approached the SALT talks with easy optimism. The issues on both sides were potentially mortal; and, therefore, a strong tendency existed for each side to provide itself with substantial margins of safety—or what passes for safety in an age of mutually "assured destruction capability."

But there was a more subtle hope about which McNamara, in particular, was highly explicit. It was that protracted negotiation would educate each side in the fears and anxieties and modes of thought of the other. And out of that mutual education might flow implicit as well as explicit agreements and the habit of taking rationally into account the probable reactions of one side to the initiatives of the other. Out of such mutual understanding the nuclear arms race might be damped even if comprehensive formal agreements were not reached.

The progress made over the twelve years from the first Sputnik to the opening of the talks was considerable—even remarkable. No more important or difficult negotiations have ever been attempted by man. They did not come about simply because American leaders worked to tame nuclear weapons in a fragile and dangerous world. They came about because American strength and will to frustrate Moscow's expansionist initiatives were combined with a stubborn appeal to the rational interests of the Soviet leadership as politicians responsible for one among many nation states—and as men.

JOHNSON'S HOPE FOR THE FUTURE

JOHNSON evolved a particular way of formulating his vision of what he hoped U.S.–Soviet relations might become. He first expressed it to me in an early-morning telephone conversation, shortly before the Glassboro meeting with Kosygin.

He said the United States and the Soviet Union should regard themselves as the two eldest children in a large family. They had the responsibility of keeping peace and order in the family. The younger children, however, were too old and independent to be ordered about. Therefore, the United States and the Soviet Union had to fulfill their joint mission by three other methods: by setting a good example in their bilateral relations; by working together with others to create an environment of peace; and, if others fought, by bringing about peace, if possible, but if not, by refusing to be drawn into the fight.

Although I had been involved in U.S.–Soviet problems since the summer of 1945, I had never read or heard the matter stated that way. I found it apt and said so, pointing out that the SALT talks represented the first method of fulfilling the joint mission; the NPT, the second; the hot-line effort on the Middle East, through which we had just passed, the third. I urged him to express his hopes to Kosygin in precisely those terms, which he did.

In Johnson's time Moscow did not wholly accept this vision of its mission; but it moved a little way, at least, down that road.

35

Europe

The Nuclear Question Again

In the spring of 1963 Kennedy had pressed hard to move the MLF to completion. In his letter to Adenauer of March 29, he envisaged rapid movement forward, so that he could present the proposed treaty to Congress in September. On April 4 Adenauer strongly agreed. After gauging in Europe the unwillingness of London to move in the spirit of the Nassau communique before the next election and the complexities in Rome and Brussels, Kennedy pulled back in degree, lengthening his timetable. But he encouraged the experimental mixed-manned ship as well as the work of a civil international planning group in Paris and a military group in Washington. The balance of Kennedy's mind was well reflected in his instructions, after the European trip (July 11, 1963): a best effort in support of the MLF proposal, but not an effort "to sell" it, leaving, rather, each European government to decide for itself.

Johnson repeated a final cycle of urgency and retraction in 1964. On April 8, 1964, he received Rusk's assessment of progress in congressional briefings and diplomacy, including a judgment that Soviet opposition was not deep and that the MLF would not interfere with any disarmament agreements Moscow might otherwise favor. He recommended a widening of congressional consultations and a carrying forward of diplomacy to permit presentation of a treaty to Congress early in 1965. At a meeting on April 10, with Thomas K. Finletter, just in from Paris, Johnson weighed the balance of the argument, including certain reservations in the Pentagon on the one hand, and the arms control agency on the other. He was informed, among other things, that British voices were telling the

Italians that Johnson was less interested in the enterprise than Kennedy. He decided that an informal but widened briefing of congressional committees should proceed; that the Europeans be told that it was his judgment that the MLF was the best way to solve the nuclear problem in the alliance. If possible, agreement on the MLF should be reached by the end of the year. But again, the plan should not be shoved down the throats of potential participants.

Johnson's judgment was framed by an assessment of the Germans and Germany, reflecting a life's experience. He said Germany could be difficult if left lonely or treated unfairly; American policy would be to stay close to Germany and assure it even-handed treatment in the alliance.

When Chancellor Ludwig Erhard came to Washington, Johnson and he agreed, in their joint communique of June 12, that "efforts should be continued to ready an agreement for signature by the end of the year." This was, perhaps, the high point of MLF diplomacy in the post-Nassau period.

On October 12 Harold Wilson was elected Prime Minister of Great Britain. De Gaulle, recognizing that the MLF might come to life in the months ahead, altered his earlier position that he would "understand" German participation and began to exert serious pressure on Bonn to stay out of the MLF.

De Gaulle linked two problems: an agricultural settlement within the European Economic Community (EEC) (needed both to protect the German farmer and to permit the Kennedy Round negotiation to go forward) and German participation in the MLF. On October 23, 1964, Premier Georges Pompidou said: "The agricultural common market must take shape, for without it the industrial common market will collapse. . . . If the multilateral force were to lead to the creation of a German–American military alliance, we would not consider this as being fully consistent with the relations we have with the Federal Republic which are based on the Franco–German Treaty."[1] This was accompanied by French threats in November of leaving NATO if the MLF was consummated and by Franco–Russian maneuvers that raised the specter of a reversal of alliances.

All this generated severe pressures within Erhard's government and party from those anxious to maintain good relations with Paris. On November 27 Erhard indicated that he was prepared to meet the French grain position, but he did not formally move away from the MLF.

On the eve of Wilson's visit to Washington the pressures on Erhard were vividly reported to Washington by the American Embassy in a cable of December 6. The problem of de Gaulle and the disarray he had generated in Bonn were much on Johnson's mind as the talks with the British opened.[2] They were underlined by those in Washington who did not believe the MLF was a wise undertaking.

Wilson did not know how far toward the MLF he would have to go to get the understanding with Johnson he needed. His tactic was to propose an Atlantic nuclear force to include U.K. submarines, the British strategic bomber force (the V-bombers), some U.S. Polaris submarines, and some jointly owned and mixed-manned Minuteman missiles. The MLF surface fleet was to be abandoned or reduced. In any case, Britain did not wish to join.

Johnson heard all this with some skepticism but urged Wilson to talk directly with the Germans and see if an agreement could be reached. To Wilson's relief, he was not pressed for an early, clear decision on the MLF. On December 17 Johnson's policy was laid down in NSAM 322: there should be no American pressure for an early agreement; the interests of Germany, Britain, France, and other European states would have to be taken into account in any nuclear agreement, as well as the U.S. veto and its interest in nonproliferation.

A good deal of care was taken in subsequent weeks and months to portray the American position as other than a withdrawal of support for the MLF. But the proposal had arisen as a means of reconciling the complex of factors listed in the new directive; there was no alternative in sight; only steady American support might have brought London and Bonn together; and as Washington's position became known, Erhard asked, in mid-January, that the MLF be put aside until after the September election. Erhard's move was designed to clear the ground for his meeting with de Gaulle on January 19. But, in effect, the MLF had run its course. The successful demonstration of mixed-manning, completed by the *Ricketts* on December 1, 1965, went virtually unnoticed; although it is still remembered among the navies concerned.

A number of factors entered Johnson's calculus.[3] Among those perceived in the bureaucracy were these: possible difficulties with Congress; the public arguments of those who believed the MLF would foreclose a nonproliferation agreement with Moscow; the urgency of moving on the NPT in the wake of the Chinese Communist nuclear explosion of the previous October; a certain compassion for Wilson with his four-vote majority in Commons; the gathering crisis in Asia.

In the short run, the desirability of avoiding a direct confrontation with de Gaulle was pressed hard on Johnson by some of his advisers. And there is a certain irony in this, given the General's later unprovoked withdrawal from NATO. But behind the whole process of disengagement from the MLF was the waning urgency of the nuclear question within the Alliance in the post-Cuba missile crisis period.

De Gaulle, his appetite whetted by what appeared an easy victory over the MLF, moved into high gear. In his press conference of February 4, 1965, he publicly pressed Bonn on the MLF, knowing the issue had, in fact, been put aside. He also called for an increase in the gold price, which confirmed the policy, previously inaugurated, of building up French gold stocks and drawing down dollar balances. In a world where international transactions were increasing more rapidly than gold available for monetary reserves, the French policy of trying to keep a relatively fixed gold reserve ratio was bound to put pressure on the dollar. On June 30, 1965, de Gaulle moved again. He launched a boycott of the Common Market in the wake of the settlement in principle of the grain question and the emergence from the Common Market Commission in Brussels of some proposals which he judged excessively supra-nationalist. When the Germans—and other EEC partners—united to use the implementation of the grain agreement as a lever on Paris, de Gaulle withdrew his boycott of Brussels at the end of the year; but in February 1966 he announced French withdrawal from the NATO structure and demanded the removal of U.S. bases from France.

A good deal of European and Atlantic policy was, then, taken up with coping with de Gaulle's enterprises in ways which permitted the EEC and NATO to survive. But there was, in each dimension of policy, also some forward movement.

So far as the nuclear question was concerned, the major development was the emergence of the nuclear planning committee of NATO defense ministers. With the MLF in abeyance, McNamara moved (May 31–June 1, 1965) to propose to his colleagues a "Select Committee" on nuclear planning. He launched the proposal with a candid and impressive initial exposition of nuclear problems. It firmly took hold in 1966. By September 27, 1966, when Erhard again met with Johnson, the joint communique did not refer to the MLF but cited the emerging concepts of a permanent nuclear planning committee as a device "which would broaden and deepen the areas of nuclear consultation and . . . bring the Allies more intimately into planning for nuclear defense."[4]

It was just a few days earlier that Rusk and Gromyko appeared to have turned the corner on the NPT in their conversations in New York (see p. 378).

Despite the fact that the MLF had been quiescent for almost two years, Johnson moved cautiously before he foreclosed a solution to the nuclear issue in the Alliance which would involve joint ownership of warheads as well as delivery vehicles. It was one thing to push the nuclear question onto a back burner, a quite different matter to rule out a future course of action. But with Bonn's agreement, the prohibition on "transfer" was included in the draft treaty. As the NPT moved forward, however, it was made clear to the Russians, as well as to the Congress, that a truly united western Europe would, as a successor state to Britain and France, have the right to be a nuclear-weapons power.

NATO and the Balance of Payments

The nuclear issue in the Alliance faded not only with the diminished urgency of the Soviet nuclear threat but also with the rise of problems from other areas. As of September 1966, Johnson and Erhard were concerned with an emerging agenda in the Atlantic quite different in emphasis from that of the period between Sputnik and the Cuba missile crisis. The headings of their communique of September 27, 1966, suggest the extent to which Atlantic priorities had shifted in new directions: toward German reunification; Western unity and East–West relations; equitable sharing of defense burdens; nonproliferation; Vietnam; space and scientific cooperation; natural resources and environmental control cooperation; the Kennedy Round; international monetary negotiations.

Of all these the most urgent was embedded in the phrase "equitable sharing of defense burdens." The chickens had at last come home to roost on the decision taken in 1961 in the wake of Brentano's talk with Kennedy. Kennedy had wished to move on a concerted basis with NATO allies to link monetary cooperation with a solution to the balance-of-payments problems arising from the presence of large U.S. forces in Germany and elsewhere in Europe. Those problems derived from the simple fact that the American military establishment spent a lot of dollars abroad which, like tourist expenditures, increased European dollar holdings and weakened the American balance of payments. They could be solved by offsetting monetary actions undertaken by NATO as a whole, on a multilateral basis, or by special bilateral arrangements. The language of the joint Kennedy–Brentano statement of February 17, 1961, looked to a multilateral monetary solution.[5] Kennedy was, however, reluctantly persuaded to take the more pragmatic and technically easier course of permitting German military purchases in the United States to offset American balance-of-payments costs arising from the American troop presence in Germany. This method kept the monetary and military problems of the Alliance in separate compartments; but it sufficed so long as the German military budget was expanding and, along with it, requirements for American equipment. It left the British, however, with substantial unrequited foreign exchange costs for maintaining their forces in Germany.

In the summer of 1964 the arrangement came under strain. In the post-Cuba missile crisis atmosphere, the priority of welfare outlays rose relative to the military budget in Germany. There was also a retardation in German growth, cutting into tax revenues.

The problem worsened over the next two years and became acute in both Bonn and Washington in the summer of 1966 when the United States appeared to confront over the coming fiscal year a gap of some $800 million in foreign exchange outlays for military purposes in Germany.

On July 5, 1966, Erhard wrote to Johnson that he faced difficult problems in meeting the bilateral offset agreement. He suggested, in general language, that consideration be given to offsets by German payments and services other than purchases of military equipment; and he indicated he would like to take up the matter on the occasion of his September visit to Washington.

In the meanwhile, Johnson felt severe pressure from two other directions: London, where Wilson was under urgent pressure to pull some of his forces out of Germany if their foreign exchange burden was not offset; and in the Senate, where Majority Leader Mike Mansfield introduced on August 31, 1966, a sense of the Senate resolution that ". . . a substantial reduction of U.S. forces permanently stationed in Europe can be made without adversely affecting either our resolve or ability to meet our commitment under the North Atlantic Treaty."

At about this time I attended a meeting at the State Department of Democratic Senate leaders, chaired by Dean Rusk. Listening to the divergent views around the table, one could see the makings of a powerful isolationist coalition: those, like Richard Russell, who felt that more than twenty years after the war Europe ought to be able to defend itself; isolationists or neo-isolationists, like Frank Church and Mike Mansfield; those obsessed with the balance-of-payments problem, like Stuart Symington; those, like John Pastore, furious with the European allies for their failure to support the United States in Southeast Asia. A failure to solve the offset problem in ways which met legitimate American financial interests and avoided a withdrawal of U.K. forces from the Continent could, evidently, set this coalition irresistibly in motion.

Erhard came in September without a plan. Johnson's affection for Erhard was real and abiding. But there was no way, consistent with American interests and the survival of NATO, to evade the need for Germany to face up to hard decisions if the alliance was to be held together. It was agreed, after some rather difficult meetings, that: NATO's force requirements for the future would be reviewed, and this review would deal simultaneously with financial problems; the offset question would be dealt with not bilaterally, as Bonn preferred, but trilaterally, with the British.

Looking back, it may be difficult to establish why the problem was so troublesome for Erhard. After all, what was at stake was money, and Germany was comfortable both in resources and in an easy balance-of-payments situation. Nothing in any way inequitable was being asked of Germany. And despite certain odd constitutional arrangements governing the German budget and central bank, there were ways to solve the problem. But a whole set of circumstances converged to produce a mood of widespread uneasiness, if not true crisis, in Bonn. First, Erhard's political position was precarious; second, German political leaders had failed to explain the offset problem, and to the German public the American insistence for full offset of foreign exchange costs appeared as a demand for payment of American mercenaries; finally, with the reduced danger from the East and de Gaulle's frustration of movement toward western European unity, German thoughts had begun to turn away from Europe and the Atlantic toward unification, but there was no clear path along which Bonn could act.

There was, in short, no firm sense of direction in German foreign policy, considerable accumulated frustration, and some self-pity. There was also an awkward delay as Erhard's government fell and his successor, Kurt Kiesinger (also from the Christian Democratic party), only gradually came to grips with the painful offset issue.

The heart of Johnson's position was that the financial problems of the United States and Britain had to be solved in ways that gave primacy to a strong and credible NATO. This judgment governed his decisions from the beginning to the end of the exercise, including his choice of the redoubtable John McCloy as his negotiator.

The final agreement of April 28, 1967, included some limited reductions in British and American forces located in Germany; a radical reduction in the foreign exchange gaps, mainly by German purchases of medium-term American bonds. Most important of all, it included a major step toward stabilizing the international monetary system—a Bundesbank commitment not to convert dollar holdings into gold. With that commitment in place, a limit was set on the French capacity to generate pressure on the dollar; and German policy was, in effect, geared to seeking with the United States and others the early creation of Special Drawing Rights (SDR's). There was a less well understood corollary to this linking of security and monetary policy in the Alliance: in degree, at least, German support for the dollar was tied implicitly to American steadiness as a NATO ally in much the same way as German support for the NPT.

Trade and Money

The successful outcome of the NATO offset crisis set the stage in a quite specific way for critical decisions on the Kennedy Round as well as the future of the international monetary system. In each capital—Bonn, London, and Washington—politicians faced a choice: they could act in classic terms of national sovereignty or act collectively. Lacking the palpable threat of Stalin's brutal thrusting to the west or Khrushchev's nuclear blackmail, it was easy for nationalist sentiments and irritations to rise. The array of divergent pressures, symbolized by the Mansfield Resolution for troop withdrawals from Europe, was matched in London and Bonn. Why should a Britain with an economy less buoyant than Germany's, carrying disproportionately heavy burdens in the world, bear additional weight in its balance of payments? Why should Germany, consigned by London and Paris to second-class nuclear status in Europe, already supplying the bulk of the European ground force contribution to NATO, buttress the pound and the dollar when British and U.S. domestic economic policies were less disciplined than Germany's?

Similar parochialism had to be overcome to bring the Kennedy Round to completion barely within the June 30, 1967, deadline (decreed by the American trade legislation of 1962) and to pass through the monetary crises of 1967–1968.

In the Kennedy Round Washington had to swallow a degree of agricultural protectionism in the Common Market, rooted primarily, but not exclusively, in German politics, that was economically unsound for Europe and inequitable to American interests. Europe had to accept an awkward agreement that would leave to subsequent congressional legislation the repeal of the American selling price system (ASP) in which certain imports, notably chemicals, were valued, for tariff purposes, in terms of their selling prices in the United States rather than their export value, the normal convention. But beyond these critical points of negotiation and decision, the whole Kennedy Round enterprise translated itself within each country into a series of domestic political struggles against local protectionist interests. On balance, those interests were well contained on the one hand by Johnson's determination to hold to a liberal trade policy, and on the other hand by the revolutionary precedent which granted negotiating powers to a Common Market officer. But, as always, the protectionist snake was only scotched, living to fight another day.

Johnson has described the monetary crises and anxieties he experienced from the devaluation of the pound, announced on November 18, 1967, to the signing of the tax bill on June 28, 1968.[6] In the aftermath of the British devaluation and then again during the March 1968 gold crisis, one could peer over the edge of the abyss as governments were torn between conventional nationalist impulses of *sauve qui peut* and the imperatives of a viable international monetary system which demanded mutual understanding, accommodation, and support.

In the case of both trade and monetary policy Johnson was blessed by effective, like-minded, well-coordinated staff support. Secretary of Agriculture Orville Freeman, for example, accepted loyally the agricultural disappointments in the Kennedy Round settlement, seeing clearly the larger interest. In monetary matters, the coordination among Treasury, the Federal Reserve, State, and the White House Staff was quite remarkable, given the radical innovation required to bring the SDR's to life and to create the two-tier gold system in March 1968.

No one who observed Johnson making the sequence of decisions he did during the Kennedy Round negotiations and the monetary crises of 1967–1968 (as well as during the McCloy tripartite negotiation) was ever likely to take seriously the notion that he was either unsophisticated or unsubtle in foreign affairs. His command of the technical issues, combined with a surefooted sense of direction, took the West forward at a time when progress was by no means inevitable. Behind it all was his deeply rooted conviction that Atlantic affairs were fundamental to American security and his memory of what disunity had brought upon the West in the 1930s and of weakness in the years after 1945. He often said, as men argued for a large reduction of U.S. forces in Europe: "It would be easy to make another Berlin crisis like 1961—or worse. I'm not going to do that." He was determined that, whatever burdens he bore in Asia and at home, he would leave to his successor a vital and viable Atlantic connection. Despite de Gaulle and a phase of respite from Soviet pressure, he succeeded.

So far as de Gaulle was concerned, Johnson had no illusions that, in his time, French policy would accommodate itself to the rest of Europe and the United States. He rigorously held the American government to a policy of avoiding overt debate or confrontation with Paris on grounds that it could only elevate de Gaulle and, perhaps, deepen the divide between France and the rest of the Atlantic Community. He understood the limits of de Gaulle's power to affect the course of events both within and outside Europe; he felt that a political base existed—if nurtured—to prevent de Gaulle from doing irreparable damage to European and Atlantic institutions; and he judged that post-de Gaulle France would become a less rigid and assertive member of the Western family.

Somewhere along the way it became clear that de Gaulle had overreached himself. He could still make difficulties—he would not alter course—but the institutions of Europe and the Atlantic could go about their business in reasonable confidence that they had seen the outer limit of his capacity to do mischief. The moment is hard to date, but the year is clearly 1966: perhaps it was the return of the French representatives to the Common Market on terms that had been steadily available; perhaps the unequivocal decision of all other members of NATO to move to Brussels and to protect the integrated military structure. In any case, by the time of Adenauer's funeral in April 1967, the sense was clear among those gathered in Bonn and at Cologne that de Gaulle had moved into a twilight period. The most vivid observation was that of German Defense Minister Franz Josef Strauss, with whom I drove from his office in Bonn to the Cathedral. He said de Gaulle had taught Europe that even a nation of fifty million—no matter how wealthy, technologically sophisticated, or brilliantly led—could not make a significant impact on Europe's problems, acting alone. Strauss cited the failure of de Gaulle's travels—from Cambodia and Iran to Latin America—to leave a mark on events; the failure of his gestures toward Peking and toward Moscow. Above all, de Gaulle had demonstrated that a European nation, acting alone, could not absorb efficiently modern technology—notably, computers and the world of aerospace. Now Europe knew, Strauss said, that it needed to unite and to embrace Britain. I asked him if he, a famous German Gaullist, was prepared to say that now. He said he was; and shortly after he did.

POLITICAL CONSULTATION: LIMITED SUCCESS ON A VERY NARROW FRONT

WHEN I went again to work at the White House on April 1, 1966, Johnson told me that, in addition to carrying forward the tasks of my predecessor, Mac Bundy, I was to make a special effort to suggest new directions and initiatives in foreign policy. Within the next two weeks, working with my colleagues, I put two major propositions to him: that he support a hemispheric summit meeting; and that he generate from the bureaucracy new proposals that would increase the cohesion of NATO and the North Atlantic Community, while moving toward détente with the East.

Knowing from fresh experience as State Department planner the schisms and lacerations in the bureaucracy over NATO nuclear policy, I suggested to Johnson that we clearly separate the nuclear issue from other less contentious matters. On these non-nuclear matters, I knew a number of ideas had been generated in the Policy Planning Council and elsewhere. As I said in a memo to the President of April 21: "One purpose of this NSAM is to make sure that what we all agree about in the U.S. Government is staffed out and made as effective an item in our policy as can be done . . . [that we] set the framework for constructive work which would unite not divide the town."

The NSAM of April 22, 1966, incorporated this perspective. It was the framework within which work went forward on McNamara's nuclear planning group, trade and monetary matters, the handling of the shift of NATO headquarters to Brussels, and the effort to balance and reconcile a strengthening of ties within the West and movement toward détente with the East. Proximately, it also gave impetus to the work of a task force on NATO policy, headed by Dean Acheson.

One of its papers forwarded to Johnson on June 10 had a striking heading to its first proposition: "NATO's Principal Political Function—Preparation for Settlement in Central Europe." This judgment was the product of hard-won experience.

Political consultation, as well as the common defense, had been viewed, from the beginning, as a NATO function—or, at least, since the NATO Wisemen's exercise of 1956. It proved a difficult task. A few members of NATO had limited major interests beyond the area itself, but on these there was no consensus about policy. None was anxious to share America's global interests and responsibilities. In the post-Cuba missile crisis period one area, however, did emerge where consultation was of universal interest and a degree of concert was possible; that is, policy toward the Soviet Union and eastern Europe. There was by 1966 an authentic agreement in the American government—and, more important, within NATO—that the central political task of NATO was to orchestrate the policy of its members in ways which would ease East–West relations and gradually prepare the way for a settlement whose ultimate shape and timing lay in a misty future.

Johnson's October 7, 1966, speech was the most complete statement of the new Atlantic agenda that evolved during his administration, a transition in which NSAM's 322 and 345 were benchmarks. It applied to Europe the four principles which emerged as Johnson's way of articulating his foreign policy: deterrence of aggression ("Our first concern is to keep NATO strong and to keep it modern and to keep it abreast of the times in which we live"); economic and social progress (the Kennedy Round, international monetary reform, the development of science and technology as a common Atlantic resource, and accelerating the growth of the developing nations); regionalism (the continued vigorous pursuit of a united western Europe); reconciliation (". . . one great goal of a united West is to heal the wound which now cuts East from West and brother from brother").

The art of the effort was to weave together abiding strands of Atlantic policy reaching back to 1947–1949; impart to them some new forward thrust; and, on that basis, to reach beyond by ameliorative action toward the East. Johnson listed what had been accomplished in East–West relations in the two previous years and then announced seven additional measures of bridge-building, around the theme: "Our aim is a true European reconciliation." The goals of a nonproliferation agreement and mutual U.S.–Soviet force reductions in Europe were reaffirmed.

It was not easy to strike precisely the right balance between strengthening the institutions of the West and reaching out to the East; and it was not easy to keep all the members of NATO in harness as each European foreign office and foreign trade ministry pressed its own Eastern interests and the United States conducted its complex dialogue with Moscow on nuclear matters.

Nevertheless, the Western club as a whole (aside from de Gaulle) managed to keep roughly together in these efforts to explore the possibilities and limits of détente, including Bonn, whose shift toward Ostpolitik carried some real disruptive possibilities as well as the haunting memory of interwar German–Soviet bilateral relations.

A symbol of this mature effort of the Alliance to remain in at least loose harness in a phase of uncertain and ambiguous détente was the "Harmel exercise." The Belgian foreign minister, Pierre Harmel, suggested at the NATO meeting of December 1966 a study by the North Atlantic Council of changes in the international situation since 1949 and ways to

TABLE 35–1
NET FLOW OF OFFICIAL DEVELOPMENT ASSISTANCE TO LESS-DEVELOPED COUNTRIES AND MULTILATERAL AGENCIES, 1960–1968
(in millions of U.S. dollars)

Country	1960	1961	1962	1963	1964	1965	1966	1967	1968
Australia	58.9	70.7	73.8	95.9	100.0	118.6	126.1	157.2	159.8
Austria	0.1	2.9	7.0	2.1	11.8	33.8	34.8	28.2	23.0
Belgium	101.0	92.1	69.8	79.7	71.3	101.6	76.1	88.8	88.0
Canada	75.2	60.6	34.5	64.9	77.9	96.5	187.1	197.9	174.7
Denmark	5.3	8.1	7.5	8.7	10.1	12.9	21.1	26.0	28.7
France	847.3	942.9	976.0	851.7	828.2	752.2	744.8	825.5	855.2
Germany	242.5	322.0	399.8	397.6	472.9	436.9	439.7	528.1	553.7
Italy	90.9	79.1	93.6	112.9	59.1	80.0	61.9	120.0	165.2
Japan	105.1	107.8	85.3	137.6	115.8	243.7	283.3	384.3	355.2
Netherlands	35.3	55.9	65.0	37.8	49.2	69.6	93.9	113.5	134.4
Norway	5.2	6.8	6.5	9.9	9.6	11.3	14.1	14.5	25.5
Sweden	6.7	8.4	18.5	22.9	32.8	38.1	56.9	59.9	71.4
Switzerland	3.5	7.9	4.9	6.2	9.2	10.7	14.2	13.0	18.8
United Kingdom	407.0	456.8	421.0	414.5	493.3	480.6	525.9	498.0	428.0
United States	2,702.0	2,943.4	3,271.5	3,627.0	3,611.0	3,570.8	3,599.0	3,559.0	3,347.0
Total	4,686.0	5,165.4	5,534.7	5,869.4	5,952.2	6,057.3	6,278.9	6,613.9	6,428.6

Source: OECD, DAC, *Statistical Tables for the 1969 Annual Aid Review.*

strengthen the Alliance "as a factor for durable peace." He was promptly made chairman of a group which filed its report on Future Tasks of the Alliance a year later.[7] Despite the sobering setback of Czechoslovakia in August 1968, the NATO Council and the governments behind it did generate sustained political consultation on East–West matters in the period 1966–1968 and a rough concert of view on how patiently to work over the long pull for peaceful change.

Aid

One little noted but substantial positive achievement of the Atlantic Community (plus Australia and Japan) in these years was to widen the circle of contributors and to achieve increasing acceptance of multilateralism and fair shares as the method and principle by which resources would flow from the more advanced to the less advanced nations. Table 35-1 suggests the changing scale and proportioning of the effort between 1960 and 1968.

The American contribution fell away marginally from the 1963 peak in the post-Cuba missile crisis period, exacerbated by the pressures of Vietnam. The French contribution also declined from a 1962 peak. The British contribution declined in 1967–1968, under acute balance-of-payments pressures. But the slack was taken up by other nations, notably, Japan, Australia, Canada, Germany, and the Netherlands.

Equally significant was the emergence and strengthening of various consortium and other multilateral arrangements: the increasing role of the Inter-American Bank and CIAP; the Asian Development Bank; The Hague Club, to support post-Sukarno Indonesia; and a good many others built on the pathfinding model of the World Bank's India and Pakistan consortia.

The principle of multilateralism and fair shares was, at Johnson's insistence, brought to bear also with respect to agricultural assistance to India during the second of its terrible drought years (1966–1967); and it was institutionalized during the Kennedy Round negotiations by a special agricultural aid agreement.

A Conclusion

European policy in Johnson's years was an exercise in trying to give shape and order to a situation of diffusing power. The forces making for diffusion were both real and psychological.

Psychologically, the outcome of the Cuba missile crisis altered expectations about the future relations of Moscow to eastern Europe. Just as the

West Berliners promptly perceived that the ultimatum which had hung over them for four years was lifted, eastern Europeans perceived that the tides had shifted and the future, long as it might be, was likely to grant increasing degrees of freedom from Moscow.

To this shift of mood in the communist world was soon added an overt and exacerbated stage of Sino–Soviet relations. This brought some real changes: a shifting of Soviet military force to its eastern frontiers; a heightened anxiety in the Soviet leadership to keep the eastern European (and other) Communist parties from playing off Moscow against Peking, as Bucharest succeeded in doing; a fragmenting tendency within Communist parties in other parts of the world.

So far as Moscow was concerned, Johnson's policy was to try to convert this changed mood and setting into concrete, limited measures of East–West agreement that would, step by step, move relations from confrontation to normalization: to substitute for the clarifying but dangerous order of intense bipolar Cold War the more benign, if not always easy, relations between nation states; to help move a balkanizing communist world toward, roughly, the norms of the U.N. Charter.

But he faced also potential balkanizing trends within the Atlantic world: a diminished fear of Moscow; a de Gaulle free and eager to play a disruptive lone hand from his January 1963 press conference forward; a Britain haunted by its own problem of grandeur, trying still to find a stable role in the face of de Gaulle's frustration of its belated drive toward Europe; a Germany, notably after Erhard's fall, willing to experiment a little with assertiveness, and whose relative economic success was a somewhat ironic affront, as Britain's immediate postwar image of its global destiny waned; a Belgium and Italy, loyal to the concepts of a United Europe and the Atlantic, but also anxious not to confront de Gaulle and endanger the Common Market. Behind this disarray was the hard fact that European (and Japanese) economic strength was growing, and economic dependence on the United States declining, as the trade and monetary negotiations reflected.

Here, too, Johnson's policy was to try to use the declining but real margin of America's influence on Europe to convert fragmentation into new patterns of order and partnership in which the European voice would be stronger but a common effort to solve specific identifiable common problems would go forward. In the end, he found responsive minds and voices in the European capitals. These permitted NATO to survive the trip from Paris to Brussels; the McCloy exercise and the Kennedy Round to succeed; the international monetary system to move to a new revolutionary basis with the SDR's and the two-tier gold system; the commitment of the more advanced nations to help the less advanced to become more firmly institutionalized; and the Alliance to remain stable in the face of the complex negotiation for an NPT.

It was a protracted and delicate exercise in transition requiring vastly more of Johnson's energy and attention than the public could perceive, at a time when a war in Southeast Asia and a multifaceted social revolution at home dominated the media.

But his task was not merely to organize power gradually diffusing among the more advanced noncommunist nations; it was also to recognize the limits of that diffusion in a world where nuclear power still was disproportionately concentrated in the hands of Moscow and Washington. There was, in the end, no substitute in the defense of Europe for the commitment, there and elsewhere, of American nuclear arms, made credible by the presence of substantial U.S. ground forces. Despite the burdens of Vietnam and the drumfire of criticism from Europe of his Southeast Asian policy, Johnson had to accept and budget for that fact, a stance mitigated a little by the understanding and quiet support of most European governments for his effort in Asia. Despite their anxiety that U.S.–Soviet negotiations might be at their expense, the European governments also had to accept America's unique nuclear role and support, even if uneasily, both Johnson's effort to achieve an NPT consistent with Alliance interests and to move toward bilateral SALT talks.

What could not be accomplished in Johnson's time was the joining of Britain to Europe and, hopefully, the emergence in such a Europe of a sense of common responsibility for encouraging stability and progress on a global basis. It was not only in Asia that Johnson felt lonely as he observed the Europeans going peacefully about their business while he struggled to hold the balance of power in the part of the world where two-thirds of humanity lived. It was he—and not some European prime minister—who had to send three C-130's to the Congo in July 1967 in order to strengthen Mobutu's capacity to deal with some mercenaries and avoid the slaughter of a good many Europeans in Katanga. I can recall few more vivid demonstrations of the holiday from responsibility enjoyed by Europe in the 1960s than the cables explaining why one after another European government could not act to meet Mobutu's request. Johnson's action stirred Senators Russell and Fulbright to protest, but the dispatch of aircraft proved remarkably successful in quieting the Congo.

The most massive demonstration of European political impotence beyond Europe was its cross-purposes during and after the Arab–Israeli war of June 1967. Great Western interests were at stake; but the lack of consensus reduced Europe to observer status. It was not difficult to explain the phenomenon in the light of British, French, and German ties to the Middle East over the previous century—ties which left painful memories and national ambitions not quite stilled. But the spectacle made clear the gap between Europe's potential role in stabilizing a volatile world and the way things stood in the 1960s.

36

Johnson and the Developing World

The End of the Honeymoon

The distinguished British economic historian M. M. Postan once remarked that Kennedy dealt with the problems of the 1960s in their honeymoon period while Johnson had to deal with them after the honeymoon. Kennedy's years were hardly the usual notion of a politician's honeymoon. But, still, there's something in Postan's bon mot.

Kennedy pioneered a reconciliation between a rapid rate of growth and price stability, including wage-price guideposts; but he could do so in a period when unemployment was still relatively high. Johnson had to struggle with the problem at a time when unemployment was low, a substantial war was being fought, and Congress was not prepared to raise taxes immediately.

Kennedy sensed in 1963 the potentially revolutionary surge of Negro feeling which gave a new urgency to the race question in America. He sought to lead and organize it within the framework of the American political tradition, and he managed well the August march on Washington. But he was killed before Watts—and all that followed—could reveal the depth and recalcitrance of the race problem in the urban North.

Kennedy was preparing to launch an attack on poverty, but it was Johnson who had to give it shape and try to solve the enormously complex problems of its operation, notably in the urban ghettos.

Although Kennedy dealt with de Gaulle's disruptive press conference of January 1963—and delivered in June his stirring response in Frankfurt—it was Johnson who had to hold the line and keep the faith when de Gaulle actually left SHAPE and did his worst against the dollar, as Kennedy always feared he would.

Kennedy moved nuclear relations with Moscow from maximum confrontation in Cuba to the 1963 test ban treaty. But that was an easy step to negotiate as compared with Johnson's NPT negotiations and the preliminaries to the SALT talks.

There is also an important element of truth in Postan's proposition when applied to American policy toward the developing world in the 1960s. Although Eisenhower's stance toward Asia and Latin America was changing in the late 1950s, there was legitimate scope for drama and rhetoric in Kennedy's launching of the Alliance for Progress; actually setting the India and Pakistan consortia in motion; welcoming gracefully the new African leaders onto the world stage; articulating policy in terms that underlined the American stake in the independence of the new nations, the American expectation of a world of ideological diversity, and the American commitment to a Decade of Development. There was among some a mood of romantic hope about the developing nations in the early 1960s —a hope that they, coming late to modernity and the arena of power, would be wiser than the old states of Europe. Perhaps they could avoid pedestrian and bloody struggles for real estate and glory and lead the whole community of nations to stable peace. And some leaders in the developing world—notably, Nehru—encouraged this vision of higher virtue. Kennedy was not vulnerable to such illusions. As President, he saw enough of the problems of the developing world to know how long, uneven, and rocky the road to modernity would prove to be in Asia, the Middle East, Africa, and Latin America; how unyielding the Indian–Pakistani confrontation; how unromantic the consequences of such romantic revolutionaries as Sukarno, Nkrumah, Nasser, Goulart, and the rest; how slow moving the task of translating the stirring objectives of the Alliance for Progress into Latin American economic and social progress. But it was Johnson who had to stare at the full potential damage Sukarno might do, as he left the U.N. and made common cause with Peking early in 1965; to try to get India and Pakistan back on the tracks when the chronic mutual ill will between them yielded war in 1965; to limit an Arab–Israeli war in the Middle East when a harassed and declining Nasser mobilized in the Sinai and closed the Gulf of Aqaba; to deal with a Latin America whose sense of independence was rising but which still lacked the capacity to achieve steady progress, economic unity, and a dignified balance with the Colossus of the North.

And, of course, it was Johnson who had to face the full consequences of the process of disintegration in Indochina, set in motion by the Buddhist demonstrations in May 1963 and by Hanoi's decision in 1964 to send its regular units south.

Putting Southeast Asia aside for later treatment, it is useful to review

Johnson's approach to the developing continents under the four headings in terms of which he tended to articulate his foreign policy: problems of aggression; economic and social progress; regionalism; and reconciliation.

Deterring or Dealing with Aggression in the Developing World

The cases of violence with which Johnson had to deal represent a wide spectrum from the water crisis at Guantanamo in 1963 and the seizure of the *Pueblo* in 1968; to the recurrent problem of Greek–Turkish tension over Cyprus, where the communist role was minor; to the aftermath of the Indian–Pakistani war in 1965 when Moscow moved parallel to Washington to end hostilities and avoid increased Chinese leverage on Pakistan.

Johnson's stance toward the endless flow of trouble was to engage the United States to the minimum consistent with his view of vital American interests. This, in fact, has been the instinctive stance of all American postwar Presidents. There is nothing an American President does more reluctantly than engage his troops, resources, domestic capital, and international prestige abroad. But it was, perhaps, a more conscious posture with Johnson than with his three predecessors. First, he had a long, urgent, and absorbing domestic agenda before him to which was added, in 1965, the heavy burden of large-scale American engagement in Vietnam. Second, he was conscious that in the developing world, as in Europe, the spirit of the middle and late 1960s was of increasing assertiveness—a desire of nations to take their own destinies into their hands in an increasingly multipolar world. It was not in the American interest to thwart this tendency but rather to encourage those who would organize it constructively. When this impulse expressed itself in unconstructive ways that did not damage vital American interests, it was Johnson's policy to step aside and minimize the possibility of confrontation. He moved only when he was thoroughly convinced that vital American interests were at stake; and then he moved to the minimum extent necessary. This is what Johnson did in Europe, with respect to de Gaulle and NATO. In the developing world the equivalent pattern was set by one of his first foreign policy crises, which led to what might be called the Guantanamo water ploy.

Guantanamo and Other Exercises in Low Posture

On February 2, 1964, Havana launched a kind of limited chess game to test the new President.[1] The pawns were four Cuban fishing boats which turned up less than two miles off the American coast. They were picked up and hauled in, their crew members acknowledging that they were engaged in a "historic venture" to "test United States reactions." After some Cuban diplomatic protests, Castro turned off the water supply to the Guantanamo naval base. Johnson's response was minimal but decisive: an alternative independent water supply was generated in accordance with contingency plans; 2000 Cubans working at the base were discharged; the fishermen who wished to go home were released after the four ship captains paid their fines. Castro's offer to turn on the tap again was refused.

Under provocation, Johnson did what was essential, but increased his distance from Castro.

A similar policy was pursued in Indonesia, as Sukarno moved toward Peking and the local Communist party and became increasingly anti-American in rhetoric and policy. In 1964–1965 the American presence in Indonesia was progressively lowered.[2] Economic aid was reduced to the barest trickle; the USIA was closed down in March 1965; after Ellsworth Bunker talked to Sukarno in April, the Peace Corps was withdrawn; Ambassador Howard Jones, who had in better days maintained close human ties with Sukarno, was succeeded in July by a cool professional, Marshall Green, who was instructed to maintain correct relations but no more. The task of dealing with Sukarno was, essentially, left to others; although, in oblique ways, Johnson's July 1965 commitment to Vietnam was a decisive setback to Sukarno's vision of the future. But it was the British Commonwealth that contained the thrust against Malaysia; and in the first days of October 1965, the Indonesian military dealt successfully with the threat to themselves and the independence of their country that the communists mounted on September 30 with Sukarno's connivance.

With respect to the 1965 war between India and Pakistan, Johnson also took his distance; but he played a more direct role than in Indonesia. Economic and social development had proceeded quite well in Pakistan since 1958, but the possibility of a Kashmir settlement appeared to be progressively receding. A sense of now-or-never gathered strength in Karachi, stimulated by Zulfikar Ali Bhutto, Ayub's foreign minister, in the wake of Ayub's re-election. Border clashes in April between India and Pakistan in the Rann of Kutch were apparently settled at the June Commonwealth conference in London; but in August Pakistan launched an invasion of Kashmir by infiltration. The Indians responded not only in Kashmir but with an offensive aimed at Lahore. By September 4 a quite substantial war was under way.

Johnson's response was first to postpone the forthcoming visit of Ayub as well as the later visit to Washington planned by Lal Bahadur Shastri, Nehru's successor. Then he left to Prime Minister Harold Wilson and his Commonwealth colleagues the task of quieting things after the clash in the Rann of Kutch. In September the United Nations took on the task of arranging a cease-fire, but Johnson brought heavy pressure to bear on both parties by suspending deliveries of military equipment and new commitments of economic aid.

In January 1966 Johnson let Kosygin take the lead as an intermediary between Ayub and Shastri in Tashkent, and he orchestrated American diplomacy in such a way as to ease Kosygin's task. (I heard Johnson several times observe: "I couldn't be seen; but I was at Tashkent.")

In 1966 more normal ties with India and Pakistan resumed; Mrs. Indira Gandhi, who had replaced Shastri as Prime Minister, came to Washington in March, and aid began to flow again to both impoverished nations.

Perhaps the most painful exercise in self-restraint came in the aftermath of the North Korean seizure of the *Pueblo* on January 23, 1968. That act was evidently geared to the attempt to assassinate President Park of South Korea and, almost certainly, represented a North Korean diversionary operation in support of Hanoi's Tet offensive, which began a week later. At stake was the possible withdrawal of the South Korean forces from Vietnam, the re-allocation of American air and naval strength away from Southeast Asia, and the dissipation of American executive attention at a crucial moment in a war. Given the pathological mood of the North Koreans, conveyed to Washington by, among others, some eastern European governments, a full-scale invasion of South Korea could not be wholly ruled out, although objectively it would have been a most unpromising undertaking. By the time Washington was informed of the *Pueblo*'s seizure, the ship and its crew were in North Korean territorial waters and the American commanders in the field had decided there was no air or naval action they could usefully take to remove them from North Korean hands. It was an ugly situation. Johnson canvassed all the options open to the United States as well as the probable intentions of Pyongyang and Moscow.

The first task was to move in ways that minimized the likelihood that North Korea would open a second front in Asia. To that end, American naval and air strength in the area was increased without drawing down forces in Southeast Asia. Additional air power was particularly important since the North Korean air force was larger than the South Korean. The second task was to decide if any retaliatory action by the United States was rational. Many possibilities were examined. None promised to get back the captured crew; some would be mere pinpricks; others (like sustained air attack or blockade) would only have been rational as part of a war against North Korea, which no one advised. Therefore, the return of the crew by diplomatic means became the limited objective. This posed a third task: reassurance to the South Koreans.

The South Koreans were understandably upset by the inaction of the United States and the relative passivity that Washington urged on them. But with the war in Southeast Asia at a critical stage, it made sense, from the American point of view, not to divert major military resources to a second front. With South Korea enjoying a remarkable stage of economic and social progress, it made sense, from Seoul's point of view, to fend off Kim's provocations rather than respond to them in ways that might distort the economic and political life of the country. Cyrus Vance's mission in Seoul during the second week of February 1968 was, nevertheless, difficult.

South Korean pride demanded some form of retribution; but, in the end, Park agreed that the major common tasks were the war in Southeast Asia, South Korean economic and social progress, and improvement in the South Korean capacity to deal with North Korean incursions. And, finally, the interminable exchanges at Panmunjom yielded a formula by which the men were returned without an apology for a violation of international waters that did not occur.

I recall few more human moments at the Tuesday lunches than the discussions, week after painful week during 1968, on the question posed for us at Panmunjom: Should the United States make a lying apology to get back the crew? We were dealing with cynical and brutal men in Pyongyang; the decision to restrict our objective to the return of the crew had been made; the temptation was real among all of us to put their welfare above all else and to lie. But, as Dean Rusk said one day: "It won't stay down." And this remained Johnson's position. For reasons none of us quite understood, the North Koreans finally agreed to a formula we could accept, and the men came home. Their brutal treatment at the hands of the North Koreans, as it emerged from their debriefings, made hard reading—so hard that I noted, in forwarding the material to the President on December 28, 1968, that I had considered not burdening him with it.

THE RELUCTANT ACCEPTANCE OF A HIGH POSTURE: THE DOMINICAN REPUBLIC

THERE were other examples of this style of minimum intervention consistent with vital American interests: Johnson's passivity as President João Goulart, with communist support and advice, brought Brazil to the brink of dictatorship in 1964; and the powerful but quiet interventions of August 1964 and November 1967 to prevent Greece and Turkey from going to war over Cyprus.

On the other hand, when a vital American interest was involved and all other remedies had been exhausted, Johnson reluctantly but firmly accepted the inevitable costs of substantial overt intervention. At the high end of the spectrum were his 1965 decisions on Vietnam; at the low end, the three C-130's for the Congo in 1967 (see page 405).

In between were the two 1965 decisions on the Dominican Republic.[3] The first, on April 28, 1965, was to land a limited force of Marines (initially, 400) to protect Americans and other foreign nationals endangered by the disintegration of order; the second, late on April 29, was to land a larger force (22,000 at peak strength) to prevent the communist-dominated forces in the center of Santo Domingo from taking over the country and to force a cease-fire and a negotiated arrangement for a provisional government that might manage new, free elections. The situation in Santo Domingo had changed markedly between the two decisions. The regular army forces under General Wessin y Wessin failed, on April 27–28, to cross the Duarte bridge and clear out the rebel citadel. They returned in disarray to their barracks. A situation of disorder rapidly became one where the danger of a communist takeover was real, since forces of Juan Bosch, the deposed President, ran for cover when it appeared Wessin y Wessin might succeed. Communist leaders dominated the citadel in the wake of his failure and the withdrawal of the more moderate rebel leaders.

The debate over Johnson's actions was complicated by the blurring, in the reporting of events and in the public mind, of the two decisions. But the debate reflected far more than that. It was, in substance and in timing, a kind of dress rehearsal for the debate on Vietnam.

Johnson's decision posed these four critical questions, each of which was to have its counterpart in the later Vietnam debate:

On what legal basis was action undertaken?

Whatever the legal basis, were vital American interests involved in the outcome?

Whatever American interests might be, was it morally right for the United States to use its military forces to frustrate the outcome of a civil war in a foreign nation?

Whatever American interests might be, were we not bound to await majority agreement in the OAS before acting?

A highly articulate minority of American opinion took the view that Johnson's action was an extralegal throwback to old-style imperialism; that no vital American interests were involved, since the communist menace was overrated; even if the communists were to take over the Dominican Republic, that was Dominican and not American business; and, finally, that in moving before the OAS had fully and formally committed itself, Johnson had undermined the collective institutions of the hemisphere and the Alliance for Progress to boot. To all of this was added the confusion about the two decisions: Were American forces sent to Santo Domingo to protect American and other foreign citizens or to prevent a second communist takeover in the Caribbean? Out of that confusion, which the American government should have done more to dissipate, the notion of a "credibility gap" quickly grew.[4]

Johnson knew well that his Dominican Republic decisions would be controversial at home and in Latin America. And before moving on his second and critical decision, late on the 29th, he had to answer these questions.

Legally, the Punta del Este decisions of January 1962 provided that "communism was incompatible with the principles of the Inter-American system," and urged the member states to "take those steps that they may consider appropriate for their individual and collective self-defense" in the face of the danger of communism.

Then there was a question of fact and judgment: Was the danger of a communist takeover real on April 29, or was the intervention merely frustrating the noncommunist forces of Juan Bosch? Here the press did not know until much later of the abdication of the moderates and of the consequent shift of the rebel forces toward communist control.

Johnson and his advisers agreed unanimously that the situation confronted on the evening of the 29th constituted a real and present danger that the communists could convert the chaos in Santo Domingo into a takeover of power. They were all conscious, moreover, of the conclusion at which Kennedy had arrived: that the United States should act to prevent a second communist state in the Caribbean. Johnson shared the view that it was a vital American interest to prevent such an outcome.

Morally, the question was not difficult. The communists were a tiny minority in the Dominican Republic. The U.S. intervention was undertaken, in conformity with an OAS resolution, not to occupy the island or to impose an American-controlled government. Nor was American force used to attack the positions held by the rebels. Force was used to isolate the rebel citadel and to achieve a cease-fire; create the conditions for negotiating an interim government; and arrange for a carefully inspected election. The balance of Dominican sentiment as revealed in the election of 1966 clearly indicated that the will of the majority would have been violated if a communist takeover had been permitted. Johnson, at the time and in retrospect, could feel that there was a clear convergence between the vital interests of the United States and what was morally right. And in this he was strongly supported by the American majority: by something like two and a half to one in December 1965.[5]

The question of the role of the OAS was more searching. The American public—as well as President Johnson—understood that this was a more difficult matter.[6] Etched in the minds and memories of even those Latin Americans closest to the United States was the history of unilateral U.S. interventions in the past. The determination to avoid such humiliation in the future was—and remains—one of the binding strands of the OAS; that is, OAS doctrine and policy includes restraints on the intervention of any nation in the internal affairs of others, and one abiding interest of the OAS is to maintain those restraints, most obviously on the United States but on the larger states of Latin America as well.

Johnson faced, however, not a doctrine but a situation. First, the only legal authorities in the Dominican Republic, frayed and bedraggled as they were, had asked for help; and the Punta del Este resolutions gave them the right to ask for and accept bilateral, as well as multilateral, aid. Second, and more important, was the image of uncertainty the Latin American governments projected to Washington in the face of a fast-moving situation. In some cases, the ambassadors in Santo Domingo took one view while the ambassadors to the OAS in Washington took another. When Johnson received the critical messages from Santo Domingo late on the 29th, he had concluded that no unified diplomatic and military position could be generated in time by the governments in the hemisphere. The danger in the Dominican Republic was not sufficiently clear in the Latin American capitals to produce the kind of unanimity Khrushchev and his missiles generated in October 1962. It was the sense of urgency conveyed from Santo Domingo about the deterioration of the situation that evidently led Johnson to move on the night of the 29th with American forces, while continuing to push the issue in the OAS. The first fruit of work in the OAS was the agreement to seek a cease-fire through the Papal Nuncio. Against the background of the arrival of American forces, this was achieved on April 30. The Secretary General of the OAS promptly assumed a central role in the process of reconciliation; and before long armed forces from five countries, plus officers from El Salvador, formed part of the OAS force, under a strong-minded Brazilian general. What happened was not, in fact, an old-fashioned unilateral American intervention; but neither was it an orderly OAS exercise. The Latin American nations were at the critical moment as split, uncertain, and unprepared to move with effective unity as they were in January 1962 in the face of the pressures from the Caribbean states harassed by Cuba. The outcome in the Dominican Republic reflected the same forces that yielded the permissive Resolution II at Punta del Este, except for the sturdy role of Brazil in 1965.

The other issue embedded deeply in the debate about the Dominican Republic was the fate of Juan Bosch. He had come to the Presidency as a clear popular choice, hopefully to supply the kind of noncommunist left leadership that had proved effective in Venezuela and Costa Rica. He faced an inherently more difficult task than Betancourt or Figueres. The post-Trujillo Dominican Republic lacked resources, democratic political institutions, and democratic political experience. Even taking into account these difficulties, he had not proved an effective President, tending to substitute rhetoric for hard work, decision, and action. The elements in the equation of political power fell out, and Bosch was overthrown. Nevertheless, he continued to have strong support among certain Latin American groups, and among elements of the American press and the Congress. Somehow, they felt, American intervention, once it had taken place, ought to re-install Bosch. It was not until the meticulously inspected election of June 1966 that the judgment was accepted that Bosch no longer represented the majority of the Dominican people.

With the orderly end to the Dominican crisis in 1966, feelings subsided. From Johnson's point of view the effort had been remarkably successful. The application of overwhelming force and skillful diplomacy to achieve a limited and lucid objective had protected a vital American interest and yielded a decent and honorable result. My old colleague at Punta del Este, Antonio Mayobre, who represented U Thant for a time in Santo Domingo, had reacted initially with some passion against the intervention, as he made clear when we met in Rio on Alliance for Progress business in November 1965. But by the early months of 1966 he had come to the view that the process of democratization in the Dominican Republic had been set forward by fifteen years, and, with rare grace, he was prepared to tell this to me and others.[7] To this outcome two men, aside from Lyndon Johnson, greatly contributed: the interim President of the Dominican Republic, Garcia Godoy, and Ellsworth Bunker.

To this day there are scars among some thoughtful Latin Americans over the Dominican affair; but, by and large, most recognize that the lesson for the OAS is the need for more responsible contingency planning, better communications between the OAS ambassadors in Washington and the Latin American capitals, and a greater willingness of Latin American governments to assume collective responsibility in the face of common problems. But in 1965 most Latin American governments were prepared to enjoy the double luxury of having the United States bear the brunt of solving a dangerous problem plus a critical stance toward Washington which eased some of their domestic political problems.

An Intermediate Case: The Middle East War of June 1967

The June 1967 war in the Middle East can be viewed in many perspectives. For example, it reflected the diffusion of power away from Washington and Moscow. Certainly, Johnson tried hard, but failed, to keep Israel from initiating hostilities on June 5. Less certainly, Moscow probably did not approve Nasser's closing of the Gulf of Aqaba on May 22, the act that made war inevitable if Nasser did not withdraw. At critical moments, the control of the super-powers over nations that vitally depended on them proved dilute.

In another perspective, the war represented the failure of the effort, launched by Kennedy in 1961, to so engage Nasser in the economic and social development of his country that the problem of Israel could be kept on the back burner.

I remember well a talk in the White House on January 14, 1967, with Ambassador Mostafa Kamel. We had worked together for seven years to try to keep alive the two strands of common interest between Cairo and Washington: that Egypt concentrate on its economic and social modernization and maintain a decent degree of independence of Moscow. Now, he reported, forces in Cairo were gathering strength which would move in other directions and a major crisis in the Middle East would result. He asked if there was any hope that the United States might grant more food aid to Egypt since the existing program was due to end in April 1967.[8] I explained the feelings in the Congress, feelings so strong that the whole aid program might be jeopardized if we pressed for assistance to Nasser at this stage. Kamel concluded that the independence of his country was at risk. I responded that I hoped and believed that Egyptian nationalism was more deeply rooted and did not, in the end, depend on the foreign aid decisions of a distant power.

We parted sadly.

Neither at the time nor in retrospect do I believe American aid was a decisive consideration in Nasser's policy in the critical months of 1967. He was galvanized into action in May by the Syrian appeal for help and the implicit challenge to his leadership of the Arab world. This, in turn, was triggered by rumors of Israeli mobilization on the Syrian frontier—rumors that Moscow originated and spread.[9] The Soviet ambassador to Israel refused an Israeli offer to inspect the frontier. Then events unfolded as follows:

May 14: Nasser mobilizes his armed forces.

May 16: Nasser asks the U.N. to withdraw its peace-keeping forces from the Sinai; U Thant agrees.

May 18: U.N. forces withdraw.

May 22: Nasser announces closure of Gulf of Aqaba.

May 24: George Thomson, British minister of state, comes to Washington to propose both a public declaration reasserting the international right of free passage through the Gulf of Aqaba and the creation of a naval task force to open the Gulf. Johnson agrees to support this course.

May 26: Johnson confers with Israeli Foreign Minister Abba Eban.

May 30: In the light of Johnson's assurances to Eban, Israeli Premier Levi Eshkol assures Johnson that he will allow up to two weeks for international action to open the Gulf of Aqaba.

May 30: Hussein flies to Cairo, signs a five-year joint defense agreement with Nasser, and accepts an Egyptian commander of United Arab forces in Jordan; Iraqi troops and Egyptian commandos enter Jordan.

May 31: After a discussion with Robert Anderson, Nasser agrees to send his Vice President, Zakaria Mohieddin, to Washington on Wednesday, June 7.

June 1: Prime Minister Harold Holt agrees that Australia will join the United States, the United Kingdom, and the Netherlands in opening the Gulf of Aqaba.

June 5: War breaks out.

Johnson regarded his message to Eban on May 26 as a fundamental statement of American policy.[10] He prepared for the meeting with care, writing out beforehand the critical portion of his message. The lovely oval Yellow Room in the Mansion, which softened almost any occasion, somehow failed this time to reduce the tension and concentration of men conscious that on their words and the precision of their communication might hinge war or peace—and, for Israel, survival. Johnson reaffirmed the American commitment to free passage in the Gulf of Aqaba, asked time to generate multilateral action and congressional support, and concluded: "Israel will not be alone unless it decides to go alone." In response to Eban's paraphrase of his policy, Johnson affirmed that it was his disposition to make every possible effort to assure that Aqaba remain open.

Eshkol's response to Johnson, after Eban's report, appeared to leave room for diplomacy until the weekend of June 10–11.

The critical question is, of course, why Israel did not wait. Like many decisions in history, that of the Israeli Cabinet on June 4 probably resulted from the convergence of many different factors, all pushing in the same direction. Above all, there were the consequences that flowed from Hussein's visit to Cairo on May 30. The subsequent arrival of an Egyptian commander and Iraqi troops in Jordan was, for Israelis, like a firebell in the night, evoking memories of 1956. There was fear that Mohieddin's visit to Washington might postpone a showdown on Aqaba or weaken the American position. There were anxieties about the steadiness of British support for an international force to open the Gulf of Aqaba and about troubles Johnson might face in the Congress. Also, perhaps, there was a sense that in the long run it might be wiser for Israel to deal with the Arab challenge alone rather than as a ward of the West.

After Hussein's trip to Cairo, there was ample evidence that the spring was coiling in Jerusalem; but, on balance, the evidence suggested, until the early hours of June 5, that we still had until, say, June 11.

On June 3 Hal Saunders, the Middle East man on the NSC staff, set out for me what we had to accomplish in the week ahead if war was to be avoided. The list included persuading Nasser that there was simply no give in the U.S. position on Aqaba but probing the terms for a broader settlement; pressing the United Nations debate and the Maritime Declaration to a conclusion early in the week; deciding if a probe to open Aqaba was required, and, if so, carrying the Congress.

Johnson has said he "was determined to honor President Eisenhower's 1957 pledge on Aqaba."[11] I have not the slightest doubt he would have done so.

It would have been a lively week of diplomacy, politics, and, perhaps, naval action, had not war on the ground intervened.

For Moscow this period may have been the most difficult of the postwar years. In the Cuba missile crisis the Soviet leaders were dealing with an enterprise they had initiated and in which there was only one other party engaged—the United States. They were in a position to control events with some confidence. In the Middle East their control over the situation was more dilute, and there were many more actors. Their clients were not only humiliated in the field but they deeply resented Soviet military restraint and Soviet diplomatic pressure for an immediate cease-fire. Arab delegations in Moscow kept the Soviet leaders in consultation day and night, while the latter sought simultaneously to deal with the United Nations negotiations in New York and the hot-line exchanges Kosygin initiated on June 5. If they had moved promptly, the Arab nations might have traded a cease-fire and an Israeli withdrawal to its June 5 borders for a lifting of the Aqaba blockade and a withdrawal from the Sinai. But their delay led, day after day, to a weaker bargaining position until a simple cease-fire resolution was finally agreed, which left Israel in control of the Syrian heights, Jordan west of the river, and the Sinai.

The Israeli tactical victory eased certain short-run problems for the United States, but Johnson's view of the long-run prospects remained somber. As he instructed us to formulate proposals for a permanent Middle East settlement, his guidance was that we develop as few heroes and as few heels as possible. To the end of his term, without rancor or moralizing, he made it clear to Israeli officials he regretted their decision to go to war on June 5.

Once started, the war posed an incredible array of urgent business. One does not fully appreciate the complex interdependencies of the modern world until they are violated by war. Some Arab nations broke diplomatic relations with the United States; American citizens and officials were endangered; hour-by-hour contacts were required with the United Nations in New York; thousands of letters and telegrams from concerned American citizens had to be answered; American military forces relevant to Middle East contingencies had to be put at readiness.

The stage for relations between Moscow and Washington during and after the June war was set by a powerful message from Johnson to Kosygin on May 22, 1967. That message underlined the danger that American and Soviet ties to nations in the Middle East could bring about difficulties that neither side sought. He urged a maximum effort in the cause of moderation.

But there was more to the message than that. Johnson spoke of dangers in Southeast Asia and in Latin America which also could get out of hand and underlined the urgency of creating an environment in which movement forward on the nonproliferation treaty could take place. The message of May 22 was, in a sense, the prelude not merely to the hot-line exchanges but to the Glassboro meeting later in June.

During the war itself American forces in the eastern Mediterranean were strengthened, and directed to within fifty miles of the Syrian coast when a message from Moscow of June 10 raised the possibility of Soviet military intervention.

But the major business between Moscow and Washington over the hot line was, in effect, a high-level review of what was going on at the United Nations in New York; that is, an attempt to achieve a cease-fire. The Arabs wanted more than diplomacy could yield, given their position in the field and Soviet unwillingness to engage its forces. A simple cease-fire emerged piecemeal: first Jordan, then Egypt, finally, on the 10th, Syria.

The tortured history of the area for twenty years, the breakdown of the fragile settlement of 1957, and the long-run instability of a situation where Israel occupied all the Sinai and Jordan's West Bank led Johnson to decide early that the proper postwar objective should be a solid peace rather than still another truce. He came to this conclusion, in fact, on June 5 itself and spoke the next day of "settled peace" in the area as the objective and of "real peace" on the 7th.[12] In making this decision, he was conscious that peacemaking would not come easily or quickly. He knew that Arab humiliation and Israeli euphoria and sense of release from immediate mortal danger were not the raw materials for a prompt accord. He personally designed the five principles for stable peace in his talk of June 19. He hoped to find in Kosygin at Glassboro the representative of a government which had concluded that the Middle East was an area of greater danger than opportunity. But he did not. Despite its immediate setback, Moscow evidently believed the Arab defeat had its advantages. Cairo was even more dependent on Moscow than before for arms and diplomatic support, so long as Nasser sought something short of stable peace. Under these circumstances, the radical Arab countries, having severed diplomatic ties with the United States, must have appeared a target for consolidation and manipulation to Moscow's purposes, in the Middle East and beyond. In any case, Moscow refused to join Washington in limiting the postwar flow of arms to the area and, with some reluctance, Johnson turned to assure Israel an adequate supply of military equipment, including the relatively long-range Phantom jet fighter-bomber.

Despite his leadership in stating the principles on which a Middle East peace might be based, Johnson resisted efforts to draw the United States too deeply into the negotiating process. In the first instance, he felt, this was a task for the United Nations but ultimately, he believed, the governments of the Middle East would have to settle the matter among themselves.

Johnson and the Romantic Revolutionaries

By the time Johnson came to the Presidency, there was little illusion in Washington about Sukarno, Nasser, Ben Bella, and Nkrumah, let alone Castro and Mao. They all appeared deeply committed to courses of action which, in different ways and in different degrees, were designed to expand their power and influence in ways that ran counter to American interests.

All engaged in passionate anti-American rhetoric. Johnson's general policy toward them was to ignore their rhetoric and to minimize confrontation or the possibilities of confrontation, unless he concluded vital American interests were actually at stake. He did not court them; nor did he engage in verbal or other crusades against them.

Meanwhile, however, they were caught up in processes that had a dynamic of their own. Their external adventures and strivings were generally frustrated; their search for external support (excepting Mao) endangered the independence of their countries; and, above all, their neglect of domestic welfare generated pressures for change. All this finally yielded pressures for either their overthrow or for a change in policy. These degenerative forces lay behind Boumedienne's coup against Ben Bella in June 1965 and the military coup against Nkrumah in February 1966. Although Goulart was not engaged in external adventure, his fall in April 1964 conforms roughly to this pattern.

The most important of these crises was that in Indonesia. There the initiative lay not with the military but with Sukarno and the Indonesian communists, linked to and supported by Peking.[13] But behind the effort to kill the army general staff was the certain knowledge that the army leadership disapproved of Sukarno's policy and would certainly seek to frustrate a communist succession to Sukarno if the latter should die. When General T. N. J. Suharto successfully emerged, however, his concentration on economic development and on assuring the effective independence of his country paralleled the postcrisis policies in Brasilia, in Accra, and, with some delay, in Algiers.

Such relatively benign resolutions did not occur in Johnson's time in the other major centers of revolutionary romanticism. But there were desperate ventures which may, with the passage of time, be regarded as peak efforts that led ultimately to a subsidence of revolutionary zeal and a turning to the more mundane tasks of economic and social progress. On mainland China there was the Cultural Revolution which began to give way in 1967 to a slow, erratic movement toward relative normalcy in domestic and foreign policy. For Castro there was the unleashing of Che Guevara, with its denouement in the Bolivian Andes in October 1967. For Nasser there was the mobilization in the Sinai and the closure of Aqaba. For Ho there was the Tet offensive, and for Kim the attempted assassination of Park and the seizure of the *Pueblo*.

History never provides neat and uniform patterns; but there is clearly a family relation here among the stories of these revolutionary leaders, captured by a vision of external grandeur they could not make happen, trying desperately to make their dreams come true, falling back reluctantly to the more homely responsibilities of government. And, of course, as this is written, the outcome is by no means yet clear in Peking and Pyongyang, Hanoi and Havana.

There was no way for Johnson to escape the consequences of Ho's ambition to take over all of French Indochina; but with the others he managed to minimize the level of friction and get on with the job of working constructively with the less enflamed leaders of the developing world.

Economic and Social Progress

TABLE 36-1 suggests the broad movements in the major components of assistance and private capital flows to developing nations during the Johnson administration. It shows an overall slight net decline in economic assistance of all kinds, more than outweighed by increases in private capital flows.

Among the major components there was:

a decline in military grants and loans, excepting special assistance to Southeast Asia (not included);

an increase in defense support largely associated with the war in Southeast Asia;

TABLE 36-1
THE CHANGING SCALE AND COMPOSITION OF AMERICAN FOREIGN AID, FY 1964–1968
(in millions of dollars)

	1964	1965	1966	1967	1968
Military aid	1485	1229*	968*	873*	601*
Defense support	371	387	500	587	433
Development loans and grants	768	754	677	662	598
Agriculture (P.L. 480)	1704	1641	1784	1452	1204
Technical assistance and cooperation	226	227	224	224	222
Contingency and other special and development assistance	816	1083	847	1147	1040
Total economic assistance (including P.L. 480 and defense support)	3885	4092	4032	4072	3467
Total official flows (DAC definition)†	3611	3571	3599	3559	3347
Total flows (DAC definition, including private investment)	4770	5524	5020	5565	5676

* Excluding special Vietnam costs.
† Calendar years.
Sources: Derived from annual budgets of the U.S. Government and from *1969 Review: Efforts and Policies of the Members of the Development Assistance Committee.*

a decline in development loans and grants, caused in part by the Indian–Pakistani war of 1965 and its consequences;

a high level of food aid, declining in the latter years of the period as the Green Revolution began to take hold.

This was a defensive period in the story of American assistance to the developing world, brought on by the outcome of the Cuba missile crisis, the 1965 Indian–Pakistani war, the burdens of Vietnam, and increasing pressures on the American balance of payments.

Johnson fought both to hold the line and to alter the direction of the aid programs. First, he assumed leadership in focusing attention on the food–population balance. A series of studies within the government made clear that, if existing trends in population and food production persisted, the world would face before 1980 a true Malthusian crisis. Population increases of over 2 percent and increased urban demand were not fully matched by increases in food production; production in the developing world was expanding mainly by increases in acreage rather than in yields; acreage that could be brought into production was limited in a number of key countries; and history suggested that a surge in yields awaited a higher level of development in general.[14] A good part of humanity seemed caught in a desperate trap. Net grain imports into the developing countries rose from 19 to 36 million tons between 1960 and 1966.

Johnson decided to use his margin of influence and leverage actively to encourage an increase in agricultural productivity and an expansion in population control policies in the developing world.[15] The authority of AID to support family planning programs was expanded short of the financing of contraceptive devices themselves and the equipment to make them.

Johnson was aided by both a disaster and new technology. The disaster was two successive droughts in India. The new technology was the emergence of new high-productivity strains of wheat and rice from protracted research by international teams conducted in Mexico and the Philippines, respectively.

The Indian drought provided the occasion for a sharp change in priorities within India and in assistance policy to India and other developing nations.[16] Meanwhile, despite the heavy budgetary costs involved, Johnson mobilized in those years a fifth of the American wheat crop to India, and some 600 ships in "the largest maritime assemblage since the Allied Forces crossed the English Channel on D-Day. For a period of two years, more than 60 million Indians were sustained entirely by American food shipments."[17]

The upshot was a revolution in agricultural productivity in critical parts of the developing world. In Asia, for example, the area planted with new seeds increased from 200 acres in 1964–1965 to 38 million in 1968–1969. The revolution posed problems as well as new possibilities. The new seeds and the investment required to make them efficient changed and polarized, as well as enriched, rural life, since only relatively well-to-do farmers could take full advantage of them. It only bought time, and perhaps not much, for population control programs to bring down birth rates.

Johnson's task in helping bring about a change in agricultural policy in the developing world was not easy. He gave to it an extraordinary amount of time, energy, and resourcefulness. When I was in the White House in the drought year 1966–1967, I helped him follow the fall of rain in India and Pakistan as closely as he did along the Pedernales. He knew the dates of shipment from American ports of grain required for timely arrival in Calcutta and the state of Indian grain stocks. He personally guided the negotiation of each tranche of food aid as well as the Indian performance in re-allocating its own resources to agriculture and population control. Amidst all the pressures of this period, abroad and at home, he never lost the sense that the fate of hundreds of millions of men, women, and children was involved, not merely in the Indian famine but in bringing about a change in policy toward food production and population. On October 21, 1967, the first day of the march on the Pentagon, he sat in the Rose Garden with Ambassador B. K. Nehru discussing the possibilities of sorghum as a substitute for wheat in the Indian diet and whether the Indian states might be willing to relax their restrictions on movements of grain surpluses to deficit areas.

A second distinctive feature of Johnson's policy was the priority he attached to the dimensions of development that bore directly on the life of human beings: education and health, as well as food and population control. This impulse clearly arose from his own experience in the past. I remember him telling Averell Harriman this story. There was in Cotulla, Texas, a road stand where truck drivers stopped for breakfast. Behind it was a garbage heap. The Mexican children would go through the pile, shaking the coffee grounds from the grapefruit rinds and sucking the rinds for the juice that was left. It was in this setting, he said, that he developed a sense of outrage at the unnecessary wastage of human beings born into the world and not provided with all the food and medical services they needed, all the education they could absorb. From FY 1966, AID shifted to a new emphasis on education and health as well as agriculture and population control.[18]

Third, Johnson pressed hard and systematically to move economic assistance to the developing world onto a multilateral basis in which others would do more, the United States less, on the principle of "partnership and fair shares." This was linked to his thrust toward regionalism because the Inter-American Bank and the Asian Development Bank were built around proportionate contributions, rooted in principles of equity. The International Development Association of the World Bank was also attractive for this reason. Johnson made special efforts to bring Japan into Asian development efforts on a basis of equality of contribution with the United States. The two nations both contributed 20 percent to the capital of the Asian Development Bank, and 30 percent to The Hague consortium in support of Indonesian development after Sukarno's overthrow. Reflecting the expanding contributions of others, the American proportion of official development assistance fell from 61 percent in 1963 to 51 percent of a higher total in 1968.

Fourth, Johnson, from his first days of responsibility,[19] gave special attention to Latin American development. Here his experience and judgment converged with a commitment to carry forward his predecessor's policies. It was both a difficult and a propitious period for renewed effort. It was difficult because the first few years of experience had revealed that there were no miracles that Washington could perform to bring about accelerated economic and social progress: the job would have to be primarily Latin American. It was propitious because the wisest Latin American leaders had accepted this fact and, with Kennedy's support, set up the Inter-American Committee on the Alliance for Progress (CIAP) at a meeting in São Paulo on November 11–16, 1963. This new instrument of the OAS provided for the possibility of Latin American leadership in the Alliance. CIAP provided for only one North American member, dramatizing the appropriate junior-partner status of the United States. In addition, by 1964 preliminary work in planning, feasibility studies, and the setting up of new institutions made it possible for Latin America to begin to absorb resources on a larger scale.

The upshot was a considerable increase in official lending to Latin America, which persisted through the Johnson administration: a rise from $981 million in 1963 to $1.7 billion in 1968.[20] By the end of the Johnson administration Latin American growth as a whole was moving forward at rates beyond the 2.5 percent per capita target set at Punta del Este; although the performance of some individual countries remained erratic.

TABLE 36–2

RATE OF GROWTH OF LATIN AMERICAN GROSS DOMESTIC PRODUCT PER CAPITA (%)

Year	%
1965	2.5
1966	1.5
1967	1.4
1968	3.3
1969	3.7
1970	3.8

Source: Organization of American States.

Having weathered the political and psychological strains of the Dominican intervention, the Alliance for Progress began to move in somewhat new directions:

—the Economic and Social Act of Rio de Janeiro (November 30, 1965) extended the life of the Alliance beyond its original ten-year span and introduced the principle of "mutual aid," in which the more advanced countries of the hemisphere (aside from the United States) undertook an obligation toward the less advanced;

—the CIAP annual country-by-country review process took hold, yielding an increasingly thorough and sophisticated process of mutual evaluation of self-help and legitimate external assistance;

—the issue of Latin American physical as well as commercial integration gradually came to the fore, leading ultimately to the summit meeting of April 1967 at Punta del Este.

Despite much economic and social progress in Latin America during the 1960s, the situation as of 1968 justified no complacency. The population problem had not yet been seized in certain critical countries; the original Punta del Este target (5 percent annual rate of increase in real GNP) proved too low to avoid substantial urban unemployment and partial unemployment; the modernization of rural life proceeded slowly and unevenly; the prospects for economic integration in the 1970s, to which the Presidents had committed themselves in 1967, were shadowed by inflation, nationalism, and political differences among and instability within some of the Latin American nations.

The most profound of these problems was political; that is, the incapacity of some Latin American nations to sustain constitutional civil government for protracted periods. In these years Brazil and Argentina passed under military rule, as did Bolivia and Peru. In stagnant Uruguay the old democratic tradition was hard pressed to survive. The fragmentation of the civil politicians and their parties, their incapacity to come together in compromise to build a foundation for viable policies, lay behind this instability.[21] An underlying social and political fragmentation was also a cause of the chronic inflation that bedeviled Latin American economic development, yielding stop-and-go policies which denied the nations the kind of inner confidence in the reality of progress enjoyed, for example, in Mexico. On this matter the United States could not do much. Economic aid could cushion a little the instabilities that flowed from convulsive political life; but only Latin Americans could fashion in each country the kind of attitudes and institutions that had yielded at least substantial passages of sustained civil government in Mexico and Venezuela, Costa Rica, Colombia, and Chile.

REGIONALISM IN THE DEVELOPING WORLD

EACH President articulates his foreign policy in distinctive terms; but there has been underlying continuity in the broad themes of the American approach to the world since at least 1947, when the Truman Doctrine and the Marshall Plan came to life. There was, however, one major change in the rhetoric and substance of Johnson's foreign policy as opposed to Kennedy's.

In Kennedy's time American objectives were usually expressed along something like the following lines: The United States would honor its commitments at the truce lines of the Second World War, but it would also seek to reach across these lines in search for stable peace. Within the truce lines the United States would seek to organize an environment of regular economic expansion and social progress by cooperation among the more advanced nations of the Atlantic and, increasingly, Japan. It would also lead the more advanced nations of the north in systematic efforts to assist the less developed continents in the southern half of the globe. The developing world of the south was not, of course, treated in a wholly undifferentiated way. For example, Kennedy launched the Alliance for Progress; and he took an interest in the special problems of emerging Africa. Nevertheless, there was a tendency, in concept and language, for his administration to think of the developing world as something like a group of nations and peoples with common problems. In the notion of *le tiers monde* the French contributed a parallel and widely accepted concept.

There was a similar tendency in communist thought and policy to group the developing continents under a broad rubric as the "anti-imperialist" crusade was conducted. In Johnson's time events and reflections on them brought a change in thought and policy, the essence of which was increasingly to treat Asia, the Middle East, Africa, and Latin America on a regional basis.

JOHNSON AND REGIONALISM

IN the wake of the Cuba missile crisis I took stock with my colleagues on the Policy Planning Council of the changes occurring on the world scene. We seemed to detect forces at work which might lead to a new impulse toward regionalism in the developing world. First, one could observe a rising priority for narrow national objectives as the fear of Moscow diminished, Peking lost prestige with the failure of the Great Leap Forward, and the Sino–Soviet split became overt. Second, we could observe the extreme limitations of the nation-state in dealing with national goals of security and development. If rich European nations of 50 million could not, alone, cope with their problems, the need for cooperation was even greater among the developing nations, most of which were smaller as well as less advanced in their mastery of modern technology. Third, one could observe growing sentiment among the American people that the United States was, in some ill-defined sense, overextended on the world scene.

With my colleagues, I examined the implications of these attitudes in each of the regions of the world, taking into account special problems and distinctive features. By the spring of 1965 I was ready to crystallize some new lines of policy as a Johnson doctrine. Here is how I set it out on March 29, 1965.

> It is our interest in each of the regions of the Free World to assist in the development of local arrangements which, while reducing their direct dependence on the United States, would leave the regions open to cooperative military, economic, and political arrangements with the U.S. This requires of us a systematic policy designed to strengthen the hand of the moderates in the regions and to reduce the power of extremists—whether those extremists are Communists or ambitious nationalists anxious to take over and dominate their regions. We are for those who, while defending legitimate national and regional interests, respect the extraordinarily intimate interdependence of the modern world and pursue policies of development and peace rather than aggrandizement.
>
> This is the appropriate central theme of U.S. policy, transcending the distinction between developed and underdeveloped areas.[22]

Johnson was, quite independently, coming to similar conclusions on the basis of insights available to him.[23] There was an easy mutual understanding, therefore, as I worked with him on new regional initiatives in the period 1966–1968.

But whatever the thoughts of Americans on this matter, the possibilities of forward movement in the regions were aided by events in 1965. Above all, the attempt of Peking and Djakarta to organize the developing world as an anti-American bloc failed at Algiers; and the communist takeover effort fell short in Indonesia. The fit of madness with which mainland China was then seized in the Cultural Revolution induced nations to draw back in fascinated horror. They turned away to more narrow national and regional objectives.

So far as Asian regionalism was concerned, the turning point was Johnson's speech of April 7, 1965, at Johns Hopkins,[24] although it was not until his July 1965 decision to save Vietnam and Southeast Asia by introducing substantial American forces that Asians could feel some ground under their feet as they looked to the future. The Asian Development Bank was then formed; the Mekong Committee came to life; in 1966, through South Korean initiative, the Asian and Pacific Council (ASPAC) met for the first time; and the Association of Southeast Asian

Nations (ASEAN) was revived in the same year, with a new nationalist government in Indonesia. And as South Vietnam began to find its feet in 1966, Johnson pressed with force the theme of Asian regionalism in his talk to the American Alumni Council on July 12, 1966, and then built his trip through Asia around that concept in October.

Asian regionalism was a viable concept for three reasons. First, each major government had a quite specific local rationale for turning increasingly to others of the region in mutual support. Korea, for example, had lived its troubled life caught among three contending giants: Japan, Russia, and China. American strength had, from 1950, protected it against this three-way vise. But as South Korea looked to a future in which the American role was likely to diminish, it made sense in Seoul to help build a larger grouping in which South Korea's relations with Japan would be intimate but Japan would not be overbearing, and it could find in the collective institutions of the region a wider political base than in the past in confronting Russia and China—and North Korea. For Japan, Asian regionalism was a way of moving out from the home islands in a setting of multilateral institutions which dimmed painful memories of the days of Japanese imperialism. The Japanese have found regional institutions congenial for reasons similar to those of the Federal Republic of Germany. For the Philippines and Thailand, Asian regionalism was a way of finding local strength and support and diluting the image of American tutelage without wholly losing the advantages of ultimate American security guarantees. For Malaysia and Singapore—and, indeed, Australia and New Zealand—Asian regionalism promised a partial substitute for the British withdrawal as well as closer political association with Japan, which was becoming rapidly the dominant trading partner of virtually all the nations of the area. For Taiwan, regionalism offered not only a widened base of support in its political confrontation with Peking, but also a long-run hedge against the possibility of Peking's entrance into the United Nations and enlarged participation in the affairs of Asia. For Indonesia, regionalism provided a base for dealing with its somewhat sensitive, smaller neighbors in an atmosphere of mutual confidence, while exercising a degree of constructive leadership.

The second reason for the viability of Asian regionalism was the problem of China. Mass and geography made China the central problem of Asia, once its unity was achieved in 1949, as Germany became the central problem of Europe once it was unified in 1871. That fact does not decree relations of permanent hostility; but it does mean there is a sensitive and abiding set of problems to be solved. In 1965 the question was neither subtle nor ambiguous: Peking, working overtly with Djakarta and Hanoi, was actively leading an explicit effort to take over Southeast Asia in a nutcracker movement, of which the attack on South Vietnam was one arm, the Malaysian confrontation the other. For those who doubt the domino theory, the situation in the region at that time is worth attention. But regionalism, as it emerged in Asia in this period, was not primarily addressed to the immediate threat. The institutions being set up for the long haul in 1966 looked beyond the war in Southeast Asia to a regional cohesion that would permit, in time, relations of dignity and balance with a mainland China which might emerge more rational and temperate than the nation caught up in the Cultural Revolution.

The third reason was the feeling, sensed clearly in Asia from 1966, that the American effort in Vietnam was transient and the United States could only buy time for Asia to organize itself. This mood was reinforced by both the antiwar movement in the United States and Johnson's urging on his tour that Asia organize so that it could increasingly shape its own destiny. The mood was caught as early as June 1966 by Premier Lee Kuan Yew in Singapore who told a student audience that ". . . if we just sit down and believe people are going to buy time forever after for us, then we deserve to perish."[25]

In Latin America, of course, regionalism was an older story. The Organization of American States emerged after the Second World War (1948), rooted initially in a Latin American consensus on two matters: the desire to prevent the military intrusion of extra-hemisphere powers into the region; and the desire to inhibit the United States in conducting the kind of interventions into the life of Latin American nations that had marked earlier years in the century. To these interests was added the hope that the United States, initially focused in the postwar years on the recovery of western Europe, would turn its attention and resources to the economic and social development of Latin America. Thus, initially, the OAS was a focal point for relations between Latin America and the United States: American military strength and resources were to be sought; American impulses to intervention were to be discouraged. There was little initial impulse to cooperation among the Latin American nations themselves. Their economic life tended to be focused on the great coastal cities built up to mobilize exports to and to receive imports from Europe and the United States rather than to trade among themselves. Most telephonic communications between Latin American countries had to pass through the United States. The development of the interior of most Latin American nations was neglected.

As the Alliance for Progress moved forward, this situation began to change. Most of the population in Latin America lived in countries whose economies were shifting from light consumer-goods industries to metals fabrication, chemicals, and light electronics. The high tariff barriers, small markets, and inefficiency which had marked the first stage of Latin American industrialization slowed down expansion in the newer sectors on which Latin American growth depended. It is one thing to have an inefficient textile plant; it is a quite different matter to have a white elephant steel mill or chemical fertilizer plant, where much greater amounts of capital are required. Thus, Latin American leaders began to look to a widening of regional markets as a way of inducing the competitive efficiency the new technologies required.

At the same time, the coastal-port mentality began to give way to the neglected development of the Latin American interior—to exploit natural resources and to open new areas for agricultural settlement. As they moved to develop their inner frontiers, the Latin American nations began, as it were, to run into each other. To build the Carretera Marginal along the eastern slopes of the Andes required, for example, cooperation among Peru and Bolivia, Ecuador and Colombia.

Johnson threw his weight behind the Latin American movement toward both trade and physical integration.

The proposals explored with the Congress before the Punta del Este meeting of April 1967 included an American contribution of $250–$500 million to a fund designed to cushion strains that might arise from movement toward a Latin American Common Market. A second proposition was for the United States to put into the Inter-American Bank (IAB) an additional $150 million earmarked for multinational projects which would more closely link the Latin American nations.

In the end, Congress balked at granting Johnson, before the event, the specific commitments he wanted. The fund to encourage and ease the transition to a common market still remains to be created; but the IAB was granted, in time, additional funds which have been used to expand resources allocated to multinational projects.

In fact, however, in the wake of the Punta del Este summit conference, the Latin Americans made little serious progress in overcoming the nationalist barriers to achieving the goal commonly agreed on. The most promising limited step forward, the building of an Andean Common Market (including Colombia, Venezuela, Ecuador, Bolivia, Peru, and Chile) foundered on Venezuelan unwillingness to risk its high-wage high-cost industrial establishment in competition with neighbors technologically advanced but lacking the bounty of large oil resources. Johnson did succeed, however, in dramatizing an authentic concern for Latin American problems; the inescapable need for Latin Americans to solve among themselves the problems of economic cooperation and unity; and the transition of the United States to a junior-partner role in the hemisphere.

His last major act in Latin American policy was to visit the Presidents of the members of the Central American Common Market in July 1968 to encourage them to go forward with their enterprise, which had accomplished far more in the 1960s than most had initially predicted, but which was beginning to confront severe difficulties as the easier gains of trade integration were accomplished and harder problems of industrial location were confronted. It was not a major diplomatic venture; but the depth and genuineness of his concern with Latin America never shone through more clearly than on his visit to a small elementary school named for him in San Salvador, and his opening of a TV facility for secondary education in a normal school at San Andrés. And it was on this valedictory trip abroad that he summarized most fully his view of regionalism in Latin America, Africa, and Asia and expressed for the first time his "hope that as the nations and peoples of the Middle East find their way to stable peace, they, too, will find dignity and hope in working together on a regional basis. . . . the resources available to them also offer unique possibilities."[26]

In Africa, regionalism had a somewhat different meaning than in Europe, Asia, and Latin America. Unlike the other continents, Africa did not confront the kind of balance-of-power problem posed by Germany and Russia in Europe, Japan and China in Asia, and the United States in the Western Hemisphere. Geography decreed that a postcolonial Africa might be able to work out its destiny without the threat of major-power intrusion or hegemony. And that is the primary political purpose of the Organization of African Unity (OAU). If that purpose is achieved, the role of the United States in the evolution of postcolonial Africa might remain, as it has mainly been, subsidiary.

Johnson perceived the possibility, even necessity, of economic regionalism and subregionalism in an Africa whose nation-states emerged from colonial history too small for the effective exploitation of much modern technology. The American interest would be satisfied in Africa, as elsewhere, if no single power threatened to dominate the area and if the problems of modernization and racial tension could be solved in ways that avoided chaos or major violence threatening to the international order.

Out of these perceptions Johnson made the only speech by an American President wholly devoted to Africa, on May 26, 1966.[27] It was the product of many prior months of prodding the bureaucracy to produce a coherent approach to African problems.

On the basis of the doctrine of regionalism stated on that occasion, Johnson instructed Ambassador Edward Korry, then assigned to Ethiopia, to recommend new proposals for the support of African economic and social development. American aid programs and those Washington could influence (for example, through the World Bank) began, in fact, to be reshaped to support regional and subregional ventures in Africa.

Like Kennedy's vision of a Grand Design for Europe and the Atlantic on July 4, 1962, and Johnson's visions of Asian and Latin American regional cohesion of 1966 and 1967, the road to African regional cooperation was obviously going to be long and erratic, full of frustrations and setbacks. The central postcolonial problem of most African nations was, in fact, the tension between central government and tribal and regional loyalties. In some cases, statehood, let alone a pervasive sense of nationhood, was fragile. And many of the initial tasks of modernization did not require much regional or subregional cooperation; for example, elementary education, road building, improvements in agricultural productivity, basic measures of public health. African regionalism made slow progress at best; but no thoughtful African or sympathetic observer of Africa failed to perceive that, in the end, regionalism and subregionalism would have to play a large role if Africa was to maintain its freedom from foreign intrusion and produce in time modern societies which, while maintaining loyalty to their old cultures, successfully absorbed what modern science and technology could offer.

RECONCILIATION: COMMUNIST CHINA

JOHNSON'S efforts to erode the barriers of the Cold War between Moscow and Washington are set out in Chapter 34. The state of affairs in Peking and Hanoi did not lend themselves in his time to moving far forward in the process of reconciliation. In 1964–1965 Peking, recovering from the failure of the Great Leap Forward, was pressing forward in coalition with Sukarno, Ho, and others to collapse the noncommunist states in Southeast Asia. In 1966–1967 the chaos of the Cultural Revolution made diplomatic communication with Peking virtually impossible for the United States and practically every other nation. In 1968 the trend toward moderation in Peking took somewhat firmer hold, as did more rational policies of economic growth, but the trend was not sufficiently advanced to permit a renewed dialogue between Washington and Peking; and, from March 31, 1968, Peking would have, in any case, been inclined to await the outcome of the American election.

As for Hanoi, Johnson had to live with the simple fact that the disintegration of the South Vietnamese political and military position from May 1963 had led to new hopes and commitments to go forward and conquer South Vietnam.

Nevertheless, he sought systematically to project to the Chinese the larger vision of an Asia in stable peace, concentrating its resources and talents on the great unfulfilled tasks of welfare and the building of a modern life for the people. In a series of public statements starting in April 1965, he spoke in terms like these.

> Sooner or later the pragmatic and compassionate spirit of the Chinese people will prevail over outmoded dogmatism.
>
> We in America look to that day with hope and with confidence.
>
> For our part, we shall do what we can to hasten its coming. We shall keep alive the hope for a freer flow of ideas and people between mainland China and the United States, as I have said so recently on so many other occasions. For only through such exchange can isolation be ended and suspicion give way to trust.

> We do not believe in eternal enmity. All hatred among nations must ultimately end in reconciliation. We hopefully look to the day when the policies of mainland China will offer and will permit such a reconciliation.[28]

Such statements were designed not merely to enunciate Johnson's policy to the American people and the world community but also to communicate a vision to the embroiled Chinese leadership to which they might someday repair. The curious, stylized, apparently sterile Sino–American dialogue in Warsaw revealed that these words were followed closely, even when they were ardently denounced as lies and deceptions.

Ambassadors John M. Cabot and John Gronouski carried forward through these tortured years the diplomatic ballet which had begun in August 1955. With variations only experts could detect, the Chinese communists, in a framework of decorum marking the beginning and close of the sessions, would denounce the United States on a good many grounds, but notably for intrusions into Chinese airspace; actions and policy toward Southeast Asia; and, above all, its "occupation" of and support for Nationalist China. The United States would, in a typical session, indicate the limits of its interest in Southeast Asia; the defensive character of its support for Taiwan; its desire to achieve the release of prisoners still held by Peking; and then propose an enlargement of travel between the two countries (e.g., doctors, scholars, newspapermen, etc.); the exchange of scientific data; the exchange of agricultural samples of mutual scientific interest; joint investigation of alleged incidents on the high seas; and discussions about arms control. The Chinese representative would typically respond that these and other constructive steps would become possible if the United States would settle the fundamental question between China and the United States—the forceable occupation of Taiwan; but until that fundamental question was settled, all attempts to deal with concrete and specific matters would be futile.

Despite the repetitive character of these dialogues, and the embarrassment to the Chinese of their location in Warsaw, as the Sino–Soviet split became increasingly violent, they permitted the American government to hold steadily before the authorities in Peking an image of limited objectives, reasonableness, and a working agenda when Communist China was ready to move forward.

The slightly changing tone of the various meetings, along with other evidence, permitted Washington to chart the fever level in Peking and to detect, as early as January 1968, the recapture of the Foreign Office by the professionals as the Cultural Revolution erratically subsided.

On May 28, 1968, the Chinese Communist Embassy in Warsaw announced it wished to postpone the 135th ambassadorial meeting until mid- or late November, evidently to await the outcome of the American election.

Perhaps the most important diplomatic communication between Johnson and Peking, however, took place in the summer of 1967, through the visit of the Romanian Prime Minister, Ion Gheorghe Maurer. He called on the President on June 26, just before going to mainland China. Johnson told Maurer that he wished neither war with China nor to change its form of government. He hoped to see Communist China join the society of nations. He believed the two countries should discuss the nonproliferation treaty and work out ground rules for avoiding nuclear war. He made clear to Maurer that he was at liberty to express his view to other governments.

The message was undoubtedly recorded in Peking, which had then not wholly emerged from the convulsion of the Cultural Revolution. It was a useful message to transmit; but there was not yet a political foundation for acting on it in Peking.

37

Vietnam: A Race between Two Political Processes

BENEATH ITS IMMENSE COMPLEXITIES HANOI'S STRUGGLE TO TAKE over South Vietnam was dominated in the 1960s by two processes: the evolution of American opinion about Vietnam; and the erratic process of political development in South Vietnam, rooted in an emergent postcolonial nationalism. The latter had profound consequences for the South Vietnamese military performance in the field. Both the American political scene and the politico-military situation in South Vietnam were subject to slow-moving forces, while the headlines and television screens were dominated by more or less conventional accounts of battle in a highly unconventional war.

Hanoi conducted an extremely sophisticated military, political, psychological, and diplomatic campaign to take over the former French colonial empire in Asia; but at the core of the effort was an assessment by Pham Van Dong late in 1962: "Americans do not like long, inconclusive wars—and this is going to be a long, inconclusive war. Thus we are sure to win in the end."[1]

When Johnson made his decision in July 1965 to commit major forces to avoid communist victory in Southeast Asia, he, too, launched a sophisticated course of military, economic, political, and diplomatic operations. But at the core, he (like Kennedy, and then, Nixon) built his policy on a faith that the South Vietnamese wanted a destiny independent of Hanoi and would develop the military, political, and institutional capacity to achieve it; and that the North Vietnamese would, in the end, have to accept the reality of a new nationalism their attack on South Vietnam had helped to create.

The war in Southeast Asia is thus to be understood as a kind of race between two historical processes, one occurring in the United States, the other in Southeast Asia, both of which were fundamental to Hanoi's willingness to pursue the war.

It did not have to be that way. Johnson (and then, Nixon in early 1969) could have taken greater risks of a larger war by applying more direct and decisive military power on the ground against North Vietnam or against the Laos infiltration routes, thus forcing the military issue; for without North Vietnamese leadership, supplies, and forces, there would have been no substantial hostilities in Southeast Asia in the 1960s. (The prompt, even desperate commitment of North Vietnamese reserves to protect the Laos corridor in early 1971 against an inadequate South Vietnamese thrust underlined the mortal significance of external supplies and men to the war against South Vietnam.) But the military dispositions made by the United States—under Kennedy, Johnson, and Nixon—were directly geared to permitting South Vietnam to emerge gradually as a viable, independent, postcolonial nation, while an essentially defensive military strategy was pursued.

There were, of course, other factors at work; for example, the nationalist responses in Laos and then Cambodia to North Vietnamese invasion and harassment, and the willingness of both Moscow and Peking to provide aid to Hanoi; but a good deal that is fundamental becomes clear when the story of Vietnam is stripped to these two essentially political processes.

They explain why Hanoi—denied military victory by close margins at the end of 1961 and again in early 1965, and by a wider margin at Tet in 1968—could nevertheless persist with faith that victory was possible. Out of its formative experience with France, its eyes were fastened not merely on the field of battle but on the impact of the battle on American political life. Hanoi could either perceive disintegration of the political base for American policy in Southeast Asia or observe symptoms, evocative of French political life at earlier times, that promised such disintegration, if Hanoi was sufficiently patient, prepared to pay the price in blood and postponed economic and social progress, and if Moscow and Peking remained willing to support the tragic adventure.

The two factors explain also why knowledgeable American officials in Vietnam and in Washington became so profoundly depressed as they watched the politico-military disintegration begun in May 1963, and why they were genuinely optimistic in, say, the two and a half years before the Tet offensive in 1968, and, then again, in the post-Tet period. The long, slow, hard process of political development was moving positively from mid-1965, rooted in South Vietnamese nationalism; and it was yielding positive military results, palpable to those prepared to examine dispassionately the inherently complex evidence.

These two factors explain, above all, the shape of the Tet offensive of 1968 and its outcome. The North Vietnamese, becoming conscious in 1967 that time might have ceased to be their friend, sought a quick decision. They scored a major success in American political life, but they suffered a major setback not only in military terms but also in terms of South Vietnamese political development.

Down to Hanoi's spring offensive of 1972, Hanoi could observe the very substantial attrition since 1965 of American political support for its commitments in Southeast Asia—including the withdrawal from combat of United States ground forces—although the United States had not yet produced in the White House a Mendès-France, prepared to negotiate, in his own phrase, a "bargain-basement settlement" against a fixed deadline.[2] Looking back to 1965, Washington could observe a remarkable strengthening of South Vietnamese nationhood, reflected in its political as well as its military institutions; although the stability of South Vietnamese political life was not assured and North Vietnamese forces were permitted by the international community[3] to wander illegally over large parts of Laos and Cambodia, using this territory as a base for attack across the borders of South Vietnam. Quite aside from its narrowly military implications, dramatized in the spring offensive of 1972, this situation constituted a threat to the whole of Southeast Asia if American political will should collapse or if the still fragile postcolonial political life of South Vietnam should yield a crisis like that of 1963.

The analysis presented in the next two chapters is built around this view of the struggle; that is, as a race between the attrition of American will in the face of an indecisive protracted war and the gathering strength of South Vietnamese (and Southeast Asian) nationalism. It is not in any sense a full history of Southeast Asian policy during the Johnson years, whose details are now known in almost compulsive detail.[4] It is an essay designed to give shape to a tangled tale, as one man sees it.

38

Vietnam, 1964–1969: From Near-Defeat to Near-Nationhood

The Shape of the Period

The struggle in Vietnam during Johnson's administration breaks down naturally into these five phases:

November 1963–July 1965: political and military disintegration;
July 1965–January 1966: the avoidance of defeat;
January 1966–October 1967: political and military progress;
October 1967–May 1968: the winter–spring (Tet) offensive;
May 1968–January 1969: recovery and accelerated pacification.

These phases are best illuminated by the accompanying charts, which reflect with rough accuracy the stages of the struggle as it grew and then declined. The charts should be examined in the light of the general observations on the use of statistical data on the Vietnamese war set out on pp. 279–280. They extend beyond January 1969 to mid-1971 in order to provide perspective on the character of the turning point at Tet 1968 and to serve as background to the discussion of Nixon's policy in Southeast Asia and Hanoi's spring offensive of 1972 in Chapter 42.

The ratio of enemy to Allied casualties and the ratio of enemy to Allied weapons losses (Charts 38-1 and 38-2) exhibit the declining fortunes of the South Vietnamese down through the first half of 1965. Here the inset annual data should be particularly noted. There is gradual improvement thereafter, including the grave military impact of the 1968 Tet offensive on the enemy. The casualty ratio moves up from its low level of early 1965 and then fluctuates with the intensity of engagement of major communist units, subsiding in periods of relatively low military activity.

The movements of the curve are meaningful, although the absolute level of enemy casualties is the least firm of the statistical series reflected in these charts. Nevertheless, I am inclined to feel, from all the evidence I have seen, including some on the North Vietnamese population structure, that communist casualties will prove to have been approximately as estimated at the time—not necessarily week by week but, say, year by year. The sharp rise in weapons losses after Tet 1968 reflects the large caches of weapons captured in the counteroffensive; then, General Abrams' systematic campaign to roll back the supply network inside South Vietnam; finally, the large caches captured in the Cambodian incursion of 1970.

Data on population status in South Vietnam (Chart 38-3) show (notably Viet Cong control) the deterioration in early 1965; the gradual improvement thereafter; the limited but real shift of population control from "relatively secure" to "contested" as a result of the Tet offensive of 1968; and, then, accelerated progress from the autumn of that year to the relatively stable position achieved by the end of 1970.

Chart 38-4 shows the expansion of Allied forces during the period, including, particularly, the leveling off and decline of American forces, as well as the rapid buildup of Vietnamese forces after the Tet offensive.

Chart 38-5 shows, first, the increasing role of the North Vietnamese, in the wake of the 1964 decision to introduce regular North Vietnamese units into the South; second, the severe losses of the Viet Cong in the Tet offensive; and third, the subsequent decline in the communist capacity to recruit in the South.

Chart 38-6 shows the rise and subsidence of the war in terms of enemy and Allied battle deaths.

November 1963–July 1965: Political and Military Disintegration

Between General Minh's assumption of responsibility after the assassination of Diem in November 1963 and Prime Minister Quat's turning over the power of the state to the Armed Forces Council at the end of June 1965, there were some eleven changes of government or attempted coups in South Vietnam. With Thieu as Chief of State and Ky as Prime Minister, a substantial period of relative political stability and peaceful evolution was then launched.

But the period of instability (which began, of course, prior to Diem's assassination) was as costly a passage in postcolonial political history as the world has seen; for it reignited Hanoi's hopes for victory and led to a decision, probably in the summer of 1964, to introduce regular North Vietnamese units into the battle for South Vietnam in the winter–spring offensive of the 1964–1965 dry season.

CHART 38–1

RATIO OF ENEMY TO ALLIED CASUALTIES

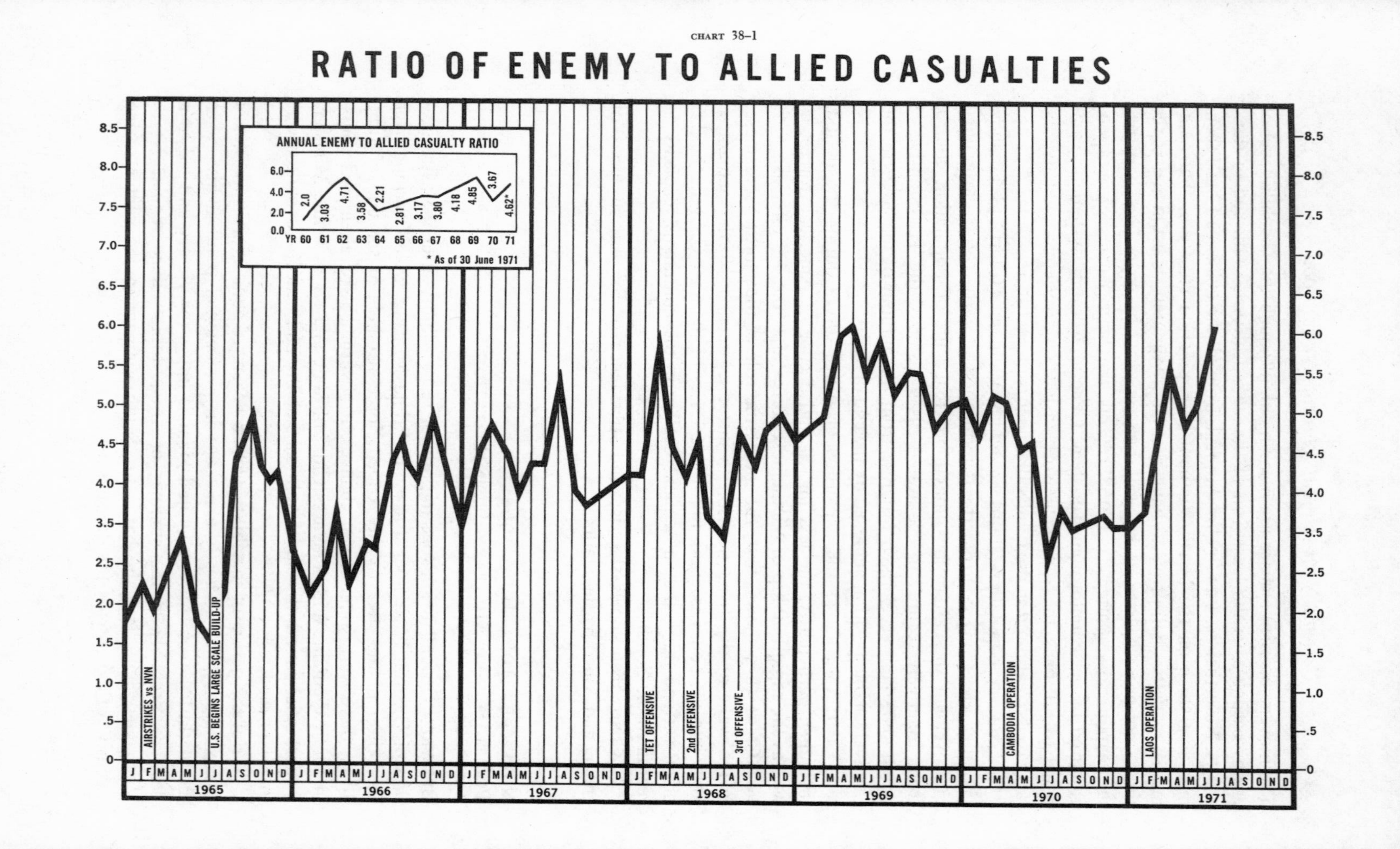

CHART 38–2

RATIO OF ENEMY TO ALLIED WEAPONS LOSSES

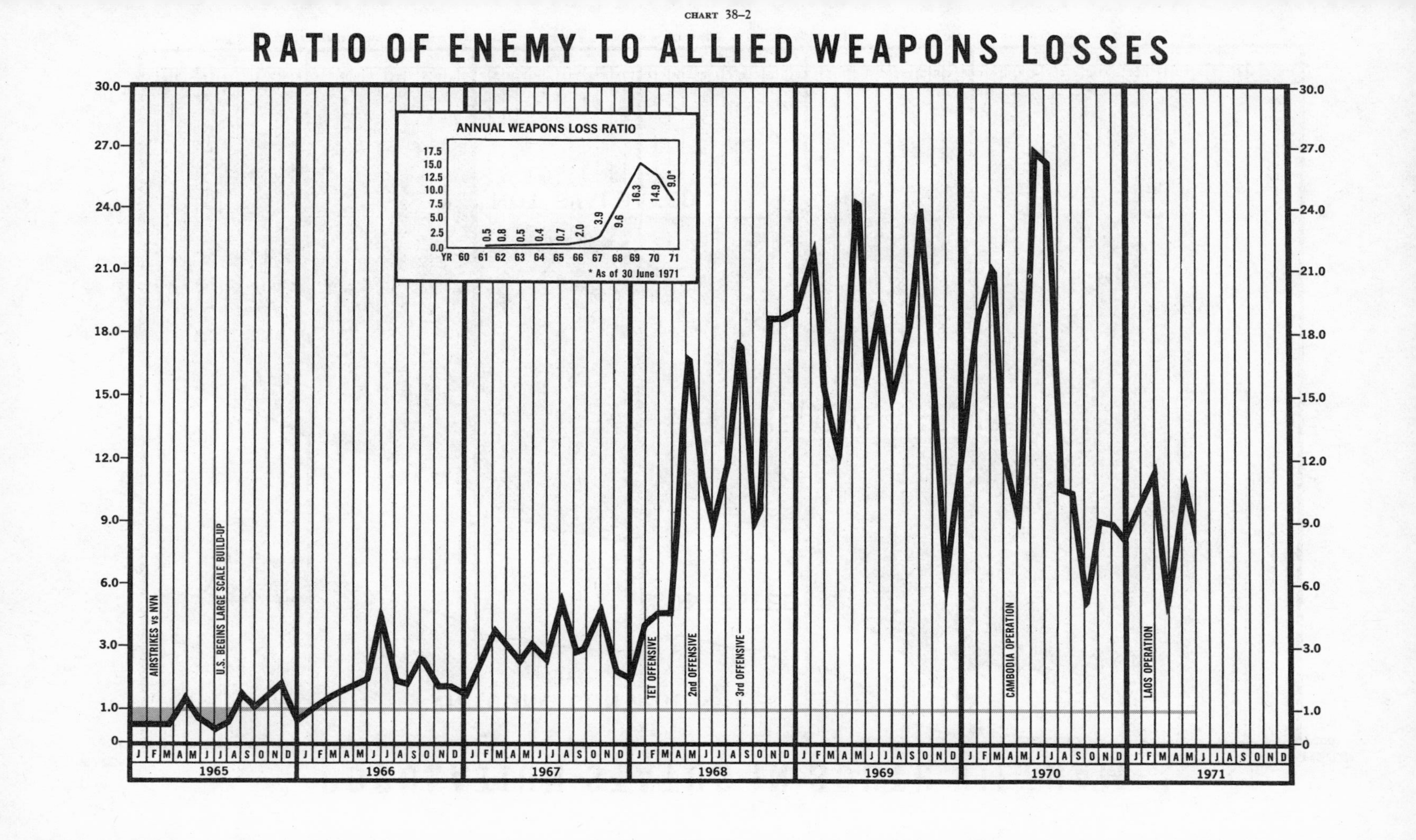

CHART 38–3

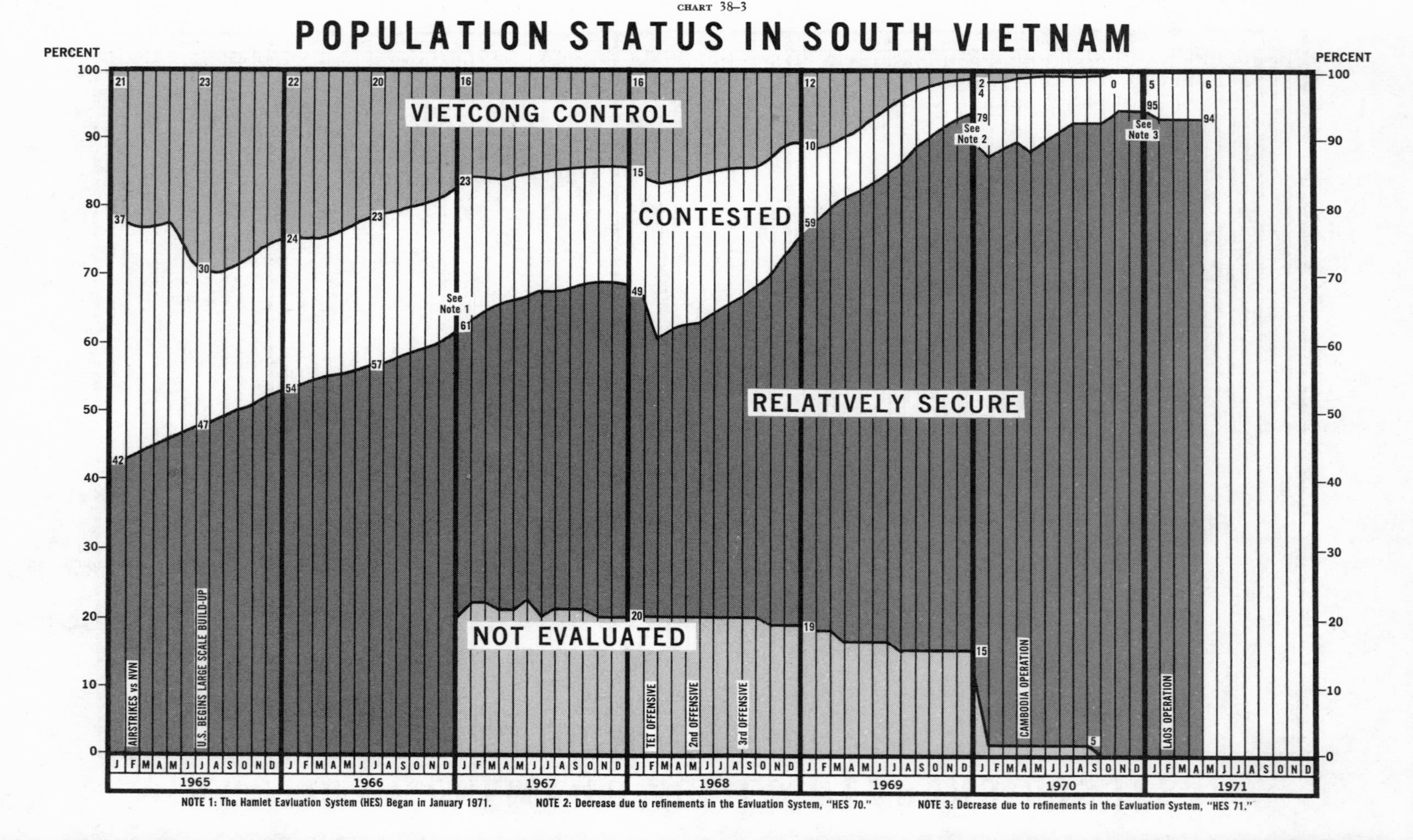
POPULATION STATUS IN SOUTH VIETNAM
PERCENT
100
90
80
70
60
50
40
30
20
10
0
VIETCONG CONTROL
CONTESTED
RELATIVELY SECURE
NOT EVALUATED
AIRSTRIKES vs NVN
U.S. BEGINS LARGE SCALE BUILD-UP
TET OFFENSIVE
2nd OFFENSIVE
3rd OFFENSIVE
CAMBODIA OPERATION
LAOS OPERATION
See Note 1
See Note 2
See Note 3
21
37
42
23
30
47
22
24
54
20
23
57
16
23
61
16
15
49
20
12
10
59
19
2
4
79
15
5
0
5
95
6
94
J F M A M J J A S O N D
1965
1966
1967
1968
1969
1970
1971
NOTE 1: The Hamlet Eavluation System (HES) Began in January 1971.
NOTE 2: Decrease due to refinements in the Eavluation System, "HES 70."
NOTE 3: Decrease due to refinements in the Eavluation System, "HES 71."

CHART 38–4

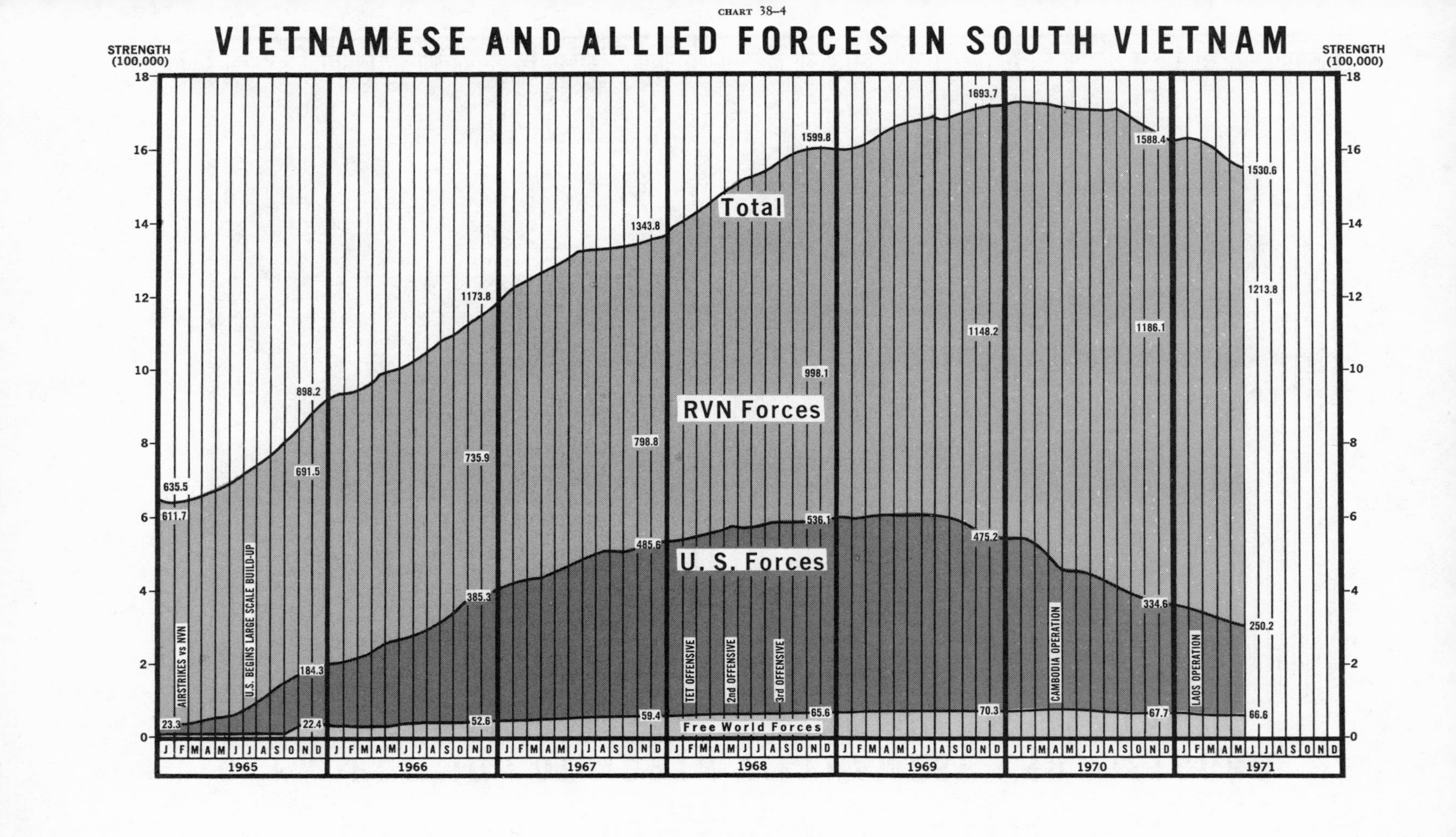
VIETNAMESE AND ALLIED FORCES IN SOUTH VIETNAM
STRENGTH (100,000)
18
16
14
12
10
8
6
4
2
0
Total
RVN Forces
U. S. Forces
Free World Forces
635.5
611.7
23.3
898.2
691.5
184.3
22.4
1173.8
735.9
385.3
52.6
1343.8
798.8
485.6
59.4
1599.8
998.1
536.1
65.6
1693.7
1148.2
475.2
70.3
1588.4
1186.1
334.6
67.7
1530.6
1213.8
250.2
66.6
AIRSTRIKES vs NVN
U.S. BEGINS LARGE SCALE BUILD-UP
TET OFFENSIVE
2nd OFFENSIVE
3rd OFFENSIVE
CAMBODIA OPERATION
LAOS OPERATION
J F M A M J J A S O N D
1965
1966
1967
1968
1969
1970
1971

CHART 38–5

PROPORTION OF NORTH VIETNAMESE AND VIETCONG MANUEVER BATTALIONS IN SOUTH VIETNAM

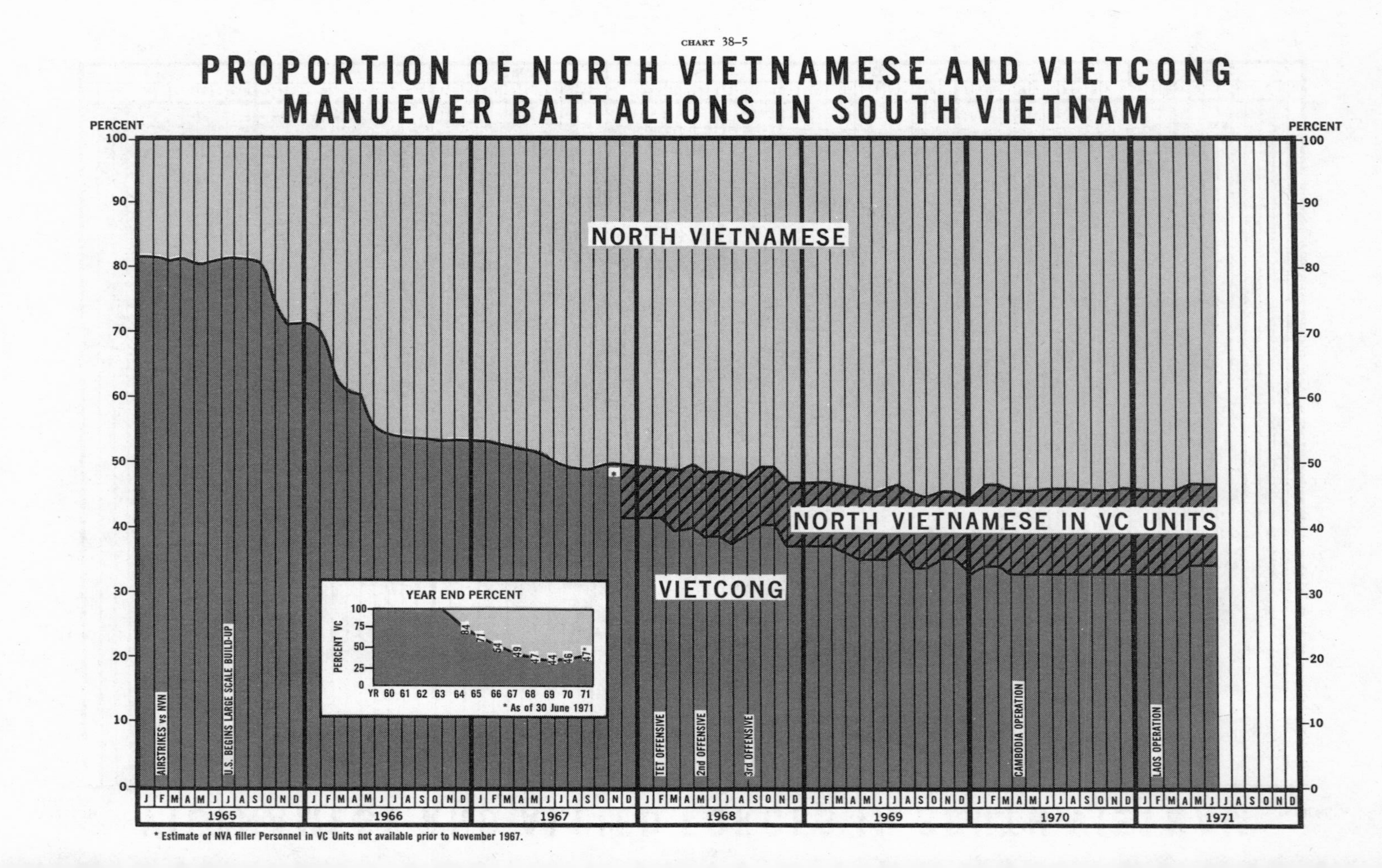

* Estimate of NVA filler Personnel in VC Units not available prior to November 1967.

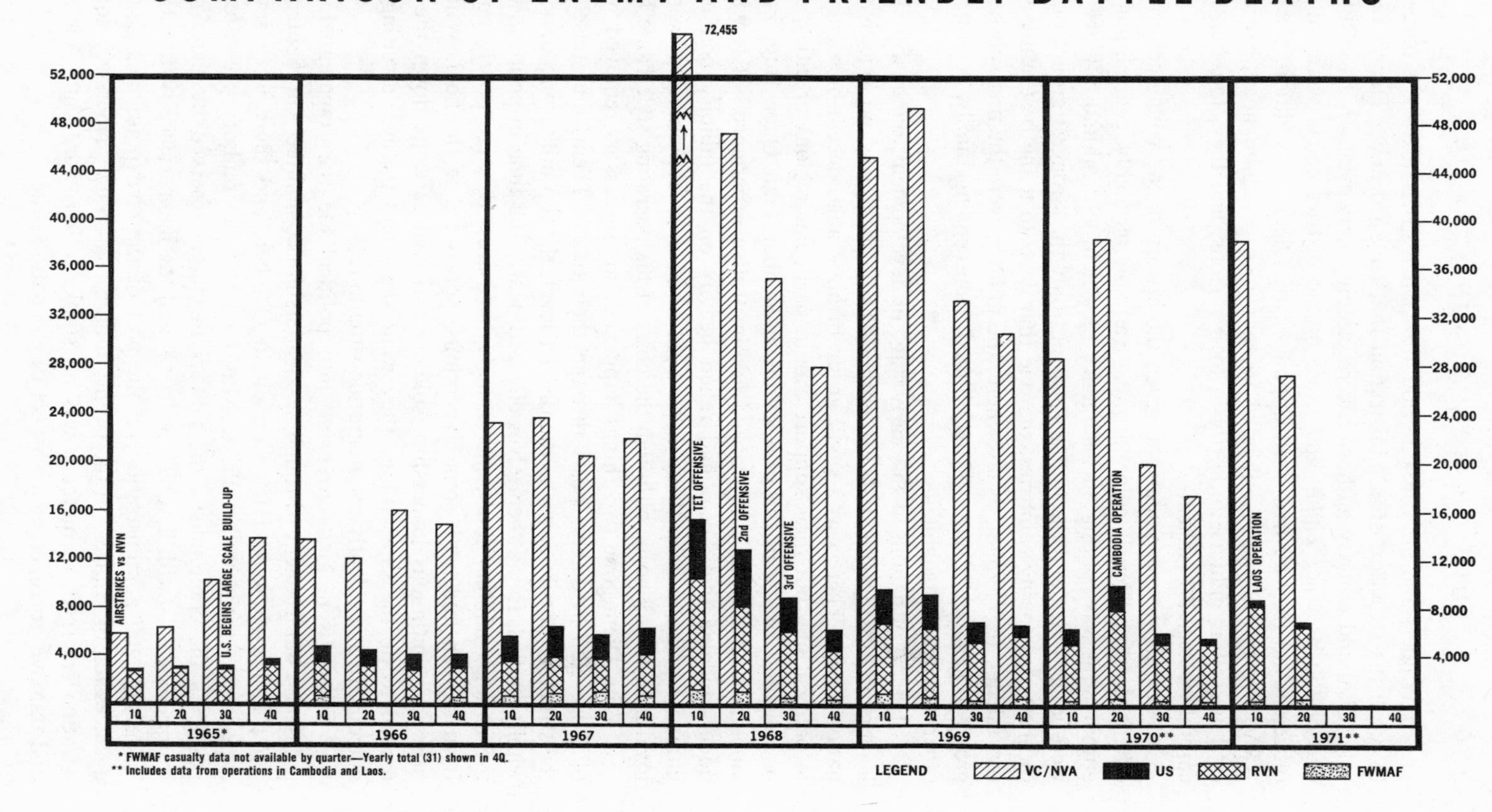

CHART 38–6

COMPARISON OF ENEMY AND FRIENDLY BATTLE DEATHS

To understand the whole period after Diem's overthrow it is necessary to recall the structure of administration that emerged under Diem's family rule. Civil and military authority were closely interwoven. In 1964 all but one of the province chiefs and most of the district chiefs were military officers. And they all had been appointed by Diem. In addition, the four ARVN (Army of the Republic of Vietnam) corps commanders exercised civil as well as military authority in their regions; and they, too, had been carefully selected by Diem.

All this was not unnatural, given the history of the young country. It inherited from French colonialism a tradition of highly central political authority; it was fighting an insurgency in which political and military acts were interwoven; and the military was not only the strongest group, but, as in many developing countries, the one that drew to it the best administrative talents. In Vietnam, as elsewhere, the military were the first substantial group to generate a sense of nationhood, transcending family, region, and other narrower attachments.

Typical of nations at this early stage of development, the civil political leadership was fragmented. Excepting Diem, there was no one with a national base. There was a small group of honorable, decent men engaged in political life, but their support was in particular regions or cities, sects or religions, or, as in the case of the influential Tran Quoc Buu, in the labor movement. And they lacked administrative experience.[1] It is wholly understandable that Diem had relied heavily on the military and taken immense pains to keep them under tight control by appointing personally loyal men to key posts, although the costs of his operating style came high.

With Diem gone two things happened: his successors removed many of those who held their posts through their ties to Diem, thus unsettling the structure of rule down to the district level; the top military leaders, not wholly unified, found themselves engaged nearly full time in politics, while the nation's military units, increasingly hard-pressed, were poorly guided from the top and, with some exceptions, poorly led in the field. Without firm and continuous leadership, soldiers and civil servants down the line tended to do the same thing: they went slack and passive, awaiting the outcome of an evidently disintegrating situation.

Efforts were made to bring into political life the fragmented civil political establishment through a "leadership committee" in September 1964 and a National High Council in October; and there were several experiments with civilian Prime Ministers. But the military pressure imposed by the communists, the powers inevitably reserved by the Armed Forces Council (with its own rivalries), and the inexperience with national leadership and administration on the part of the civil politicians decreed a succession of failures. In the twenty months before the Thieu–Ky administration emerged, then, there was no stable authority in South Vietnam, and this fact corroded every aspect of the nation's life.

Hanoi, which had failed to exploit effectively the unsettled period at the time of the unsuccessful coup of November 1960, was determined to make the most of the post-Diem period, as Lansdale and other observers in 1961 had predicted they would.

The communist political infrastructure in South Vietnam pressed its control through rural areas; communist military forces were re-equipped with standardized weapons, including the excellent Soviet AK-47 rifle; Viet Cong main-force units were built up to regimental and then divisional strength; by July 1964 first reports were received by American intelligence that North Vietnamese regulars were entering the battle as key military cadres; by December three regular North Vietnamese regiments (the 95th, 32d, and 101st) were reported on their way. By the late spring of 1965 the South Vietnamese Army was losing about one battalion a week to enemy action, as the North Vietnamese fully engaged their forces.

The trend of events through this period is clear enough, in retrospect; and it was generally clear at the time, although there were brief intervals of hope. Early in 1964 there appeared to be some prospect that General Khanh might provide energetic and effective political leadership. The adoption of a constitution in October and the appointment to office of two respected civil politicians, Phan Khac Suu and Tran Van Huong, yielded two generally hopeful months. Moreover, there were a few elite South Vietnamese military units that consistently performed well, and, from time to time, there were successful South Vietnamese military operations; for example, in March 1964 in the Plain of Reeds, along the Cambodian border.

Finally, with the arrival on the battlefield of the three North Vietnamese regiments and the activation of a fourth, after infiltration across the DMZ, the stage was set for movement to Mao's third stage of guerrilla warfare; that is, mobile warfare by conventional units commanding the countryside, followed by the isolation and capture of the cities. All of this might be calculated to produce a small-scale repetition of the communist victory in China of 1949.

The statistics of the period reflect uniformly the deterioration of South Vietnamese fortunes, but they do not adequately catch the sense of crisis that suffused Saigon and Washington in the early months of 1965. Technically, the primary immediate objective of Hanoi was to cut South Vietnam in half along the line from Pleiku in the highlands to Qui Nhon on the coast—precisely the objective South Vietnamese military leaders had described to Maxwell Taylor and me on our 1961 trip. This is where the North Vietnamese regiments were initially applied, and the plan nearly succeeded. At the worst period in 1965, the vital Route 19 corridor was cut by the enemy, and traffic could move only in heavily armed convoys.

Johnson has described in detail the process by which his advisers in early 1965 came, painfully and reluctantly, to the conclusion that time was fast running out and that American military power would have to be applied massively if South Vietnam was to be saved.[2] The key dates and events are now familiar.

January 27: A McNamara–Bundy memorandum asserts "the time has come for harder choices" and leans toward the "use of our military power in the Far East . . . to force a change of Communist policy."

February 7: Bundy, back from a trip to Vietnam in wake of attack on U.S. barracks in Pleiku and the retaliatory air strike on North Vietnam, urges "graduated and continuing reprisal" through air and naval action.

February 13: Johnson decides in principle on "measured and limited air action jointly with GVN" against military targets below the 19th parallel, 120 miles deep into North Vietnam.

March 13: Regular bombing of North Vietnam begins.

March–May: Marine and Army airborne units are dispatched to protect key U.S. air bases.

May–June: ARVN suffers major military setbacks in battles against regular North Vietnamese units; Nguyen Van Thieu and Nguyen Cao Ky take over government and ask for additional U.S. forces.

July: McNamara goes to Vietnam and recommends on July 20 that Johnson "expand promptly and substantially the U.S. military pressure against the Viet Cong in the South," including increased U.S. ground forces; Johnson announces prompt dispatch of an additional 50,000 troops, July 28, 1965, with "additional forces" to follow.

On that day—July 28, 1965—the die was cast. It was cast, however, in a particular form, at a particular time.

First, the decision was reached a full year after Hanoi's decision to commit regular North Vietnamese units to the battle, move to Mao Stage Three, and seek straightforward military victory. Washington had failed to respond decisively to Hanoi's systematic violation of the Laos Accords of 1962. The infiltration trails had been harassed but remained open since October 1962, when the Accords went into effect. As in 1917 and 1941, 1947 and 1950, the American weight was thrown into the scales late, long after the aggressors had committed themselves to the venture.

Second, Johnson's decision was taken in extremis. Politically and militarily the South Vietnamese were almost beaten to their knees in mid-1965—a fact palpable to the South Vietnamese public as well as the civil and military leadership. This meant that the first urgent task had to be the avoidance of defeat, rather than the application of American military power in ways that might have cut off Hanoi's access to the South. It also meant that the road back for the South Vietnamese armed forces was likely to be long.

Third, after canvassing the alternatives, Johnson decided, as with the application of air power against North Vietnam, to bring American ground forces to bear gradually and to avoid a sharp political and psychological change in course. His diplomatic advisers urged strongly that this was the route best calculated to minimize the likelihood of Soviet or Chinese Communist military intervention.[3] Johnson's nuclear responsibility bore heavily upon him. As he had said before, he was determined to defend American security interests and honor the nation's treaties in ways consistent with the survival of civilization. The memory of Chinese intervention in Korea also played a part, although there were significant differences between the two situations.

These three factors taken together decreed a pattern of military operations that was initially defensive. In McNamara's terms, the American "strategy for 'victory' over time is to break the will of the DRV/VC by denying them victory."[4] As General William Westmoreland read his political instruction it was: "to defeat aggression so that the people of South Vietnam will be free to shape their own destiny."[5] These factors, and the strategy that flowed from them, inherently committed the United States to a protracted engagement, in which American and North Vietnamese staying powers were pitted against one another, with the South Vietnamese capacity "to shape their own destiny" the critical variable in the outcome. Given Hanoi's view of protracted war and the strains it would impose on American life, this was a difficult course to undertake.

July 1965–January 1966: The Avoidance of Defeat

In August the Marines engaged, trapped, and decimated a major Viet Cong unit south of their base at Chu Lai; and in October–November a major battle was successfully fought by the American 1st Cavalry Division troops against a North Vietnamese division in the Ia Drang Valley, close by the Cambodian frontier. By the end of the year it was clear that U.S. forces were operating with great success in the field. This was immensely stabilizing in both Saigon and Washington, given anxieties about the Vietnamese terrain and climate and the long experience of the communist forces encountered.

These developments were reflected in the statistics of battle. In the first seven months of 1965 more than two friendly weapons were lost for every enemy weapon captured. In the last five months the ratio shifted to something like 1.2 enemy weapons captured for every friendly weapon lost. There was a similar favorable shift in relative casualties.

There were failures as well as successes in these months; for example, a bad setback in November for the ARVN 7th Regiment, which was operating in the Michelin Plantation northwest of Saigon. But by the close of 1965 the danger that South Vietnam would be severed was ended; the political and military morale of the South Vietnamese was lifted; 184,000 American troops had arrived along with South Korean, Australian, and other Allied units; and the logistical base for larger operations was being built. The stage was set for the long road back.

On the other hand, having committed its regular units a year earlier, Hanoi did not draw back in the face of the new situation. As the Laos trails dried with the coming of autumn, the flow of North Vietnamese regulars accelerated sharply. As of mid-1965 about 20 percent of the communist battalions in South Vietnam were North Vietnamese; by January 1966, 30 percent. As of that time, communist forces totalled 221,000, including main forces, local forces, and guerrillas.

In January 1966 General Giap published an article in *Nhan Dan*, a government newspaper in Hanoi, in which he listed some ten points which he claimed would guarantee North Vietnamese victory, despite the American commitment of ground forces.[6] Of these, the first three probably represented real hopes in Hanoi as of that time: first, that the United States would not be able to put into South Vietnam the number of troops required; second, that United States forces would antagonize the Vietnamese people as time went on; third, that pressure against the war would grow in the United States and throughout the world and the costs of the war would be very high.[7]

Giap's first proposition was based on a calculation of the scale of South Vietnamese and Allied forces required to deal with the North Vietnamese and Viet Cong buildup. We do not know precisely what ratios Giap applied, but they are likely to have been something like the traditional 10–1 required by a defending government coping with a guerrilla insurrection. There was at least one indication that Hanoi may have calculated something like 2,000,000 American military would be required to frustrate the communist effort on the scale planned. This calculation of American troop requirements proved excessive because of the mobility that helicopters provided, the firepower brought to bear from aircraft and with artillery, and the fact that a good deal of the fighting in which the North Vietnamese units were engaged—particularly in the North and along the Laos and Cambodian frontiers—proved to be less guerrilla warfare than sporadic conventional combat without a fixed front. The proportion of communist to Allied forces in those regions was nearer 1–1 than 1–10.

Giap's second proposition represented a fair initial hope for Hanoi. In fact, there was considerable initial anxiety among Americans about the impact on the South Vietnamese of the presence of large American forces in the country. But significant friction did not develop in the period of most intense American military engagement, 1965–1968.

Giap's third proposition, about American opinion, did represent a valid insight whose consequences are traced in detail in Chapter 39.

We now have available a large volume of captured enemy documents covering the war years, some of which were acquired at the time, others only in 1969–1970. The communist leadership in the South met from time to time to take stock and receive directives for the next phase of the struggle. The resulting documents are a mixture of propaganda and exhortation, shrewd analysis and operational guidance. Like most communist documents, they are set out in opaque ideological jargon which is, nevertheless, a recognizable medium for communicating concepts and situations. When one becomes accustomed to the jargon, one can trace without difficulty the communist view of how the war was going year by year, or even over shorter intervals. There was a period of gathering optimism and confidence in 1959–1961; a reflection of the communist setback down to about mid-1963; a sense of renewed hope and effort down to the middle of 1965, but with anxiety about American intentions reflected in the spring of that year. And then at a meeting in January 1966, the Military Affairs Party Committee concluded:

> As a result of the major combat forces sent by the U.S. imperialists to SVN in the middle of 1965, the U.S. imperialists saved the Puppet Government and troops from heavy losses. From late 1965 to early 1966, on the SVN battlefield, they formed a new strategy using a defensive system, attacks, and many mobile forces which created favorable conditions for the enemy to counter our forces.[8]

In their own terms, the communists had forced the United States from "special warfare" (United States advisers and military aid) to "limited war." And deeply committed by their decision of 1964 to introduce regular North Vietnamese troops into the struggle, Hanoi fully accepted the challenge of this next phase.

January 1966–October 1967: Political and Military Progress

MEETING August 2–19, 1966, the top communist political committee set the hard, defensive tone for the year ahead in these terms: "The war is very fierce and full of difficulties and hardships which will become fiercer with even more difficulties and hardships. . . . We have to frustrate the counteroffensive plans of the Americans for the coming dry season at any cost."[9]

In a discussion with Johnson in February 1968 at Palm Desert, Eisenhower remarked that Westmoreland's task in Vietnam was vastly more complex than his as a commander of Allied forces in Europe during the Second World War. He added that while he was dealing with much larger forces, his operational tasks were relatively straightforward compared to Westmoreland's, and his political problems, even as leader of a coalition force, much easier than dealing with a young, inexperienced government like that in Saigon.

As Westmoreland's task changed from the avoidance of defeat to helping lift the communist weight from the life of South Vietnam, he and his colleagues confronted these necessities in 1966: protecting Saigon and other densely populated areas from the enemy main-force units by spoiling operations; expanding and protecting bases for American forces; penetrating the major enemy base areas within South Vietnam; improving the quality and encouraging the expansion of South Vietnamese forces; assisting the South Vietnamese in the organization of new pacification programs, virtually in abeyance since the collapse of Diem's regime in 1963.

Meanwhile, forces under command of Admiral Ulysses S. Grant Sharp, Commander-in-Chief, Pacific, applied air and naval pressure against North Vietnam to reduce the flow of men and supplies to the South below the level they would otherwise attain. This was done by attrition in transit and by forcing upon the communists increased allocations of men and resources to air defense, the repair of essential facilities in the North, and transport.

By 1967 all these enterprises had acquired real momentum, but they were only instruments, often crude instruments, for achieving two larger objectives: the creation of a constitutional political system in South Vietnam that would reconcile legitimacy with order and continuity; and the progressive extension of security and reliable government administration to the rural areas.

One of the most remarkable political sequences in a modern post-colonial nation was that set in motion by Prime Minister Ky's speech of January 15, 1966. He pledged a referendum in October on a new constitution, to be followed in 1967 by "genuine democratic elections," yielding a new structure of civil government. The initiative was remarkable because it was undertaken at a time of war, only six months beyond a period of mortal danger. It reflected not merely a sense that military fortunes had improved, but also two other judgments. First, if the government of South Vietnam were to face negotiations for a peace settlement, it ought to stand before its adversaries, its own people, and the world community with greater legitimacy than its origins in June 1965 had provided.[10] Second, Ky, in a vivid statement at Honolulu on February 7, 1966, argued that economic, social, and political progress could not await the coming of peace, concluding:

> . . . we must have a record of considerably more progress than we have been able to accomplish so far. We must, if we are to be assured of a lasting peace, create a society which will be able to withstand the false appeals of communism. We must create a society where each individual in Vietnam can feel that he has a future, that he has respect and dignity, and that he has some chance for himself

and for his children to live in an atmosphere where all is not disappointment, despair and dejection.

Johnson's purpose at the Honolulu meeting of February 7–8, 1966, was to assess the seriousness of the Thieu–Ky commitment to political, economic, and social development; to consolidate that commitment; to throw behind it American resources; and to dramatize to the American people and to the world the constructive dimensions of the effort going forward in Vietnam.

There is an understandable skepticism in the press about high-level meetings—a combination of the view that nothing has been accomplished and a suspicion that important matters were settled without being revealed. The Honolulu meeting of February 1966 was more important than it looked, although less was decided than might have been suspected. It was unusual, because it was not long prepared or sharply focused on a narrow range of issues. It simply brought together the senior members of the two governments to consolidate a mutual commitment to press forward with the nonmilitary aspects of the problem in Vietnam and to set in motion new initiatives. The objective was to translate a shared sentiment that there was a great deal of business to be done to develop the political, social, and economic life of Vietnam into concrete and more effective policies. Orville Freeman, John Gardner, and David Bell were there, as well as Rusk and McNamara. On the Vietnamese side there were the ministers of economy, health, and rural reconstruction, as well as the governor of the Central Bank.

There was an unstructured spontaneity about the occasion that reflected more than a lack of detailed preparation. Six months had passed since Johnson's decision to introduce major American forces. One sensed among all the participants a feeling that the immediate military crisis had been successfully passed; that there had been a rare meeting of minds of the nonmilitary dimensions of the common task; but that a great deal of hard work over a wide front would be necessary if the consensus was to yield significant results.

For me the Honolulu meeting marked a return to operational engagement with the Vietnam problem after more than five years. Johnson called me off the eastern slopes of the Peruvian Andes, where I was visiting with President Fernando Belaúnde Terry the frontier area around Tarapoto. I returned to Washington and flew immediately to Honolulu. As a planner at the State Department, I had, of course, followed the evolution of events and policy in Vietnam from the middle level of the bureaucracy. And I had occasionally been asked or volunteered my views. But it was not until the Honolulu meeting that I had a chance to meet the South Vietnamese team that had emerged from the chaos of post-Diem politics. They were just the kind of second-generation figures I had hoped in 1961 Diem would find and bring forward—young, intensely nationalist, inexperienced, energetic.

The most urgent post-Honolulu task was to make good on the Thieu and Ky pledge "to formulate a democratic constitution in the months ahead, including an electoral law; to take that constitution to our people for discussion and modification; to seek its ratification by secret ballot; to create, on the basis of elections rooted in that constitution, an elected government."

Like most political enterprises in Vietnam, or anywhere else, things did not go smoothly. On March 10 General Thi was removed from the military National Leadership Committee and relieved of his command of I Corps. Thi, a colorful and energetic man with a strong political base in the northern part of the country, had as early as August 1965 indicated to Ky that he could provide better national leadership than the Prime Minister. He had resisted orders from Saigon and, among other things, was accused of making his own appointments of province and district chiefs without central government approval. He was also a Buddhist. In all this Thi was expressing the strong sense of regional identity that exists in central Vietnam.

For more than three months South Vietnam was in a rolling crisis involving regional resistance to central rule, which centered in Hue and Danang, and a wider insistence, led by activist Buddhist organizations but embracing students and others, that a constituent assembly be elected to draft a new constitution.

Ky met the demand for rapid movement to constitutional government by convoking a Political Congress, which met April 12–14. There was some anxiety that the meeting would be substantially boycotted. In the end, however, the major groups were well represented and even the radical Buddhists acknowledged that their substantive demands were met. If the Political Congress did not quite match the deliberations at Philadelphia in 1787, it proved a lively and pragmatic political body. Its ten recommendations were: national elections for a constituent assembly should be held within three to five months; the government should pledge to resign as soon as the constituent assembly was elected; the government should convene within ten days a body to draft an election law and hold elections; the government should prevent the constituent assembly from being infiltrated by communists and neutralists; freedom of the press should be established; the government should encourage the growth and development of minor parties; the government should pledge not to punish antiregime demonstrators and should use political not military solutions to end rebellious conditions in such areas as Danang and Hue; the government should promote the education of the people in democracy and elections; all religious groups and parties should halt antigovernment demonstrations; all factions in the country should work for national unity. Thieu and Ky promptly approved the elections for a constituent assembly; and a thirty-two-member committee began drafting an election law on May 5.

With this political process under way, Ky moved on May 15 to bring Danang under control. It had been in a state of virtual independence since March. He flew 1000 South Vietnamese Marines to Danang from Saigon. With some local assistance, the Danang rebellion was ended on May 23. The following day Thieu said: "It is unacceptable to have an army within an army, a government within a government and a state within a state."

There was further difficulty with the radical Buddhists who wished to force the Ky government to resign. They resorted to immolations and less dramatic demonstrations, but clearly the South Vietnamese majority, including the moderate Buddhists, was satisfied by the commitment to an orderly constitutional process. There were further difficulties in Hue and Quang Tri. But when Ky signed a decree on June 20, setting September 11 as the date for the election of the constituent assembly, the crisis passed.

I went back to work at the White House on April 1, 1966, as the crisis was reaching its height. The anxiety of my colleagues, all of whom had lived more intimately than I through the traumatic events of 1963, was acute. This time, moreover, the capacity of the Vietnamese for political suicide appeared to be operating just when massive American forces were deeply and irreversibly committed. But there were two differences: in 1963 there was a generalized revulsion against the rise of Nhu, whereas in 1966 there was a clear and concrete demand to set in motion a constitutional process; in 1963 Diem could see no viable alternative to continued family rule, whereas in 1966 Thieu and Ky were prepared to move forward to constitutional rule.

When I suggested one day at a meeting with the President that we were not seeing a recurrence of 1963 but the pangs of a nation being born, an old friend almost shouted across the Cabinet table: "Walt, are you mad?"

Johnson took a philosophical view of the political process in South Vietnam. On May 21, for example, he said: "The South Vietnamese are trying to build a nation. They have to do this in the teeth of Communist efforts to take the country over by force. It is a hard and a frustrating job, and there is no easy answer, no instant solution to any of the problems they face."[11] He was comforted somewhat by the judgment he had reached at Honolulu that Thieu and Ky were patriots who had meant what they said in their commitment to go forward with the election process. There was something quite moving—as well as precarious—in observing a great nuclear power, involved in a major military commitment, allied with and very much dependent on a young postcolonial nation struggling to move forward to constitutional government. While the Americans in Vietnam did everything they could to prevent political disintegration,[12] the essential decisions were taken by the South Vietnamese.

By and large, Johnson's faith in the Vietnamese and their leaders was well rewarded. The Constituent Assembly was duly elected on September 11 and proceeded to draft a constitution. Some 5.3 million registered and

81 percent of these voted despite communist intimidation. The new Assembly convened in Saigon on September 27, 1966, and a copy of the constitution which emerged was presented at Guam on March 20, 1967, by Thieu and Ky to Johnson. They did so with real pride, after a long night session with the leaders of the Constituent Assembly. Knowing how much Thieu and Ky wanted to present an agreed document to Johnson, they exacted some significant concessions diluting executive power in the constitution. It was at Guam that the two men, evidently rivals for the Presidency, promised Johnson that they would conduct honest elections and not permit any personal differences to damage the essential unity of the nation.

In the end, of course, Ky ran for Vice President with Thieu; and their ticket won with a plurality of 34.8 percent in the election of September 3, 1967. Voter registration was 11 percent higher than in the election a year earlier, and almost 84 percent of those registered turned out. This represented 57 percent of the total voting-age population in the country, about the same proportion that votes in Presidential election years in the United States.

The election also reflected the endemic political problem of underdeveloped nations: there were ten civilian Presidential candidates. The civilian politicians evidently preferred to stay with their limited constituencies and small party groupings rather than constitute themselves as factions of a larger national party or parties. Article 100 of the Vietnamese Constitution states that "the Nation encourages progress toward a two-party system." After the election, Thieu experimented with efforts to build a national coalition that would bring together a good many of the old parties and groups. In this he failed and fell back to reliance on the military and civil bureaucracy as a political and electioneering structure.[13] On the other hand, the election process moved forward vigorously at the village level, providing new long-run foundations for a democratic South Vietnam if fragmentation at the national level can gradually be overcome.

One of the key characteristics of government in a developing nation is its limited executive and administrative energy and talent. Maxwell Taylor, Henry Cabot Lodge, and Ellsworth Bunker, as ambassadors, were all forced to remind a hard-pressing Washington bureaucracy that if it urged too many high-priority tasks on the South Vietnamese at the same time, none would be accomplished. The election process was clearly the highest-priority administrative effort of 1966–1967 in Saigon, and it was accomplished with purposefulness and attention to detail. Even the most determined noncommunist critics of the South Vietnamese (for example, in Paris) acknowledged the relative lack of corruption; the physical organization of arrangements throughout the country; the effective representation at the polling places of each of the candidates; and the scale of the voter turnout. The latter represented, in part, government propaganda and local pressure for participation, but no one could read the reports from the field or hear the account of the distinguished team of observers sent by Johnson[14] without knowing that the people of South Vietnam wanted an honest one-man one-vote political process. And no one could read the returns without knowing they voted with confidence that the ballot was secret: the Thieu–Ky ticket received under 40 percent of the vote.

Next to these steps in political development, the most significant process undertaken in 1966–1967 was the progressive buildup of the machinery for pacification of the countryside.

Once the threat of defeat had been removed in 1965, it was clear to all thoughtful observers that as the North Vietnamese and Viet Cong main-force units were pushed back, the villages had to be secured and a political structure developed in which the villagers could take an increasing hand in their own destiny with educational, health, and economic services supplied by the central government.

The insight, of course, was by no means new. In 1959–1960 Diem had tried to consolidate rural security through his "agrovilles," including the resettlement of families in more secure areas.

The 1961–1963 strategic hamlet program, which collapsed after the assassination of Diem and Nhu, was based on a similar concept. Even during the worst disintegration of the post-Diem period Westmoreland mounted with the South Vietnamese a pacification program called Hop Tac in the area around Saigon. Its results were extremely disappointing, but Westmoreland's controversial judgment, after a most candid review of its failings, is not lightly to be set aside: "I believe that Hop Tac—in spite of its many shortcomings—probably saved Saigon from enemy control."[15] In addition to American Army and Allied contributions to the pacification program, the Marines in I Corps experimented extensively in areas surrounding their bases with Combined Action Platoons. Although they lacked an administrative structure that would fully engage the South Vietnamese military and civil authorities, they did succeed in dramatizing the need for pacification, not least in the Pentagon. Contrary to a widespread view, no knowledgeable South Vietnamese or American official I ever knew, military or civil, ever believed the war could be won (once the 1965 strategy of operating primarily within South Vietnam was adopted) simply by large-unit military actions, search and destroy missions, and the penetration of base areas. These were all viewed as instruments to permit pacification slowly to spread and be consolidated.

As early as August 1965 the Thieu–Ky government established a Ministry of Rural Reconstruction and a Central Rural Reconstruction Council. This was clearly a South Vietnamese rather than American initiative. The vital but somewhat mercurial General Thang emerged as the central figure in this enterprise. It was he who made the presentation at Honolulu of pacification problems and plans. It was a realistic proposal: to restore public security and then carry forward political, economic, and social development. He outlined concrete, modest, practical targets for 1966, on the basis of commitments from the provinces, and emphasized that rural pacification was a long-term operation. From the central government side, the heart of Thang's Revolutionary Development program was the training of special fifty-nine-man teams to go to work in the villages on both security and developmental tasks.

Thang impressed me most, perhaps, by saying something about village development I had long since learned in other less harassed developing nations. He said if the villagers were not involved in the choice of their projects and if they did not invest their own resources, the projects had limited meaning. If the central government built a school and the Viet Cong burnt it down, the people would shrug their shoulders. If they built it at their own choice with their own labor, they would fight for it.

On the American side, Honolulu launched a series of decisions that progressively elevated the role of pacification to which Johnson systematically accorded a very high priority. After Honolulu, William Porter, deputy ambassador, was charged with coordinating all American civil agencies in Saigon in support of pacification. Then, in April 1966, Robert Komer, with the full status of a special assistant to the President, was made Washington coordinator of all civil actions in support of the Vietnam effort, including pacification but going beyond to such issues as inflation, congestion in the Saigon port, refugees, etc.

At Manila, in October, Ky announced that half the regular ARVN battalions would be assigned to rural security tasks in 1967, and in December Porter's operation in Saigon was shifted from coordination to unified management, in a new Embassy Office of Civil Operations. The South Vietnamese target plan for pacification in 1967 was markedly more ambitious than in 1966.

At Guam, in March 1967, Johnson decided that the American role in pacification should be put under overall military management, with Komer, as Westmoreland's deputy, having the status of ambassador. This arrangement went into effect in May, with military and civilians interwoven at every level. To the surprise of a good many, this structure, which persisted under the Nixon administration, worked well, providing both men and resources to back effectively an effort that, of its nature, had to be primarily Vietnamese.

At Johnson's direction, I had a hand in persuading Komer at Guam to go to the field and drive forward the pacification program on the spot. It was not an easy decision for him, but once it was made, he threw himself into the task, making one of the most significant identifiable American contributions to the whole effort in Vietnam.

Progress in pacification during 1966–1967 was modest but real: the re-institution of hamlet and village self-government, including the reservation of local taxes for disposition by the villages; a radical expansion of hamlet schools and local medical facilities; the spreading of the new rice strains and the enlarged use of chemical fertilizers and irrigation pumps; the encouragement of land reform, climaxed finally by the June 1970 Land Reform law; the improvement of communications, including the upgrading of roads. In addition, an American woman working in a Vietnamese refugee camp initiated modern methods for mass production of chickens—methods that spread out rapidly over the Vietnamese countryside.

But there was also a war going on and progress in pacification would remain fragile unless sustained security was provided. All previous efforts at pacification had failed because the communist main force units could attack at times and places of their choice. Even with the North Vietnamese units held near the frontiers and the Viet Cong main force units forced to remain in unpopulated redoubts, the tasks of local security were formidable. Therefore, the pacification effort, as it crystallized in 1967, required the buildup of the regional and popular forces; the slow improvement of rural police; efforts to defect Viet Cong members and to root out the shadow Viet Cong political and administrative apparatus.

Johnson's decision to put the American contribution to pacification under military command, with a civilian acting as deputy to Westmoreland (and, then, General Abrams), was a major act of policy. There were, essentially, three reasons. First, the civilians in Saigon could not generate sufficient advisory personnel, transport, and communications to handle efficiently their part of the effort. Although there were something like a hundred Vietnamese engaged for every American, the American part in pacification was, in itself, a large-scale enterprise. There are 44 provinces in Vietnam, 2000 villages, and over 10,000 hamlets. The scale of the problem lay beyond civilian management and resources, operating alone or in loose coordination with the military. Second, the military and civil tasks were so intimately interwoven that normal methods of coordination would not suffice. In a given district or village there had to be a single plan behind which Vietnamese and Americans, military and civil, threw their weight. Third, Johnson knew that the military would take the pacification effort much more seriously if its own chain of command was directly engaged.

Taken altogether, the South Vietnam which faced the winter–spring offensive of 1967–1968 and the massive assaults at Tet and in May was a much stronger country than it had been in mid-1965.

October 1967–May 1968: The Winter–Spring (Tet) Offensive

Sometime in the late spring or early summer of 1967 the leaders in Hanoi took stock.[16] They recognized that the North Vietnamese units were being held at the frontiers, that the internal base structure was being shattered and rolled up, that the Viet Cong main-force units were being held away from the population centers, and that an internal governmental structure and pacification effort was slowly but unmistakably extending security in the countryside. A captured document in 1967 confirmed the rough estimate in Saigon that the communists had lost control to the government of about a million of the rural population over the previous year. The 1964–1965 movement from guerrilla operations to large-scale mobile warfare to isolate the cities was failing. As early as the summer of 1966 there was evidence of a debate between the communist commander in the South, General Nguyen Chi Thanh, and General Giap on whether to press forward with the strategy launched in 1964–1965 or return to protracted warfare at lowered cost in men and supplies. Giap won out, but a year later it was evident to all in Hanoi that more of the same would not do. The communists were on a losing course. (There was at least one intelligence report of this period suggesting that experts from all over the communist world were called in to assess the situation and arrived at this conclusion.)

Undoubtedly, the leadership in Hanoi, thinking, as always, in political terms, gave particular attention to the danger represented by the consolidation of constitutional government in South Vietnam, as the elections of 1967 proceeded, and to the hope represented by the rising pressures on Johnson of the peace movement in the United States.

The decision reached in Hanoi was extremely bold. It aimed to destroy both the emerging political structure in South Vietnam and the political support in the United States for Johnson's policy. Operationally, Hanoi's aim was to draw American forces to the frontiers through massive attacks by radically expanded North Vietnamese units; to leapfrog the rural areas and attempt to overthrow the government in the cities by inducing a "general uprising." For the latter purpose, a maximum recruitment effort to expand Viet Cong units was required from the rural areas where communist control over the population was still effective; for it was judged that except in Hue, where large North Vietnamese as well as Viet Cong forces were employed, local communists would be required successfully to infiltrate Saigon and the other cities in the southern part of the country. Tet 1968 was chosen as the period for the climactic attack, on the assumption that it would afford surprise and that South Vietnamese units would be substantially on leave. The end of January was also a good time for such an offensive since it follows some four prior months of dry weather in Laos, during which there was time to build up supplies and bring in the North Vietnamese units, and precedes another four months of good weather in South Vietnam, during which there would be time to exploit the hoped for victory.

The plan required secrecy, political preparations to exploit and consolidate the urban uprisings the attacks were expected to detonate, and a willingness to invest every unit in the North that could be spared plus the maximum manpower that could be mobilized in the South. It also required a massive increase in Soviet military equipment, including larger rockets for urban attacks than had ever been used in the past. Moscow granted in the summer of 1967 the requisite military supplies on a lavish scale. It was a go-for-broke effort.

In concept, the plan was a violation of Maoist guerrilla doctrine. It sought a quick political victory in the cities, achieved before the countryside had been methodically consolidated. It was rooted in the judgment and faith that if the communist units could penetrate the cities, the latent support for communism would assert itself, overthrow the local administration, and confront the United States with an irreversible fait accompli. The concept had something of the flavor of the communist effort of 1927 in China to seize power in the cities—a concept with Leninist roots, encouraged at the time by Soviet advisers; although there were also precedents in Vietnamese history and Vietnamese communist tactics against the French. The captured documents and briefings suggest that Hanoi thought of the plan in grandiose terms as matching Lenin's victorious strategy of 1917 and Mao's of 1948–1949.

A great deal is known of the plan from the many prisoners, including some of quite high rank, captured during the Tet offensive. With the exception of Khe Sanh, it did not call for tactical military defeat of American forces. It envisaged, rather, that they would be left isolated in a communist-controlled political sea; and a "red-carpet withdrawal" would be offered. Many reports suggested that Hanoi looked to early negotiations from the position of political and military strength victory at Tet would provide. The interim government, when Thieu's administration collapsed, was to be a communist-dominated coalition. When the Americans left, communists would take over more explicitly and unity with Hanoi would be arranged.

Such were Hanoi's hopes for success in the offensive that those who were sent into the cities to fight or as political commissars were given no plan for withdrawal. The military plan, however, provided for keeping substantial forces (e.g., the North Vietnamese 7th Division) out of the initial battle and available for a second wave of attack. When the desperate plans for direct assault were revealed to the communist units (generally about two weeks before Tet), the leadership promised, in some cases at least, an early end to the war.

Within the American government—in Saigon and Washington—a sense of the impending climactic effort gradually developed during the autumn. Heavy North Vietnamese pressure came to bear in late October at Loc Ninh, along the Cambodian border, and then in November at Dak To in the same region, the latter involving four North Vietnamese regiments. Simultaneously, heavy pressure was brought to bear by North Vietnamese units against Allied positions south of the DMZ. Although American reinforcements were brought in at Loc Ninh and Dac To, they were quickly withdrawn as the South Vietnamese and Americans successfully frustrated the attacks at great cost to the enemy. American units were not pulled away from the densely populated areas for substantial periods.

By early December the scale, range, and objectives of the impending enemy effort were increasingly clear. I asked for a summary (dated December 8) of the view from Saigon and for a commentary on it (dated December 15) from the intelligence community in Washington. I forwarded both to Johnson on December 16, 1967, with a brief covering note.

The Saigon document is worth quotation in some detail, indicating both the extent to which the structure of the Tet offensive was appreciated as early as December 8 and the kind of data available to Johnson at that time; for he had been receiving regularly and following closely the piecemeal evidence on which this summation was based.

> Numerous recently captured documents have brought into focus Viet Cong (VC) and North Vietnamese (NVN) plans and ambitions for their 1967–68 winter–spring campaign. This campaign is to consist of three phases: a first phase from October to December, 1967; a second phase from January to March 1968; and a third phase from April to June 1968. The campaign entails military and political ambitions which surpass anything previously attempted in such a relatively short period of time by the VC/NVN in South Vietnam. Moreover, thus far VC/NVN activity indicates that they are indeed attempting to implement these plans at their intended levels of intensity.
>
> . . . the U.S. is viewed as being increasingly isolated politically abroad and torn by mounting dissension from within. The VC/NVN state that the present U.S. administration feels itself under pressure to end the war before the 1968 elections in order to guarantee its political survival. . . .
>
> VC/NVN strategy for this campaign is described as an "all-out attack." This is a departure from the traditional VC/NVN three-phase strategy "of resistance, general offensive, and general uprising." The immediate objective is to step up military and political offensives "on all battlefronts" and to create favorable conditions for a "turning point" which will result in "a general counter-offensive and general uprising." . . .
>
> Viet Cong/North Vietnamese military and political missions for the winter–spring campaign can be broken down as follows—
>
> A. Military:
>
> (1) Conduct large-scale continuous, coordinated attacks by main force units, primarily in mountainous areas close to border sanctuaries.
>
> (2) Conduct widespread guerrilla attacks on large U.S./GVN units in rural/heavily populated areas.
>
> (3) Attack key U.S./GVN agencies and rear service bases.

(4) Destroy lines of communications.
(5) Conduct terrorist activities in the cities by special action and sapper units.

B. Political:
(1) Consolidate and strengthen VC/NVN organizations at province, district, and village levels throughout South Vietnam.
(2) Coordinate military actions with political activities to promote political turmoil and struggle movements.

Through these tactics, the VC/NVN hope to force the redeployment of major Allied military units to the border areas where the VC/NVN enjoy sanctuary and will be able to inflict heavy casualties on them. According to the VC/NVN plan, this will tie the Allied forces down in static defensive positions and, equally important, will relieve the pressure on the VC/NVN activities in the populated areas. . . .

The VC/NVN state that if they are successful in the above activities, the conditions will have been created for the overthrow of the present GVN and its replacement by a regime which will consent to form a coalition government with the National Front for the Liberation of South Vietnam (NFLSV) and will follow the program of the NFLSV. Moreover, in these circumstances, the VC/NVN state that they would assume control of the country's armed forces and would ensure that they exercised control at the local administrative level. The second major expectation on the part of the VC/NVN is that if they are successful, this will break the "aggressive will" of the Americans and force them to agree to withdraw from South Vietnam in a short period of time. . . .

In sum, the one conclusion that can be drawn from all of this is that the war is probably nearing a turning point and that the outcome of the 1967–68 winter–spring campaign will in all likelihood determine the future direction of the war.

Washington intelligence analysts, whose comments Johnson also read, were inclined to think the coming campaign was less "decisive" than Saigon, rather more a continuation of the basic strategy pursued throughout the year and, in fact, since early 1966: a policy of eroding American will to pursue a protracted war, despite unfavorable trends on the ground. They saw no early turning point. They agreed that Hanoi was taking "serious risk" in promising its cadres in the South an early, "decisive," and victorious end to the war.

The Washington analysts were quite correct in their judgment of Hanoi's view of American politics; but they did not quite capture the scale and spirit of the extraordinary effort which was to take place at Tet.

Without viewing the outcome of the coming offensive as determining an early end to the war, Johnson correctly sensed its maximal character and its possible link to negotiations when the offensive subsided. He instructed McNamara to get to Westmoreland before Christmas all the fighting forces he had been promised by mid-1968—bringing the total to 106 combat battalions. Two brigades of the 101st Airborne Division and the 11th Light Infantry Brigade (amounting in all to some 10,000 men) were flown out to Vietnam in December, ahead of schedule. The Army refused, however, to send four additional battalions until their training was completed in the spring of 1968, resisting Johnson's suggestion that they finish training in Vietnam so as to be available in reserve when the storm broke.

During December the movement of two additional North Vietnamese divisions to the South was noted and correctly associated with a likely effort to invest Khe Sanh.

All this was in Johnson's mind when he spoke to the Australian Cabinet on December 21, 1967, while attending the memorial service for Harold Holt.[17] His warning of the dark days ahead, of "kamikaze" attacks, and a desperate effort by Hanoi to achieve a breakthrough took some of the Australians by surprise. One senior Australian politician sought me out at the Canberra airport before our departure to ask more details about the two divisions heading south for Khe Sanh.

The gathering weight of the winter–spring offensive was obvious in both statistical and nonstatistical evidence on the war. Forward momentum in pacification halted. The ratio of enemy to friendly weapons lost dropped in November and December. And, as January unfolded, Westmoreland sensed and reported the likelihood of a major offensive at the time of Tet and made special dispositions, particularly for the protection of Saigon. He also asked and received permission to cancel the Tet truce in I Corps and to maintain bombing attacks in the area north of the DMZ where major forces were evidently poised for attack. Nevertheless, there was a real element of surprise at the breadth of the attacks that came at the end of January: 39 of the 44 provincial capitals, 5 of the 6 autonomous cities, 71 of 242 district capitals, and 50 hamlets. The concept of "a general uprising" to be detonated by military action was quite familiar; but no one quite envisaged so grandiose an effort conducted on so wide a front against the main strength of the Allied forces. And the South Vietnamese could not bring themselves to accept fully the notion of an attack during Tet itself, so that many units were at half strength because of leaves.

Some 84,000 communist troops were committed to battle, which started on January 29; by the end of February 45,000 had been killed. The Tet offensive was a military disaster for Hanoi.

Meanwhile, a strange drama was unfolding at Khe Sanh, where Hanoi evidently had maximum and minimum objectives. At the maximum it hoped to inflict there a major defeat on American forces that would have psychological consequences in American political life equivalent to the French defeat at Dien Bien Phu in 1954. At the minimum, it hoped to draw massive U.S. forces from the defense of the coastal populated areas out to the frontier and open up Quang Tri, Hue, and Danang for communist military and political takeover.

There was, from Westmoreland's point of view, a straightforward and symmetrical reason for accepting the test at Khe Sanh. If the 6,000 Americans and South Vietnamese could tie down 20,000 North Vietnamese regulars before Khe Sanh, those forces (plus an almost equal number elsewhere in the DMZ area) would be kept away from the populated areas of I Corps.

As a table included in the footnotes[18] indicates, there were marked similarities between the situation of Dien Bien Phu in 1954 and Khe Sanh in 1968. These similarities extended to the terrain, weather, the scale of forces engaged on each side, and fire power on the ground.

The confidence of the American military rested on certain key differences in the two situations: a massive difference in air power (1–20 in bomb tonnage) and air supply capabilities (1–8 in supply tonnage) plus the existence of large, airmobile reserve forces available to lift the siege if the base should find itself endangered. There was a further minor, but not trivial, difference: at Dien Bien Phu the French were in a valley; at Khe Sanh the Americans and South Vietnamese were on a plateau, with some, at least, of the mountain positions around held by friendly artillery units.

For seventy-seven days Khe Sanh was supplied by air. The North Vietnamese forces used precisely the techniques applied at Dien Bien Phu, including the construction of elaborate protected trenches for secure approaches to the base, with the added purpose at Khe Sanh of getting inside the B-52 bomb line. But full-scale assault was never mounted on Khe Sanh; and because of American spoiling actions, the exact relation in Giap's plans of the timing of the attack on Khe Sanh to the rest of the winter–spring offensive has never been quite clear. It is evident that the application of air power threw the North Vietnamese off balance at certain critical moments. It is known, for example, that their underground command headquarters in Laos was torn open at one point and that a B-52 strike destroyed perhaps 75 percent of one regiment of the 304th Division.

Early in April—with Hue cleared since February 27, pressure relieved from the populated areas in I Corps, and the Allies generally on the offensive—Westmoreland's troops moved in to relieve Khe Sanh against only sporadic opposition. He applied the contingency plan formulated in January for relief of the base if it got into bad trouble. Rarely have major forces been neutralized and decimated at less cost at a critical stage of a major battle than the North Vietnamese before Khe Sanh in January–March 1968. The North Vietnamese maximum and minimum objectives were both frustrated. No reliable figures exist for North Vietnamese killed in action at Khe Sanh. Estimates range between 6,000 and 20,000. At least one division was put totally out of action.

Johnson was aware of what an American failure at Khe Sanh might cost, but he decided to leave the choice of staying or pulling out to Westmoreland. He backed the decision to stay to the hilt, following the course of the struggle through daily reports covering weather, supply movements, rate of fire, and casualties.

But the heart of Hanoi's failure in South Vietnam at Tet was political, not military. The great uprising did not occur. Evidently, the South Vietnamese were hurt. I said at a press conference on February 18, 1968, at Indian Wells, California (where Johnson was conferring with Eisenhower):

> The cities have been hit hard. There is a great deal of human suffering. There are refugees. The people were frightened. That is a part of it.
>
> The other part of it is that . . . the effect of the first wave of attacks was to force people [in the cities] to take a clearer view of where they stood, vis-à-vis the VC on the one hand and the government on the other.
>
> As for the VC, the first and most primitive fact is that they came in proclaiming they were coming to take over the cities and they failed. They were trying to eliminate from the equation in Vietnam the two institutions . . . which distinguish their struggle with the Americans from their struggle with the French.
>
> The two institutions are, first, a national army, the ARVN, the Armed Forces of the Republic of Vietnam; the other is the Constitutional Government. In all their propaganda, they never cease to refer to the Government as the Thieu–Ky clique. They never refer to the ARVN except as a puppet force.
>
> They are obsessed with their memories of 1954. . . . We are not there to maintain a colonial empire. We are there to help a nation find its feet and to make its decisions, relieved of aggression.
>
> That is their greatest concern—the fact that a legitimate government, supported by the people, might emerge; that a national army with a national spirit might emerge.
>
> . . . they failed to achieve their strategic objective, and may have left the ARVN and the Government stronger institutions than before they attacked.

I would not alter that assessment.

The government elected in October 1967 had been proceeding somewhat sluggishly. Tet suddenly put it to a maximum test. The cities and towns were cleared; refugees looked after; and emergency housing built. The Vietnamese military emerged with a new confidence. Even when under strength, they fought and defeated the best attacks the communists could mount with the advantage of the tactical surprise Tet afforded. Above all, Tet made politically possible the general mobilization (voted on February 9 by the Vietnamese lower house) which, along with increased volunteers, increased South Vietnamese forces by 122,000 in the first half of 1968.

The government, the military, and the nation emerged stronger than before the assault.

From the beginning of the Tet offensive, intelligence indicated Hanoi planned a "second wave" of attacks. The date suggested was initially in the first week of February, but it kept sliding forward. There were on February 18 concerted mortar attacks, but no serious efforts to get into the cities. Meanwhile, Hanoi accelerated infiltration, bringing to the battlefield a mass of inadequately trained men. The second wave actually occurred on May 7. Attacks along the Cambodian frontier and in I Corps were preempted by Allied offensive military action; but there was again a substantial attack on Saigon. The VC units were unable to recover their strength by May. The attacks were conducted mainly by North Vietnamese units, hastily rebuilt by large-scale post-Tet infiltration. As the statistics show, the losses suffered in May were extremely high, although they did not reach the February peak; nor could the effort be sustained as long as the Tet attacks.

The May effort was evidently designed to fill the American and world press with a demonstration of communist strength at precisely the time the Paris peace talks opened—once again a throwback to 1954. In an extraordinary piece of bad luck for Hanoi, the May riots in France almost totally blanketed the military news from Vietnam. On the whole, the press underplayed the communist effort in May, and there were no substantial additional repercussions in American public opinion.

By mid-year the communists had lost 120,000 men, half their total strength at the beginning of the year. A rather feeble effort was mounted in August, apparently timed to the Democratic Convention; but it was evident that the winter–spring offensive had failed militarily and politically in South Vietnam. Hanoi's residual hope lay in what American politics might yield.

May 1968–January 1969: Recovery and Accelerated Pacification

With the failure of the second wave in May, the 1967–1968 winter–spring offensive was, essentially, over. Saigon and Washington turned to regaining the ground lost in the countryside, dealing with the refugees, and expanding the South Vietnamese forces as the negotiating process moved laboriously forward in Paris.

Johnson's basic military decision on March 31 had been to throw his full weight behind the new sense of confidence and capacity that emerged among the South Vietnamese in the wake of Tet. The production bottleneck of the M-16 rifle was broken and plans made to equip not only the South Vietnamese regulars but the regional and popular forces with that effective weapon. Johnson refused to commit his successor by agreeing to Thieu's proposal at Honolulu in July that American troop withdrawals be announced for 1969[19]; but as the South Vietnamese forces rapidly expanded, that option would clearly be open to the next President, as Westmoreland had predicted it would be as early as November 1967 in his speech before the National Press Club in Washington.

There was an easy consensus at Honolulu in July 1968 that the time was ripe for an accelerated pacification effort. There had been great anxiety in the early days of the Tet offensive that, as South Vietnamese units came in to defend the cities, the countryside would be lost to and consolidated by the communists. This had not happened. The slippage in pacification was real enough, but it was limited and quite quickly repaired. By October a plan for accelerated pacification was agreed on; and on October 29 Johnson gave Abrams a written instruction to maintain maximum, unrelenting pressure on the enemy.

On the eve of Tet the proportion of the South Vietnamese population under reasonably reliable and secure government administration was 66 percent, with 16 percent contested, and 18 percent under Viet Cong administration. At the low point after Tet, the figures were, respectively, 59 percent, 21 percent, and 20 percent. At the end of January 1969 they were 80 percent, 8 percent, and 12 percent. The net gain in government population control over the year was more than 2 million, about twice the gain during 1967. The precision of the numbers can be debated; but there is no doubt whatsoever that the last four months of Johnson's administration saw the most rapid progress in consolidating the countryside in the whole history of the war in Vietnam. It was then (and in subsequent months) that the South Vietnamese victory at Tet was fully exploited and the long, slow process of building the foundations for pacification in 1966–1967 brought to something like fruition. One of the best evaluations of what had transpired was published by The Institute for Strategic Studies in London:

> The main "success" for the United States [in 1969] was the revelation of the extent to which North Vietnam and the Viet Cong had suffered during 1968. The enormous losses incurred by North Vietnamese units during their major offensives of February and May 1968 destroyed the elite of North Vietnam's army. That army showed little sign of complete recovery during 1969. The rapid decline of the infiltration rate from North Vietnam during the spring and summer of the year, accelerated by the urgent need for manpower to repair heavy flood damage in the North, demonstrated the difficulty which the government in Hanoi undoubtedly had in providing replacements for the men killed in 1968. When infiltration gathered pace again in the autumn, it served only to reveal the relatively low quality of the human material now available. . . .

> The Viet Cong also experienced increasingly serious recruiting difficulties during 1969. They had been forced in 1968 to abandon much of their rural power base, in the form of territory under their control, in order to launch the assault upon the cities. That assault having failed, they found in retreat that their rural base, once neglected, had begun to crumble. Moreover, the South Vietnamese Government, encouraged by the United States, had seized the opportunity to fill the vacuum left by the Viet Cong march on the towns. The programme of "accelerated pacification" was paying rich dividends to Saigon. . . .
>
> The effect on the size of Communist forces in South Vietnam was great enough. . . . The effect on the morale of Communist forces was, if anything, even greater. Despite a determined campaign of political education, it was difficult to conceal the failure of the 1968 policy of assaulting the towns. . . .
>
> Apart from the erosion of their political influence, the Viet Cong, by losing control of many of their "popular bases" in the countryside, had sacrificed much of the logistic organization which had permitted them to live off the land. In particular, their indigenous sources of food had been seriously reduced, both by neglect and by the determined efforts of American and South Vietnamese forces to find and destroy them. As a result, they had become heavily dependent upon external sources, especially in Cambodia, for vital rice supplies.[20]

Despite an awareness of progress in 1966–1967 and of these post-Tet developments in 1968, Johnson was skeptical that Hanoi would seriously negotiate a settlement on terms even minimally acceptable to the United States. He believed that they had invested so much in victory and could see so much in the United States evocative of France of the early 1950s that they would hold out. When he explained to the Australian Cabinet at Canberra in December 1967 that an effort to induce a negotiation by a bombing cessation would have to await the failure of Hanoi's impending offensive, he also indicated doubt that they would in fact move toward peace until after the American election.

Nevertheless, Johnson could not be sure of his own skeptical assessment. He felt he had a duty to see if his judgment was wrong. And throughout his administration, he and his chief advisers devoted what must be judged in retrospect a disproportionate amount of energy, talent, and time to one contact or alleged negotiating possibility after another. In our hearts we knew that Hanoi would let us know, and knew how to let us know, if it was ever serious. The only reward, and it is not trivial, is a certainty that no stone was left unturned in trying to find a formula that would reconcile Johnson's view of minimum American interests and the maximum legitimate interests of Hanoi.

So as we worked intensively from May 1968 forward on the negotiating process, we thought of the likelihood that the next President would still have a war on his hands. Johnson's objective, if he could not achieve peace, was to leave a situation in South Vietnam with such forward momentum and such palpable assets that, when the new administration independently took stock, as it had the duty to do, it would decide to remain loyal to the American treaty commitments in Southeast Asia. The accelerated pacification program begun in October 1968 contributed to that objective; but it was rooted in the process of political development launched by Ky's speech of January 15, 1966, the organizational structure developed by the Vietnamese and Americans in 1965–1967, and, above all, the response of the people of South Vietnam to the Tet offensive.

FROM PRECONDITIONS TO THE EVE OF TAKEOFF

THE developments and policies of the 1960s, the human responses of the South Vietnamese to them, and the evolution of South Vietnam as a society in the widest sense moved the young nation rapidly forward in modernization from where it was in 1954 to the spring of 1972.

Colonialism in Vietnam, as elsewhere, was both a modernizing and a distorting force. The distortions included a system of education that failed to train the engineers, economists, and entrepreneurs required for rapid economic growth. The most powerful distortion of colonialism, however, was to concentrate men of talent on the process of ending it. And this familiar phenomenon was joined with endemic military conflict from the Japanese occupation of 1940–1941 to the present.

Nevertheless, South Vietnam was, in 1954, a nation more modern than, say, Cambodia or Laos. It had acquired unevenly some elements of modernization; but it emerged from colonialism in a relatively early phase of what I have called the preconditions for takeoff: that is, the period of preparation before the first sustained phase of industrialization.

From that initial position it moved forward rapidly to a situation where, with reasonable political stability and security, it could soon enter takeoff. War imposed on the South Vietnamese great casualties and human suffering. Along with massive mobilization, it also slowed and distorted the process of modernization in certain directions. But war accelerated modernization in others.

The data available on this evolution are incomplete; but they permit brief summary notes at least under the headings one would use to describe the transition of any other developing nation at this stage: agriculture; urbanization; education; public administration; infrastructure; early industrialization; foreign exchange.

AGRICULTURE[21]

WAR and public policy caused a deterioration of Vietnamese agriculture in the mid-1960s, after reasonably steady progress from 1954. Danger in the countryside and the attraction of jobs in the cities (as American installations expanded) led to flight from the land. The GVN gave urban interests priority over rural, anxious, in particular, about the possible disruptive effects of inflation in the cities. Low prices paid to farmers were not a sufficient incentive to expand production. In the winter of 1966–1967 the GVN faced a crisis: total farm production had fallen by 24 percent since 1963; land planted to rice had decreased by a half-million acres; the cities were becoming dependent on American rice imports. In response to this crisis, and the increased emphasis on rural pacification, priorities were reversed: the price of rice received by farmers was raised; special measures were taken to increase imports of fertilizers and pesticides and improve the efficiency of their distribution. The year 1967 was one of real progress: some 40,000 irrigation pumps were sold, probably ten times the total number in the country a few years before. The harvest of early 1968 was almost 10 percent larger than the previous year. Professor Ton That Trinh (later minister of land reform and agriculture) had experimented with the new IR-8 rice seeds. South Vietnam was on the eve of mass distribution of the new seeds when the Tet offensive struck. The disruption of transport between Saigon and the Delta set things back for some months. By the late fall of 1968, however, with transport links restored, the first major Green Revolution rice harvest was gathered, achieving 90 percent of the pre-Tet target. Since then, agricultural production has gone forward with great momentum, yielding 5.6 million tons of rice in 1971, the largest crop in South Vietnamese history, 30 percent over the 1967 level. South Vietnam, despite its rapid increase in population and urbanization, is almost certain to achieve self-sufficiency with the rice harvest of 1971–1972. This should result in more rapid agricultural diversification. Diversification is needed to meet urban demands for animal protein and vegetables. It is also required because increased rice production in Asia, stimulated by the new rice strains, limits the prospects for large-scale Vietnamese exports.

The agricultural boom in South Vietnam brought the city and countryside together in new ways: increased use of fertilizers, pesticides, pumps, and farm machinery; the spread to the increasingly affluent countryside of radio and television, sewing machines and motorcycles; the development of vaccine production to back the chicken revolution; a doubling of vegetable production for urban consumption.

Economically as well as administratively, psychologically as well as politically, the classic barriers between urban and rural life in a country undergoing the preconditions for takeoff were rapidly lowered in the period 1967–1972.

The rural boom was underpinned by a massive land reform program. It was formulated by Vietnamese technicians assisted by the Stanford Research Institute in the latter part of the Johnson administration; adopted by Thieu and his Cabinet in June 1969; sent to the National Assembly on July 2; finally passed after a grueling struggle on March 16, 1970. It is one of the few serious land reform schemes ever passed in a developing nation by a democratically elected legislature, which contains, as such bodies inevitably do, a good many landlords. Something like a half of the one million hectares scheduled for redistribution had been transferred to tenant farmers by early 1972. Aside from its other long-run consequences, the measure clearly strengthened Thieu's hand with rural voters, notably in the Delta.

Meanwhile, self-government was re-installed in virtually all the 10,655 hamlets and 2174 villages of South Vietnam. In June 1970 the first province and city council elections since 1965 took place. These developments were accompanied by programs in which national and local resources were mobilized on a roughly equal basis to carry out projects of local interest.

The requirements of pacification and Thieu's political strategy converged to produce this rural revolution. It left unsolved many problems; e.g., the rapid development of the Delta versus the slower expansion in the less well endowed northern rural provinces, and the dim prospects for rice exports. But as South Vietnam looked to its takeoff in early 1972, it did so from an agricultural base that could provide two essentials lacking in many underdeveloped nations: a prosperous countryside capable of serving as a market for locally produced industrial products; and a capacity for feeding a greatly expanded urban population.

URBANIZATION

FOR a nation at its early stage of economic development, South Vietnam is heavily urbanized. It has moved from a prewar situation when 15 to 20 percent of the population was urban to a current position of 35 to 40 percent—the result, as noted earlier, of the push and pull of wartime circumstances. The reduction of American bases and personnel since 1969 caused a rapid decline in the number of those employed directly or indirectly as a result of the American presence. There may have been some return to the countryside in 1968–1972 with improved rural security; although the urban labor market was generally tight, with more than a million men under arms and some 20,000 inducted monthly into the armed forces. The coming of peace would require rapid industrialization to sustain the level of urban employment. In fact, a problem of unemployment began to emerge in 1972, notably in some of the northern urban areas.

EDUCATION[22]

STARTING in 1954 South Vietnam has undergone an educational revolution which has transformed the colonial heritage and the manpower base for modernization. In 1954, 401,000 Vietnamese children were enrolled in primary schools; in January 1972, 2.7 million—about 91 percent of the estimated primary school population, as opposed to 15 percent when colonialism ended. Over a similiar period, secondary school enrollment expanded from roughly 53,000 to over 710,000, about 30 percent of secondary age children in the country, a low but creditable figure by standards of contemporary developing nations.

The first university in South Vietnam was founded in 1955 in Saigon by professors and students who had left Hanoi the previous year. There were seven universities in 1972. Enrollment rose over these seventeen years from 2,900 to some 76,000.

Like the Chinese and Koreans, the Vietnamese have exhibited an avid interest in taking advantage of expanded educational opportunities.

Urbanization, combined with work on military bases (including equipment maintenance), has helped develop the mentality and skills needed for an industrial working force. Some 300,000 Vietnamese received some mechanical, secretarial, or professional training as a result of employment with American institutions or installations in Vietnam. These trends were institutionalized by a large-scale program to expand vocational and technical training. Such schools had over 21,500 students in early 1972. In addition, the Vietnamese government has launched engineering and agricultural colleges which are likely to become part of the university system.

PUBLIC ADMINISTRATION

THE tasks of war itself, of pacification reaching out to every village, of organizing national elections, of mounting a massive land reform program to eliminate tenant farming, of dealing with the infinite complexities of American aid, of decentralizing rural government—all required a forced-draft development of South Vietnamese administrative capabilities. South Vietnam is one of the few developing nations using computer equipment to assist in tax collection, a fact reflected, for example, in a 38 percent rise in domestic revenues in 1970 and 30 percent in 1971. The bureaucratic apparatus in Saigon as of 1972 was not exactly as efficient as that in, say, Stockholm or The Hague. It still bore marks of its rather rigid

French heritage as well as the endemic problems of poorly paid, unevenly trained bureaucrats in the developing world. Much of the best administrative talent was in the military services. On the other hand, it had come a long way since the days of Diem and, indeed, since the shock of Tet in 1968. It certainly had the capacity, under conditions of security and political stability, to mount a vigorous and coherent program of sustained economic development, enriched by some of the 4000 Vietnamese who received professional training abroad during the 1960s.

INFRASTRUCTURE

THE period of massive American engagement in Vietnam endowed the country with a virtually unique infrastructure base for further development. The port of Saigon, for example, discharged 3.8 million tons of cargo in 1969 as compared with 2.5 million tons in 1965, against a previous average of 1.5 million tons. Major new ports were constructed at Cam Ranh Bay and Newport, while Saigon and others are now thoroughly modernized—notably at Danang and Qui Nhon.

Similar developments have occurred in highways, airports, and the telecommunications system. A large and quite efficient national airline (Air Vietnam) has emerged, carrying in 1969 more passengers than the combined total over the previous ten years.

Electric power requirements in South Vietnam are growing at about 20 percent per annum and a single national power company now operates these rapidly expanding installations, planning as well an integrated network for the future.

Some of the American infrastructure heritage may be indigestible in the short run; but South Vietnam should emerge from war with an ample physical base for rapid industrialization.

INDUSTRY

THE major industries of South Vietnam during the 1960s were the classic array for a country in the preconditions for takeoff—like those to be found, for example, in the more advanced African nations: textiles, beer, soft drinks, sugar refining, glass bottles, cement, paper. This small industrial sector grew at a rate of about 14 percent per annum in the period 1963–1967. Industrial production was set back by about 9 percent due to the Tet offensive in 1968 but moved well above the 1967 levels in 1969; and it has continued to advance quite briskly since. The critical task is to move beyond the initial industrial array to sectors of more advanced technology capable of lifting South Vietnam into takeoff.

This should involve: the assembly, component production, and then full production of hitherto imported consumer goods such as bicycles, motorcycles, sewing machines, radios, pumps, etc.; the manufacture of major chemical inputs to agriculture, as well as a broad range of pharmaceuticals; the processing of fish, wood, rubber, and other agricultural products for export. The movement into these sectors requires, in the usual case, collaboration with foreign firms. As of early 1972, a good many Japanese and American firms were tentatively exploring the possibilities of such ventures, and a few were under way.

Foreign Exchange

The greatest economic challenge facing South Vietnam is, of course, to move to a viable long-run balance from its present extreme dependence on American aid (and local expenditures by Americans) to finance its high import level. This structural adjustment will take time and require the first serious phase of South Vietnamese industrialization as well as a sustained export drive.[23]

Large external resources are now required to balance a diversion of about 15 percent of the labor force and gross domestic product of South Vietnam to the armed forces and defense outlays. Exports in 1969, for example, were only $27 million, imports $809 million. As in the case of South Korea, which successfully managed a similar structural transition in the years since 1963, South Vietnam will require sustained external assistance, private as well as public, combined with extremely vigorous programs of import substitution and export promotion.

The point to be made here is, simply, that in the midst of a terrible war—with enormous human and physical costs—the government and people of Vietnam met their challenges and seized their opportunities in ways that took them rapidly forward in economic and social as well as political modernization. They have exhibited a formidable stubbornness and will to survive and prosper. It took South Korea almost a decade after the end of the war in 1953 to bring itself, as a society, to the eve of takeoff. Passing through a similar sequence during a more protracted war, South Vietnam, despite continuing heavy military burdens and diversions, was, in early 1972, roughly where South Korea stood in the early 1960s. This quiet, slow-moving, but highly important development has been virtually unreported in the American press, and has been studied and understood by only a handful of Americans outside government.

A Conclusion

As of early 1972 the outcome in Southeast Asia is still to be determined. It is already clear, however, that a rather grand irony will frame the history of

Southeast Asia in the 1950s, 1960s, and 1970s. Ho came to power in North Vietnam as an anticolonial communist leader who had rallied to his side a good deal of Vietnamese nationalist sentiment. He was widely applauded in Asia as the leader who had lifted French colonial rule from Indochina. He lost much support between 1954 and 1956 as he consolidated North Vietnam in blood and fully revealed his communist orthodoxy. He then moved to fulfill his ultimate dream of taking over the rest of the former French colonial empire in Asia. His intrusions into Laos, South Vietnam, and Cambodia—and the protracted exertions required to contain and repel them—stirred and strengthened nationalist feelings in those countries. In Southeast Asia, as elsewhere in the world over the past two centuries, reaction to external intrusion has proved to be the basis for the emergence of modern nationalism. After further vicissitudes that we cannot predict, I believe that Hanoi's dream of hegemony over Indochina will ultimately be frustrated by the modernizing nationalism its tragic adventures helped to create. For an interim analysis of Hanoi's offensive of the spring of 1972, see pp. 556–562.

The Tet offensive of 1968 was a critical test of the viability of that dream, of Hanoi's political appeal (as well as of its military virtuosity) set against the strength of South Vietnamese nationalism. The great uprising never happened; the South Vietnamese proceeded to an accelerated phase of modernization; and Hanoi was left to rely primarily on the confusions and ambiguities of American thought and feeling about Asia, and their consequences for U.S. military dispositions and policies in Southeast Asia.

39

Vietnam and American Political Life

The Consequences of Two Discontents

In dealing with presidents, at least with the two I have personally worked with, one spends little time during the working day in philosophical dialogue. In the case of Lyndon Johnson, there were occasions for spacious telephone conversation early in the morning when he took stock of the coming day from his bedroom and there was time for talk again toward the close of the day, before his usually late dinner, when the formal schedule had run its course. In between, business was conducted with maximum terseness and relevance to the task in hand. Long thoughts were often embedded in those tasks, and all hands were conscious of that fact. But one did not spend a great deal of time in their unnecessary elaboration.

One day in 1967 Johnson was going over a message to a chief of government, drafted initially in the State Department. He found the language excessively bureaucratic and involuted. He made a good many changes, and I suggested some others. The message was then given to one of his secretaries for retyping before final scrutiny. He turned to the two tickers in his office to catch up with the flow of news. The results of the latest poll on Presidential popularity were coming in. Without turning toward me, he said: "In this job you must set a standard for making decisions. Mine is: What will my grandchildren think of my administration when I'm buried under the tree at the Ranch, in the family graveyard. I believe they will be proud of two things: what I have done for the Negro and in Asia. But right now I've lost twenty points on the race issue, fifteen on Vietnam."

Chart 39-1[1] shows the course of Johnson's popularity as measured by the Gallup poll. Down to mid-1965, his polls held between 65 and 70 percent. Over the next two years, with only occasional interruption, they fell to the range of 40 to 45 percent, dropping to below 40 percent under the impact of the urban riots of 1967, rising briefly to about 50 percent as the Paris peace talks opened and, again, as his administration ended.

I make this point to emphasize once again a central fact about the Johnson administration: the unique convergence of a social revolution at home with a protracted and difficult war abroad. It is impossible to assess precisely the degree to which domestic concerns and anxieties exacerbated the inherent difficulties of conducting the protracted strategy in Vietnam. Certainly, domestic unrest and inflation (from, say, mid-1966) heightened popular dissatisfaction with the apparently endless effort in Southeast Asia. Certainly, the point was pressed hard by an articulate minority (including, for example, Martin Luther King) that the war in Vietnam was drawing resources away from what should have been the overriding tasks of American society. Nevertheless, the public opinion polls of the period, without question, indicate that the decisive factor, so far as overall rising popular discontent on Vietnam was concerned, was the failure to achieve victory or palpable progress toward victory; and that the reaction to the Tet offensive and its aftermath, as it was popularly understood, was the critical crossover point.

POPULAR OPINION TOWARD THE WAR IN VIETNAM: 1965–1967

CHART 39-2[2] shows the proportion of Americans believing it was a mistake to send troops to Vietnam. It begins in 1965 at the classic level for a minority view, around about 25 percent; rises slowly in 1966 to 31 percent in November; rises more rapidly in 1967 to 46 percent in October; and then moves to over 50 percent in June 1968.

The anxiety of Americans to get it over with is indicated by the sharp temporary increases in Johnson's popularity when there were dramatic moments in the bombing of North Vietnam and also when there was apparent hope for a negotiated movement toward peace, like the Glassboro meeting of June 1967.

The percentage of Americans feeling the war would go on a long time rose as follows[3]:

October 1965	54%
July 1966	72
February 1967	71
May 1967	81

CHART 39–1
JOHNSON'S POPULARITY AS MEASURED BY THE GALLUP POLL

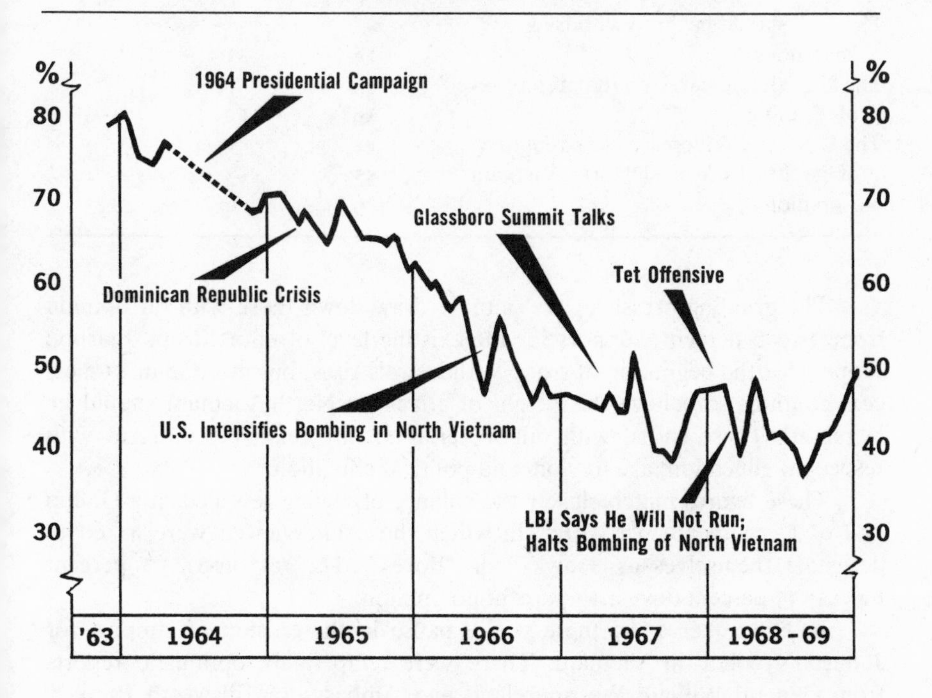

In the face of these frustrating prospects and a rising sense of prior error, the proportion who felt Johnson's intermediate strategy was correct (always low) fell in the course of 1967, as Table 39-1 indicates.[4]

CHART 39–2
PERCENT SAYING U.S. INVOLVEMENT IN VIETNAM A MISTAKE

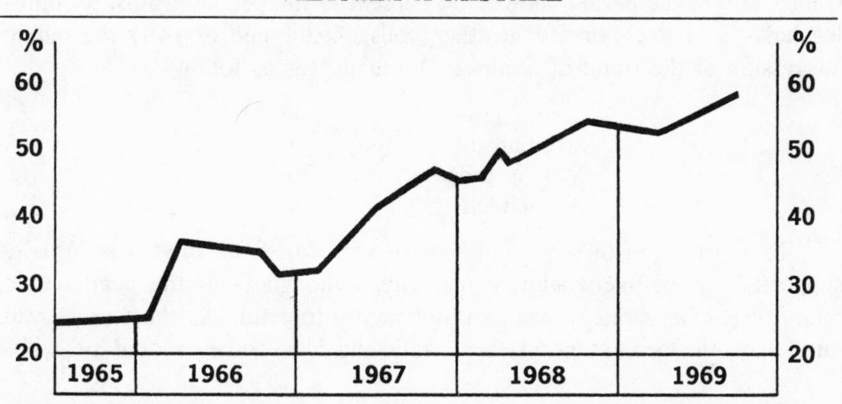

TABLE 39–1

	November (%) 1966	October (%) 1967	Differences (%)
The U.S. should begin to withdraw its troops	18	31	+13
The U.S. should carry on the present level of fighting	18	10	− 8
The U.S. should increase the strength of its attacks against North Vietnam	55	53	− 2
No opinion	9	6	− 3

The grinding pressures of Vietnam draw down those with no opinion from 9 to 6 percent; support for the existing level of effort drops sharply; support for the beginning of troop withdrawals rises; but more than 50 percent continue to believe the weight of attack on North Vietnam should be increased. These shifts, with minor variation, are relatively uniform with respect to education, age, region, and political affiliation.[5]

These figures match closely the balance of feeling revealed in a Gallup poll of December 9–13, 1967, in which those interviewed were asked to designate themselves as "hawks" or "doves." The response: 52 percent hawks; 35 percent doves; 13 percent no opinion.

In November 1967 there was a pause in the erosion of support for Johnson's policy in Vietnam. There were temperately optimistic reports from General William Westmoreland and Ambassador Ellsworth Bunker, home from Saigon. Westmoreland's suggestion that American troops might begin safely to withdraw within two years was noted with some skepticism in the press; but it represented in the worst case—of neither a negotiated settlement nor a clear military victory—a significant element of hope. Johnson's rating on the conduct of the war rose in the wake of an effective press conference of November 19; and between October 1967 and January 1968 his overall favorable rating rose ten points (from 38 to 48 percent). A Gallup poll of the period showed 69 percent of the people against a bombing halt—a view confirmed in other polls. At the end of 1967 the public impression of the trend of affairs in Vietnam was as follows:

Losing ground	8%
Standing still	33
Making progress	50
No opinion	9

In short, Johnson's commitment of U.S. forces in 1965 was initially supported by an overwhelming majority, although from the beginning a majority felt his strategy was not sufficiently forceful. As the war moved on slowly, the percentage of those believing U.S. forces should be withdrawn rose and the percentage believing the U.S. commitment in 1965 was a mistake rose even higher. But despite these trends and the frustrations and dissidence they reflected, there was a hawkish majority as 1967 drew to a close and a sense among half the people that progress was being made.

The Impact of the Tet Offensive

It was in this setting of weary but not hopeless doggedness that the Tet offensive struck. A good many background briefings had been given to the press on the coming effort in both Saigon and Washington. Earle Wheeler, chairman of the Joint Chiefs of Staff, told the Economic Club of Detroit on December 18, 1967, that a desperate Battle of the Bulge effort by the communists was expected. But in a matter of this kind, only the President's voice would have been effective. Albert Cantril's summation is, therefore, just; and, given the knowledge of the coming storm in the government, it represents a major charge against the Johnson adminstration: "The public was completely unprepared for the offensive. . . ."[6] Johnson, in retrospect, agrees:

> Looking back on early 1968, I am convinced I made a mistake by not saying more about Vietnam in my State of the Union report on January 17, 1968. In that address I underscored how intensely our will was being tested by the struggle in Vietnam, but I did not go into details concerning the build-up of enemy forces or warn of the early major combat I believed was in the offing. I relied instead on the "background" briefings that my advisers and I, as well as the State and Defense departments, had provided members of the press corps for many weeks. In those briefings we had stressed that heavy action could be expected soon. This was one of those delicate situations in which we had to try to inform our own people without alerting the enemy to our knowledge of its plans. In retrospect, I think I was too cautious. If I had forecast the possibilities, the American people would have been better prepared for what was soon to come.[7]

In the initial reaction to the Tet offensive, those designating themselves as hawks rose from 52 percent (December 9–13, 1967) to 61 percent (February 3–7, 1968).[8] The Gallup poll of February 18 showed the drop in Johnson's rating came almost exclusively from hawks. But between February and June 1968 there was a marked shift: those supporting a pullback or pullout rose from 28 percent to 49 percent; those supporting an enlarged military effort fell from 53 percent to 35 percent; those supporting the existing level of effort fell from 10 percent to 8 percent.[9]

Behind this dramatic shift were, I would estimate, four factors.

First, Johnson's strategy did not build on the immediate post-Tet impulse for a strong military response. He sorted out his next moves carefully, but even by March the hawkish mood had waned. (In a poll of March 16–20 only 41 percent designated themselves as hawks.) His basic decision was to throw his weight behind the expanded and more confident South Vietnamese effort. This was wholly consistent with his strategy since 1965, but promised no quick solution. The American press was systematically drawing a quite different (and less optimistic) portrait of the performance and prospects of the South Vietnamese than Bunker's and Westmoreland's assessments from Saigon, which, along with the daily flow of intelligence, guided Johnson.

Second, partly in consequence but partly also because the buildup of the South Vietnamese took time, the image of the trend in Vietnam shifted dramatically from the temperate optimism of, say, November 1967.[10]

TABLE 39–2

	November (%) 1967		March (%) 1968		June (%) 1968	
Losing ground	8	41	23	61	25	72
Standing still	33		38		47	
Making progress	50		33		18	
No opinion	9		6		10	

Third, the opening of negotiations in Paris in May appeared to signal some kind of probably unsatisfactory compromise settlement, arrived at after a painful and protracted repetition of the Korean War negotiations at Panmunjon in 1951–1953. This turn of events undoubtedly changed and soured the mood of many hawks.

Fourth, Johnson's March 31 announcement that he would not seek re-election was almost universally read as some kind of admission of defeat in Vietnam. Interpretations in the press and media virtually took it for granted that he had made the decision primarily because of the rise of Eugene McCarthy and Robert Kennedy on his anti-Vietnam flank within the Democratic party and because of his discouragement with the prospects of the war.

In fact, Tet and its aftermath gave Johnson more confidence than he ever had before in the South Vietnamese; it opened the way for the accelerated forward movement in pacification which actually occurred in his last four months in office; it promised a long-term reduction in the communist capacity to fight in Southeast Asia; and, as he has since made clear, his motives in withdrawing from the race had much longer and different roots than those deduced by commentators of the time. But the fact was that Tet, the timing and nature of Johnson's response to it, and the popular interpretation of what had happened and why he had made the decisions he did, altered radically the structure of American public opinion toward the war.

The 60–25–15 Split

In studying American public opinion while writing *The United States in the World Arena* in the 1950s, I was much struck by a tendency for polls to crystallize around the proportions 60 percent pro, 25 percent anti, 15 percent don't know.[11] The proportions held on many issues, domestic as well as foreign. In foreign policy one could expect about 60 percent of the American public to take what might be called an "internationalist" position, about 25 percent an "isolationist" position, and about 15 percent a "don't know" position. These figures vary, of course, from issue to issue and from time to time; but something like this breakdown in basic attitudes appears to exist, independent of party allegiance and of region. This does not mean that 60 percent of Americans wish actively to become more involved in the world and its affairs. On the contrary, there is ample evidence that Americans remain reluctant to assume international responsibility. What these recurrent poll figures do demonstrate is that a substantial majority of Americans will support military and foreign policy measures when they become convinced that they are absolutely necessary for the maintenance of the nation's world position; that a substantial majority will shy away from positions they believe associated with an isolationist retreat or an abandonment of major alliances. On issues like Vietnam, of intense interest and concern, the group with no opinion tends to fall from 15 percent to under 10 percent.

Down to Tet, despite the burdens and frustrations of the war, public opinion on Vietnam tended to approximate this norm. In November 1966, for example, 73 percent believed the United States should carry on at existing or higher levels of military activity, 18 percent believed troops should be withdrawn, 9 percent had no opinion. After a year's further struggle, the figures were still in this range, which provides a solid basis for the conduct of a national policy: 63 percent, 31 percent, and 6 percent, respectively.

The impact of Tet, Johnson's withdrawal, and subsequent events (as they were interpreted) produced a new, more even balance: in June 1968 43 percent wished to continue at existing levels or apply more American military power; 49 percent wished to pull back forces to enclaves or begin to withdraw them; 8 percent had no opinion.

The great middle group of both parties, which, until Tet, had held together in support of the President's Vietnam position (or even supported stronger measures), split. And it was that split and its structure with which Nixon had to deal.

THE ANTI-VIETNAM MOVEMENT

THE shift in American public opinion can be charted and analyzed with reasonable clarity in terms of gross shifts in the balance of public opinion in the face of a protracted and apparently indecisive war and then the shock of Tet and its aftermath as it was interpreted in the United States. Impatience with the war (and the apparently dim post-Tet prospects) was a central phenomenon at work in American political life. But American political life is not a simple reflex of public opinion, on a one-man one-vote basis. Some groups are more articulate and volatile than others. There are the powerful media. There are the leaders of business and labor, educational institutions and religious groups. These elite elements in American political life cannot determine popular attitudes, but they can influence them and create a political atmosphere that rests heavily on a President even if it does not accurately reflect the breakdown in popular sentiment.

Therefore, large questions remain about Vietnam and American political life that go beyond the polls. What of the ardent and assertive "peace movement" and the focusing of student radicalism on Vietnam? The rise of the anti-Vietnam senators, led by William Fulbright? The passionately anti-Vietnam intellectuals? The shift to a systematic anti-Vietnam stance of *The New York Times*, *The Washington Post*, *Newsweek*, the television networks, and finally, the Luce publications? The split in the foreign affairs establishment on the Vietnam issue, notably after Tet?

Except for the procommunists, the failure to produce quick, decisive military results suffused the attitudes of these groups and institutions as well as the less sophisticated mass of public opinion. But the elite debate raised different, less pragmatic questions: Was the SEATO treaty a legitimate definition of American interests in Asia? Indeed, did the United States have any abiding interests in the structure of power in Asia? Was the conduct of the war illegitimate or immoral?

The debate on these more fundamental questions did not engage a statistically high proportion of the nation, but it did deeply engage the nation's intellectual and policy leadership. What, then, was the content of the debate?

THE INTELLECTUAL AND MORAL CONTENT OF THE VIETNAM DEBATE

A recent analyst of the nation's division over Vietnam identified six more or less distinctive sources of opposition to Johnson's policy as follows[12]: pacifists, ideological anticommunists, procommunists, old-fashioned isolationists, those believing that America should only support progressive democracies, and those believing America is overcommitted in the world and must withdraw to concentrate on domestic problems.

As a first approximation, I agree with these broad categories. But the strands of pacifism, ideological moralism, and isolationism, deeply rooted in the American past, had a particular cast when applied to the affairs of Southeast Asia in the 1960s. And they took on a particular intensity, since the grueling struggle that began in mid-1965 occurred in the post-Cuba missile crisis period when there was a widespread sense that the Cold War was waning and the nation, after an arduous and dangerous quarter-century, was eager to turn inward.

As noted in the Appendix (p. 609), it appears to be the case that the United States cannot be effective in military and foreign policy unless a majority believes that both its security interests and its commitment to certain moral principles require the nation to act.

In effect, there emerged an anti-Vietnam position which asserted that vital American security interests were not involved in the outcome of the struggle in Vietnam and that moral principles required the nation to desist in its effort to protect the area from communist takeover.

Here is a summary of a generalized anti-Vietnam position. The emphasis of various individuals and groups varied a good deal within it, and the range of positions is suggested.

Security

The view of the American security interest in Asia by those opposing Johnson's position covered a wide spectrum.

There were those, for example, who held flatly that the United States has no vital interest in who controls Southeast Asia. Control by Peking is natural and acceptable. The United States should confine its commitments in Asia either to peoples who share with us a common culture or to the protection of the sea lanes and island states of the area.

Others acknowledged that the United States might have a vital interest in keeping the control of Southeast Asia out of the hands of a single major potentially hostile power. But they asserted the outcome in Vietnam would not determine the control of Southeast Asia either because: a united Vietnam under Hanoi would be independent of Peking; Peking is not an expansionist power and would not move to seek control of Southeast Asia if Vietnam and Laos fell to Hanoi; Thailand, Burma, Cambodia, Malaysia, Singapore, and Indonesia could maintain their independence if Vietnam and Laos fell to Hanoi.

Then there were those who agreed that the loss of all or part of Southeast Asia would be damaging, in some degree, to American security interests, but that the outcome was either impossible to avoid, or could be achieved only at excessive cost in resources expended abroad, domestic programs, and domestic disarray. They tended to argue that, in any case, the loss of the area to a hostile power would not damage American security interests in the more vital parts of the world, notably Europe, Japan, and Latin America.

Pursuing this point of view, it was often asserted that the credibility of the American commitment elsewhere in the world would not be affected if the SEATO treaty was not honored because the treaty, unlike the NATO treaty, calls only for "consultation" in the case of attack. The relevant language of Article IV follows:

> 1. Each Party recognizes that aggression by means of armed attack in the treaty area against any of the Parties or against any State or territory which the Parties by unanimous agreement may hereafter designate, *would endanger its own peace and safety, and agrees that it will in that event act to meet the common danger in accordance with its constitutional processes.* Measures taken under this paragraph shall be immediately reported to the Security Council of the United Nations.
>
> 2. If, in the opinion of any of the Parties, the inviolability or the integrity of the territory or the sovereignty or political independence of any Party in the treaty area or of any other State or territory to which the provisions of paragraph 1 of this Article from time to time apply is threatened in any way other than by armed attack or is affected or threatened by any fact or situation which might endanger the peace of the area, the *Parties shall consult immediately in order to agree on the measures which should be taken for the common defense.* [Author's italics]

Finally, there was the New Left position: that authentic American security interests in Asia, as elsewhere, are nonexistent, but are simply fabricated by the economic and other vested interests of the private and public bureaucracies that control American life. Therefore, the defeat of the United States in Southeast Asia is required to destroy the grip of these institutions so that American society can move forward, restructured, on a more humanistic basis.

MORALITY

THIS array of positions on America's security position in the world was linked in debate to a parallel array of assertions about the moral aspects of Johnson's policy in Southeast Asia. It was asserted that a whole series of actions by the executive branch of the American government negates the moral commitments of the United States under the SEATO treaty and the Southeast Asia [Tonkin Gulf] Resolution of August 1964 and lift from

Hanoi its responsibilities under the Geneva Accords of 1954 and 1962. For example, the United States did not insist on the Vietnamese election of 1956 envisaged at Geneva in 1954; there was no second attack on August 4, 1964, and, thus, the legal and moral basis for the Southeast Asia Resolution is flawed; American air and other operations in Laos balance Hanoi's violation of the Geneva Accords of 1962.

On less formal grounds, some felt American use of air power, artillery, and herbicides, and atrocities committed by Americans fighting in Vietnam, have caused such damage and represent such violations of moral behavior that it would be better for the people of South Vietnam to be taken over by Hanoi, whatever the consequences, than to achieve independence by such methods at such cost.

This view was often linked to certain political propositions: that the United States was intervening immorally in a domestic civil war in Vietnam; and that the only authentic nationalist political force in Vietnam is the communist government in Hanoi and the Communist party in Indochina, which it leads. The United States was thus viewed as trying to save an inept and corrupt regime of its own creation: aside from the fact the effort would fail, it was judged morally wrong to try.

In various combinations and formulations, the anti-Vietnam position represented, in typical American style, an argument in which the nation's security interests and moral values appeared to converge in ways that justified American withdrawal of commitment and effort from Vietnam and Laos, leaving the outcome to the forces at work within the area itself, including the continued supply of arms and economic aid by communist capitals to Hanoi.

There were within the Johnson administration differing formulations in support of the President's policy, as well as some dissidence; but Johnson's position can be set out in something like these parallel terms.

Security

The United States has a vital and abiding interest that Southeast Asia not pass into the control of a single potentially hostile power. The SEATO treaty correctly reflects that interest. Moreover, if the United States withdrew its commitment to the area, it would, in extremis, later recognize its interest and re-engage in vastly more dangerous circumstances. As Johnson puts it in *The Vantage Point*:

> I was too young at the time to be aware of the change in American mood and policy between the election of Woodrow Wilson in November 1916 ("He kept us out of war") and our reaction to unrestricted German submarine warfare in the Atlantic in April 1917. But I knew the story well. My generation had lived through the

> change from American isolationism to collective security in 1940–41. I had watched firsthand in Congress as we swerved in 1946–47 from the unilateral dismantling of our armed forces to President Truman's effort to protect Western Europe. I could never forget the withdrawal of our forces from South Korea and then our immediate reaction to the Communist aggression of June 1950.
>
> As I looked ahead, I could see us repeating the same sharp reversal once again in Asia, or elsewhere—but this time in a nuclear world with all the dangers and possible horrors that go with it. Above all else, I did not want to lead this nation and the world into nuclear war or even the risk of such a war.[13]

Johnson was also quite explicit about the process he feared would be set in motion in Southeast Asia by the loss of South Vietnam. At San Antonio in September 1967 he said:

> I cannot tell you tonight as your President—with certainty—that a Communist conquest of South Vietnam would be followed by a Communist conquest of Southeast Asia. But I do know there are North Vietnamese troops in Laos. I do know that there are North Vietnamese trained guerrillas tonight in northeast Thailand. I do know that there are Communist-supported guerrilla forces operating in Burma. And a Communist coup was barely averted in Indonesia, the fifth largest nation in the world.
>
> So your American President cannot tell you—with certainty—that a Southeast Asia dominated by Communist power would bring a third world war much closer to terrible reality. One could hope that this would not be so.
>
> But all that we have learned in this tragic century suggests to me that it would be so. As President of the United States, I am not prepared to gamble on the chance that it is not so.[14]

Stable peace in Asia as a whole was thus seen to depend on the defeat of Hanoi's aggression against Laos and South Vietnam; and the United States was judged to have abiding interests in the stability of Asia where two thirds of humanity live.

A failure to honor fully American commitments in Asia would, in Johnson's view, damage gravely the credibility of American commitments elsewhere. In Dean Rusk's often repeated formulation, approved by Johnson: "If our adversaries find our word is not good in Southeast Asia, they are unlikely to stay their hand elsewhere."

MORALITY

JOHNSON, and those who supported him, believed that morality, as well as national interest, required that we honor our treaty commitments in Asia and the cumulative policies of three Presidents based on these commitments.

Men and governments have built their lives and policies on those commitments. American withdrawal from them would be profoundly dishonorable. As for charges that certain U.S. actions had negated the moral basis of our intervention in Vietnam:

> The United States and South Vietnam never committed themselves to the 1956 elections; and well-documented events in North Vietnam between 1954 and 1956 fully validated their reservation.
>
> Absolutely reliable intercepts and other hard information confirmed the second attack in the Tonkin Gulf of August 4, 1964, and the record of congressional consultations and the published Senate debate make clear that Congress knew precisely the wide scope of the Southeast Asia Resolution of August 1964.
>
> The United States fully honored the Laos Accords when they went into effect in October 1962; Hanoi did not. American air and other operations in Laos were undertaken only after the continued presence of North Vietnamese forces in Laos, in violation of the agreements, was confirmed; after the continued use of Laos as a transit corridor for men and supplies to be deployed against South Vietnam was confirmed; and with the agreement of Souvanna Phouma, installed as Prime Minister as the result of the Geneva negotiations of 1962.

The human and physical costs of the war in Vietnam were, of course, recognized as real and tragic, as in all wars. But American forces operated under, and by and large have strictly obeyed, severe restraints on the use of military power. The damage done by the use of herbicides is clearly exaggerated.[15] More fundamentally, despite the costs and casualties imposed on the South Vietnamese by the communists and the course of the battle, they chose to fight for their independence of Hanoi, raising and arming well over a million men in a population of 18 million—the fourth largest army in the world. These men could not fight—nor could the communists—if arms were not supplied from outside the area. Those of this mind concluded that since the United States made a commitment to support the struggle against the North Vietnamese invasion, and the people of South Vietnam committed their lives and their future to the struggle on the basis of the American commitment, it would be immoral for the United States to decide unilaterally to withdraw on the grounds that the pain suffered by the South Vietnamese exceeded the benefits of an independent future.

The Johnson administration recognized, of course, that there was an element of civil strife within South Vietnam; but the struggle was externally directed, supplied, and supported by illegal (mainly) South Vietnamese re-infiltrators down to 1964; and then, by regular units of the North Vietnamese armed forces. Overwhelming evidence, including communist assessments of the period 1954–1958, indicates the communist movement in the South could not and would not have mounted an effective struggle without illegal support from Hanoi. Despite its civil element, the struggle in Vietnam was as much a struggle against external aggression as the war in Korea of 1950–1953.

The government and political life of South Vietnam were judged to be rooted in an authentic nationalism. Its problems and evolution parallel closely that of other former colonial states; e.g., South Korea. Its performance since 1965, including the introduction of a significant degree of constitutional democracy, exceeds that of most postcolonial nations. By any objective standard, it can claim a higher degree of democratic legitimacy than the single-party dictatorship Ho installed in Hanoi between 1954 and 1956, a period whose terrors are well documented and acknowledged by the communist leadership at the time.

Those who supported Johnson felt, then, an authentic convergence of American security interests with a sense of moral legitimacy.

THE INTELLECTUALS

A good many American intellectuals have played a lively role in the anti-Vietnam movement and the cast of their argument deserves a special word.

The word "intellectual" is difficult to define. Irving Kristol has produced an apparently ironic but serious definition: "An intellectual may be defined as a man who speaks with general authority about a subject on which he has no particular competence."[16] Kristol's point is that a significant segment of the American intellectual community holds to a definable ideological vision, independent of special fields of professional specialization; and it has been prepared to apply that vision to public policy, including policy toward Southeast Asia.

Kristol defines the prevailing American intellectual tradition as rooted in "two profound commitments: to 'ideals' and to 'the people.' It is the marriage of these two themes that has made the American mind and given it its characteristic cast—which might be called *transcendentalist populism.*"[17]

The commitment to "ideals" makes it difficult for intellectuals to accept the role of power in domestic as in international affairs, except under special circumstances. The intellectual would like the world to be a place in which his particular skill—the logical elaboration of ideas—holds sway, and in which the role of raw power is minimized, unless power is linked to the ideas he supports. And, indeed, a world where conflict is settled by the arbitration of logical debate rather than resort to military force or other forms of raw power might be vastly more congenial than the one we know. The attraction of Adlai Stevenson to intellectuals was, in part, his image as being somehow above politics, just as the initial intellectual reaction to John Kennedy, who patently reveled in politics, was generally negative. It only turned favorable as it appeared he might be a vehicle for bringing to life and action certain ideas favored by intellectuals.

As for "the people," intellectuals are prone to accept the claim of those who raise banners in their name. As Kristol puts it:

> Is it conceivable for American intellectuals ever to approve of their government suppressing, or helping to frustrate, any popular revolution *by poor people*—whatever the nature or consequences of this revolution? The answer would obviously have to be in the negative; and the implications of this answer for American foreign policy are not insignificant. This policy must work within a climate of opinion that finds the idea of a *gradual* evolution of traditional societies thoroughly uninteresting—which, indeed, has an instinctive detestation of all traditional societies as being inherently unjust, and an equally instinctive approval, as being inherently righteous, of any revolutionary ideology which claims to incorporate the people's will.[18]

It was easy, from this ideological base, for a good many intellectuals to view the American action in Southeast Asia as an "imperialist" and illegitimate use of power, while viewing the communists with active sympathy.

In this, American preachers, men of letters, academics, and journalists were repeating a familiar pattern of reaction that accompanied the War of 1812, the Mexican War, the Spanish-American War, and the aftermath of the First World War. (In the Civil War, those in this intellectual tradition tended to be abolitionist hardliners.[19]) And, as Dexter Perkins noted in the *Yale Review* of June 1951, historians in this tradition tend to conclude "that the foreign policy of the United States has been almost uniformly inept; that every war in which this country has been engaged was really quite unnecessary or immoral or both; and that it behooves us in the future to pursue policies very different from those pursued in the past."[20]

In the case of Vietnam, this perspective was heightened by some of those with human or scholarly ties to China. Out of their knowledge of history, they shared an understandable sense that China has suffered greatly since the 1840s in its contacts with the more advanced nations of the West and Japan; that it was the seat of a mighty culture; and that, somehow, it would not be a bad outcome for the smaller states of Southeast Asia to fall under Chinese dominance.

Against this background, Johnson's strategy in Vietnam raised a particular problem. Central to the outcome was the laborious process of political, economic, and social development in a postcolonial nation. A few Americans, including American academics, understood this process and had studied it with objectivity and human sympathy in other settings; for example, Samuel Huntington, Henry Kissinger, Ithiel Pool, Lucian Pye.

They and other professional political scientists interested themselves in Vietnam, visited there, and made constructive suggestions. Most American intellectuals, however, including a great many journalists and commentators, had spent little time in the study of political development and tended to approach Vietnam in terms of concepts derived from American or European intellectual life. The substantial, if not predominant, role of the military in the political life of most developing nations was taken in Vietnam to be a pathological result of American intervention. The endemic problem of corruption in poor nations making their way from orientation to family and clan to nationhood was taken as a sign of peculiar evil. South Vietnam's educational revolution of these years was ignored as were many other indexes of economic and social progress. The quite extraordinary, even unique, effort of the South Vietnamese to install constitutional government during a war was systematically denigrated. The slow, hard task of building an effective armed force on a massive scale in a small developing nation was mocked and poorly and unfairly reported. Above all, the response of the South Vietnamese military and civilians to Tet, which literally saved the American commitment to Southeast Asia, was never conveyed by the media to the American people, although it was the basis for Johnson's policy in the balance of 1968 and, subsequently, for Nixon's policy.

And so the difficult, precarious, but serious process of helping the South Vietnamese gradually to build up their own strength, which lay at the heart of American strategy, was never understood or reported with accuracy, except by a very few; and the accepted intellectual cliché was that the government in Saigon was hopelessly corrupt, incompetent, and unrepresentative. The profoundly irrelevant categories of left and right, derived from continental European history in another century, were freely applied: Saigon was right and therefore bad; Hanoi was left, and therefore good.

The Split in the Establishment

THE American establishment in foreign affairs can be traced back to the days of Theodore Roosevelt, Henry Cabot Lodge, Elihu Root, and the doctrines of Admiral Alfred Thayer Mahan. It acquired another generation of men from those engaged at Versailles with Woodrow Wilson; for example, John Foster Dulles and Allen Dulles, Christian Herter, and Walter Lippmann. Proximately, however, the foreign affairs establishment dates from 1940 when Henry Stimson joined the Roosevelt administration and men of both parties took posts of responsibility, accepting George Marshall's 1945 dictum: "It no longer appears practical to continue what we once conceived as hemispheric defense as a satisfactory basis for our security. We are now concerned with the peace of the entire world."[21]

The establishment contained men of many talents, of both parties, from every part of the nation: businessmen and bankers, labor leaders and academics, foundation officials and journalists. They had served in high places and low, on every continent, and were bound together by a conviction that, working with others, the United States could only secure its safety and move the world toward stable peace by active commitment on the world scene. They were an establishment in the sense that the term derives from British life: they systematically supported the chief of state when he led the nation in accepting the burdens of global responsibility.

The predominant interest of this group was Europe. The Second World War was fought with priority given to the defeat of Germany. The principal enterprise in the first five postwar years was the Marshall Plan and the building of NATO. Asia, of course, could not be ignored: the struggle in China and the communist victory of 1949; the Korean War; the troubles in Indochina; the Japanese Treaty. But some of the key decisions in Asia were made substantially in reflex to problems in Europe. The decision to fight in Korea was urged on Truman by some of his principal advisers primarily to deter the Soviet Union in Europe and to make NATO, just coming to life, credible. It was the Korean War that, in effect, created SHAPE, NATO's integrated military command. Truman's financial support for the French in Indochina, despite deep reservations about the viability of its colonial rule, was meant not only to protect the balance of power in Asia, but also to secure French support in the enterprises of the West.

In general, there was much less conviction within the foreign policy establishment that the balance of power in Asia was intrinsically important to the United States than there was with respect to the balance of power in Europe. Many elements contributed to this asymmetry. Large parts of Asia were poor and seemed to lack the technological strength to threaten the United States. Asian cultures seemed alien and remote to some. They did not feel the links to a common civilization which heightened the ties of common security interests across the Atlantic. Deep in the American ethos were images of "Asian hordes," "the Yellow Menace," Hindu masses caught up in poverty so deep that nothing the West could do would really help.[22]

In addition, there was a history of American bafflement, frustration, and even failure in Asia. It started, perhaps, with the Boxer Rebellion in China and the painful Philippine guerrilla insurrection after the Spanish-American War, which ended America's brief flirtation with conventional imperialism. Then there was the turning of the Japanese to naked militarism in the 1930s. The long missionary, educational, and cultural courtship with China, and the wartime alliance with the Nationalists, culminated in the communist takeover of 1949. Finally, there were the miseries and frustrations of the Korean War which, for some time, obscured the success achieved in anchoring Japan to the West and in laying the basis for one of the most remarkable success stories of the postwar period: South Korea's economic, social, and political development.

Nonetheless, from 1940 to 1941, when Franklin Roosevelt cut off the flow of oil and scrap metal to Japan as it moved into Indochina, down through the Korean War and the SEATO treaty, the United States recognized that when the chips were down, it had a vital interest in avoiding the seizure of the balance of power in Asia by a single potentially hostile nation. In that spirit, Eisenhower gave his farewell advice to Kennedy on January 19, 1961, to fight, if necessary, for Laos; Kennedy made his decisions in Asia, and flatly reaffirmed the domino theory as late as September 9, 1963; and Johnson reaffirmed his policy and bore the heavy burden of seeing it through. The public opinion polls and the votes in the Congress show that view was supported by the American people and their representatives.

But Truman's experiences in Korea and then Johnson's in Vietnam demonstrated that there was a kind of geological fault line that emerged in the establishment as well as in American public opinion when the pressures and costs of commitment in Asia mounted, although the establishment generally supported Truman in his constitutional confrontation with MacArthur, mitigating somewhat its disaffection over the war in Korea itself.

Aside from the historical factors cited above, there was in the 1960s a narrower reason for this asymmetry with respect to Asia. Many of those who came to Washington to work on military problems with Kennedy and stayed on when Johnson became President were products of what I called earlier the bipartisan consensus of the late 1950s. Some had been trained in modern economic theory and knew little of the economics (or politics) of development. Some had been trained, in part, at Oxford or Cambridge; and they knew Europe well. But few had ever studied Asia or set foot on that continent before 1961. In the 1950s they had focused their minds sharply on problems of nuclear deterrence and arms control; on the need for highly mobile conventional forces in a nuclear world; on how to reorganize the Pentagon and the military budget to produce a rational force structure. And when they took posts of responsibility, they felt comfortable with this array of problems, even in such acute forms as the Berlin and Cuba missile crises of 1961–1962.

But they found themselves caught up overwhelmingly in a problem for which they were ill-prepared—guerrilla warfare—in a region where their knowledge was shallow, in a setting of postcolonial political development that few had studied deeply or personally experienced. They could and did skillfully help to organize the movement of conventional forces to Asia and their supply. But they experienced cumulative frustration in confronting the men in Hanoi, whose belief in the doctrines of protracted war was heightened by their prior experience with the French. The inherently slow, erratic, and often frustrating process of political development in South Vietnam did not interest them greatly and, when the fortunes of their government's enterprise became dependent on it, they were, again, frustrated and irritated by the pace at which things could move and by the behavior of allies whose political setting and problems were so alien to their own. And so, also, with the pace at which the ARVN could improve.

Their view of the war was influenced by a type of debate familiar to those who have worked in either intelligence or academic life. They felt the judgments of the military were both unscientific and overoptimistic. Instead of constructing an alternative, systematic analysis of the course of the battle, they tended to do something more limited, but wholly legitimate; that is, to debate critically the views (or believed views) of the military. A kind of vested interest in pessimism gradually grew up among some of the Pentagon civilians in 1966–1967. Its most serious consequence, however, was not merely skepticism, for that, if not overdone, is useful in a wartime headquarters, but a failure to follow closely in the period November 1967–January 1968 the intelligence on the winter–spring offensive. As a result, the Pentagon civilians were peculiarly shaken and disoriented by the Tet offensive of 1968. They produced evaluations at a critical moment that were grossly at variance with the day-to-day evidence flowing in from Westmoreland and Bunker in the field. The Pentagon civilian assessments were viewed at the time as excessively pessimistic by Johnson,[23] and they are patently so in retrospect.[24] These misinterpretations not only affected the judgment of some high officials, but also seeped out to the Washington press corps in the osmotic social life of that small company town.

All these elements played a part in the fact that the Tet offensive, as it was interpreted in the press and some parts of the government, opened up a chasm in the foreign policy establishment with important consequences in the Congress and the media. The line of division was basically between those who regarded the fate of Asia and the balance of power there as intrinsically important to the United States, and those who had supported the President's policies in Southeast Asia primarily on the grounds that a failure to honor treaties in that part of the world would affect the security structure in Europe and the Middle East. The line was real, if not always sharp, or even wholly conscious.

Johnson, Rusk, and some others (including myself) had long since concluded that the fate of Asia and, in particular, the balance of power in Asia were intrinsically important to the United States—looking to the future, as important as the balance of power in Europe. And some members of the establishment shared that view.

Johnson, and those who supported him in the post-Tet crisis of opinion, were also influenced, of course, by the global repercussions of an American failure in Southeast Asia. But his steadiness arose from a deeply rooted concern with Asia and the meaning of its future for the security of the United States. He was always conscious that something like two thirds of humanity lived in Asia, a proportion that would, if anything, rise with the passage of time. He understood that, though the standards of living there were low in comparison with Europe, modern technology was being rapidly absorbed. Like Kennedy, he was sensitive to the long-run meaning of Mao's decision to build a national nuclear capability. Having lived with the inner architecture of the nonproliferation treaty, he knew that American steadiness in Asia was the primary counterweight to the impulse of India and Japan to manufacture nuclear weapons in the face of a nuclear China. He knew well how close South Vietnam and Indonesia had come to communist takeover in 1965. He had talked privately and solemnly with almost every Asian noncommunist chief of government, and each had impressed on him the consequences for his country of an American withdrawal of commitment to Southeast Asia. Day after day he followed the intelligence on communist operations in Laos and Thailand, Burma and Malaysia. The domino theory was not a bookish abstraction, but a living network of interconnections decreed by geography, by history, by evident communist activity, and by the balance of forces at work in Southeast Asia.

There was still another dimension to Johnson's view and the opposition to it. I heard him several times tell the story of a conversation with a well-known senator in the small room just off the Oval Office. Arguing against Johnson's policy in Vietnam, the senator put his hand on the President's knee and said: "Lyndon, they're not our kind of people." Johnson, in telling of the encounter, said that he understood at that moment more clearly than ever before the depth of his own commitment. Asians, he said, were just as much our kind of people as Europeans: they cared about their families, they wanted good food, education, and health for their children; they wanted independence for their countries and peace in the world around them. This was the strand of human empathy for the travail of Asia that had emerged when I had first heard him speak in support of foreign aid in 1961 and the impulse that led him to insert in his Honolulu speech of October 18, 1966, a long autobiographical passage on the transition in his own approach to Asia.[25]

Johnson's transition in his attitude toward Asia was closely related to his transition toward the problem of race in the United States. Embedded in the opposition to Johnson, there was a distinct racial component whose weight is difficult to estimate and distinguish from other factors. The attitude erupted in phrases referring to Vietnam as a "remote and alien country"[26] or in passages like this from an interview with Eugene McCarthy:

> I asked him the final question about Vietnam: "How are we going to get out?" He said "Take this down. I said that the time has come for us to say to the Vietnamese, We will take our steel out of the land of thatched huts, we will take our tanks out of the land of the water buffalo, our napalm and flame-throwers out of the land that

scarcely knows the use of matches. We will give you back your small and willing women, your rice-paddies, and your land."

He smiled. "That's my platform. It's pretty good, isn't it?"[27]

To Johnson South Vietnam was a struggling postcolonial nation, its farmers eagerly adapting to new rice seeds, the chicken revolution, chemical fertilizers, small tractors, diesel pumps, radios, television, and motorcycles. South Vietnam was going through a revolution in education and land tenure, politics, and its view of itself and the world outside. It was, to him, a young, modernizing nation with familiar growing pains, suffering a cruel invasion that required the mobilization of more than a million men. South Vietnam produced no military equipment. But the withdrawal of American steel and tanks and napalm would not lead to a quiet lapsing back to the peaceful round of life of a stagnant traditional society; it would lead to a takeover by Hanoi, amply supplied with modern arms from other sources.

The women of Vietnam are small and, no doubt, as willing as women in other lands, although Vietnamese society had traditionally allowed a major, active role for women; but they, too, were undergoing a revolution as they struggled to bring up their families in an environment both dangerous and modernizing, as the proportion caught up in urban life increased, urban communications with the countryside intensified, and the role of women in the society expanded under the pressures of both war and an educational revolution.

The point here is not to assert the correctness of one view or the other —although my perspective is quite clear—but to identify conflicting images, rarely brought to the surface and examined critically. These images lay embedded in a debate that not only split off a significant portion of the intellectual community from the government, but also, to a degree, split the government itself—the executive as well as the congressional branches —and a foreign policy establishment that had, by and large, maintained its unity in support of a succession of Presidents from 1940 to 1968.

The Dissident Youth

In this schismatic process the anti-Vietnam young played a special role. As a favorite target, I am something of an expert on their views. As a public servant, I took part in teach-ins and visited universities around the country on a number of occasions—both private and public—where Vietnam was the inevitable focus of questioning and discussion. In Washington I had many quiet, if impassioned, discussions in my home, as well as discussions at American University (where my wife taught), beyond the reach of the press or television. Since January 1969 I have had literally scores of such meetings in many parts of the country, in large groups and small, many lasting up to three hours, some running five or six.

The first thing to be said is that student views on Vietnam are just as wide-ranging and subject to variation and nuance as those of everyone else.

The second thing to be said is that by and large there is much less difference in the pattern of views among the young (as opposed to other age groups) than is often supposed. This impression, strongly borne in on me from personal experience, is now well documented.

> Another generally accepted impression about public opinion is that the younger generation has been the vanguard of discontent and frustration. The assumption has been that the younger generation has been represented in the wave of protests across the country.
>
> However profound the protests of students have been, the data suggest that those under 30 years differ little from the population as a whole in either their reaction to events or their basic views about what should be done in Viet-Nam.
>
> In Gallup's three-alternative question asked in November 1966, differences between age groups were hardly significant:

	21–29	30–49	50 & over
Begin to withdraw its troops	17%	15%	20%
Carry on the present level of fighting	24	17	16
Increase the strength of its attacks against North Vietnam	55	60	51
No opinion	4	8	13

> As late as May 1970, age differences in the Gallup four-alternative question are hardly noticeable:

	21–29	30–49	50 & over
Withdraw all troops from Vietnam immediately	23%	22%	25%
Withdraw all troops by the end of eighteen months	29	25	23
Withdraw troops but take as many years as needed to turn the war over to the South Vietnamese	32	31	30
Send more troops to Vietnam and step up the fighting	11	16	11
No opinion	5	6	11[28]

Cantril has documented carefully the proposition that variations in views on Vietnam have been somewhat less subject to level of education than many have thought[29]; but also that the less educated have been somewhat more dovish, less volatile and suggestible in their views than the more educated.

Nevertheless, the views of the young Vietnam dissidents have been significant in a number of ways. They assumed violent and photogenic forms capturing a volume of journalistic and television attention disproportionate to their statistical weight in the balance of opinion. Linked as they often were to New Left doctrines critical of the whole structure and institutional life of the United States, they raised wide-ranging questions about the appropriate future directions for American society that transcended the war in Vietnam. In a society long remarked as vulnerable to the worship of youth, these views had a disproportionate and unsettling impact on some, not least on some who bore governmental responsibilities in both the executive branch and the Congress. But, above all, the methods of violence sometimes used, coming at a time of increased concern with urban riots and a rise in the crime rate, helped push the balance of American political sentiment toward a heightened priority for law and order over other dimensions of political life.

In my experience there is a particular pattern in the way the anti-Vietnam youth argue their case and respond to debate.

A typical discussion begins with the set of moral propositions set out beginning on page 486: the setting aside of the election of 1956, the corrupt government in Saigon, the Vietnam struggle as a civil war, etc. When these are patiently countered, or set in a different perspective, the bulk of the students will by no means necessarily agree, but it becomes evident that they are conscious of having derived their initial arguments secondhand, they realize that their initial case is at least arguable, and there is a tendency to move on. A moment of truth comes, perhaps an hour or more into the debate. Someone will say: "But we don't give a damn about what happens in Asia."

A more temperate exchange of views then transpires about the threat that Asia may or may not represent to the United States at present or in the future. The ins and outs of the dominos will be explored and debated; the nature of Chinese interests and intentions in Southeast Asia; the implications of the Sino–Soviet split, etc. Again, from my experience, most students are certainly not promptly persuaded, but two new pragmatic themes emerge. First, someone will ask: "If Southeast Asia is all that important to the United States, why didn't we use all our military power and get it over?" I have had that question put to me on a good many occasions by the most orthodox of student dissidents: barefoot, beads, ragged jeans, peace symbols, and all. Second, they ask: "If the future of all Asia is at stake in Vietnam, why haven't Asians done more to support the struggle?"

When these matters have been explored, I have been inclined to pose a question independent of the views being debated; that is, the tendency of the United States, since 1916–1917, to oscillate between isolationism and engagement, acting decisively only late in the day, after the other side had committed itself to expansion and the balance of power in Europe or Asia was actually endangered. The typical—and wholly legitimate—question at the end of that sequence is: "But will we react that way again?"

At that point, many hours along, the debate is likely to shift to domestic matters of lesser contention.

I describe this stylized generalization of personal experience simply to make a point I know to be true: the view of the typical student antiwar dissident was more complex, less monolithic, and less confident than his initial debating posture would suggest, when it was quietly explored in private.

My specific conclusions about young anti-Vietnam dissidents (putting aside the small hard core of professional or semi-professional agitators) are these:

Lacking in their own lives any visceral sense of the case for collective security, they are drawn strongly to arguments that would reject a war that might distort or destroy their own lives and that, on the face of it, does not appear to involve a direct and immediate threat to American security. Shocked—and properly so—by the ugliness of war, they are strongly drawn to views that would assert the war is immoral as well as unnecessary. The defection of a substantial part of the intellectual community and the split in the establishment on Vietnam provided the young dissidents with specific arguments and a sense of legitimacy in taking a vigorous if not violent antiwar position.

On the other hand, they are conscious that their arguments are second-hand, derived from members of the older generation and they are less confident of their ground than they often appear. More deeply influential than they would like to admit, given the idealistic cast of their overt case, is the fact that the war has been protracted and thus far inconclusive. They are profoundly ignorant of Asia and vulnerable to the image of a dynamic China surrounded by stagnant United States puppets. They lack almost totally a sense that an authentic nationalism exists in South Vietnam, Laos, Cambodia, and the other parts of Asia and are equally ignorant of the movement forward in economic and social modernization. They are more uneasy about the potential future threats to the United States from Asia than they easily acknowledge. They lack almost universally a sense of the connection between the nonproliferation treaty and the reliability of American commitments in Asia. They may initially respond to the point with the question: Why shouldn't everyone have nuclear weapons? But this is not a position they hold with conviction.

In general, the student anti-Vietnam position, at the peak of the Vietnam debate, was a variant on that of the intellectual dissidents; but, in the end, less moralistic, more groping and uncertain.

A CONCLUSION ABOUT THE DEBATE

IN writing this book I have read and re-read as objectively as I could the views of those who opposed or came to oppose Johnson's policy in Southeast Asia. As I have tried to suggest, that opposition, formed in the minds of many men with differing values and views of the world, was articulated in a variety of ways. Since the issue was one of war, with men dying every day, much of the debate was understandably impassioned. Positions were often asserted in the most evocative and persuasive language the debater could summon rather than developed in an orderly and coherent way.

Putting aside pro-communist positions, I would conclude that the heart of the debate centered on two questions capable of reasonably dispassionate analysis. First, was there an authentic South Vietnamese (or Lao or Cambodian) nationalism that deeply opposed Hanoi's effort to take over the French colonial empire in Asia, or was the nationalist strand in the North Vietnamese effort the only serious political element in play? This was Kennedy's critical question as he made his dispositions toward the close of 1961. It remains a critical question.

Second, does the SEATO treaty correctly reflect an abiding interest of the United States? This question, in turn, poses three underlying issues: does the fate of Southeast Asia hang on the outcome in Indochina? Will the fate of Southeast Asia significantly affect the balance of power in Asia? Does the balance of power in Asia matter greatly to the United States?

Under differing circumstances, six successive American Presidents between 1940 and 1972 painfully answered these three questions affirmatively. With greater or lesser clarity, the anti-Vietnam position would render a negative verdict.

The critical issue that emerged from these differing perspectives was never joined: those holding the anti-Vietnam position were, in the end, content to accept whatever consequences flowed from American withdrawal from Southeast Asia, in the name of peace; Kennedy and Johnson believed the outcome would be a larger war.

Vietnam and the American Style

The Vietnam debate, with all its dramatic manifestations, heightened the inherent strain imposed on the national style by the war and the manner in which Johnson conducted it.

In relating the national style to the Cold War more than a decade ago, I made this observation:

> . . . the character of the Cold War, as decreed by Communist strategy and method, has denied us the opportunity to react to national threat in the style with which we were most comfortable; that is, a clean and total switch from peace to a war which could be fought with the widespread conviction that both our interests and our ideals were at stake. We have been forbidden a convulsive once-and-for-all resolution; the nature of modern weapons and the

> strength of the enemy, in the end, eliminated total crusade as unrealistic, despite its evident and understandable temptation as a method. In consequence, we have faced a sequence of dangerous but not definitive crises which force us to explore the character of our abiding interests, the limits of our power, and the limits of our idealism.[30]

Vietnam imposed the most painful and searching strain on the national style of all the major Cold War episodes. This was so for at least five distinct reasons.

First, the crisis confronted by Johnson and the United States in 1965 was not palpably mortal to American interests. It was real enough to Johnson and his advisers, but was not as self-evident to the American public as the Cuba missile crisis, the attack on South Korea, or the blockade of Berlin in 1948–1949, let alone Pearl Harbor or Hitler's conquest of western Europe in the spring of 1940. The alternative to introducing American forces in 1965 as seen by Johnson was a fairly complex sequence of events which was likely to yield a larger war fairly soon. Kennedy had seen the alternative to holding Southeast Asia in similar terms in 1961. But the alternatives facing Johnson were not as easy to project as on some earlier occasions when vital national interests were more visibly challenged.

Second, the form of Hanoi's attack, via infiltration, was less clear-cut than on other occasions of communist military challenge, like the invasion of South Korea.

Third, the method for dealing with the challenge chosen by Johnson was slow-moving. And without a fixed front, the solid progress made in the period 1965–1967 was hard to dramatize. Similarly, the Tet offensive and its outcome were hard to understand and easily subject to misinterpretation. It is fair to add that the massive uninhibited reporting of the complex war was generally undistinguished and often biased[31]; and neither military nor civil authorities were effective in penetrating the daily screen of unhelpful journalism with a clear and persuasive picture of the course of events. The complex interweaving of military, political, social, and economic developments—of short-run crises and slow-moving long-run trends—proved beyond the capacity of the government to synthesize and project.

Fourth, the South Vietnamese government and military forces did not project a clear-cut and attractive image. In part, this was because they were struggling with difficult slow-yielding problems in a postcolonial setting few understood. (The image of South Korea and South Koreans was quite similar in reportage of the early 1950s.) But in part it resulted from a sharing by many American reporters of the biases imputed above to intellectuals.

Fifth, the counterpoint of domestic difficulties, notably the race question and urban violence, strengthened the strands of dissidence among both the restless hawks, who wanted a more forceful military policy, and those who wanted the American effort in Southeast Asia to cease.

The Tet offensive of 1968 thus had converging effects on the components of the national style: to those who had by and large supported Johnson it appeared to deny that the actions taken after the 1965 crisis were solving the problem; and to the opposition it seemed to proclaim that Johnson's policy was failing as well as wrong.

Under these circumstances, the fate of the American stake in Southeast Asia was thrown back on the initial gamble that Kennedy made and Johnson reaffirmed—a gamble on the gathering strength and ultimate viability of South Vietnamese and Southeast Asian nationalism, with the dynamics of life in the communist world a possible reinforcing or weakening component in the equation.

40

Southeast Asia, 1963–1969: A Personal View

Reflections on Southeast Asia, 1963–1966

When Johnson came to the presidency I, as a planner at the State Department, was in a position to follow quite closely the course of affairs in Southeast Asia. But I was not reading the most tightly restricted cable traffic nor did I attend the critical sessions on Southeast Asia with Secretary Rusk or President Johnson. The Planning Council was fully engaged on other matters. Only our continuing work on Asian regionalism and political development bore on day-to-day matters in Vietnam. Nevertheless, we gave a good deal of thought to what was obviously the most dangerous problem on the nation's agenda.

In the wake of the coup overthrowing Diem, I suggested to Rusk that "we consider promptly bringing to a head the issue of infiltration from North Vietnam via both Laos and Cambodia, in defiance of the Geneva Accords of 1962." I urged that we assemble publishable evidence and warn Hanoi either to comply with the Accords or expect retaliatory action against the North. I repeated three propositions deeply engraved on my mind:

> It is difficult, if not impossible, to win a guerrilla war with an open frontier.
>
> Given the inherent political problems of South Vietnam—or any country with so complex and uncertain a political history—we are taking great risks in permitting the war to be prolonged.
>
> Ho Chi Minh's strategy is explicitly based on the fact that he has been able to keep the war going at little cost, no threat to his

industrial complex around Hanoi, playing for time, a political upset in Saigon, and U.S. boredom with the effort.

My next involvement with the subject of Vietnam was at the meeting with Johnson on December 23, 1963, when he outlined to his advisers what he wanted to say in his first State of the Union Message. I suggested that his address should contain reference to the illegal shipment of arms and men across international frontiers by Havana and Hanoi. (Castro had been quite active at that time, notably in his effort to prevent a peaceful Venezuelan election.) Johnson told Ted Sorensen to note and include the point, which was done.

Johnson's reference to the problem in his message of January 8, 1964, was the following:

> In 1964 we will be better prepared than ever before to defend the cause of freedom, whether it is threatened by outright aggression or by the infiltration practiced by those in Hanoi and Havana, who ship arms and men across international frontiers to foment insurrection.[1]

Following that statement, I discussed with Rusk the advisability of undertaking contingency planning, should Johnson decide to act more strongly against Hanoi. I listed the major headings for a military–political–diplomatic plan in a memorandum of January 20. On February 12 and 13 I raised with Rusk the advisability of an approach to Congress and a congressional resolution; and I outlined the case that could be made to the congressional leaders. Even this early in the Johnson administration word had gotten back to the bureaucracy that Johnson disapproved of Truman's failure to seek a congressional resolution in the Korean War. We understood that, should the occasion arise, he intended to be governed by Eisenhower's precedent in the Formosa and Middle East resolutions, where broad congressional support was sought before policies that might lead to military confrontation were carried out.

With U. Alexis Johnson and William Sullivan taking the lead in the State Department, systematic contingency planning was begun at this time and linked to work in the Pentagon. Because of my long-held and familiar view, I confined myself to helping set the effort into motion and investing in it considerable talent from the Planning Council, including one member profoundly skeptical that South Vietnam could be salvaged.

I soon had occasion to report directly to the President what I had been doing. The occasion was neither important nor propitious; but it is worth recounting because it reveals clearly that the contingency planning of this period in no way reflected a decision by Johnson to engage American forces in Vietnam.

I was on a ski holiday in Aspen. I was called from my bath on March 4, after a long afternoon on the slopes. Without preliminary warning, the voice I heard was the President's. Evidently not told by the White House operator where I had been found, he asked in no uncertain terms what I had been saying to Elie Abel and what was Rostow's "Plan Six." When I told him that I had not heard any broadcasts in Aspen he told me that Abel was reporting that the President was about to adopt Rostow's "Plan Six." The President had never heard of "Plan Six," he was not about to adopt that or any other plan, and he did not want any of his officials lobbying with the press. I told him I had not seen Abel in many months and that I had not been lobbying with the press. I indicated briefly the 1961 origins of Rostow's "Plan Six" (see above p. 278). On returning home, I sent him a note on March 9, restating at greater length what I said on the telephone.[2] I described the planning under way and observed:

> . . . neither with the press nor within your Administration have I been conducting a personal crusade. I have been trying to assure what I presume the taxpayer and you wish me to assure; namely, that contingency plans are prepared in advance of crises so that, in the event, you will have the benefit of the most careful forethought possible.
>
> I do, of course, have convictions about the war in Southeast Asia, which have developed over a decade of experience and thought. I do not believe a guerrilla war can be won with as open a frontier as that which now exists in South Viet Nam. These views I have shared with Secretary Rusk, Secretary McNamara, and General Taylor. I should be pleased to lay them before you if there were an appropriate occasion.
>
> But I wish you to be confident that I am trying to serve as a planner in your Administration, not as advocate of a policy which is not yours.

As planning proceeded, I kept out of Southeast Asia except for a rather despairing memorandum to Rusk on April 23, 1964, entitled "On How Much Flesh and Blood Can Stand: Laos and Vietnam." It tried to evoke the impossible political and human situation in which the leaders of both countries found themselves, fighting without any clear hope, as the international community callously permitted the continued violation of the Geneva Accords of 1962. The analysis concluded:

> In short, in both Laos and Viet Nam our policy of delaying decision or action to force Hanoi's conformance with the 1962 Accords risks posing us with the dilemma, in both Laos and Viet Nam, of either accepting a major setback; or acting vigorously to salvage the situation from a base of apparent political disarray if not disintegration.
>
> We may be saved by some egregious Communist aggressive act in Southeast Asia; but we must reckon that Hanoi, Peking, and (I would guess) Moscow all understand well that in Southeast Asia they

have a game of salami tactics going which has a fair chance of denying to us the lucid basis for reaction we had in the other great postwar crises, from Berlin to Korea to Cuba.

I briefly attended Presidential assistant Bill Moyers' thirtieth birthday party on June 4 in Washington, but had to leave to speak at the Haverford commencement before the President arrived. Moyers and Jack Valenti told me Johnson wished me to set down my views on Vietnam. I spent most of June 6 complying in a fifteen-page single-spaced memorandum, which I sent to Rusk as well as to Johnson. It argued the case for a showdown on the Accords of 1962; defined the stakes as I saw them in Southeast Asia, the Indian subcontinent, and elsewhere; outlined a scenario for action; discussed likely communist reactions. I concluded that no one could promise this course of action would not lead to substantial engagement of U.S. forces in Southeast Asia, but prompt and determined U.S. action might persuade Hanoi to desist. The next day I forwarded, on my own initiative, a draft speech suggesting how a decision to confront the infiltration issue might look in public presentation. Johnson did not respond to the memorandum; but he sent it to the Pentagon for study.

It was at just about this time that Hanoi, surveying the promising situation in Southeast Asia, made the decision to introduce regular North Vietnamese units into battle in the forthcoming winter–spring offensive.

In the months that followed I helped a bit on Johnson's Syracuse speech of August 5, 1964, explaining his reprisal for the second Tonkin Gulf attack—a speech that fully elaborated the reasons for his commitment to the defense of Southeast Asia. It should be carefully read by those who believe Johnson misled the electorate during the campaign period. On November 23, 1964, I sent a memo to Rusk urging the introduction of ground forces into South Vietnam and, possibly, into the Laos corridor, plus the beginning of retaliatory attacks on North Vietnam. I had mentioned in my June 6 memorandum the potentialities of joint economic development of the Mekong Valley. I now added that, if the President decided to move, he should go beyond this point and hold out a vision for Southeast Asia of peace, accelerated economic development, Asians taking a larger hand in their own destiny, and as much peaceful coexistence between Asian communists and noncommunists as diplomacy could generate.

Johnson's attention in the critical period from February to July 1965 was properly fastened on the facts and choices emerging before him, and on the advice of Dean Rusk, George Ball, Robert McNamara, McGeorge Bundy, and General Earle Wheeler in Washington; of General Maxwell Taylor, General William Westmoreland, and Ambassador U. Alexis Johnson in Saigon; of Admiral U. S. Grant Sharp in Honolulu.[3] I had argued since the autumn of 1962 that the longer the delay in facing the violation of the Geneva Accords of 1962, the greater the cost was likely to be. I had failed to persuade Kennedy in 1962; and I failed to persuade Johnson in 1964. I understood—and understand—with compassion why Johnson waited until all hopes short of American military engagement were exhausted. Like his predecessors, Johnson conformed to Tocqueville's dictum: ". . . it is extremely difficult in democratic times to draw nations into hostilities. . . ."[4] This admirable aspect of democracy always carried potential costs in a world where ambitious autocracies exist, and it carries special dangers in a nuclear age. But the pain of deciding that Americans must fight and die is so great—and war itself so ugly in so many ways—that one cannot be sure that any American political leader, no matter how prescient, would have taken a course different from Johnson's. But my nightmare since 1961 had come true; that is, the United States acted to save Southeast Asia late in the day, in a waning situation (see above page 287).

As for my conviction that a prompt effort ought to be made to interdict the infiltration trails on the ground as well as to impose air attacks on the North, I know of no evidence that the matter was considered at a high level in 1965. I raised it in a memorandum to Bill Moyers of February 7, 1965, urging sustained pressure on the North in the wake of the attack at Pleiku. I said the forms of pressure might include—but might go beyond —bombing. The weakness of bombing is that it is both sanguinary and episodic, and, therefore, incapable of being maintained if formal negotiations begin. I argued that naval blockade or the placing of ground forces in the infiltration corridors south of the 18th parallel might be more effective and serve as bargaining counters in a negotiation. In July U.S. ground forces were introduced into South Vietnam at such a precarious and defensive stage of the battle, with an inadequate logistical base, that the possibility of cutting and holding the Laos routes or those in southern North Vietnam had to be set aside for the time being.

What I said in 1965 differed, of course, from 1964, as it became evident that Johnson was facing his crucial decisions on the application of American military power. As early as January 9, 1965, I filed with Rusk and Bundy the outline for a Presidential speech proposing an Asian Alliance for Progress, embracing the then contentious proposal for an Asian Development Bank. Other long-run peacekeeping institutions in Asia were suggested. Some of these thoughts flowed into the stream that yielded Johnson's speech at Johns Hopkins on April 7, 1965, with its conciliatory offer to Hanoi to join in a regional effort to develop Southeast Asia.

In 1965 Johnson opened a channel through which I was urged regularly to address memoranda to him. On September 27, October 23, and December 23 I set out reflections on problems that were to absorb a good deal of my time and effort over the following three years:

the need for the South Vietnamese to begin to generate a long-range plan for reconstruction and development;

the need to develop in South Vietnam a large but not monopolistic political party to embrace the major groups that constitute a majority, and thereby overcome the dangerous fragmentation in Vietnamese politics;

the desirability of establishing an early direct and quiet contact with Hanoi, rather than using intermediaries;

the need to overcome the diffuse character of the bombing of North Vietnam by more systematic and concentrated attack on the transport routes to the South;

the desirability of a systematic attack on the oil and electric power facilities of North Vietnam.

I never believed that bombing operations alone, short of the mass destruction of population, could induce Hanoi to end the war, and I know of no member of the government who ever recommended such mass destruction. I did believe selective systematic air attacks could reduce the weight that Hanoi could bring to bear against the South and could contribute, if other factors moved in the right direction, to shortening the war. What concerned me in 1965 (and for the next two years) was our tendency to use air power in ways that dissipated its effects through attack on too many target systems; for the one solid lesson of the Second World War and after was that concentration of effort was the key to the effective use of air power.

In short, once Johnson made his critical decisions of 1965, my thoughts turned to making the civil and military effort more effective in ways that would bring the war to a satisfactory end at the earliest possible time. Behind each of these lines of thought lay the reflections my planning post had provided. These reflections I brought to the White House on April 1, 1966.

THE WHITE HOUSE, 1966–1967

THE work of a Presidential assistant was, of course, quite different from that of a planner. There is, nevertheless, a high degree of continuity in the suggestions I made to Johnson as his assistant and the perspectives on Vietnam I had generated as a planner.

Economic development planning was a good example. In the wake of the 1966 Honolulu meeting, as the nonmilitary tasks were explored, the need for a Vietnamese planning team naturally emerged. It was headed by Professor Nguyen Dang Thuc of Saigon University. By December 16, 1966, the White House was able to announce that, in response to a request of the South Vietnamese government, David Lilienthal had agreed to organize an American counterpart group. Both Thuc and Lilienthal were at the Guam meeting in 1967. Lilienthal's willingness to throw himself into this joint venture, involving much air travel he found physically awkward, was gallant; and his insistence from the beginning that the Vietnamese be the senior partners in the enterprise, in fact as well as in theory, was wise.[5]

Encouraging the South Vietnamese to build a large but not monopolistic national political party was more complex, more sensitive, and less successful. I discussed it with Ambassadors Lodge and Bunker, as well as with Vietnamese officials on a number of occasions. (When Lodge told me the Vietnamese were reading *The Federalist Papers*, I told him they should not be distributed without a notice like that on cigarette packages: "This prescription for democracy is dangerous if taken without large but not monopolistic political parties.") After his election as President, Thieu moved in the direction of a less fragmented party system. The Tet offensive and its aftermath both postponed political initiatives and created a sense of national unity that made such a coming together of fragmented political groups in a large framework more conceivable.

In similar circumstances, President Park of Korea had used one of his most able and energetic colleagues, Kim Chong-Pil, to build a government party. Thieu found no equivalent colleague. Those who then and later tried to form a government coalition party under Thieu lacked the force and competence to do the job. It might have happened only if Thieu had taken the task in hand himself. The effort failed, and a potentially important stabilizing institution in Vietnamese political life was not created. Vietnamese political life remained fragile and vulnerable at the top, although village and legislative politics progressed surprisingly well on a quite reputable democratic basis.

So far as Asian regionalism was concerned, there was an easy convergence between Johnson's own bent and the ideas I had developed in the Planning Council since early 1962. I had ample opportunity to support this strand in his policy, notably from the time of his trip to Asia in the autumn of 1966 forward. In particular, I worked closely with Eugene Black, whom Johnson appointed to encourage Asian regional development.

Bombing, especially the bombing of North Vietnam, was a major matter for Presidential decision in 1966–1967, as well as of political debate in the United States and abroad. Johnson personally cleared the targets for attack in the Hanoi–Haiphong area. They were systematically argued before him in terms of the military results expected; expected losses of aircraft and men; estimated civilian casualties; and the risks of damage to foreign shipping in the ports.

My view was that the small industrial complex in the Hanoi–Haiphong area could be hamstrung most economically by taking out the electric power installations on which they depended. It was not necessary to attack all the particular plants in the region. I was skeptical that transport bombing in the northern part of North Vietnam (between Hanoi and the Chinese border) could be sufficiently regular and systematic to yield more than a harassing result, achieved at high cost. I thought it best to use strategic bombing in the most limited way possible and to focus on raising the costs of infiltration to the battlefield by concentrated and systematic air attack on the transport routes in the southern part of North Vietnam and Laos.

In addition to electric power, I believed the oil storage facilities in the Hanoi–Haiphong area should be attacked. Clearly, oil storage could be dispersed; but the increased reliance on truck transport for infiltration to the South (which had become massive in 1965) made the harassment of oil supplies an appropriate operation if systematically pursued.

Mine was neither the only nor the most influential voice arguing the case for such operations in 1966. The oil attacks began on June 29; the Haiphong and Hanoi electric power plants were attacked in April and May 1967. There were also attacks on steel, cement, and transport facilities, including those between Hanoi and the Chinese frontier.

As of March 1967, the best estimate in the government was that the air and naval bombardment of North Vietnam had tied up from 600,000 to 700,000 North Vietnamese who were diverted from other tasks to repair, reconstruction, dispersal, and transport programs, and to civil defense activities. The figure also includes about 83,000 military personnel, or 20 percent of North Vietnam's military strength, who were directly engaged in air defense activities, and an additional 27,500 personnel who were indirectly involved.

These diversions of manpower limited North Vietnam's capability for sustained large-scale conventional military operations against South Vietnam. Additionally, air attacks destroyed or inactivated significant percentages of direct military or war-supporting targets, like military bases, ammunition depots, petroleum storage, electric power, radar sites, explosives manufacturing, and communications facilities. And there was ample evidence that the bombing slowed transit to the south and inflicted attrition on men and supplies in transit of up to 20 percent.

There were, of course, costs for this effort: the loss of planes and pilots; the killing of some North Vietnamese civilians; the development of political opposition in parts of western Europe and Japan, as well as among a minority of Americans; and a diversion of attention from the refinement of tactical bombing along the infiltration routes.

On May 6, 1967, with the Hanoi power station on the agenda but not yet attacked, I reviewed my thoughts on Vietnam strategy in general and bombing policy in particular in a memorandum for the President, sent also to my senior colleagues in the government—a memorandum which, in selective quotation and paraphrase, has received some public attention.[6] My conclusion was that the Hanoi electric power plant should be attacked, but from that point on air attacks should be concentrated overwhelmingly in the southern part of North Vietnam and on the Laos infiltration trails; and that the advantages of keeping the large pool of North Vietnam's manpower pinned down in air defense be maintained by occasional attacks in the Hanoi–Haiphong area, if the targets made sense.

I believed that the major advantage of the attacks in the far north—manpower diversion—could be maintained at lower cost, while attacks on the infiltration routes, affecting the course of the battle in the short run, could be made more efficient. Johnson rejected this view on the grounds that an ending of bombing attacks in the Hanoi–Haiphong area would weaken his political support at home and deny him a possible negotiating asset.[7]

It was late in 1966 that the concept of "the barrier" was proposed and accepted. The barrier involved a series of heavily protected strong points in the flat eastern portion of South Vietnam, just below the DMZ, and the use on the western infiltration trails of a variety of sensors which would permit countermeasures against infiltration to be more effective. I supported the concept on two grounds: that any method that promised a significant reduction in infiltration was worth trying; and that the technology involved might be extremely important in developing postwar monitoring of the frontiers of Vietnam and Laos against renewed infiltration.

With respect to my view that the war could best be shortened by closing off the Laos corridors on the ground or invading the southern part of North Vietnam, I did not press Johnson on these points. By the time I went to the White House he had formed a clear military and political strategy. In a memorandum of May 6, 1967, I summarized that strategy as follows:

> We have been seeking to frustrate the effort by the Communists to take over South Vietnam by defeating their main force units; attacking the guerrilla infrastructure, and building a South Vietnamese governmental and security structure—rural and urban—strong enough to stand on its feet as a reputable independent nation.
>
> To hasten the decision in Hanoi to abandon the aggression, we have been trying to do two other things:
>
> (1) to limit and harass infiltration; and
>
> (2) to impose on the North sufficient military and civil cost to make them decide to get out of the war earlier rather than later.

In the course of 1966 and 1967 the strategy was working, slowly but steadily. Hanoi's strategy was also working, slowly but steadily, in the sense that American support for the Vietnam effort was eroding. This was troubling not only to me but to others, notably McNamara. We talked several times of moves that might, without excessive risk of enlarging the war, force the issue in Hanoi. An important decision bearing on this option was made by Johnson, after discussions over the period April–July 1967.[8]

In April General Westmoreland submitted alternate proposals for expanding American forces in Vietnam: a minimum essential force involving an increase of about 80,000 men and an optimum force involving an increase of about 200,000 men. The latter would permit him to harass the sanctuaries in Laos and Cambodia and to capture the southern part of North Vietnam. Pressed hard by McNamara on how long the war would last in each case, Westmoreland reluctantly estimated: three years with the optimum force; five years with the minimum force.

It was in discussing these alternatives, on April 27, that I indicated to Johnson my preference. It was to invade the southern part of North Vietnam in order to block infiltration routes and to hold the area hostage against North Vietnamese withdrawal from Laos and Cambodia as well as from South Vietnam. On balance, I thought this a more effective way to proceed than going into the difficult terrain of Laos during the dry season, which, in any case, lay a half-year or more in the future. I did not believe Communist China would march the length of Vietnam, risking long supply lines, vulnerable to air and sea harassment, if American forces moved in south of Vinh. Intelligence evaluations supported this assessment. Not only would Hanoi not be anxious to have massive Chinese units on its soil, but every bit of evidence we had in 1967 suggested that the internal struggle over the Cultural Revolution and Peking's anxiety about both the growing Soviet force on its frontiers and its emerging, but vulnerable, nuclear capability would be paramount considerations.

So far as American opinion was concerned, I argued that it would be difficult to justify further large increases on a more-of-the-same basis. An effort to force a conclusion to the war was desirable.

I went to the map set up in the Cabinet Room of the White House and briefly made this case. Westmoreland indicated he had developed contingency plans for such an enterprise. He talked also of the weather factors that would affect the timing of such an invasion and of the forces required. Johnson took it all in and bided his time, chewing over the problem for many weeks.

In the end, McNamara, Wheeler, and Westmoreland agreed on an increase of some 45,000 men, well below the minimum figure. As Johnson makes clear, fears of enlarging the war played a large role in his refusal to expand forces beyond that level or to use them outside South Vietnam.

I believed then—and believe now—that those fears were exaggerated, but in a matter of this kind I felt a profound reticence in pressing the case. First, in a nuclear age the margins of error should not be estimated too fine. Second, Johnson had an acute ear and a remarkable memory: repetition was not required. Third, and above all, the positions of a President and an adviser are quite distinct. The best formulation of the problem was Rusk's. He used to say: "If I urge a course of action on the President, he adopts it, and things go wrong, I can call up and say 'Sorry, sir,' resign, and disappear. The President must live with his decisions and their consequences."

I did not withhold my opinions from Johnson on this or any other question, but I did not press or lobby. I worked cheerfully within the framework of the decisions he made because I believed the basic thrust of his policy was right.

The aspect of Vietnam that absorbed far more of my working time than any other was dealing with negotiating initiatives or alleged negotiation openings. Johnson lists in an appendix in *The Vantage Point* some seventy-two such pieces of business between June 18, 1964, and the opening of the Paris peace talks in May of 1968. Of these, forty-three took place when I worked at the White House. Some took relatively little time or Presidential attention. Others generated thick cable files, in which every significant American communication was carefully guided and controlled by Johnson after interdepartmental staffwork.

Working with me on this and other aspects of Vietnam in 1966–1967 were two first-class men with long experience of the American diplomatic position and the negotiation process: William Jorden and Robert Ginsburgh. I had been working with Jorden, in one way or another, since early 1961. He was the senior man on the NSC staff for Far Eastern problems, with a rare historical and human knowledge of Asia and Asians. Ginsburgh, a scholarly Air Force officer with a temperate and sure judgment, was White House liaison with the Joint Chiefs of Staff; but he had also served with me on the Policy Planning Council, and done special work on negotiating problems in a State Department committee. He was in every sense a full member of the NSC staff as well as a liaison officer. Like-minded in our view of Asia and the abiding character of the American interest in Asia, with years of common experience behind us, we were a congenial team.

We had concluded that a negotiated settlement, if it came, was likely to have two tracks: an American negotiation with Hanoi on the terms of mutual U.S. and North Vietnamese troop withdrawals from the area; and a negotiation among South Vietnamese concerning the terms on which those supporting the Viet Cong would enter South Vietnamese political life. Given Hanoi's domination of the Viet Cong, confirmed almost daily by an overwhelming body of reliable evidence, the latter negotiation would, in fact, be between Hanoi and Saigon. But if peace came on terms satisfactory to the United States, we were inclined to believe that Hanoi would prefer to remain in the background in such a negotiation, since the terms available were unlikely to go beyond what was known as the "Greek formula"—an arrangement that had given a place to the communists in Greek political life after the civil war. This meant that South Vietnamese communists could enter constitutional political life as a party, run candidates in elections, and take part in the critical supervising election commission—all this despite the formal bar to communists written into the Constitution. Thieu, in effect, accepted this position, at Johnson's urging.

From the beginning to the end of contacts during Johnson's Presidency, Hanoi took the view, with respect to the first track, that the only relevant negotiating subject was the withdrawal of American forces. With respect to the second, the communist view was what might be called classical, going back, for example, to the method of takeover used in Poland in the period 1944–1947. Knowing (as in Poland) that communists could not win a one-man one-vote election, Hanoi sought an interim coalition government in which their men would hold key posts and be in a position (as in the Polish parliamentary election of February 1947) to rig the results or otherwise take over the country while holding "interim" power.

During 1966 and 1967 the diplomatic networks were filled with suggestions emanating, or allegedly emanating, from Hanoi that a serious negotiating process was possible. In some cases these hopes—expressed through third parties—were encouraged by Hanoi to create an environment of false hope and to try to erode the American negotiating position. In others, there was simply wishful thinking by third parties. When a moment of truth arrived, as it occasionally did, and a clear and authoritative statement of position was required from Hanoi, the North Vietnamese authorities were consistent and candid: they held to terms which, in effect, amounted to unilateral American troop withdrawal and a turning over of power in the South to the communists.

As one after another of these exercises proceeded, Johnson concluded toward the end of 1967 that perhaps the best way to initiate negotiations was within South Vietnam, among South Vietnamese. This was the emphasis in his taped television interview, broadcast December 19, 1967: "The political future of South Vietnam . . . must be worked out in South Vietnam by the people of South Vietnam."[9] And at Canberra, on December 21, he found that Thieu and he agreed on the approach to such a negotiation.

Historians will find that as Johnson doggedly pursued or initiated this long series of fruitless contacts and proposals there were moments of hope as well as skepticism. The rational case for hope was that in 1966–1967 the Viet Cong control of the countryside was being palpably diminished; VC defections were increasing; VC morale and expectations about the outcome of the war were slowly eroding. The long-run political foundations for the communist position in the South were being reduced. In this sense, time was not their friend.

On the other hand, as the war dragged on—with progress slow, real, but hard to dramatize—the political base for the war in the United States was also eroding, although it was temporarily stabilized, and even strengthened, toward the end of 1967. The American scene obviously weighed heavily in Hanoi. For example, I sent to Johnson on December 13, 1967, a report of the interrogation of a relatively high-ranking Viet Cong defector. He had attended a meeting in July 1967 that discussed a resolution passed by the North Vietnamese Communist party some five months earlier.

After reviewing antiwar agitation and racial troubles in America and communist efforts to heighten them, the meeting was informed that "VC policy was that the longer the war continued, the stronger the U.S. doves would become and the VC were, therefore, dedicated to fight at least until the 1968 Presidential election. The VC felt the Johnson administration was losing prestige and President Johnson will lose the 1968 election in favor of a dove candidate."

The waning political base for the war in the United States strengthened my view that we should force the issue on the ground by action against the southern part of North Vietnam or in the Laos corridors. It also influenced those, like McNamara,[10] who by the autumn of 1967 had concluded that some formal and announced stabilization of the American effort plus a bombing halt was required to hold the American political base steady.

It was to the dangers of an improving situation in South Vietnam and to the hopes of increased public disenchantment in the United States that the North Vietnamese addressed themselves in the Tet offensive.

THE TET OFFENSIVE

As the year ended and January unfolded, awareness of the gathering storm shifted in Saigon from intelligence analysis to operational evidence, and, on Westmoreland's part, to operational preparations. Tet became increasingly the likely time for the assault. Johnson has described this period, including his assent to continued bombing in the area of North Vietnam south of Vinh during the Tet truce.[11] Throughout this period, with Johnson's knowledge and encouragement, I briefed the press in detail on a background basis on what was afoot. And there were some strikingly accurate briefings and reports from Saigon, notably those of Hanson Baldwin, published in *The New York Times* of December 26–28, 1967. But the effort to prepare the public was inadequate; and I must assume some responsibility for not urging Johnson to speak out in January as he had to the Australian Cabinet at Canberra in December.

The period from January 30 to March 31, 1968, was as intensive a period of work as any I had known in government. My first task was to help keep Johnson fully informed of events as they unfolded so that he could command an independent feel for what was happening in Vietnam. We were greatly strengthened because Johnson himself was well prepared for the communist attacks at Tet, although the number of cities attacked in the effort to achieve "the great uprising" was a surprise. The White House staff team working on Vietnam was not only prepared, but hopeful that Hanoi's decision to make this extraordinary effort might lead, if it were set back, to a shortening of the war.

For example, I sent this memo to Johnson on February 5:

Monday, February 5, 1968—9:00 A.M.

Mr. President:

Responding to a question from Elspeth [my wife] last night, I explained events in Vietnam as follows.

The war had been proceeding in 1967 on an attritional basis with our side gradually improving its position, the Communists gradually running down: like this

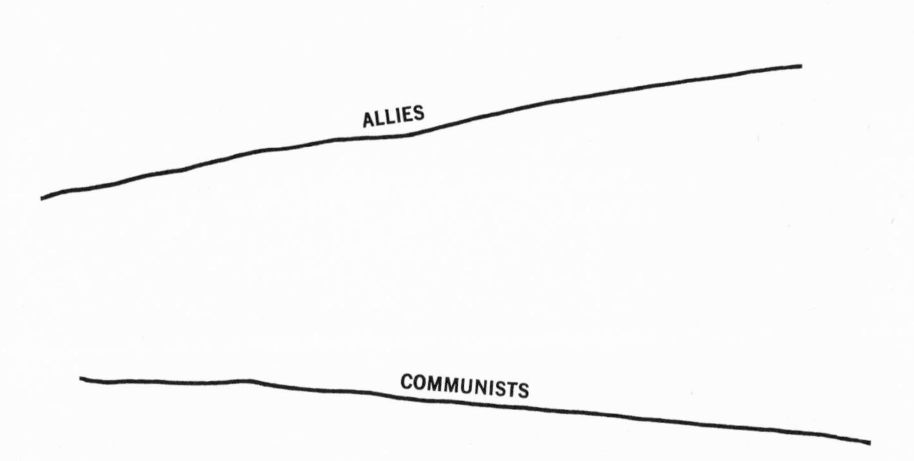

Behind these curves were pools of military forces and fire power which represented the working capital available to the two sides.

As the documents forecast, the Communists decided to take a large part of their capital and put it into:

an attack on the cities;

a frontier attack at Khe Sanh and elsewhere.

In the one case their objective was the believed vulnerability of the GVN and the believed latent popular support for the Viet Cong.

In the other case, the believed vulnerability of the U.S. public opinion to discouragement about the war.

So the curves actually moved like this:

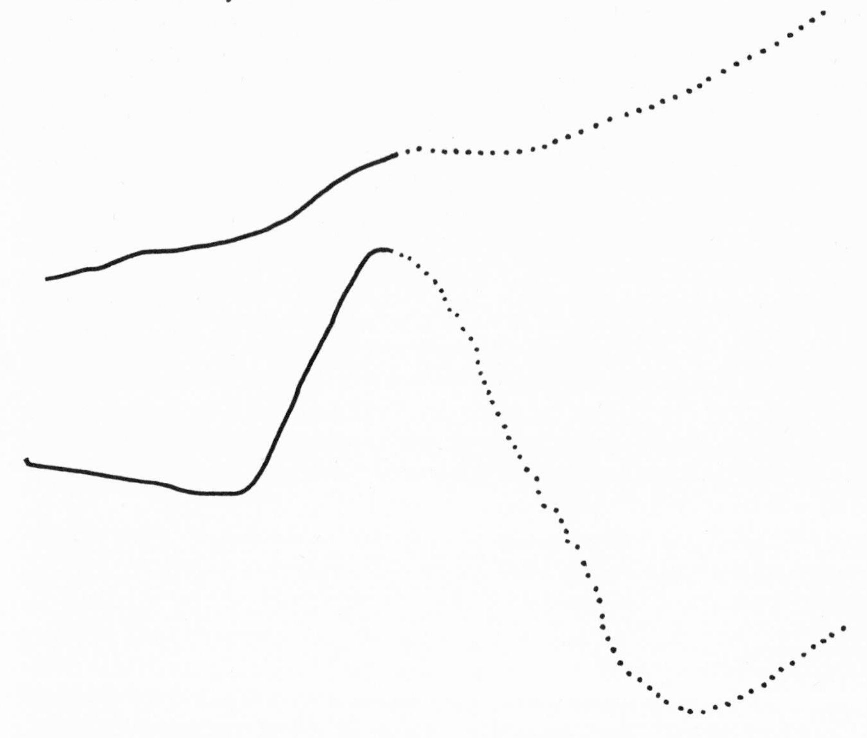

The dotted portions indicate the potentiality if:

the cities are cleared up and held against possible follow-on attacks;

the GVN demonstrate effective political and relief capacity;

we hold Khe Sanh;

we keep U.S. opinion steady on course.

In short, if all on our side do their job well, the net effect could be a shortening of the war.

The news from Saigon was by no means all hopeful from the beginning. The communist forces had got into Hue and had to be rooted out at heavy cost. There was initial alarm about losses of rural population in the Mekong Delta to the communists—estimates that soon proved excessive. There was an immense increase in refugees in Saigon, as well as problems of emergency housing repair, feeding, and garbage collection. And there were the four concerns reflected at the end of my memorandum of February 6, 1968, on which the ultimate outcome depended: frustrating a second attack; performing well in civilian relief; holding Khe Sanh; keeping American opinion steady.[12]

So far as the political and military situation in Vietnam was concerned, it became clear to Johnson and those most responsible for government policy by the second week in February that the Tet offensive had, essentially, failed. The key question became: What could the South Vietnamese and their allies do to exploit that failure, to convert a successful but somewhat disheveled defensive position into forward momentum? It was at this time that Westmoreland requested additional troops, ". . . not because I fear defeat if I am not reinforced, but because I do not feel I can fully grasp the initiative from the recently reinforced enemy without them." By this time also, the South Vietnamese government, supported by a groundswell of popular sentiment, was moving to mobilize an additional 65,000 men—later expanded to 135,000.

It was also about this time, however, that a gap opened up between the assessment of the situation made by, say, Bunker, Westmoreland, and Johnson, and the assessment made by others, in and out of government. *The Washington Post*, for example, published on February 11, 1968, an article written from London by Sir Robert Thompson entitled "Viet Reds' Drive Was a Giap 'Masterstroke,' " which asserted, inter alia: "As for nation-building and pacification, years of work are now in ruins. To start again from scratch with a new approach in a time frame of at least 20 years is not exactly an attractive prospect." The next day, the *Post* reported that one congressman, who heard a secret CIA briefing, "said he drew as grim a picture of the war's progress 'as anything the Kennedys are saying.' " On February 23 *The Wall Street Journal* concluded: "We think the American people should be getting ready to accept, if they haven't already, the prospect that the whole Vietnam effort may be doomed. . . ." Day by day, hour by hour, the television networks projected a portrait of communist strength and a beleaguered American effort, including a precarious position for the men at Khe Sanh. On February 27 some nine million Americans heard Walter Cronkite, after a visit to Vietnam, render his glum verdict: "To say we are mired in stalemate seems the only realistic, yet unsatisfactory, conclusion."

On February 28, as the question of additional troops was posed in Washington, a memorandum, written by Daniel Ellsberg and launched into wide circulation within the government, asserted:

> In terms of our earliest, most ambitious objectives . . . or even, most of our less ambitious goals—I think that the war is over; those aims are lost. I expect the Tet offensive—and those events I am quite sure will follow in the next two months—to have decisive impact on the course of the war, decisively foreclosing most evolutions favorable to us. . . . By that time things are going to get much worse; and then, they will not get better. . . . The TET offensive and what is shortly to come do not mark a "setback" to pacification; it is the death of pacification, as it has been conceived. . . . If Khe Sanh has not already been attacked by then, it will probably be in even

> greater danger than now, with tension increasing. . . . I am forced to predict not only that the "blue" area will contract in the next few months and the "red" zone expand . . . but that the new red on the maps will *never go back*. Not without, say, 400,000 more U.S. troops. . . .[13]

These items catch accurately the deeply rooted pessimism among some that formed part of the setting within which Johnson—who did not share these assessments—made his critical decisions on Vietnam policy in March.

On February 27 Johnson received the Westmoreland–Wheeler preliminary proposal for mobilizing an additional 206,000 men for possible dispatch to Southeast Asia.[14] My initial reaction was to support the proposal. I set down my reasons in a memorandum.[15] The heart of my argument was: "The outcome (say) two months from now of the whole battle since Tet depends on what happens between now and then. If we send some forces now—and Westy knows others are on their way—he will be able to do much more than if he has to work off thin margins." And in the following weeks, in memoranda to Johnson, I included among the options that of forcing the end of the war by movement of American forces into North Vietnam and Laos.

To consider the important question of sending more troops to Vietnam, the President set up a planning procedure that called for me to operate as organizer of data and alternatives for his decision, rather than as an adviser. And that is what I did. I made sure that every facet of the troop decision was canvassed, drafting under Johnson's guidance the February 28 directive that guided the work of the committee headed by Clark Clifford.

The only substantial comment I can recall making in the first meeting of that committee on the afternoon of February 28 was that a sharp distinction should be made between troops that might be made available to Westmoreland before the end of the winter–spring offensive (say, June 1) and those that could only be made available at a later time. The former, I suggested, we ought to provide; the latter proposition ought to be examined with the greatest care, for all its implications.

As the military and political situation brightened day by day, the President came to the decision to throw his weight behind modernizing the South Vietnamese armed forces, and to send only extremely limited additional forces to Westmoreland. I fully accepted his reasons for that course. Perhaps if Johnson had gone to the country in early February to demand a maximum effort to respond to the Tet offensive and to force an early end to the war, an alternative path might have been developed, including the critically important passage of the tax bill required to stabilize the international position of the dollar. But the changing political environment at home and the international financial crisis of March reduced that possibility. The evidence in March was that Johnson could not have gotten the tax increase of 1968 if he had been a candidate or if the Republican leadership in the Congress thought he was a candidate. It appeared to require more bipartisanship than the American political system could manage in an election year. Meanwhile, the improvement in the situation in Vietnam made a costly surge in the American effort less necessary.

As for a negotiating initiative, I had felt for a long time that an initiative should be undertaken in 1968 and the proper time was toward the end of the winter–spring offensive, when the communists had tried their hardest and failed. Several of my memoranda to Johnson of this period mention May as the appropriate time. I confess to a rather complete failure to link the possibility of Johnson's not running to a negotiating initiative. On October 3, 1967, I had heard him tell a group of his senior advisers that he was inclined not to run.[16] On one other occasion in the autumn of 1967, at a small meeting in the Cabinet Room, he reacted sharply when someone referred to his running in 1968. He said: "I don't want any of you to plan in terms of my being a candidate next year." He mentioned to me in November his conversation with Westmoreland about the likely reaction of troops in the field to his not running. After he decided not to make the announcement in his State of the Union message in January, I recall his asking an aide to check the exact date that Truman had announced his withdrawal of candidacy in 1952, because he owed the Democratic candidates at least that much time. I should have circled Truman's date, March 29. But I didn't. I did not relate the clear possibility of his not running to the intense day-to-day business in hand. Except for Johnson himself, I believe only Rusk did.

Nevertheless, as it became clear that Johnson leaned to Rusk's proposition—to try to induce a negotiation by a bombing halt at the 20th parallel—I had less and less reserve about its timing. The military and political situation was clearly improving in March. If Hanoi was going to enter a negotiation on the basis of the outcome in Vietnam of the Tet offensive, the returns were pretty well in by March 31.

It was my impression from intelligence before Johnson's speech, from the prompt response from Hanoi, and from later information from visitors to Hanoi at the time that Johnson's initiative came at a time when the North Vietnamese were just about prepared to launch a negotiating initiative of their own.

The improvement of affairs during March was not clearly projected by the press. The feeling that gripped a good many Americans in February seemed impervious to facts. Technically, the issue in February was the relative staying power of the communist offensive versus the resilience of South Vietnamese civil and military capacities. In March there was no doubt the latter were coming on strong. But this verdict of the evidence seemed difficult even for some in the government to accept[17]; and it certainly did not get through to the group of distinguished outside advisers who met in Washington on March 25–26. With certain exceptions, they came with their minds hardened in pessimism not only about the situation in South Vietnam but, I would guess, even more by their assessment of the impact of Tet on the mood of the country. As I heard their comments around the table in the State Department on the night of March 25, I wrote a note to Dick Helms sitting next to me: "Only the men in the field can save us." And they pretty well did, as the course of the war and pacification in the following ten months demonstrated; although, as indicated in the previous chapter, Tet had longer-run consequences in the United States.

Johnson's decision not to run in no way diminished the intensity of work. In a few days we had a kind of positive response from Hanoi; and then, after a month's test of will over a negotiating site, there was a delegation in Paris to be supported.

It is hard to recapture the peculiar quality of the period from April 1968 to January 20, 1969, as seen from inside the administration. There was the assassination of Martin Luther King and the burning of part of Washington; then the assassination of Robert Kennedy. There was the violence at the Democratic Convention in Chicago. There was also the Soviet invasion of Czechoslovakia and pressure on Romania to which Johnson reacted with a public warning to Moscow.

In the midst of all this Johnson kept himself and his administration focused on efforts to break the negotiating deadlock in Paris; maintain momentum in the pacification drive in South Vietnam; retrieve honorably the *Pueblo* crew from North Korea; move the Middle East cease-fire to negotiation; consolidate the nonproliferation treaty and start the SALT talks with the Soviet Union; manage an efficient transition to a new administration.

We carried forward these pieces of business against a background that sometimes suggested the nation and, indeed, the world community were about to become unhinged. One of my abiding impressions from eight years in Washington is, in fact, how fragile modern civilization is; how close the margin is between minimal order and uncontrolled violence; how much effort by men of good will everywhere must be endlessly expended to preserve the possibility of civilization. That impression was never more acute than in the spring and summer of 1968. The last four months or so of the Johnson administration were quieter and more hopeful, despite the odd but still interesting task of turning things over to men of another party.

In the matter of the war, the major question was the terms that tortuously emerged in Paris for a total bombing cessation. Explicitly, the terms included the acceptance by Hanoi of the GVN as a negotiating partner—a valuable legitimizing of the South Vietnamese political process of 1965–1967. They also included the understanding that bombing could be resumed if there was infiltration across the DMZ or major attacks on cities in the South. In addition, it was understood that aerial reconnaissance of the North would continue.

These conditions on Hanoi fulfilled, and a little more, Johnson's May instructions to the mission headed by Averell Harriman. That Hanoi chose the form of "an understanding" about the resumption of bombing rather than an "agreement" was substantially irrelevant; for we knew from painful experience that any agreement negotiated with Hanoi would be honored only so long as Hanoi judged it to be in its interest. The terms having been set in innumerable formal and private meetings with the North Vietnamese and in full accord with the government in Saigon, his advisers urged Johnson to proceed with the cessation of bombing. We felt we had a duty to the peoples of Southeast Asia, the American and Allied forces in the field, and to the American people to find out if an end to the war on honorable terms was negotiable.

In those days we gave considerable thought to our successors, whoever they might turn out to be. We were anxious to leave them the best situation possible. Johnson's refusal to join Thieu in announcing American troop withdrawals in 1969[18] had given his successor the freedom of action either to use American forces to help force an early decision in Hanoi or to ease domestic tensions in the United States by their phased withdrawal. The progress of the accelerated pacification program, stiffened by Johnson's directive to Abrams of October 29 to conduct a maximum effort,[19] guaranteed the next administration the best possible position in the field on January 20, 1969. And if Hanoi was, in fact, prepared to negotiate, there was the chance, at least, that the heavy burden of war in Southeast Asia could be removed before January 20, 1969.

On the other hand, we knew we were putting the difficult problem before the new administration of resuming the bombing, if Hanoi failed to comply with the understandings that underlay the October 31 decision to halt the bombing of North Vietnam.

In fact, the October 31 decision did not yield a serious negotiating process. And this violated the most fundamental understanding behind the bombing cessation: namely, that serious talks would begin when the bombing had ceased. By no stretch of the imagination did Hanoi engage in "serious talks" in the three and a half years following the bombing halt. On this ground it is my view that Richard Nixon was free at any time he thought necessary to resume the bombing of North Vietnam, quite aside from the gross violations of the DMZ and major attacks on the cities of South Vietnam that led to the resumption of the bombing in April 1972.

In the short run, the bombing halt was, perhaps, a necessary test of Hanoi's willingness to negotiate an end to the war. It may have imposed some inhibition on Hanoi with respect to the DMZ which helped de-escalate the war in the I Corps area for three and a half years. In more subtle ways, it may have contributed to a reduction in the scale of combat in Southeast Asia over that period. Whether a longer perspective will judge Johnson's October 31 decision wise or unwise is moot. It can only be recorded that at the time Johnson and his advisers judged it to be, in Abrams' phrase, "the right thing to do."

In briefing my successor, Henry Kissinger, I underlined one aspect of the situation in Southeast Asia that could easily be forgotten in the focusing of attention on Vietnam; that is, the continued presence of large North Vietnamese forces in Laos and the dangers of a communist thrust to the Thai border on the Mekong. It had been Kennedy's decision to fight the battle for the destiny of Southeast Asia, if it came to that, with South Vietnam, rather than Laos, as the fulcrum. As the expansion of government control in South Vietnam moved forward rapidly in the waning months of the Johnson administration, as the North Vietnamese were pushed back to the borders and the attack on the Viet Cong political infrastructure made some progress, it was clear that Hanoi would have another card to play before the war was over—and Peking, too, quietly engaged as it was in building a road from the Chinese border to the Mekong through northern Laos. That card was to seize all of Laos, bypassing South Vietnam. I passed along to Kissinger such recommendations as I could offer to deal with this contingency (as well as other problems and possibilities) in a memorandum of December 23, 1968.

Asia in early 1969 was a different and more hopeful place than it had been in mid-1965: Peking was moving out of the Cultural Revolution toward more rational domestic and foreign policies; Djakarta was the scene of energetic and intelligent efforts to move forward in economic and social development with the backing of the world community; Singapore, Malaysia, Thailand, the Philippines, Taiwan, and South Korea were more confident that they had a destiny to forge and they were working, along with Japan, Australia, and New Zealand, in a gathering network of regional ventures; Burma, the critical buffer state, was still independent and its chronic guerrilla insurgencies manageable; Laos was still beleaguered, but the Pathet Lao were a much less significant force, and somehow the armed forces of Laos each year contained the dry-season thrust of the North Vietnamese, regained ground in the rainy season, and gradually moved toward a sense of nationhood. Their capacity to fight the North Vietnamese—psychological as well as technical—had improved considerably since the dismal months of early 1961. Cambodia, however, was under greater direct pressure from Hanoi in 1969 than in 1965. The Viet Cong had lost much of their recruiting capacity as well as their control over population and territory in the aftermath of Tet, notably in the Delta. Cambodia thus became an increasingly important route of supply and infiltration for the North Vietnamese forces, which had to carry an increased share of the battle.

On the whole, however, Nixon had important assets in Southeast Asia. He also had an American public more divided than in 1965, and still confused about what had happened at Tet and about the character of American interests in Southeast Asia.

Believing as I did—and had for almost twenty years—that the balance of power in Asia was a vital and abiding interest of the United States, and that it was at stake in the fate of Southeast Asia, I left the White House just before noon on January 20, 1969, with the hope that Nixon would decide to stay the course and that, in so doing, he would find his assets outweighed his liabilities.

41

Johnson as President

As we gain perspective on our times, the 1960s will emerge as a peculiarly difficult and testing decade for the United States and the world community. Life on the planet was being shaped by two overriding issues: the nuclear question and the destiny of the volatile developing continents. There were men in Moscow and Peking, Hanoi and Cairo, Havana, Djakarta, and elsewhere, with clear visions of what they wanted to see transpire. And they moved to bring their sometimes converging, sometimes disparate visions to life. If successful, their efforts would have yielded a world quite different from that of 1972, less hopeful for those who believe in the independence of nations, the possibilities of human freedom, and the cause of stable peace. Despite the diffusion of power from Washington, as well as from Moscow, despite the rising claims of a new agenda in American domestic life, only the United States in the 1960s had the capacity to organize resistance to those efforts and to strengthen the forces making for a more benign outcome. That was Kennedy's mission and Johnson's—and their administrations will increasingly be seen as a continuum. Kennedy took the full brunt of nuclear blackmail, turning it back, while he launched at home and in the developing world a set of new policies and a beginning of the long, slow process of caging the nuclear beast. Johnson carried forward these policies in years of even greater difficulty, facing domestic and foreign crises whose convergence was unique in American history. His time as President was one of tragedy and violence, but also of heroic labors of construction.

Johnson preserved and advanced the national interest in a complex and difficult time. Under his leadership, the balance of power in Asia was held by a painful commitment of American forces, and the basis was laid, through support for Asian regionalism, for its maintenance in the future with a progressively diminished share of effort by the United States. Johnson not only fought the war in Southeast Asia in ways that avoided a nuclear confrontation, but also carried forward the effort to tame nuclear weapons with the nonproliferation treaty, while laying the foundations for the SALT talks and otherwise moving to make U.S.–Soviet relations more rational. He accomplished more in this direction than had previously been achieved—certainly since 1945, perhaps since American diplomatic relations with the Soviet Union were established in 1933.

He held the balance of power in Europe by preventing a disintegration of NATO at a time of temptation to laxness in the wake of the Cuba missile crisis, pressure for fragmentation from de Gaulle, balance-of-payment difficulties, and division in the Atlantic community over American policy in Asia.

At the same time, Moscow's attempt to seize the balance of power in the Middle East was checked by steady U.S. support for both Moslem moderates and Israel and by effective efforts to discourage the engagement of Soviet forces during the Arab–Israeli war of June 1967.

Johnson acted with a mixture of decisiveness and restraint in the Dominican crisis, using American military power not to crush the rebellion but to achieve a truce. Then, working within the OAS, he encouraged negotiation of an interim government and a carefully inspected election.

While fighting a complex war in Asia, Johnson recognized the underlying forces which required a limited retraction of the American role on the world scene and an expanding role for those who were gathering strength and wanted a larger and less dependent role in fashioning their destiny. In Latin America, Africa, and Asia he threw his weight behind the forces making for regionalism. He understood that regional organizations were required to make effective the endemic aspiration for greater independence; and they could also permit the safe reduction of effort and responsibility clearly sought by the American people since the Cuba missile crisis.

Johnson's perspective on his task, as stated on January 10, 1967, was that: "We are in the midst of a great transition: from narrow nationalism to international partnership; from the harsh spirit of the Cold War to the hopeful spirit of common humanity on a troubled and threatened planet." He moved the world community some considerable distance through that transition in his time.

Johnson's care to avoid a larger war in Asia had its cost. The inevitably protracted nature of the engagement gradually eroded the initial basis of public support and left him and the nation particularly vulnerable to the confusions attendant upon the Tet offensive and its aftermath—confusions for which his administration and American journalism jointly bear responsibility.

In terms of stages of growth, Johnson recognized that the nation's agenda had gone beyond the diffusion of the automobile and all its works to the tasks of the search for a society of higher quality. He carried out a set of revolutionary changes in the structure of American life that Kennedy had foreshadowed but did not live to achieve: changes in education, health, civil rights, and the struggle to eliminate poverty. He brought every residual piece of wilderness he could into the domain of the national parks; began the long, slow battle to retrieve the air and water from pollution; and, with Mrs. Johnson's help, made Americans conscious that their environment could be enhanced in small local ways as well as by large measures of public policy.

Federal law and federal funds (including massively expanded grants-in-aid to the states) accomplished some remarkable things in Johnson's time: historic changes in the federal role in education and medical services; the virtual end of Jim Crow; a lift in Negro voter registration in the South sufficient to change irreversibly the political tone of the whole region. The cities—and the ghettos—yielded improvements less quickly. Here Johnson initiated wide-ranging experiments and focused the talent of the nation on the problem; but there was clearly still much to be learned, as Johnson's administration ended, before the solution to the ghetto problem could be reduced to an ongoing process. But in engaging the Negro urban poor in efforts to shape their own destiny—confused as the efforts may have been —Johnson may well have provided "the rope on which our society crossed over a chasm and survived."[1]

It may take some time to compare with confidence the results of the New Deal and Great Society legislation. But, clearly, they will remain the two great peaks of creative structural change in American society during the first two thirds of the century.

In facing a war and simultaneously conducting a social revolution, Johnson shifted about twice the volume of additional resources to welfare as to military purposes. The dual task was made manageable by the maintenance of a high rate of growth in the American economy—a surge detonated in part by his 1964 success in getting Kennedy's tax cut through the Congress. By 1966 it was clear the tax cut ought to be at least partially reversed; but Johnson could not persuade the Congress to raise taxes substantially until mid-1968. The two-year delay was costly. The gap between the government's commitments (both executive and legislative) and congressional reluctance to generate the tax resources necessary to cover those commitments, yielded accelerated price increases and a break in Kennedy's wage-price guideposts which had worked well for some five years.

The price increases in Johnson's time were, by international standards, remarkably modest. Only the Germans did better between 1963 and 1968. Nevertheless, the rise in prices was corrosive, given the special role of the dollar in the international monetary system, the special requirements of the United States for a balance-of-payments surplus, and the underlying pressure on the American trading position since the late 1950s. The latter resulted from the coming of western Europe and Japan into high mass-consumption (and their efficient exploitation of technologies that America had dominated since the 1920s), while American society was moving off into sectors (e.g., education, health, travel, recreation) which did not link with technologies that helped earn increased foreign exchange.

The convergence of war and social revolution yielded not only price acceleration but another symptom of unresolved social tension—radical violence. Along with the rise of crime in urban areas, this phenomenon shifted the balance of feeling and priority in the country, yielding a typical conservative shift by 1968 in the constitutional balance between canons of justice on the one hand, and law and order on the other. In pursuing simultaneously his view of the national interest and the requirements of welfare and justice in American life, Johnson consciously expended his capital as a political leader; and this, along with other more personal considerations, led to his decision to withdraw from the election of 1968.[2]

Coming to responsibility in a sea of troubles—and of opportunities—Johnson acted in ways typical of the national style. Like his predecessors back to Woodrow Wilson in 1917, he waited until the military situation had degenerated to a point where the choice was narrowed to defeat or massive engagement before putting substantial American forces into Vietnam. Having defined his domestic objectives in terms of long-neglected problems (education, health, race, the cities)—and with a sense of transient opportunity—Johnson threw his weight into their solution with drama, energy, and a resourcefulness reflecting a lifetime of governmental experience.

Where will Lyndon Johnson stand in the gallery of Presidents? No one as close to his years as we are can speak with confidence, least of all a member of his administration. But my view is this: His domestic achievements are clearly among the most impressive in American history. If Southeast Asia retains its independence without another major war, Johnson will emerge, along with Harry Truman, as a principal architect of modern Asia. Indeed, Truman's painfully achieved stabilization of South Korea and Japan was endangered in 1965, as authorities in both Seoul and Tokyo clearly recognized. It had to be revalidated by a successful stabilization of Southeast Asia.

As he took on himself the burden of decision in 1965, Johnson held out a larger vision of its meaning and of Asia's future. He sketched the outline of an Asia strong and cohesive enough to balance the weight of mainland China, in a position to seek reconciliation, with a diminishing

American role. In all this—within South Vietnam and beyond its borders—Johnson built his policy on his assessment of the vitality and staying power of Asian nationalism and on the clearly demonstrated capacity of the Asian states to move forward in economic and social modernization. If something like this vision comes to pass, through the efforts of Asians and others, Johnson's Vietnam policy will be vindicated in history; for without his dispatch of American forces in 1965, no such Asia could have evolved.

Whether Johnson's tactical policy in Vietnam will be judged too cautious will, undoubtedly, be debated. As the reader is now well aware, I would have preferred an earlier American confrontation with Hanoi on the issue of the violation of the Geneva Accords on Laos of 1962; and a more direct use of American military power to interdict infiltration on the ground, in Laos or the southern part of North Vietnam. But I am not prepared with hindsight to say his caution and primary reliance on the slow, painful buildup of South Vietnamese capabilities was wrong. The conflict was certainly longer than it might have been. It wracked American domestic life more profoundly. But if the policy succeeds, it will leave behind a stronger and more self-reliant South Vietnam, Laos, and Cambodia. The ultimate resolution will be more Asian and, perhaps, more stable.[3]

Johnson's policy did have the consequence of leaving to his successor the task of playing a difficult end-game that is still not resolved. If Nixon's policy fails, and Indochina and Southeast Asia are thrown into protracted crisis and danger, history is likely to judge more critically Johnson's tactics and Kennedy's failure promptly to confront the violation of the Laos Accords of 1962.

Historians may also debate whether Johnson's ardent domestic leadership promised too much too soon, especially to the Negro trapped in the vicious circle of ghetto life. Could America have come to grips with these deep intractable urban problems in ways that less inflamed domestic life? I doubt it. Just as the momentum of the race question in the South struck John Kennedy with surprise and force in 1963, Watts, and all it meant, was generated not out of the White House but out of the dynamics of American society and the pathology it had permitted to develop in the heart of the great cities. Like Kennedy in the spring of 1963, Johnson had a bear by the tail, starting with the explosion in Watts in August 1965. Perhaps only a phase of ghetto violence which revealed its sterility and of experiment revealing the long and complex road that lay ahead in the cities could have produced the more temperate mood that began to appear in 1968.

Something of the same may well prove to be the case with the revolt of the white affluent dissident youth. Time and experiment and the frustration of bright dreams of a quick fix may have been required to reveal that happiness did not lie in the lonely corrosive world of drugs; that affluence for some did not mean that the problem of allocating scarce resources had been lifted from the society; that global peace could not be made to happen by wishing or even demonstrating passionately for it; and that, while the private pursuit of lives of higher quality could provide reward as well as frustration, there was no way for modern man to exorcise the need to work through the instruments of bureaucracy and politics, compromise and diplomacy.

The American version of this international revolt against the values and institutions of high mass-consumption was joined with peculiar strength, after 1965, to the antiwar movement, and Johnson became its focus. There was little he—or anyone else bearing the responsibilities of the Presidency—could have done to mitigate this hostility in the period 1965–1968. The fever of New Leftism, with its profound antirationalism and elevation of violence as a purifying, sanctifying experience, made dialogue difficult.

There will also be debate about Johnson's leadership. There is no doubt that he himself felt grave inhibitions arising from his Texas and southern background.[4] He felt early in his Presidency (well before the issue of Vietnam became enflamed) that the media and the intellectuals of the East would come to harass him systematically. He knew they did not represent the American majority; but he recognized their power to destroy. This defensiveness had a particular consequence. Except on rare occasions, Johnson was more formal in television press conferences than he was in private interviews with the press. (Students of such matters will find, I believe, that his sentences were more grammatical, his exposition more logical and sustained than either Kennedy's or Eisenhower's.) Many members of the press, some of whom wrote with hostility about Johnson, sought me out after private sessions with him and urged me to persuade him to talk to the nation as he had just done to them. Their judgment was: "He is great, but it doesn't come across in speeches or press conferences." The advice was unnecessary. Virtually every Johnson aide I know wrote memoranda to him suggesting that he go on television in an informal setting or that he revive the Rooseveltian fireside chat. In private, Johnson was wise and colorful, perceptive and humorous, compassionate and worldly, with a range, vividness, and precision of language beyond the capacity of his best speech draftsmen. He was also as good a raconteur as any of us had ever heard. No one could listen to him in the long sessions in the evening, before his usually late dinner, without knowing he had been in the presence of a remarkable political leader—and that men and women in every part of the country would know this if they could share the experience.

Johnson quietly but firmly resisted these efforts to change the format and style of his public expositions of policy. He had evidently thought it through and concluded that the risks of informality outweighed the possible advantages. He was troubled, in particular, by the dangers of misstatement in a complex international environment; and he felt his natural style was too discursive for television. When the point was pressed, and the possibility suggested of tapes edited down in length, he doubted the networks would accept such editing, and that, in any case, it would raise more problems than it would solve. He broke through once—in a memorable press conference of November 17, 1967. Using a lavaliere microphone, he strode about, speaking with vividness and force on a wide range of issues. The effect was electric. But he never did it again.

And so there remained a gap between Johnson as he appeared to the public and Johnson as he was in private. It was a loss to all concerned.

But the question is: Did Johnson's sense of hostility from the East inhibit his performance as President and make his leadership less effective than it might otherwise have been?

Again, time may provide more wisdom than we now can muster. If I had tried to answer that question at the end of January 1969, my answer would have been unequivocably affirmative. Now, some three years later, I am less sure. His loss of popular support, from its remarkable level during and just after the election of 1964, can be attributed mainly to the protracted character of the war in Vietnam, to the sense among some that he was pushing too fast toward racial equality, to the law-and-order backlash against white and black resort to violence, and the rising crime rate in the cities. Nonetheless, popular assessment of Johnson as President never fell as low as Truman's 23 percent under the frustrations of Korea and the confusions of his dismissal of General MacArthur.

On the race issue, just as Kennedy had felt sharply the impact of his policies on popular support from the South in 1963, so there was no way Johnson could press for what he believed was right for the Negro without accepting the backlash costs.

I still believe Johnson was too defensive toward what he regarded as the eastern establishment, which is neither as eastern nor as established—and not nearly as formidable—as he imagined. And I still regret that his reticence denied the American people a clearer image of what he was really like. But I am also inclined to believe his growing problems in holding popular support were substantially inescapable, given the issues he faced and his policies toward them.

Of one matter I am sure: as Johnson approached his major decisions, all lesser impulses and concerns were stripped away. He brought to bear all that experience and judgment and a prodigious intellect could provide; and he did what he thought was right in the highest interests of the nation and humanity, with a stoic disregard of short-run political costs. At critical moments he was quiet, concentrated, and devoid of irrelevance. Despite his bold enterprises, he was a judicious and careful President, with a sense of history and a passionate vision of what America should be.

Only a truly extraordinary figure could have dealt simultaneously with a war in Southeast Asia and a struggle to move Moscow towards more normal and rational relations with the United States and the West; with the enacting of legislation which brought the Negro closer than ever before to full citizenship, while the cities burned and exploded with violence; with the management of revolutionary change in health and education, while a margin of disaffected youth challenged the underlying values and structure of the society. It took brute energy and balance, perspective and maturity to ride these years through to quieter times.

I would guess that Lyndon Johnson's Presidency will rank among the greatest, as well as the most turbulent, in American history.

BOOK FOUR

The Present and the Future

42

The Nixon Administration: A Preliminary Sketch

Introduction

As this book is completed in June 1972, it is too soon to cast up the accounts of the Nixon administration with confidence. With the important exception of the SALT agreement announced in Moscow on May 26, all its major enterprises, at home and abroad, are still under way and their outcome is uncertain. This chapter is, then, a brief preliminary sketch of Nixon's policies under the headings used for the three previous administrations.

Growth, Price Stability, and the Balance of Payments

The Nixon administration was advised by its predecessor to move strongly in the wake of the June 1968 tax increase to reinvigorate the wage-price guideposts. Specifically, it was urged to seek something like a 5 percent norm for wage settlements in 1969, with prices set on the basis of profits no higher than those of 1967–1968.

In his first press conference of January 27, 1969, Nixon rejected this advice:

> I do not go along with the suggestion that inflation can be effectively controlled by exhorting labor and management and industry to follow certain guidelines. . . . the primary responsibility for con-

> trolling inflation rests with the national administration and its handling of fiscal and monetary affairs. . . . We assume that responsibility.[1]

Nixon accepted the advice of those who argued that wage-price guideposts were clumsy and had never worked effectively except for limited periods. Some of Nixon's advisers also argued that more vigorous and stubborn use of controls over the money supply could do a great deal more than in the past to reconcile a high rate of growth and price stability. And so a major experiment was attempted: to put aside the wage and price guideposts of the 1960s, returning to an early postwar reliance on fiscal and monetary policy that left wage and price decisions to the private sector; and to devise a carefully phased fiscal-monetary strategy which would gradually drain the inflationary impetus, without excessive unemployment, and then yield a high noninflationary growth rate.

In 1969 budgetary restraint and a rapid deceleration in the money supply began to slow down the economy from the 5 percent real growth rate of 1967–1968 to a zero growth rate in the last quarter of 1969. But prices did not respond as expected. They increased more in 1969 than in the previous year and continued to rise in 1970. As compared to the administration's plan for 1970, real GNP fell, rather than increased, by about 1 percent; prices and unemployment rose more than planned, the latter reaching the level of 6.2 percent by December 1970. The combination of declining real income, falling profits, and rising prices cut radically into the real resources available to federal, state, and local governments. There was a substantial federal budget deficit instead of the planned surplus. High unemployment led the Nixon administration to expand the money supply, especially in the first half of 1970. Thus, fiscal policy (because of declining revenues) and monetary policy were eased before inflation was brought under control.

Slowly, and with obvious reluctance, the Nixon administration began to move toward a reinstallation of wage-price guideposts. On June 17, 1970, Nixon announced that the Council of Economic Advisers would issue periodic "inflation alerts." After an unsatisfactory congressional election in November, in which the economic issue at least balanced law and order, a second "inflation alert" (December 1, 1970) acknowledged that the wage-price spiral was unbroken and that the problem lay in wage and price setting in the private sector. Nixon's December 4 speech to the National Association of Manufacturers reflected a new position:

> If business and labor expect public policy to help stimulate real expansion, then business and labor should be prepared to offer the public some real help in curbing inflation. . . . Government has done its part . . . to hold the line. Now this is the critical moment for business and labor to make a special effort to exercise restraint in price and wage decisions.

In January 1971 Nixon persuaded Bethlehem Steel to cut back by about half a 12.5 percent price increase for structural steel products; and in February he launched the first serious effort to bring order and rationality to wage policy in the fragmented construction industry. But these measures did not get at the heart of the matter. Major collective bargaining negotiations yielded wage and benefit increases of 7.4 percent in 1969 and 8.9 percent in 1970, as opposed to 6.0 percent in 1968; in the critical industries which had been "jawboned" in the Johnson administration, prices rose 6 percent in 1969 and 4.6 percent in 1970, as opposed to 1.7 percent in 1968.[2]

The initial laissez-faire posture of the Nixon administration had unleashed price policies, in not wholly competitive markets, which assumed there would be continued inflation. Organized labor fought to correct for past as well as expected future price increases in collective bargaining agreements. Political inhibitions prevented the Nixon administration from throwing the economy into a recession sufficiently severe and protracted to break these inflationary expectations. By 1971 the United States was caught in a version of inflation long familiar in Latin America. With wage settlements far exceeding productivity increases, and with the government troubled by the impact of high unemployment on politics and the public revenue, it was clear that inflation would continue. Business and labor acted on that basis. The American economy was like a dog chasing his tail.

All this had its impact on both the American balance of payments and on confidence abroad that the dollar would remain a viable currency at existing exchange rates. After a period in 1969–1970, when the slowdown in American production reduced imports relative to exports, the trade surplus turned into a deficit. The balance of payments deteriorated further as capital moved abroad, responding to multiple signs that inflation was not under control, and the relative position of the dollar, already fragile in 1968–1969, was steadily weakening.

The gathering international crisis centered on the dollar triggered the drastic measures announced on August 15, 1971, including the wage-price freeze and the 10 percent surcharge on imports.

As the second-quarter balance-of-payments data became available in the government, the administration found itself with the first deficit for goods and services since 1959; a vast unrecorded outflow of private capital; an overall quarterly balance-of-payments deficit of $5.7 billion (on both a net liquidity and official reserves transaction basis[3]). The American deficit was running in the first half of 1971 at something like an annual rate of $20 billion—twice the amply dangerous level of the previous year.

Out of these developments there evolved not only the emergency measures of August 1971, but also the full-scale machinery for price and wage control announced on October 7. If ever there was an example of the American style of innovation by crisis, this was it.

THE ALLOCATION OF PUBLIC RESOURCES

TABLE 42-1 exhibits by broad categories the scale and allocation of public resources for the first two years of the Nixon administration. These figures reflect:

TABLE 42–1
GOVERNMENT EXPENDITURES
AS PROPORTIONS OF GNP, 1968–1970

	1968	1969	1970
National security	10.7	10.1	9.3
Interest	1.4	1.4	1.5
Law, order, and administration	2.5	2.7	3.0
Economic and environmental services	4.6	4.4	4.4
Social welfare	14.2	14.6	16.4
	33.4	33.3*	34.6

* Due to rounding, total differs slightly from sum of components.

1. the reduction in national security expenditures permitted by the beginning of Nixon's withdrawal of American forces from Southeast Asia plus a reduction of spending on the space program;

2. an increase in outlays for social security, reflecting both past legislation and increases in social security benefit rates;

3. a tendency of the public expenditure proportions for the recession year 1970 to rise, since government outlays did not slow down as fast as the economy.

A new administration, especially one succeeding an extremely innovative legislative period, is likely to find itself committed by law to many budget increases it cannot control. It must struggle to free resources to pursue policies of its own. In the federal budget for FY 1971, for example, something like $10 billion of the $14 billion increase was "largely uncontrollable"[4]; discretionary increases for FY 1972 rose to $14 billion of the $16 billion planned increase.[5]

The Nixon administration did manage, then, over its first two years to begin to put its own stamp on the federal budget, although Congress, too, left its mark on the pattern of federal outlays. In part, the Nixon administration did so by changes in military policy. It sought further to conserve budgetary resources for new purposes by a postal rate increase and increased payments by recipients in the Medicare and Medicaid programs. In line with the legislation of 1968, it increased outlays for housing and community development, including a new emphasis on rural housing and housing for low- and moderate-income families. It expanded outlays for water development and water pollution control; and it spent more for the improvement of mass transport facilities and, marginally, for crime control.

Its two major innovations were proposals for revenue sharing between federal and state governments and for welfare reform. But as of early 1972, the Congress had acted on neither.[6]

Both innovations reflected gathering concern over weaknesses in the welfare structure that had emerged in the Kennedy–Johnson years. They also reflected the not unliberal spirit of Senator Robert Taft when he once said to President Eisenhower:

> "You know, I hate federal bureaucracy. . . . The best way I can think of to combat its growth and at the same time help people would be to have the federal government pay a flat fee to the states for every child in school, and automatically to send out a monthly pension check, also of a fixed amount, to every man and woman who reached the age of sixty-five."[7]

Revenue sharing represented a device to use the efficiency of federal tax-collecting machinery and the relatively greater equity of the federal tax structure than that of some of the states (which are excessively reliant on property and excise taxes) to decentralize responsibility for many of the welfare programs which proliferated in the 1960s. The massive grant-in-aid programs, aimed at specific problems of national concern, would give way, in degree, to the judgment of state governments on how resources should best be allocated. The proposal ran into resistance on two major grounds: first, congressional jealousy of its constitutional prerogative in controlling the purse strings; second, there was a judgment by some that the political structure of state governments would yield too diffuse an allocation of federal resources, thus diminishing efforts to ameliorate some of the most acute urban problems.

Nixon's proposed welfare reforms were an effort to break out of a system whose administrative burden was rapidly escalating. It incorporated the simple, powerful notion that what the poor needed most was more money; and, that if cash benefits were granted by family size for those with less than minimum incomes, and if work incentives were assured, a better system would emerge. In concept, this proposal moved away from the older notion of welfare (to assist particular categories of disadvantaged persons) to the doctrine that no family in a rich society should have an income below a certain minimum level. It also reflected a certain despair at the failure of existing programs to bring families that had fallen out of reach of the society's socializing institutions into the mainstream of the nation's life. Essentially, the proposal said: "We have not been very successful in engineering people out of the ghettos step by step; let's see if they can do it by themselves if they have higher incomes."

This effort to cut the Gordian knot of the welfare tangle by family assistance payments (leaving aid to the aged, blind, and disabled on the old basis) would expand welfare expenditures by something like $3.4 billion, notably to assist the working poor. Its fate is still to be determined as Congress probes the inequities it would create as well as solve.

Whatever their fate, Nixon's revenue-sharing and welfare proposals were serious efforts to reduce the administrative burden on Washington of the social revolution of the 1960s, while accepting its permanence. They were creditable—even imaginative—initiatives by an administration whose fundamental political base was conservative and consolidating rather than innovative.

In addition, Nixon's Health Message of February 18, 1971, recognized and dramatized the crisis of spiraling medical costs. It proposed a compulsory health insurance plan to be financed by employers and employees, with modified Medicare and Medicaid programs looking after those outside the working force or on welfare. Whatever the final legislative outcome, the Nixon administration did not remain passive in the face of a situation where medical expenditures (private and public) were moving up toward 8 percent of GNP—a disproportionately high level as compared to that in other developed nations.

Nixon responded to another problem and lesson of the recent past; but, in this case, with evident reluctance. In addition to a high rate of growth, the Kennedy and Johnson administrations experimented with a wide range of measures for job training and placement, including measures to shift labor from surplus to deficit areas. Although hard to evaluate, these did not appear to make a dramatic dent in the problem of structural unemployment. Thought turned to the use of public funds to provide socially useful jobs or to subsidize additional jobs in the private sector. Nixon accepted finally, at reduced levels, congressional proposals for expanded public employment.

While proposing welfare policies that required expanded outlays for the future, Nixon made several major moves that inhibited his capacity to generate public revenues. He recommended that Johnson's hard-won 10 percent tax surcharge be reduced to 5 percent by January 1, 1970, and permitted to expire on June 30, 1970. Congress gladly acquiesced. The Tax Reform Act of 1969 and the further tax reductions of 1971 substantially cut back the capacity of the federal government to generate tax revenues over the longer future. Nixon's budget message for FY 1973 made his choice clear, philosophically and politically:

> . . . over the past 3 years, *the rate of increase in Government spending has been cut nearly in half* compared to the 3 comparable years before this Administration took office. . . .
>
> By putting the brakes on the increase in Government spending, we have been able to leave more spending power in the hands of the individual taxpayer. . . . I believe that the members of . . . [a typical] family can use that money more productively for their own needs than Government can use it for them.[8] [italics in original]

In short, Nixon's approach to growth and inflation as well as his tax policies conflicted seriously with his efforts to rationalize and improve the nation's welfare system and to deal with the nation's problems over a wider range. Stimulation of private expenditures was given priority over essential public outlays. As Richard L. Strout reported on January 3, 1972:

> The great social problems of America are being postponed. . . .
>
> . . . Judging by reports from over the nation, cities are frantic for funds, school sessions are being shortened to save money, crime does not seem to be giving way, unsolved racial problems are moving up from the South into the North, and environmental issues still pile up. . . .
>
> Practically every physical problem on the domestic front comes down ultimately to a question of money: more funds for schools, prisons, health, more for law enforcement, more assistance for the city ghettos. But instead of that, Congress under White House initiative has been cutting taxes to give a boost to the economy.[9]

Over the longer pull, should expanded military outlays be required, Nixon's tax structure threatened to put welfare and security expenditures into head-on competition.

Justice and Order

Only a small proportion of Negroes voted for Nixon in 1968. He received the vote of those Americans who believed Johnson had gone too fast and too far in moving toward racial equality, and who reacted strongly against the rhetoric and the militant posture of Negro extremists. As he looked to 1972, with the aim of gathering a greater popular proportion of the vote than in 1968, he obviously took seriously the problem of drawing to his support some of those who had voted for George Wallace. All this inevitably affected his approach to race questions.

On the other hand, he could not move to reverse the trends in race policy of the 1960s without losing excessively in the great urban areas and risking a revival of explosive tension. Besides, he had sworn to execute the laws, and he had become President of all the people.

Nixon's dilemma was eased by two significant trends that emerged in the late 1960s: the changing political mood of the South, as the voting legislation of 1965 cumulatively worked its effects, and the realization by most of the Negro community that violence was no answer to the race problem in America. In this period of stock-taking and reflection, the Black Panthers became a relatively isolated group. The American Negro and his leaders were by no means content, but they were not prepared to plunge ahead on a path of revolution and destruction. Unlike Kennedy and Johnson, Nixon did not face a strong, purposeful Negro drive toward new objectives which had to be brought by Presidential leadership within the political process if grave distruption of the society was to be avoided. He could afford, for a time at least, a low posture.

Nixon's economic policy denied him, in 1970–1971, the most powerful solvent in diminishing racial inequality; that is, a high and regular economic growth rate. Negro unemployment rose disproportionately. The problem was peculiarly acute among the young, where white as well as black unemployment was excessive, even at maximum employment levels. The drastic decline in profits, moreover, did not create a setting in which efforts to encourage Black Capitalism, which Nixon strongly backed, were likely to prosper.

The thrust of Nixon's welfare policies, moreover, tended to shift the focus from hard-core ghetto problems to wider categories. The older functional programs were not, for the most part, abandoned. The Office of Economic Opportunity survived. The management of welfare remained in the hands of Republican liberals who took the cities and ghetto problems seriously. But, on balance, there was a relaxation of efforts to liquidate by head-on action the Negro ghetto. And the most promising initiative of Johnson's time—Model Cities—was not pressed forward on a scale capable of testing its viability.

This posture stemmed, in part, from an awareness that none of the policies of the 1960s had proved capable of achieving quick results and, in part, from the hope that the Family Assistance Plan, if accepted, might do more for the ghetto Negro with less administrative burden. Edward Banfield's critique of the Johnson programs and Patrick Moynihan's reflections on the wound-stripes he had earned in the struggles of the 1960s played their part in this re-assessment.

Meanwhile, the Negro community fell into a mood well described as "cool but tough and self-reliant."[10] The underlying sources of discontent were not easing as the 1970s began: crime levels remained high, linked to the unrelenting corrosion of drugs; schools were turbulent; unemployment got worse. But there was an acceptance that there was no magic key to liberation from the ghettos. The battle for improvement was one that had to be fought from the inside; violence would hinder and not help; politics, in the classic American sense, was proving a better route to black power than many Negros had earlier supposed. And there was the solvent of growing pride in the uniqueness of the Negro's history, his qualities, his dignity. To a degree, separation, which could not be quickly overcome, was made a virtue.

In the South, however, there was forward motion. With Jim Crow lifted and Negro voter registration on the rise, white leaders—reluctantly, gratefully, or simply realistically—accepted the fact that an irreversible change had occurred. And the southern cities, whose Negro population was generally less concentrated than in the northern cities, moved into authentically easier times, even when bedeviled by the busing problem.

The American Negro had not expected much of a Nixon administration but by 1972 he probably found things somewhat better than he had anticipated, with two exceptions. First, of course, the state of the economy in 1970–1971 struck disproportionately at the Negro and reversed the forces making for a narrowing of the economic gap between whites and nonwhites. Second, Nixon's initial candidates for empty places on the Supreme Court appeared ominous. But down to early 1972 the Burger Court, as it was in fact constituted, remained loyal to the basic decisions of its predecessor on race in America.

Nixon benefited by and his policies somewhat reinforced a tendency to subsidence among the radical affluent white youth. First, there was Nixon's election itself, which helped set in motion a tendency to self-examination in radical groups. Most had been acting on the implicit assumption that the political struggle in America was, somehow, between the left and right wings of the Democratic party—that if Johnson and Humphrey could be brought down, their heroes would triumph. Their performance at Chicago in August 1968 did, indeed, weaken Humphrey's candidacy. As with the Republicans in 1964, many moderate voters drew the conclusion that a party so riven by ugly conflict could not provide responsible national leadership. Nixon's victory, plus the proportion of voters who backed Wallace, enforced on some of the young a more realistic view of the real balance in American political life. As a university teacher in the spring of 1969, sought out for extensive dialogue by ardent student groups, I can attest that this factor was at work and played a part in the fragmentation of the SDS.

A second factor, paralleling a tendency in the Negro community, was the emergence of the Weathermen and the rejection of violence by the majority of dissidents. This was an interacting process: the extreme radicals, observing the weakening of fervor, abandoned the effort to hold the more moderate dissidents together and struck out on their own; and this fact, in itself, helped accentuate a tendency already under way.

A third factor that mitigated the force of white radicalism was American troop withdrawals, reduced draft calls, and a decline in the intensity of fighting in Southeast Asia. The antiwar movement did not disappear from the campuses, but it gradually waned. The flare-up over Cambodia and the killings at Kent State in the spring of 1970 ran counter to a stronger trend in the other direction. Those released from classes and examinations did not, by and large, plunge into politics and the congressional elections of 1970: they went off on their summer vacations a little early. And some of the activist young reflected on that fact.

Fourth, there was the recession of 1970 and the realization that affluence and economic security could not be taken quite as much for granted as New Left doctrines implied. The awareness that jobs were scarce was sobering.

With all this went a gathering sense that the New Left slogans of the 1960s were becoming a bit old hat. The underlying (and, in my view, legitimate) concerns of the young were not dissipated: the meaning of a university education; the inequities of American society; the human values to be sought beyond the routines of work in a complex bureaucratic society; the problems of peace in a still-nuclear world where war in Southeast Asia and explosive tension in the Middle East persisted. But Woodstock and marches on the Pentagon no longer appeared to be responsive courses of action. The period from 1969 to 1972 became increasingly a time for quiet reflection, a tentative probing of religion, a finding of increased satisfaction in disciplined work, a pulling back from hard drugs.

Except for the effort in May 1971 by antiwar agitators to halt the operations of government, and Daniel Ellsberg's transfer of the Pentagon Papers to *The New York Times*, the Nixon administration faced no major legal or constitutional problems arising from conflicts between justice and order generated by the affluent white dissidents.

As in the case of Negro moods, it was too soon to know whether this was a transient phenomenon—a downswing in a cycle—or a more substantial trend.

MILITARY AND ARMS CONTROL POLICY

TABLE 42-2 exhibits the major changes in the American force structure for key fiscal years between 1961 and 1972.

Nixon designed and constructed a post-Vietnam military force before the war was over. It was on about the same scale as Eisenhower's, containing, however, a larger strategic component, a slightly larger component of general-purpose forces, greater airlift, and a smaller but more sophisticated naval component.

In terms of resources, rather than men and hardware, the allocation of total expenditures, in real terms, as among strategic forces, general-purpose forces, and Vietnam, is shown in Table 42-3.

There was a decline in Vietnam expenditures of some $20 billion in 1972 dollars from the FY 1968 peak and the difference was mainly made available for civil purposes; although there was a slight rise in military outlays in FY 1972 and a more substantial increase proposed for FY 1973. As a proportion of GNP, military expenditures fell below 7 percent, the lowest figure since the period just before the Korean War.

There is a family resemblance between Nixon's military cutbacks of these years and Eisenhower's in the wake of the Korean War. Then, too, the essential decision was to cut back conventional forces sharply and the Navy to a lesser extent, and to maintain the strategic deterrent. Then, too, the overall decline of the military budget was about 20 percent (from 1953 to 1956).

The major difference in the military budget revisions of the early Eisenhower and Nixon years was doctrinal. In cutting back conventional forces, Eisenhower announced a policy of increased reliance on nuclear deterrence, with its threat of "massive retaliation." Nixon justified his cutback on the premise that America's allies were in a position to carry more of the burden of deterring or dealing with conventional or guerrilla attack; although it may be that his administration also assumed a conventional Chinese Communist attack was less likely than in the past, given the tension on the Sino–Soviet border and the Chinese forces committed to its defense. In crude terms, the American military establishment in conventional forces was geared to deal with one and a half wars (Europe or Asia plus a small additional contingency) as opposed to the two-and-a-half-wars posture generated during the Kennedy administration.

In addition, Nixon pursued Johnson's SALT initiative, and the talks were begun in November 1969. Reversing an older Soviet position—for example, Kosygin's at Glassboro in 1967—Moscow appeared to place primary emphasis on an ABM agreement. It appeared to be at American insistence that the May 20, 1971, joint announcement contained reference to the negotiation of "certain measures" to limit offensive as well as defensive weapons. The agreement reached a year later promised to permit certain future expenditures to be avoided; but it did not foreshadow any mutual reductions in outlays for strategic defense. It limited the strategic arms race, but did not end it.

Nixon did not alter American treaty and other commitments. He resisted pressures from the Senate to reduce American forces committed to NATO and pressed the Allies to enlarge and modernize their NATO forces. He insisted that a Berlin agreement, formalizing West German and Allied access and other rights in West Berlin, precede the conclusion of a pact between the German Federal Republic and the German Democratic Republic, a meeting on European security, or a negotiation of mutual and

TABLE 42–2

STRUCTURE OF DEPARTMENT OF DEFENSE MILITARY FORCES, SELECTED YEARS, FY 1961–1972*

Description	Last Eisenhower year, 1961	Pre-Vietnam, 1964	Peak Vietnam, 1968	1970	Estimated 1971	Estimated 1972
Military personnel (thousands)	2,484	2,685	3,547	3,066	2,699	2,505
Civilian personnel (thousands)	1,042	1,035	1,287	1,161	1,104	1,082
Strategic offensive forces						
Land-based missiles	28	654	1,054	1,054	1,054	1,054
Sea-based missiles	80	336	656	656	656	656
Strategic bombers†	1,654	1,277	648	517	569	521
General-purpose forces						
Divisions (Army and Marine Corps)	14	19⅓	23⅔	20⅓	16⅔	16⅓
Tactical air wings						
Air Force	21	22	28	23	21	21
Navy	16	15	15	13	12	11
Marine Corps	3	3	3	3	3	3
Attack carriers	15	15	15	15	14	13
Antisubmarine carriers	9	9	8	4	4	3
Nuclear attack submarines	13	19	33	46	53	56
Total number of ships	819	932	932	743	710	658
Airlift and sealift forces						
C-5A squadrons	—	—	—	1	2	4
All other squadrons	31	33	30	17	15	13
Total obligational authority (billions of constant 1972 dollars)	68.1	74.3	96.1	85.5	78.0	79.2

Sources: *The Budget of the United States Government*, various years; *The Budget of the United States Government—Appendix*, various years; Department of Defense, News Release 72–71, Jan. 29, 1971; *Defense Report: Statement of Secretary of Defense Melvin R. Laird before the House Armed Services Committee on the Fiscal Year 1972–1976 Defense Program and the 1972 Defense Budget* (March 9, 1971); unpublished data from the Department of Defense.

* All figures, except those for total obligational authority, are for the end of the fiscal year.

† Includes, before 1968, some medium-range bombers, forward based, that were used in the strategic role. The FB-111 is included in the 1971 figure.

TABLE 42–3
FUNDS AUTHORIZED FOR STRATEGIC AND GENERAL-PURPOSE FORCES, BY CATEGORY, SELECTED YEARS, FY 1961–1972
(in billions of 1972 dollars)

Category	1961	1964	1968	1970	1971	1972
Strategic nuclear forces	23.8	24.8	21.4	19.7	19.3	19.7
General-purpose forces (other than additions for Vietnam)	44.3	49.5	45.6	46.2	45.7	50.9
Vietnam additions	—	—	29.1	19.6	13.0	8.6
Total	68.1	74.3	96.1	85.5	78.0	79.2

balanced force reductions as between the NATO and Warsaw Pact organization. His activist stance in the search for a Middle East settlement foreshadowed increased, rather than reduced, security commitments in the area. In Asia, of course, there were important changes centered on the problem of Vietnam and the process of Vietnamization, discussed below. But American treaty commitments were reaffirmed. The expectation was asserted that the nations of the area would carry a larger part of the burden of maintaining conventional forces and would, in general, have to count on dealing with guerrilla aggression without the assistance of American ground forces. On this basis, military aid programs were expanded in Southeast Asia and South Korea.

All this, too, was evocative of Eisenhower's first term, with its emphasis on making and supporting security agreements, backed by military aid programs which would permit nations on the periphery of the communist world to maintain larger conventional forces than they could otherwise support. As the Guam doctrine said: ". . . we shall look to the nation directly threatened to assume the primary responsibility of providing the manpower for its defense." As with Eisenhower's first term dispositions, the consistency of this posture with American treaty commitments was still to be tested.

SOUTHEAST ASIA, JANUARY 1969–MARCH 1972

THE Nixon administration evidently conducted a thoroughgoing review of the situation in Southeast Asia before making its dispositions. It was greeted in February by a fairly vigorous North Vietnamese offensive which was quite easily turned back; and under Johnson's directive of October 29, 1968, Abrams kept up a maximum American effort in the accelerated pacification program. In 1969 the proportion of the population under reliable government administration moved up from about 80 percent to well over 90 percent.

On May 14, July 25, and November 3, 1969, Nixon defined his Vietnam policy in the context of his policy toward Asia. In May he rejected the two alternatives Kennedy and Johnson had faced and rejected before him:

> We have ruled out attempting to impose a purely military solution on the battlefield.
>
> We have also ruled out either a one-sided withdrawal from Vietnam, or the acceptance in Paris of terms that would amount to a disguised American defeat.

He chose Vietnamization, "a plan in which we will withdraw all our forces from Vietnam on a schedule in accordance with our program, as the South Vietnamese become strong enough to defend their own freedom."

Nixon defined his objective as "a just peace" and recommitted himself to his campaign pledge to end the war in Vietnam "in a way that would increase our chances to win true and lasting peace in Vietnam, in the Pacific, and in the world."

Noting the possibility that Hanoi might increase its military effort as American forces withdrew, he said:

> Hanoi could make no greater mistake than to assume that an increase in violence will be to its advantage. If I conclude that increased enemy action jeopardized our remaining forces in Vietnam, I shall not hesitate to take strong and effective measures to deal with that situation.

Nixon committed himself to the American electorate, however, to disengage U.S. forces (about eleven divisions) from ground combat and not to reintroduce them. He acted on this pledge. He thereby limited his capacity to respond to "an increase in violence" initiated by Hanoi to American sea and air forces.

This military posture was accompanied by a public negotiation position essentially identical with that of the Johnson administration, including Thieu's reaffirmation of the "Greek formula": that communists could run for office as well as vote in an inspected Vietnamese election, and take their place in supervising the election. The only innovation was Thieu's agreement of January 25, 1971, to stand down for the month before a Presidential election in which the communists might participate. Nixon also reaffirmed in public (July 25, 1969, Guam press conference) Johnson's position that the supervision of a Southeast Asian cease-fire (and, presumably, a settlement) should be done by Asians.

In July 1969, while in Vietnam, Nixon altered Johnson's October 1968 orders to Abrams to conduct a maximum American effort in support of accelerated pacification. The primary mission of American forces became: "to enable the South Vietnamese forces to assume full responsibility for the security of South Vietnam."

Fulfilling Westmoreland's prediction of November 1967, American forces in Vietnam began to be drawn down in the second half of 1969.

Nixon clearly faced a situation in 1969 of potentially redundant forces within South Vietnam. He could have decided to use American forces to interdict the Laos corridors or to invade the southern part of North Vietnam. This is, presumably, what is meant by the somewhat ambiguous phrasing of his rejected option: "a purely military solution on the battlefield." I do not know, of course, why, like Johnson, he rejected this course. The possibilities of Chinese intervention, increased domestic dissidence, and the budgetary cost of the effort may have weighed heavily.

The path of Vietnamization must have seemed attractive precisely because it minimized the possibility of a larger war, calmed the American scene, and saved money.

The question was undoubtedly considered: Will Vietnamization increase or decrease the chance of an early negotiated settlement? Obviously, Hanoi would be tempted to keep the war going at a moderate rate until American withdrawals were complete—or virtually complete—and then mobilize for a second maximum effort, as at Tet in 1968. On the other hand, Hanoi might judge that the inevitably increased authority of Saigon in the negotiating process (as it carried an increased relative military burden) and the calming of American dissidence (as casualties fell) might make it wiser to negotiate sooner rather than later. Down to the spring of 1972, Hanoi persisted—awaiting the end of American withdrawal from a combat role on the ground, pressing against Laos and Cambodia, hoping for a breakdown in South Vietnamese political life or for a break in the continuity of American economic and military aid to South Vietnam. It then launched its second maximum effort.

The adverse impact on troop morale of American forces assuming a secondary military role, with withdrawal foreseeable, may or may not have been weighed. I had heard both Westmoreland and Abrams attribute the extraordinarily high morale of 1965–1968 to the fact that the troops were fully engaged; and I assume they would have been sensitive to an obverse situation. This judgment accorded with experience in the Second World War. It may be that the degenerative effects of a pullback from combat, withdrawal from a war not yet ended, and the wholly understandable desire not to be killed on the eve of American withdrawal were underestimated.

Nixon's Vietnam policy contained certain presumably purposeful ambiguities. First, by linking our reaction against increased communist military pressure to the safety of American forces, it left open the question of what American guarantees to South Vietnam would remain after troop withdrawals were complete. In reaffirming, in general, the continuity of American treaty commitments, did Nixon include the protection to protocol states provided in the SEATO treaty?

The ambiguity had a special meaning in American politics. American troop withdrawals could be supported as a pragmatic step wholly consistent with an abiding commitment to Southeast Asia; or they could be regarded as a once-for-all liquidation of the American commitment to use military forces on the ground in Southeast Asia. The ambiguity in Nixon's policy permitted support by men of both views. It had the cost of leaving the Asian governments uncertain about the American posture and commitment over the longer run. It also reinforced the continued lack of clarity in the United States about the abiding American interest in the balance of power in Asia.

It is not difficult to understand why an American administration might accept these costs rather than answer clearly a contingent question that might stir controversy at home. The danger lay, as on a number of occasions since 1945, in these ambiguities encouraging the authorities in communist capitals to attempt to alter the status quo by military action. The problem was heightened by the situation in which Laos and Cambodia found themselves.

Cambodia came under increasing pressure in the wake of the communist failure during the 1968 Tet offensive. The weakening of the Viet Cong and the loss of communist recruiting capacity in the South Vietnamese countryside meant that the Cambodian lines of supply, infiltration routes, and base areas became of increased importance to Hanoi. As Hanoi exploited these assets more intensively, it affronted Cambodian nationalism. Prince Norodom Sihanouk spoke out increasingly against what was rapidly becoming a North Vietnamese invasion and occupation of a significant portion of the thinly inhabited countryside. In May 1969 he embargoed shipments through Cambodia to communist base areas, but he relented in September.

With Sihanouk's departure for Peking early in 1970 there were two reactions: a nationalist military coup in Phnom Penh; and then, the South Vietnamese–American invasion of the communist redoubts in Cambodia in the spring. The results of the latter were the hobbling of the North Vietnamese capacity to bring military weight against the III and IV Corps areas in South Vietnam (roughly, the Saigon area and the Mekong Delta); the diversion of communist forces against the Cambodians; and a subsequent situation where South Vietnamese forces could fight the North Vietnamese in the thinly populated areas of Cambodia rather than the densely populated areas of South Vietnam.

These events also plunged Cambodia fully into the Indochina war. The decision was clearly Cambodian, and it was backed by a remarkable expansion of the Cambodian armed forces from 35,000 to about 200,000. There is no doubt that the bulk of the Cambodian population regarded the North Vietnamese as an invading enemy. But relations with the South Vietnamese were awkward both because of traditional tensions and the freewheeling behavior of South Vietnamese troops in the Cambodian countryside. Nevertheless, there emerged a degree of military collaboration of a kind unthinkable in the past, given the historic tension between Cambodians and Vietnamese. The ARVN brought pressure on the North Vietnamese at critical moments to help keep the essential Cambodian communication routes open, clearly an interest of Saigon as well as Phnom Penh.

The issue posed in Washington by the new Cambodian stance was, of course, the extent of the support the United States should render. Down to the present, military and economic aid have sufficed and the congressional inhibition on American troop engagement in Cambodia has not been onerous. The Cambodians have not been able to drive the North Vietnamese out of the more remote parts of the countryside; but the North Vietnamese have, despite considerable efforts, not been able to generate a strong antigovernment movement from the old Cambodian communist base, the Red Khmer organization. Nevertheless, the North Vietnamese invasion of Cambodia bore heavily on the life of that young, fragile, underdeveloped nation—notably during the winter–spring offensive of 1971–1972.

The cutting off of the communist supply route through the port of Sihanoukville had important implications for the situation in Laos. When hard evidence emerged, it appeared that the Cambodian supply route had been vastly more important and larger in scale over the period from the end of 1966 to the spring of 1969 than American intelligence had estimated at the time. To sustain their forces in South Vietnam and Cambodia after this route was lost required Hanoi to increase greatly its supply effort through the Laos Panhandle.

It was this development—plus the improved situation inside South Vietnam—that led to the South Vietnamese invasion of the Laos corridors early in 1971. This was an attack on a route of unique importance during the October–May dry season. Evidently, the attack was anticipated by Hanoi; it was prepared to invest some of its divisions normally held in reserve to contest it; exceedingly heavy losses were accepted, since the communist forces were exposed to American air power; but the South Vietnamese operation fell short of its full objective, which was to hold the key infiltration routes for the balance of the dry season and systematically mop up the supply caches in the area. On the other hand, quite aside from severe losses taken by some of its best forces, Hanoi's whole military effort in 1971 was enfeebled by the South Vietnamese initiative. The engagement demonstrated clearly that the Laos supply route was, indeed, viewed by Hanoi as absolutely essential to its effort to seize Indochina.

Nixon's policy in Indochina over his first three years permitted essential American interests to be preserved, with a radical decline in American casualties and expenditures in the region. It did not succeed in inducing a negotiated settlement; and it left unanswered some critical questions for the future. By exploiting the post-Tet communist disarray and the slowly rising tide of effective nationalism in the region, Nixon was able for three years to lift a good deal of the burden of Vietnam from American life without the sacrifice of vital American interests.

Turning to the two critical variables—the translation of South Vietnamese nationalism into a viable political life, and American public opinion—the election process of 1971 in South Vietnam was clearly marred by Thieu's unique candidacy.

Thieu failed to develop in his first term a government political party, on a national but nonmonopolistic basis, which could provide a political base like that generated in South Korea by Park. After several experiments failed, he decided to rely mainly on the administrative and military apparatus he controlled. Similarly, neither Ky nor Minh set about organizing opposition political parties. They sought support in the typically fragmented civil political groupings of South Vietnam. I do not know what pre-election political polling showed or would have showed. I assume it would have indicated that Thieu's strength was considerable. But, in an environment lacking political parties of any stature or vigor, Ky and Minh judged their chances negligible so long as Thieu controlled the machinery of government. It was logical, therefore, that they should call for his removal in the pre-election period and equally logical that Thieu should refuse to step down.

Seen from a distance, it would appear that Thieu overplayed his hand in the sense that a less vigorous use of his assets might have made the Presidential race competitive while not endangering his re-election. He may have been led to the course he followed, in part, because of his judgment that he would have to rely increasingly on his own wit, political strength, and resources as support in Washington waned. Evidently, he was in no mood in the pre-election period of 1971 for noblesse oblige.

In terms of the development of South Vietnamese constitutional life, the October 3, 1971, Presidential election was a disappointment and a setback. It reflected, above all, the failure of Thieu to develop the party substructure that has marked the very few successful examples of operating democracy in the developing world. It also revealed that the active opposition was small and fragmented; although, under the circumstances, many South Vietnamese must have voted in apathy or to conform to the wishes of local officials.

In any case, 1971 did not see a repetition of the disastrous internal political events of 1963, in part, perhaps, because their disastrous consequences were remembered—in Washington as well as in South Vietnam.

As for American public opinion, Nixon's support varied with the course of events and the public mood; but, on the whole, he held a majority with him on Vietnam, although there was a sag during the South Vietnamese invasion of the Laos infiltration corridors.[11]

Behind this support lay cross-strands and ambiguities. On the one hand, those believing it was a mistake to get involved in the Vietnam war continued to grow slowly from the level of just over 50 percent at the end of the Johnson administration to something over 60 percent by June 1971. On the other hand, there remained a strong residual feeling that the United States should not act in ways that might turn South Vietnam over to the communists.[12] Nixon's course reconciled these thoughts and feelings quite successfully over the first three years of his administration.

But Nixon's decision not to clarify and reassert the nature of Amer-

TABLE 42–4
PRESIDENT NIXON'S HANDLING OF SITUATION IN VIETNAM

	Approve (%)	Disapprove (%)	No Opinion (%)
March 1969	44	26	30
June 1969	52	24	24
October 1969	58	32	10
November 1969	64	25	11
January 1970	65	24	11
February 1970	53	32	15
March 1970	47	43	10
April 1970	46	41	13
May 1970	53	37	10
July 1970	55	32	13
February 1971	46	41	13

ica's abiding interests in Southeast Asia—his focusing on the safe withdrawal of American forces—left him vulnerable to pressure from all those who, in various formulations, urged that total U.S. withdrawal should be promptly executed.

SOUTHEAST ASIA, APRIL–JUNE 1972

THE massive North Vietnamese invasion of South Vietnam launched on March 30, 1972, yielded results that cannot be fully assessed as this book goes to press. However, the rationale and initial course of the attack are reasonably clear.

As Hanoi took stock in the spring and summer of 1971, it could perceive a gradual strengthening of South Vietnamese military and economic capacity and a consolidation of Thieu's administrative structure deep into the countryside. While the South Vietnamese election of October 1971 was imperfectly democratic in American eyes, it was, in Vietnamese terms, a demonstration of Thieu's strength. The military and political capacity of the Viet Cong was progressively eroding. Nixon's Vietnam policy was emerging as a source of political strength, permitting as it did a withdrawal of U.S. forces and a virtual ending of U.S. casualties while maintaining American interests and commitments in Southeast Asia.

In addition, Hanoi followed with ill-concealed anxiety the rapprochement between Washington and Peking, which not only promised to dilute Peking's support for North Vietnamese objectives but also outflank the anti-Vietnam forces in the United States and strengthen Nixon's hand. Hanoi tended to agree with spokesmen of the Nixon administration that if things went on as they were, Vietnam would not be a significant issue in the election of 1972.

Both of the critical variables appeared to be moving against Hanoi as Vietnamization progressed: the strains on American political life of protracted war were easing; and South Vietnam was consolidating its nationhood.

Evidently, a blow that would destroy the South Vietnamese military and political structure, discredit Nixon's Vietnamization policy, and bring men into power in Washington already committed to abandon U.S. commitments in Southeast Asia seemed attractive in Hanoi.

As Moscow observed all this, there was at least a partial overlap with Hanoi's interests. Whether the United States stayed in Southeast Asia or not, Moscow was not about to abandon the field to Peking. Its old interest in contesting for Hanoi's friendship within the communist movement remained. In addition, Moscow was engaged over a wide front in exploiting the openings and anxieties created by the developing Washington–Peking rapprochement and the drama of Nixon's trip to Peking (announced as early as July 15, 1971). Moscow appeared ready and eager to move into the empty chairs left by American policy. A blow that would bring Hanoi closer to Moscow and simultaneously weaken both Washington and Peking must have seemed quite intriguing to Soviet strategists. And if Hanoi's effort failed (as did Nasser's Middle East venture of June 1967), Moscow would still have been the partner who had helped the North Vietnamese and the one to whom Hanoi would have to turn to reconstruct its army and its economy, in a posture of even greater dependence.

As for the invasion's effects on American politics, Moscow, assessing the rhetoric of the various major Democratic candidates for the 1972 election, must have regarded Nixon's defeat as a supportable political event, although Nixon's policy of retraction in Asia and elsewhere was already offering the Soviet Union some interesting possibilities for the expansion of its power.

All this had to be weighed against Soviet interests in the summit, for Moscow must have calculated that Hanoi's invasion might set in motion forces and events that would make the summit difficult for Washington, Moscow, or both. But, as with Johnson in 1968, Moscow could regard the summit as postponable, if it came to that. After all, every postwar President had participated in or planned a summit with the Soviet leadership. A SALT agreement could wait, particularly if the next American administration was committed to a further unilateral reduction in the American military budget. The German treaties were more precarious, but represented the long-run direction in which things were moving in Europe. A collapse of Nixon's Asian policy, a firm consolidation of Moscow's position in Hanoi, and a strengthening of its prestige throughout Asia were real and immediate matters of power. In this light, a summit must have appeared secondary, although its cancellation was not a positive Soviet interest.

The London *Economist* put the matter well on May 6, 1972:

> No doubt they have measured the risk that Mr. Nixon may now refuse to come across with his side of the assumed bargain. But they may reckon that with the election campaign already beginning, and with the expectations he has built up in American minds about his visit to Moscow, he will have no choice but to proceed with the agenda as if Vietnam did not exist: they can get Vietnam and still get the other things they want too. . . . The Russians do not often gamble, but they may be playing it the gambler's way this time, and if it works they may even try it somewhere else. If they are right, Mr. Nixon may be faced with more than the failure of his Vietnam policy. He may also have to contemplate the failure of the United States as a power capable of operating a coherent worldwide policy towards the Soviet Union, a policy which balances events in Europe with those in Asia and Latin America and Africa, and insists on the principle of give and take, and requires an accounting at the end of the day. There is no other country in the non-communist world that can do that, if the United States cannot. It may not be only the map of Vietnam that is beginning to be rolled up.

But why was the North Vietnamese military plan judged potentially viable in both Hanoi and Moscow? Three factors made victory in a conventional invasion conceivable. First, the U.S. withdrawal from combat since 1969 of the equivalent of eleven full divisions. However one rated the improved ARVN, it was difficult to believe that their twelve divisions (substantially smaller and less well equipped than American divisions) could have improved over three years enough to compensate for such a massive reduction in American strength on the ground.

Second, the regular units of ARVN (plus South Vietnamese marines) constituted a smaller force than the North Vietnamese army, because the requirements of defending the South Vietnamese countryside diverted a large part of South Vietnamese military manpower to the regional and popular forces and to the rural police. The relative strength of the regular armed forces on the two sides was about fifty-four versus forty-five regiment equivalents, or six to five in favor of Hanoi. The actual gap, as it emerged in key combat areas, was greater, owing to Hanoi's ability to attack from bases all around the periphery of South Vietnam's long borders.

Third, Nixon had firmly committed himself before the American electorate to limit his support of the South Vietnamese to air and naval power. He had withdrawn not only virtually all U.S. combat units from South Vietnam, but also reduced the Marine and Army forces in Okinawa and Hawaii, which had for many years constituted the strategic reverve in the Pacific. Although Hanoi had to count on facing American air and naval power in mounting its invasion, it could reasonably assume that Nixon would not reintroduce U.S. fighting units. In fact, it is doubtful that Hanoi's all-out offensive of the spring of 1972 would have been attempted if, say, two American divisions had remained in South Vietnam as an operational strategic reserve, as in post-1953 South Korea.

To increase its strength and to achieve tactical surprise, Hanoi negotiated with Moscow for long-range artillery and tanks. To diminish the weight of the air power it would have to confront, Hanoi took two steps: it obtained large supplies of Soviet mobile antiaircraft weapons; and it timed the invasion carefully to the transition of the monsoons. The offensive in I Corps was launched during poor flying weather; similarly, the effort in the highlands and against Saigon was geared to the deteriorating May–June weather of that region. But the shifting weather meant also that, if the initial blitzkrieg across the DMZ failed to roll in one lunge to Hue, the second effort would take place under clear skies and heavy, sustained pressure from American and South Vietnamese air power.

And so, with full Soviet support, Hanoi threw virtually its entire army (plus partially trained recruits) into a second maximum effort to destroy the ARVN and the government in Saigon. It was essentially a straightforward invasion like that launched against South Korea in 1950. Its ultimate targets, however, were the political life of South Vietnam and the United States, and additionally, for the Soviet Union, the power and prestige of Peking.

Technically, it turned into an attritional battle, patiently conducted by Hanoi so as to exhaust Saigon's forces and achieve a politico-military collapse. After the failure of Hanoi's initial effort to burst through Quang Tri to Hue, there was a month of grinding conflict with heavy losses on both sides. For a time the South Vietnamese line in the north held; An Loc also held on one of the major approaches to Saigon. The attack on Kontum and Pleiku remained in abeyance while the North Vietnamese moved to prepare for the gambit (feared in 1961 and almost achieved in both 1965 and 1968) of cutting South Vietnam in half on the line from the highlands to the coast in Binh Dinh province, where Viet Cong strength, always great, survived to a considerable extent the post-Tet 1968 period. This required, however, that the substantial and competent South Korean forces around Qui Nhon be bypassed.

A second major wave of North Vietnamese effort was launched in the last week in April, as Hanoi's last reserve division (the 325th) was brought down to the DMZ from the north. Quang Tri was surrounded, pulverized by long-range artillery, and captured on May 1. The critical battle for Hue was being prepared in the second week of May, as both sides consolidated their forces and the North Vietnamese initially set May

19, Ho Chi Minh's birthday, as the target for the capture of the old imperial capital—the home town of Ho and Diem, as well as of Giap. The North Vietnamese outnumbered the South Vietnamese by almost two to one at Hue, with air power the potential equalizing element. Meanwhile, the North Vietnamese began to move slowly against Kontum and Pleiku. They also began shifting some of their forces into the invasion route towards Saigon, via Tay Ninh province and the Saigon River, confronting, however, strong local resistance.

Thoughtful military men in Washington assessed South Vietnamese chances of politico-military survival in the first few days of May as, at best, 50–50.

Meanwhile, responding to Hanoi's clear violation of the agreements and understandings that led to the bombing cessation of October 31, 1968, Nixon resumed air and naval attack on North Vietnam. Haiphong was attacked for the first time by B-52s on April 16. In apparent response, Moscow sought and achieved briefly a return to negotiations in Paris. It may be that Nixon's statement of April 26 (after Kissinger's hasty visit to Moscow) was a quite exact paraphrase of Moscow's assurance, the language recalling similar assurances from the highest Soviet levels in October 1968: "We are resuming the Paris talks with the firm expectation that productive talks leading to rapid progress will follow through all available channels." When, on May 2, Kissinger secretly met Le Duc Tho in Paris, however, he confronted an unyielding North Vietnamese position, in no way reflecting the Moscow agreement or an interest in serious negotiations. As at Tet 1968, Hanoi demanded a communist-dominated coalition in Saigon. Perhaps the fall of Quang Tri the previous day altered Hanoi's policy; perhaps Hanoi's agreement to the language Kissinger brought back from Moscow was infirm or ambiguous, as in the past; perhaps the whole exercise was a Hanoi–Moscow ploy to keep the weight of American bombardment off Hanoi and Haiphong, even if for a short time, in the midst of a climactic battle. But a good deal hinged on whether Le Duc Tho's performance in Paris on May 2 was private enterprise by Hanoi, its hopes elevated by the fall of Quang Tri, or a posture agreed between Hanoi and Moscow. In the former case, Hanoi put Moscow at risk of acute confrontation with the U.S. without Soviet agreement; and this was not likely to be well received in Moscow. But with Kissinger's return from Paris, it was clear—as it had been for more than three and a half years—that there was no negotiating option for Washington short of unconditional surrender by South Vietnam and the United States.

This was the hard military and diplomatic situation Nixon confronted as he made his decision, announced on May 8, to mine the harbors of North Vietnam. The plan envisaged also that supplies off-loaded by freighters outside the harbors would be attacked as they attempted to move to the beaches. In that sense, Nixon's decision was to blockade rather than merely to mine. Nixon's actions were supported by 59 percent of the American public, with 24 percent against, 17 percent with no opinion—the classic proportions of public response to a strong presidential initiative.

In addition, the rail lines between Hanoi and the Chinese border were attacked. With the failure of the Kissinger–Le Duc Tho meeting, attacks resumed on supplies already ashore in northern storage areas and were continued in the region north of the DMZ, in southern North Vietnam. In terms of my memorandum of May 6, 1967 (see above, pp. 511–512), Nixon's decision was to act simultaneously on all three major options: to close the top of the supply funnel; to attack supplies within the funnel; and to hammer away at the bottom of the funnel, close to the battlefield, in North Vietnam as well as in Laos. So far as air power was concerned, this risked a certain diffusion of effort at a critical time on the battlefield—a factor that had to be weighed against longer-run leverage on Hanoi, a strengthening of South Vietnamese morale, and possible effects on petroleum supplies for the North Vietnamese forces, notably those in I Corps. Excepting petroleum products, the supplies for many weeks of battle on the ground were probably already in place in South Vietnam or in the logistical pipeline. They were likely to be accessible, if at all, only to tactical bombing. Nevertheless, Nixon's decision of May 8 obviously put important questions to Hanoi, Moscow, and Peking.

It is hard to believe that American mining of the North Vietnamese harbors was a wholly unforeseen contingency when the North Vietnamese invasion was planned. Nevertheless, for Hanoi it meant turning at a critical stage of the struggle for additional help from Moscow, Peking, or both. Specifically, Nixon's decision meant putting to Moscow the question of what military or other action it was prepared to take to assure the continuity of supplies by sea to Hanoi. It also posed a question of some delicacy: should Peking be asked to cooperate, as in the period 1965–1968, in trans-shipping Russian supplies and protecting the rail lines between Hanoi and the Chinese border? In the earlier period, large Chinese engineering and antiaircraft forces were introduced into North Vietnam for that purpose. Would Hanoi and Moscow wish to see that happen again to support an offensive which Peking probably did not plan, may well not have approved, and which was clearly aimed in part at diminishing Peking's role in Hanoi as well as in Asia generally? And if the request were made of Peking, what would be its response and the terms it would ask in return for such assistance? Above all, Moscow had to decide what risks, if any, to take with a direct naval confrontation with the United States in Southeast Asia. The area was a secondary arena of Soviet initiative, not nearly as important, for example, as the northwest Pacific bordering on Siberia, central Europe, or even the Middle East. Throughout the whole postwar period—from the Iranian crisis of 1945—Moscow had drawn back when it met the credible threat of American military power in Soviet thrusts beyond the truce lines of the Cold War. On the other hand, the Soviet role in the 1972 invasion was more overt than in the Tet offensive of 1968, and more of its prestige was on the line; Moscow had generated increased prestige in Asia because of its role in the India–Pakistan war of 1971, and the momentum of its rise in Asia was endangered; and there was, finally, the question of whether its enhanced naval and nuclear power permitted Moscow to reverse in the South China Sea the verdict of October 1962 in the Caribbean.

The debate on what course to follow must have embraced assessments of North Vietnamese prospects on the field of battle, including supplies already ashore, as well as Nixon's will and political capacity to face down whatever challenges might arise from both the communist response and from the American opposition to Nixon's policy.

The upshot in Moscow was an initial decision, at least, to avoid a U.S.–Soviet confrontation over the mines and to permit a still-confident and fully supplied North Vietnamese army to seek victory on the battlefield in the weeks ahead. The longer run issue of maintaining imports for North Vietnam was put aside. It remained to be seen how tight the noose would be, and when, if at all, it would begin to have significant effects on North Vietnamese military capacity or its capacity to operate as a society. Peking took a similar but presumably independent stance.

With the international crisis postponed, attention came again to focus on the battlefield. Recognizing that he faced a protracted struggle, Thieu took a whole series of measures to expand military recruitment, to tighten and improve civil and military administration, to deal with some 700,000 refugees the conflict had generated in its first six weeks, and to increase taxes and bond sales.

During May, the strategic tide in the bitter attritional struggle slowly turned. An Loc and Kontum held. The battle for Hue remained to be fought, and there was the possibility of raids on Saigon; but the relative position of the South Vietnamese had greatly improved. Meanwhile, the mining and bombing of North Vietnam gradually weakened Hanoi's logistical capacity, without significant countervailing action by Moscow or Peking. Neither was prepared to assume the costs of rescuing a North Vietnamese military operation failing on the ground.

In the wake of the Moscow summit, Hanoi appeared to move toward serious negotiations. But with at least one major Democratic candidate promising, if elected, to overthrow the GVN, it was obviously in Hanoi's interest to postpone a settlement until after the November election. On the other hand, the mines and bombing would be hard to live with for another five months, if Nixon used his leverage fully.

In this setting, as of June 15, both sides seemed to be approaching a resumption of diplomatic dialogue.

Like the Tet offensive of 1968, Hanoi's spring offensive of 1972 failed to produce decisive military or political results in Southeast Asia. Hanoi was, once again, thrown back on the hope that American politics would grant a victory it could win by neither its political appeal nor its military strength.

Nixon's Foreign Policy in General

Taking stock in 1969 and gambling on a successful deflation of the war in Southeast Asia, if not its complete ending, Nixon chose to dramatize in his foreign policy, themes of negotiation, reduced American engagement, and partnership. For this purpose he used lengthy annual reports to the Congress on foreign affairs, delivered February 16, 1970, February 25, 1971, and February 9, 1972. These provided an opportunity for more spacious exposition of doctrines and policies than the foreign affairs passages in a conventional State of the Union message.

For a member of the Johnson administration, these (and some other) Nixon expositions of policy make slightly uneasy reading. A good deal that is continuous with the past is presented as innovation, but that is a minor matter. If drawing a somewhat exaggerated distinction between past and present policies is judged by a President to strengthen his hand, and the policies are good, the device is legitimate—or, at least not unknown in American political life.

Nixon's three dramatized themes of policy were closely interrelated: if negotiations with Moscow and Peking eased communist pressures on the noncommunist world, the total burden of defense, in its widest sense, would be eased and American efforts could safely be diminished. As a result, the sharing of burdens with America's allies would be more manageable, since they would not require sharp increases in efforts by others.

With respect to the Soviet Union, Nixon moved ahead with the SALT talks. As these complex negotiations laboriously progressed, shadowed by the continued Soviet expansion in nuclear submarines as well as land-based missiles, progress was made on other fronts: a treaty demilitarizing the seabeds; the elimination of biological weapons; the conversion of the hot line to a satellite link; a formal agreement covering the status of West Berlin and confirming Western rights of access, evidently regarded in Moscow as a preliminary to both an accord between East and West Germany and the possible negotiation of mutual force reductions in Europe between NATO and the Warsaw Pact organization. Aside from the SALT agreement, the Moscow summit of May 1972 was taken as the occasion to sign a further group of significant bilateral agreements, each reflecting sustained prior negotiation. These included a joint venture in space and collaboration on environmental problems; but expanded economic relations evidently required further negotiation.

Any change or potential change in the balance of military forces is inherently unsettling. It was inevitable that Nixon's initiatives (as well as the parallel *Ostpolitik* of Brandt) should stir anxiety as well as hope. Would the development of Soviet strategic capabilities produce a gap that would make a first strike "rational" or would it set the framework for a confrontation of U.S. and Soviet forces in the Middle East or elsewhere? Was the quasi-isolationist mood (symbolized, for example, by pressure in the Congress to set a firm public date for the withdrawal of U.S. forces from Southeast Asia and for a reduction of U.S. forces in Europe) likely to encourage another phase of expansionist policy in Moscow? Would the Berlin agreement, the agreement between East and West Germany, and talk about mutual force reductions lead to a progressive reduction in western Europe's capacity to stand steady in the face of Soviet power?

Parallel but more intense anxieties were stirred in Asia by the ambiguities in Nixon's Southeast Asian policy, combined with the dramatic, unilateral opening of high-level diplomatic contact with Peking. The possibility of such a new development became evident with the subsidence of the Cultural Revolution and the rise to authority of the more moderate military and technocrats in Peking. It was a rational move for Peking, given the tension on the Russian frontier, Soviet movement into the Indian Ocean, concern about the future stature of Japan, and the possibility of entering the United Nations on terms that would, at the minimum, weaken the fabric of the Nationalist government on Taiwan. It was a rational move for Washington if it induced a period of restraint on the part of Peking in Southeast Asia and ended the unnatural position of the Chinese communists in the international community, without endangering the security of those associated with the United States in vital areas.

Although the revelation of Henry Kissinger's first secret visit to Peking was a piece of diplomatic theater, Nixon had signaled clearly the direction in which he was moving. He stated his broad intentions and undertook a series of ameliorating measures climaxed by the visit of the American Ping-Pong team to China.

Nevertheless, there were questions, as in the case of developments in Europe: Why were the Japanese not treated as full partners in a matter of such vital importance and such acute domestic political sensitivity? Were there sufficient prior assurances on Peking's future dispositions, notably in Southeast Asia, to justify the costs, in Taipei and elsewhere, of a Presidential visit rather than a more cautious exploration of possibilities? Was there sufficient awareness of the costs in New Delhi (including strain on the nonproliferation treaty) of this radical shift in American diplomacy?

It would be a poor return for the drama of a Presidential visit to Peking if the Chinese were to continue their active support for aggression in Southeast Asia and if Japan and India were to decide that the uncertainty of American policy required them to produce nuclear weapons.

As for the visit itself, no one, including the major actors, is in a position to assess confidently all its results. It must be viewed as part of a process set in motion by the failure of the Cultural Revolution and the pragmatic cast of Peking's domestic and foreign policy which emerged in its wake. The process will continue as Peking widens its ties with the United States and other nations. It is a potentially hopeful process, although history suggests that close cultural, diplomatic, and commercial ties in themselves do not prevent war.

Dangerous cross-purposes evidently remain over Taiwan. Its strategic importance to Japan, as well as to the United States, will remain. Its internal evolution, marked by the inevitable rise of the Taiwanese, in an economic and social setting wholly different from that on the mainland, may or may not accord with the Nationalist and communist insistence that it must remain a province of China. The option of an independent Taiwan cannot and should not be foreclosed. The issue of Taiwan may, therefore, have been complicated, rather than eased, by the awkward symbolic American concession in Peking and the subsequent sturdy reaffirmation of the American security commitment to the island's defense.

But Southeast Asia remains still the heart of the matter, if the joint agreement to oppose the hegemony of any single power in Asia is to have substance. A stable settlement there requires that a series of abiding and legitimate long-run interests be recognized by all the parties concerned. It is a legitimate interest of Peking that no major power emplace itself permanently in Southeast Asia in ways that might threaten China's borders. India has a dual legitimate interest in Southeast Asia: that no major power dominate the region and thereby the eastern portion of the Indian Ocean; and, more narrowly, that Burma, India's potential Ardennes, remain independent and not be dominated by China or any other major power. The United States, Australia, Japan, and other nations have a legitimate interest that no major power be in a position to dominate the Southwest Pacific from Southeast Asian bases, both for narrow security reasons and to assure the freedom of the seas in this critical area. Above all, the peoples of Southeast Asia, together amounting to a population the size of Africa or Latin America, have the right to shape their independent destinies without the movement of arms and men illegally across their frontiers.

No dialogue with Peking is likely to be meaningful and no understandings fruitful in the long run unless these propositions are frankly aired, agreed on, and implemented. In the wake of Nixon's visit to Peking, it was by no means clear that substantial progress had been made along these lines.

Nixon's transitional diplomacy was cross-cut, in 1971, by the American economic crisis and the disruptive measures Nixon felt impelled to take in cutting the official tie of the dollar to gold and in imposing the

10 percent surcharge on imports. These measures weighed heavily on America's major allies. They sent a signal of American weakness at precisely the time when our allies were trying to assess the meaning for their own security of Nixon's dealings with Moscow and Peking, and of the Nixon Doctrine in general. Having unilaterally gathered its bargaining weight into its own hands, Washington asked its allies to adopt economic measures that would end the American balance-of-payments deficit. There was legitimacy in the American claim that Japan was conducting a trade policy more appropriate to a poor developing nation than the third industrial power in the world; and there was legitimacy in the pressure on Europe to ease certain American financial burdens in connection with NATO. More generally, it is true that those who generate balance-of-payments surpluses, as well as those who generate deficits, bear responsibilities to the international community for corrective action.

The problem in Washington's dealings with its allies was that the crisis had been brought on by an inappropriate domestic policy over the previous two and a half years; and the legitimacy of Washington's claims on its partners was, for a time at least, overshadowed by the manner in which American bargaining leverage was employed.

The outcome could, in the end, be constructive, as the December 1971 reconcilation of exchange rates and opening of trade discussions suggested. For both western Europe and Japan, America's market and its military strength were indispensable elements in the equations of both prosperity and security, and these factors carried weight. Nevertheless, the economic crisis of 1971 made more precarious the environment in which the negotiations with Moscow and Peking were conducted. The image most required for such imaginative diplomacy was of an America managing its internal affairs well, capable of balancing carefully the benefits against the costs of détente, and shifting burdens to others gradually through orderly negotiation. A dramatic retraction of the critical role of the dollar in the international monetary system and a powerful protectionist threat were not helpful in 1971.

All this encouraged a Soviet diplomacy already moving to make the most of the possibilities opened up by Nixon's shift in China policy. Moscow had long feared an American–Chinese rapprochement. It responded in classic balance-of-power style to exploit the anxieties created by Nixon's moves. Russia moved closer to India, which was already drifting away from the United States in an atmosphere of what New Delhi regarded as Washington's neglect. The new Soviet–Indian understandings played their part in the tragic India–Pakistan war of December 1971. Moscow also approached Tokyo with a new sense of possibilities, including the bait of disgorging some of the Japanese islands seized after the Second World War. It explored in Ottawa the possibilities of exploiting Canadian concern over its colossal partner to the south, and Brezhnev went to Paris.

In riposte, perhaps, to Nixon's visit to Romania, Moscow expanded its economic and military assistance to Allende's Chile. Cautious about assuming another massive economic liability like Castro's Cuba, Moscow did not appear prepared to underwrite the consequences of a total Chilean break with the inter-American system. Above all, Moscow moved strongly to exploit Hanoi's anxiety over the Peking–Washington rapprochement to increase its influence and generously to support Hanoi's spring offensive of 1972.

Fluidity is the technical diplomatic word for the confusion and uncertainty, hope and anxiety, generated by Nixon's foreign and military policy of the period 1969–1972—a policy that might yield more stable and peaceful balances in Europe and the Far East, or increase the possibilities of chaos and violence.

Aside from the ultimate verdict of the battlefields of South Vietnam, the outcome would depend heavily on Nixon's (or his successor's) ability to generate long-run domestic political support for continued loyalty to the alliances the Nixon doctrine explicitly reaffirmed; the image of American reliability held by both America's allies and Moscow, Peking, and Hanoi; and the successful renegotiation of a stable, viable, and liberal international system of money and trade.

Nixon and the Developing World

The tendency of the nations and regions of the developing world to go their several ways was evident before Nixon came to responsibility. The failure of the Algiers Conference to take place in June 1965 was an important bench mark in that process. It reflected, as well as heightened, the lack of homogeneity in what was once called the Third World. The nations of Asia, the Middle East, Africa, and Latin America were turning inward, caught up increasingly in the long, hard struggle to build nations and a sense of nationhood and to move forward in economic growth—tasks they had to perform essentially for themselves. In Southeast Asia an important degree of regional cohesion emerged out of the crisis of 1965, and the fighting brought Thailand, Laos, Cambodia, and South Vietnam together in new ways. In the Asian subcontinent, however, Pakistan moved into acute and tragic crisis as the unevenness of economic and social development exacerbated the underlying tensions between the east and west wings of the country—a crisis bringing with it war and the dismemberment of Pakistan. In the Middle East the chronic incapacity of the Arab states to sustain cooperation, even in relation to Israel, continued. In Africa the Nigerian civil war ended and the healing began faster than most had expected, but little progress was made in regional and subregional organization as the several states struggled with their particular problems of political and economic development. Latin America failed to move toward effective economic integration. This failure compounded the inherent frustrations of development and encouraged a surge of anti-Yankee nationalism—in part, escapist, in part, reflecting unresolved problems in the flows of international private capital.

The one common strand of interest in these regions remained economic development, and Nixon appointed in 1969 a Task Force on Economic Development. Following its recommendations, the President threw his weight behind an enlarged role for multilateral lending institutions. He also moved to reduce restrictions on the use of American loans. He recognized the importance of liberalized access to the American market but could do little in this direction given the state of the domestic economy and the consequent rise of protectionist sentiment. Nevertheless, in his 1970 report to the Congress Nixon could point with pride to a reversal of the downward trend of the late 1960s.[13]

Since I took office, appropriations for bilateral economic aid have risen as follows (in millions of dollars):

FY	Development Assistance	Supporting Assistance	Total Economic Assistance
1969	$ 878	$ 385	$1,263
1970	917	395	1,312
1971	1,049	570	1,619

The trend has also been upward in our contributions to the international financial institutions and other multilateral development agencies (in millions of dollars):

	Inter-American Development Bank			World Bank			
FY	Hard Loans	Soft Loans	Asian Development Bank	Hard Loans	Soft Loans (IDA)	UNDP and Others	Total
1969	$206	$300	$20		$160	$118	$ 804
1970	206	300	20		160	113	799
1971	387	100	20	$246	160	116	1,029

Our total economic aid, bilateral and multilateral, has now been restored to a level nearly equivalent to that of the early 1960s. This is a firm foundation for undertaking the effort that is required.

In dollars, total economic aid during the Nixon administration rose from $2,067,000 in FY 1969 to $2,111,000 in FY 1970 to $2,648,000 in FY 1971.

The momentum of this development was broken, however, with the 10 percent reduction in the foreign aid budget announced along with the other crisis measures on August 15, 1971. The important long-standing request of the Congress for $100 million for the soft-loan window of the Asian Development Bank still had not been granted; and the manner of nationalizing certain American companies in Latin America cast a shadow over future U.S. development relations to the south. In the end, however, Congress did act on the request for additional funds for the Asian and Latin American regional banks, reflecting the inherently viable political base for multilateral development enterprises.

The most substantial effort to maintain the flows of assistance to the developing world during these years was that of the World Bank, under the leadership of former Secretary of Defense Robert McNamara. Using its borrowing capacity to the limit and forcing the pace in other directions as well, McNamara managed to expand the flow of development loans as follows:

FY 1968	$1.0 billion
1969	1.9
1970	2.3
1971	2.6

McNamara set out to double the flow from the World Bank in his first five years; and he seemed likely to exceed his target. It was a rare demonstration of what effective leadership could accomplish from the difficult political base of an international organization. It was by no means inevitable that this cushioning expansion of aid, at a difficult time, would occur.

The period 1969–1972 was an awkward interval in the American relation to the developing world. The developing nations pursued their interests in rather conventional nationalistic ways, while the United States was asserting its intention to retract, in degree at least, its responsibilities on the world scene while focusing on diplomacy among the great powers. Thus, the area of overlapping interest between the United States and many parts of the developing world appeared to contract.

This taking of distance was made somewhat more precarious than necessary by certain failures of the Nixon administration. While Nixon, for example, threw considerable public support behind CIAP, as the executive mechanism for the Alliance for Progress, he failed to invest the energy and quiet leadership required to make it an effective day-to-day instrument. And Latin Americans tended to follow Washington's lead in this matter, leaving a sturdy but hard-pressed secretariat to hold the fort in an important institution.

Similarly, during the period from 1969 to 1972 there was no American in New Delhi of sufficient stature to convince the Indians that they had not been written off in Washington. Over the years, United States and Indian policy had at times, converged; at others, conflicted; and at still others, been without close linkage. The period 1969–1972 was relatively barren, as had been the case during a good part of the 1950s. Nevertheless, Eisenhower, recognizing the abiding importance of India, appointed three extremely able ambassadors: George V. Allen, John Sherman Cooper, and Ellsworth Bunker. They conveyed effectively, without excessive drama, the continuing American interest in India's problems and destiny. There was no equivalent link in Nixon's time. And this compounded the perhaps inevitable costs of Nixon's posture during the Indian–Pakistani war over what became Bangladesh.

There may have been, as well, a tendency to underrate the long-run strategic importance of the Indian subcontinent—a tendency reflected, for example, in talk of a five-power world comprising western Europe, the Soviet Union, Communist China, Japan, and the United States. There did not appear to be great sensitivity in Nixon's Washington to the Indian potentiality to produce nuclear weapons or to the critical strategic links between the independence of the nations of Southeast Asia and the security of the Indian subcontinent.

The period 1969–1972 was also marked by the further decline of the romantic revolutionaries of the developing world. The ending of the Cultural Revolution in China was, of course, the most dramatic event. There was the beginning of a parallel change in Pyongyang. Having failed to kill President Park in January 1968 and with the North Korean infiltration effort rather successfully frustrated, Kim Il Sung recognized that South Korea was moving ahead at a much more rapid rate than North Korea. He began to focus attention on accelerating growth in the North, and the first beginnings of a dialogue—like that between East and West Germany—were undertaken. Similarly, in the Mediterranean, Boumedienne turned away from his former intense involvement in the struggle against Israel and fastened the attention of his people on the unfulfilled tasks of Algerian economic and social development. Even Castro, in an extraordinary masochistic speech of July 26, 1970, detailed for his people the failures in Cuban economic development of the previous decade and, thereby, committed his government to giving these matters a higher priority.

There was also a beginning of such a turn in Egypt. It may have begun in Nasser's final months as he contemplated the unprofitability of another Arab–Israeli war in the immediate future, the corrosive effect on Egyptian independence of excessive reliance on Moscow for military equipment and the massive presence of Soviet advisers, and the unsatisfactory state of Egyptian economic and social development. His successor, President Anwar el Sadat, elevated the priority of Egyptian modernization as he sought a dignified settlement of the 1967 war, which included a more explicit acknowledgment of Israeli sovereignty, territorial integrity, and political independence than Cairo had been prepared to offer in the past.

Reacting to this new climate, Nixon moved away from the format of bilateral talks with Moscow and four-power discussions on the Middle East to an American initiative. On June 25, 1970, a cease-fire proposal was suggested, as well as a structure for negotiations by Israel, Jordan, and Egypt, within the framework of the U.N. Security Council Resolution of November 22, 1967. Its acceptance in principle in Amman and Cairo triggered a flare-up of violence by the fedayeen (Arab guerrillas), backed by Syria. The independence of Jordan under King Hussein was, once again, in danger, as well as the fate of the negotiating possibilities. As Syrian forces moved into Jordan to support the fedayeen revolt, Israeli and American forces were positioned in defense. The Jordanian military did the essential work of forcing Syrian withdrawal and then turned to a virtual liquidation of the fedayeen. But the American posture was a reminder in Moscow and Cairo, as well as in Amman and Jerusalem, that the Nixon Doctrine did not involve a withdrawal of the kind of American concern and commitment for the Middle East that Eisenhower had displayed in 1958, and Johnson in 1967.

Although the drastic reduction in the power of the fedayeen freed Sadat's hands to a degree, he still faced a most complex situation in moving to negotiate a settlement with the Israelis. He acquired from Moscow sufficient arms and direct military assistance to make unprofitable deep Israeli air penetrations, which were evidently eroding his bargaining position. He also acquired amphibious transport and long-range artillery. With the threat of another war made somewhat more credible, Sadat more or less committed himself before his people to resolve the issue either by negotiation or military action before the end of 1971, thus hoping to put pressure on Israel and the United States to move to a more forthcoming negotiating posture. For Egypt, the immediate object of negotiations, derived from the 1970 American initiative, became not a general settlement but an opening of the Suez Canal; an Israeli pullback in the Sinai peninsula; and some kind of Egyptian presence on the eastern bank of the Canal.

For Israel, the immediate question was whether an agreement on the Suez Canal would lead to the deployment of massive Egyptian forces on the east bank for an easier jump-off into the Sinai. The longer-run question was whether the abandonment of its forward positions gained in 1967 could be compensated for by a peace settlement backed by a more firm and reliable American commitment to the defense of Israel. Here the isolationist temper of American political life exacerbated the vulnerability Israel felt.

For Washington, it was clear that the cease-fire proposal June 25,

1970, had set a course which, if it were to succeed, would require a greater (as well as more specific) commitment to peacekeeping in the Middle East than was made in the unsatisfactory agreements of 1957.

For Moscow, the Middle East remained an area of apparent opportunity and long-run dilemma. The dependence of Egypt (as well as Syria and Iraq) on Soviet arms continued to provide the kind of political leverage it had enjoyed since the arms deal of 1955. But that leverage was well short of Moscow's long-run requirements, if the Middle East was to be a Soviet strategic bastion. Sadat, like Nasser, had demonstrated that he was not prepared to see Soviet influence translated into political subservience to Moscow. The difficulty of translating military dependence into a reliable quasi-satellite government was further underlined for Moscow by the debacle in the Sudan in 1971. There the Soviet Union engaged itself deeply in the civil war between the Sudanese government and the southern rebels. But a communist coup was vigorously suppressed, and Soviet relations with Sudan were re-established only on a more difficult arms-length basis. Sadat reacted swiftly and negatively to this Soviet venture in the Sudan.

Quite aside from an intractable nationalism in Cairo was the inherent dilemma of a peaceful settlement. Presumably, Moscow did not want another war in the Middle East. Despite the arms buildup since 1967, the Egyptian outlook in another full-scale engagement with Israel was not hopeful. The initial battle lines were less advantageous; and there was no evidence that Egyptian pilots had overcome the qualitative superiority of the Israelis, which was based on much longer training periods and operational experience. And Moscow was less likely than in 1967 to be susceptible to over-sanguine reporting from its representatives in Cairo.

Presumably, Moscow did not yet feel safe in engaging its own forces directly against Israel. Nixon, by word and action, indicated that he was prepared to move with military force to avoid Soviet hegemony in the Middle East. The buildup of Soviet capabilities in the Mediterranean was real. But there was no evidence that the Soviet Union was prepared for a war with the United States in the Middle East, although the American Navy watched anxiously the Soviet expansion of its naval forces.

Stable peace, on the other hand, would release Egypt from the real but limited bondage that went with dependence on a flow of Soviet arms in circumstances of chronic confrontation with Israel. Cairo's behavior would become less easy to predict and control; and it might not wish to see the enlargement of Soviet influence in the Horn of Africa, the Persian Gulf, and the Indian Ocean, which were evident objectives of Moscow's global strategy.

Therefore, a deal to open the Suez Canal before a final peace appeared a reasonably promising interim move from the Soviet perspective. But Washington did not appear capable of delivering Israeli agreement on terms Sadat found acceptable. There was a hiatus in the American intermediary role, as Washington stood back to give U.N. mediator Gunnar V. Jarring another try—a possibility encouraged by the United Nations General Assembly and permitted by Sadat's quiet acceptance of his failure to resolve his problem by the end of 1971.

Meanwhile, with enlarged opportunities for Soviet initiative emerging from the Horn of Africa to Southeast Asia, thought in Moscow may have been shifting toward ways of keeping its leverage in the Middle East, even under conditions of an Arab–Israeli settlement; for the opening of the Suez Canal was becoming day by day more desirable for Soviet strategic purposes.

Nixon as President: An Interim Evaluation

The preceding analysis makes clear my view of Nixon's defense of the national interest. As of June 15, 1972, there had been no major breakthroughs in the balance of power during his administration; but serious unresolved questions overhung Southeast Asia and the Middle East, South Asia, Europe, and Latin America. The military balance between the Soviet Union and the United States and the state of international monetary and trade negotiations also posed questions whose answers would suffuse all other matters.

In committing himself to summit meetings in Peking and Moscow, Nixon had gained great potential political advantage as a Presidential election approached. And there were sound bases for pursuing these openings, if the foundations of American strength and will were maintained as well as stability in the alliance structure. The outcome of this critical equation could not be predicted as of June 1972. The state of the alliances had not been more precarious in Asia since the early months of 1965 or in Europe since the time of Suez, only partially mitigated by Nixon's series of fence-mending meetings with the heads of governments of important allies in December 1971 and January 1972. It was not to be ruled out that the net outcome of Nixon's initiatives would be salutary, despite the gambles they incorporated and underpinnings one would wish to see more firm. A "generation of peace" was a decent hope, a goal worthy of effort, risk, and sacrifice; but it was too soon to make it a promise.

In terms of stages of growth, Nixon recognized that the objectives of American society had shifted since the mid-1950s; and he recognized also the widespread desire for a pause, consolidation, and regrouping in the wake of Johnson's social and legislative revolution of the 1960s. There was in his approach a typically conservative tendency to substitute apparently tidy government reorganization for serious movement forward on concrete problems. Nevertheless, there was substance, or potential substance, in some of his domestic initiatives. He moved ahead on problems of air and water pollution; and he placed before the Congress two proposals which, if accepted, could cast long shadows: revenue sharing with the states and the family assistance plan, with its underlying concept of a negative income tax.

But down to 1972 the combination of Nixon's tax policy and the disheveled state of the economy slowed the flow of revenue to federal, state, and local governments, inhibiting efforts in every direction to move forward in the search for quality. In the wake of the exhausting efforts of the 1960s, the political life of the nation accepted with relative passivity this setback; but, I would guess, not for long.

In terms of the allocation of resources (including the President's political capital), Nixon's performance in his first three years was colored, like the other dimensions of his policy, by the way he initially handled the problem of growth and inflation. Within that framework he reduced allocations to national security. But Nixon's dissipation of the 1968 surcharge and his tax reforms promised to make more difficult the generation of public revenues over the longer future. In this, Nixon's policy conformed to the classic conservative choice between the allocation of resources between the private and public sectors.

In the balance between justice and order Nixon correctly reflected the election verdict of 1968, with its evident national concern with disorder and crime; and he benefited by the less volatile moods among Negro and white dissidents that became evident in 1968. He used openings for appointment to the Supreme Court to shift the balance sharply in a conservative direction, with the proviso, of course, that the behavior of Supreme Court justices, once on the bench, has not always proved predictable. With respect to the hard-knotted problems of the cities and their ghettos, he expended little of his political capital, excepting the proposal for family assistance whose fate remained obscure and whose consequences, if put into effect, remained uncertain.

On November 6, 1968, the day after the election, I met with a group of German political figures who had been scheduled for some time to visit various branches of the government. Commenting on the election, I told them of Arthur Schlesinger, Sr.'s, famous hypothesis that defined cycles of activist and conservative phases running the full length of American history. I said we had clearly entered a conservative phase, not unexpected in view of the ardent and turbulent period through which America had passed since Kennedy's inauguration. And in his political base and history, Nixon belongs among the conservative American Presidents; and his hope for a larger mandate in 1972 lay primarily in drawing to his cause many who in 1968 had voted for George Wallace—a figure whose support was complex but, on the whole, conservative.

In terms of the American style, Nixon falls generally among those whose instinct is to deal with problems by institutionalizing their handling rather than by introducing major experimental initiatives.

On the other hand, the problems he confronted did not permit the passivity of a Warren Harding or Calvin Coolidge. And, by temperament, he is more activist than Eisenhower, and, perhaps, more of a gambler. Tactically, his style is more dramatic. As a matter of conviction, Eisenhower felt that issues should be presented in less rather than more dramatic form, designed to minimize conflict and maximize consensus. Nixon has evidently enjoyed the *coup de théâtre*.

Nixon is evidently concerned, in the best sense, with his place in history. The areas of greatest opportunity lay in seeing Southeast Asia and the Middle East through to stable peace; completing successfully the SALT talks; stabilizing the situation in central Europe; and opening a new relationship with Peking. These opportunities had emerged from tangled events and confrontations of the past, reaching back, at least, to the post-Sputnik communist offensive and its frustration. But Nixon set about to make the most of the opportunities before him.

He did so in his first three years in a purposeful and systematic way. In terms of the American style, he was not reacting to crisis but trying to reduce the pursuit of peace to an ongoing process. He recognized the potentialities opened by Hanoi's setback in Tet 1968, the victory of the pragmatists in the Cultural Revolution, the Soviet interest in the SALT talks, and the shift in Cairo's political temper. The fate of his pacific ventures hinges on whether the military, political, and economic foundations for America's world position remain sufficiently sturdy to avoid the re-opening of temptations in adversary capitals—as Vietnamization, at the pace it was conducted, tempted Hanoi to launch and Moscow to support the spring offensive of 1972.

With respect to the domestic scene, Nixon's ambitions were less majestic. There did not appear to be within him the outrage Johnson felt at the wastages of talent and vitality that came with inequalities of opportunity in American society; and, even if there were, the time was not propitious for dramatic advances. His visceral instinct seemed to come from another old strand in the American tradition; namely, that a man should expect to move forward by his own efforts, that obstacles and set-backs were a part of life, but that American society was sufficiently flexible and yielding to grant success to the persevering. But in a nation already deeply committed to the search for quality, Nixon did not turn back the clock in major matters. I doubt, however, that his dispositions will prove adequate for the longer pull. The United States is not matching the scale of its unresolved problems with adequate resources. And, of their nature, the problems require Presidential definition and public education before the foundations for effective action can be laid. All this may require either a lifting of the fatigue of the late 1960s or the re-emergence of acute crisis;

but, in the meanwhile, 1972 might be a prosperous year, and, for a time, Nixon's dispositions, like Eisenhower's in his first term, might well suffice. Nevertheless, a good deal of thin ice had to be transited before November.

Putting aside domestic matters and particular tactical situations and choices in foreign policy, Nixon was seeking to organize in new ways a world of diffusing power. This was the meaning of his diplomacy with Peking, of Vietnamization, and the Guam doctrine; of his enlarged contacts with Romania and Yugoslavia; of his willingness to contemplate negotiations between NATO and the Warsaw Pact organization on mutual force reductions; less felicitously, of his stance toward Latin America and the Indian subcontinent. Basically, the diffusion of economic power, exacerbated by Nixon's initial domestic policy, lay behind the broken link between the dollar and the gold price and the 10 percent surcharge.

Nixon perceived that a world of more diffuse power could be a more peaceful world. But it could also be a world of increased disorganization and violence, as the outbreak of war on the Indian subcontinent in December 1971, Hanoi's offensive of 1972, and the danger of further nuclear proliferation suggested. It is to the longer-run characteristics of a world of diffusing power and the American role within it that we now, finally, turn.

43

The American Agenda

THE DIFFUSION OF POWER AS SEEN IN 1960

SPEAKING TOWARDS THE CLOSE OF THE PUGWASH CONFERENCE IN MOSCOW in December 1960, I said:

> As an historian, I am convinced that the central historical fact of our time is this: power is being rapidly diffused away from Moscow and Washington. What we are seeing in the world is an equivalent of the process which occurred after 1815. In 1815 Great Britain was the only country in the world which had absorbed the tricks of then modern technology. It alone had experienced an industrial revolution. In the century after 1815, the industrial revolution took hold in Belgium, France, Germany, Russia, Japan, and North America.
>
> Now the industrial revolution is taking hold in the areas which were skipped during the century after 1815—that is to say the industrial revolution is taking hold in China and Eastern Europe; and it is occurring—or it will soon occur—in the whole southern half of the globe.
>
> The inevitable result is that industrial potential, military power, and influence on the world scene are being diffused and will continue to be diffused.
>
> Faced with this fact, there are three choices open to the Soviet Union and the United States. We can stumble into a war and destroy a large part of what man has built on the face of the earth and a large part of the world's population. We can continue the Cold War

> until the diffusion of power removes the capacity to decide from Moscow and Washington. Or, working constructively together, we can create the terms on which power will become diffused.
>
> This is the limit of the historical powers of the Soviet Union and the United States. I would hope that we would choose the third path. This is the historical responsibility we owe to our peoples.[1]

I recall this perspective of more than a decade ago to underline a fact sometimes forgotten: in a world marked by rapid, apparently shapeless, and kaleidoscopic change there are also identifiable forces at work which move at a slower pace but with great power and consistency.

Despite an important continuing element of bipolarity in nuclear matters, the diffusion of power has quietly proceeded so far in these twelve years that the capacity to decide on the terms of its further diffusion has, in some areas, almost passed from the hands of Moscow and Washington, even in areas where they may be prepared to work in concert.

The diffusion of power in a democratic society is the foundation for human liberties. In the global community, it is the basis for national independence, because it renders less realistic dreams of global or regional hegemony. But human liberty without an ordered structure of law would make democratic life chaotic and violent within national societies, and so it is with uninhibited and unstructured national independence on the world scene. Therefore, the central question on the international scene remains this: Can the intimately interconnected world community of nations organize the diffusion of power in ways that lead to relatively stable peace; or will the diffusion of power lead to increased violence and choas?

THE NUCLEAR QUESTION: THE CONDITIONS FOR NONPROLIFERATION

THE most sensitive form of power diffusion is, of course, the production of nuclear weapons; and a common interest in limiting nuclear proliferation has been, for more than a decade, the strongest link between Moscow and Washington, short of their responsibility to avoid nuclear war itself.

Three powers produced nuclear weapons in 1958, five in 1971. In addition, a good many nations have acquired over these years the economic and technological capacity to produce nuclear weapons within a reasonably short time, if they should decide to do so—among them, Japan, India, Israel, and the Federal Republic of Germany. Of these, neither India nor Israel has signed the nonproliferation treaty; Japan and Germany have signed but not ratified the treaty. The fate of the NPT is, then, undecided.

As the diplomacy of nonproliferation unfolded, it became clear that those states without nuclear weapons commanded considerable bargaining leverage over those producing nuclear weapons; and that leverage had its effect.

First is the commitment exacted in the preamble of the nonproliferation treaty, in which the nuclear weapons states declare "their intention to achieve at the earliest possible date the cessation of the nuclear arms race." Preambular rhetoric is not notably influential in international affairs. But, in fact, Moscow as well as Washington recognized that the acceptance of the nonproliferation treaty around the world was unlikely unless the United States and the Soviet Union appeared to be making an effort in good faith to control the bilateral strategic arms race.

Second is the question of nuclear blackmail. Moscow and Washington came to understand that nations capable of producing nuclear weapons were not likely to deny themselves that option for long if they themselves were subjected to nuclear blackmail. Thus, the commitments of the Soviet Union, the United Kingdom, and the United States to the United Nations Security Council of June 1968 to provide assistance to any non-nuclear weapons state party to the nonproliferation treaty that is a victim of active aggression or the threat of aggression involving nuclear weapons.

The third condition is that non-nuclear weapons states suffer no technological or economic disadvantage by signing the treaty. Although some problems are still to be resolved, the diffusion of nuclear technology for nonmilitary purposes has, in fact, gone forward in a reasonably even-handed way through intergovernmental cooperation as well as commercial channels.

The fourth condition is American reliability as an ally. The NPT permits withdrawal if "extraordinary events, related to the subject matter of this Treaty, have jeopardized the supreme interests" of a signatory nation. The negotiating history of the NPT made clear that continued steadiness in American security commitments would be required if the "supreme interests" clause was not to be evoked at some time.

In addition to these four reasonably formal conditions for the maintenance of the nonproliferation treaty, two questions may have to be answered if the production of nuclear weapons is not to be extended.

First is whether possession of even a small national nuclear capability is to be regarded as "a ticket to the top table." After the Berlin and Cuba missile crises of 1961 and 1962, the nuclear question in Europe abated. The nuclear status of France and Britain has created less tension in Germany and Italy than in the early 1960s, although I doubt we have seen the end of the nuclear problem in Europe. Barring a remarkable breakthrough toward stable peace, it will certainly arise when the British movement into Europe is fully consummated and, perhaps, sooner. But the lack of nuclear weapons did not prevent Germany from continuing to rise in economic and diplomatic stature in the decade after the Cuba missile crisis; nor did possession much mitigate the vicissitudes of Great Britain in recent years or enlarge the stature of France vis-à-vis its European partners.

In Asia, however, things are potentially different as Peking enters the U.N. Security Council. At the end of the Second World War it was natural that China occupy the only permanent Security Council seat for Asia. But more than a quarter-century later, Japan, the third industrial power in the world, and India, the second largest nation in the world—and its largest democracy—equally deserve seats on the Security Council. The Asia of 1972 is not the Asia of 1945; and three seats for Asia, where two thirds of humanity live, are not excessive.

The major ground on which Communist China can claim a unique position in Asia is that it has produced nuclear weapons. If it emerged that this is the foundation for a special status for Peking in world councils, the pressure in Tokyo and New Delhi to join the nuclear weapons club will increase.

Second, there is the question of guerrilla harassment across international frontiers. The world community in the 1960s was exceedingly casual about dealing with this problem, leaving the victims alone or supported by those friends willing to help—whether it was Laos, Cambodia, and Vietnam, Malaysia, Venezuela, Bolivia, or Israel. If this casualness persists in a world where nations acquire the technical bases for producing nuclear weapons, and if this technique of guerrilla aggression is still applied, pressure to break the nonproliferation barrier could increase. This could happen through a process of escalation we have already observed in the Middle East. Protracted and systematic guerrilla harassment of Israel led in 1967 to Israeli reprisals by conventional forces. This, in turn, led to the mobilization and clash of large armies. The likelihood of a repetition of this sequence has already brought Israel close to a nuclear weapons capability. In time others might be drawn by a similar logical sequence to consider a nuclear riposte, even if it promises no more than to pull down the pillars of the temple around them; for men do not generally accept defeat passively without using up the weapons in hand or those for which they can reach.

Nations will not decide lightly to produce nuclear weapons. The nontechnological barriers are quite high. If a nation decided to make nuclear weapons, it might, for example, face an awkward and even dangerous interval—when ties with the United States would be weakened, but before an adequate national deterrent force had been built. For Germany and Japan there would, in addition, be extremely heavy diplomatic pressure from abroad derived from memories of the Second World War; and for India, the danger that Pakistan might invite Chinese Communist nuclear power into the subcontinent.

Nevertheless, over time something like these six conditions will have to be fulfilled if nuclear proliferation is to be contained within its already dangerous limits. Taken together, these six conditions, if met, would move the world a long distance toward stable peace.

It is quite possible that the wisdom and foresight required to avoid further nuclear proliferation will prove beyond the capacity of conventional statesmen, operating under conventional nationalist political pressures, in a still highly competitive world arena of diffusing economic and technological capacity. The global community would then risk a dangerous fragmentation of its political and economic, as well as security, arrangements. There is no aspect of contemporary diplomacy more important or less well understood than the rules of concert and coordination required for an alliance (or diplomatic friendship) to operate successfully in a nuclear age. If nuclear proliferation proceeds, the maintenance of such ties would, somewhat ironically, require that those rules be even more rigorously honored than at present.

The Diffusion of Economic Power

Quite aside from the nuclear question, modern science and technology are being progressively diffused throughout the world as nations move forward—some swiftly, others fitfully—through the stages of economic growth. Tables 43-1 and 43-2 suggest roughly how things might look in the year 2000 for major groupings in terms of population and per capita GNP.[2]

TABLE 43–1
POPULATION, BY MAJOR REGIONS, 1965 AND 2000
(millions)

	1965	2000
Less developed world		
Africa	311	779
Asia less Japan	1,791	3,558
Latin America	233	615
	2,335	4,952
Developed world		
Japan	98	123
United States and Canada	227	383
Oceania	14	25
Europe	648	886
	987	1,417

World total 1965: 3,322; 2000: 6,369

TABLE 43–2
PER CAPITA GNP, IN DEVELOPED AND LESS DEVELOPED WORLD, 1965 AND 2000

	1965	2000
Less developed world	143	373
Developed world	1,826	5,155

In terms of per capita income, the projected progress of the less developed world may appear disappointing. Per capita GNP of $373 doesn't seem like much (an average brought down by the heavy weight of China and India, starting as they do from present levels of about $100 per capita). But GNP per capita does not accurately reflect the degree to which national economies have or have not absorbed technologies relevant to military power. Japan, for example, conquered most of East Asia and mounted the attack on Pearl Harbor with a GNP per capita (in 1965 dollars) of about $300.

At a GNP per capita of about $100, Communist China has developed both nuclear weapons and missiles. At a similar level, India commands a sophisticated atomic energy establishment as well as substantial engineering and chemical industries. Three decades of further development should permit the Chinese and Indians to absorb virtually all then-current technologies, even if the average standard of living for the people is still relatively modest and large regions in both societies remain relatively impoverished. The point is that in terms of stages of growth, many nations of the less developed world will attain technological maturity about the year 2000 and, with it, the potential to amass vastly increased powers of destruction. Whatever the gap in income between rich and poor nations, the gap in military potential is likely to narrow over the next three decades, heightening the already strong case for making the nonproliferation treaty viable.

The movement forward in the stages of growth will have significant consequences in the various regions of the world as well as globally. In the Western Hemisphere, for example, Brazil may well be a nation of more than 200 million, with a GNP per capita of about $560 (in 1965 dollars), beyond technological maturity, enjoying an early phase of high mass-consumption. Mexico may well have a population of 120 million and a GNP per capita of $750. Nations within the hemisphere will, evidently, be able to generate significant military potential of their own. Obviously, more mature relations between the United States and Latin America will have to evolve if the fundamental security understandings within the hemisphere are to be maintained. The classic posture of the United States toward the hemisphere will have to change.

Advances through the stages of growth will not be smooth and uneventful for either the presently developed or less developed nations. The latter confront, above all, the desperate necessity of lowering their birth rates. The time bought by the discovery and diffusion of new wheat and rice strains is likely to be short. The likelihood of major food crises in India, East Pakistan, China, and Java is great unless there is a breakthrough in birth control methods—of high acceptability and capable of rapid and efficient diffusion—equivalent to that in agricultural productivity.

Continued industrialization at its present pace, moreover, will pose massive environmental problems, of which the world community is only now becoming conscious, as well as the possibility of raw material and energy bottlenecks. It is not difficult, given the pace of both population increase and industrialization, to project gross tragedies of starvation, pollution and resource exhaustion for the twenty-first century on the basis of present trends.[3] One aspect or another of such projections is debatable. What is not debatable is the urgency of international cooperation to generate and apply new technologies of birth control; resource substitution; recycling and other antipollution measures; and power generation.

A new agenda of balance will gradually supersede the old agenda of uninhibited growth which, in all its manifestations, dominated the global community over the past two centuries. The necessity for global cooperation in dealing with that new agenda is heightened by a particular probability.

The requirements for oil, natural gas, and basic minerals between the older industrial nations (whose take-offs occurred before 1900) and younger countries (whose take-offs have occurred since, say, the 1930s) could increasingly conflict under circumstances where the latter feel a sense of inequity at the advantages granted the former by accidents of history.

The older industrial nations, on the other hand, could well feel a sense of inequity at the abnormally high rates of population increase (by historical standards) that have come about in the newer nations as the result of the rapid diffusion of modern medicine and public health and the failure to allocate sufficient resources and political priority to population control. Current rates of population increase could produce unbearably high claims on international resources and impose heavy burdens of pollution on air and water as industrialization and urbanization proceed along presently conventional lines.

In an effort to avoid such conflict, quite specific responsibilities would fall on both the old and new industrialized nations, which I shall not try to elaborate here. It is sufficient to underline that next to the need to seek a world consistent with nuclear nonproliferation, the foreseeable imperatives of avoiding a Malthusian–Ricardian doomsday argue most strongly for a struggle to organize a world of diffusing power, rather than permitting that diffusion to yield the anarchy and chaos of which it is evidently capable.

The diffusion of economic power has consequences quite aside from its relation to military potential and the task of balancing equitably man and his limited physical environment. The rise of western Europe and Japan as holders of monetary reserves, trading partners, and sources of international aid dramatically altered over the past fifteen years the terms on which economic negotiations were conducted and political dispositions made. These shifts affected not only dealings within the rich man's monetary and trade clubs (e.g., the Organization for Economic Cooperation and Development [O.E.C.D.] and the Kennedy Round negotiations completed in 1967), but also diplomacy with the developing world and even the dispositions made in Moscow and Peking, where the rapid emergence of Germany and Japan, in particular, was noted and taken into account. This process also made possible the shift in the proportion of aid resources allocated to multilateral organizations; e.g., the World Bank complex, and the Latin American and Asian regional banks. The leverage of the United States was systematically reduced and an increasing amount of American diplomacy shifted from a bilateral to a multilateral basis. From Truman's support of the Marshall Plan and western European unity to the present, American policy actively supported these efforts to diffuse economic and political power in the noncommunist world and to organize it on a multilateral basis.

Partially related to this process has been a diffusion of political power. As noted above, the rising political importance of Bonn and Tokyo, including Chancellor Willy Brandt's role in negotiations with the East and the uneasy courting of Tokyo by Peking as well as Moscow, clearly relates to the emerging economic stature of Germany and Japan. The capacity of the countries of east Asia to begin the building of regional institutions is related to gathering economic strength and confidence, as is the role of Iran in trying to build understandings in the Persian Gulf to maintain that area's independence as the British withdraw. But political assertiveness emerged in Africa even when its economic foundations were frail, rooted in a determination to cut back and limit the role of non-African nations on the continent. And the assertiveness of Latin American countries toward the United States has sometimes been a function not of emerging economic strength but of domestic frustration and an incapacity to move forward in Latin American economic integration.

In general, the diffusion of power within the noncommunist world proceeded in reasonable order in monetary and trade affairs down to the crisis of 1971. The monetary agreement of December 1971 opened up the possibility of restoring concert in trade and, hopefully, in aid policy as well. Britain's entry into the Common Market, when consummated, would greatly strengthen that organization and open the way to a more even balance across the Atlantic. Despite its vicissitudes, the OAS structure has survived the crisis of a communist Cuba and adjusted to the Latin American thrust for accelerated economic and social development, although its future is not assured. The attempt to organize a regional structure in Asia, seriously begun in 1966, is too new and the structure of Asia still too unsettled for the outcome to be judged certain. In Africa a structure exists of regional and subregional institutions as well as a common will to exclude major external powers; but its strength is still to be acquired, and its capacity to adapt to new problems still to be tested. The Middle East remains essentially fragmented, still incapable of organizing around any stable, agreed security, welfare, or political objectives.

One can conclude, then, that the noncommunist world has worked since Bretton Woods and the Marshall Plan to generate structures within which power can safely be diffused. Of these, the most important and the most fully elaborated are those that keep constructively in harness western Europe, North America, and Japan: notably, NATO, the Japanese Security Treaty, and the OECD. The regional and subregional structures of the developing world will assume increased importance with the passage of time. But all these enterprises, even the most deeply rooted and substantial, remain fragile and incomplete.

The Diffusion of Power in the Communist World

The central advantage in the Cold War thus far enjoyed by the United States has been the fact that the diffusion of power posed less difficult problems for Washington than for Moscow. Major American security interests were satisfied by three essentially negative conditions; namely, that no single power dominate Europe or Asia or emplace itself within the Western Hemisphere. American policy could honestly support the efforts to gather strength and maintain independence of those nations which shared one or another of these negative objectives. That included all the noncommunist countries of western Europe, Asia, and Latin America, except those which, for reasons of local or regional ambition, sought to exploit the possibilities of close association with Moscow; e.g., for a time, Sukarno's Indonesia and Nasser's Egypt. The United States could also throw its weight behind regional developments—like the Common Market and the movement for Latin American integration—whose inherent structures assured that no single power was likely to achieve dominance. Ideologically, while American interests were real, they could be fully satisfied by a world of great diversity.

The problem for Moscow was that it was driven by Russian history, geography, ideological commitment, and the international organization of

Communist parties to seek a positive objective: the domination of both ends of Eurasia, and the regions beyond, by communist states.

This proposition requires careful elaboration, for the relation between ideological and national power objectives has always been complex in Soviet policy; and that also has been the case for Peking since 1949.

From earliest days, the Soviet regime's priority was the maintenance of communist power in Russia. As it looked abroad, its policy was influenced by the ideological vision of a communist world dominated by Moscow; and this vision was institutionalized in the Comintern and subsequent linkages to communist parties in every part of the world. But systematically, Moscow has put its own interests as a regime controlling a nation-state above those of foreign communist parties when such interests came into conflict. The first and formative test came with the Treaty of Brest–Litovsk. Lenin decided to accept the "annexationist-peace" rather than "to start at once a revolutionary war." The "actual conditions and the interest of the Socialist Revolution" in Russia came first; and the German Communist party was left to fend for itself. This general policy has persisted.

The nationalist imperatives in Soviet foreign policy substantially derived, as in the case of the United States and others, from geography. As an island off the land mass of Eurasia, the United States could be content unless threatening constellations of power emerged across the seas in Europe or Asia, or intruded into the Western Hemisphere. As a nation in the center of Eurasia, with open plains to the west and southeast, Russia had lived its life endlessly threatened and tempted by strengths and weaknesses in Europe or Asia. Whereas the threats to the United States emerged sporadically, Moscow has always lived with a sense of chronic danger. When serious concentrations of power generated in central or eastern Europe or in Japan or China, Moscow was concerned; when weaknesses emerged in either direction, Moscow's instinct was to exploit them.

The Russian Revolution of 1917 did not change all this except to heighten the sense of danger and to provide a reinforcing ideological sense of legitimacy in exploiting opportunities to expand the power Moscow could exercise around its periphery and beyond.

Thus, when the interests of communism abroad converged with—or were thought to converge with—Russian interests, Moscow has been willing to invest resources and take risks in advancing the communist cause. Moreover, the ideological impulse to continue to lead the world communist movement and to resist those who would contest or dilute that leadership has remained strong. As we have seen since 1957, the challenge of Peking has influenced Soviet policy on many critical occasions; and despite all the high-level visitors who go from Moscow to Belgrade, Yugoslavia's independence remains a deep affront.

Finally, to be a communist carries with it a conviction that the appropriate end product of history, no matter how long delayed, is the emergence of communist-controlled states. A Finland or an Austria can be accepted; a close relation with a noncommunist India can be regarded as a legitimate tactical phase. But the impulse to move to the end of the line remains strong, as the stories of Indonesia in 1965 and Sudan in 1971 suggest.

There is, then, an abiding communist strand in Soviet foreign policy. This element of ideological compulsion does not yield a fixed plan for Soviet expansion; but it is a real and vital factor in Soviet policy that plays its part from day to day without determining in any simple way how Moscow will act in the face of a given situation.

The role of ideology is further complicated by another dimension of Soviet experience. Even where communist governments were installed or independently acquired power, their national interests ran counter to the grand vision of a communist empire led and dominated by Moscow. Thus, the eastern European base created by Stalin came under strain as early as 1948 with Tito's defection. Eastern Europe gradually became a source of continuing defensive anxiety. The nationalist and liberalizing forces at work, set back by the 1968 invasion of Czechoslovakia and the Brezhnev Doctrine, will certainly gain strength over time. Thus, Moscow's concern to achieve a degree of international legitimacy for East Germany and to contain the assertiveness of Belgrade and Bucharest.

The relation between the Soviet and Chinese Communist parties, uncertain since 1927, was ruptured by the nuclear issue as well as the question of who should lead the world communist movement. Although Sino–Soviet relations may in time become less enflamed, a pattern of mutual hostility and anxiety has been set and bit deep.

The diffusion of power over the past fifteen years has, then, not only tended to make the noncommunist world less vulnerable to communist penetration, but it has also weakened the cohesion of the communist world. The overwhelming fact is that the diffusion of power in the world has reduced Soviet power and will continue to do so.

All this has not denied Moscow openings for a vigorous foreign policy. Cross-purposes among the states of the Middle East permitted Moscow to penetrate and gain considerable leverage in the area. India's problems and interests permitted a quite close association to develop between Moscow and New Delhi, aided by a somewhat myopic American policy. Cuban history yielded Castro and the expensive, sometimes baffling, but still interesting, relationship between Moscow and Havana. The vagaries of Chilean politics produced Allende. I have no doubt that, as it surveys an inherently volatile world scene, the secretariat to the Presidium will continue to find openings for Soviet initiatives that might expand Soviet power at the expense of Washington or Peking—or, as in the case of Hanoi's 1972 offensive, at the expense of both. These will continue to be seriously considered by Soviet rulers; and on some of them they will act.

In general, however, what we have observed over the years since Sputnik is a gradual, erratic rise in the role of conventional national interests in Soviet policy, as the power of nationalism elsewhere deflated the hopes for a united, expanding communist empire which Mao had stated so forcefully in Moscow in November 1957. And the Russian national interest in a world of diffusing power counsels increasing concern for dangers that might come upon the Soviet Union—thus, the nonproliferation treaty and all that must follow if nonproliferation is to be brought about.

The diffusion of power does not guarantee that Moscow will work with Washington and others to make the world more safe for the Soviet peoples; but it makes that outcome more possible. Similarly, the diffusion of power, as it appears to a Peking confronting massive Soviet forces on its inner frontiers and a Japan emerging as the third industrial power in the world, makes the achievement of a stable balance of power in Asia conceivable. But once again, American policy and Peking's view of the society that sustains it remain critical variables.

THE AMERICAN AGENDA: AN APPROACH

THE world of diffusing power I have tried to evoke is clearly capable of moving toward more order than we have known since 1914—or more violence and anarchy. What are America's tasks if we try to tip the balance in the right direction? I shall try to get at these matters by bringing to bear successively the four concepts which shape this book: the stages of growth; the generation and allocation of resources among the three abiding tasks of government; the national interest; and the national style.

THE STAGES OF GROWTH: CAN AMERICA REMAIN A GREAT POWER IN THE SEARCH FOR QUALITY?

THE Treasury's gold stock stood at $24 billion in 1949, only a billion dollars lower in 1957. It then fell rapidly to $18 billion by 1960. A decade later it was $11 billion. These figures symbolize the gathering balance-of-payments crisis of the United States from the quiet anxieties of 1958 to the desperate measures of August 1971 and the precarious resolution of December of that year.

In breaking the link between the dollar and the price of gold, Nixon proclaimed, in effect, that the United States was a nation like any other; and that it would not and could not sustain the commitment to surrender gold for dollars in official transactions at $35 an ounce—the commitment on which the international monetary system had rested since the Bretton Woods agreement went into effect.

But the United States in 1971 was not a nation like any other. It was the nuclear guarantor of western Europe; and the presence of substantial American forces in Europe was required to make that guarantee credible. It was also the nuclear guarantor of Japan, Taiwan, Australia, and New Zealand; and the security of South Korea and Southeast Asia had to be assured (as explicit American commitments required) if those guarantees were to remain credible. Less formally, the United States had accumulated commitments to Iran and Lebanon, Jordan, Saudi Arabia, and Israel. For these to remain credible—and the ample explosive potentials of the Middle East to be contained—the Sixth Fleet had to be near at hand with bases available permitting the quick bringing to bear of additional American forces, should circumstances so require. Finally, like other major rich nations, the United States had come to accept the common law commitment to maintain substantial assistance to the developing world; and, although its relative performance in this role weakened in the late 1960s, substantial outlays were required to permit the South Vietnamese, Lao, and Cambodians to resist the North Vietnamese aggression financed with military and economic aid by Moscow, Peking, and other communist capitals.

A nation with these responsibilities, which also wished to avoid nuclear proliferation, needed a balance-of-payments surplus—or, at least, a deficit that added only modest and mutually acceptable amounts to the dollar reserves of other nations.

This requirement places before the American economy and national policy an inherently difficult challenge exacerbated by three technical factors[4]: the shift in leading sectors in directions unlikely to expand the nation's export potential; e.g., education, medical services, travel, recreation, environmental and urban policies; the structure of American research and development, unevenly distributed among the sectors, with an extraordinary concentration in electronics, chemicals, and the aerospace industries; the lack of export-mindedness in all but a small proportion of American firms.

These technical factors heighten the already acute need for highly disciplined wage and price policies. The United States must master and institutionalize the difficult problems of labor, industry, and government cooperation (including, above all, cooperation among labor leaders) required to make wage-price guideposts work as a supplement to fiscal and monetary policy. If one thing is now certain, after the Nixon experiment of January 1969-August 1971, it is that fiscal and monetary policy alone are incapable of steering successfully within the narrow path bounded by a politically unacceptable level of employment and an economically unacceptable level of inflation. It is by no means clear that the price and wage decisions emerging from the complex machinery created by Nixon in October 1971 are sufficiently rigorous to do the job. Without an effective wage-price policy, the exchange rate and trade concessions negotiated by the United States with its major trading partners will soon be dissipated.

In as large and resourceful an economy as that of the United States, where price and wage discipline is maintained, there are, surely, the possibilities of generating the increases in productivity required to pay our way. In a trillion-dollar economy, the margins on which balance-of-payments strain or viability hinge are small. Despite the new directions in which resources are likely to be allocated in a society engaged in the search for quality, the critical factor is likely to be whether an effective national consensus is developed on the society's purposes, at home and abroad, rather than the technical constraints imposed by the new stage of development.

When a substantial American majority agrees on what needs doing, we will find we still command the means to do it.

THE GENERATION AND ALLOCATION OF PUBLIC RESOURCES: IS THE UNITED STATES LIKELY TO MAKE PROGRESS IN SEARCH FOR QUALITY?

As always and everywhere, a nation's purposes are reflected in the public budgets—for the United States, the federal budget above all, not only because of its size, but also because it helps determine the level and composition of state and local outlays.

The two fundamental questions that have to be answered are: How much of their income are the citizens prepared to surrender for public purposes? And how should public resources be allocated as among competing possible uses?

The answer to both questions is strongly colored by the state of the economy: its real rate of growth and the rate of price increases. A slowdown in growth hits simultaneously both sides of the budget: it cuts tax revenues; adds to unemployment relief and other welfare payments; and it also strengthens resistance to tax increases. Similarly, inflation both increases costs of government (often disproportionately) and, by putting pressure on real wages, strengthens resistance to tax increases.

Clearly, the most basic task of American society is to find its way to regular growth without inflation.[5] Unless this objective is achieved, the prospects for the American position on the world scene and at home are exceedingly dim.

In what follows I shall assume the problem of wage-price discipline is tolerably solved. I shall also set aside for later the problem of the American national interest and the policies required to sustain it. The purpose here is to consider the question: Is the United States likely to make progress in the search for quality?

A society of quality involves, of course, much more than the allocation of public resources; but the concept is stripped of meaning unless progress is made in dealing with certain problems that will not yield unless large public resources are applied to their solution.

On the domestic side, the major problems are clear[6]: revenue sharing, welfare and family assistance, job creation, social security, financing medical care, environmental quality, transportation, housing, and agriculture.

I would make three general observations about this range of problems which cannot be fully explored here. First, national policy is now moving along lines that promise to reduce the solution of some of these problems to an ongoing process. The legislative foundations are there or, at least, a common recognition that a major problem exists. A consensus exists, based on experience, as to how the problem should be approached. Argument, of course, proceeds and will continue; but there is reason for confidence that the American political process is, in the widest sense, committed to act. The critical question is: Will the American political process generate the resources required to diminish the weight of the problem with the passage of time?

Second, the problem of the urban ghetto deserves a different status because we do not know how to solve it. I am not wise enough to outline with confidence a program to liquidate the urban ghettos,[7] but I do know the period of experiment has been too short to justify despair.[8] I believe, moreover, that a serious and effective program must have these characteristics: it must be a long-term program, for there are no quick solutions; it must exist in an environment of rapid noninflationary growth, which will create incentives to recruit ghetto labor and provide a feasible setting for Black Capitalism; it must involve the opening up of the suburbs to Negroes as well as an improvement in the conditions of the cities themselves; it must involve experiment until we learn what works, notably experiment with Model Cities as originally conceived, day care, and family assistance; it must involve revision of present boundaries to permit efficient planning of metropolitan areas.

We need, in effect, a combination of functional and development approaches to the ghetto, combined with high, noninflationary growth.

Third, any serious effort to set in motion a constructive spiral in the ghettos will cost a lot of money—more money than now appears available. Looking ahead to 1976, the Brookings study of the budget and its future concludes:

> Economic growth, combined with reduced costs in Vietnam, will make available substantial additional resources to the federal government over the next several years. But most of these additional resources have already been implicitly committed under existing or

> proposed expenditure programs. Indeed, between now and 1974, it is likely that all of the funds made available by economic growth and savings in Vietnam will be absorbed by expenditures to which we are already committed and new programs already proposed in the budget. Only in the years after 1974 will uncommitted resources become available, and then only in relatively small amounts. Although the federal budget accounts for roughly 20 percent of GNP, by 1976, under present tax laws, the amount available for discretionary use by the President and the Congress will amount to only $17 billion (1 percent of GNP), and even some of that may have to be held as a full employment surplus. . . .
>
> As a consequence, the pursuit of new and expanded high-priority objectives by the federal government, including substantial further increases in aid to state and local governments, will require some difficult choices. To have more of some things we must sacrifice some of others, either in private goods and services or existing public goods and services. One such choice was made in 1969, when, through the Tax Reform Act, it was judged that private spending should take priority over public spending. Those who believe that certain public needs should now take top priority must seek either to reverse that decision through tax increases, or find low-priority areas of public spending from which resources can be withdrawn.[9]

The challenge raised by this conclusion bears not only on programs that aim to resolve the ghetto problem, but also on programs of wider focus where we know pretty well what we ought to do; e.g., health insurance, education, environmental measures, transportation.

Putting aside for the moment the question of further reduction in military outlays and assuming that large savings are not likely from reductions in older government programs, the further development of the search for quality is likely to pose the first question with which this analysis began: How much of their income are the citizens prepared to surrender for public purposes?

In the short run, the mood is clear enough: the taxpayer feels put upon; the President and the Congress reduced the tax-raising potential of the federal government through the Tax Reform Act of 1969 and further tax measures of 1971. The 1969 legislation cut by $9 billion revenue flowing to government (at "full employment," in 1971 dollars). The 1971 measures cut a further $6 billion. There is a serious gap in American life between rhetorical and legislative commitments and the resources the political process is now prepared to mobilize to match those commitments. From where we stand in early 1972, I would guess that a second-stage booster—a renewal of leadership and a regathering of political consensus —will be required during the 1970s if we are to do what public policy can do to carry forward the search for quality in America.

The National Interest: Can America Play Its Proper Role on the World Scene?

In a world of diffusing power, the United States is, in one sense, engaged in a systematic process of retreat; and a well-conducted, orderly retreat has always been recognized as the most difficult of maneuvers to execute. The retreat is an inevitable product of the revival of Japan and western Europe and the emergence of increasingly assertive nations, new and old, in the southern continents. It was also, from Truman's administration forward, a positive object of American policy.

The central issue of American foreign and military policy is, therefore, how far and how fast the United States can retract its role on the world scene without endangering the movement toward stable peace or endangering the security of the United States. The limits to safe retraction are set by four factors: the nature of abiding American interests on the world scene; the American nuclear role and its stake in nonproliferation; the extent to which western Europe and Japan, notably, but other nations as well, assume responsibility for their security and prosperity through regional cooperation; the evolution of domestic as well as foreign policy in Moscow, Peking, and other communist capitals.

Whatever the changing rhetoric of our leaders, the United States has consistently acted in this century at critical moments on the proposition that it has an abiding interest that no major power dominate Europe or Asia or emplace itself in the Western Hemisphere in a posture of potential military pressure or hostility. Our existing commitments, military and foreign aid budgets, military force structures, and day-to-day diplomacy are geared to the proposition. I believe it is, essentially, correct. And I believe that the United States can only play its full role in moving the world toward stable peace if it continues to act effectively on it.

This limit to retraction is strongly reinforced by the role of American nuclear strength. It is the foundation on which:

> NATO and other American alliances and understandings are maintained in the face of non-nuclear threats (e.g., in South Korea, Thailand, the Middle East, Latin America);
>
> American allies are willing to support substantial conventional forces for their own defense, in the face of potential Soviet or Chinese Communist pressure or threats;
>
> and a number of nations forego producing their own nuclear weapons.

But a quarter-century of painful experience—in Europe, the Middle East, Asia, and the Caribbean—has taught us that nuclear weapons do not suffice, that the deterrence of aggression requires the likelihood of confronting American conventional strength. This does not mean American overseas commitments of conventional force are sacrosanct. They have been reduced, for example, in South Korea, Southeast Asia, and western Europe. But the deterrence of aggression, the viability of alliances, and the viability of the nonproliferation treaty all decree that the commitment of American conventional, as well as nuclear, forces remain persuasive in the parts of the world critical for the balance of power.

It is also surely true that American allies can and should carry more of the complex burdens of both defense and the pursuit of stable peace in the broadest sense.

The problem of burden sharing is suffused by the asymmetry in the diffusion of power noted by Kennedy when he observed, on July 2, 1962, that in the 1950s the United States had spent its time collecting nuclear bombs, while Europe had been rounding up gold (see above, p. 235).

But now, and for the foreseeable future, western Europe lacks the political and economic cohesion to generate military forces capable of substituting effectively for the American nuclear and conventional component of NATO. And in a world moving toward East–West détente, even if uncertainly and erratically, it would be irrational to build such forces so long as American political life and will do not disintegrate into a grossly unreliable isolationism. But it is no easy thing for nations, now rich and relatively stable, to accept the degree of dependence implicit in the nuclear asymmetry of the alliance.[10]

The American presence in NATO is so critical to the effectiveness of the enterprise that it is also difficult for each of the other partners to persuade its parliament that its modest component is vitally important. It was, therefore, a considerable achievement of the Nixon administration, aided by pressure in the Senate for American troop withdrawals, to persuade ten European members of NATO to initiate late in 1970 a five-year program costing about $1 billion to improve the NATO infrastructure.

The popular American image of the disproportion in burden sharing in NATO is probably exaggerated: of ready NATO forces, the United States provides only 10 percent of ground forces, 20 percent of air forces, and 30 percent of naval forces.[11] The total budgetary cost of all U.S. forces (home and abroad) maintained specifically for the defense of Europe is less than the combined military outlays of the European members of NATO. The American figure is about $25 billion, somewhat over 2 percent of GNP.

Furthermore, the foreign exchange outlays associated with U.S. forces in Europe run to about $1.9 billion, of which $650 million are offset by purchases of American military equipment. Something like $200 million in American military expenditures are in the less developed countries of Europe (notably Greece, Turkey, and Spain) where offsetting is less realistic. The net figure to be offset is, therefore, about a billion dollars. Since

1967 Germany has offset a substantial part of this net figure by purchasing medium-term U.S. Treasury bonds and conducting an international monetary policy in which it was prepared to hold large dollar balances rather than convert dollars into gold. From 1967 to 1971 this linking of the NATO offset problem to international financial policy helped stabilize the international monetary system in important ways.

Overall, with per capita income about twice that of western Europe and bearing unique global responsibilities, the United States spends about 7 percent of GNP on defense; the European NATO nations, about 4 percent. The Soviet Union, also with global interests, allocates about 10 percent of GNP to defense.

Unless one is prepared to reduce the total U.S. forces committed to NATO, there are no substantial budgetary savings involved in troop withdrawals from Europe: American units cost at least as much to support at home as abroad. The first object of a stable NATO policy should, therefore, be the complete elimination of the foreign exchange burden carried by the United States in fulfilling its NATO obligation. This can be done in various ways; for example, by European assumption of certain infrastructure costs for American forces in Europe and/or by making it possible (through exchange rate and trade policy adjustments) for the United States to sell more in Europe and elsewhere.

This linkage of military and economic policy is not easy for two basic reasons. First, psychologically Europe has not yet fully shaken off the habits of past economic dependence on the United States and of continuing military dependence. Second, both technically and politically the linkages between security and economic relationships are not sufficiently understood.

Japan was even less well prepared than Europe to face this intermingling of security and economic issues. History and geography made military partnership with Japan less substantial than with western Europe. Japan was in a position to take its protection as a by-product of American interests and to concentrate on its economic development; although many Japanese understood well that its safety was assured not only by the American nuclear guarantee, but also by the honoring of American commitments to South Korea, Formosa, and Southeast Asia. The Japanese, from the Korean War forward, were large foreign exchange beneficiaries of American military outlays in Asia. While the Japanese government and political leadership were coming increasingly to understand the two-way requirements of partnership with the United States, this understanding did not penetrate deeply in Japanese political life.

In the wake of the monetary settlement of December 1971, a group of twelve western European, North American, and Japanese private experts gathered in Washington and outlined, in a report of December 21, the technical agenda that still lay ahead if the European community, the

United States, and Japan are successfully to "order their relationship."[12] That agenda includes complex issues of money and trade, capital flows and aid, and the monetary aspects of mutual defense arrangements. It is clear that the monetary settlement of December 1971 was the beginning, not the end, of a new chapter in sustained partnership.

For the long pull much more is required in resolving the financial and trade crisis of 1971, and all that lay behind it, than acceptable, well-balanced economic negotiations. More, even, than a willingness of American partners to make concessions in economic policy in return for American willingness to continue to carry the burdens that only a massive nuclear power can support. In the end a large vision of what the Atlantic and Pacific partnerships are about must emerge. For western Europe and Japan this will require a freeing of minds from the simple image of a dominant United States, committed to look after the world's problems out of its own interests and natural hegemony—a freeing of minds also from the traumas of the Second World War, the painful liquidation of colonialism, Suez, etc. Positively, a new consensus must be developed on what is required from all if a world of tolerable order and peace is to emerge from the process of power diffusion. Once the issue is posed in that way—and the familiar tasks of security become, simply, a minimum condition for the pursuit of stable peace—it becomes clear that there is more than enough for all to do: in helping to assure that Peking's arrival on the stage of Asia and the world community is a constructive rather than a disruptive event; in helping to assure that Moscow's détente in Europe is a stabilizing process, not the prelude to new and dangerous imbalances; above all, perhaps, in helping to convert a phase of pragmatic stirring in the developing world into successful and sustained economic and social development.

As a development economist I am convinced that the world community is taking unnecessary risks by not expanding substantially the flow of resources in the 1970s from the more advanced to the less developed nations. The capacity to absorb resources efficiently has increased; the balance between success and failure in a number of critical areas is close; even where growth rates are quite high and steady, the expansion of the urban working force is outstripping the pace of industrialization, yielding chronic and corrosive levels of unemployment and partial employment. Moreover, it is from the developed world that new technologies for birth control must come if the world community is not to experience massive Malthusian crises; for the present course of birth rates promises nothing but disaster, and even in the rare case where the problem is locally accorded high priority, existing birth control methods do not appear appropriate for rapid acceptable mass diffusion.

There is a tendency in much of the literature on the developing world to stop there: with an appeal for the rich nations to continue to help the poor on a large scale.

But the diffusion of power extends to the developing continents as well as to the richer nations; and power carries with it responsibility. There are two areas (aside from inadequate attention to population control) where the developing nations have responsibilities of their own, often unfulfilled. Both relate to the development of regionalism in Asia, the Middle East, Africa, and Latin America.

First, peacemaking. For too long peacemaking has been regarded as business for major powers, while lesser powers felt free to indulge, with acts of force across international frontiers, their resentments and painful memories from the past. There has been a tendency to cherish old quarrels rather than to accept the domestic political pain and discipline of settling them. This is true of the Indian subcontinent and the Middle East. It remains true of a few old costly quarrels in Latin America and Africa. It was true of noncommunist Southeast Asia, but under the pressure of common danger the situation there has somewhat improved.

A concerted effort to settle these disputes is necessary as part of the process of moving toward stable peace. It is also required for these nations and regions to attain greater independence vis-à-vis the major powers; for efforts to strengthen their position versus their local adversaries often take the form of soliciting additional arms or asking the major powers to exert pressure on their behalf. All this has its price and dilutes the capacity of the *demandeur* to conduct national and regional policies rooted in positive local interests.

Second, the developing nations bear a major responsibility if a political basis is to be created for enlarged and sustained flows of development assistance from the richer nations. I believe that the most likely basis for appeal is the demonstration that they are willing and capable of curbing their own nationalism, not only by regional peacemaking, but also by regional economic cooperation. Regional (and subregional) economic cooperation is desperately needed if major obstacles to accelerated development are to be removed in Latin America, Africa, the Middle East, and the Far East. Evidently, India, Pakistan, and Bangladesh, among the poorest of the developing nations, require a normalization of their economic relations and active collaboration on such projects as the joint development of the Ganges–Brahmaputra river system—an enterprise that ought promptly to be translated into reality as a small compensation for the tragic India–Pakistan war of December 1971.

Although the developing nations bear unfulfilled responsibilities, I conclude that foreign aid ought substantially to expand. Even now, the United States is not carrying a fair share. Among the sixteen major donors, the United States now ranks twelfth in the proportion of economic aid to GNP.

As for the American military budget, there is an array of possible levels more or less consistent with the maintenance of existing American commitments. The range of these possibilities is suggested in Table 43-3 (from the Brookings study) which costs out three options, one above, the other below Nixon's proposed military budget for FY 1972.[13]

TABLE 43–3
PROJECTIONS OF OPTIONAL DEPARTMENT OF DEFENSE BUDGETS, BY MILITARY PROGRAM, FY 1972 AND FY 1976

Option and program	1972	1976*
Option 1		
Austere Nixon Doctrine	44	52.5
Diversified strategic deterrent with only essential modernization	17	20.5
All-volunteer Army	†	1.5
Vietnam	8.5	1
Total	69.5	75.5
Option 2		
General-purpose forces as in 1972 budget	51	61
Strategic forces as in 1972 budget	20	24
All-volunteer Army	†	2
Vietnam	8.5	1
Total	79.5	88
Option 3		
Nixon Doctrine with heavy modernization	55	65.5
Diversified strategic deterrent with rapid modernization	23	27.5
All-volunteer Army	†	2
Vietnam	8.5	1
Total	86.5	96

Source: Brookings authors' estimates.
* Outlays other than for the cost of the all-volunteer Army and Vietnam have been adjusted for projected increases in pay and prices.
† The $1.5 billion provided in FY 1972 budget for the volunteer force is included in the 1972 costs of the general-purpose and strategic forces in each option. The figure shown for this purpose in 1976 is the estimated additional cost that will be required to put the proposal into effect: $1.5 billion for Option 1 (with a smaller number of troops) and $2 billion for Options 2 and 3.

I have worked through a number of military budgets in government and studied a good many more as a private citizen. That experience underlined the dangers of dogmatism about any particular item; the inertia of habits and commitments out of the past; and the usefulness of trying doggedly and skeptically to relate the mass of detail about men and hardware, physical installations, and research and development, to the abiding requirements of the national interest. Without dogmatism, I would conclude that, given the increased reliance on nuclear deterrence in Option 1 and the temptations it might offer to expansionist adventures, notably in Asia, it would be unwise to succumb to the temptation of Option 1 and the $10 to $12.5 billion cut it would grant. The savings might prove as illusory as Truman's pre-Korean War budgets. Under present unsettled conditions in the Middle East, the Indian Ocean, and Southeast Asia, and with a definitive SALT agreement still to be reached on offensive strategic systems, Option 2 already involves some substantial risks.

It is, of course, possible that international agreements would make rational something like Option 1. For example:

—A full SALT agreement that would break the momentum of the Soviet strategic buildup and end the qualitative race still proceeding;
—A firm Middle East settlement that would greatly diminish the flow of Soviet arms to the Middle East and make possible a substantial withdrawal of the massive Soviet advisory team in Egypt;
—A firm Southeast Asian settlement involving the withdrawal of Chinese Communist engineering units from Laos as well as a general withdrawal of North Vietnamese forces behind their borders—a settlement monitored by Asians, including, say, Japanese, Indonesians, and Malaysians.

But until such settlements are realities rather than possibilities, there is little rational basis for further radical cuts in the American military budget.

What, then, are the prospects for policy in Moscow, Peking, and the other communist capitals? Are they likely to accept the implications of the diffusion of power; sign and honor agreements that would reduce or remove the role of force from international affairs; and leave to the tests of nonmilitary history the ideological competition which, for a time at least, is likely to persist? The diffusion of power within both the noncommunist and the communist worlds makes that outcome more possible. But the readjustments required by the United States and its partners as the American role contracts and that of others expands poses a danger. Those readjustments could open up possibilities for the expansion of Soviet or Chinese Communist power, notably if the American pullback from responsibility is premature or excessive. Under such circumstances it must be assumed that Moscow or Peking would act. Neither past performance nor current dispositions justifies the view that Russian or Chinese communism is a self-containing phenomenon. On the other hand, each, for different reasons, is in a situation where détente with the noncommunist world and a freeing of resources and energies for domestic development make sense

—for a time at least—unless opportunities for expansion are presented to them so attractive as to be beyond bearing. Put another way, we are in a phase in communist history unlike the concerted activist mood of the November 1957 summit meeting. If the noncommunist world goes about its business in reasonable order and, on that basis, the slow, hard work is steadily conducted of isolating limited areas of common interest with both Moscow and Peking (as well as Hanoi, Pyongyang, and, perhaps, Havana), the movement toward stable peace has a reasonable chance of being consolidated. Although events in Moscow and Peking—and trends in Soviet and Chinese societies—will play their part, the key to peace lies mainly in the hands of the noncommunist world, whose weaknesses, real or apparent, provided the temptations which yielded the Cold War itself and all its major crises—from Iran in 1945 to Vietnam in 1972.

THE NATIONAL STYLE: WILL AMERICA GROW UP?

MATURITY consists in knowing who you are and pursuing steady purposes in the light of your capacities, limitations, and the environment you confront. If some such definition is accepted, America in the twentieth century cannot be said to have come to maturity in its relations with the world. We have not generated a steady view of our interests and acted steadily upon it. We have oscillated systematically between a moralistic isolationism and active military commitment when interests were violated we had failed clearly to define before the event.

This pattern began during the First World War.[14] In 1916 Wilson won re-election on the platform: "Too proud to fight"; "He kept us out of war." But five months later the United States went to war in the face of unrestricted German submarine warfare and the threat it represented to American control over the Atlantic, as well as to the survival of Britain and France.

For the next generation, the United States remained essentially isolationist, acutely and purposefully so in the 1930s. In the spring of 1940, 65 percent of the American people supported aid to the Allies under the condition that it be short of involvement in the war. Then Paris fell, Britain was beleaguered, the French coast became a base for German submarines; and by January 1941, about 70 percent of the American people were for aiding Britain even at the risk of war.

In Asia, America passively observed the Japanese takeover of Manchuria in 1931, and then the major cities of China. In 1940–1941 the Japanese moved into Indochina and toward Indonesia. As Cordell Hull wrote: ". . . Japanese troops on July 21 [1941] occupied the southern portions of Indo-China and were now in possession of the whole of France's strategic province, pointing like a pudgy thumb towards the Philippines, Malaya, and the Dutch East Indies. . . . When Welles telephoned me, I said to him that the invasion of Southern Indo-China looked like Japan's last step before jumping off for a full-scale attack in the Southwest Pacific."[15] Franklin Roosevelt had every interest at that time in concentrating American attention and American resources on rearmament at home, and aid to Britain and Russia. But he could not bring himself to accept passively the Japanese takeover of the balance of power in Asia, including control of the sea routes to the Indian Ocean and to Australia and New Zealand. He cut off shipments to Japan of scrap metal and oil, and froze Japanese assets in the United States.

Indochina was the substance of the diplomatic dialogue with Japan right down to the eve of Pearl Harbor.

At Yalta Roosevelt told Stalin that the American people would not support the presence of substantial military forces in Europe for more than two years. And the postwar dismantling of American armed forces appeared to support Roosevelt's assessment. Only when the balance of power in southern and western Europe was clearly threatened, by a mixture of economic weakness and communist pressure, did Truman respond in 1947. And he did so only after surrendering hard-won wartime commitments to the political freedom of Poland in particular, and eastern Europe in general—thus helping to bring about a situation where American interests in the European balance of power could only be assured by the confrontation of two power blocs.

With respect to Korea, the Joint Chiefs of Staff, and then, in public, the secretary of state in January 1950, drew the line of the American defense perimeter through the Tsushima Straits after American forces began to withdraw in 1949. Six months later South Korea was invaded. The United States responded both to protect the balance of power in the Northwest Pacific and to give newborn NATO, now confronted with a nuclear Soviet Union, some credibility. But there was an element of truth in Andrei Vichinsky's statement to a group of diplomats at the United Nations: "The Americans deceived us on Korea."

Out of the Korean experience other pacts and arrangements were developed to make explicit the American commitment to hold the balance of power in the Middle East, South Asia, and Southeast Asia; and thus to deter further overt aggression across international frontiers. After their failure in Korea, the communists turned to guerrilla warfare as a primary tool. Hanoi decided that it could proceed with success in Southeast Asia, despite the SEATO treaty and, later, the Geneva Accords on Laos of 1962. The United States did not react promptly and decisively to the violation of the Laos Accords. And in 1965, in consequence, Johnson confronted a choice of fighting or seeing an area judged critical to the American interest fall to aggression.

Thus, for more than a half-century we have rocked along from crisis to crisis. In the face of acute crisis we have behaved as if the nation understood its abiding interest in avoiding the passage of the power balance in Europe or Asia into the hands of a single power. Through this series of convulsive reactions to crisis we have managed to survive. But we have not been able to formulate a concept of our interests and policies based upon them which permitted us to avoid costly crises. We have, in short, not been able to translate into a successful working process the task of protecting the national interest under twentieth-century conditions.

As these words are written, an American President once again confronts a heavy undertow of isolationism in America—in part, reflecting a corruption of American idealism into a shallow moralism; in part, a corruption of American power interests into a hardhanded isolationist temper. That was the convergence that yielded the Senate vote to destroy the foreign aid program in November 1971. The vote was undone, but the mood remains. This unhappy convergence emerged at a moment when the possibilities of movement toward stable peace are more real than they have been since 1945—or, perhaps, 1914.

If my analysis is correct, it is not beyond the capacity of fallible men and governments to organize diffusing power in relatively stable ways; meet the minimum conditions required to avoid further nuclear proliferation; stabilize the U.S.–Soviet arms race on relatively secure terms for both nations; and gradually find the terms for reasonable stability in the Middle East and Southeast Asia. By complex routes the diffusion of power has, in different ways, made all this conceivable.

For the United States to make its contribution to these possible but not certain outcomes requires something new: sustained popular support for an active effort to achieve a positive goal—the peaceful organization of a world of diffused power. This positive objective is what should unite us by bringing together in a coherent and stable way the abiding strands of idealism and power interests that any satisfactory American policy must continue to satisfy.

America cannot be itself if it builds its relations to the world solely on a projection abroad of its ideals or solely on a projection of its narrow national interests. Maturity requires a stable synthesis.

A maturing of the American style is required in other directions as well. A major lesson of the 1960s is that rational solutions to the major domestic problems we face ought not to await the coming of acute crisis. If we are rational, we cannot wait until cost-push inflation is upon us before we act to achieve wage-price discipline. We cannot wait for the cities again to flame before acting with vigor and purpose to deal as a national community with their problems. We cannot wait until great environmental crises are fully developed before allocating sufficient resources to their amelioration. And, on the world scene, we ought to play a role of leadership in generating this anticipatory perspective. Aid to the developing world at its best has always had as part of its rationale the objective of heading off dangerous economic, political, or military crisis. Rational men ought to be able to act to reduce birth rates before Malthusian horrors and disciplines are enforced. And so also with potential global catastrophes in the environment as well as possible raw material bottlenecks as industrialization spreads.

My argument comes to this. The United States, child of the Enlightenment, favored adolescent of the nineteenth century, powerful but erratic youth of the first half of the twentieth century, assumed in the third quarter of the twentieth century extraordinary burdens in holding the balance of power against determined thrusts in Europe and Asia, Latin America, the Middle East, and Africa. It did so in its own interest, but also in the cause of national independence and of freedom and diversity among men. History is likely to record the years 1941–1968 as the interval of maximum American exertion and authority on the world scene; although, if things go badly, America may sometime in the future have to play the kind of role Britain did in 1939–1941. As we come toward the last quarter of the century, both the world environment and America are changing. The environment of diffusing power permits and requires a retraction in degree of the American role; but the retraction must be gradual and limited if the diffusion of power is to yield an approximation of stable peace. Concluding a study of American life and foreign policy in 1958, I stated the critical questions for the future as follows:

> Will the United States mobilize the strength, will, and imagination to bring about the process of persuasion in the Communist Bloc which, by denying all other alternatives, would permit without major war the gradual evolution and release of the forces for good within it? Will the United States mobilize the strength, will, and imagination to bring about the emergence of the new nations in Asia, the Middle East, Africa, and Latin America as congenial open societies in a world structured for order rather than for racial and ideological hostility and nuclear anarchy? Will the United States mobilize the strength, will, and imagination to hold firm, with a new common understanding and new lines of common action, the Western coalition and the links to Japan on which both historical transitions depend?[16]

While progress has been made in response to each, none of these questions can be answered with a flat affirmative. In my view the three questions are still the right questions. What has changed is that the further diffusion of power, combined with the exertions of the United States and others, has made constructive outcomes more possible and also reduced in degree the role the United States can and should play in those outcomes.

The successful conduct of the American role requires, however, a shift in the national style—from a convulsive oscillation between moralistic isolationism and the military defense of vital interests to a new steadiness based on a mature blending of abiding strands of idealism and concern for the structure of power.

The agenda set out in this chapter requires not change but strengthening in one strand of the American experience—the finding of compromise among diverse groups and interests, and the experience of federalism in its widest sense. Recall the major tasks which emerge from this analysis. At home, the maintenance of the social contract required for a reconciliation of steady growth with price stability; the generation of a balance-of-payments position consistent with the nation's irreducible tasks on the world scene; the interweaving of public and private, federal, state, and local efforts to deal with problems of the environment, poverty, and the cities; the movement to completion of the Negro's drive for full and unencumbered citizenship. Abroad, the management of global arrangements in monetary affairs, trade, and aid; the maintenance with the other nuclear weapons powers of the conditions required to make viable the nonproliferation treaty; the adjustment in the terms of partnership with western Europe and Japan; the evolution of changing terms in America's links to Latin America, Africa, Asia, and the Middle East as, hopefully, they build and strengthen regional structures; and beginning the long task of finding the terms of equity between the more advanced and less advanced nations as they jointly confront the globe's limited capacity to sustain population and industrialization.

In domestic life the elaborate and subtle partnerships that already suffuse the working of American society require refinement—if possible, refinement where power and authority can be diffused to state and local institutions capable of bearing increased responsibility. Similarly, on the world scene, the stable organization of a system of diffusing power is, in the end, an exercise in federalism. In this sense, the Italian economist could be prophetic who once wrote: "America has the key to the historical enigma which Europe has sought for centuries in vain, the land which has no history reveals luminously the course of universal history."[17] Western Europe may be close to solving the enigma in its own way; but the task has hardly been begun on the other continents.

If Americans can come to see clearly what they, and the world, have been through since 1914—where we stand; what remains to be done; what burdens we can safely relinquish and which we must continue to carry—America may yet help to give creative meaning to the injunction of one of her poets:

> One thought ever at the fore—
> That in the Divine Ship, the World,
> breasting Time and Space,
> All peoples of the globe together sail,
> sail the same voyage,
> Are bound to the same destination.

APPENDIX

The National Interest

NOTE: The concept of the national interest that runs through this book is so central to the judgments made that it is worth stating explicitly, permitting the reader to examine critically my presuppositions.

A DEFINITION

IT is the American interest to maintain a world environment within which American society can continue to develop in conformity with the humanistic principles that are its foundation. This definition, in terms of the development of the quality of American society, includes, of course, the physical protection of the country; but the protection of American territory is essentially a means to a larger end—the protection of a still-developing way of life.

The operational meaning of this definition derives from the geographic position of the United States. It is, essentially, part of a continental island off the greater land mass of Eurasia. The security, economic welfare, and political life of the United States have, from the beginning, been linked to Eurasia. For no substantial period in the nation's history has the American interest been automatically assured by geographic isolation. Contrary to a mythology that still strongly affects American attitudes and the nation's performance, the American interest has been chronically in danger from the late eighteenth century forward. From the beginning, this danger arose from an abiding fact: the combined resources and military potential of Europe were and are capable of threatening the security of the United

States. A united Britain and France could have stifled the American Revolution. American independence was achieved in the eighteenth century only because Americans could exploit a conflict between Britain and France. During the nineteenth century the nation, shielded by Britain's strength and policy, expanded and consolidated American power on the North American continent by exploiting the power conflicts of Europe, while it protected its southern flank by asserting and defending the Monroe Doctrine.

Initially, traditional Asia represented merely an arena within which more advanced nations could compete for commerce and power; the missionaries, for converts. But as Asia modernized in reaction to these intrusions, a potential threat, parallel to that from Europe, emerged in the twentieth century. As early as 1905 Theodore Roosevelt at Portsmouth foreshadowed the American balance-of-power interest in Asia by leaning against Japan, after the Russo–Japanese War. But Franklin Roosevelt's resistance to Japan's consolidation of Asia, as it moved into southern Indochina in 1940–1941, marks the clear beginning of modern American policy in the Far East, risking as it did direct military confrontation with the major power in Asia.

Thus, in the twentieth century, as the structure of Eurasia changed with the march of industrialization, and Britain could no longer contain and balance the new powers that emerged, the United States has been placed in jeopardy, instinctively sensed that jeopardy, and actively threw its weight into the balance when a single power or combination of powers threatened to dominate Europe, Asia, or to intrude its power into the Western Hemisphere; e.g., 1917, 1941, 1947, 1950, 1961–1962, 1965.

The continuing American interest in the balance of power in Europe is institutionalized in NATO and related commitments in the Middle East.

The continuing American interest in avoiding the military presence of another major power in the hemisphere is institutionalized in multilateral understandings with Latin America, which also set limits on the power of the United States to intervene in Latin America.

The continuing American interest in the balance of power in Asia is institutionalized in a more complex and less widely agreed on set of bilateral and multilateral treaties, understandings, and policies. They reflect the fact that the balance of power in Asia is made up of four major elements: China, Japan, Southeast Asia, and India. As in the case of Europe, Russia and the United States are significant and interested elements in the equation. The Asian balance of power was threatened when Japan neutralized China and then moved to take over Southeast Asia; when, with Japan neutralized, Russia and China encouraged Kim Il-sung to take over South Korea; and, again, when China (in concert with Hanoi and, for a time, Djakarta) sought to take over Southeast Asia. The Asian balance could conceivably be threatened by other combinations.

Southeast Asia has been and will remain a critical area for these reasons: its resources and population (now approaching 300 million); its relation to the sea routes of the southwest Pacific and the eastern Indian Ocean; and its role as a buffer between India and China. Its fragmentation into relatively small national units makes it a natural target for larger powers. Stability in Asia requires that no single power dominate Southeast Asia or try to dominate it. That is the interest of the peoples who live there and the legitimate interest of China and India, the United States, Japan, and Russia.

There is, then, much in the whole sweep of American history that denies the notion of an America safely isolated by act of God and geography. In the first century and a quarter of the nation's life there is an underlying continuity in the American interest in exploiting the Eurasian power balance: from the American Revolution itself, through the Louisiana Purchase, the enunciation of the Monroe Doctrine, the purchase of Alaska, and the maneuvering in the Far East to assure a place for the United States among the contending trading powers. In this century the American need to throw its weight directly into the power balance emerged, as first Europe (from 1914) and then Asia (from 1941) failed to maintain power balances of their own that precluded dominance by a single power. Stable power balances within Europe and within Asia may be constructed in the future that will permit diminished direct American involvement. That has been a major objective of American policy since 1947. But the relevance of the Eurasian power balance to American security, which has made itself felt in different forms for two centuries, is likely to persist.

The Dual American Interest in Eurasia

If the national interest is viewed as a question of protecting not only the nation's territory but also its basic values as a society, it follows that the United States has a second distinct but connected interest in Eurasia. Whatever the military situation might be, a Eurasia coalesced under totalitarian dictatorships would threaten the survival of democracy both elsewhere and in the United States. Under modern conditions it is difficult to envisage the survival of a democratic American society as an island in a totalitarian sea. It is, therefore, the American interest that the societies of Eurasia develop along lines broadly consistent with the nation's ideology.

This general proposition must be clarified and tempered in three significant respects. First, the United States need not seek societies abroad in its own image. The United States does have an interest that societies abroad develop and strengthen those elements in their respective cultures that elevate and protect the dignity of the individual as against the claims of the state. Such elements of potential harmony with the Western democratic tradition exist in different forms everywhere. But the forms of legitimately democratic societies can vary widely.

Second, the democratic process must be viewed as a matter of aspiration, trend, and degree—not as an absolute. The pure democratic concept is compromised to some extent in all organized societies by the need to protect individuals from each other, by the need to protect the society as a whole from other sovereignties, and by the checks required to protect the workings of the society from man's frequent inability to define wisely his own long-run interest. Even when societies strive for the democratic compromise, the balance between liberty and order which any society can achieve and still operate effectively, and the particular form that balance will take, are certain to vary. They will vary not only from society to society, but also within each society in response to the state of education of its citizens, its constitutional and party structure, and the nature of the specific problems it confronts as a community at different stages in its history.

The legitimate American ideological interest is not that all societies become immediately democratic in the degree achieved in the United States or western Europe, but that they have as a goal a version of the democratic value judgments consonant with their culture and their history and that they move toward their realization with the passage of time.

Now, a third limitation of the American ideological interest. Since the American interest does not require that all societies at all times accept democratic values and move toward their achievement, the nation is concerned not with total ideological victory, somehow defined, but with the balance and trend of ideological forces in Eurasia and Latin America. Therefore, the application of the limited, but real, margin of American influence on the course of other societies can and should be selective. Given the nation's geographic circumstance, its history, and the quality of its society, the American interest demands, in a sense, that Americans continue to be crusaders; but the American ideological crusade must be tolerant, long term, and directed toward areas of importance where the nation's inevitably limited margin of influence may be significant. The United States is concerned not with absolutes but with the direction of political trend. American society can live and develop in a world of great diversity.

The Interweaving of Power and Ideological Interests

If this view of the American interest is correct, the endemic debate as to whether the nation's interests should be defined in power terms or in terms of the ideological principles to which American society is attached is somewhat misguided. This is so in two respects.

First, if the essential American interest is to preserve a world environment within which its chosen form of democratic society can persist and develop, then the nation's stake in the ideological and political balance in Eurasia is as legitimate as its interest in the military balance of power in Eurasia. Two national efforts, one military and the other political and economic, interacting intimately, must go forward together as part of a total effort to protect the interests of American society.

There is a second sense in which the debate appears misguided. It appears to be a characteristic of American history that this nation cannot be effective in its military and foreign policy unless it believes that both its security interests and its commitment to certain moral principles require the nation to act. From the Spanish-American War to the present, the nation has acted effectively only when both strands in its interest were believed to be involved—in the Spanish-American War itself, in the First and Second World Wars, in the effort to reconstruct and defend western Europe in 1947–1950, in the early phases of the Korean War and the war in Vietnam.

When idealism alone seemed to be the basis for the positions taken, the nation did not back its play, as, for example, in Wilson's ideological formulation of the American interest at Versailles and after. Equally, the nation has not been effective when confronted with situations where its power interests might be involved but where a persuasive moral basis for American action was not present. The notion of American imperialism, popular in certain American circles at the turn of the century, died quickly when it confronted the abiding American instinct in support of political independence in the case of the Philippines and elsewhere. Similarly, a major reason why the United States was ineffective in the Indochina crisis of 1954 was that it was then extremely difficult simultaneously to deal with the communist threat to Southeast Asia and to disengage from French imperialism in that area. In the summer of 1956 the United States was gravely inhibited in dealing with Nasser because his claim to national sovereignty over the Suez Canal had resonance in the American image of its historic role on the world scene as the friend of those struggling for independence. Again, in 1961 Kennedy could not bring American military power to bear to retrieve a covert operation that was failing against Cuba.

Whether a nation's ideals are or are not involved in a given military action is an arguable proposition, as American debates about the War of 1812, the Mexican War, the Spanish-American War, the wars in Korea and Vietnam, and the Dominican intervention of 1965 suggest. Nevertheless, it is unrealistic to expect American society—given its history and values—to perform effectively in terms of pure power criteria alone.

The art of American statesmanship is, therefore, to formulate and sustain courses of action that harmonize, in specific settings, abiding American interests and abiding American ideals, steadily preserving the dual power balance in Europe and Asia, maintaining a safe environment in the Western Hemisphere, preventing by forehanded effort the emergence of such crises as those which hitherto have been required to evoke a major American effort at self-preservation.

The requirements of protecting the military balance of power and developing the ideological balance of power do not always converge. Foreign policy, like other aspects of the human condition, is full of painful choices. There are times, for example, when, in order to maintain military positions, short-run action must be taken in conflict with the American ideological interest. But if the dual character of the national interest—as a democratic island off a potentially threatening Eurasian mainland—is accepted, and if the interrelations of the two objectives are understood, courses of action still appear open to the United States in a world of diffusing power that will protect and sustain the quality as well as the existence of the nation's life in the face of current and foreseeable challenges.

The United States and the Pursuit of Stable Peace in a Nuclear Age

THE pursuit of stable peace is a moral objective. It is also a military objective, because the possible use of nuclear weapons is a danger to the national interest sufficiently grave to justify acceptance of important constraints on the nation's sovereignty, as others accept balancing constraints. This we have already done in the test ban treaty of 1963, the commitments made in the context of the nonproliferation treaty, entrance into SALT talks, and the quiet acceptance (along with the Soviet Union) of satellite reconnaissance.

Put another way, it is a legitimate American national objective in the narrow military sense, as well as in terms of universal human aspiration, to see the world arena organized for stable peace, where powerful and effective constraints are built against the use of force across international frontiers.

The pace at which means of communication and ties of mutual economic dependence are now developing argues, further, that nations will move into relations of increasing intimacy and interaction. The need to bring the world's population under control and to find a viable balance between man and his physical environment on a planet of limited size and physical resources will heighten these tendencies.

Between them, the need to tame military force and the need to deal with peoples everywhere on the basis of growing interdependence argue strongly for movement in the direction of federalized world organization under effective international law. This could take place by agreements among still formally sovereign nations—as in the European Common Market or NATO; or, new, larger political units could emerge. Should effective international control of military power be achieved, it might prove convenient and rational to pass other specific functions upward from unilateral determination to an organized arena of international politics, dealing with some problems on a universal basis, others regionally. Indeed, something like this process is under way in monetary affairs, trade, aid, and, regionally, in the European Common Market. It is latent in the regional and subregional strivings in Latin America, Africa, and Asia.

It is not easy or particularly useful to peer beyond the time when the great human watershed of effective constraint on military power is actually attained, and a world of diffuse power is safely organized on federal principles. That watershed may lie generations ahead, if, indeed, men are capable of achieving it. Nevertheless, it can be said that the American national interest would still continue to embrace elements from the long sweep of the past. Relationships of geography, of cultural connection, of economic interest, would in substantial measure be simply transferred from a setting where military force enters the equation of negotiation to one of regional and global politics. The agenda of international politics would look not unfamiliar. Much in the historic relation of the United States to the balance of affairs in Eurasia would remain. The still great continental island would remain the natural friend of the smaller nations of Eurasia, also anxious that no single power politically dominate their region; and the special concern for Latin America and Canada would persist. There would be, however, a special dimension to global politics with a particular meaning for Americans—the problem of so conducting the world's affairs as to avoid a dissolution of the federal machinery and civil war.

A nation's definition of its interest ought to be compatible with those of other nations when drawn up in parallel terms, if it is not to yield dangerous conflict. Such definitions will, of course, vary with geography, history, and ideological and cultural commitment. But a nation should not ask for more than it is prepared to grant to others. I have, therefore, tested this definition of the American interest by translating it, as it were, into western European, Russian, Chinese, Japanese, Latin American, and Indian terms. I believe it meets that test. I invite the interested reader to conduct the experiment for himself.

Notes

Introduction

1. *Essays on the British Economy of the Nineteenth Century,* Oxford, 1948, p. 144.
2. Arthur M. Schlesinger, Jr., *A Thousand Days,* Boston, 1965, p. ix.

Chapter 1: *Prologue: The Concentration and Diffusion of Power, 1940–1957*

1. George F. Kennan, *American Diplomacy, 1900–1950,* Chicago, 1951, p. 77 (Mentor edition).
2. W. Averell Harriman, *America and Russia in a Changing World,* New York, 1970, 1971, p. 44.
3. W. S. Churchill, *The Second World War,* Vol. 6, *Triumph and Tragedy,* Cambridge, Mass., 1953, p. 227.
4. *Ibid.,* pp. 234–235.
5. W. Averell Harriman, *op. cit.,* pp. 37–39.
6. *Foreign Relations of the United States, the Conferences at Malta and Yalta, 1945,* Washington, D. C., 1955, p. 235.
7. Harry S. Truman, *Memoirs,* Garden City, N. Y., 1955, p. 78.
8. *Ibid.,* pp. 245–246.

9. Robert E. Sherwood, *Roosevelt and Hopkins,* New York, 1948, p. 909.
10. J. C. Campbell, *The United States in World Affairs, 1945–1947,* New York, 1947, p. 72.
11. Lloyd C. Gardner, Arthur Schlesinger, Jr., and Hans J. Morgenthau, *The Origins of the Cold War,* Waltham, Mass., 1971, p. 43.
12. *Ibid.,* pp. 44–45.
13. For a fresh perspective on the possibility of a large American postwar loan to the Soviet Union, see E. V. Rostow, "The Revisionists," *Art International,* September 20, 1971, pp. 16–19.
14. For reflections of the extreme sensitivity and suspicion of Stalin to what the Allies were up to as the war ended and the occupation of Germany began, see, for example, G. K. Zhukov, *The Memoirs of Marshal Zhukov* (Novosty, tr.), London and New York, 1971, pp. 659 ff. Stalin's not very promising instruction to Zhukov (p. 659) is reported: "All the decisions of the Control Council will be valid on condition of unanimity. You will probably have to act alone against the other three in settling a number of questions. But it won't be the first time we've had to fight alone. . . ."
15. Arthur H. Vandenberg, Jr., ed., *The Private Papers of Senator Vandenberg,* Cambridge, Mass., 1952, p. 134.
16. *Ibid.,* pp. 136–137.
17. See, notably, V. Dedijer, *Tito,* New York, 1953, p. 322.
18. For Khrushchev's account of the planning in Moscow of the invasion of South Korea by Stalin, Mao, and Kim, see *Khrushchev Remembers,* (Edward Crankshaw and Strobe Talbott, eds.), Boston and Toronto, 1970, pp. 367–369.
19. *Ibid.,* pp. 481–483.
20. For a vivid linking of Budapest and Mao's ultimate response to the Hundred Flowers movement, see János Rádvanyi, "The Hungarian Revolution and the Hundred Flowers Campaign," *The China Quarterly,* July–September, 1970, pp. 121–129.

Book One: From Sputnik to Kennedy

Chapter 2: *Sputnik and After: The Communist World*

1. The most vivid portrait of Khrushchev's ambiguous primacy is that of Michel Tatu, *Power in the Kremlin: From Khrushchev to Kosygin,* (Helen Katel, tr.), New York, 1969, especially for 1957–1960, pp. 19–37.
2. See, for example, Alice Langley Hsieh, "The Sino–Soviet Nuclear Dialogue: 1963," in R. L. Garthoff (ed.), *Sino–Soviet Military Relations,* New York, 1966, p. 165. Also, John Gittings, *Survey of the Sino–Soviet Dispute, 1963–1967,* London, 1968, p. 106. The initially forthcoming—or apparently forthcoming—position of Moscow toward nuclear assistance to China, contrasting sharply with later hardening, raises the question of why Moscow moved as far down the road as it did in 1957. Halperin poses some of the possible considerations, without settling the matter (Morton

H. Halperin [ed.], *Sino–Soviet Relations and Arms Control,* Cambridge, Mass., 1967, pp. 121–123):

There were at least six factors that may have combined to make Khrushchev feel that it was desirable for him to acquiesce in Chinese demands for aid to their nuclear program:

1. Khrushchev was faced with the fact that the Chinese were determined to go ahead with the development of nuclear weapons whether or not they received extensive Soviet assistance. Hence, Krushchev's choice was not between a China equipped with nuclear weapons or a China dependent on the Soviet Union for nuclear deterrence. Rather it was between a Chinese nuclear program carried out in defiance of, or at least without the aid of, the Soviet Union, or a nuclear program carried out in cooperation with the Russians. . . .

2. During 1957 Khrushchev was engaged in a power struggle for the leadership of the Soviet Communist Party that was to see him purge first the anti-Party group in June and then Marshal Zhukov in October. Khrushchev undoubtedly was interested in securing at least the neutrality, and if possible the support, of the Chinese Communist Party in his effort to deal with opposition in the Soviet Union. . . .

3. The Chinese had played a critical role during the latter part of 1956 and in early 1957 in helping to resolidify Soviet influence in Eastern Europe following the events in Hungary and Poland. Nuclear aid might have been in part a repayment for Chinese favors and support.

4. The Sino–Soviet agreement on advanced technology for defense was signed on the eve of the Moscow Conference, at which the Soviets hoped to have a manifesto approved that would form the basis for the unity of the international Communist movement. . . . Stepped-up nuclear aid could have been part of the price that Khrushchev paid to the Chinese to secure at least their partial cooperation at the November conference and their willingness to compromise on key issues in dispute.

5. Khrushchev was seeking closer military cooperation with Communist China during this period, and was to propose, in 1958, various kinds of joint military arrangements, including . . . an agreement to station Soviet nuclear weapons on Chinese territory. It is possible that he viewed the granting of aid to the Chinese nuclear weapons production program as a useful backdrop with which to negotiate closer military cooperation with Peking.

6. Although there was a hiatus in negotiating forums in October 1957, Khrushchev had already taken the first steps toward a nuclear test ban agreement with the United States, and was to take further steps in 1958. A test ban at this time required the active participation of China. . . . He may have concluded that the most effective way to secure Chinese public and private support for the test ban treaty was to make such support a precondition for the granting of nuclear assistance.

3. D. S. Zagoria, *The Sino–Soviet Conflict, 1956–1961*, Princeton, 1962, p. 146.
4. John Gittings, *op. cit.,* p. 82.
5. *Ibid.,* pp. 81–82.
6. *Ibid.,* p. 82.

7. The best account of the debate beneath the surface of the 1957 conference is that of Kevin Devlin, "The Secret Confrontation of 1957," unpublished manuscript, January 22, 1970.
8. *Ibid.*, p. 16.
9. *Ibid.*, p. 18. For the possible role of Ho Chi Minh's 1956 formulation of this doctrine, see Chapter 4, note 5. For the linkage of the 1957 Moscow communique to the reopening of war against South Vietnam, see below, Chapter 4, note 4.
10. *Ibid.*, p. 20. Italics in original.
11. *Ibid.*, p. 21.
12. *Ibid.*, p. xi.
13. Arnold L. Horelick and Myron Rush, *Strategic Power and Soviet Foreign Policy,* Chicago and London, 1966, p. 35. Horelick and Rush trace in detail the strategy and tactics of Khrushchev's great bluff from 1957 through the Berlin and Cuba missile crises down to his removal from power on October 14, 1964.
14. "Department of Defense Statement on U.S. Military Strength," April 14, 1964.
15. Quoted, Arnold L. Horelick and Myron Rush, *op. cit.*, p. 64.
16. *Idem.*

	Great Britain February 1960	*West Germany February 1960*	*Norway June 1960*	*France February 1960*	*Italy February 1960*
Number of cases	613	599	1,020	608	591
U.S. ahead (%)	15	22	15	16	38
U.S.S.R. ahead (%)	59	47	45	37	32
Both equal (%)	4	8	17	16	5
No opinion (%)	22	25	23	31	25

The scale of the professional mis-estimate of the missile gap is suggested by the following table, based on *The New York Times* interviews with "numerous persons having intimate knowledge of the defense effort," published January 17, 1959 (Arnold L. Horelick and Myron Rush, *op. cit.*, p. 51, n. 7):

	USSR ICBMs	*US ICBMs*
1960	100	30
1961	500	70
1962	1,000	130
1963	1,500	130
1964	2,000	130

In 1959 it was estimated the gap would narrow only after 1964 with the rapid buildup of Polaris and Minuteman missiles.

In one sense, of course, the missile gap—and the publication of figures such as these—was a self-disproving hypothesis. Khrushchev's post-Sputnik posturing and inadequate American intelligence yielded an acceleration in the ICBM program; but behind the extraordinary outcome was also the Soviet decision to produce initially many fewer ICBMs than their capabilities suggested was possible.

17. Lincoln P. Bloomfield et al., *Khrushchev and the Arms Race,* Cambridge, Mass., 1966, pp. 94–95. See also Roy E. Licklider, "The Missile Gap Controversy," *Political Science Quarterly,* December 1970, pp. 600 ff.
18. Quoted, Lincoln P. Bloomfield et al, *op. cit.,* p. 97.
19. *Microcosmographia Academia,* Cambridge, 1933. Preface to Second Edition.
20. At the Pugwash Conference of November–December 1960, my first concern was to form an assessment from my Soviet contacts, some of whom were deeply involved in the nuclear business, as to whether they believed Russia commanded or would foreseeably command a first-strike capability. At that time I did not have access to official U.S. intelligence on relative U.S.–Soviet capabilities. In a Washington debriefing in December 1960, after the conference, I made the following observations:

> The smell of these twelve days to me was . . . that we are at the other end of the gap. The kinds of issues they were raising [suggested] . . . they had concluded they would not get a first-strike capability. . . .
> Katz [Amrom Katz of the RAND Corporation] had the same feeling. He had the feeling that if we both had to reveal in the First Stage [of a general disarmament plan] what our weapons totals are they would shudder to reveal what the relative sides look like. Just watching their reactions and the kind of conviction that went into them I had the feeling that they [the Soviet scientists] had done very hard work; they were proud of it; they had a respectable and serious deterrent; but not a first strike.

Chapter 3: *Four Interwoven Crises in Sino–Soviet Relations, 1958–1960*

1. John Gittings, *Survey of the Sino–Soviet Dispute, 1963–1967,* London, 1968, pp. 106–109.
2. Harold P. Ford, "The Eruption of Sino–Soviet Politico–Military Problems, 1957–60," in Raymond L. Garthoff [ed.], *Sino–Soviet Military Relations,* p. 102. Morton H. Halperin [ed.], *Sino–Soviet Relations and Arms Control,* Cambridge, Mass., 1967, New York, 1966, pp. 128–129, notes references to this shift toward self-reliance as early as February 1958; Malcolm Mackintosh (*ibid.,* p. 207), before the end of January.
3. Harold P. Ford, *op. cit.,* pp. 102–103.
4. See, in particular, John Gittings, *op. cit.,* pp. 102–105, and Harold P. Ford, *op. cit.,* pp. 100–113. On the Sino–Soviet nuclear issue see also Morton H. Halperin, *op. cit.,* especially Chapters 2 (Oran R.Young); 4

(Helmut Sonnenfeldt); 5 (Morton H. Halperin); 6 (Walter C. Clemens, Jr.); 7 (Harold C. Hinton); and 8 (Malcolm Mackintosh).

5. John Gittings, *op. cit.,* p. 103. For other speculations on the content of the Soviet proposition, see Morton H. Halperin, *op. cit.,* pp. 130–131, and Malcolm Mackintosh, *ibid.,* pp. 203–208. In Khrushchev's account, Moscow asked only for a Russian radio station in China to keep in touch with the Soviet submarine fleet. He also refers to Moscow's right to use Chinese airfields for layovers and refueling, presumably also denied by Mao. (John Gittings, *op. cit.,* pp. 472–473.) Given the inherent nature of the issues involved for the Soviet Union in granting the kind of nuclear assistance Mao wanted, including a sample nuclear weapon, I am skeptical that Soviet counter-requests of Mao were as limited as Khrushchev suggests.
6. See, for example, Harold C. Hinton, Chapter 8 in Morton H. Halperin, *op. cit.,* p. 177.
7. Quoted by Harold P. Ford, *op. cit.,* p. 105. Moscow's anxiety about an independent Chinese nuclear capability was later made even more pointed by its advocacy, on January 27, 1959, of an atom-free zone in Asia.
8. John Gittings, *op. cit.,* pp. 104–105.
9. See, especially, Morton H. Halperin, *op. cit.,* pp. 135–143; and Walter C. Clemens, Jr., *ibid.,* pp. 145–148.
10. Subsequent polemics indicate 1,390 Soviet specialists were withdrawn from Communist China in 1960. Agreements of August 1958 and February 1959 committed the Soviet Union to assist in the construction of 125 industrial projects, in addition to 211 projects in progress or completed. (John Gittings, *op. cit.,* p. 131.) Sino–Soviet trade moved as follows in the period 1957–1965 [*idem.*]:

	Soviet exports to China (millions of old roubles)	Soviet imports to China (millions of old roubles)
1957	2,176	2,952
1958	2,536	3,525
1959	3,818	4,401
1960	3,270	3,390
1961	1,470	2,200
1962	930	2,065
1963	749	1,651
1964	541	1,257
1965	756	891

11. Kevin Devlin's unpublished manuscript of May 20, 1970, is the best available account of the meeting ("Conference and Conflict: The Moscow Meetings of 1960"). See also Edward Crankshaw, *The New Cold War: Moscow v. Pekin,* Baltimore, 1963, evidently based on European Communist Party documentary sources.
12. Donald S. Zagoria, *The Sino–Soviet Conflict, 1956–1961,* Princeton, 1962, p. 365. On the Moscow Conference, see, in particular, Zagoria's Chapter 15; Klaus Mehnert, *Peking and Moscow,* London and New York, 1963, Chapter XVI, especially (Mentor edition) pp. 540–552; William E. Grif-

fith, *The Sino–Soviet Rift,* Cambridge, Mass., 1964, pp. 3–20; John Gittings, *op. cit.,* Chapter XVIII.

13. Quoted, Donald S. Zagoria, *op. cit.,* p. 198.
14. *Ibid.,* pp. 258–260.
15. *Ibid.,* pp. 206–207. On this crisis, see also John Gittings, *op. cit.,* Chapter X, pp. 89–92.
16. Zagoria (*op. cit.,* pp. 206–208) arrays as follows the factors that may have influenced Mao's decision to launch the Quemoy–Matsu crisis.

    First, the West was preoccupied with the Middle East crisis. . . . Second, the Chinese believed that they had an unbeatable hand. The evidence strongly suggested they . . . believed that, by interdiction, they could force the Quemoy garrison to surrender . . . which, in time, would lead to the automatic collapse of the other offshore islands. The Chinese seemed to base their calculations on a judgment . . . that once air and sea interdiction became effective the offshore islands could not be supplied, unless Nationalist and American forces were prepared to bomb the coastal provinces on the Chinese mainland.

    . . . The flaw in the calculation was that the blockade did not work; it did become feasible to supply the offshore islands without bombing the Chinese mainland.

    A third Chinese Communist calculation in initiating the venture has already been suggested. Mao probably believed sincerely that the West needed to be given a sobering lesson in brinkmanship in return for its intervention in the Middle East.

    Fourth, one of Peking's intentions may have been to extract from Moscow expanded military commitments, including tactical nuclear weapons to oppose those that might be brought to Taiwan.

    Fifth, the stimulation of greater popular effort for the leap forward and the commune program may have been expected from military action in the Taiwan Strait.

    Sixth, the offshore island venture must also be looked upon as a calculated Chinese Communist probe of U.S. intentions. How far would the Americans go in defending these islands? . . .

    A final and not least important Chinese Communist calculation was that the initiation of another crisis over the offshore islands would badly shake the Nationalist confidence in the American alliance and thus serve as a major stepping-stone to . . . incorporating Taiwan into mainland China. . . . If one recalls the great pressures in both the United States and Western Europe for an evacuation of the offshore islands, one will see that the Chinese calculation was wrong only in not allowing for the obduracy of Secretary Dulles.

17. "Statement by Spokesman of Chinese Government . . . ," September 1, 1963, quoted, John Gittings, *op. cit.,* pp. 91–92. For a contrary view of Sino–Soviet relations in the Quemoy–Matsu crisis see Morton H. Halperin and Tang Tsou, "The 1958 Quemoy Crisis," Chapter 10 in Morton H. Halperin [ed.], *op. cit.* Halperin and Tsou argue, in effect, that Moscow and Peking were pretty well aligned during the crisis and Peking's complaints are ex post.
18. Donald S. Zagoria, *op. cit.,* p. 283. With respect to Taiwan, Peking subsequently accused Khrushchev of advocating a two-China policy on his

post-U. S. visit to Peking (John Gittings, *op. cit.*, p. 118). On the Sino–Indian border dispute, see John Gittings, *op. cit.*, pp. 110–115.

19. Donald S. Zagoria, *op. cit.*, p. 278.

Chapter 4: *Three Crises in the Developing World*

1. In a top secret directive of November 1, 1951, the leadership in Hanoi explained the change of name from Indochinese Communist party to Vietnamese Communist party as a device to meet the nationalist susceptibilities of their Lao and Cambodian comrades. But the directive went on to inform the Vietnamese cadres that these parties would continue to receive secretly their orders from Hanoi and that "later on, when conditions permit this to be carried out, the three revolutionary parties of Vietnam, Cambodia, and Laos will be reunited to form a single party." There has never been any question that the Communist party in South Vietnam is a part of the Vietnamese Communist party run from Hanoi; although this fact did not preclude some friction between its southern and northern members. P. J. Honey, *Communism in North Vietnam,* Cambridge, Mass., 1963, pp. 25, 169–170.
2. On the 1956 crisis see *ibid.,* pp. 43–47. Also the vivid contemporary account (January 1957) reprinted in Bernard Fall, *Viet-Nam Witness, 1953–66,* New York, 1966, pp. 96–104.
3. Among other things, Giap said:

   > We made too many deviations and executed too many honest people. We attacked on too large a front and, seeing enemies everywhere, resorted to terror, which became far too widespread. Whilst carrying out our Land Reform program we failed to respect the principles of freedom of faith and worship in many areas. In regions inhabited by minority tribes we have attacked tribal chiefs too strongly, thus injuring, instead of respecting, local customs and manners. When reorganising the party, we paid too much importance to the notion of social class instead of adhering firmly to political qualifications alone. Instead of recognising education to be the first essential, we resorted exclusively to organisational measures such as disciplinary punishments, expulsion from the party, executions, dissolution of party branches and calls. Worse still, torture came to be regarded as a normal practice during party reorganisation.

   Quoted from *Nhan Dan,* No. 970 (October 31, 1956), in Hoang Van Chi, *From Colonialism to Communism,* New York, London, 1964, p. 210. Chi takes the quite possible view that the extreme violence with which land reform was carried out was planned, as in the case of Mao's post-1949 land reform, for deep psychological and political purposes. The period of apparent moderation signaled by Giap's speech is, in this perspective, a pre-planned and essentially cosmetic relenting of pressure. Chi's book is the most full account in English of the stages by which the North Vietnamese countryside was placed in its present dreary, inefficient, collectivized framework. See also Ho on "shortcomings" and the "correction of errors" in this period (Bernard Fall [ed.], *Ho Chi Minh on Revolution,* New York, 1967, pp. 304–322).

4. P. J. Honey, *op. cit.,* p. 57. The following three passages suggest that the doctrine of "non-peaceful transition to socialism," accepted at the Moscow meeting of 1957 (and again in 1960) may have been rooted in Ho's basic position articulated as early as April 24, 1956:

   Speech Closing Ninth Plenum of the Central Committee of the Lao Dong Party, April 24, 1956.

   While recognizing that in certain countries the road to socialism may be a peaceful one, we should be aware of this fact: In countries where the machinery of state, the armed forces, and the police of the bourgeois class are still strong, the proletarian class still has to prepare for armed struggle.

   Declaration of the Conference of Communist and Workers Parties of Socialist Countries, Moscow, 1957.

   In conditions in which the exploiting classes resort to violence against the people, it is necessary to bear in mind another possibility—nonpeaceful transition to socialism. Leninism teaches and history confirms that the ruling classes never relinquish power voluntarily. In these conditions the severity and forms of class struggle will depend not so much on the proletariat as on the resistance of the reactionary circles to the will of the overwhelming majority of the people, on the use of force by these circles at one or another stage of the struggle for socialism.

   Declaration of the Conference of Communist and Workers Parties of Socialist Countries, Moscow, 1960.

   [The paragraph cited above from the 1957 Declaration is repeated virtually verbatim and the following conclusion drawn:]

   In each country the actual possibility of one or another means of transition to socialism is determined by the specific historical conditions. . . .

5. Douglas Pike, *Viet Cong,* Cambridge, Mass., 1966, p. 78.
6. *Ibid.,* p. 79.
7. *Ibid.,* p. 82.
8. Bernard Fall *loc. cit.,* p. 77. Given the policies conducted in the North, it is clear that a good deal of Ho Chi Minh's political capital in the South, as of 1954, was dissipated in the subsequent two years. Those who quote the following passage from Eisenhower's *Mandate for Change* (New York, 1963, p. 372) often omit the italicized reference to the timing of his dictum: "I have never talked or corresponded with a person knowledgeable in Indochinese affairs who did not agree that had elections been held *as of the time of the fighting,* possibly 80 per cent of the population would have voted for the Communist Ho Chi Minh as their leader rather than Chief of State Bao Dai." It is often implied that Eisenhower's judgment would have applied to 1956 or even later, on the basis of this quotation.
9. *The New York Times,* January 23, 1955.
10. P. J. Honey, *op. cit.,* pp. 66–92, makes the most extensive effort to relate

the timing of Hanoi's decisions with respect to the attack on the South to Ho's relations with Moscow and Peking. He dates the most critical decision as probably taken in May 1959. For a foreshadowing of the May pronouncements see Harold C. Hinton, *Communist China in World Politics,* Boston, 1966, p. 342.

11. *Khrushchev Remembers*, Edward Crankshaw and Strobe Talbott (eds.), Boston and Toronto, 1970, pp. 480–487.
12. It has been argued that a fifth factor was at work: Hanoi's food requirements. Agriculture under communism and collectivization did not flourish in North Vietnam. Hanoi had to look to rice imports; and, on so politically sensitive a margin, it would not wish to rely on a non-communist source. But reliance on Communist China also carried with it hostages to fortune. In the long run, control over the Mekong Delta must have appeared the right solution; but, if realistic, the leadership would also have to weigh the adverse effects of communist methods on the South Vietnamese rice surplus. In general, so fundamental an objective as the unification of Vietnam under Hanoi is unlikely to have been seriously influenced, one way or another, by economic considerations. P. J. Honey, *op. cit.*, argues this point extensively; e.g., p. 120.
13. The two most complete accounts of the post-1954 period in Laos are: Arthur J. Dommen, *Conflict in Laos*, New York, 1964; and Hugh Toye, *Laos*, London, 1968.
14. Arthur J. Dommen, *op. cit.*, p. 79. See also Harold C. Hinton, *loc. cit.*, especially pp. 341–344.
15. Arthur J. Dommen, *op. cit.*, pp. 114–116.
16. *Ibid.*, pp. 134–136.
17. Arthur Dommen's analysis of the motives and role of the military in Laos is typical of the military position in many nations at an early stage of economic and political development (*op. cit.*, p. 126):

> Their putsch was a natural consequence of their genuine disgust at the political situation. . . . Had they, the generals of the Royal Army, not spent the last six months battling a rebellion whose leaders were sympathetic to the Communists? And here were these civilian politicians, many of them old-time masters at corruption and graft, arguing hotly about how long their terms should run. Was this not madness?
>
> Besides frustration, another factor motivating the generals was their conviction that they alone could prepare the country to resist the Communist menace. The army has a peculiar status in Laos. It is the only organization that reaches every part of the territory and that involves the life of virtually every Lao family. It is the country's greatest unifier. . . . The army may be slipshod and lazy, but without it there would be little to make the villages feel the existence of the monarchy, the flag, and the government.
>
> Also, in economically underdeveloped Laos, the national army represents a reservior of manual skills and practical training. . . .
>
> Third, the army is the Lao economy's only sizable source of circulating currency. In the army, many Lao are paid in cash for the first time. . . . The Lao soldier with his monthly pay, equivalent to about $10, is a rich man compared to his peasant brothers who will still live in a barter economy.

18. Edward Crankshaw and Strobe Talbott (eds.), *op. cit.*, pp. 483–484.
19. See, notably, Theodore Draper, *Castroism: Theory and Practice*, New York, 1965, pp. 3–56; for a contrary interpretation, see Herbert L. Matthews, *Fidel Castro*, New York, 1969, especially pp. 165–198. Also Hugh Thomas, *Cuba: The Pursuit of Freedom*, New York, 1971, especially pp. 1037–1090, 1193–1299.
20. Dwight D. Eisenhower, *Waging Peace, 1956–1961*, New York, 1965, pp. 520–525.
21. Arthur M. Schlesinger, Jr., *A Thousand Days*, New York, 1965, pp. 363. For Schlesinger's own sensitive evaluation of this matter see pp. 216–220.
22. Ernest Halperin underlines Castro's early caution with respect to anti-Americanism, a caution that extended to the basic stance of the July 26 Movement in the two years after its program was announced in Mexico in November 1956. For example, in the wake of the Lebanon landings Castro released American military personnel kidnapped in late June 1958, ostensibly on the grounds of "the need your army has for each one of your members in these moments." ("The National Liberation Movements in Latin America," June 1969, draft manuscript, Center for International Studies, M.I.T., Cambridge, Mass., especially pp. 34–37.)
23. For one of a number of parallel exercises, see Bernard Fall, *The Two Viet-Nams* (second revised edition), New York, 1967, pp. 130–138, on Ho Chi Minh's 1946 consolidation of power by techniques "to be repeated from North Korea to Czechoslovakia."
24. For evidence on the formal character of the Cuban Communist party's decision in 1958, see Theodore Draper, *Castro's Revolution*, New York, 1962, pp. 53–56. Also, Draper's *Castroism: Theory and Practice*, New York, 1965, pp. 31–34, where he dates the first communist "half turn" toward Castro in February 1958 (p. 31), with sources indicated in footnotes. On the evolution of Castro's relations with the Communist party, see also Hugh Thomas, *op. cit.*, pp. 1005–1007; and the detailed analysis of K. S. Karol, *Guerrillas in Power*, New York, 1970, pp. 138–186. Khrushchev's memoir (Edward Crankshaw and Strobe Talbott [eds.], *op. cit.*, pp. 488–489) states flatly that Raul Castro was known in Moscow as "a good Communist" who concealed his true convictions from his brother; Che Guevara and "some of the others" were communists; Rodriguez resigned as secretary of the Central Committee of the Communist party to join Castro; Moscow did not know what policy Castro would follow when he came to power. It is implied, therefore, that Moscow did not know of or follow closely the protracted negotiations between Castro and the Cuban communists in the course of 1958. Without firm evidence, I am inclined to be skeptical that Moscow was unaware of the decision of the Cuban communists to join Castro and supersede his noncommunist base of support. There is no evidence that Rodriguez lost his role in the Cuban Communist party by joining Castro; and there is much evidence of Rodriguez's faithfulness as an orthodox agent of Moscow, both before and after the 1958 negotiations with Castro.
25. See, in particular, for these events Theodore Draper, *Castroism: Theory and Practice*, pp. 142–146.

26. "For New Victories for the World Communist Movement," *World Marxist Review*, January 1961, p. 19.
27. It was not difficult to conclude in December 1960, after talking with Russians day and night for almost two weeks: ". . . we must prepare for a major and probably accelerated struggle in the underdeveloped areas. I have the sense that the Communist victory in Cuba has substantially increased their optimism." (From my report to Kennedy on the Pugwash meeting in Moscow.)
28. Herbert L. Matthews, *op. cit.*, p. 197.
29. Communist optimism about prospects in the developing world was endemic in those years, and included economic arguments shared by some Western economists. In May 1959 I was in Warsaw on an eight-week tour of Europe presenting to academic colleagues the set of ideas later published as *The Stages of Economic Growth*. Michael Kalecki, Polish economist and planner, invited me to debate before his graduate seminar in the University of Warsaw the question: "Will communist or noncommunist methods triumph in the developing world?" His optimism was expressed on that occasion in these terms: only strong dictatorial communist governments could generate the high level of investment required for regular growth in the face of low levels of income and the consequently low levels of saving that would prevail without central compulsion in developing nations. The political and economic policies that worked in western Europe and North America would simply not work in, say, India. I replied that: communist methods in agriculture would limit working capital available for industrialization; and that adequate foreign aid plus private incentives in agriculture would give the advantage to noncommunists. He responded by agreeing frankly about the communist weakness in agriculture but argued that bourgeois governments were too obtuse to generate adequate foreign aid for, say, India. I pointed to the Kennedy–Cooper Resolution then moving slowly through the Congress, looking toward a Western consortium in support of India and Pakistan. Kalecki expressed skepticism. I said I was optimistic; we could clearly not settle the matter between us; and it was on such differences in assessment that horse races were based.

    For a formal expression of Kalecki's views at this time, see "The Problem of Financing of Economic Development," *Indian Economic Review*, Vol. II, February 1955.

Chapter 5: *The Eisenhower Second Term: The Domestic Scene*

1. Dwight D. Eisenhower, *Waging Peace, 1956–1961*. New York, 1965, p. 226.
2. The phrase is from the title of Chapter VIII, "Sputnik and a Sputtering Economy," *ibid.*, p. 205.

3. Arthur F. Burns and Paul A. Samuelson, *Full Employment, Guideposts and Economic Stability*, Washington, D. C., 1967, p. 8. For a view of the Eisenhower policy in this period in somewhat different terms, see Arthur M. Okun, *The Political Economy of Prosperity*, Washington, D. C., 1970, especially pp. 37–40. Okun contrasts the Eisenhower view that fiscal policy should only be applied to resist major depression with the Kennedy–Johnson use of fiscal policy to promote sustained growth. I am inclined to agree with Burns that balance-of-payments anxieties played a substantial role in fiscal policy of the late 1950s without denying a considerable shift in perspective toward growth and fiscal policy (in domestic terms) after 1961.
4. With respect to welfare, Eisenhower believed the defense of social security benefits against the erosion of rising prices was his most urgent task (Dwight D. Eisenhower, *op. cit.*, p. 386):

   > In health, education, and welfare, I insisted that spending more money did not necessarily hasten progress. Preventing deterioration of our currency was not only an economic necessity but a *humanitarian goal as well*, because failure to preserve the purchasing power of the dollar spells hardship for those who will one day live on pensions, insurance policies, and savings in government bonds.

   The Economic Report of the President for January 1960 foreshadowed the concept of wage-price guideposts in both the President's letter of transmittal (p. iv) and the Council of Economic Advisers Presentation (pp. 7–8); but, in fact, the Eisenhower administration relied to the end on fiscal and monetary policy as the virtually exclusive tools for managing the economy and constraining prices.
5. For the author's view of the connection between the depth and intractability of the depression after 1929 and the inherent nature of the stage of high mass-consumption, see *The Stages of Economic Growth*, Cambridge, 1960 and 1971, pp. 77–79, and *Politics and the Stages of Growth*, Cambridge, 1971, p. 220.
6. See, for example, H. G. Vatter, *The U.S. Economy in the 1950's*, New York, 1963, especially pp. 158–163, on deceleration in the automobile industry.
7. For the flavor of Eisenhower's feeling on this issue at the time and in retrospect see Dwight D. Eisenhower, *op. cit.*, pp. 305–310, 377–382, 385–388, and Appendix U, pp. 699–701. For earlier, pre-recession anxieties that budget cuts would go "beyond the bone," see pp. 127–132.
8. For the method used in making these calculations and similar calculations for the Kennedy, Johnson, and Nixon administrations, see my *Politics and the Stages of Growth*, pp. 386–387, n. 8.
9. Expanded public investment in roads was a major feature of the first phase of the stage of high mass-consumption in the United States as well as its second, post-1945 phase. See, notably, R. A. Musgrave and J. M. Culbertson, "The Growth of Public Expenditures in the United States, 1890–1948," *National Tax Journal*, June 1953, pp. 102–103.
10. William Brink and Louis Harris, *The Negro Revolution in America*, New York, 1963, p. 39.

11. Dwight D. Eisenhower, *op. cit.*, p. 154. For a politically somewhat more earthy account of Eisenhower's race policies in 1957, see Sherman Adams, *First Hand Report*, New York, 1961, pp. 331–359.
12. Theodore C. Sorenson, *Kennedy*, New York, 1965, pp. 49–50.
13. Dwight D. Eisenhower, *op. cit.*, p. 161.
14. *Ibid.*, pp. 162–175.

Chapter 6: *Sputnik, Military Policy, and Space*

1. For full discussion see my book *The United States in the World Arena*, New York, 1960, pp. 301–309.
2. *Ibid.*, especially pp. 206–210.
3. Trevor Gardner's evaluation in the spring of 1956, a year and a half before the first Sputnik, was impassioned but accurate on the whole ("Our Guided Missiles Crisis," *Look*, May 15, 1956, pp. 46 ff.):

   1. The Army, the Navy, and the Air Force, each working on its own parochial guided-missiles program, are vying with each other in an intolerable rivalry.

   2. The over-all missiles program is smothering in an administrative nightmare of committees and subcommittees competing with each other for influence and appropriations.

   3. The ICBM project, which two and a half years ago was given a top-priority status, now shares top priority with many subsidiary missiles projects and the result is that there is no such thing as "top priority."

   4. The executive personnel of the missiles program is notable for its preponderance of management experts recruited from private business, and for its poverty of fulltime scientists who qualify as missiles experts and know what they're talking about.

   For a fuller evaluation of missile development in the United States, 1953–1958, see my book *The United States in the World Arena*, pp. 314–316.
4. On interservice rivalry, see notably Michael H. Armacost, *The Politics of Weapons Innovation: The Thor–Jupiter Controversy*, New York, 1969.
5. The Soviet research and development effort was probably somewhat more substantial in the years 1945–1952, among other reasons because the intermediate-range ballistic missile was immensely significant for Soviet but not for American strategy. A Soviet IRBM could strike at population centers in western Europe and Japan as well as at American strategic air bases around the periphery of the communist bloc; but there was nothing particularly urgent that an American IRBM could strike which could not already be hit with some efficiency from airplanes.

   It is clear that down to 1953 Moscow also pursued at the research and development level a major effort to create the long-range aircraft required for a modernized Soviet version of SAC. But until the thermonuclear bomb was created, the long-range ballistic missile appeared as a relatively limited instrument. The vastly enlarged area of destruction by the H-bomb, once it could be reduced in size to fit the nose cone of a rocket, elevated the military status of missiles. In the course of 1953 the long-range rocket for the first time became a weapon of urgent operational interest.

6. A Ministry of Defense Production, charged with the manufacture of missiles, was set up in 1953; a special Committee on Space Travel, at the highest scientific level, was set up in 1954; and the ablest minds in the four most relevant fields of basic science evidently turned with increased operational emphasis to the missile problem: fluid dynamics and heat transfer; fuel chemistry and combustion; structures and materials; and electronics and communication theory. In 1954 missile technology invaded the Soviet engineering curriculum on a large scale. In 1955 a crash effort to produce MRBMs and ICBMs was probably launched. (For discussion and evidence on this point, see Lincoln P. Bloomfield et al., *Khrushchev and the Arms Race*, Cambridge, Mass., 1966, pp. 40–41.)

7. The historians of NASA (Robert L. Rosholt et al., *An Administrative History of NASA*, 1958–1963, Washington D. C., 1966, p. 5.) described the Vanguard enterprise as follows:

   This project, designed to place a 20-pound sphere in a 300-mile orbit around the earth, was to be mainly a civilian scientific effort. However, most of the national services and their contractors, and thus the military, had to be brought into the picture. With the help of a committee of civilian scientists, the DOD Committee on Special Capabilities was to work out the details for the satellite project. The Committee canvassed the three military services for proposals. After what would seem to have been adequate investigation and review, the decision was made to use most of the elements of the Naval Research Laboratory proposal, which was based on the Navy's Viking/Aerobee-Hi launch vehicle technology. Thus, Project Vanguard, as it was named, became for all practical purposes a Navy-civilian project under the Navy's Office of Naval Research. Its scientific aspects were under the purview of the U.S. IGY Committee of the National Academy of Sciences.

   Subsequent events have revealed that Project Vanguard suffered from the decisions which gave it a "shoestring" status in terms of national priorities and resources.

8. Dwight D. Eisenhower, *Waging Peace, 1956–1961*, New York, 1965, pp. 206–209. The NASA historians note, however, that in May 1955 Nelson Rockefeller argued as follows in a memorandum that circulated through the various branches of the government and to the National Security Council as a whole:

   I am impressed by the costly consequences of allowing the Russian initiative to outrun ours through an achievement that will symbolize scientific and technological advancement to people everywhere. The stake of prestige that is involved makes this a race we cannot afford to lose.

Subsequent NSC action did not accept Rockefeller's evaluation. It approved the Vanguard program on the condition that it not interfere with urgent work on military missiles. (*Preliminary History of NASA, 1963–1968*, Chapter 1, pp. 4–5, and relevant footnotes.) William Leavitt ("The Air Force and Space," in *Air Force and Space Digest*, September 1970, p. 92) notes that a RAND memorandum as early as May 2, 1946, observed:

> The achievement of the satellite craft by the United States would inflame the imagination of mankind and would probably produce repercussions in the world comparable to the explosion of the atomic bomb.

9. I was invited late in 1959 by Keith Glennan to serve on an advisory committee to examine the space program in general and the pros and cons of manned flight to the moon in particular. The chairman was Crawford Greenewalt of Du Pont. The committee included scientists like Jerome Wiesner and Edward Purcell, as well as laymen like Frank Stanton, Paul Nitze, and myself. Views were divided. Some argued that all the scientific advantages of flight to the moon could be achieved by unmanned missions with adequate instruments. Others argued the political, psychological, and scientific advantages of manned flight. The committee met for dinner with Vice President Nixon in the White House mess and discussed their findings. The Vice President appeared to side with those who supported manned flight.

   On balance, I supported manned flight for a narrow reason. It emerged from the work of the committee that the technological intensity and creativity of the space effort as a whole was radically increased when those engaged had not only to mount a space flight but to do so under conditions where the lives of men had to be sustained and preserved. I concluded the scientific and technological dividends of a manned trip to the moon would be substantially greater than an unmanned venture. In response to a casual solicitation of my view in the spring of 1961, I reported this net judgment to President Kennedy.

10. For the origins, membership and (unclassified) conclusions of this committee, see *In the Matter of J. Robert Oppenheimer, Transcript of Hearing before Personnel Security Board*, Washington, D. C., April 12, 1954, through May 6, 1954, U.S. Atomic Energy Commission, Washington, D. C., 1954, p. 95. With official permission, Oppenheimer incorporated three of its major conclusions in "Atomic Weapons and American Policy," *Foreign Affairs*, July 1953, pp. 530–532. For more full discussion of the committee's conclusions and the Eisenhower administration's reaction to them, see my book *The United States in the World Arena*, pp. 316–319.

11. For an account of this conversion, see Dwight D. Eisenhower, *Mandate for Change, 1953–1956*, New York, 1963, pp. 251–255. Also, Sherman Adams, *First Hand Report*, New York, 1961, pp. 111–114.

12. Among the recommendations of this panel was the Open Skies proposal, subsequently carried forward by Rockefeller into the heart of government and accepted by Eisenhower at Geneva. (Dwight D. Eisenhower, *Man-*

date for Change, pp. 519–521; also, Sherman Adams, *op. cit.*, pp. 177–179.)

The Quantico group included: Frederick Dunn, director, Center for International Studies; C. D. Jackson, TIME–LIFE; Ellis A. Johnson, director, Operations Research Office; Paul Linebarger, School of Advanced International Studies; Max Millikan, Center for International Studies; Philip Mosely, director, Russian Institute; George Pettee, deputy director, Operations Research Office; Stefan Possony, air intelligence specialist, Department of the Air Force; Hans Speier, RAND Corporation; Charles A. H. Thomson, Brookings Institution. I was chairman. With the failure of the Summit Conference to yield substantive movement toward a German settlement or arms control, Rockefeller assembled a second Quantico group toward the end of 1955. The rejection of its proposals, which included recommendations for expanded security and aid budgets, led to Rockefeller's resignation and the setting up of the Rockefeller Brothers Fund panels. For an account of these initiatives see, especially, James Desmond, *Nelson Rockefeller: A Political Biography*, New York, 1964, pp. 142–153.

13. Dwight D. Eisenhower, *Waging Peace, 1956–1961*, p. 220.

Chapter 7: *Sputnik and the Atlantic Alliance*

1. This and other experiences with the Joint Atomic Energy Committee rankled deeply with Eisenhower. Among his major reflections, as he passed responsibility to Kennedy, was his feeling the Joint Atomic Energy Committee of the Congress should be abolished as "worse than silly." (Dwight D. Eisenhower, *Waging Peace, 1956–1961*, New York, 1965, pp. 714–715.)
2. The Eisenhower administration began U-2 photographic intelligence missions in 1956. Their limited coverage did not permit a firm estimate of the actual rate of production and deployment of Soviet ICBMs; although intelligence gradually provided evidence that was progressively more reassuring than theoretical projections based on Soviet technical and economic capabilities, such as those in the Gaither report. But when pressed, Defense Secretary Neil McElroy and his successor, Thomas Gates, did not wholly eliminate the sense that a "missile gap" of some sort might exist or emerge. This was true even in 1960 when it was becoming clear that Moscow had not engaged in a crash program to deploy ICBMs.

   See, for example, A. L. Horelick and Myron Rush, *Strategic Power and Soviet Foreign Policy*, Chicago and London, 1966, p. 68. In the wake of the U-2 crisis of May 1960 Khrushchev moved to modify his claims in the direction of parity rather than strategic superiority over the United States (*ibid.*, pp. 78–82); although Khrushchev noted that the U-2 had passed only over the Soviet missile test range, not over operational bases (*ibid.*, pp. 73–74).

3. See, notably, John Newhouse, *De Gaulle and the Anglo–Saxons*, New York, 1970, pp. 14–16.
4. *Ibid.*, pp. 23–24.
5. Macmillan's difficulties with the pre–de Gaulle French government on economic issues relating to British entrance into Europe suggest, however, that the negotiating problem in any case would have been difficult. See, for example, passages from Macmillan's memoirs, London *Sunday Times*, November 8, 1970.
6. On the French nuclear problem as it emerged in 1958–1961, see for example, John Newhouse, *op. cit.*; also, Robert E. Osgood, *NATO, The Entangling Alliance*, Chicago, 1962, pp. 222–229, 256–259, 267–269, 283–285, 288–289, 350–351.
7. Quoted, Robert E. Osgood, *op. cit.*, p. 258.
8. John Newhouse, *op. cit.*, p. 249.
9. On an extended trip through eastern Europe and to the Soviet Union in the spring of 1959, and on a trip to Moscow at the close of 1960, I found the routine and virtually uniform initial approach of communist officials was the assertion: "The realities of power have now shifted against you. You must accept the new reality." This theme did not wholly disappear from the American–Soviet dialogue until after the Cuba missile crisis of 1962.
10. John Newhouse (*op. cit.*, pp. 90–92) summarizes precisely the nuances on the Berlin question among the Western capitals, in the shadow of Khrushchev's nuclear blackmail, which were well understood in Moscow and were to keep the Berlin crisis alive down to the end of October 1962:

    Berlin had a purifying quality; in the harsh light of a showdown with Moscow the real attitudes and purposes of the four Western capitals were revealed. . . . Principally, Eisenhower wanted to maintain a firm Western position while minimizing the risk of nuclear war and making certain that the issue of war and peace was clearly set forth in political terms. This meant that Washington would not, say, declare war if Moscow delegated to East Germany the right to stamp Western passports.

    West German policy was characteristically paradoxical. Adenauer's real concern was to preserve Bonn's sovereign pre-eminence vis-à-vis East Germany; he was in no case prepared to risk a war over the status of Berlin. Franz-Josef Strauss was equally reluctant to risk war. He lacked confidence in the Americans' judgment and frankly feared they might use tactical nuclear weapons on German soil. He felt that maintaining a position in Berlin, a city far from Western defenses, suited an offensive strategy but not the defensive strategy imposed by geography. Together, Adenauer and Strauss sought to harden the Western position while discouraging plans to keep open by force the Autobahn linking Berlin to the Federal Republic, as Washington was prepared to do if it became necessary.

    For de Gaulle, Berlin was an opportunity—he never really saw it as a crisis. From the start he assumed—doubtless correctly—that Khrushchev was bluffing; and he arrived at a tacit understanding with Adenauer. In return for Adenauer's support for French policies favoring limits on the development of the EEC and France's pre-eminent role in it, de Gaulle would back Adenauer's position vis-à-vis East Germany. This understanding served as an ideal means for turning Adenauer against Washington and London; at the same time, de Gaulle was trying to catch Moscow's eye.

Great Britain was chiefly concerned with defusing the situation, and to accomplish this Macmillan was willing to pay a higher price than the others. In the end he held firm, but he wobbled often. The role of peace-broker attracted him strongly—and not just because it suited the British political climate. So in December Macmillan arranged to have himself invited to visit Khrushchev in Moscow, and he notified Bonn, Paris, and Washington of his plans without specifying his intentions.

It was this gesture which inspired Dulles's final voyage to Europe; he felt obliged to test the firmness of Macmillan's position and to reassure the West Germans, for whom the British initiative was an unwelcome surprise, to put it mildly. And, of course, . . . Dulles met with de Gaulle. Nobody can say for certain, but it seems at least possible that de Gaulle's hard Berlin position, in contrast to the ambiguity at 10 Downing Street, might have been the factor that moved Dulles to go as far as he did in offering de Gaulle a de facto veto on American nuclear weapons in Europe.

11. *Waging Peace, 1956–1961*, pp. 339–340, 397–412. Eisenhower (pp. 405–407) describes a failure of communication between himself and Robert Murphy in setting the terms for the invitation to Khrushchev, which was conveyed orally via Kozlov as he departed from New York on July 12. Eisenhower wanted the visit to be conditional on progress at the Geneva negotiations and prelude to a summit meeting, but Murphy delivered the message as unconditional. Given the pace and complexity of postwar diplomacy, it is remarkable that there have not been more such breakdowns; but it is an interesting object lesson in the virtues of written, as opposed to oral, diplomatic instructions.
12. *Waging Peace, 1956–1961*, pp. 445–446. On October 6, 1959, at Vladivostok, after his talk with Mao, Khrushchev, in a speech, stated:

    We shall produce many cars, but not at the moment.

    We want to set up a different system for the use of cars than the one in capitalist countries, where one reasons according to the principle: It is a lousy car but at least it is my own! Cars will be used in our country more rationally than is done by the Americans. Common taxicab parks will be widely developed in our country, where people will take cars for essential purposes. Why should one rack one's brains over where to park the car, and to be bothered with it? Such a system will be more satisfactory to meet the needs of people, to meet the interests both of society as a whole and the individual.

    FBIS, October 8, 1959, p. BB 16.
13. See Michel Tatu, *Power in the Kremlin*, New York, 1969, pp. 19–37, for a summary statement.
14. Tatu, *ibid.*, p. 122, poses an interesting question concerning the appro-

priate determinants of American policy in a world where the interplay between foreign policy and the domestic politics of other nations so intimately interact:

> An embarrassing political reverse (the U-2 incident) served as a catalyst for the latent opposition. Grievances long suffered in silence came tumbling forth, both from the military, who had been by-passed in appropriations, and from the top planners yearning for greater centralization. All their demands, which constituted the background of the struggle for power, found political expression in the Party Presidium where the balance of profits and losses was swiftly drawn. Thus 1960 witnessed a serious blow to Khrushchev's ambitions and forced him to accept some sharing of power. His decline seems definitely to date from this period.
>
> Whether all this would have happened if the U-2 had not overflown Soviet territory a fortnight before the summit meeting and if President Eisenhower had not accepted responsibility for it is a moot point. It is likely that the detractors of Khrushchev's policy, ranging from the Chinese to the Soviet marshals and including the conservatives within the state and party apparatus, would eventually have found an opportunity for action. But the best chance was given them by a foreign country. . . .
>
> No opinion will be expressed here as to whether this event was salutary from the Western point of view. United States policy was in any case influenced by domestic motives, particularly the fact pointed out by Allen Dulles [*The Craft of Intelligence*, New York, 1963, pp. 197–198], that secrecy could not have been maintained for long under American conditions. But such motives should not have been the only ones. No policy of relations with Moscow can be planned intelligently without regard to the capital question of how it affects the struggle for influence at top level in the Soviet Union. For this purpose, the symptoms of that struggle which are visible to the outside world must be taken seriously however slight they may seem. Even before May 1, 1960, these signs showed clearly enough that Khrushchev, despite his self-assurance and the cult that surrounded him, was far from being the absolute master he had been taken for. This fact seems to have been generally underestimated. Before considering whether or not it was in the Western interest to help him consolidate his power, it would have been useful to have been aware of its limitations.

In the bilateral U.S.–Soviet talks following the December 1960 Pugwash Conference, Amrom Katz put the question of the U-2 and the détente issue to our Russian counterparts in a somewhat different way (text supplied by Mr. Katz):

> About the U-2, much has already been said. Let me say only the following—it is quite clear by now that Mr. Khrushchev and our Soviet colleagues knew much more about the U-2 during its entire history than did anyone sitting on the American side of the table. Did the U-2 fly over the Soviet Union for four years? Apparently the answer is yes.
>
> Which U-2 flights did the Soviet more damage by their standards, the U-2's which flew over and returned safely, or the U-2 which they shot down? Clearly it must be the U-2 that returned, not the one that was shot down.

Yet I must point out that during this entire period the Soviet Union was engaged in serious negotiation and friendly conversation, and the spirit of Camp David was flying almost as high as the reputed height at which the U-2's flew. There is only one question I have then. Why did the Soviets shoot down the U-2 and spoil this nice situation and end this era of good will?

The joke was too good not to be appreciated by the Soviet delegates, and the point too sharp to be accepted. Federov replied, in effect, that the USSR had to have irrefutable proof of the flights to force the issue of their legitimacy and, therefore, had to shoot one down at first opportunity.

15. In a vivid but somewhat overdrawn passage, Emmet John Hughes comments on this linkage in *The Ordeal of Power*, New York, 1963, pp. 299–305, 314.

Chapter 8: *Eisenhower's Policy Toward the Developing World*

1. See, for example, my book *The United States in the World Arena*, New York, 1960, pp. 293–298.
2. The only retrospective reference to Jackson's effort of which I am aware is in Sherman Adams, *First Hand Report*, New York, 1961, pp. 115–116. It is somewhat vaguely described, but basically consistent with my memory and records. The *New York Post* (June 8, 1954) and *The Wall Street Journal* (August 27, 1954) carried contemporary references.
3. Those present were: Samuel W. Anderson, assistant secretary of commerce; George B. Baldwin, Center for International Studies, M.I.T.; Lloyd V. Berkner, president, Associated Universities Inc.; Robert Cutler, special assistant to the President; Allen W. Dulles, director, Central Intelligence Agency; Arthur Flemming, director, Office of Defense Mobilization; Robert Garner, vice president, The International Bank; Gabriel Hauge, administrative assistant to the President; C. D. Jackson, TIME Incorporated; John K. Jessup, TIME Incorporated; Edward S. Mason, Harvard University; David J. McDonald, president, United Steel Workers of America; Thomas McKittrick, Chase National Bank; Max Millikan, Center for International Studies, M.I.T.; H. Chapman Rose, assistant secretary of the treasury; Harold E. Stassen, director, Foreign Operations Administration; Charles L. Stillman, vice president, TIME Incorporated; Abbott Washburn, United States Information Agency; Wal Mackenzie, Atomic Energy Commission; and myself.
4. Millikan and I (and our colleagues, notably Paul Rosenstein-Rodan and Everett Hagen) went on to write our book and lobby in the Congress, which yielded, among other things, our association with John Kennedy.
5. *Public Papers, 1957*, Washington, D. C., pp. 63–64. Sherman Adams (*op. cit.*, pp. 375–380) attributes to congressional pressures Eisenhower's inability to move forward with development. And the yearly vicissitudes

of the Mutual Security program, with its limited development features, justify Adams' view up to a point. Adams says (p. 375): "The President argued himself hoarse trying to explain the need for assisting neutral countries that were not allied to the United States in defensive military agreements." On the other hand, Eisenhower did not in 1957 end the division on this matter within his administration and later he was recurrently haunted in moving to expand development aid by his concern for the budget at a time of slow increase in growth and public revenues.

6. For an excellent account of the foreign aid debates, struggles, and triumphs of the Eisenhower administration, see Russell Edgerton, "Sub-Cabinet Politics and Policy Commitment: The Birth of the Development Loan Fund," Syracuse, 1970 (The Inter-University Case Program). Like all accounts of the bureaucratic process underlying major policy decisions I know and can assess, Edgerton's is incomplete and, to a degree, inaccurate. But it is certainly one of the best.
7. Eisenhower invited Adlai Stevenson to assist in preparing the post-Sputnik NATO meeting and to participate on the American delegation. He served as a consultant but decided not to attend. As he had for some time, Stevenson, in private as well as in public, urged the importance of an enlarged development effort by the United States and other developed nations. As consultant at a sensitive period, he may have strengthened the hand of like-minded men in the Eisenhower administration and the American stance at Paris. I worked closely with Stevenson in the immediate post-Sputnik period and the early months of 1958. For an account of Stevenson's activities and frustrations as a consultant in these days see, especially, Kenneth S. Davis, *The Politics of Honor: A Biography of Adlai E. Stevenson*, New York, 1957, pp. 370–375. Stevenson's marginal role in strengthening the line of thought and policy in the government which finally yielded the OECD and, especially, the Development Assistance Committee, may have been somewhat more substantial than he (or his biographer) suggests.

Chapter 9: *Crisis in the Middle East*

1. Dwight D. Eisenhower, *Waging Peace, 1956–1961*, New York, 1965, p. 180.
2. *Ibid.*, pp. 269–270.
3. *Ibid.*, p. 237.

Chapter 10: *Crisis in Latin America*

1. Dwight D. Eisenhower, *Waging Peace, 1956–1961*, New York, 1965, p. 520.

2. March 1959 is a useful bench mark in measuring the progress of the communist takeover. At the end of February Castro announced the postponement for two years of his promised free election. By March 26 Allen Dulles reported to Eisenhower that "the Castro regime is moving toward a complete dictatorship," with communists operating openly and legally, working their way into the unions, armed forces, and other organizations. (Dwight D. Eisenhower, *op. cit.*, p. 523.) Arthur Schlesinger, Jr., (*A Thousand Days*, Boston, 1965, pp. 218–219) reports a conversation with Jose Figueres of Costa Rica. Figueres supported Castro with arms and was invited to visit Havana, which he did in March. Scheslinger reports:

   > On his arrival . . . he found the atmosphere curiously sullen and hostile. Castro put off seeing him, but they finally met at a great mass meeting of the Cuban Trade Union Confederation. When Figueres called on the revolution to keep its independence and not become the instrument of extra-continental powers, David Salvador, the secretary-general of the confederation, rushed to the microphone and denounced him as a lackey of Wall Street. Castro himself followed with a bitter speech against the imperialists.

   Nevertheless, there was an apparent hiatus in Castro's move to the extreme left during his travels abroad in April and May 1959.
3. Herbert L. Matthews, *Fidel Castro*, New York, 1969, p. 158.
4. Hugh Thomas, *Cuba: The Pursuit of Freedom*, New York, 1971, pp. 974–1271.
5. See, for example, *ibid.*, pp. 1204–1209. Castro's negative attitude was foreshadowed as early as February, despite his April 2 broadcast.
6. The best single account of this process is in *ibid.*, pp. 1226–1271. As Thomas notes (pp. 1263–1268), Eisenhower's conciliatory statement on Cuba of January 26, 1960, and Castro's limited positive response to it, may have offered a last occasion to avoid confrontation; but by this time he was far down the road, with Mikoyan on his way to Havana.
7. Philip W. Bonsal, *Cuba, Castro, and the United States*, Pittsburgh, 1971, especially Chapters 15 and 16, pp. 133 ff.
8. Dwight D. Eisenhower, *op. cit.*, p. 536.

Chapter 11: *The Crisis in Indian Economic Development*

1. See, for example, my book *Prospects for Communist China*, New York, 1954, pp. 258–259.
2. For a succinct account, see Government of India: Planning Commission, *Third Five Year Plan*, New Delhi, 1961, pp. 107–109.
3. John P. Lewis, *Quiet Crisis in India*, Washington, D. C., 1962, pp. 248–264, perceptively traces the evolution of American aid to India in the 1950s.

4. *Ibid.*, p. 257. The following table shows the scale and character of American aid to India in the fiscal years 1952–1959.

U.S. Government Aid Programs to India, Obligations, FY 1952–1959

(Dollar items in millions)

Program	Grants	Loans repayable in rupees	Blocked rupee sales	Loans repayable in dollars	Total
Technical cooperation	70.3				70.3
Development assistance*	140.1	130.0			270.1
Other TCM-administered†	18.9	20.0			38.9
1951 Wheat Loan				189.7	189.7
Wheat Loan Education	5.0				5.0
Export–Import Bank				151.9	151.9
Development Loan Fund		175.0			175.0
Subtotal					900.9
Farm surplus, MSA, Sec. 402			66.7		66.7
P.L. 480, Title I			658.2		658.2
P.L. 480, Titles II & III	99.5				99.5
Subtotal: Farm surplus					824.4
Totals	333.8	325.0	724.9	341.6	1725.3

* Excludes $66.7 million of surplus wheat and cotton rupee sales under MSA, Sec. 402 administered by TCM and classified by it as "Development Assistance."

† Includes $22.2 million from the Asian Development Fund ($20.0 million loan, $2.2 million grants) and $16.7 million of Special Assistance for Malaria Eradication.

5. *Review of Foreign Policy, 1958*, Part 1, pp. 284–286.

Chapter 12: *Crisis in Southeast Asia*

1. Dwight D. Eisenhower, *Waging Peace, 1956–1961*, New York, 1965, pp. 133 and 145.
2. *Ibid.*, p. 294.
3. *Ibid.*, p. 607.
4. *Idem.*
5. See *ibid.*, pp. 421 and 431 for the flare-up of trouble in August–September 1959; and pp. 607–612 for the Laos crisis of 1960–1961.
6. *Ibid.*, p. 611.
7. *Ibid.*, p. 612.

Chapter 13: *From Eisenhower to Kennedy*

1. Taft was much more prepared than Eisenhower to see the federal government undertake responsibilities in the fields of education and housing, although Eisenhower cited Taft's position in defending his 1957 school construction bill (Dwight D. Eisenhower, *Waging Peace, 1956–1961*, New York, 1965, pp. 139–140). Eisenhower (in *Mandate for Change*, New York, 1963, p. 219) concludes:

   > In some things I found him [Taft] unexpectedly "liberal," specifically in his attitudes on old-age pensions, school aid, and public housing—attitudes, incidentally, which were miles away from those of some self-described "Taft stalwarts." One day after a Legislative-leaders meeting, he walked into my office to continue the discussion.
   >
   > "You know, I hate federal bureaucracy," he said. "The best way I can think of to combat its growth and at the same time help people would be to have the federal government pay a flat fee to the states for every child in school, and automatically to send out a monthly pension check, also a fixed amount, to every man and woman who reached the age of sixty-five."
   >
   > When I heard these things, I had to chuckle. "Why, Bob, with those views you're twice as liberal as I am. How did you ever come to be called a conservative?"
   >
   > "Oh, you know how it is," he replied. "A label like that gets applied to you, and afterwards you just have to live with it."

2. *Mandate for Change*, p. 131. Although Taft was initially adamant in pressing Eisenhower for a tax cut and a sharp downward revision of the budget inherited from Truman, his basic position was that the federal budget should not exceed 20 percent of GNP except during times of war. By and large Taft's rule of thumb has held over the past decade.
3. *Waging Peace*, p. 622.
4. See, for example, Eisenhower's evaluation of progress in the period 1953–1960, *Waging Peace*, pp. 464–465.
5. Richard M. Nixon, *Six Crises*, Garden City, N. Y., 1962, pp. 309–311.
6. *Waging Peace*, pp. 712–716.
7. *Ibid.*, p. 715. Although Eisenhower formed in these meetings a higher view of his successor than he had expected, he observes, after noting his twenty-minute briefing on the balance of payments and Robert Anderson's forty-five minute exposition: "I pray that he understands it." In fact, Kennedy by this time was exceedingly knowledgeable about the balance-of-payments problem.
8. *Prospect for America*, New York, 1961.
9. *Goals for Americans*, New York, 1960.
10. Edited by Allan Nevins, New York, 1960.
11. *Goals for Americans*, pp. 42–48.

12. *Prospect for America*, especially pp. 261–262, 269–271; *Goals for Americans* (John J. McCloy), p. 353.
13. John F. Kennedy, New York, 1960, pp. 166 and 173–176.
14. *The United States in the World Arena*, p. 321.
15. See, for example, *The Strategy of Peace*, pp. 57–65.
16. *Ibid.*, pp. 37–38.
17. W. W. Rostow, *The Stages of Economic Growth*, Cambridge, 1960 and 1971, p. 16.
18. *New Frontiers of the Kennedy Administration, The Texts of the Task Force Reports Prepared for the President*, Washington, D. C., 1961, p. 28.
19. Galbraith's view is set out in his *The Liberal Hour*, Boston, 1960, pp. 59–70. His activities on behalf of this view in the early days of the Kennedy administration are reflected in his *Ambassador's Journal*, Boston, 1969, pp. 8, 21–22, 25–26.
20. *The Process of Economic Growth*, Oxford, 1953 and 1960, p. 237 (1960 edition). The political economy of inflation control is discussed at some length, pp. 220–237, including (p. 237) the "problem of generating the attitudes and creating the forum within which the major groups in the society might negotiate equitable agreement to sacrifice a real or apparent short-run interest to a common longer-run interest."
21. *Ibid.*, p. 259.
22. Otto Eckstein and Gary Fromm had dramatized the critical role of the steel price in setting the pattern for prices in general in their study "Steel and the Postwar Inflation," Study Paper No. 2, U.S. Congress, Joint Economic Committee, *Study of Employment, Growth, and Price Levels* (Washington, D. C., U.S. Government Printing Office, 1959).
23. For Kennedy's activities the rest of the day, see Arthur M. Schlesinger, Jr., *A Thousand Days*, Boston, 1965, p. 162; Theodore Sorensen, *Kennedy*, New York, 1965, pp. 233–234.
24. In retrospect, it is a little difficult to recall the widespread doubts that Kennedy could be an effective President. When it was reported in the press that I was working with Kennedy, James Reston and Walter Lippmann, for example, sought me out and, somewhat incredulous, probed at length why I regarded Kennedy as a serious prospect for the Presidency.
25. Sorensen, *op. cit.*, especially pp. 71–223.

Book Two: The Kennedy Administration

Chapter 14: *Introduction to Book Two*

1. For an excellent analysis of the 1960 crisis, see George P. Packard III, *Protest in Tokyo*, Princeton, 1966.
2. Walter W. Heller, *New Dimensions of Political Economy*, New York, 1966, p. 20. I talked to the Seventieth Annual Convention of the Farm

Equipment Institute at New Orleans on October 1, 1963. The firms represented embraced virtually every major engineering company between the Appalachians and the Rockies. I chatted informally with many of the delegates. Their universal message on the tax bill was: "Don't worry. We have told our Republican friends in Congress we want it with or without an expenditure cut." I so reported to Kennedy.

3. *Public Papers, 1962*, Washington, D. C., p. v.

Chapter 15: *Growth, Price Stability, and the Balance of Payments*

1. Sorensen catches accurately the mixture of considerations that made Kennedy appear excessively sensitive to the balance-of-payments problem (*Kennedy*, New York, 1965, p. 408):

   "I know everyone else thinks I worry about this too much," he [Kennedy] said to me one day as we pored over what seemed like the millionth report on the subject. "But if there's ever a run on the bank, and I have to devalue the dollar or bring home our troops, as the British did, I'm the one who will take the heat. Besides, it's a club that De Gaulle and all the others hang over my head. Any time there's a crisis or a quarrel, they can cash in all their dollars and where are we?"

2. For the twists and turns in the process, see, especially, T. Sorensen, *op. cit.*, pp. 393–469; Arthur M. Schlesinger, Jr., *A Thousand Days*, Boston, 1965, pp. 620–656; Walter W. Heller, *New Dimensions of Political Economy*, New York, 1966, pp. 1–83. Also, Seymour E. Harris, *Economics of the Kennedy Years*, New York, 1964, including, especially, his summary of the views of the critics of Kennedy's economic policies, Chapter 18, pp. 217–230.
3. *Public Papers, 1961*, Washington, D. C., 1962, pp. 592–594 and 604–605.
4. Kennedy himself confined his statement of the guideposts to this terse passage (*Economic Report of the President*, 1962, Washington, D. C., p. 17): "If labor leaders in our major industries will accept the productivity benchmark as a guide to wage objectives, and if management in these industries will practice equivalent restraint in the price decisions, the year ahead will be a brilliant chapter in the record of the responsible exercise of freedom." The Council of Economic Advisers elaborated the guideposts in quite sophisticated terms (pp. 185–190), triumphing over considerable bureaucratic resistance, and achieving acquiescence in their publication only just before their report went to the printer. For a summary of the CEA formulation, see note 12, below.
5. Reuther, in fact, was of two minds. He understood well the kind of case I had made and its advantages for labor, as a way of avoiding the burdens of inflation and permitting higher levels of employment and

growth, higher public revenues for welfare purposes, etc. In another part of his mind he was tempted to seek wage increases higher than the increase in productivity and to try to achieve a favorable shift in the proportion of wages to profits. As late as May 1962 he was still splayed between these two positions. See, for example, Roy Hoopes, *The Steel Crisis*, New York, 1963, pp. 240–241.

6. The passage in the text on the government role in the automobile negotiation is based on a reminiscent conversation with Arthur Goldberg on November 20, 1970, in the course of which he also confirmed my memory and memorandum of conversation of our exchange at lunch on February 1, 1961.
7. *Congressional Record—Senate*, August 22, 1961, pp. 16679–16688; 16694–16705. Before the field day was over—replete with statistics on prices, productivity, capacity utilization, etc.—the following senators had held forth against a steel price increase: Gore, Moss, Neuberger, Douglas, Symington, McGee, Clark, McCarthy, Monroney, Kefauver, Long, Gruening, Humphrey, Young of Ohio, Sparkman, and Carroll. Republican Senators Dirksen, Javits, and Keating merely reserved their positions in the face of the learned and passionate onslaught.
8. Roy Hoopes, *op. cit.*, p. 44.
9. *Public Papers, 1961*, p. 590.
10. *Ibid.*, pp. 593–594.
11. *Ibid.*, p. 605.
12. *Economic Report of the President, 1962*, p. 189. The heart of their formulation, which is likely to stand the test of time, was the following:

> The general guide for noninflationary price behavior calls for price reduction if the industry's rate of productivity increase exceeds the over-all rate—for this would mean declining unit labor costs; it calls for an appropriate increase in price if the opposite relationship prevails; and it calls for stable prices if the two rates of productivity increase are equal.
>
> These are advanced as general guideposts. To reconcile them with objectives of equity and efficiency, specific modifications must be made to adapt them to the circumstances of particular industries. If all of these modifications are made, each in the specific circumstances to which it applies, they are consistent with stability of the general price level. Public judgments about the effects on the price level of particular wage or price decisions should take into account the modifications as well as the general guides. The most important modifications are the following:
>
> (1) Wage rate increases would exceed the general guide rate in an industry which would otherwise be unable to attract sufficient labor; or in which wage rates are exceptionally low compared with the range of wages earned elsewhere by similar labor, because the bargaining position of workers has been weak in particular local labor markets.
>
> (2) Wage rate increases would fall short of the general guide rate in an industry which could not provide jobs for its entire labor force even in times of generally full employment; or in which wage rates are exceptionally high compared with the range of wages earned else-

where by similar labor, because the bargaining position of workers has been especially strong.

(3) Prices would rise more rapidly, or fall more slowly, than indicated by the general guide rate in an industry in which the level of profits was insufficient to attract the capital required to finance a needed expansion in capacity; or in which costs other than labor costs had risen.

(4) Prices would rise more slowly, or fall more rapidly, than indicated by the general guide in an industry in which the relation of productive capacity to full employment demand shows the desirability of an outflow of capital from the industry; or in which costs other than labor costs have fallen; or in which excessive market power has resulted in rates of profit substantially higher than those earned elsewhere on investments of comparable risk.

13. For a retrospective analysis of the economics of the settlement and the battle that followed, see, especially, John Sheahan, *The Wage-Price Guideposts*, Washington, D. C., 1967, pp. 33–38. Also Grant McConnell, *Steel and the Presidency, 1962*, New York, 1963, especially pp. 16, 28–33, 105–115.
14. See, notably, Theodore Sorensen, *op. cit.*, pp. 447–459; Wallace Carroll's account in *The New York Times* of April 23, 1962; Roy Hoopes, *op. cit.*; Grant McConnell, *op. cit.*
15. See Theodore Sorensen, *op. cit.*, p. 446. He notes Goldberg's conversation on March 6 with Blough in which Goldberg presented the 2½ percent increase as "well within the capacity of the industry to absorb without a price increase, a conclusion which neither Blough nor other industry leaders disagreed with."
16. Roy Hoopes, *op. cit.*, p. 44.
17. John Sheahan, *op. cit.*, p. 38.
18. *Ibid.*, pp. 40–41.
19. *Ibid.*, pp. 39–40.
20. David C. Smith, *Incomes Policies: Some Foreign Experiences and Their Relevance for Canada*, prepared for the Economic Council of Canada, Ottawa, 1966, p. 90, where sources are indicated.
21. *Ibid.*, p. 14.
22. For the inner debates of the administration leading to this decision see, especially, Theodore Sorensen, *op. cit.*, 421–433.

Chapter 16: *The Allocation of Public Resources*

1. See, notably, Sorensen's listing, *Kennedy*, New York, 1965, pp. 759–760;
   1. The Nuclear Test Ban Treaty (required Senate approval only)
   2. The Civil Rights Act
   3. The Tax Reduction Act
   4. The Trade Expansion Act
   5. The Peace Corps

6. The Mental Health and Mental Retardation Acts
7. The Higher Education and Medical Education Acts
8. The depressed communities Area Redevelopment Act
9. The Manpower Development and Retraining Act
10. The authority and funds for:
    a. A full-scale outer-space effort, focused on a manned moon landing in the 1960s
    b. The largest and fastest military buildup in our peacetime history
    c. New tools for foreign policy: the Disarmament Administration, a revamped Foreign Aid Agency, an independent Food-for-Peace program and a UN bond issue
    d. The Alliance for Progress with Latin America
    e. More assistance to health, education, and conservation than had been voted by any two Congresses in history
    f. A redoubled effort to find an economical means of converting salt water to fresh
    g. The world's largest atomic power plant at Hanford, Washington
11. Modernization of New Deal–Fair Deal measures:
    a. The most comprehensive housing and urban renewal program in history, including the first major provisions for middle-income housing, private low-income housing, mass transit, and protection of urban open spaces
    b. The first major increase in minimum wage coverage since the original 1938 act, raising it to $1.25 an hour
    c. The most far-reaching revision of the public welfare laws since the original 1935 act, a $300 million modernization which emphasized rehabilitation instead of relief
    d. A revival of Food Stamps for the needy, plus increased food distribution to the impoverished and expanded school lunch and school milk distribution.
    e. The most comprehensive farm legislation since 1938, expanding marketing orders, farm credit, crop insurance, soil conservation, and rural electrification
    f. The first accelerated public works program for areas of unemployment since the New Deal
    g. The first major amendments to the food and drug safety laws since 1938
    h. The first full-scale modernization and expansion of the vocational education laws since 1946
    i. A temporary antirecession supplement to unemployment compensation
    j. The first significant package of anticrime bills since 1934, plus a new act on juvenile delinquency
    k. The first major additions to our National Park System since 1946, the provision of a fund for future acquisitions, and the preservation of wilderness areas
    l. A doubling of the water pollution prevention program, plus the first major attack on air pollution

m. The most far-reaching tax reforms since the New Deal, including new investment tax credit
n. Major expansions and improvements in social security (including retirement at age sixty-two for men), library services, hospital construction, family farm assistance, and reclamation

12. The Twenty-fourth Amendment to the Constitution, outlawing poll taxes
13. The Community Health Facilities Act
14. The Communications Satellite Act
15. The Educational Television Act.

See also Arthur M. Schlesinger, Jr.'s summary of Kennedy's legislative achievements, *A Thousand Days*, Boston, 1965, pp. 712–713.

2. *Ibid.*, p. 760n.
3. *Public Papers, 1963*, Washington, D. C., p. 849.
4. Hugh Sidey (*John F. Kennedy, President*, New York, 1963 edition, pp. 32–33) dates this perspective from the period between the election and Kennedy's inauguration:

> And suddenly the talk of legislative activity like Roosevelt's 1933 "100 days" began to vanish. Before the election there had been such an expectation by some within the Kennedy camp, by journalists even more. But the victory had been too narrow. The temper of the Congress, streaming back into Washington, had been tested. Now came the first clear symptoms that the New Frontier's program would be a hard, foot-by-foot struggle.
>
> There was born a new theory. Kennedy's power would increase year by year until it reached its peak perhaps at the start of his second term, in 1964. This expectation was contrary to every political pattern. But Kennedy had already shattered an assortment of political myths—he was too young, he was too rich, he was Catholic. People would see, the thinking went, how good a man he was. By the 1962 congressional elections, he might reverse the tradition of a loss of seats by the party in power in off-year elections and actually increase the Democratic margin. By 1964 Kennedy would have shown his mettle enough to make further gains in Congress and to come back to the White House with confidence, stature and, yes, power.

For a careful analysis of Kennedy's problems with and perspective on congressional resistance to his domestic programs, see also James L. Sundquist, *Politics and Policy*, Washington, D. C., 1968, pp. 471–495.

Chapter 17: *The Race Crisis of 1963*

1. *Public Papers, 1963*, Washington, D. C., pp. 468–469.
2. It may be that the true peak of tension came in the summer of 1967, with the widespread urban riots. See p. 311.
3. This considerable setback to morale in an 82nd Airborne unit led a Negro soldier to remark: "If we go to Cuba, I bet we'll be on the first team." Source: a company commander of the time. Tension centered on Cuba was already rising in September 1962.

4. Gunnar Myrdal, *An American Dilemma*, New York, 1962 edition, especially pp. 75–78, and Appendix 3 (pp. 1065–1070). Myrdal's analysis of cumulative causation was, in effect, an extension of the analysis of the economy (in his *Monetary Equilibrium*) which led him (and other Swedish economists) to produce a view of business cycles and policy to avoid them which substantially anticipated John Maynard Keynes. In his analysis of a whole society in terms of the race question, Myrdal could have built in the equivalent of the constraints which set limits on the rate of growth (due to cumulative causation), thereby producing a somewhat more realistic theoretical structure than he did—perhaps even a cyclical theory of racial progress. For an attempt to introduce the notion of ceilings and floors into a cumulative process in another field, see my *Politics and the Stages of Growth*, Cambridge, 1971, especially pp. 60–63.
5. In this context, Arnold Rose's "Postscript Twenty Years Later," printed in the 1962 edition of *An American Dilemma*, is an interesting document (pp. xxvii–xlv). It was completed in June 1962, which was a relatively quiet moment in American race relations. Rose reviews the extraordinary progress since the 1940s, starting with the Negro movement to the cities and the mechanization of cotton growing. He finds the progress broadly confirming Myrdal's analysis, in which he had participated. He is skeptical of additional civil rights legislation, since the political negotiations involved in the Civil Rights Acts of 1957 and 1960 had damaged the possibilities of passing other legislation (e.g., education bills) which might have helped the Negro more (pp. xxxiv–xxxv). He noted the problem of "permanent unemployment" that might emerge for Negroes in the age of automation; the de facto segregation of Negroes in urban slums as "the most serious aspect of the race problem, certainly in the North" (p. xxxvii); and the heightened activism of the younger generation of Negroes, including the revival of Garvey-like doctrines (pp. xxx–xxxii). But there is no foreshadowing of the explosive potentialities of these trends which were to be revealed within twelve months. And in this Rose faithfully mirrors the mood of the times and of the Kennedy administration.
6. For an illuminating debate on this matter, see Richard Young, "The Irony of Negro Progress in America," and Nathan Glazer's reply in *Encounter*, December 1969, pp. 80–87.
7. *Ibid.*, p. 82. For a balanced and careful portrait of Negro attitudes as of approximately this period (1964), see Gary T. Marx, *Protest and Prejudice*, New York, 1967. Marx catches well the mixture of frustration, belief that demonstrations were helpful, opposition to Negro extremists, moderation, and long-run optimism of the majority of Negroes at this time.
8. See, notably, Theodore Draper's account and analysis of this surge in the search for nationhood, *The Rediscovery of Black Nationalism*, New York, 1969.
9. Gunnar Myrdal, *op. cit.*, p. 1068.

10. George Plimpton (ed.), interviews by Jean Stein, *American Journey, The Times of Robert Kennedy*, New York, 1970, p. 121. See also Arthur M. Schlesinger, Jr., *A Thousand Days*, Boston, 1965, p. 967.
11. See, for example, Arthur M. Schlesinger, Jr., *op. cit.*, p. 963; also, Theodore Sorensen, *Kennedy*, New York, 1965, pp. 505–506.
12. Theodore Sorensen, *op. cit.*, p. 505.
13. The Belden poll, *Beaumont Journal*, September 23, 1962.

Chapter 18: *The Organization of National Security Affairs, 1961*

1. George Kennan, *Memoirs, 1925–1950*, Boston, 1967, p. 480.
2. Dwight D. Eisenhower, *Waging Peace, 1956–1961*, New York, 1965, p. 634.
3. Dean Acheson, *Present at the Creation*, New York, 1969, p. 455.

Chapter 19: *Military, Arms Control, and Space Policy*

1. For McNamara's presentation of these initial changes see, especially, *Department of Defense Appropriations for 1962*, Hearings before the Subcommittee of the Committee on Appropriations, Eighty-seventh Congress, First Session, Part 3, U.S. GPO, Washington, D. C., pp. 1–150.
2. *Department of Defense Appropriations for 1965*, Hearings before the Subcommittee on Department of Defense Appropriations, Part 4, Eighty-eighth Congress, Second Session, U.S. GPO, Washington, D. C., 1964, p. 291.
3. *Department of Defense Appropriations for 1963*, Hearings before the Subcommittee on Department of Defense Appropriations, Eighty-seventh Congress, Second Session, Part 2, U.S. GPO, Washington, D. C., 1962, pp. 49–50.
4. *Department of Defense Appropriations for 1964*, pp. 98–102 and 109.
5. *Ibid.*, pp. 101–102.
6. Another problem was the danger of leaks. This was borne in on us vividly by the publication in the *Chicago Tribune*, on June 17 and 18, 1962, of out-of-context passages from a draft of the BNSP paper as well as flat misstatements of its contents. The implication drawn was that I was dangerously soft on communism. Similar leaks had begun to appear over the previous month. Senator Everett Dirksen, goaded by a journal prominent in his constituency and, perhaps, smelling a little political blood, called for the Senate to look into the matter on June 18. I was telephoned

by a staff member and asked if I was prepared to appear before the Senate Foreign Relations Committee. I immediately agreed. A closed session was held on June 26, to which Senator Dirksen was invited as well as Senators Goldwater and Saltonstall, who were also not members of the Committee. Before going up, Kennedy, George Ball (in Rusk's absence), McGeorge Bundy, and I met to plan strategy. Kennedy had carefully read the quoted passages and concluded that in full context they were unexceptionable. He believed it was an Air Force leak. It was agreed that it would be inappropriate for me to discuss an executive branch working paper before a congressional committee; but I should respond to questions about my own views. Ball and Bundy counseled minimum brief replies. Kennedy immediately said: "No. Tell them exactly what you think." With Senator Fulbright in the chair the session was fully attended, and lasted some three hours. It became clear before long that my views—no different from those incorporated in books I had written—were not likely to supply interesting political ammunition to the Republicans. The session then became a rather broad review of foreign policy problems. At the close Fulbright noted the rare full attendance. (I believe only Senator Hickenlooper was not there.) He somewhat wistfully asked why an odd occasion of this kind was required to generate a full committee discussion of foreign policy. It proved a thoroughly unimportant one-day wonder, of interest only in Washington.

The time between the announcement of the Senate hearing and the time the harmless outcome became clear was, however, a troubling week in the State Department. I could sense in my colleagues, in their faces and their manner with me, a sudden fear that, perhaps, the early 1950s were upon them again. Was Rostow vulnerable? Was a new wave of McCarthyism about to be launched? It was good to see the mood subside.

Over the years that followed, my relations with Senator Dirksen were wholly amiable. I remained, however, a recurrent target for the Republican right as well as, a bit later, for the Democratic left.

7. *Public Papers, 1961*, Washington, D. C., p. 622.
8. The phrase is from Arthur M. Scheslinger, Jr., *A Thousand Days*, Boston, 1965, p. 505.
9. *Ibid.*, p. 895.
10. See, especially, Michel Tatu, *Power in the Kremlin*, pp. 352–353.
11. This account is from *Preliminary History of the National Aeronautics and Space Administration during the Administration of President Lyndon B. Johnson*, Washington, D. C., November 1, 1968 (unpublished manuscript), pp. 1–23. For a published account of space policy in the latter days of the Eisenhower administration and the early critical decisions of the Kennedy administration, see Robert L. Rosholt et. al., *An Administrative History of NASA, 1958–1963*, Washington, D. C., 1966, pp. 183–196.
12. *Public Papers, 1963*, Washington, D. C., p. 883.
13. See Chapter 6, note 9.

Chapter 20: *Kennedy's Policy toward the Developing World in General*

1. *Public Papers, 1961*, Washington, D. C., pp. 204–205.
2. *Ibid.*, p. 205.
3. *Ibid.*, pp. 212 and 623. I do not know who the original source was for the concept of the 1960s as the Economic Development Decade. I called it to Kennedy's attention on March 2, 1961, in the following memorandum:

   1. A new idea has formed up within your staff. It is likely to be present in the submissions to you of the Latin American proposals and the proposals for foreign aid in general. You may wish to have a word in advance.

   2. The idea is to present our aid proposals in the context of an Economic Development Decade. Since some of my ideas as an economist underlie this notion, I thought it might be useful for me to explain the sense in which the notion is not a gimmick. (Incidentally, Dick Goodwin and the Latin American task force first surfaced it.)

   3. Barring a catastrophe, it is likely that a good many of the countries in the underdeveloped world will, during the 1960's, either complete the take-off process or be very far advanced in it. When take-off is complete a nation may be poor but it is normally in a position to draw its external capital requirements from private commercial sources. Post-take-off countries should be off the international dole. For example, this is now the case with Mexico.

   4. To be specific, it should be possible, if we all work hard, for Argentina, Brazil, Colombia, Venezuela, India, the Philippines, Taiwan, Turkey, Greece—and possibly Egypt, Pakistan, Iran and Iraq—to have attained self-sustaining growth by 1970 and to be drawing from special international sources either no capital or much diminished volumes of capital. In population these nations would include more than 80% of Latin America and well over half of the other underdeveloped portions of the Free World.

   5. In short, in the 1960's we face the peak historical requirement for special external aid. More important politically, we can honestly say to the American people and to the world that we are not entering onto an endless job; but that if we work hard for a decade we will get well over half the peoples of the underdeveloped areas into self-sustained growth and off the dole.

   6. I believe such a concrete goal for the 1960's—of moving the majority of the underdeveloped areas into take-off and sustained growth—could have enormous power in catching the public imagination in all countries. It should also reassure the Congress that we are not getting onto an endlessly expanding demand for American resources for development purposes.

4. John F. Kennedy, *Strategy of Peace*, New York, 1960, pp. 57–65.

5. *Ibid.*, pp. 65–81.
6. See *ibid.*, pp. 124–132.
7. See *ibid.*, pp. 132–141.
8. *Ibid.*, pp. 141–158 and above, pp. 104–107.
9. *Public Papers, 1961*, pp. 203–212.

Chapter 21: *Some Crises in the Developing World*

1. See, especially, for a short account of the evolution of the Congo crisis, Roger Hilsman's *To Move a Nation*, New York, 1967, pp. 233–271. Also, Robert C. Good, "The Congo Crisis: A Study in Post Colonial Politics," in Lawrence W. Martin (ed.), *Neutralism and Nonalignment*, New York, 1962; and Ernest W. Lefever, *Crisis in the Congo: a U.N. Force in Action*, Washington, D. C., 1965.
2. For elaboration of this concept, see my *The Stages of Economic Growth*, Cambridge, 1960 and 1971, pp. 112–114, and *Politics and the Stages of Growth*, Cambridge, 1971, pp. 279–282.
3. Dean Acheson, *Present at the Creation*, New York, 1969, p. 930.
4. The diplomatic history of the matter was set out for Kennedy as follows in a memorandum forwarded by me of November 30, 1961:

   At the Round Table Conference of November 1949 at which Indonesia was granted its independence from the Netherlands, the two sides were unable to agree upon the future of New Guinea. They agreed that its status should be determined by negotiations within a year of Indonesian independence. The Indonesians were under the impression that the Dutch had tabled the issue as a face-saving device to facilitate ratification of the Round Table agreement by the Dutch Parliament and that once ratification had been obtained, the Dutch would yield the territory to Indonesia. Negotiations in 1950–55 failed to produce agreement. Indonesia bases its claim to the territory primarily on the grounds that it was part of the Netherlands East Indies to which the Republic of Indonesia became the successor state. Indonesia's claim is essentially that of any nationalist movement to the territory it identifies, because of past association, with the nation. The Dutch argue that geologically, ethnically and culturally the territory is distinct from Indonesia.

   Indonesia has consistently sought UN action on a resolution calling for bilateral talks between Indonesia and the Netherlands. When it failed in 1957 to get a two-thirds majority, Sukarno took over all Dutch assets in Indonesia. When the Dutch sent an aircraft carrier and military reenforcements to West New Guinea in mid–1960, Indonesia broke diplomatic negotiations and concluded a $500 million arms deal with the USSR. This arms aid has been subsequently increased to over $830 million.

   The issue of West New Guinea has been central to Indonesian politics, has diverted attention from Indonesia's main task of nation building, has been exploited by the Communist Party (which is nearly the largest outside the Bloc) and has been exploited by Sukarno as a means of frustrating opposition to himself and his policies. Thus a very heavy price has been paid by the Dutch and by the West more generally. We are approaching the point where the stake may be the future orientation of Indonesia itself.

5. The ties built up between the American and Indonesian military men were deep and authentic. It was not a question of Americans persuading Indonesians to fight communism. It was, on the one hand, the satisfaction of the Indonesians at being received with dignity and respect in American staff schools and, on the other, the wholehearted and sensitive manner in which American advisers entered into the Indonesian civic action program mounted in the countryside. The CIA association with the Indonesian revolt of the 1950s made the American military extremely sensitive to entering into Indonesian politics.
6. Roger Hilsman, trying, with Harriman, to engineer a constructive outcome, details that aspect of the story well. (*Op cit.*, especially pp. 394–405.) And he describes the final effort in the Kennedy administration to pick up the pieces by keeping Sukarno from full-fledged military confrontation by designing a limited package of economic assistance and persuading Kennedy to announce an Asian trip, including an Indonesian visit, which might have kept things quiet for a while.

   In my view, Hilsman's account does not quite catch the balance of forces at work on Sukarno and in his mind. American policy was, in my opinion, properly addressed to maximizing the chance that Sukarno would accept Malaysia, join his neighbors in Maphilindo as a long-term venture in regional cooperation, and turn to the long-deferred task of Indonesian economic and social development. But there were others in Indonesian political life—or with influence upon it—who opposed this course. They were of two types. First, there were communists, who looked to regional conflict, exacerbated United States–Indonesian relations, and economic disintegration as the matrix for a communist effort to take over the country. They also wished to get the Indonesian army engaged in a distant confrontation so that the military ability to influence the course of political events in Djakarta would be diminished. Second, there were noncommunist Indonesian politicians—Sukarno and Subandrio, above all—to whom the attractions of confrontation, and rallying the people around external grievances, were all but irresistible. The turn away from the pattern of West Irian was too difficult. It ran against the grain of their temperament, experience, and skills.
7. The best account of the Yemen crisis and American policy toward it is in John S. Badeau, *The American Approach to the Arab World*, New York, 1968, Chapter VII, "Yemen—A Case Study," pp. 123–151.
8. *Public Papers, 1963*, Washington, D. C., p. 850.
9. W. Howard Wriggins, *The Ruler's Imperative*, New York, 1969, p. 164.
10. *Public Papers, 1961*, Washington, D. C., p. 161. See also Arthur M. Schlesinger, Jr., *A Thousand Days*, Boston, 1965, pp. 571–572.
11. Ernest W. Lefever (*Spear and Scepter*, Washington, D. C., 1970, p. 52) describes the incident and its outcome as follows:

While he was decreasing Western military advice and assistance, Nkrumah for the first time turned to the communist states for security aid. During his summer trip to communist states [in 1961] he ordered Alexander [Ghana's Army chief] to select 400 cadets immediately for officer training in the Soviet Union. In a "cry from the heart," a letter to Colonel J. A. Ankrah who five years later became the first chairman of the National Liberation Council, Alexander expressed the misgivings of the officer corps, British and Ghanaian alike. It was written September 22, 1961, the day he was dismissed: ". . . The President proposes to send 400 potential officers to the Soviet Union for training. I have done all I can to persuade him that such action is neither necessary nor prudent. It is not necessary because it will in no way speed up the rate of Africanization which by doubling the size of the Academy I have already put at a gallop. . . . It is unwise for several reasons. Firstly, it splits the training and outlook of the officers into two camps, and can breed neither contentment nor efficiency. Secondly, I consider that such action may in the long-term prove dangerous to the President himself."

Alexander's judgment was ratified by subsequent events. In October 1961, Ghana sent 68 cadets who had been rejected by its own academy to the Soviet Union for military training. The men returned within six months, dissatisfied with their training and disillusioned by their total experience in Russia. After careful screening, many of them were admitted to the Ghana Academy. Eventually one-third of the group became officers. It was a disaster from the beginning and, perhaps more than any other single development, demoralized ranking Ghanaian officers. Alexander's warning that the opening to the Soviet Bloc "may in the long-term prove dangerous to the President himself" was elegant prophecy.

12. Here is how I formulated the argument on October 2, 1961, for Kennedy:

Pro-Cancellation.

—Nkrumah's foreign and domestic policies have taken an ugly lurch to the left since your letter of June 29.

—His domestic economic and political position is less stable than it was five weeks ago.

Anti-Cancellation.

—The dam is a long-range project for the people of Ghana and Africa. It should not be handled off-again, on-again in a country that is bound to suffer from various instabilities in the course of its building.

—The long-range prospects for Ghana fetching up an independent African country are reasonably good: it has political elements which are not yet cowed; its trade is heavily tied to Britain and the West. There is risk; but less risk over coming years than, say, the risk of Nasser's taking Egypt into Communism in 1956.

—If we pull out on what will be interpreted as political grounds, we shall place extremely heavy pressure on Nkrumah to make any terms with Moscow he can get to build his dam; and Africans (who dislike him) will, on this account, be sympathetic. . . . We shall probably have a second Aswan Dam problem on our hands and have given Nkrumah powerful grounds for justifying his Moscow connection.

—The deal itself represents an extremely complex consortium of government, private business, and the International Bank. And, as the memo from the Legal Adviser's office at State indicates, it is extremely hard to find justifiable grounds for breaking it up now. Nkrumah may give us a clean-cut provocation, but his unsatisfactory behavior at Belgrade and Moscow wouldn't hold up in court—or in African and world opinion.

Conclusion.

a. We should buy a little time to assess where Nkrumah is going; to bring maximum external and internal pressure on him to settle down. . . .

b. The weight of the argument is for going ahead with the project unless things turn radically for the worse in Ghana.

c. If we go ahead, we should do so—and say so— in ways which make clear this is being done for Ghana and Africa—despite Nkrumah, not because of him.

13. To illustrate in a trivial context the problem of historians lacking written records: Arthur M. Schlesinger, Jr. (*op. cit.*, p. 573) quotes Kennedy as follows: "The Attorney General has not yet spoken, but I can feel the hot breath of his disapproval on the back of my neck"; I recall the critical phrase as "I can feel the cold wind of his disapproval. . . ."
14. Here is my report to Kennedy, on April 8, 1963, on the India–Pakistan conversations:

India–Pakistan Conversations, April 1–7, 1963:
The Impending Negotiating Crisis.

The message was delivered loud and clear in the two countries; and they may have marginally helped our Ambassadors set the stage for the presentation of Principles and Round Five. In any case, as we left, the two parties and the assorted doves of peace were girding themselves for what they know to be a fateful period.

The reactions to our messages and the emotional and political posture of the various principal actors followed a well-worn script wholly familiar to those in the Kashmir business and even to observers at one remove like myself.

But one reaction emerged, which I had not anticipated. It took different forms with different men: it almost always surfaced as the final thought, the last sentence; it was expressed at high levels and low almost unconsciously, always in a moment of sincerity, by Indians and Pakistani, British and Americans; with fatalism, scepticism, or anxiety; and in the case of a few bitter die-hards, with anticipation.

The reaction was this: no one can yet see by what process the negotiation over Kashmir—any negotiation over Kashmir—can be brought to a politically viable conclusion. Nehru, after agreeing the case for a settlement, asked aloud: "But how can it be done without creating more tension than we now have?" Ayub, after warning that a Kashmir settlement might raise tensions, went through his concept of moving by stages, closing in on the Vale only at the end. Ken Galbraith's last thought was: "Perhaps the lines will never meet, but we've got to try." The Indian High Commissioner in Karachi said: "We'll discuss the Vale all right in the Fifth Round; but we won't settle it; and then what do we do?"

And so it went.

This prevalent vision of a stone wall ahead arises from a complex of psychological, political, and technical negotiating problems.

First, of course, Indian minds run into a real block in surrendering any substantial part of the Vale; and Pakistani minds run into an even greater block in ceding once and for all any part of the Vale to India. Quite aside from political pressures, the issue is so highly charged and men's minds have run so often over the tracks which rationalize their respective present positions that it is literally difficult and literally painful for them to visualize a change in the way things are (for Indians) or anything short of the fulfillment of their dream and crusade (for Pakistani).

In addition, back in a more rational world, both sets of politicians see trouble as they contemplate any conceivably negotiable Kashmir compromise; and tolerably objective observers concede the possibility of trouble—for example, the Pakistan High Commissioner in Delhi concedes Nehru's problem, and the Indian High Commissioner in Karachi, Ayub's. At the same time, men perceive that Ayub and Nehru both retain, if they are determined, very large potential influence to alter the political scene. Their problem, as I see it, is that they cannot afford to move off their present political postures until two conditions are satisfied: the terms of the whole deal are known; and each is satisfied that the other will wholeheartedly commit himself before his own people to that deal. By "the whole deal" I mean the terms of economic coexistence and at least implicit military collaboration (as well as disengagement), not merely the Kashmir deal. The dilemma, then, is this: only a radical change in political atmosphere, plus economic and military ameliorations, can justify the inevitable pain of a possible Kashmir settlement; but it is possible that the change in atmosphere cannot be brought about until Ayub and Nehru see the whole package; and our present negotiating sequence, for good and sufficient reasons—notably the Pak desire to get at the Vale before being diverted to other issues—does not permit the other, softening issues to be gripped and the vested interests in both countries connected with them, to be brought effectively into play.

The problem may well be complicated by the emergence of negotiating postures, designed to put the other fellow in the wrong and to impress Washington and world opinion rather than to move forward.

Ayub, for example, is so deeply convinced of Nehru's political unreliability (not without recent reinforcing ammunition) that only very hard commitments by the Indians are likely to lead him to defend reconciliation before his people. Similarly, Desai asked us: "Why should we give anything to the Pakistani if their hostility to us is so deeply rooted and fixed that reconciliation is impossible?"; and after I heard Dehlavi, I was damned if I knew what I could have replied to Desai. Thus, the Indians will require very firm assurances that they will, in fact, get the advantages of a new relation to Pakistan before surrendering any part of what they hold.

It is quite clear that thoughtful men on both sides appreciate the irrationality of the present arrangements and the advantages of sensible coexistence; although the economic advantages are, I suspect, even greater than most political figures now understand. But the Pakistani dare not expound these nor evoke the political forces that are directly interested (e.g., East Pakistan) until something substantial in the Vale is sewed up; and the Indians dare not give up something substantial in the Vale until it is clear that Pakistan is broadly committed to a policy of conciliation and that the military benefits of that policy will be available to India.

The vicious circle will operate, I suspect, even within the narrow orbit of the Kashmir and Vale discussions. The complexities are inherently such that "clean surgery" is either likely to lead to events which will produce the higher tensions Nehru and Ayub fear; or it will require for its success a degree of intensive and sympathetic Indo-Pak cooperation which, in turn, is only possible if the two leaders had already committed themselves before their own peoples to a fundamental change in policy.

I conclude, therefore, that if the principles are accepted or if the Vale gets gripped in negotiation by other means, we are likely to run into a dangerous *cul-de-sac.* At the moment the notion is, as I understand it, that under such circumstances various high-level Anglo–American chaps might be rushed into the breach to hold appropriate hands and try to bring the lines closer together; or, in the last resort, to trot out an internationalized Vale. If this analysis is correct, any amount of pressure and hand holding about Kashmir will not then do the trick. Two other elements must then be introduced, perhaps in sequence, before a Kashmir settlement could become viable:

a. While the Kashmir discussion proceeds on some sustained basis, the other issues must be brought into negotiation in a separate but equal forum (or forums) with an understanding that a total package will be brought together and no part of the negotiated deal is final until all elements are brought together.

b. At a certain point, when the deal as a whole is clear, but before it is signed and announced, Nehru and Ayub would have to enter into a solemn commitment, verifiable by what they say and do before the sign off, to take the case for reconciliation to their people and to be prepared to deal with violent dissidents on a ruthless basis, if necessary.

The latter provision may appear farfetched; but the mutual suspicions go so deep and the interactions of the two governments' policies are so sensitive, that until the deal is consummated—and perhaps for sometime thereafter—it could spiral off into a debacle unless each government performs its part of the bargain with unexampled consistency and rigor.

I would only add this: assistance to Ayub and Nehru in finding their way through this political and psychological maze will be vastly more important than any direct bargaining pressure or exhortation we can mount in getting a solution. Or, put another way, bargaining pressure and exhortation at the right moment may prove useful, but only if there is a workable track that these two highly responsible politicians can perceive. Right now the central fact about Nehru and Ayub is that they do not see such a track, embracing the full complexity of the problem—and neither does anyone else on the subcontinent.

Chapter 22: *The Bay of Pigs and Latin American Policy*

1. I had, of course, known a refugee operation to invade Cuba was in the works. There was much talk in the press and I could see my colleagues going to and coming from what were, from the cast of characters involved, palpably high-level Cuba meetings. On April 12 a respected State Department officer called on me and expressed his anxieties about the operation. I conveyed them to Bundy. He told me something about the plan but said the President was keeping his options open and, in his (Bundy's) judgment, was inclined to be negative.
2. Arthur M. Schlesinger, Jr., superbly evokes this mission, *A Thousand Days*, Boston, 1965, pp. 279–284.
3. SUBJECT: *The Problem We Face.*

   1. Right now the greatest problem we face is not to have the whole of our foreign policy thrown off balance by what we feel and what we do about Cuba itself. We have suffered a serious setback; but that setback will be trivial compared to the consequences of not very soon regaining momentum along the lines which we have begun in the past three months.

   2. How did we begin? Our central aim has been to bind up the northern half of the Free World more closely and begin to link it constructively to the south. We began by seeking to associate ourselves more powerfully with the constructive aspirations of the peoples in the underdeveloped areas. This was done in the Alliance for Progress; in the foreign aid message; in our position on Angola; etc. [A whole series of further illustrations followed.]

   3. The action in Cuba has temporarily damaged the grand alliance in all its dimensions.

   4. In Latin America we run the risk of posing an almost impossible dilemma for those politicians whose success and collaboration we need most. . . .

   5. In Asia we have posed a similar and even more dangerous problem for Nehru and other neutrals. Nehru can and will support us in dealing with overt aggression. . . . But we have not found the means and the legal basis for dealing overtly with infiltration and covert aggression. The trouble with our Cuban operation was and remains that it was mounted on simple ideological grounds. Given the common law of the contemporary world, those grounds cannot be generally acceptable. . . . I suspect overt action of a useful kind can be developed on a case-by-case basis; and, as I have suggested to you earlier, the crucial element may be forms of international action on the question of Communist arms shipments.

   6. To Europeans our recent action on Cuba seems much like the obsessive reaction of the British on Egypt; the French on Algeria;

the Netherlands on Indonesia; etc. We have appeared to move with violence, on a unilateral basis, in an area where historically we had deep commitments and deep emotions. Their anxiety is on three scores:

First. Because our prestige appears somewhat to be damaged and our prestige is important to each of them in his own situation.

Second. We did not consult with them and they will bear a part of the consequences.

Third. Their confidence in our judgment has been, at least temporarily, shaken.

All of this, it seems to me, is reparable, if we do not get further driven in on ourselves with respect to Cuba, and if we resume with vigor the lines of action we have launched with the Europeans, including especially the technique of intimate and candid consultation, which Acheson has proposed.

7. What, then, must we do? The answer should be in two parts: What we do about policy in general, and what we do about Cuba.

8. *First, policy in general.* I believe we must resume with intensified vigor and perhaps more boldness than we have heretofore envisaged, the lines of action already under way. [Seven items are then set out covering the Atlantic Alliance, the Alliance for Progress, the India and Pakistan consortium meetings, Laos, Vietnam, and the United Nations.]

9. As for Cuba itself, I have little background and little wisdom. There are, evidently, three quite different threats which Cuba poses, which are now mixed up in our minds and in our policy. There is the military question of Communist arms and of a potential Soviet offensive base in Cuba. If we are not immediately to invade Cuba ourselves, we must decide whether we shall permit Castro, so long as he remains in power, to acquire defensive arms; and we must decide what the touchstones are between defensive arms and the creation of a Communist military base threatening to the U.S. itself. I assume that evidence of the latter we would take virtually as a cause of war, although we should bear in mind what the placing of missiles in Turkey looks like in the USSR. Second, there is the question of Cuba as a base for active infiltration and subversion in the rest of Latin America. Here, evidently, we must try to do more than we are now doing, and we should seek active hemispheric collaboration—wherever we can find it—in gathering and exchanging information on the networks involved and on counter-measures. Third, there is the simple ideological problem. Cuba is a Communist state, repressing every value we treasure. But on that ground alone we are prevented by our treaty obligations from acting directly and overtly. . . .

10. As I said to the Attorney General the other day, when you are in a fight and knocked off your feet, the most dangerous thing to do is to come out swinging wildly. . . . we must think again clearly and coolly in the light of the facts as they are and are likely to be. We may emerge with a quite different approach to the Castro problem after such an exercise, or we may proceed with more of the same. But let us do some fresh homework.

11. In the meanwhile, what we must do is to build the foundation and the concepts, in Latin America, the North Atlantic Alliance, and

the UN, which would permit us, next time round, to deal with the Cuban problem in ways which would not so grievously disrupt the rest of our total strategy. . . .

4. *United States in the World Arena*, pp. 547–548.
5. Haynes Johnson, *The Bay of Pigs*, New York, 1964, p. 115.
6. For a post-Bay of Pigs, pre-missile crisis statement of American policy toward Cuba in terms of "specific threats," see my interview in *U.S. News and World Report*, May 7, 1962, p. 68.
7. See, notably, Arthur M. Schlesinger, Jr., *op. cit.*, pp. 292–297; Theodore Sorensen, *Kennedy*, New York, 1965, pp. 294–309; and Haynes Johnson, *op. cit.*, pp. 349–355.
8. Theodore Sorensen, *op. cit.*, p. 301: ". . . he would have been far wiser, he told me later, if, when the basic premises of the plan were already being shattered, he had canceled the entire operation. . . ." The context is the famous cancellation of the second air strike on Monday, April 17, when the first strike failed to eliminate Castro's air force.
9. Ernest K. Lindley (ed.), *The Winds of Freedom: Selections from the Speeches and Statements of Secretary of State Dean Rusk, January 1961–August 1962*, Boston, 1963, p. 156. The phrase is from a talk given by Rusk on April 25, 1962 at the School of Advanced International Studies of Johns Hopkins University, Washington, D. C.
10. *CIAP Policy Statement: The State of the Alliance for Progress and Prospects for 1965*, 4 November 1964, OEA Serv. H/XIII, CIAP/170, Washington, D. C. For the text of the OAS Resolution of November 15, 1963, creating CIAP, see *American Foreign Policy, Current Documents*, Washington, D. C., 1963, pp. 342–347.

Chapter 23: *The Nuclear Question: Vienna, Berlin, and the Atlantic Community*

1. Edward Crankshaw and Strobe Talbott (eds.), *Khrushchev Remembers*, Boston, 1970, pp. 454–457. Khrushchev says, in part (pp. 454–455):

   Meanwhile, Walter Ulbricht and our other comrades in the GDR were facing serious troubles directly stemming from the ambiguous status of West Berlin. Berlin was an open city, which posed two problems: First, there was the problem of people crossing from East Berlin into West Berlin. The GDR had to cope with an enemy who was economically very powerful and therefore very appealing to the GDR's own citizens. West Germany was all the more enticing to East Germans because they all spoke the same language. An East German with adequate professional qualifications had no difficulty finding a job if he moved to West Germany. The resulting drain of workers was creating a simply disastrous situation in the GDR, which was already suffering from a shortage of manual labor, not to mention specialized labor. If things had continued like this much longer,

I don't know what would have happened. I spent a great deal of time trying to think of a way out. How could we introduce incentives in the GDR to counteract the force behind the exodus of East German youths to West Germany? Here was an important question—the question of incentives. How could we create conditions in the GDR which would enable the state to regulate the steady attrition of its working force?

The second problem was the problem of the West Berliner's easy access to East Berlin. Residents of West Berlin could cross freely into East Berlin, where they took advantage of all sorts of communal services like barbershops and so on. Because prices were much lower in East Berlin, West Berliners were also buying up all sorts of products which were in wide demand—products like meat, animal oil, and other food items, and the GDR was losing millions of marks.

2. Michel Tatu, *Power in the Kremlin*, p. 232.
3. My own contribution was the following memorandum of May 26, 1961:

SUBJECT: *Medium Level Conversation With Mr. Khrushchev.*

1. Mr. Khrushchev is a pragmatic politician, with a broad faith in the success of his ideology, and a quite particular view of history. He believes three things about history. First, that in time the expansion of the economy of Russia and the Communist Bloc will outstrip the West; second, that the techniques he has now adopted will gain victory for communism in the underdeveloped areas, probably without major war; and, third, that the United States lacks a coherent and effective historical concept of how to oppose his strategy.

2. Cuba and Laos have recently confirmed him in the second and third propositions; that is, he takes these two events as evidence that we do not know how to deal with his tactics and will thrash about ineffectively. But he also fears that war may come because the United States will not gracefully accept the defeat he plans by salami tactics.

3. In view of this outlook, I believe the President must not merely talk about Berlin and the test ban treaty. He must also make Khrushchev realize that we understand his tactics; that we have a strategy as well as a faith of our own; and, above all, we must radically heighten his fear that his present technique—and notably its guerrilla warfare component in Southeast Asia—may lead to war unless he exercises much more caution than he has exhibited in Laos and Vietnam.

4. The President should state that the common problem we face in the underdeveloped areas is how to conduct the current ideological struggle without starting a war that could lead on to a nuclear exchange.

5. Evidently Mr. Khrushchev believes that the underdeveloped areas will go Communist. Evidently the President believes that, in the end, they will choose independence and political freedom. We can live with these cross purposes if the historical conflict is confined to propaganda, aid, trade, space, diplomacy, etc. But the technique of guerrilla warfare mounted, supplied, and led from outside an independent country is a threat to the peace.

6. The President might say as a fact that, if the Mekong Valley towns had been attacked by the Pathet Lao, American forces would have moved in despite the political, logistical, and military difficulties.

He is quite well aware that this might have led to a widening of the conflict. Viet-Nam presents an even more dangerous problem.

7. The only safe course is to make Laos truly neutral, with effective ICC control, and to deflate the Viet Cong offensive in Viet-Nam.

8. Mr. Khrushchev will probably reply with two propositions.

a. It was the U.S., not the USSR, that upset the Laos arrangement under the Geneva Accords.

b. He is likely to deliver a paternal lecture on how the U.S. always backs unpopular rulers like Boun Oum and Diem.

Here the President should reply:

a. He has no brief for U.S. policy in Laos before he assumed responsibility.

b. The fact is that under Geneva Accords the Pathet Lao were confined to two northern provinces and they now spread out aggressively over the whole Lao landscape.

c. We are prepared to make an honestly neutral Laos but are not prepared to a face-saving arrangement which would be tantamount to a Pathet Lao take-over; and an essential ingredient in that settlement must be an effective ICC not subject to veto.

d. The President should then turn to Diem. He should point out that the ability to conduct a guerrilla war successfully, supplied and directed from outside, is not an acceptable test of the legitimacy of a government. Continuation of this method can only lead to chaos and risk of peace. What we need to get through this period without war is a most serious understanding between the U.S. and the Soviet Union about the limits within which force shall be used.

9. The President should point out that the Viet Cong operation in Viet-Nam is not designed to win popularity among the people; it is designed to terrorize the people and make them unsure of their government. The Viet Cong do not go about spreading ideas about agrarian reform. They murder the government officials in the village, notably health, education and agriculture officers. Khrushchev should be made aware that the American commitment to the independence of South Viet-Nam is a serious commitment; and that in the President's view the continued or enlarged activity of the Vietminh, who are now operating that offensive from Hanoi, is a major danger to the peace.

10. More generally, the President should say that in his view the revolutionary course of events in Asia, the Middle East, Africa and Latin America is going to yield in time governments which are under the effective control of neither the Soviet Union nor the U.S. Moreover, they will tend to create their own institutions and their own ideologies. The President believes that the historical vision of world Communist domination projected after the December meeting of the Communist parties in Moscow is an inaccurate vision. The underlying historical forces are not making for uniformity and central control of nations but for diversity and independence. These forces are working equally within the Communist Bloc and in the Free World. It is the President's hope that the Chairman will consider this matter seriously; because, if the President is right, the proper policy for both the Soviet Union and the U.S. is not to contest for power and influence in these areas, but to work together to organize a world system which can safely contain the many new assertive nations which are emerging.

11. Although the U.S. will continue to use its power and influence to protect the right of individual nations to make their own choice as they modernize and develop, he looks forward to the time when Russians and Americans will agree that it is their common interest to cooperate, and not to compete, in the underdeveloped areas.

4. For example, Arthur M. Schlesinger, Jr. (*A Thousand Days*, Boston, 1965, pp. 366–367) concludes:

> Where he perhaps erred was in beginning by engaging Khrushchev in abstract discussion. Ideological debate was bound to be fruitless; Khrushchev was not likely to forswear the faith of a lifetime. Moreover, Khrushchev was a veteran dialectician. Though Kennedy held his own, he was fighting on his opponent's familiar terrain. He might have done better to seek the realm of concrete fact, the pragmatic rather than the ideological debating ground, and concentrate, as he had tried increasingly to do through the day, on particular situations in particular countries.

This judgment parallels the somewhat diverse views of the three major American Soviet experts of the modern Foreign Service: George Kennan, Charles Bohlen, and Llewellyn Thompson. Their views are recorded in the Kennedy Oral History Project.

Kennan felt Kennedy was a tongue-tied young man at Vienna whose failure to reply with sufficient force to Khrushchev's arguments helped lead to the emplacement of missiles in Cuba. Bohlen and Thompson are less critical and dogmatic but believe it was a mistake for Kennedy to raise the ideological issue because Khrushchev could not retreat and this was a field where he was a master. I do not find Khrushchev's exposition at Vienna masterly even by communist dialectical standards; and, because of the nature of his Vienna adversary, he could not even be wholly candid as he could be, for example, in attacking Mao at Bucharest in 1960. His primary ideological assertion was that American policy stood in the way of the diffusion of ideas and found itself backing unpopular leaders—neither a novel nor particularly brilliant position, for which his examples proved something less than prescient.

My basic reason for disagreeing with this view, however, is that the relation of ideological to power interests was, in fact, the critical question of the 1960s; e.g., the fate of politically free West Berlin, a politically neutral Laos, the ideological acceptance of Castro if Cuba did not become a base for aggression in the hemisphere, etc. When Kennedy argued that he could accept diverse ideological outcomes if they were not brought about by external means and did not shift the balance of power, he was explaining the heart of the policy on which he was acting. Khrushchev could not, of course, accept it as an abstract position. But it was important that he understand it; for it governed American behavior over the decade that followed.

After all, the encounter at Vienna was not a high school debate, to be scored by judges. Kennedy had two objectives: to get a feel for Khrushchev, as Thompson counseled; and to inform Khrushchev of the touchstones for his policy, so that the chance of misunderstanding would be minimized.

I suspect Kennedy's three distinguished critics might take a somewhat different view of the transcript, reread with the benefit of hindsight, knowing in particular the outcome in Berlin, the Cuba missile crisis, Iran, and the various other parts of the developing world discussed at Vienna. Kennedy was much more sensitive to the power implications of the ideological struggle—and outcome—in the developing world than most Soviet experts, who tended to look on the tension between Moscow and Washington as focused on central Europe and the arms race. This may explain, in part, Kennedy's impulse to explore the ideological question with Khrushchev, and Bohlen and Thompson's view that it was redundant or counterproductive.

5. Edward Crankshaw and Strobe Talbott (eds.), *op. cit.*, p. 457. The first sentence quoted is, as Crankshaw notes, remarkable for a Soviet politician—so remarkable that I am inclined to think it may have been inserted by another hand.
6. *Ibid.*, p. 458.
7. For an engaging account of how Kennedy persuaded Gromyko and Khrushchev in October 1961 to drop their general proposal for a troika in the U.N. Secretariat, see Norman Cousins, "President Kennedy and the Russian Fable," *Saturday Review*, January 9, 1971, pp. 20–21.
8. In private, with Macmillan and Adenauer, de Gaulle exploited the Berlin question in 1962 to heighten Bonn's suspicion of the Anglo–Saxons. See, for example, John Newhouse, *De Gaulle and the Anglo–Saxons*, New York, 1970, p. 150.
9. Despite his generally flesh-creeping effort on July 17, Menshikov slipped in a modification of Khrushchev's Vienna position which suggested some growing anxiety in Moscow. He suggested that East Germany would not block access to Berlin but would trade access rights for an enhanced degree of recognition from the West plus the cessation of certain "offensive" activities emanating from West Berlin. He also flatly stated the German peace conference would take place in the last two weeks of November.
10. On August 2 Senator William Fulbright had said, "I don't understand why the East Germans don't close their border because I think they have a right to close it." When the border was closed, however, he viewed the act "in a most ominous light." (*The New York Times*, August 3 and 13, 1961.)
11. *Public Papers, 1962*, Washington, D. C., p. 538.
12. The debate Kennedy had to settle was between those who regarded OECD as inherently an Atlantic club of culturally similar nations and those who believed it should be a club for the more advanced industrial nations in general. Functionally, neither aid, trade, nor monetary affairs could rationally be dealt with without Japan, as it was emerging in the 1960s. Moreover, some of us felt it urgent that, as Japan moved from the trauma of defeat, occupation, and isolation into roaring prosperity, it ought to be brought fully into the work of the global community. It was clearly on its way to world stature. It was unnatural for Japan to be locked

up in bilateral diplomacy with the United States. I argued with Kennedy and my working colleagues the case for supporting full Japanese membership in the OECD on these grounds. The Europeanists in the State Department, who generally found my views congenial, were troubled. Jean Monnet was in town and they thought he might bring me back to an uncorrupted Atlantic view. I was invited to discuss the matter with him and some of my State Department friends. When the case for Japanese membership was laid before him, Monnet, who had never lost interest in Asia since his work as a young man in China, supported Japanese membership. The matter was settled, of course, by Kennedy who finally observed that if we needed a pure Atlantic club, beyond NATO, we would have to create another organization.

13. *Public Papers, 1961*, Washington, D. C., p. 385.
14. Michael Lewis, *The Navy of Britain*, London, 1948, pp. 312–313.
15. Richard E. Neustadt, *Alliance Politics*, New York and London, 1970, captures in a masterly way the crosscurrents in this critical month, Chapter III: "The Skybolt Affair," especially pp. 40–50.
16. See, especially, John Newhouse, *op. cit.*, pp. 184–212. Technically, de Gaulle's position was foreshadowed by the rigid French position in early December 1962 on the issue of British agriculture, the formal stumbling block in the Brussels negotiations.
17. *Public Papers, 1963*, Washington, D. C., p. 518.
18. For an even stronger criticism of Kennedy's posture on the MLF, see George W. Ball, *The Discipline of Power*, Boston and Toronto, 1968, pp. 207–209. For a serious academic effort to analyze the political and bureaucratic history of the MLF, see John Steinbruner, *The Mind and Milieu of Policy-Makers: A Case Study of the MLF* (unpublished M.I.T. doctoral thesis), Cambridge, Mass., 1969.

Chapter 24: *The Cuba Missile Crisis: "Khrushchev at Bay"*

1. See, notably, Arthur M. Schlesinger, Jr., *A Thousand Days*, Boston, 1965, pp. 794–841; Theodore Sorensen, *Kennedy*, New York, 1965, pp. 667–718; Elie Abel, *The Missile Crisis*, Philadelphia and New York, 1966; and Robert Kennedy, *Thirteen Days*, New York, 1969.
2. Elie Abel, *op. cit.*, pp. 34–37.
3. With some revisions I presented that assessment at the Free University of Berlin on October 18, 1962, under the title "The Present State of the Cold War" (*Department of State Bulletin*, November 6, 1962, pp. 675–677).
4. Michel Tatu (*Power in the Kremlin*, p. 171) poses the interesting question: "It is hard to tell whether it was the Berlin crisis that brought about an increase in military expenditure, as the official version has it, or con-

versely whether the need of the military to strengthen the armed forces prompted the crisis. In other words, was the crisis the pretext or the cause of the armed forces' good fortune?" In any case, at the beginning of July 1961 Khrushchev announced the suspension of 1960 demobilization measures and a defense budget increase of some 3 billion rubles.

5. In an interview with Dr. A. McGehee Harvey (LIFE, December 18, 1970, p. 48B) Khrushchev is reported as saying in 1969: "Things were going well until one event happened. From the time Gary Powers was shot down in a U-2 over the Soviet Union, I was no longer in full control. . . . Those who felt America had imperialistic intentions and that military strength was the most important thing had the evidence they needed, and when the U-2 incident occurred, I no longer had the ability to overcome that feeling." Also, see Chapter 7, note 14.
6. See *Power in the Kremlin*, pp. 125–225, for Tatu's analysis of the unfolding of the Twenty-second Party Congress. See also Andre Fontaine, *History of the Cold War: From the Korean War to the Present*, New York, 1969, pp. 425–430.
7. There are also reports of Castro asserting he requested the missiles to frustrate a believed invasion. For a fair summary of the various scraps of evidence, see Hugh Thomas, *Cuba: The Pursuit of Freedom*, New York, 1971, pp. 1385–1393.
8. Edward Crankshaw and Strobe Talbott (eds.), *Khrushchev Remembers*, Boston and Toronto, 1970, p. 494.
9. The most complete attempt to reconstruct the setting of Khrushchev's Cuban decision is Michel Tatu, *op. cit.*, pp. 229–243. See also, Andre Fontaine, *loc. cit.*, pp. 437–439.
10. Tatu independently reports these Chinese diplomatic observations (*op. cit.*, p. 235).
11. A quiet period emerged in Sino–Soviet relations which ran roughly from February to September 1962. This muted phase may be related, to some degree, to the emerging Soviet plan; but it may also have had independent roots. See *ibid.*, p. 235; William E. Griffith, *The Sino–Soviet Rift*, Cambridge, Mass., 1964, pp. 33–42; John Gittings, *Survey of the Sino–Soviet Dispute*, London, 1968, pp. 169–173.
12. In a speech of December 12, 1962, Khrushchev stated that the agreement on the installation of the missiles was made when Guevara was in Moscow; but the scale of the enterprise suggests it must have been set in motion much earlier—quite possiblly, as Tatu argues, in the last week of April.
13. Theodore Sorensen, *op. cit.*, p. 667.
14. Michel Tatu, *op. cit.*, p. 241.
15. *Ibid.*, p. 233.
16. *Public Papers, 1962*, Washington, D. C., p. 674.
17. Lazar Pistrak, *The Grand Tactician*, New York, 1961, Chapter 8, pp. 88ff.
18. Edward Crankshaw and Strobe Talbott (eds.), *op. cit.*, p. 497.
19. *Ibid.*, p. 495.

20. As Kennedy noted, this inhibition was enhanced by the Soviet desire to avoid American examination of the highly sensitive military equipment being transported. Theodore Sorensen, *op. cit.*, p. 711.
21. There is no doubt that Kennedy regretted acutely that the Turkish missiles were still in place during the Cuba missile crisis. He had asked Rusk to initiate negotiations for their removal in the spring of 1961. Kennedy was informed of the difficulties of the Turkish government in accepting removal of the missiles and, notably, of its desire that they remain in place until Polaris submarines could be deployed in the Mediterranean. This was not possible until the spring of 1963. With this knowledge, Kennedy did not press the issue of removal to a showdown prior to the Cuba missile crisis.
22. At least one other man in Washington shared our perspective. Professor Samuel L. Sharp of American University conveyed through my wife, a colleague of his, the following view shortly after Kennedy's speech of October 22: "The whole thing is, essentially, a cheap trick; it is based on the principle you can't shoot a guy for trying; if we are steady, the missiles will go home." It was one thing to believe this, on balance, as I did: another thing to act on it responsibly when the consequence of being wrong might be nuclear war, as Kennedy had to do.
23. V. A. Sokolovsky (ed.), *Military Strategy, Soviet Doctrine and Concepts,* with an introduction by Raymond L. Garthoff, New York, 1963.
24. *Ibid.*, p. xiv.
25. Michel Tatu, *op. cit.*, pp. 273–297.
26. *Ibid.*, p. 332.
27. *Ibid.*, p. 346n.
28. For an interpretation of the timing of the India–China clash as essentially independent of the Cuba missile crisis, see Neville Maxwell's scholarly study, *India's China War,* New York, 1970. Maxwell noted (p. 367n.): "It is impossible to be certain" that the timing of the Chinese attack was linked to the Soviet adventure in Cuba, but leans strongly to the view that it can be explained in its own terms. Given quite good evidence that the Chinese became aware of the Soviet plan in the spring of 1962, it would be odd if Peking did not take this factor into account. I lean, therefore, to the latter view, without dogmatism, and recognizing that the Indian–Chinese border dispute had a history of its own.
29. J. K. Galbraith, *Ambassador's Journal*, Boston, 1969, pp. 494–502.

Chapter 25: *Southeast Asia*

1. See above, p. 116. In a CBS interview on November 28, 1967, Eisenhower was asked: "How did you see [Vietnam] at the time? Did you envisage a military operation?" Eisenhower: "Well, I didn't at that time. . . . For this reason: Laos was causing much more trouble than

Vietnam, and when I turned over to President Kennedy, I had two long talks with him about that situation. But at that time, Vietnam was not giving us real concern. Except that Diem—he believed in nepotism. He trusted his sister-in-law and his brother, and that's about all the people he would talk to. And we were trying to correct that situation. Otherwise, we weren't going to worry at that time."

2. *Public Papers, 1961*, Washington, D. C., p. 214.
3. Memorandum to the President, March 10, 1961:

   I believe you should reflect on the deeper lesson of our experience in Laos thus far. That lesson is that the Department of State has an understandable instinct to conduct pure diplomacy with minimum involvement with . . . the military until an acute crisis occurs. The tendency is then to turn the problem over almost wholly to those who control force, and to get the hell out. Concretely, first we listened to Brown; then we listened to Felt. We never faced them—and what they represent—together. This is the pattern which produces the uneasy relations between State and the Pentagon which surfaced yesterday.

   This is the exact opposite of Communist policy which is to orchestrate force and diplomacy intimately at every stage.

   The instinctive American position, in the face of Communist tactics, is dangerous on several grounds. When we are being nice diplomats we tend to lose ground. We lose opportunities along the way to strengthen our diplomatic position. When we turn to force, after diplomatic setbacks, we have to use more force than would otherwise be necessary, and we bring closer the moment when our position must be defended by direct U.S. military intervention.

   There is another weakness. When the diplomats withdraw and we begin to think, as we did yesterday, in terms of military hardware, we tend to forget that, in the end, most of the situations we confront are, in their essence, political and can only be settled by diplomatic and political formulae. You yourself noted the vagueness of the Department's conception as to what kind of a political settlement in Laos is possible that we could live with.

   I think we must put our minds steadily to work—in general and on each particular problem—on how to orchestrate diplomacy and force better all the way along the line. In the case of Laos, we must have a much sharper notion as to what our political objective is; and the Department of State should be instructed to go to work on this and report.

4. I had in one way or another known the American military establishment in various contexts since the late summer of 1941. I had seen it perform well and badly. I knew that it was made up of fallible human beings like all the other institutions of American society. I also felt that given the predominant values of American society—and the nation's recurrent oscillation between isolationism and tardy military engagement—the United States had drawn into the military better, abler, and more dedicated men than, in a sense, it deserved. I did not accept professional military judgments uncritically; but I did not share the view of some that the military were inherently less intelligent or less wise than civilians. Against that general background, I must observe that I never saw the American military less clear in mind, less helpful to a President,

than in the first four months of Kennedy's administration. The phenomenon is capable of dispassionate analysis and explanation; but since this book is an essay on the main contours of national policy rather than an account of the evolution of the bureaucracies of the executive branch, I shall not attempt that assessment here. The fact should be noted because it had a distinctly unsettling effect on Kennedy in his first year.

5. I do not know whether Kennedy ever set down in writing his view of the alternative to a policy of holding Southeast Asia. I discovered in 1967 that Johnson had come to a remarkably similar judgment on the sequence that would follow American abandonment of Southeast Asia. It is roughly articulated in his San Antonio speech of September 29, 1967, which also evokes a third world war as a possible ultimate outcome of American withdrawal from Southeast Asia. Kennedy's view had a particular nuclear dimension. He felt historians might well record Chinese acquisition of nuclear weapons as the most important event on the world scene of the 1960s. He canvassed coolly various routes, diplomatic and other, that might deny China a nuclear capability. The most promising, he concluded, was Soviet (or U.S.–Soviet) pressure in the wake of the test ban agreement of 1963. That is why Harriman was instructed to raise with Khrushchev the Chinese nuclear question at the end of his Moscow talks. Khrushchev was unresponsive. (See Arthur M. Schlesinger, Jr., *A Thousand Days*, Boston, 1965, p. 908.)
6. Lucian Pye, *Guerrilla Communism in Malaya, Its Social and Political Meaning*, Princeton, 1956.
7. For a discussion of differences in the timing of the downturn in these data, see Roger Hilsman, *To Move a Nation*, New York, 1967, p. 467, n. 2.
8. Roger Hilsman, *op. cit.*, p. 464.
9. *An American Policy in Asia*, Cambridge, Mass., and New York, 1955, p. 5. *The Prospects for Communist China* was reserved on the long-run viability of the Moscow–Peking tie; and *The United States in the World Arena* made the diffusion of power away from Washington and Moscow its central closing theme, including a probable widening of the gap between the Soviet Union and Communist China. I did not—and do not—believe, however, that the diffusion of power in the communist world ended the danger to American interests in Asia. First, as noted above (p. 44), the Moscow–Peking schism made easier—not more difficult—Ho's revival of war against South Vietnam. Second, the threat of Chinese control over the Asian balance of power is not dependent on Peking's alliance with Moscow.
10. *An American Policy in Asia*, p. 42.
11. Kennedy did raise the issue of the Laos Accords with Khrushchev in April 1963, in the course of a visit by Harriman to Moscow. This yielded a public joint statement of April 26, 1963, in which Khrushchev reaffirmed his support of the 1962 Geneva agreement (*American Foreign Policy, Current Documents, 1963*, Washington, D. C., p. 8). But the Soviet reaffirmation was empty. Hanoi continued to violate the Geneva agreement.

For a rationale for American acceptance of North Vietnamese violation of the Laos Accords, see, especially, Roger Hilsman, *op. cit.*, pp. 152–155. It includes this passage (p. 154):

> To those who felt that a showdown between Communist China and the United States was inevitable and believed that it was to the advantage of the United States that the showdown came sooner rather than later, any such tacit agreement to put the question of Laos to one side for a time seemed dangerous. And there is, of course, a respectable argument for this position. But to those who saw the long-run interest of the United States best served by an accommodation between Communist China and the United States and the goal in Southeast Asia as limited to denying the area to Communism rather than making it an American ally, a postponement seemed better than the obvious alternatives—a large-scale military intervention or surrendering it to the Communists. To those who sought this more limited goal, in other words, Laos was a victory—of sorts.

To the best of my knowledge, there was no significant (or insignificant) adviser to Kennedy who sought "a showdown between Communist China and the United States"—soon or late. The question was whether a denial of South Vietnam to communism was a viable objective, at acceptable cost, if the Laos trails remained open. In my discussions with Hilsman in 1962, I supported his emphasis on pacification but expressed doubt that pacification could be sustained against main-force Communist units supported by a continued infiltration flow through Laos. Hilsman's net judgment on the Laos Accords is somewhat ambiguous, including, as it does, a dictum I fully share, which was at the heart of my position at the time: "The lessons of the Laos crisis are many—that agreements with the Communists can be kept by and large intact, for example, but only if one is willing to keep up the same level of commitment to keep the agreement as one was willing to use to obtain it in the first place" (p. 155).

12. *Public Papers, 1963*, Washington, D. C., p. 652.
13. Theodore Sorensen, *Kennedy*, New York, 1965, p. 661.

Chapter 26: *Kennedy as President*

1. Johnson notes (*The Vantage Point*, New York, 1971, p. 566) his first reaction to Nixon's taking the oath as follows: "I would not have to face the decision any more of taking any step, in the Middle East or elsewhere, that might lead to world conflagration—the nightmare of my having to be the man who pressed the button to start World War III was passing. . . ."
2. Sidney Hyman, "Why There's Trouble on the New Frontier," *Look*, July 2, 1963, pp. 30, 33–34, and Louis J. Halle, "Appraisal of Kennedy as World Leader," *The New York Times Magazine*, June 16, 1963, pp. 7–8, 40 and 42.

3. Following Kennedy's instruction, I drafted an article on the central theme of this memorandum. It was scheduled for publication in a national weekly in the spring of 1964. After his death, I included the essence of the argument in the introduction to my *View from the Seventh Floor*, New York, 1964.

Chapter 27: *Johnson Before the Presidency and at the Beginning: A Personal Impression*

1. Arthur M. Schlesinger, Jr., *A Thousand Days*, Boston, 1965, pp. 10–11, provides his own retrospective account of this meeting, which conforms closely to my memory of his immediate report. See also reference in Rowland Evans and Robert Novak, *Lyndon B. Johnson: The Exercise of Power*, New York, 1966, pp. 104–105.
2. See, for example, Stewart Alsop, "Lyndon Johnson: How Does He Do It?" *Saturday Evening Post*, January 24, 1959; Henry A. Zerger, *Lyndon B. Johnson: Man and President*, New York, 1963; William S. White, *The Professional: Lyndon B. Johnson*, Boston, 1964, and *The Responsibles*, New York, 1972; Rowland Evans and Robert Novak, *op. cit.*; Philip Geylin, *Lyndon Johnson and the World*, New York, 1966; Hugh Sidey, *A Very Personal Presidency*, New York, 1968; Alfred Steinberg, *Sam Johnson's Boy*, New York, 1968.
3. James Gould Cozzens, *By Love Possessed*, New York, 1957, p. 353.

Book Three: The Johnson Administration

Chapter 29: *Growth, Price Stability, and the Balance of Payments*

1. The effort to reconcile a high rate of growth with price stability in these years has been analyzed, notably, by: Walter W. Heller, *New Dimensions of Political Economy*, New York, 1966, especially Chapter II; John Sheahan, *The Wage-Price Guideposts*, Washington, D. C., 1967, especially Chapters V–VI; Arthur F. Burns, *The Business Cycle in a Changing World*, New York, 1969, especially Chapters X and XI; Arthur M. Okun, *The Political Economy of Prosperity*, Washington, D. C., 1970, especially Chapters II and III. The story can also be traced, of course, in the annual *Economic Report of the President*, submitted to the Congress early in the years 1964–1969.

2. From Arthur M. Okun, *op. cit.*, p. 67.
3. *Annual Report*, Council of Economic Advisers, Washington, D. C., 1965, p. 107.
4. See, especially, John Sheahan, *The Wage-Price Guideposts*, Washington, D. C., 1967, pp. 40–41, 44, 128. The Council of Economic Advisers noted this dangerous failure, *op. cit.*, pp. 57–58.
5. Arthur M. Okun, *op. cit.*, pp. 66–69. It is, in particular, difficult to understand the special message on the reduction of excise taxes (of about $4 billion) sent forward as late as May 17, 1965 (*Public Papers, 1965*, Washington, D. C., pp. 540–546). Although Johnson's troop decision was made in July, the possibility of enlarged military outlays in Southeast Asia should have begun to color economic policy by mid-May.
6. See, notably, Walter W. Heller, *op. cit.*, pp. 85–99; also, Arthur M. Okun, *op. cit.*, pp. 69–84.
7. In a statement before the Joint Economic Committee, February 1, 1971, Joseph A. Califano, Jr., a major participant, lists the following examples of federal intervention in the market in this period:

   —The stockpile provided important assistance in rolling back or holding the price of copper, aluminum, mercury and other materials. The Federal government today holds some $6 billion in stockpile materials, many of which can be sold on the open market to ease temporary shortages or roll back proposed price increases. In other words, the government has the capability of providing competition in some concentrated areas where none exists today.

   —Import quotas can be lifted or relaxed largely by the stroke of a Presidential pen—as was done with respect to oil and hides during the Johnson Administration and as President Nixon has done with respect to Canadian oil and threatened with respect to steel.

   —As lumber prices increase, the President has the authority to open up more timberland. Both Presidents Johnson and Nixon have exercised this authority.

   —With the price of food increasing, the Department of Defense, with its enormous purchasing power in this area, can have a major impact. You may recall that by merely withdrawing from the butter market for a few months in 1966, the Secretary of Defense was able to roll back an increase in the price of butter. Similarly, as egg prices increased in 1966 and 1967, the Department of Defense, simply by shifting from the purchase of large eggs to the purchase of medium-sized eggs, was able to reduce and stabilize the price of eggs in the private consumer market. The Agriculture Department, of course, can have enormous impact on food prices, for example, through marketing orders and price support programs.

   —In the late summer and early fall of 1966, furniture prices began to rise sharply. In talking to furniture manufacturers, we discovered that the shortage of hardwood available for furniture was largely responsible. On October 7, 1966, a few weeks after that discovery, we ordered the General Services Administration to stop purchasing high-grade furniture, thus relieving the hardwood shortage and, incidentally, saving about $3 million per year for the American taxpayer.

   —Each year, prior to automobile pricing decisions, the Chairman of the Council of Economic Advisers and I met with representatives of the three major auto companies to impress upon them the public interest in their pricing decisions.

—The Secretary of Transportation was directed by the President to contact all Federal transportation regulatory agencies to ask them to hold rate increases to a minimum. In turn, those agencies with counterparts at the state level, like the Federal Power Commission, contacted state regulatory agencies and asked them to do the same.

—Verbal persuasion itself was of enormous assistance. For example, meetings with representatives of the newsprint, molybdenum, gypsum and nickel industries, as well as others, resulted in rollbacks, eliminations or delays in price increases.

—On word of an impending price increase, telegrams were sent from the White House urging price restraints to manufacturers as diverse as those of sulphuric acid, cartons, cellulose, chlorine, castors, soda, glass containers, air conditioners, household appliances and even men's underwear and women's hosiery. There were at least fifty such product lines contacted in 1966 alone.

—Meetings were held by Cabinet Officers, members of the Council of Economic Advisers and White House staff with hosts of manufacturers, including manufacturers of textiles, television sets, fertilizers, farm machinery and household appliances.

—In the copper industry, several programs were combined: copper was released from the stockpile to ease the immediate shortage and relieve the price pressures; the Office of Emergency Planning invested funds to encourage long-range copper exploration; Ambassador Harriman and State Department officials were dispatched to Chile to reach an agreement concerning the world market situation of copper.

—When excise taxes were reduced, the President set up a team to monitor industry activities to make certain the tax reductions granted by the Congress were passed along to the American consumer.

—With respect to interest rates, beginning in September of 1966, every issue of government securities was reviewed by a task force composed of representatives of the Treasury Department, the Council of Economic Advisers and the White House staff, and then submitted to the President for his personal approval before issuance. As a result, we deferred in time or reduced in amount several projected issues of government bonds and notes.

—When there was pressure on the capital markets, governors, mayors and large corporate presidents were called to the White House and sent personal notes urging them to forego and delay projected capital investments—and to report back to the President what they had done.

—Federal pay increases were carefully reviewed to make certain they were non-inflationary and on at least one occasion—the star route carrier bill—the President vetoed legislation which contained an inflationary wage increase.

8. Arthur M. Okun, *op. cit.*, p. 71.
9. *Economic Report of the President*, January 1969, Washington, D. C., p. 301.
10. Seasonally adjusted quarterly figures for federal government receipts and expenditures in terms of national income and product accounts move as follows for 1966–1967 (in billions of dollars, annual rates):

		Receipts	Expenditures
1966	I	137	135
	II	142	138
	III	146	146
	IV	148	151
1967	I	148	159
	II	148	162
	III	152	165
	IV	156	169

Source: *Economic Report of the President*, January 1969, p. 301.

11. Lyndon B. Johnson, *The Vantage Point*, New York, 1971, Chapter 19.
12. *Economic Report of the President*, February 1970, Table 8, p. 50.
13. *Ibid.*, Table 9, p. 50.
14. John Sheahan, *op. cit.*, p. 60.
15. Arthur M. Okun, *op. cit.*, pp. 84–86.
16. *Economic Report of the President*, January 1969, pp. 11–13.
17. *Ibid.*, p. 59.
18. Gardner Ackley, *Stemming World Inflation*, Paris, The Atlantic Institute, 1971, p. 49. For the year 1971 as a whole, unemployment averaged 5.9 percent; the price increase, 4.6 percent (*Business Week*, December 11, 1971, p. 74).

Chapter 30: *The Allocation of Public Resources*

1. *The Budget of the United States Government*, Fiscal Year 1970, Washington, D. C., p. 27.
2. *Ibid.*, pp. 50–51.
3. Richard A. Musgrave, *Fiscal Systems*, New Haven, Conn., 1969, p. 94.
4. Lyndon B. Johnson, *The Vantage Point*, New York, 1971, Chapter 4.
5. The goings-on within the Republican party in 1964 are best caught by Theodore H. White, *The Making of the President, 1964*, New York, 1965, pp. 61–221.

Chapter 31: *Problems of Race, 1963–1969*

1. Theodore Sorensen, *Kennedy*, New York, 1965, pp. 470–472.
2. See Lyndon B. Johnson, *The Vantage Point*, New York, 1971, Chapter 4, for some observations on the evolution of Johnson's view of the race issue.

3. At his own insistence, Johnson linked this initially domestic incident of American political life to his policy toward Asia in a passage of his talk on October 17, 1966, at the East–West Center in Honolulu, at the beginning of his trip through Asia. (*Public Papers, 1966*, Vol. II, Washington, D. C., pp. 1220–1221.) See also *The Vantage Point*, p. 360.
4. This point is noted by Kenneth Clark in George Plimpton and Jean Stein (eds.), *American Journey, The Times of Robert Kennedy*, New York, 1970, p. 121.
5. *Public Papers, 1963–1964*, Washington, D. C., pp. 1285–1286. William S. White (*The Professional: Lyndon B. Johnson*, Boston, 1964, pp. 43–44) evokes well how Johnson dealt in this matter with his southern colleagues:

   In his mind, the President begins at the bottom of this scale; at first his sole concern is to draw his consultants totally and irrevocably away from the worst possible solution; the quite intolerable one. This he will do by calmly and deliberately throwing them intellectually off-balance, a process of which he is master, combining both high audacity on his part and understanding on his consultant's view. For an illustration, say he is dealing with civil rights legislation and his audience is one or more powerful deep southern senators. He will say to them in substance: "Now, I understand your problems; I know that from where you sit you cannot vote for an all-out civil rights bill and remain alive politically. In me, you are not dealing with some fellow who is eagerly urging you to commit political suicide. But I know you to be reasonable men, and responsible men. I concede that you cannot go all the way with me here. Still, I know and you know that we must do something in this country about this problem; this is not because I am saying it; it is because history is saying it—and you know it is saying it. We are talking together as reasonable men, and all of us love and value our country. So I know you are not now going to say to me that you will accept nothing whatever in this field.

   "A senator owes a duty to his state and to the opinions, and even prejudices of its people; and you know that I know this. But, after all, a senator is, in the end, a senator of the United States—*all* the United States."
6. I was, of course, only rarely brought into domestic matters operationally. But one day Johnson asked my view of Andrew Brimmer as an economist. I said he was excellent. He said he planned to appoint him to the Federal Reserve Board, as he did some time later. Johnson explained that it would mean a great deal to the Negro community to have a Negro located "where the money is"—perhaps more, even, than a Negro in the Cabinet or on the Supreme Court.
7. *Public Papers, 1965*, p. 291.
8. *Report of the National Advisory Commission on Civil Disorders*, Washington, D. C., 1968, p. 6. The following table for the years 1964–1966 shows the underlying structure of the poverty problem and that part of it in which the nonwhite population was caught up in the major cities (Standard Metropolitan Statistical Areas [SMSAs]):

Poverty by Location and Race 1964–1966
(thousands of persons)

Location	Total				White				Nonwhite			
	1964	1965	1966	% Incidence 1966	1964	1965	1966	% Incidence 1966	1964	1965	1966	% Incidence 1966
Farm	4,375	3,294	2,458	22.5	3,046	2,093	1,566	16.2	1,329	1,201	892	70.4
Nonfarm	29,877	28,935	27,511	15.0	20,568	19,606	18,903	11.7	9,309	9,329	8,608	39.2
Outside SMSA	13,531	12,911	12,261	21.0	9,799	9,468	8,726	16.7	3,732	3,443	3,535	56.9
Rural Nonfarm	9,000	8,202	7,443	22.9	6,725	6,284	5,443	18.8	2,275	1,918	2,000	56.2
Urban	4,531	4,709	4,818	18.5	3,074	3,184	3,283	14.0	1,457	1,525	1,535	57.9
Inside SMSA	16,024	16,024	15,250	12.3	10,769	10,138	10,177	9.4	5,577	5,886	5,073	32.2
Central City	10,056	10,355	9,501	16.2	5,625	5,431	5,392	11.7	4,431	4,924	4,109	33.1
Poverty Areas	—	—	4,461	32.4	—	—	1,559	23.7	—	—	2,902	40.3
Fringe	6,290	5,669	5,749	8.7	5,144	4,707	4,785	7.7	1,146	962	964	28.7
Poverty Areas	—	—	1,041	21.8	—	—	690	18.5	—	—	351	33.8
Total	34,252	32,229	29,969	15.4	23,614	21,699	20,469	12.0	10,638	10,530	9,500	40.9

Source: Office of Economic Opportunity, reprinted in Robert A. Levine, *The Poor Ye Need Not Have With You*, Cambridge, Mass., 1970, p. 22.

9. *Ibid.*, p. 81.
10. Robert A. Levine, *op. cit.*, 44–45. See also, James L. Lundquist, *Politics and Policy*, Washington, D. C., 1968, Chapter IV. Lundquist's Chapter III is excellent on the foreshadowing in the Kennedy administration of elements in the poverty program. Lundquist and David W. Davis pursue the community action aspect of the poverty program in their later work, *Making Federalism Work*, Washington, D. C., 1969, especially Chapter 2. On the politics of the community action program, Daniel P. Moynihan's *Maximum Feasible Misunderstanding*, New York, 1970, is, of course, necessary reading.
11. Robert A. Levine, *op. cit.*, p. 105. The scale and complexity of the total effort is indicated in the following breakdowns of the major categories (pp. 106, 133, 156, and 179).

Federal Antipoverty Budget, FY 1969: Community Betterment

Program	Fund Source	Management	Funds (millions of dollars)
"Catalytic" Programs	—	—	517
CAP	OEO	OEO	443
Legal Services	OEO	OEO-CAP	42
VISTA	OEO	OEO	32
Housing	Mainly Department of Housing and Urban Development	Mainly Department of Housing and Urban Development	405
Economic Development	Many Agencies	Many Agencies	293
Miscellaneous	—	—	288
Total Community Betterment			1,503

Source: Office of Economic Opportunity.

Federal Antipoverty Budget, FY 1969: Manpower

Program	Fund Source	Management	Funds (millions of dollars)
JOBS (Job Opportunities in the Business Sector)	OEO and Labor Department	Labor Department and National Alliance of Businessmen	200
Concentrated Employment Program	OEO and Labor Department	Labor Department and Local Community Action Authorities	115
Manpower Development and Training Act	Labor Department and Office of Education	Labor Department and Office of Education	226
Work Experience Work Incentive	OEO HEW	HEW and Labor Department HEW and Labor Department	128
Job Corps	OEO	OEO (through 7/1/69)	280
Out-of-School Neighborhood Youth Corps	OEO	Labor Department	129
Miscellaneous	—	—	996
Total Manpower			2,114

Source: Office of Economic Opportunity.

Federal Antipoverty Budget, FY 1969: Individual Improvement

Program	Fund Source	Management	Funds (millions of dollars)
Education			2,301
Head Start	OEO	OEO (through 7/1/69)	318
Follow Through	OEO	Office of Education	30
Upward Bound	OEO	OEO (through 7/1/69)	30
In-School Neighborhood Youth Corps	OEO	Department of Labor	51
Summer Neighborhood Youth Corps	OEO	Department of Labor	122
Elementary and Secondary Education Act (Title I)	Office of Education	Office of Education	1,123
Miscellaneous Education	—	—	623
Health			7,002
Neighborhood Health Centers	OEO	OEO (CAP) (through 7/1/69)	60
Medicare	Social Security Admin.	Social Security Administration	2,553
Medicaid	Social and Rehabilitation Services Administration	Social and Rehabilitation Services Administration	2,400
Miscellaneous Health	—	—	1,989
Nutrition			702
Food Stamps and Commodity Distribution	Department of Agriculture	Department of Agriculture	273
School Lunch Program	Department of Agriculture	Department of Agriculture	59
Emergency Food and Medical Program	OEO	OEO	17
Miscellaneous Nutrition	—	—	353
Total Individual Improvement			10,005

Source: Office of Economic Opportunity.

Federal Antipoverty Budget, FY 1969: Income Maintenance

Program	Fund Source	Management	Funds (millions of dollars)
Old Age, Survivors, and Disability Insurance (Social Security)	Social Security Fund	Social Security Administration (HEW)	5,782
Public Assistance (Federal contribution)	Social and Rehabilitation Services Administration (HEW)	Social and Rehabilitation Services Administration (HEW)	3,459
Unemployment Insurance	Employment Insurance Fund	Department of Labor	422
Miscellaneous (primarily other pension systems)	—	—	2,507
Total Income Maintenance			12,190

Source: Office of Economic Opportunity.

12. Joseph A. Califano, Jr., address, "The Politics of Innovation," at the Department of Commerce, Washington, D. C., May 15, 1967.
13. See, especially, *The Model Cities Program, A History and Analysis of the Planning Process in Three Cities: Atlanta, Georgia, Seattle, Washington, Dayton, Ohio* and *The Model Cities Program, a Comparative Analysis of the Planning Process in Eleven Cities*, Department of Housing and Urban Development, May, 1969, Washington, D. C. Also, James L. Lundquist and David W. Davis, *op. cit.*, Chapter 3.
14. Andrew F. Brimmer, "Economic Integration and the Progress of the Negro Community" in *Ebony*, Special Issue, August 1970; and "An Economic Agenda for Black Americans," Remarks at the Charter Day Convocation, Atlanta University, October 16, 1970. On the limitations of an approach focused exclusively on the ghetto, see also John H. Kain and Joseph J. Persky, "Alternatives to the Gilded Ghetto," *The Public Interest*, Winter 1969, pp. 74–87.
15. Andrew F. Brimmer, "Economic Progress of Negroes in the United States," Remarks at the Founder's Day Convocation, Tuskegee Institute, March 22, 1970.
16. *Ibid.*, Table 3.
17. Edward C. Banfield, *The Unheavenly City*, Boston, 1970, pp. 245–246. Banfield's injunctions are:

    1. Avoid rhetoric tending to raise expectations to unreasonable and unrealizable levels, to encourage the individual to think that "society"

(e.g. "white racism"), not he, is responsible for his ills, and to exaggerate both the seriousness of social problems and the possibility of finding solutions.

2. If it is feasible to do so (the disagreement among economists has been noted earlier), use fiscal policy to keep the general unemployment level below 3 percent. In any case, remove impediments to the employment of the unskilled, the unschooled, the young, Negroes, women, and others by (a) repealing the minimum-wage and occupational licensure laws and laws that enable labor unions to exercise monopolistic powers, (b) ceasing to overpay for low-skilled public employment, and (c) ceasing to harass private employers who offer low wages and unattractive (but not unsafe) working conditions to workers whose alternative is unemployment.

3. Revise elementary and secondary school curricula so as to cover in nine grades what is now covered in twelve. Reduce the school-leaving age to fourteen (grade 9), and encourage (or perhaps even require) boys and girls who are unable or unwilling to go to college to take a full-time job or else enter military service or a civilian youth corps. Guarantee loans for higher education to all who require them. Assure the availability of serious on-the-job training for all boys and girls who choose to go to work rather than to go to college.

4. Define poverty in terms of the nearly fixed standard of "hardship," rather than in terms of the elastic one of "relative deprivation," and bring all incomes above the poverty line. Distinguish categorically between those of the poor who are competent to manage their affairs and those of them who are not, the latter category consisting of the insane, the severely retarded, the senile, the lower class (inveterate "problem families"), and unprotected children. Make cash income transfers to the first category by means of a negative income tax, the rate structure of which gives the recipient a strong incentive to work. Whenever possible, assist the incompetent poor with goods and services rather than with cash; depending upon the degree of their incompetence, encourage (or require) them to reside in an institution or semi-institution (for example, a closely supervised public housing project).

5. Give intensive birth-control guidance to the incompetent poor.

6. Pay "problem families" to send infants and children to day nurseries and preschools, the programs of which are designed to bring the children into normal culture.

7. Regulate insurance and police practices so as to give potential victims of crime greater incentive to take reasonable precautions to prevent it.

8. Intensify police patrol in high-crime areas; permit the police to "stop and frisk" and to make misdemeanor arrests on probable cause; institute a system of "negative bail"—that is, an arrangement whereby a suspect who is held in jail and is later found innocent is paid compensation for each day of confinement.

9. Reduce drastically the time elapsing between arrest, trial, and imposition of punishment.

10. Abridge to an appropriate degree the freedom of those who in the opinion of a court are extremely likely to commit violent crimes. Confine and treat drug addicts.

11. Make it clear in advance that those who incite to riot will be severely punished.

12. Prohibit "live" television coverage of riots and of incidents likely to provoke them.

18. *Ibid.*, pp. 67 and 69. John F. Kain and Joseph J. Persky (*op. cit.*, pp. 75–76) document the fact that, on the basis of income distribution, a much higher proportion of the urban Negro population would live in the suburbs than is, in fact, the case. They conclude: "Central cities are poor largely because they are black, and not the converse." On this basis they argue strongly for the suburbanization of Negro life.
19. See *Weekend Magazine*, November 1, 1969, Montreal, pp. 4–6; also Edward C. Banfield, *op. cit.*, p. 198.

Chapter 32: *The White Affluent Radicals*

1. There is even a positive Negro view of the consequences of the war in Vietnam. Echoing Louis Lomax's dictum: "War, if American history is to be believed, is the great integrator" (*The Negro Revolt*, New York, 1962, p. 223), Ralph Ellison has written:

   I would like to say something which is unpleasant about the Negro in Vietnam. Speaking historically, our condition has been bettered in this country during periods of national disaster. This was true of the Spanish-American War when there was the beginning of the migratory movement. It was true to a large extent during World War I. . . . As much as I dislike warfare, and I would like to see this thing in Vietnam ended, but from a Negro point of view, from one Negro's point of view, I know that the people who are going to rule the South together under the new political situation there will be the black and white Southerners who are fighting together in Vietnam, getting to know one another in a way that was not possible before, to know one another without the myths of racial inferiority or superiority.

   Quoted, Albert and Roberta Wohlstetter, " 'Third Worlds' Abroad and at Home," *The Public Interest*, Winter 1969, p. 98. The insight is not unique. For example, Sanche de Gramont develops the hypothesis: "In France, wars are greater agents of social change than revolutions." (*The French*, New York, 1969, pp. 115–116).
2. Daniel Bell and Irving Kristol (eds.), *Confrontation*, New York and London, 1968, 1969, p. 51.
3. Nathan Glazer, " 'Student Power' in Berkeley," in *ibid.*, Chapter 1, p. 21.
4. François Crouzet, "A University Besieged: Nanterre, 1967–69," *Political Science Quarterly*, June 1969, pp. 349–350.
5. See, notably, the analysis of Richard M. Scammon and Ben J. Wattenberg, *The Real Majority*, New York, 1970.
6. My notes on that point read as follows: "Speaking subjectively, the President said that he thought he had done more for the young via education; for the Negro; and for the colleges—via the higher education bill—than any other President. But the fact is they feel a detachment from the President."

Chapter 33: *The Organization of National Security Affairs*

1. For the continuity of diplomatic contacts on Vietnam from January 1965 to January 20, 1969, see Lyndon B. Johnson, *The Vantage Point*, New York, 1971, pp. 579–591.
2. The balance of the NSC meetings in this period of the Johnson administration were focused on urgent operational matters. There were, in all, seventy-six NSC meetings during Johnson's Presidency, of which thirty-eight took place in the period April 1966 to January 1969.
3. The most continuous of all these groups was the meeting of planners, chaired by the head of the Policy Planning Council. It hardly missed a single weekly session in the eight Kennedy–Johnson years. Having had a hand in Kennedy's decision of 1961 to abolish the OCB and to press leadership on State for interdepartmental coordination, I felt a responsibility to use such influence as I had over the subsequent eight years to encourage State to exercise that leadership. I had some direct influence on the interdepartmental planning group, both at the White House and at State. I persuaded Edward Martin and then Mennen Williams to experiment with the first IRG's, covering Latin America and Africa—a procedure extended later by executive order to the other regions.
4. Although I never enjoyed a job more, my initial choice in the matter was somewhat limited. When Johnson told a group of Latin ambassadors that he wanted to appoint me, I was in the air returning from a talk at Kenyon College. An assistant of George Ball's was at the airport. He said I had the time it took to walk from the ramp to the manager's office to decide to accept or reject: I was to call George Ball out of the Cabinet Room and let him know which.

Chapter 34: *Military Policy and Arms Control*

1. Michel Tatu, *Power in the Kremlin*, 1969, pp. 363–423, analyzes these and other aspects of the setting for Khrushchev's removal.
2. *Ibid.*, pp. 394–398.
3. Khrushchev (*Khrushchev Remembers*, pp. 484–485) discusses Hanoi's shift to Peking when the Sino–Soviet split "came into the open" in 1963. For a full account of affairs within the communist world from 1963 to the end of Khrushchev's tenure, see Kevin Devlin, Chapter VI ("Khrushchev's Showdown") in his forthcoming book.

4. Arthur J. Dommen, *Conflict in Laos: The Politics of Neutralization*, New York, 1964, pp. 262–263.
5. John Gittings, *Survey of the Sino–Soviet Dispute, 1963–1967*, London, 1968, p. 232.
6. Gittings (*ibid.*, pp. 254–257) argues that Hanoi was, briefly, prepared to acquiesce in a Soviet proposal for a reconvening of the Geneva Conference in January–February 1965, and that the United States was unwilling to contemplate a negotiation. The facts are that on February 18–19, 1965, Rusk indicated to the British ambassador (Lord Harlech) that the United States was willing to accept such a conference. Subsequent U.K.–Soviet contacts indicated that at no time was Moscow able to deliver Hanoi—a fact Gittings acknowledges as the case from March 1965.
7. The most explicit linking of the Indonesian debacle and the beginning of the Cultural Revolution is that of Arnold C. Brackman, *The Communist Collapse in Indonesia*, New York, 1969, pp. 151–153:

> In studying the impact of the Indonesian Communist collapse on the policies of the Chinese Communists, the question of the Great Proletarian Cultural Revolution necessarily arises. The evidence suggests that the total failure of Chinese policy in Indonesia may have been the straw that broke, in this instance, the dragon's back. By the end of 1965, a purge in China was "inevitable," to quote Marcuse again: things had to be explained away, mistakes acknowledged, scapegoats found, and at such a high administrative and party level that the mistakes would take on the appearance of criminal negligence bordering on deliberate treason. In the aftermath of the Cultural Revolution, Liu, Peng Chen, Lo Jui Ching, and many other Chinese luminaries associated with Chinese foreign policy generally, and Indonesian policy in particular, were swept from the scene. It may be worth recording, within this framework, that the opening shot in the Cultural Revolution was fired on November 10, a few weeks after the Indonesian debacle. In any event, during the upheaval which racked China for more than three years, Liu was attacked as a revisionist, as "China's Khrushchev," and, among other things, was accused of supporting collaboration with radical nationalist leaders such as Sukarno. Liu's wife, Wang Kuang-mei, was fiercely assailed for wearing a sumptuous gown when she visited Indonesia in 1963, of walking arm-in-arm with Sukarno, and of indulging in a "bourgeoise life" in Indonesia. Mao's wife, Chiang Ching, ordered the film on the Indonesian visit of Liu and his wife to be shown privately so that the Red Guards, in the vanguard of the Cultural Revolution, could "criticize" it. Within China, the ensuing virulent anti-Indonesia campaign was directed by Red Guards.
>
> While the defeat in Indonesia obviously could not have triggered so titanic an upheaval in China as the Cultural Revolution, it appears to have been a factor in the Cultural Revolution's development. Moreover, the PKI is identified with the most important document in the history of contemporary Chinese communism. This is the thesis promulgated by Field Marshal Lin Piao, who replaced Liu as Mao's heir apparent. Entitled "Long Live the Victory of the People's War," it developed the theme that underdeveloped Asia, Africa, and Latin

America constituted the rural areas of the world taken as a whole, while Europe (both West and East), Japan, and North America were its cities. To achieve victory in the world revolution, the rural areas must become the bases for the encirclement and capture of the cities. Vietnam was singled out as the "most convincing example" of this thesis.

Essentially, the Lin Piao thesis applied the strategy Mao developed during the Chinese civil war to the world situation, i.e., encircling the cities from the countryside accompanied by the armed seizure of political power. Fascinatingly, the evidence suggests that the idea of such an application may have been Indonesian in origin. Indeed, this is probably Aidit's most important "contribution" to Marxism–Leninism and explains his election into the Chinese Academy of Sciences. On May 23, 1965, more than three months before Lin Piao published the celebrated doctrine, the Chinese Communists publicly acknowledged that Aidit was the source for this variation on a Maoist theme. The recognition was made at the level of the Chinese Politburo by Peng Chen, who was subsequently purged during the Cultural Revolution. Lin Piao, of course, was not. This debt to Aidit might partly explain—other than direct Chinese complicity in the Gestapu affair—Peking's fidelity to Aidit. Following the PKI debacle, *People's Daily* termed Aidit the "outstanding helmsman" of the Indonesian Communist Party, although, with Aidit's hand on the tiller, the PKI foundered. The fidelity weakened in 1967.

For a more cryptic linkage of this kind, see W. A. C. Adie, "China's 'Second Liberation' in Perspective," in *China After the Cultural Revolution*, a selection from *The Bulletin of the Atomic Scientists*, New York, 1969, pp. 50–52. The most complete study of the Cultural Revolution is Robert S. Elegant, *Mao's Great Revolution*, New York, 1971.

8. "Report of an Investigation Into the Peasant Movement in Hunan," *Selected Works of Mao Tse-tung*, London, 1954, Vol. I, pp. 21–59. For the context of this essay, see, for example, my *Prospects for Communist China*, New York, 1954, pp. 24–27.
9. In "A Conversation With Mao Tse-tung," *Life*, April 30, 1971, p. 46, Edgar Snow reports Mao (as of December 18, 1970) to the following effect: In 1965 "a great deal of power—over propaganda work within the provincial and local party committees, and especially within the Peking Municipal Party Committee—had been out of his [Mao's] control. That was why he had then stated that there was need for more personality cult, in order to stimulate the masses to dismantle the anti-Mao party bureaucracy." Throughout the history of communism, ideological debates have concealed brute struggles for power. There was certainly such an element in the Cultural Revolution. Whether Mao was as cynical as this statement implies—as well as callous about the fate of his Red Guard and extreme-left supporters during the Cultural Revolution—is not clear. Nor is the general atmosphere of complacency about the outcome of the Cultural Revolution, projected in Snow's interview, wholly convincing. But his description of the Cultural Revolution as a campaign "to stimulate the masses to dismantle the . . . party bureaucracy" is quite exact.

10. *Public Papers, 1966*, Washington, D.C., p. 974. Also, see below, pp. 104–107.
11. Lyndon B. Johnson, *The Vantage Point*, New York, 1971, pp. 464–465.
12. *Ibid.*, pp. 478–479.
13. See, for example, John Newhouse, *De Gaulle and the Anglo-Saxons*, New York, 1970, pp. 16–18, 66, and 240.
14. *Documents on Disarmament, 1968*, Government Printing Office, Washington, D. C., p. 440. The full text of the U.S. declaration follows:

United States Declaration on Security Assurances to Non-Nuclear Nations, June 17, 1968

The Government of the United States notes with appreciation the desire expressed by a large number of States to subscribe to the treaty on the non-proliferation of nuclear weapons.

We welcome the willingness of these States to undertake not to receive the transfer from any transferor whatsoever of nuclear weapons or other nuclear explosive devices or of control over such weapons or explosive devices directly or indirectly; not to manufacture or otherwise acquire nuclear weapons or other nuclear explosive devices; and not to seek or receive any assistance in the manufacture of nuclear weapons or other nuclear explosive devices.

The United States also notes the concern of certain of these States that, in conjunction with their adherence to the treaty on the non-proliferation of nuclear weapons, appropriate measures be undertaken to safeguard their security. Any aggression accompanied by the use of nuclear weapons would endanger the peace and security of all States.

Bearing these considerations in mind, the United States declares the following:

Aggression with nuclear weapons, or the threat of such aggression, against a non-nuclear-weapon State would create a qualitatively new situation in which the nuclear-weapon States which are permanent members of the United Nations Security Council would have to act immediately through the Security Council to take the measures necessary to counter such aggression or to remove the threat of aggression in accordance with the United Nations Charter, which calls for taking "effective collective measures for the prevention and removal of threats to the peace, and for the suppression of acts of aggression or other breaches of the peace." Therefore, any State which commits aggression accompanied by the use of nuclear weapons or which threatens such aggression must be aware that its actions are to be countered effectively by measures to be taken in accordance with the United Nations Charter to suppress the aggression or remove the threat of aggression.

The United States affirms its intention, as a permanent member of the United Nations Security Council, to seek immediate Security Council action to provide assistance, in accordance with the Charter, to any non-nuclear-weapon State party to the treaty on the non-proliferation of nuclear weapons that is a victim of an act of aggression or an object of a threat of aggression in which nuclear weapons are used.

The United States reaffirms in particular the inherent right, recognized under Article 51 of the Charter, of individual and collective self-defense if an armed attack, including a nuclear attack, occurs against a Member of the United Nations until the Security Council has taken measures necessary to maintain international peace and security.

The United States vote for the draft resolution before us and this statement of the way in which the United States intends to act in accordance with the Charter of the United Nations are based upon the fact that the draft resolution is supported by other permanent members of the Security Council which are nuclear-weapon States and are also proposing to sign the treaty on the non-proliferation of nuclear weapons, and that these States have made similar statements as to the way in which they intend to act in accordance with the Charter.

15. *Department of Defense Appropriations for 1966 and 1969*, Hearings before a subcommitee of the Committee on Appropriations of the Eighty-ninth Congress, First Session, Part 3, p. 330, and of the Ninetieth Congress, Second Session, Part 1, p. 468. For a brief, clear account of the issues involved in the Soviet strategic force posture and the Soviet view of the SALT talks, see Thomas W. Wolfe, "Soviet Interests in SALT: Political, Economic, Bureaucratic and Strategic Contributions and Impediments to Arms Control," The Rand Corporation, Santa Monica, Calif., September 1971.
16. When the American military budget began to rise in response to the expansion of the war in Vietnam, various Soviet officials complained privately that the United States had violated an informal understanding arrived at with Kennedy that military budgets on both sides would be limited. Given Soviet unwillingness to provide budget data as full and candid as that generated by the American political process, the agreement was not only informal but vague. Moreover, the Soviet attitude about the United States budgetary increase was somewhat disingenuous. If the agreement meant anything, it meant that, so far as the United States–Soviet military balance was concerned, neither side would substantially increase its military budgets for either strategic or conventional forces. Moscow could not have believed seriously that the United States would forego honoring its treaty commitments to Southeast Asia because of this informal budgetary understanding. It is, nevertheless, possible that the Soviet military to some extent used the occasion of the expansion of United States general-purpose forces to fight the war in Southeast Asia as an occasion to press the Soviet civil leadership for an expansion in Soviet strategic and naval forces.
17. *Department of Defense Appropriations for 1966*, Part 3, p. 47.
18. The irony implicit in the creation of nuclear weapons was evident from the beginning. For example, as early as November 1946, I said in an inaugural lecture at Oxford (*The American Diplomatic Revolution*, Oxford, 1946, pp. 7–8):

    The new and awful weapons may well, in the last analysis, forestall this outcome [a U. S. return to isolationism]. For it lies clearly within the potentialities of modern aircraft and atomic weapons to inflict grievous national damage on the United States from bases deep in Europe or Asia, and to impose such damage by the mobilization of a relatively limited pool of resources, as compared with those required to inflict comparable damage during the Second World War.

The great cheapening which has come about in the cost of inflicting human and physical destruction has thrown in doubt whether, in a future war, the total amount of resources commanded on either side will in fact be relevant. The atom bomb is not only a weapon of great efficiency against concentrations of human beings; it is also capable of destroying industrial facilities and stopping production with a thoroughness, and for periods of time, far beyond the capabilities of any air weapon of the Second World War. After a thousand atom bombs have been delivered, what significance has the second thousand? Professional soldiers may still be capable of envisaging the need to land and to deploy armies in the wake of such attack; and professional sailors may well look to their transport and supply. But there is probably military wisdom in the laymen's suspicion that the new powers of destruction have caused not simply a relative change in the nature of war, but an absolute change. In a happier day students of history may be entertained by the irony of America's final acts in a victorious war, which compromised perhaps fatally the two great props of American military security—distance and a preponderance of economic resources.

I was, of course, by no means alone in reflections of this kind at the time.

19. An excellent brief account of the evolution of thought and planning in this field is that of Alain C. Enthoven and K. Wayne Smith, *How Much Is Enough?*, New York, 1971, Chapter 5, pp. 165 ff.
20. *Ibid.*, pp. 174–175.
21. *Department of Defense Appropriations for 1968*, Hearings before subcommittee of the Committee on Appropriations, House of Representatives, Ninetieth Congress, First Session, 1967, Part 2, especially pp. 153–179.
22. *Ibid.*, pp. 166 and 167.
23. *Department of Defense Appropriations for 1968*, Part 2, pp. 177–179.
24. For a somewhat similar view, see Z. Brzezinski, "USA/USSR: The Power Relationship," paper contributed to a study undertaken by The Brookings Institution, reprinted by the Subcommittee on National Security and International Operations, *The Impact of the Changing Power Balance, Selected Comment*, G.P.O., Washington, D. C., 1971, p. 9:

Had such symmetry prevailed, it might have proven much more difficult for the United States to achieve its principal objective in Cuba (the removal of hostile missiles) through the exercise of its conventional superiority (naval blockade) while simultaneously offsetting its own conventional inferiority in a politically sensitive and vital area (West Berlin) by the inhibiting threat of American strategic superiority. That potential American losses in a nuclear war may have been subjectively "unacceptable" to the American policy-makers was no reassurance to the leaders in the Kremlin who *knew* that such a war would mean the almost complete devastation of the Soviet Union. It was this asymmetry that inhibited the Soviet Union from responding to the American blockade of Cuba with a blockade of Berlin.

25. *Khrushchev Remembers*, Edward Crankshaw and Strobe Talbott (eds.), Boston and Toronto, 1970, pp. 367–371.

Chapter 35: *Europe*

1. John Newhouse, *De Gaulle and the Anglo–Saxons*, New York, 1970, pp. 272–273.
2. The MLF issue generated in the period before Wilson's visit one of the liveliest debates within the bureaucracy in the whole postwar period. Various efforts to describe and analyze the in-fighting have been made, notably John Steinbruner's doctoral thesis, *The Mind and Milieu of Policy-Makers: A Case Study of the MLF* (M.I.T., 1968). The anti-MLF group did a good job in the autumn of 1964; but Johnson's decision was not, in my view, the product of advocacy and counteradvocacy in the bureaucracy, but the independent weighing of the real factors in play as he saw them. The bureaucratic process did what it ought to do: guarantee to the President that all aspects of the problem were canvassed and laid before him. For an interesting perspective on the British dimension of the problem, see Richard E. Neustadt's report of his pre-election assessment of Labour attitudes published in *The New York Review of Books*, December 5, 1968, pp. 37–46; also in the *New Left Review*, September–October 1968, pp. 11–21. See also, Harold Wilson, *The Labour Government, 1964–1970*, London, 1971, pp. 45–51, reflecting the former Prime Minister's pride in having, as he saw it, torpedoed the MLF.
3. For his own retrospective evaluation, see Lyndon B. Johnson, *The Vantage Point*, New York, 1971, p. 477.
4. *Public Papers, 1966*, Washington, D. C., p. 1079.
5. *Public Papers, 1961*, Washington, D. C., pp. 103–104.
6. Lyndon B. Johnson, *op. cit.*, pp. 314–321 and 449–460.
7. The Harmel Report was published in *Atlantic Community Quarterly*, Spring 1968.

Chapter 36: *Johnson and the Developing World*

1. For a fuller account, see Lyndon B. Johnson, *The Vantage Point*, New York, 1971, pp. 184–187.
2. For an account of this process, see, especially, Howard Jones, *Indonesia: The Possible Dream*, New York, 1971, pp. 340–367.
3. Lyndon B. Johnson, *op. cit.*, pp. 187–205.
4. As nearly as I can ascertain, the author of the corrosive and, in my

view, inaccurate phrase "credibility gap," as applied to the Johnson administration, was Murrey Marder, in *The Washington Post* of April 5, 1965.

5. Gallup poll, American Institute of Public Opinion, release of December 17, 1965. Johnson's popular support was even greater at the time of the crisis itself.
6. *Idem.* The December 1965 Gallup poll indicated that 32 percent of the American people thought the Dominican intervention hurt the United States in its relations with Latin America, although 52 percent thought it was right. Twenty-six percent thought it would help; 42 percent thought its effects would be neutral or had no opinion. For Johnson's view, see *op. cit.*, p. 204.
7. See, for example, *The New York Times*, March 7, 1966.
8. Richard P. Stebbins, *The United States in World Affairs, 1967*, New York, 1968, p. 85.
9. Lyndon B. Johnson, *op. cit.*, p. 289. See also Randolph S. Churchill and Winston S. Churchill, *The Six Day War*, Boston, 1967, p. 28.
10. Lyndon B. Johnson, *op. cit.*, pp. 293–294.
11. *Ibid.*, p. 297.
12. *Public Papers, 1967*, Washington, D. C., pp. 598 and 599.
13. See, notably, Arnold C. Brackman, *The Communist Collapse in Indochina*, New York, 1969, Chapter 4, pp. 43–62.
14. Lester R. Brown, *Increasing World Food Output*, United States Department of Agriculture, Washington, D. C., April 1965, p. vii.
15. The transition in policy in 1964–1965 was described in these terms in the Annual Report to the Congress for FY 1965, *The Foreign Assistance Program*, p. 9:

> Fiscal year 1965 also saw the formal evolution of AID activities in the field of population dynamics. The Agency has long given assistance in developing health services and population statistics and in training health personnel. AID is now prepared to supply technical assistance as well as commodity assistance for such things as vehicles or equipment for educational purposes in family planning programs, when requested by aid-receiving countries and where the programs in question are based on freedom of choice. Local currency projects to support national efforts are also being considered. AID will not finance contraceptive devices nor the equipment to make them.
>
> A special unit on population has been established in AID's Office of Technical Cooperation and Research and population officers appointed in all Regional Bureaus and Missions. The Latin American Bureau, in particular, has placed great stress on the development of a positive program of assistance to governments to undertake population projection and analysis as an integral part of development planning. Contracts have been negotiated, under which the Universities of California, Notre Dame, Johns Hopkins, and North Carolina are developing a capacity to backstop AID population projects by providing training personnel for overseas work, and research.
>
> In the last months of the fiscal year, survey teams visited India, Pakistan, the UAR, and Turkey; central training courses in vital statistics, demography, midwifery, and family planning were given.

16. Lyndon B. Johnson, *op. cit.*, pp. 226–231.
17. Lester R. Brown, *Seeds of Change*, New York, 1970, p. 7. Even more than starvation was involved. Medical research in the 1960s demonstrated that periods of hunger (and, especially, protein deficiency) experienced by children under five years of age permanently diminished their physical and mental potential. One of the most satisfying enterprises in the Policy Planning Council in my time was to stimulate work on the production and efficient distribution, through commercial channels, of low-cost protein, derived notably from fish meal and soybeans. (The member of my staff who carried forward this work was a naval officer, William Behrens.) AID undertook from 1965 to encourage developments of this kind.
18. Annual Report to the Congress for FY 1966, *The Foreign Assistance Program*, p. 1, defined the shift as follows:

    Fiscal year 1966 marked a basic shift in emphasis in United States assistance programs abroad. American attention and resources were focused on the most fundamental needs of developing countries—enough food for their citizens, more and more from their own production; health facilities that assure at least the minimal benefits of modern medicine and population control technology; educational systems able to equip the young to meet the challenge they will inherit. . . .

    These commitments comprised nearly a third of AID's total fiscal 1966 commitments of $2.665 billion. They included:

    $561 million for agriculture, compared with initial planning of $393 million.

    $126 million for health, compared with the earlier plan calling for $114 million.

    $137 million for education, compared with $109 million first projected.
19. *Public Papers, 1963–1964*, Washington, D. C., p. 6.
20. *External Financing for Latin American Development*, published for the General Secretariat of the Organization of American States by The Johns Hopkins Press, Baltimore and London, 1971, p. 5.
21. The phenomenon is analyzed at length in Chapter 7 in my *Politics and the Stages of Growth*, Cambridge, England, 1971.
22. A full statement of the argument was set out in a paper entitled "Some Reflections on National Security Policy," April 1965, circulated widely throughout the United States government and to embassies abroad. Its prefatory note follows:

    This paper was generated in the early months of 1965 as an attempt to take stock of our position on the world scene as it has unfolded since the Cuba missile crisis: a scene marked by some decline in the pressure being exerted from Moscow on the outside world; a heightening in various Communist efforts in subversion and guerrilla warfare; and a marked rise in assertive nationalism within both the Communist and non-Communist worlds.

    The principal operational theme is the possible role of regionalism in the resolution of the triangular dilemma observable in many parts of the Free World; that is, the clash between simple nationalism, on the one hand, and, on the other, collective security and the requirements for collective action in the solution of welfare problems.

23. Lyndon B. Johnson, *op. cit.*, p. 347.
24. *Public Papers, 1965*, Washington, D. C., pp. 394–399.
25. As *The New York Times* of June 15, 1971, revealed (p. 19), a memorandum of mine to Dean Rusk, of November 23, 1964, suggested that if the President moved with military strength to hold Southeast Asia, "he should hold up a vision of an Asian community" and "the hope that if the 1954 and 1962 Accords are reinstalled, these things are possible: a. peace; b. accelerated economic development; c. Asians taking a larger hand in their own destiny; d. as much peaceful coexistence between Asian Communists and non-Communists as the Communists wish."
26. *Public Papers, 1968–1969*, Washington, D. C., pp. 783–784.
27. *Public Papers, 1966*, Washington, D. C., pp. 556–560.
28. *Ibid.*, pp. 1222–1223. See also, *Public Papers, 1965*, pp. 397–398; *ibid., 1966*, pp. 721–722 and 974.

Chapter 37: *Vietnam: A Race between Two Political Processes*

1. Bernard B. Fall, "Master of the Red Jab," *The Saturday Evening Post*, November 24, 1962, p. 20. I kept this extremely interesting article at my side in the State Department, at the White House, and, indeed, in my office when I returned to academic life. On the basis of his interviews in Hanoi, Fall advised the United States to bring into play two factors in order to achieve an early settlement and to avoid a painful and protracted war: American air power and Hanoi's fear of Chinese Communist intervention in North Vietnam (p. 21).
2. The phrase is from a private conversation with the former French Prime Minister when he was visiting Cambridge, Massachusetts, in the late 1950s.
3. It can be argued that the "international community" undertook no commitment to the Geneva Accords of 1962: there were only the communist governments in Hanoi, Peking, and Moscow which signed the agreement with total cynicism; the new, bedeviled government of Laos; and the United States. On this view, the British signature as co-chairman of the Geneva Conference can be regarded as cosmetic, as can the commitments of New Delhi, Warsaw, and Ottawa to man the International Control Commission.

   On this proposition I would make two observations. First, there is precious litle hope for the human community if commitments of this gravity—whose violation yielded war on the scale that followed such violation—are regarded as scraps of paper. Second, given all the circumstances, it would be unrealistic to expect all the parties concerned (including the communist governments) to stand by the agreement unless the American government had been prepared to make violation promptly an issue of war or peace.

I conclude, therefore, that the "international community" had a real stake in the viability of the Geneva Accords of 1962; and that, severally as well as collectively, the nations of the community, in different ways and by different routes, have paid a high price for their violation. But the principal failure was that of the American government promptly to insist on conformity to those Accords; for, barring rare statesmanship, it could not be expected that London, New Delhi, and Ottawa—let alone Warsaw, Moscow, Peking, and Hanoi—would stand up for the 1962 Accords if Washington was turning a blind eye to their violation, despite the supplementary Pushkin–Harriman agreement.

4. The publication, in several versions, of the Pentagon Papers provides massive factual background on the evolution of American policy in Southeast Asia from Roosevelt's time to March 1968. The material poses two problems for the historian.

First, it is incomplete. For the Kennedy–Johnson period, for example, neither the White House files nor those of the secretary of state or the secretary of defense were available. Although a much less serious weakness, the exchanges of view among middle-level bureaucrats are also incomplete. For example, only a small proportion of my memoranda on Southeast Asia were available to the authors. Moreover, the authors did not know on some occasions the exact operational context in which a given piece of paper was written; and they were denied the possibility of interviewing those who wrote the papers before them.

Second, at least some of the authors of the analysis brought quite powerful biases to their work which were implicit in their selection of materials and conclusions. Leslie Gelb, director of the Pentagon study, states in his covering memorandum to the final report: "Of course, we all had our prejudices and axes to grind. . . ." This is, I believe, too extreme a statement. Of some thirty-five authors, a high proportion, conscious of the limited evidence before them, confined their presentations to a factual summary of the data. This is not analytic history of a high order; but it is useful. Others felt free to interpret the motives and outlook of the Presidents and some of their advisers without adequate evidence; and there are other forms of "axe grinding" as well.

In time, when the passions of the Vietnam debate have spent themselves, I do not believe historians will have great difficulty correcting for the conscious and unconscious prejudices of the authors. And the material as a whole will be a useful but limited part of the nation's historical archive.

Putting aside matters of law (and also embarrassment to American diplomacy), the evil of publication lay in the manner in which the data were presented—notably, by *The New York Times.*

First, instead of presenting the data sequentially, from the Roosevelt administration forward, the *Times* plunged into the period of intense contingency planning in the spring of 1964.

Second, the headline, lead, and editorial writers of the *Times*, along with several *Times* columnists, projected systematically a set of conclusions not borne out by the evidence of the Pentagon Papers as a whole, nor even by that small proportion of them published by the *Times*. For example:

1. Routine contingency planning was projected in terms like these: "The Johnson Administration began planning in the Spring of 1964 to wage overt war—a full year before it publicly revealed the depth of its involvement." A rereading of the press of the period will reveal that the question of using U.S. air and/or ground forces in Vietnam was actively discussed; e.g., after Johnson's warning of February 22, 1964, at Los Angeles: ". . . those engaged in external direction and supply would do well to be reminded and to remember that this type of aggression is a deeply dangerous game." No major decision of the period 1964–1965 was taken without extensive congressional consultation and public announcement. All this was accompanied by a counterpoint of press stories and discussion that accurately reflected the issues under consideration. I doubt that history will support James Reston's characterization of June 13, 1971: ". . . the deceptive and stealthy involvement in the war under President Kennedy and President Johnson."

2. Specifically, the *Times* implied that Johnson in early 1964 prepared a congressional resolution and simply awaited an occasion to lay it before the Congress. This is consistent neither with Johnson's response to the first Tonkin Gulf attack of August 2 (which was simply a warning) nor with his delay of nearly a year before major ground forces were introduced into the battle. The restraint and moderation of Johnson's response to the August 4 attack and his motives in laying the Southeast Asia (Tonkin Gulf) Resolution before the Congress were fully understood and widely applauded at the time, not least by *The New York Times*.

3. The "consensus" to bomb North Vietnam, which allegedly developed before the election of 1964, turns out, on examination, to be an agreement in September about contingency planning; namely, that "we should be prepared to respond as appropriate against the DRV in the event of any attack on U.S. units or any special DRV/VC action against SVN." There was a consensus on bombing reached on September 9, 1964: it was a consensus shared among Johnson, Rusk, McNamara, Bundy, and the chairman of the Joint Chiefs of Staff. The consensus was *against* bombing North Vietnam. Occasions to bomb North Vietnam were set aside on November 1, 1964, and December 24, 1964. Bombing was only undertaken after the decision of February 13, 1965. This decision, in turn, came in the wake of the reappraisal triggered by the Bundy–McNamara memorandum of January 27, 1965, and Bundy's subsequent trip to Vietnam.

4. The dispatch of limited additional U.S. forces after Johnson's decision of April 1, 1965 (primarily for airfield defense, after the regular bombing of North Vietnam had begun), was interpreted by the *Times* in presenting the Pentagon Papers as "secretly opening the way to ground combat." The arrival of these forces in Vietnam was routinely announced

and widely reported in the press. Their freedom to assist a South Vietnamese unit in trouble in the vicinity of the base was noted in a press briefing in Saigon in May; announced in the White House on June 9; and first used by Westmoreland during the last week of June 1965.

The press, including *The New York Times*, clearly and accurately reflected in the preceding days the momentous nature of the troop decision then under debate, finally announced by Johnson on July 27, 1965.

I would not pretend to assess the motives of *The New York Times* and its various writers in this systematic distortion of the Pentagon Papers. A rereading of *The New York Times* itself for the period 1964–1965 would have demonstrated that nothing essential was concealed by Johnson, as he made his decisions; and that the American press projected accurately to the public the issues at stake and under debate.

What the record shows, including *The Vantage Point*, is that Johnson committed himself upon assuming the Presidency to honor the commitments to Southeast Asia incorporated in both the SEATO treaty and the acts taken under that treaty by his predecessors. He did so both as a trustee of Kennedy's policy and because he believed the policy of his predecessors faithfully reflected the national interest. The mounting pressures on South Vietnam that followed upon Hanoi's 1964 decision to introduce regular North Vietnamese forces—in an environment politically unstable since May 1963—required increased U.S. counterforce if the defeat of South Vietnam was to be avoided. Johnson acted late and reluctantly to avoid that defeat. His actions of 1964–1965 were fully understood and overwhelmingly supported in the Congress and, at the time, by something like two to one of an exceedingly well-informed public opinion. (On this latter point, see, notably, *Gallup Opinion Index*, "Public Opinion and the Vietnam War, 1964–1967," Princeton, New Jersey, December 1967, p. 17. This special thirty-five page Gallup supplement is worth careful study because it relates public opinion polls at each stage to what was known to the American public. It is a useful reminder of how well informed public opinion was and how sensitively it reacted to the changing course of events in Southeast Asia.)

Chapter 38: *Vietnam, 1964–1969: From Near-Defeat to Near-Nationhood*

1. For a sophisticated analysis of civil and military leadership, attitude, and experiences in a situation roughly parallel to that of South Vietnam, see Hahn-Been Lee, *Korea: Time, Change, and Administration*, Honolulu, 1968.
2. Lyndon B. Johnson, *The Vantage Point*, New York, 1971, pp. 122–153.
3. *Ibid.*, p. 149.
4. *Ibid.*, p. 141.

5. *Report on the War in Vietnam (as of 30 June 1968)*, U.S. GPO, Washington, D. C., 1969, p. 98. In a message to Wheeler of June 24, 1965, Westmoreland stated his underlying appreciation as follows:

   . . . the premise behind whatever further actions we may undertake, either in SVN or DRV, must be that we are in for the long pull. The struggle has become a war of attrition. . . . I see no likelihood of achieving a quick, favorable end to the war. The fabric of GVN civil functions and services has been rendered so ineffective and listless by successive coups and changes, and the military arm is in such need of revitalization that we can come to no other conclusion. . . .

   I do not believe that we should make any major change . . . in our policy of supporting the RVNAF. In my opinion, it is important that we stick with the principle that it is a Vietnamese war; that the Vietnamese must fight it; and that they are the only ones that can win it.

   . . . U.S. troops, by virtue of their ethnic background, are not as effective as RVNAF troops in a pacification role. When deployed in highly populated areas, U.S. troops must be used with discrimination. I again underline my conviction that the main contribution that could be made by U.S. ground forces, in addition to securing vital U.S. bases, is to take the fight to the main VC and PAVN forces by reacting sharply to VC initiatives and/or by offensive operations into base areas.

   Even as American forces poured into South Vietnam, Westmoreland's concept for their use was as a supplement to Vietnamese efforts.
6. Westmoreland, *op. cit.*, p. 113, summarizes the last seven of Giap's ten points as follows:

   (4) The morale of South Vietnamese forces would decline.
   (5) U.S. weapons and equipment were not suited for this kind of war, geography, or climate.
   (6) U.S. troops were then being encircled so they could not move about freely.
   (7) U.S. troops were demoralized.
   (8) U.S. infantry was weak and cowardly.
   (9) U.S. commanders were incompetent.
   (10) U.S. tactics were ineffective.
7. *Idem.*, as paraphrased by Westmoreland.
8. Report No. 6 028 0080 70, A707.00, captured 29 April 1969, date of information January 1966, p. 3.
9. Report No. 6 208 0069 70, A707.00, captured 29 April 1969, date of information August–September 1966, pp. 12 and 25.
10. In his address of January 15, 1966, to the Armed Forces Congress, Ky spoke with candor about the post-Diem period:

    My viewpoint in this problem has not originated from my subjective conception but from an objective situation of the two-year period following the November 1, 1963, events. Two years which saw the profound division of the people, the decomposition of our society, the internal subversion, along with a war that reached its highest intensity—all this caused a loss of confidence in this part of land, increased the people's suspicion and sowed confusion among them. No one had confidence in anything and every theory, policy, program submitted was regarded with distrust and cynicism.

In pure theory, democracy is the only factor which can defeat communism; if there is no democracy we lose the reason for our struggle, let alone the means of victory.

A genuine concept of democracy, however, should be based on the true situation of the country, the real circumstances of the society, the political maturity level of the population and, in this case, the subversive war being waged by the communists.

In fact, in these two years, there was no basic document which could serve as a basis for building democracy. A provisional convention which was in effect no longer than three months was violated, amended, and some months later, completely buried, only to be replaced by what was called "the Vung Tau Charter." This "Charter" had been the cause of a troubled, dark period before a civilian government came into being with a Provisional Charter. But the fate of this document was no different from that of its predecessors. Now, with the national leadership committee, we have a convention, but this is no more than a temporary statute which comes from the government not from the people.

When one speaks of democracy, everything should come from the base, that is, the people—the entire people, or at least the majority of them—and not dictated from the government and forced on the people.

A democratic regime should begin with a democratic constitution. But a constitution is not the work of a few days, and also it is not an experiment in a laboratory. Thus, the main point of the problem is to build democracy.

Without such a basic medium, a constitution, no matter how ideal, will wilt and fade away, if it is not torn up by the uprisings.

11. *Public Papers, 1966*, Washington, D. C., p. 532.
12. See, for example, the account of Lewis W. Walt, *Strange War, Strange Strategy*, New York, 1970, Chapters 10 and 11. Walt's position was peculiarly difficult. He commanded Marines who were located in the dissident area, and Thi was a close military colleague.
13. For a discussion of political parties and democratic politics in the developing world, against the background of the political history of more advanced nations, see, for example, my *Politics and the Stages of Growth*, Cambridge, 1971, especially Chapter 7.
14. Lyndon B. Johnson, *op. cit.*, pp. 264–265.
15. Westmoreland, *op. cit.*, p. 86.
16. The best published account of the background to the Tet offensive in Hanoi is that of Don Oberdorfer, *Tet*, New York, 1971, Chapter II. Oberdorfer flatly dates the decision to launch the Tet offensive from July 1967. In this prescient message of December 20, 1967, Westmoreland dated the decision in Hanoi in late September:

. . . The enemy has already made a crucial decision concerning the conduct of the war. In late September, the enemy decided that prolongation of his past policies for conducting the war would lead to his defeat, and that he would have to make a major effort to reverse the downward trend. The enemy was forced to this grave decision by the deterioration of his position over the last six months, and a realization that the trends were running heavily against him. His forces were taking heavier losses than he could replace. His coastal divisions were badly hurt. He failed to disrupt the GVN elections. His infiltration could be hampered in the near future. . . . Most important, he continued to lose control of the population, with almost 900,000 additional people coming under GVN security control in the first nine months of the year. His decision therefore was to undertake an intensified countrywide effort, perhaps maximum effort, over a relatively short period. We fix the date of this key decision from a study of enemy documents and subsequent implementing actions. Shortly after the 14–16 September publication of General Giap's article (proclaiming a protracted war of attrition and conservation of forces), captured documents began to indicate a change in policy. His forces were exhorted to make a maximum effort on all fronts (political and military) in order to achieve victory in a short period of time. If the enemy is successful in winning a significant military victory somewhere in SVN, or gaining even an apparent position of strength, he may seek to initiate negotiations. If, on the other hand, he fails badly, we do not believe that he will negotiate from weakness, but will continue the war at a reduced intensity. In short, I believe that the enemy has already made a crucial decision to make a maximum effort. The results of this effort will determine the next move.

. . . In case a negotiation phase should materialize in the next few months, we should not delude ourselves into believing that the enemy will enter into negotiations in good faith. Their willingness to negotiate will necessarily be a result of unacceptable pressure or the view that they can attain their essential objectives by negotiation. Past experience with the Communists amply illustrates that they will continue to pursue their basic objectives with whatever means they are permitted, in spite of any outward manifestations of good faith. We must continue military and political pressure to retain control of the situation and deny the enemy the opportunity to violate the agreement.

. . . In sum, the enemy has already made a crucial decision to make a maximum effort to achieve a victory of some sort in a short period of time. If he chooses to negotiate in the near future, we must be ready to react quickly. To do this, we must retain the ability to move our forces where they can best occupy and secure the country, have an effective surveillance system, both air and ground, maintain a mobile strike force capability to react to contingencies, and continue to maintain pressure on the enemy by every available means.

Without firm evidence, it is my impression that preparatory work leading up to Hanoi's decision reached back into the spring of 1967.

17. Lyndon B. Johnson, *op. cit.*, p. 379.
18. The following table exhibits the similarities and differences between the situation at Khe Sanh and that at Dien Bien Phu, as calculated by a knowledgeable American officer and forwarded by me to Johnson on February 21, 1968.

Location—Setting	*Dien Bien Phu*	*Khe Sanh*
a. Terrain	Open valley with jungle-covered mountains on two sides	Open plateau with overlooking jungle-covered mountains
b. Access	No open roads	No open roads

c. Distances	288 KM to nearest air and logistic base, Hanoi	64 KM to Quang Tri; 160 KM to Danang
c. Weather	NE monsoon rain-reduced visibility	NE monsoon rain-reduced visibility
Enemy Forces		
a. Infantry	5 divisions (−) (43,000)	4 divisions (+) (38,590)
b. Artillery*	96 Tubes 48 120" mortars 16 122-mm rockets	48 Howitzers (+) 24 120" mortars 36 122-mm rocket launchers; 105 recoilless (75 or 90 mm)
c. Anti-aircraft*	36 37-mm guns 80 12.7" machine guns	24 37-mm guns 34 12.7" machine guns
Friendly Forces		
a. Infantry	7,235 French and African 3,579 auxiliaries Vietnamese & Thai	5,906 USMC 400 VN Rangers 500 irregulars
Total friendly	10,814	6,806
b. Artillery on position	28 Howitzers 24 120-mm mortars	24 Howitzers 6 4.2-mm mortars
c. Armor	10 light tanks	None
d. Other artillery in range	None	12 175-mm guns
Supporting Reinforcing Forces		
a. Combat air		
Fighter/fighter bombers	77	200+
Bombers	47 (B-26)	B-52 (30 sorties per day)
Sorties (maximum in one day)		
(1) Fighter	99 maximum	500 (+)
(2) Bomber	38 combined	40
Ratio bomb tonnage delivered per day (approximate)	1 to	20
b. Logistical Air		
Fixed Wing	43 C-119s 29 C-37s (Maximum one-day delivery 123 tons)	60 C-123s 108 C-130s + necessary cargo helicopter augmentation (up to 1,000 tons)
Helicopter	Utility only	500+ including CH-54, CH-56 heavy lift as required

* Estimated.

c. Mobile Reserves	6 or 7 Infantry Bns (parachute delivery only)	17 USMC Bns 22 USA Bns All capable of airmobile introduction

19. Lyndon B. Johnson, *op. cit.*, p. 512. Thieu sought an official announcement of 1969 troop withdrawals in part to increase his leverage in reforming and improving the South Vietnamese military establishment. He had earlier translated and circulated Westmoreland's November 1967 speech, with its prediction of future American troop withdrawals, to provide his forces with the goal of taking the place of the Americans.
20. The Institute for Strategic Studies, *Strategic Survey 1969*, London, 1970, pp. 44–45.
21. The best published account of the turnaround in Vietnamese agriculture is William J. C. Logan, "How Deep is the Green Revolution in South Vietnam?" in Vietnam's Postwar Development: A Symposium, *Asian Survey*, April 1971, pp. 321–330. I have updated some of the statistical data in this passage from more recent published materials.
22. This section and that on infrastructure draw heavily on Solomon Silver, "Changes in the Midst of War," *Asian Survey*, April 1971, pp. 331–340. But see also the annual *Report to the Ambassador* from the Director of A.I.D. in Vietnam, in particular, the report for 1970. For a nongovernmental analysis of the remarkable expansion in the Vietnamese educational system and a discussion of its weaknesses as well as strengths, see Chester and June Bain, "Education in South Vietnam," *Texas Quarterly*, Winter 1970, pp. 137–149.
23. For a clear account of the structural problem confronted by South Vietnam, see, for example, Buu Hoan, "The South Vietnamese Economy in the Transition to Peace and After," *Asian Survey*, April 1971, pp. 305–320.

Chapter 39: *Vietnam and American Political Life*

1. Gallup Opinion Index, Report No. 43, January 1969, cover page.
2. Gallup Opinion Index, Report No. 52, October 1969, cover page.
3. See, especially, Albert H. Cantril, *The American People, Viet-Nam and the Presidency*, American Political Science Association, 1970, p. 4. The passage in the text owes a good deal to Cantril's analysis of the polling data.
4. *Ibid.*, p. 5.
5. *Ibid.*, pp. 38–39. Those advocating increased attacks on the North rose among Republicans, in farm areas, and among those with annual incomes under $3,000.
6. *Ibid.*, p. 5.
7. Lyndon B. Johnson, *The Vantage Point*, New York, 1971, p. 380.
8. Albert H. Cantril, *op. cit.*, p. 7.

9. *Ibid.*, p. 6.
10. *Ibid.*, p. 7.
11. *The United States in the World Arena*, pp. 511–512.
12. E. V. Rostow, "L.B.J. Reconsidered," *Esquire*, April 1971, p. 160:

    The first is the Pacifist School, expounding a doctrine of innocence for which we have always had a special place in our hearts. . . .

    The Second School is at the other extreme of the spectrum—the party of all-out ideological anti-communism. These critics of our foreign policy regard the cautious efforts of the American government since the war to build a balance of power, and to reach an understanding with the Soviet Union and with China, as dangerous appeasement. . . .

    Third, I note the School of those who are consciously or unconsciously identified with one branch or another of the Communist movements of the world. These men, now as always, find ways of justifying anything done by one of the Communist states. Whatever happens, they tell us, is our fault, or the fault of the bankers and industrialists who in their view pull the strings of American power. And, as good Puritans, we half believe them. . . .

    The Fourth Party in my classification is that of old-fashioned isolationism. Nobody admits he belongs to that party. Nonetheless, it has influential members who, in effect, wrap themselves in the classic mantles of the late Senators Borah, La Follette and Wheeler, and of Professor Charles A. Beard. They contend that we do not need a foreign policy at all. We should not participate in the wickedness of world politics, they argue, but devote all our energies to the struggle for social improvement at home. . . .

    All members of School Five find it difficult to become enthusiastic over the idea of the balance of power. Indeed, they find both the phrase and the idea odious. Some would have us engaged in the world not to support a general system of equilibrium but only to uphold governments they could characterize as progressive, democratic and forward-looking. . . .

    As for the Sixth School, its eloquent spokesmen stress, and stress heavily, that the United States is over-committed and must retreat. . . . They admit that a general American withdrawal could lead to neutralism or reorientation, both in Europe and in the Far East, but are willing to risk even so drastic a change in the balance of power rather than face the alternative.

    . . . I have great difficulty in distinguishing many members of both the Fifth and Sixth Schools from true isolationists of the pre-1941 type.
13. Lyndon B. Johnson, *op. cit.*, pp. 152–153.
14. *Public Papers, 1967*, Washington, D. C., p. 878 (San Antonio address, September 29, 1967).
15. The polemics about the real and terrible human costs of the war in Southeast Asia are not easy to deal with rationally for several reasons:

    —the data on civilian casualties and refugees are inadequate; and it is, in particular, extremely difficult to establish which side has been immediately responsible for their generation;

    —those opposing the war have often used data on these and other problems in exaggerated forms in the no doubt honest conviction that the war itself was so unjustified that any politically effective argument was legitimate.

The anguish of Dr. David R. Goddard as he gave up his effort to form a "Committee on Environmental Alteration" of the American Association for the Advancement of Science, will evoke well for historians the environment of the debate on these issues:

> One might think that professional scientists would not expect the committee to reach conclusions before it has received scientific evidence, but this is clearly not the case. The correspondence reaching my desk, and the telephone calls—many of them from very distinguished scientists—indicate that many people have prejudged the issue before any committee can be formed. Outsiders are trying to determine the composition of the committee, and the conclusions that it will reach.

(Reprinted in *A Technology Assessment of the Vietnam Defoliant Matter*, prepared by the Science Policy Research Division, Legislative Reference Service, Library of Congress, Serial F, August 8, 1969, p. 37.)

The argument over the use of herbicides can illustrate the problem, since the data are reasonably clear. (In what follows, I have been much aided in reviewing the debate by John H. Moellering and George K. Osborn, "A Report on the 'Thirty-Three Books' Reviewed by *The New York Times*," unpublished paper, West Point, New York, July 1971.)

Herbicides were used starting in 1961 for clearing the foliage from jungle base and infiltration areas and, to some degree, for crop destruction in areas from which communist forces drew food supplies. A National Academy of Sciences study on the effects of herbicide use is scheduled to be available by the time this book is in print. I have no knowledge of its findings; but I am confident, from data already available, that these points are essentially true:

—Defoliation was mainly carried out in thinly populated areas which were systematically exploited as communist bases and infiltration routes; notably, the Demilitarized Zone and the mountainous regions of I Corps; the western highlands bordering Cambodia; the great forest bases known as War Zone C and D of III Corps—the U Minh Forest, the Ca Mau Peninsula, the mangrove swamps of Rung Sat, etc.

—Crop destruction was conducted on a much more limited basis, mainly in the thinly populated highlands of I and II Corps. At no time were crops targeted in the food-producing center of IV Corps. Perhaps 3 percent of the total population of South Vietnam lives in defoliated areas; less than 1 percent in areas where crops were destroyed. Altogether, in the period 1962–1970, herbicides were probably sprayed on less than 10 percent of the land area of South Vietnam—the bulk for purposes of defoliation. Professor Arthur H. Westing's adversary estimate of the area subjected to crop destruction through the first half of 1969 (2500 km^2) is likely to prove a maximum since it makes no allowance for respray which may involve up to 20 to 25 percent of the total area sprayed. (In Barry Weisberg, *Ecocide in Indochina: The Ecology of War*,

San Francisco, 1970, p. 95.) The total acreage of South Vietnam is, on one estimate, 171,940 km². This yields a figure of 1.45 percent of the nation's area sprayed for crop destruction—mainly low-productivity regions, in some cases regions for long outside the market economy.

The fact is, of course, that the decline of agricultural production in South Vietnam in the mid-1960s was due to effects of the war quite apart from the use of herbicides; and the dramatic rise in food production since 1967 (the peak year of herbicide use) has causes quite independent of the declining use of herbicides (see above, pp. 471–472). As for defoliation, aerial photography of early 1971 showed a recovery of dense canopy in the hardwood forested area north and west of Saigon with approximately 10 percent of the trees dead. There is recovery also—but less marked—in the frequently sprayed mangrove swamp of the Rung Sat Special Zone in the Delta.

These relatively firm facts contrast with the image projected by opponents of the government's Southeast Asian policy: an image of irreversible ecological disaster caused by the use of herbicides against the jungle canopies and crop areas of South Vietnam, leading to permanent dependence on imported foodstuffs, if not genocidal starvation, and to permanent loss of the nation's timber resources.

I am not prepared to make a judgment on the costs to South Vietnam of the use of herbicides as against their military effectiveness. Still less would I ignore the vastly more serious cost of the war in military and civilian casualties and refugees—throughout Indochina, including North Vietnamese casualties. And I would underline—not deny—that in Vietnam, as in every other war of which I know, bullets and shells (as well as bombs and herbicides) did not always hit their targets; some men violated the rules of engagement; and there was human suffering far beyond that casualty statistics can measure. (We do not know the civilian casualty level on both sides in either the Korean or the Vietnamese war; but the best rough estimates for casualties on both sides during the Korean War are: 2 million civilians as against 2.5 million military personnel killed, wounded, or missing [David Rees, *Korea: The Limited War*, New York, 1964, Appendix C, pp. 460–461].) The inherent case for pacifism is strong. Like a great many others, I only turned away from pacifism when I reflected on all the consequences that might well flow from never fighting; and an acceptance of all the consequences is implicit in serious pacifism. The struggle in Southeast Asia has been no more and no less savage and sanguinary than most wars—probably less so (but more protracted) than the war in Korea, where the armies twice swept through the cities of both the North and the South. Putting pacifism aside, I believe the questions at stake are not those raised in the genocide and ecocide polemics but:

—Do the peoples of Laos, Cambodia, and South Vietnam wish to be run from Hanoi; or do they wish an authentic independence?

—Are the judgments and commitments built into the SEATO treaty a correct reflection of the American national interest?

—What would be the consequence of an American withdrawal of economic and military aid (and long-run treaty commitment) to Southeast Asia?

As one who would answer the first two questions affirmatively and who believes the answer to the third is a much larger and quite possibly nuclear war fairly soon, I was—and am—prepared to accept the costs of the war in Southeast Asia, in all their dimensions, as the tragic but legitimate price for achieving large purposes and avoiding greater horrors. Much more important, the people of South Vietnam have borne these costs and continued to fight for their independence—and so have the still more vulnerable people of Laos and, latterly, Cambodia.

16. Irving Kristol, "American Intellectuals and Foreign Policy," *Foreign Affairs*, July 1967, p. 594.
17. *Ibid.*, p. 600.
18. *Ibid.*, p. 599.
19. For an explicit comparison of the "doves" of the war in Vietnam and those in the post-Spanish-American War period, see Robert L. Beisner, "1898 and 1968: The Anti-Imperialists and the Doves," *Political Science Quarterly*, June 1970, Vol. LXXXV, No. 2, pp. 187–216.
20. Dexter Perkins, "American Wars and Critical Historians," *Yale Review*, June 1951, p. 686.
21. General George Marshall's report: *The Winning of the War in Europe and the Pacific*, New York, 1948, p. 118.
22. See, notably, Harold Isaacs, *Scratches on Our Minds*, New York, 1958.
23. Lyndon B. Johnson, *op. cit.*, p. 402.
24. The basic pessimistic appreciation written by the Pentagon civilians on February 29, 1968, for presentation to the President is extensively summarized in Book 5, Volume III, *U.S. Ground Strategy and Force Deployments, 1965–1967*, pp. 33–42, *United States–Vietnam Relations, 1945–1967*. Study prepared by the Department of Defense, printed for use of the House Committee on Armed Services, Washington, D. C., 1971. See also pp. 26–28 for background materials bearing on this view. In phrasing as well as tone and conclusions, it reflects, in part, the unclassified memorandum for the record by Daniel Ellsberg, dated February 28, 1968, entitled "Impact of the VC Winter–Spring Offensive." For further reference, see above, pp. 519–520.
25. Lyndon B. Johnson, *op. cit.*, p. 360. The full passage referred to follows (*Public Papers, 1966*, Washington, D. C., pp. 1220–1221):

> My forebears came from Britain, Ireland, and Germany. People in my section of the country regarded Asia as totally alien in spirit as well as nationality. East and West meant to us that Texas was west of where Sam Gilstrap lived—Oklahoma.
>
> We, therefore, looked away from the Pacific, away from its hopes as well as away from its great crises.
>
> Even the wars that many of us fought here were often with left-overs of preparedness, and they did not heal our blindness.
>
> I remember we felt we would get some planes out here after they had all they needed in Europe in the early forties.

One consequence of that blindness was that Hawaii was denied its rightful part in our Union of States for many, many years.

Frankly, for two decades I opposed its admission as a State, until at last the undeniable evidence of history, as well as the irresistible persuasiveness of Jack Burns, removed the scales from my eyes.

Then I began to work and fight for Hawaiian statehood. And I hold that to be one of the proudest achievements of my 25 years in the Congress.

There are still those who cannot understand the Pacific's role in America's future. But their voices, shrill though they may be, are becoming few and tired, and small.

Most of us who were blind two decades ago can now begin to see.

Only by answering these questions with candor can we build solid foundations for our future relations with Asia. Only then can we really understand the depth of the desire in Asia for independence, for modernization, and for dignity.

26. Arthur M. Schlesinger, Jr., CBS broadcast of July 13, 1971. The full context of Schlesinger's phrase was: ". . . why anyone ever supposed that Vietnam so involved the American national interest or so threatened the security of the United States as to justify the frightful slaughter and destruction we have brought to this remote and alien country."
27. Interview with Eugene McCarthy, *The New York Times Book Review*, August 4, 1968, p. 24.
28. Albert H. Cantril, *op. cit.*, pp. 18–19. See also Seymour M. Lipset, "The President, the Polls, and Vietnam," a chapter in Robert J. Lifton (ed.), *America and the Asian Revolutionaries*, Chicago, 1970, p. 116.
29. Albert H. Cantril, *op. cit.*, pp. 18–19.
30. Elting E. Morison (ed.), *The American Style*, New York, 1958, pp. 297–298.
31. See, for example, Edith Efron, *The News Twisters*, Los Angeles, 1971, p. 37. Also see Don Oberdorfer, *op. cit.*, pp. 237–277.

Chapter 40: *Southeast Asia, 1963–1969: A Personal View*

1. *Public Papers, 1963–1964*, Washington, D. C., p. 116
2. After a trip to Europe, I took some time in April to find out how the issue had blown up and sent Bill Moyers my findings on April 25. The origins appeared to be a warning by Johnson in February 21, at Los Angeles, that Hanoi, through its external direction and supply of the war in South Vietnam, was engaged in "a deeply dangerous game." Probably in response, two dispatches went out from Saigon on February 22, referring to plans to carry the war to the North. Building on these and Johnson's remark, Joseph Alsop did a column on the subject; and some ten days of noise about bombing and invading the North followed.

3. Lyndon B. Johnson, *The Vantage Point*, New York, 1971, Chapter 6.
4. Alexis de Tocqueville, *Democracy in America*, New York, 1954, Volume II (Vintage books), p. 297. For a discussion of the limitations of American democracy in facing another more massive aggressive effort in Asia, in terms that recall Tocqueville's dictum, see *The Memoirs of Cordell Hull*, New York, 1948, pp. 1100–1105. Hull makes a case for a policy of procrastination in 1940–1941—namely, the need for American rearmament—which cannot, however, be made for 1962–1965.
5. For a summary and analysis of the current relevance of the Thuc–Lilienthal report see Albert P. Williams, Jr., "South Vietnam's Development in a Postwar Era: A Commentary on the Thuc-Lilienthal Report," *Asian Survey*, April 1971; pp. 352–570.
6. *Pentagon Papers, The New York Times*, New York (Bantam Edition), 1971, pp. 573–577. The author of this part of the Pentagon Papers did not quote or paraphrase the following portion summarizing "what we agree upon" in the government: "We must encourage the South Vietnamese to the most forthcoming posture possible towards those fighting with the Viet Cong in the South and look to reconciliation and, ultimately, negotiating among the South Vietnamese to help settle the war." For background to this view, see above, p. 514.
7. Lyndon B. Johnson, *op. cit.*, pp. 366–369.
8. *Ibid.*, pp. 369–370.
9. *Ibid.*, p. 378.
10. *Ibid.*, pp. 372–378.
11. *Ibid.*, pp. 381–382.
12. It was in precisely these terms that I briefed the press at this time, as this report to Johnson of February 8 indicates:

    Today I met with *John Steele and Jess Cook, TIME magazine; Richard L. Wilson, Cowles publications; and Winston Churchill, London Evening News,* all on the Vietnam situation.

    I took them all through the documents: prisoner of war reports; reports from the field on cooperation and revival in the Delta; material on casualties; an account of reorganization of the Vietnamese government; etc. I took the same line as yesterday: we are in the middle of an important battle; the first stage has not gone badly for our side; the battle is not yet over and its outcome would depend on the scale of further attacks on the cities and how they are handled; the continued vitality of the Vietnamese government; the outcome of Khe Sanh and other frontier battles; and the steadiness of U.S. public opinion.
13. Those who agreed with Ellsberg's projections and incorporated passages from them verbatim in official memoranda generally failed to note his own cautionary observations: "I am more confident of some projections than others but all are speculative. Most were formed in the first days of the Tet offensive without any access to official reporting. . . ." Ellsberg had not been in Southeast Asia since July 1967.
14. Lyndon B. Johnson, *op. cit.*, Chapter 17.
15. I have no record that I ever sent this memorandum to the President. Its primary purpose was to clarify my own thought.

Memorandum for the Record as of February 29, 1968

1. I believe the Wheeler recommendation should be accepted for four reasons:

—The forces are required in Viet Nam if we are to avoid excessive military and political risk.

—The further U.S. commitment in Viet Nam and the build-up of reserves are required to deflate the widespread view we are too thin and pressure or aggression might be successful in the Middle East, elsewhere in Asia, and perhaps even in Europe.

—This is a Presidential election year and a classic period for Communist adventure: we should not go into this period over-extended—either in Viet Nam or in general.

—Our two most responsible men in the field have asked for additional forces: Westmoreland and Bunker.

2. Specifically in Viet Nam:

—The Communists are acting on the assumption that 1968 is the year of decision: we must accept that and make the decision turn the right way.

—The Communists are engaging their forces at more than twice the average rate of 1967—quite aside from the Tet peak. Westy is, therefore, thin on the ground in terms of his minimum requirements. The pressure may ease in May; but we cannot be sure; and post-May he will need more forces to retrieve losses suffered in the winter–spring offensive and to have bargaining weight should negotiations emerge.

—These forces are needed in part to give the ARVN both the assurance about the security of the cities and to make possible joint U.S.–ARVN operations in the Delta and elsewhere in the countryside. We could face a disastrous political situation if the enemy consolidated the countryside and then called for negotiations with the majority of the people in his hands.

The present situation—for us and the enemy—is one of both losses and opportunities, since the Tet offensive began. The outcome (say) two months from now of the whole battle since Tet depends on what happens between now and then. If we send some forces now—and Westy knows others are on the way—he will be able to do much more than if he has to work off thin margins.

—Right now the enemy may be introducing an additional two divisions from the North. The intelligence is uncertain, but somewhat firmer than a few days ago.

3. If we accept the Wheeler recommendation we face, of course, many problems.

—We must develop a precise list of concrete things we want the GVN and ARVN to do, and use maximum leverage to get the South Vietnamese to do them on schedule. (Incidentally, I regard the GVN performance since Tet as B+, in fact remarkable for a developing nation confronting a desperate attack of this kind. We cannot set impossible standards.)

—Since negotiations may be thrust upon us—and we certainly want them if they promise an honorable peace—we must face up to what we think and begin consultations with Thieu. We do not intend to sell them down the river; but we cannot postpone peace—if it is reachable—until every VC is killed or until in some psychological sense the GVN is "ready."

4. The dispatch of additional forces could be the occasion for a new directive to Westy setting the limits of his mission in terms of concrete U.S. political objectives in SVN and Southeast Asia.

5. There may be strong political forces generated in directions we do not wish to go:

—Invade Laos, Cambodia, North Viet Nam. We may wish to mount such operations at some time. We should not rule them out. But as I read Westy's situation, he has his hands full for the next months inside South Viet Nam. I see no reason that, if we recover equilibrium in the late spring, the President should be forced to move where he does not believe it wise to go.

—Mine Haiphong. We may (or may not) wish to hit Haiphong and Hanoi harder; but for coming months the weather is bad; we need our air in ground support; the arguments about our engaging the USSR and making Communist China the primary route for supply are still relevant. If the President makes his decisions now, I do not think he can be realistically forced into a policy which cannot now be executed. Several months from now I believe he will still command the capacity to maintain his freedom of decision.

—Pull troops out of Europe. This must be met by making our case not merely in terms of Viet Nam but thickening up our total deterrent position. We don't want a Berlin or NATO crisis. But we have a right to demand of NATO Europe—and Germany in particular—the fullest possible financial and balance of payments cooperation.

6. Taxes.

From my limited knowledge, Joe Fowler's assessment—that these moves could break the tax stalemate—makes sense. But, as he has suggested, the whole enterprise—Viet Nam forces, global reserves, taxes—must be put as an Act of National Will, in terms which transcend Viet Nam and even Southeast Asia.

7. Public Opinion.

I am no expert; but I sense three things:

—frustration at our defensive posture, and real fear;

—a hawkish balance in the country;

—a desire to do something about the situation.

With appropriate prior consultation with leading citizens—as well as Congressional leaders—I believe the package is viable.

16. Lyndon B. Johnson, *op. cit.*, p. 428.

17. Townsend Hoopes (*Limits of Intervention*, New York, 1969) indicates a possible reason why the evidence which unfolded in these weeks on the course of the battle was not absorbed: "In the Pentagon, the Tet offensive performed the curious service of fully revealing the doubters and dissenters to each other, in a lightning flash" (p. 145). In shifting, on the basis of these long-held doubts, to passionate advocacy of a policy of American retraction, there may have been a tendency among some to see the evidence flowing from Vietnam in a somewhat unbalanced way. It should, perhaps, be noted that, in retrospect, the best balanced, published evaluation of the Tet offensive and its week-by-week evolution was that of the London *Economist*. Its analyses were a considerable comfort to me at the time.

18. Lyndon B. Johnson, *op. cit.*, pp. 211–212.

19. *Ibid.*, p. 523.

Chapter 41: *Johnson as President*

1. Quoted from Paul Ylvisaker in Daniel P. Moynihan, *Maximum Feasible Misunderstanding*, New York, 1970 (paperback edition), p. xxxv.
2. On one major matter I lack evidence if, indeed, evidence exists; that is, the manner in which Johnson viewed the war in relation to his domestic objectives and domestic politics in general—notably, congressional relations. It is fundamental and inescapable that a President—or any other chief of government—live amidst the inherently competing claims of foreign and domestic affairs. It is not discreditable for the chief of government in a democratic state to take into account domestic politics, in the widest sense: it is his duty to do so. Under the American Constitution, where the President and Vice President alone are elected officials in the executive branch, a President may not share his political concerns with his Cabinet and staff in the way a Prime Minister does, whose Cabinet is made up of members of parliament.

   In any case, my work with Johnson did not regularly involve domestic affairs and politics; and I was not in the White House when the basic strategy on Vietnam was formed in 1965.

   Against this background I cannot, for example, answer confidently the question many have asked: Did Johnson's domestic objectives lead him to conduct a more gradualist military strategy in Vietnam than he otherwise would have chosen? I would assume, without evidence, that he took into account the relation between his problem in Vietnam and his Great Society objectives. Indeed, he spoke of the relation often, notably in State of the Union messages. But from my knowledge of Johnson and his military decisions in the period 1966–1969, I am confident that the overriding factor was his determination to minimize the possibility of a larger war. There is not the slightest doubt that senior diplomatic advice to him was in this vein; and as *The Vantage Point* (New York, 1971, pp. 148–151) makes clear, he took it most seriously. He fully shared the options before him with the bipartisan congressional leadership on the evening of July 27, 1965 (*ibid.*, p. 150); and the weight of opinion lay with a low key approach to the great decision before him.

   On a lesser issue, some have argued that the Honolulu conference of February 1966 was the product of Johnson's desire to upstage Fulbright's Vietnam hearings of the period. Again, any responsible President must take into account what the chairman of the Senate Foreign Relations Committee is up to, although I have not the slightest evidence of how, if at all, Fulbright's posture bore on Johnson's Honolulu decision. What I do know is that from the Johns Hopkins speech, through Honolulu and Guam, down to January 20, 1969, Johnson never ceased to regard the economic, social, and political development of South Vietnam (and Southeast Asia generally) as a dimension of the conflict co-equal at least to its military dimension. No one who saw Johnson operate at Honolulu and thereafter on the civil side of the Southeast Asian effort can believe his interest in these matters was a cosmetic reflex of domestic politics.

3. Some critics have argued that Johnson put too many troops into South Vietnam; and he himself raises that question, among others, for historians to debate (*The Vantage Point*, p. 531). They may well. My own view is that the timing of American entrance into the conflict, on the eve of South Vietnamese defeat, and the defensive, peripheral strategy adopted on the ground inherently decreed a very large American troop commitment. The most subtle form of argument for a smaller American force would be that Hanoi geared its force buildup after mid-1965 to the American force level; and that a smaller U.S. commitment would have yielded a smaller buildup in response and a smaller war altogether. Tet 1968 throws grave doubt on this proposition. I believe it represented a truly maximum effort by Hanoi (including the Viet Cong). It was turned back; but there were uncomfortable moments in certain places in early February 1968. There is no magic justification for the peak U.S. force-level figure in Vietnam; but, given American strategy in 1965–1968, the Tet offensive may not have been survivable with a much lower American force level, notably since a good many South Vietnamese units were under strength because of the holiday leave.

   On the other hand, I do believe the Regional and Popular Forces might have been given higher priority earlier; and the failure to produce enough M-16 rifles sooner than they were remains a major puzzlement.
4. Lyndon B. Johnson, *op. cit.*, pp. 88–89, 95–96.

Book Four: The Present and the Future

Chapter 42: *The Nixon Administration: A Preliminary Sketch*

1. *Public Papers, 1969*, Washington, D.C., 1971, pp. 22–23.
2. *Economic Report of the President*, February 1971, p. 58; and Goldman Sachs, *Economic Comments*, August 25, 1971, p. 4 (Table prepared by Arthur Okun).
3. Department of Commerce *News*, September 16, 1971, "U.S. Balance of Payments Developments: Second Quarter 1971 (Revised)."
4. Charles L. Schultze et al., *Setting National Priorities, The 1971 Budget*, The Brookings Institution, Washington, D.C., 1970, p. 14.
5. Charles L. Schultze et al. *Setting National Priorities, The 1972 Budget*, The Brookings Institution, Washington, D.C. 1971, p. 15.

6. For a careful analysis of both proposals, see, especially, *ibid.*, Chapters 6 ("General Revenue Sharing") and 8 ("Welfare and Family Assistance").
7. Dwight D. Eisenhower, *Mandate For Change*, p. 219.
8. *The Budget Message of the President, 1973*, p. 8.
9. *The Christian Science Monitor*, January 3, 1972, p. 14.
10. Gil Scott, *The Christian Science Monitor*, September 30, 1971, pp. 1 and 8.
11. Albert H. Cantril, *The American People, Viet-Nam and the Presidency*, p. 10.
12. *Ibid.*, pp. 11–15. See, also, Albert H. Cantril and Charles W. Roll, Jr., *Hopes and Fears of the American People*, New York, 1971, p. 40:

    . . . we asked:

    "Thinking about all that the United States has done over the years to help the South Vietnamese fight the war, suppose that the entire effort failed as the United States continued to withdraw its troops. Which of these things would really bother you the most—that the communists would be expanding their influence by taking over one more country, or that we had been defeated in Vietnam, losing our first war in this century?"

    Over half of those surveyed—58 percent—replied that they would be more bothered by the possible expansion of communist influence. Only 18 percent expressed more concern about an American defeat. The remainder gave either qualified responses (13 percent) or expressed no opinion (11 percent).

    These findings point to a strong residue of anticommunism, at least at the ideological level, among the American people. Yet, as noted earlier, 55 percent of those surveyed indicated that they would be willing to risk a communist takeover in South Vietnam in order to end the fighting.
13. *U.S. Foreign Policy For the 1970's: Building for Peace*, A Report to the Congress by Richard Nixon, President of the United States, February 25, 1971, pp. 146–147.

Chapter 43: *The American Agenda*

1. My 1960 statement in Moscow was rooted in convictions which formed up in the late 1950s, as I sought to peer beyond the stage of acute post-Sputnik confrontation. For example, as I completed *The United States in the World Arena* in the summer of 1958 and looked to the tasks ahead, I took as my theme (p. 414):

    The central fact to which all nations must accommodate their policies . . . is the likelihood not only that the enlarging world arena will become more intimately interconnected but also that the centers of effective power within it will increase in number.

    After considering the bases for optimism in Moscow as Khrushchev conducted the first year of his lively post-Sputnik offensive, I concluded (pp. 428–429):

> . . . when projected in the longer future, the prospects of the Communist Bloc as of 1958 looked somewhat different from what they would if they were assayed in terms of the present and more immediate future. The military and diplomatic momentum of the Soviet Union, the primacy of Moscow's power within the Communist Bloc, the evident potentialities for tactical exploitation of the transitional societies of Asia, the Middle East, and Africa were offset by the limited usefulness of the new weaponry as long as the nuclear stand-off was maintained; by the likelihood that power would be progressively diffused away from direct Moscow control both within and outside the Communist Bloc; and by forces making for the diffusion of power within Soviet society, the Eastern European satellites, and even Communist China which, if permitted to work themselves out over a substantial period, could radically modify communism.

Surveying the American options in a world of diffusing power, I urged (pp. 436–438) that the nation actively use its

> . . . real, if limited, margin of influence on the course of history to yield with the passage of time a multipolar world held in order by effective international control of armaments, its individual societies structured around their own versions of government by consent. There is no guarantee that such a policy will succeed. The forces at work on the world scene are only partially susceptible to influence by American policy. The nation may at some stage be required to face, for a time at least, some version of a policy of withdrawal. But, as of 1958, the national interest requires, and the state of the world arena does not yet rule out as beyond the nation's reach. . .

a policy of partnership "embracing both the older and newer nations of the non-Communist world." (The diffusion of power is also the central theme in Chapter 9, *The Stages of Economic Growth*, Cambridge, 1960 and (2d edition) 1971, "The Relative Stages of Growth and the Problem of Peace.")

2. These figures are derived from P. N. Rosenstein-Rodan's "The Have's and the Have-not's around the Year 2000," presented at the World Law Conference, June 1969, (mimeographed). They are based, in turn, on the calculations of Herman Kahn and A. J. Wiener, *The Year 2000*, New York, 1967.
3. See, notably, Dennis Meadows, Donella Meadows, Jørgen Randers, and William Behrens III, *The Limits to Growth*, New York, 1972.
4. For further discussion, see my *Politics and the Stages of Growth*, Cambridge, 1971, pp. 233–238.
5. Without arguing the case here, my preference would be a regime of constant (average) money wages and falling prices. That is a natural outcome for a society where technological progress is proceeding. Historical periods where this result roughly emerged (e.g., Britain in the three decades after the Napoleonic wars and the quarter-century after 1873) were marked by rapid increases in real wages and productivity. The major effect of such a regime would be to diminish the role of labor unions and their leadership, since the market mechanism rather than collective bargaining agreements would mainly assure real wage increases; and historically, such periods have seen not only an increase in real

wages but also a shift in the distribution of income in favor of labor. In any case, the goal of stable prices (or prices increasing at 2–3 per cent per annum) is quite arbitrary in a society undergoing regular technological progress. Also, see above, p. 121.

6. See, notably Charles L. Schultze et al., *Setting National Priorities, The 1972 Budget*, Washington, D.C., 1971.
7. For a statement of ten basic propositions required to underpin an effective approach to the cities, see Daniel P. Moynihan, "Toward a National Urban Policy," *The Public Interest*, Fall 1969, No. 17.
8. In this connection, the wide range of results in American cities should be noted. See, for example, the evaluation of Kenneth B. Clark and Jeannette Hopkins, *A Relevant War Against Poverty*, New York, 1968, 1969, especially Chapter V.
9. Charles L. Schultze et al., *Setting National Priorities, The 1972 Budget*, pp. 331–333.
10. John Newhouse et al., *U.S. Troops in Europe*, Washington, D.C., 1971. For the interweaving of trade, monetary, and security relations in more general terms, see Edward R. Fried, "U.S. Foreign Economic Policy: The Search for a Strategy," in Henry Owen (ed.), *U.S. Foreign Policy for the 1970's*, Washington, D.C. 1972.
11. For an account of the offset problem, its evolution, and future alternatives, see, notably, John Newhouse et al., *op. cit.*, pp. 125–144.
12. *Tripartite Report on Reshaping the International Economic Order*, Washington, D.C., December 21, 1971. This excellent document resulted from a conference jointly sponsored by The Japanese Economic Research Center, the European Community Institute of University Studies, and The Brookings Institution.
13. Charles L. Schultze et al., *loc. cit.*, p. 67.
14. Frank L. Klingberg traces the oscillation of the American view of the world back to the origins of the nation in "The Historical Alternation of Moods in American Foreign Policy," *World Politics*, January 1952, pp. 239–273. He identifies, as follows, four introvert phases since 1776, averaging about 21 years in length; three extrovert phases, averaging about 27 years.

INTROVERT AND EXTROVERT PHASES

Introvert dates	*Extrovert dates*
1776–1798	1798–1824
1824–1844	1844–1871
1871–1891	1891–1919
1919–1940	1940–

In the early 1950s Klingberg concluded (pp. 271–272) quite correctly: ". . . it seems logical to expect America to retreat, to some extent at least, from so much world involvement, and perhaps to do so sometime in the 1960's."

In a later article ("Historical Periods, Trends, and Cycles in International Relations," *Conflict Resolution*, Vol. XIV, No. 4, December 1970, pp. 505–511) Klingberg dates the end of the "extrovert" phase beginning in 1940 as 1966–1967. As indicated above (p. 184), I am inclined to date the beginning of a mood of retraction in the 1960s from 1963, in the wake of the Cuba missile crisis. Klingberg examines the possible reasons for this apparent cyclical pattern with some subtlety; but no conclusive single explanation emerges or firm basis for prediction.

15. *The Memoirs of Cordell Hull*, Vol. II, New York, 1948, pp. 1013–1014. See, also, James MacGregor Burns, *Roosevelt: The Soldier of Freedom*, New York, 1970, pp. 154–159. Burns notes that on December 6, 1941, Roosevelt was drafting a personal message to the Japanese emperor. Burns paraphrases one of the critical passages as follows (p. 158): "The President dwelt on the influx of Japanese military strength into Indochina. The people of the Philippines, the East Indies, Malaya, Thailand were alarmed. They were sitting on a keg of dynamite." The message, a final effort to break the diplomatic deadlock, was held up by a Japanese military censor and was delivered after war had begun (p. 161).
16. W. W. Rostow, *The United States in the World Arena*, p. 538.
17. Achille Loria, quoted in F. J. Turner, *The Frontier in American History*, New York, 1920, p. 11.

Index

Index

Abel, Elie, 251, 506
ABMs, *see* Antiballistic missiles
Abrams, Gen. Creighton W., 439, 468, 523
  pacification efforts of, 523, 550
  on troop morale, 552
Acheson, Dean, 72, 112, 162, 165, 362
  in Berlin task force, 169, 224
  economic proposal of, 11
  foreign-policy orientation of, 164
  on Great Britain, 244
  on his duties, 167
  NATO task force headed by, 400
  on Truman's leadership, 193
Adenauer, Konrad, 229, 230, 391
  Franco-German hegemony and, 246–247
  funeral of, 399
Adoula, Cyrille, 191
AID (Agency for International Development), 422, 423
Aid programs, federal
  foreign, *see* Foreign aid
  local and state grants, 328, 592
Air Vietnam, 374
Airline machinists strike (1966), 321–322
Alabama, University of, 154
Albania, 223, 379
Algeria, 81, 186, 371, 570
  civil war in, 211, 226
  1965 coup in, 420
Algiers Conference (June 1965), 371, 567
Alliance for Progress, 91, 216–217, 252, 407
  initial focus of, 216
  launching of, 188, 215
  new direction of, 425
  See also Inter-American Committee on the Alliance for Progress
American Dilemma, An (Myrdal), 155
American Policy in Asia, An (Rostow), 283
American Revolution, 606
American Style, The (Morison), xvi
American University speech (June 10, 1963), 180
An Loc, 559, 562
Andean Common Market, 430
Antiballistic missiles (ABMs), 384–388, 563
  limited system of, 386–388
  Soviet, 369, 384
Antipoverty program, *see* Poverty program
Antiwar movement, 429, 482, 484–503, 531, 557
  intellectual members of, 490–492
  major demonstration by, 423
  moral content of, 484–487

Viet Cong stimulation of, 516
waning of, 545–546
See also Youth—antiwar actions of
APAG (Atlantic Policy Advisory Group), 236–237, 257
Aqaba, Gulf of, 407, 415–418
Arab–Israeli relations
culminating in 6-day war (June 1967), 415–419, 527
causes, 407, 416–417, 580
cease-fire negotiated, 418, 570–571, 572
European impotence, 405
example of diffusion of power, 415
U.S.–USSR dialogue, 376–377
Eisenhower's recommendations for, 97
negotiated settlement of, 571–573, 599
quiescent, 196–197
Arkansas racial crisis (1957), 66
Armed Forces Council, 439, 446
Arms control, *see* Nuclear diplomacy—nuclear arms control; SALT Talks
Arms Control and Disarmament Agency, 176
ARVN (Army of the Republic of Vietnam), 271, 495, 553, 558, 559, 560
under Diem, 446
elite units of, 447
peasant criticism of, 273
as puppet force, 466
relative strength, 558
rural pacification under, 282, 458
setbacks of, 448, 449
Asian Development Bank, 423–424, 568, 569
formation of, 427
proposal of, 508
"Assured destruction" capability, 384–386, 388, 389
Aswan Dam (Egypt), 196, 199, 203
Atlantic Policy Advisory Group (APAG), 236–237, 257
Atomic Energy Act (1958 revision), 81–82
Atomic Energy Committee, 75, 79, 239
Atomic weapons, *see* Nuclear weapons
Australia, 416, 464, 469
foreign-aid expenditures of, 402, 403
Vietnam policy meeting in, 515
in Vietnam War, 464
Automotive wage–price guideposts, 139, 140–143
Ayub Khan, 107, 204, 205, 206
in 1965 war, 409–410

Badeau, John, 197
Baghdad Pact (1955), 35, 87, 97
break in, 95
Baldwin, Hanson, 516
Ball, George, 246
Banfield, Edward C., 348–349, 544
Barnett, Ross, 153
"Barrier, the," concept, 512
BASC (Berlin Air Safety Center), 233–234
Basic National Security Policy (BNSP) paper, 174, 175–176
Batista y Zaldívar, Fulgencio, 49–50, 100
Bay of Pigs invasion (April 1961), 116, 209–215, 609
genesis of, 210–213
training of guerrillas, 102–103, 116
moral dilemma of, 212–213
political aspects of, 213–214
space program not boosted by, 183–184
Belgium, 404
aid program of, 401–403
Congolese colony of, 52–53
Belgian armed forces, 191
as MLF participant, 240, 248
NATO headquarters in Brussels, 400
Bell, David, 236, 296, 453
Berkeley campus demonstrations (1964), 120, 333, 352–353
Berle, Adolf, 210
Berlin, divided, 229–234, 246
Allied access to, 37, 38, 83
formal agreement, 563–564
East German treaties and
Soviet treaty, 83–84, 228-229
East–West treaty, 547
Kennedy–Khrushchev discussion of, 218, 222–224, 228–229
1961–1962 crisis in, 26, 173, 228–233, 630–631
Berlin Wall erected, 231–233
earlier crisis revived, 222–223
flow of refugees, 231
Soviet gamble for leverage over, 253–255
task force on, 169
Berlin Air Safety Center (BASC), 233–234

Berlin blockade (1948–1949), 13, 69, 388
Berlin Control Council, 7, 12, 13
Berlin Viability program, 232
Bethlehem Steel, 539
Birmingham demonstrations (April–May 1963), 153–154
Birth control, 423, 583, 597
Bissell, Richard, 169, 209, 210
Black, Eugene, 510
Black Muslims, 157
Black Panthers, 157, 356, 544
Black power, 157, 340, 544–545
Blacks, *see* Racial crisis
Blough, Roger, 142, 143–144, 299
BNSP (Basic National Security Policy) paper, 174, 175
Bohlen, Charles E., 245, 365
Bonsal, Philip W., 100, 101, 102
Borneo, 195
Bosch, Juan, 207, 412, 414
Boun Oum, Prince of Laos, 48, 109
Boumedienne, Houari, 371, 420, 570
Bowie, Robert, 238
Brandt, Willy, 232, 584
Brazil, 411, 414, 582
Brentano, Heinrich von, 236, 395
Brest-Litovsk, Treaty of, 586
Brezhnev, Leonid I., 566, 587
  comes to power, 370
  military policy of, 372–373
Brimmer, Andrew, 346, 347
Brinkley, David, 295
Brookings budget study, 591, 598
Bruce, David, 247
Buddhist activists (radicals), 454–455
  constitutional demands of, 454
  repression of, 290–293, 294
    protests causing, 291, 292
Bulgarian–Soviet communique (May 21, 1962), 253
Bundy, McGeorge, 167–168, 169, 177, 232
  advisory function of, 167–168
  in Bay of Pigs fiasco, 209, 215
  as national-security planner, 358, 359
  as Vietnam adviser, 448
Bunker, Ellsworth, 105, 199, 409, 415
  Dutch–Indonesian talks conducted by, 194
  as Indian ambassador, 570
  present at NSC Tuesday lunch, 358
  as Vietnamese ambassador, 456, 480, 510, 519
Burma, 15, 205, 496, 565
  guerrilla movement in, 13, 283, 488, 524
  as nonaligned nation, 225
Burns, Arthur, 61, 115
By Love Possessed (Cozzens), 304
Byrnes, James F., 7, 10
  treaties negotiated by, 11

Cabell, Pearré, 209
Cambodia, 553–554, 567
  contingency planning on, 513
  infiltration route through, 504, 524, 554
  U.S. invasion of, 352, 439, 546, 553
Camp David meeting (Oct. 1, 1966), 378
Canada, 402–403, 566
Cantril, Albert, 481, 498
Carretera Marginal, 430
Castro Ruz, Fidel, 49–52, 99–103, 217, 505
  in Bay of Pigs fiasco, 208, 211–212, 214–215
  charismatic nature of, 100–101
  domestic economic policy of, 56–57, 58
    admission of failure, 570
  Guantanamo Base ploy of, 408–409
  in missile crisis, 253, 257
  political ideology of, 49–51, 101–102
Castro Ruz, Raúl, 100, 101, 102
  Moscow visited by, 254
Central American Common Market, 430
Central Intelligence Agency, *see* CIA
Central Rural Reconstruction Council, 457
Chamoun, Camille, 95–96
Chile, 567, 587
China, Communist, 13, 15, 261–263, 270, 606
  Asian regionalism and, 428–429
  civil war in, 13, 16
  diplomatic reconciliation with, 432–434, 564–566, 576
    Hanoi's fear of China–U.S. rapprochement, 556, 564, 566
    high-level, xv, 564, 573
  emerges as power, 18
  as example of U.S. problems in Asia, 493
  economic development of, 55–56, 57, 275
    decline in production, 372

India contrasted, 104–106, 582
future of, 584, 599–600
Indian border conflict of, 204–206, 261–262
Indonesian alliance of, 371, 407
in nuclear club
Asian power base, 580
French program compared, 82
nonproliferation involving, 379, 434, 496
testing begun, 369, 370, 380
USSR policy differences, 26–27, 29–35, 36–37, 38, 615
research on, 361
M.I.T. project, 282–283
role of, in Vietnam War, 42–44, 45, 270, 565
advisory capacity, 40–41
application of domino theory, 295
Hanoi's alignment, 262–263, 428–429
Laotian involvement, 46–47, 524, 599
Soviet role vs., 22–23, 43–44, 49, 370–371, 557
U.S. provocation potential, 266, 286–287, 513
U.S. public opinion, 485–486, 492
Sino–Soviet relations, 13, 16, 252, 370–371, 587
Algiers Conference, 371
over developing states, 86
failure of Soviet policy, 4
four critical areas, 28–38, 94, 96
Franco–American relations compared, 77–78, 79
Moscow–Peking debate, 21–24
trade relations, 51
Sino–Soviet split, 404, 587
border conflict, 370, 547
cessation of polemics, 370
documentation, 181
over missile crisis, 262
See also Cultural Revolution; Great Leap Forward; United Nations—Chinese admission to
China, Nationalist (Taiwan), 14, 88, 428
dependence of, 1
Khrushchev's comment on, 226
mainland diplomacy and
overtures to Taiwan, 433
unsettling western détente, 564, 565
See also Quemoy–Matsu crisis
Chou En-lai, 23, 36
Christian, George, 358
Churchill, Sir Winston S., 4–5, 6
"Iron Curtain" speech by, 12
CIA (Central Intelligence Agency), 202, 519
Bay of Pigs directed by, 209, 214
training of guerrillas, 102–103
Guatemalan coup staged by, 212
intelligence data flow from, 364
in national-security planning, 358
CIAP, *see* Inter-American Committee on the Alliance for Progress
Civil defense, 72
Civil rights, *see* Racial crisis
Civil Rights Act of 1957, 337, 338, 339
enactment of, 65–66
Civil Rights Act of 1960, 339
Civil Rights Act of 1964, 338–339, 350
Civil Rights Act of 1965, 339–340, 350
Clark, Kenneth, 158
Clay, Gen. Lucius, 232
Clayton–Acheson proposal (1946), 11
Clifford, Clark, 305, 520
Clifton, Ted, 209
Cline, Ray, 259
Clough, Arthur, 150
Cold War, 4–15, 90, 124, 562, 577
American style strained by, 501–502
beginning of, 4–7
pause in, 14–15
revisionist debate on, 7–8
turning point in, 298
unfavorable balance in, 301
unfolding of, 12–14
U.S. advantage in, 561–562, 585
Cominform, 13
Common Market, *see* Andean Common Market; European Economic Community
Communist countries, 12–14, 21–38, 54–58, 370–377
contrasting political styles in, 38
developing-world strategy of, 87–88, 185–186
domestic economic problems of, 55–58
eastern bloc of, 8–10, 12, 587
Balkan states, 6
breakup, 16
economic dependence, 51
formation, 2–3
see also Czechoslovakia; Poland

future of, 599–600
meeting of leaders of (1957), 74
1963–1969 policy shifts in, 370–372, 403–404
peaceful vs. nonpeaceful ideologies of, 22–24
regional policy toward, 426–427
rise of "factionalism" in, 27
Stalinist control over, 12–13, 16
Warsaw Pact countries, 180, 223, 253
NATO mutual troop reductions, 547–548, 563, 576
See also Albania; China, Communist; Cuba; Soviet Union; Vietnam—North; Yugoslavia
Communist Party, International, 367
Castro's relation to, 49, 50–51, 102
CPSU leadership of, 21, 29
of Indonesia, 193, 194, 409, 420
Party Congresses
19th, 15
20th, 87
22nd, 252
23rd, 371
positive objective of, 585–586
Sino–Soviet split affecting, 34
unambiguous leader of, 54
See also National Liberation Front; Pathet Lao; Viet Minh
Congo, 190–192, 228
Katangan independence from, 53, 190
revolution in (1960), 53
U.S. aircraft dispatched to, 405, 411
Congress, U.S., 17, 182, 333, 540–542
Atomic Energy Committee of, 75, 79, 239
civil-rights laws enacted by, 338–339
congressional delegates to OAS, 218
defense measures approved by
ABM debate, 386–387
military budget, 69, 71, 171–172, 173
MLF proposal, 391–392
Skybolt appropriations, 244
development programs before, 91, 568
congressional suspicions, 199, 202–203
foreign-aid requests, 186–188, 430, 569, 602
Economic Report to (1962), 323
foreign-affairs reports to, 563, 568
foreign trade policy before, 234
legislative record of President Kennedy, 149–150, 298–299
civil-rights legislation, 152–153, 154–155, 159, 332, 338
Southeast Asia question before
Executive policy opposed, 268, 484, 496, 519
isolationist sentiment, 564
resolution on the war, 505
space program before, 182, 184
strike-breaking legislation before, 321
tax measures before, 317, 318, 528, 542, 592
negative income tax, 574
See also Senate
Connor, T. Eugene ("Bull"), 153, 333
Conservation, *see* Ecology
Constituent Assembly of S. Vietnam, 455–456
Constitution, U.S., 152
Consumer protection legislation, 331
Cornford, F. M., 26
Court of Appeals, Fifth Circuit, 153
Credibility gap, 412
Cronkite, Walter, 294, 519
Cross, James E., 119
Crouzet, François, 354
Cuba, 54
arms shipments from, 505
domestic economy of, 56–57, 58, 570
missile crisis in, 179, 251–263, 297, 562
alleged request for missiles, 253
blockade ("selective quarantine"), 257, 258, 259
causing MLF defeat, 250
political benefits, 177, 243, 250
"society survival" and, 388
Soviet objectives, 254–255
outline of Cuban revolution, 49–52
U.S. involvement in, 49–52, 54, 100–103, 208–215, 654–656
apprehension over Cuban showcase, 217–218
Cuba expelled from OAS, 218, 221
economic exploitation, 51
Guantanamo naval base, 409
Khrushchev's criticism, 49
land reform touching, 101
U.S.-trained guerrillas, 102–103, 116
see also Bay of Pigs invasion
Cultural Revolution, 361, 372, 420, 427, 680–681

ending of, 570
origin of, 372
precluding communication, 432
Cyprus, 411
Czechoslovakia, 51
Soviet invasion of, 377, 521, 587

"Damage limiting" capability, 384, 386, 388
Danang, 465, 474
regional resistance in, 454
Defense, Department of (Pentagon), 161–162, 166, 386
on arms trade, 236
civilian management of, 171
Establishment members of, 494, 495
March on the Pentagon (Oct. 1967), 423
Pentagon Papers, 546, 689–691
reorganization of, 71, 162
See also Joint Chiefs of Staff
De Gaulle, Charles, 302, 365
in Algerian crisis, 211
deterrence arrangements with, 245–246
Franco-German pact proposal, 246
MLF, 240, 241–242, 248, 392, 393–394
on German negotiations, 405
leadership of
estimate of his abilities, 80–81
overwhelming political victory, 243
twilight of his career, 399
as U.S. policy problem, 77, 79–82, 310, 367, 404, 406
Democratic Party, 152–153, 303, 521
polarized over leftist students, 356
strained over Vietnam War
1968 Convention, 311, 487, 545
party schism, 311, 482
Desegregation, *see* Racial crisis
Development Loan Fund (DLF), 91, 105
Diem, Ngo Dinh, 42–43, 109–110, 271–273, 275–279, 439, 446
deficiencies of, 43, 109, 272, 286
military program of, 269, 282
in 1963 political crisis, 290–294, 455
his assassination, 135, 292, 294
pacification program of, 281, 457
reports written about, 265, 270, 275, 276
Dillon, Douglas, 103, 126, 137
on German arms trade, 236
Dirksen, Everett, 339
Disarmament, *see* German problem—disarmament phase of; Nuclear diplomacy—nuclear arms control; SALT Talks
DLF (Development Loan Fund), 91, 105
Dobrynin, Anatoly F., 178–179, 254
Dodd, Thomas, 180
Dominican Republic, 207
OAS investigation of, 103
U.S. intervention in, 411–415, 527
Domino theory, 108–109, 295, 429, 494, 496
Dong, Pham Van, 435
Dorticós, Osvaldo, 219
Duan, Le, 41, 43, 371
Dulles, Allen, 49, 88, 112
in Bay of Pigs debacle, 209, 214
as Establishment figure, 492
Kennedy briefed by, 116
Dulles, John Foster, 36, 96–97, 126, 166
development initiative of, 89–90
as Establishment figure, 492
European diplomacy of, 79–80
Durbrow, Elbridge, 109
Dutschke, Rudi, 354

Eban, Abba, 416–417
Ecology (pollution, conservation), 334, 528, 574
fiscal outlays for, 541
future of, 583
legislation to promote, 331
water pollution first acknowledged, 62
Economic Advisers, Council of, 137, 142
annual reports of
1962, 138
1965, 316
"inflation alerts" announced by, 538
wage-price guideposts enunciated by, 143, 323
Economic aid, *see* Aid programs; Foreign aid
Economic and Social Act of Rio de Janeiro (Nov. 30, 1965), 425
Economic Commission for Europe, 11, 16, 214
"Economic Conditions in the United States" (Samuelson), 120
Economic Development, Task Force on, 568
Economic inflation and recession, *see* Inflation; Recession

Economic power, diffusion of, 576, 581–585
population control essential to, 583
by 2000 A.D., 581–582
Economist, London, 558
EEC, *see* European Economic Community
Egypt, 196–200, 570–572, 585, 599
neutralist position of, 197
role of, in Lebanon–Jordan crisis, 94–96
in 6-day war, 415–417, 419
cease-fire negotiations, 570–571, 572
Eisenhower, Dwight D.
memoir of, *see: Waging Peace*
as Supreme Allied Commander, 451–452
Eisenhower administration, 37, 59–124, 237
author's service in, xvii
developing-nations programs of, 86–92, 187, 207, 407
great debate, 88–92
primary objective, 86–87
domestic programs of, 59–67
economic, 60–64
racial, 64–66
Indian economic development programs of, 88, 91, 104–107
barren Indian relations, 570
ideological testing ground, 104–105
interregnum phase of, 111–124, 264
briefing sessions, 116, 136, 494
shift from conservatism, 111–113
Johnson's importance to, 366
later administrations vs., 296, 575, 578
Latin America policy of, 49, 99–103, 211
Cuban invasion mounted, 102–103, 214
land reform affecting, 101
Latin anti-Americanism, 99–100, 102
Middle East policy of, 94–98, 571
basis of, 94
military alliance system, 87
President's UN address, 96–98
military/space objectives of, 68–73, 115, 182, 547
BNSP paper on, 175
conservative bias, 112–113
criticism of military policy, 71–73
first satellite launched, 71
interservice rivalry in missile development, 69
view of manned lunar flight, 181
in Quemoy–Matsu crisis, 37
security arrangements of, 18, 165–166
Southeast Asia policy of, 108–110, 115, 265, 494
strains within, 126
West European allies of, 75–84, 238
Europe's frustration with U.S., 74
sharing nuclear secrets, 75
Ellsberg, Daniel, 519, 546
Employment Act of 1946, 62
England, *see* Great Britain
Erhard, Ludwig, 394
MLF arrangements with, 392–393
NATO troop reductions and, 395–397
Eshkol, Levi, 416
Establishment, U.S., 492–497, 532
history of, 492–494
military, 381
European Atomic Energy Community (Agency) (EURATOM), 382, 383
creation of, 74
European Economic Community (Common Market) (EEC), 234, 246, 394, 398, 404, 610–611
agricultural settlement by, 392, 398
British entry into, 234, 241–243, 244–245, 584
creation of, 74
de Gaulle's boycott of, 394
French return to, 399
U.S. weight behind, 585
European recovery program, *see* Marshall Plan
"European Trip and 'Greatness' in the 1960s, The" (Rostow), 300–301
European unity as postwar goal, 17
ExCom, 257–258

Fall, Bernard B., 42, 289
Family Assistance Plan, 544
Faubus, Orval, 66
Fedayeen, 571
Federal Reserve Board, 317
Federov, E. K., 178, 179
Fidel Castro (Matthews), 54
First World War, 600
Force Publique, 53
Foreign aid, 305, 402, 403
to Arab states, 97, 98

to Cuba, 51, 101
to developing nations, 186–189, 421–425, 431
comparative table, 402
development policy debate, xviii, 88–92
food–population balance, 422
fundamental task, 185
Latin American investment, 216, 424–425, 430
military aid, 88, 187, 262
"mutual aid" concept, 425
Nixon administration, 568–569
responsibility of recipients, 597
tables showing changes, 92, 187, 421
Egyptian aid expanded, 197–198
expansion of military aid, 550
to India, *see* India—development aid to
to Laos, 46, 48
power diffused through, 18, 584
resources for, 112
to South Vietnam, 108, 291
See also Marshall Plan
Forrestal, Michael, 282
Fort Bragg speech by W. W. Rostow (June 28, 1961), 284, 286
France, 244–246, 273, 600
aid program of, 402, 403
in Berlin crisis, 230, 231
communist party of, 12
Franco–American relations, 77–81, 606
independent nuclear program, 78–80, 81
Johnson's assessment, 399
Kennedy's pithy appraisal, 367
MLF arrangements, 237, 241, 392, 393–394
nonproliferation including, 380, 579–580
pressure on the dollar, 394, 397
over Southeast Asia, 266
de Gaulle's 1962 single-party majority, 243
French–Algerian war, 211
health of democracy in, 243
May 1968 riots in, 467
nuclear testing by, 228
radical youth in, 354
See also French Indochina War; NATO—Paris summit meetings of; Paris talks on Vietnam
Franks, Oliver, 249
Freeman, Orville, 398, 453
French Indochina War, 14, 272, 609
decisive battles of Vietnam and, 465
financing of, by U.S., 493
settlement of, *see* Geneva Accords (Conference) (1954)
See also Vietnam War
Fulbright, J. William, 405, 484

Gagarin, Yuri, 182
Gaither Report (April 1957), 73
Galbraith, John Kenneth, 120, 121
as Indian ambassador, 262
Gallup polls, 480
measuring Johnson's popularity, 479, 481
of support for the war, 480, 498
Gandhi, Indira, 410
Ganges–Brahmaputra river system, 597
Geneva Accords (Conference) (1954), 14, 267
failure of, 42
on Laos, 45, 46
violation of, 487
Geneva Accords (Conference) on Laos (1962), 252, 290
convening of, 268, 370–371
on infiltration route, 287–289, 448, 504
memorandum on, 506–507
as morally binding, 487, 489
Soviet commitment under, 376
German problem, 82–84
disarmament (neutralization) phase of
Allied defense problems, 235, 236
Cold War issue, 5, 7, 9–12
nonproliferation including, 492, 578, 579, 580
U.S. troop reductions, 395–397
divided Berlin as, *see* Berlin
fear of German revival, 80, 82, 240
Franco–German pact as, 246
historical problem, 428
monetary parochialism as, 397–398, 404
Ostpolitik as, 401, 564
of rearmament (MLF participation), 237, 240–242, 247, 391–392
reunification phase of, 228–229, 246
emergence as issue, 4
unilateral German peace treaty, 83–84, 223, 228–229
Germany, 584, 600
communist party of, 586

foreign-aid expenditures of, 402, 403
1953 revolt in, 16
U.S. bonds purchased by, 595
Ghana, 200–203
Convention People's Party (CPP), 200
financing of dam in, 202–203
independence of, 200
Ghetto life, profile of, 156, 341, 348
Giap, Gen. Vo-Nguyen, 41–42
military strategy debated by, 460
victory formula of, 450
Ginsburgh, Robert, 514
Gittings, John, 31
Gizenga, Antoine, 53, 191
Glassboro meeting (June 1967), 387, 479, 547
Goals for Americans (Commission on National Goals), 117, 118
Goldberg, Arthur, 122, 358
his role in steel negotiations, 138–139, 141–142
Goldwater, Barry, 333, 355
Goodpaster, Andrew, 166, 264
Gordon, Kermit, 137, 142
Goulart, João, 310, 411, 420
Grand Design, 236, 247, 302
Grand Tactician, The (Pistrak), 225, 256
Great Britain, 400, 579, 584, 601
aid program of, 402, 403
Anglo-American relations, 74, 234, 240–246, 606
MLF arrangements, 237, 240–242, 247, 248, 249, 392–393
over Southeast Asia, 266, 267
Skybolt development, 242–245
2-key nuclear agreement, 32, 76, 77
Anglo-French relations
brief history, 78
over Common Market, 241–242, 244–245
nuclear asymmetry, 78–80, 82
British Crown colonies, 195
in Cold War, *see* Churchill
domestic economy of, 397
devaluation of the pound, 398
industrial revolution, 577, 606
fading grandeur of, 404
German question before
Berlin crisis, 230, 231
British troops in Germany, 395–397
in India–Pakistan conflict, 204, 205
Middle East policy of, 380
crisis settlement, 416, 417
intervention, 95, 96, 97, 98
nonproliferation including, 380–381, 382
Great Leap Forward, 27, 32, 38, 56
failure of, 57, 426
Great Society, 328, 333, 528
Greece, 247, 411
civil war in, 12–13, 16, 286
"Greek formula," 514, 551
Green, Marshall, 409
Gromyko, Andrei A., 377, 378
on Cuban missile installations, 179
Guam conferences on Vietnam
1966, 456
1967, 458, 509
Guam doctrine, 550, 576
Guantanamo water crisis (1963), 409
Guatemala, CIA-backed coup in, 212
Guerrilla warfare, 52, 169, 264, 283–286, 488
as Cold War tool, 12
counterinsurgency training by U.S.
Cuban guerrillas, 102–103, 116
South Vietnamese forces, 269
in defense budget, 172
ending U.S. imperialism in the Philippines, 493
Establishment response to, 494–495
measuring progress in, 279
in Middle East, 571
nonproliferation threatened by, 580
"Plan Six" on, 506
research tools on, 265
special problems of, 119
third stage of, 447
See also National liberation—wars of
"Guerrilla Warfare in the Underdeveloped Areas" (Rostow), 284, 286
Guevara, Ernesto (Che), 52, 54, 254
Bolivian campaign of, 420
Castro influenced by, 100, 102
at Punta del Este conference, 217
study of his works, 265

Haiphong–Hanoi bombing raids, 510–512
Haiphong raids (1972), 560
Haiti, 219
Hammarskjold, Dag, 191, 228
Hanoi-Haiphong bombing raids (1966–1967), 510–512
"Harmel exercise," 401
Harriman, Averell, 165

in arms negotiations, 180–181, 262
in Southeast Asia tangle, 267, 268, 523
closing off infiltration routes, 287–289
on Stalin, 3
Head Start program, 341
Heller, Walter, 137, 142, 236
Herter, Christian, 77, 116
as Establishment figure, 492
MLF proposal of, 238
Hilsman, Roger, 282
Ho Chi Minh, 287, 476
domestic economic policy of, 56, 57
Geneva Accords affecting, 14, 42
Sino–Soviet diplomacy of, 43–44, 49
South Vietnam's view of, 273
Ho Chi Minh Trail, *see* Laos—infiltration route through
Holland, *see* Netherlands
Holt, Harold, 416, 464
Honolulu conferences on Vietnam
1963, 292
1966, xviii, 452–453, 455, 457–458
1968, 468
Hoover, Herbert, Jr., 88, 89
Hop Tac, 457
Hopkins, Harry, 5, 7
Hornig, Donald, 181
Hue, 460, 465
in 1972 offensive, 559–560, 562
regional resistance in, 454
Tet offensive in, 518
Hull, Cordell, 600
Humphrey, George, 88, 90
Humphrey, Hubert H., 339, 358, 545
as arms-control crusader, 180
in 1960 campaign, 127
Hungarian Revolution (1956), 16
Huntley–Brinkley Report (television program), 295
Hussein, King of Jordan, 95, 417

IAB, *see* Inter-American Development Bank
IAEA (International Atomic Energy Agency), 72, 382
ICBMs, *see* Nuclear weapons—ICBM development
ICC, *see* International Control Commission
I.D.A., *see* International Development Association
Ikeda, Hayato, 237
Imports, surcharge on, 539, 566
India, 15, 35, 362, 587
communist party of, 13
development aid to, 88, 104–107
campaign issue, 128
consortium arrangements, 91, 188
drought years, 403, 422–423
economic normalization, 597
ideological testing ground, 104–105
table for 1952–1959, 636
future growth of, 582
geopolitical conflicts of
Chinese border dispute, 204–206, 261–266
with Pakistan, *see* Pakistan—Indian conflict with
as nonaligned nation, 225
nonproliferation including, 379, 380, 381, 496, 564, 578, 580
Southeast Asia interest of, 565
in UN, 580
U.S. myopia toward, 570, 587
Indochina
Japanese occupation of, 470, 600, 606
See also Cambodia; French Indochina War; Laos; Thailand; Vietnam; Vietnam War
Indonesia, 15, 18, 192–196, 200, 585, 648–649
economic development of, 428, 524
the Hague consortium, 403, 424
politics vs., 193
review of development, 361
guerrilla movement in, 13, 488
increasing U.S. distance from, 409
overthrow of Sukarno in, 420
Peking alliance of, 371, 407
Inflation, 118, 120, 315–320, 323, 537–538, 574
cost-push, 112, 121
dissidence stemming from, 479
earnings increase during (1965–1968), 318–320
growth without, 590
"inflation alerts," 538
Latin American, xvii, 425
military outlays causing, 315
Nixon statement on, 537–538
price stability to curb, 323, 325–326
unacceptable level of, 589–590
welfare spending during, 543
Influence, spheres of, 8
Integration, *see* Racial crisis

Inter-American Committee on the Alliance for Progress (CIAP), 216, 218
author's service on, xvii, 363
country-by-country review of, 425
creation of, 216, 424
neglect of, 569
Inter-American Development Bank (IAB), 423, 430, 568
creation of, 91, 99
Inter-American Economic and Social Council, 215, 217
Intercontinental ballistic missiles, *see* Nuclear weapons—ICBM development
International Atomic Energy Agency (IAEA), 72, 382
International Control Commission (ICC), 45, 266, 285
Laos policed by, 287–288
supra-nationality of, 228
International Development Association (I.D.A.), 423, 568
formation of, 91
International Monetary Fund, *see* World Bank
Iran, 53, 207, 584
Khrushchev's view of, 225–226
Iraq, 87
coup in (1958), 35, 36, 94–96
Irian, West, 193–195, 561
Israel
nuclear potential of, 578
See also Arab–Israeli relations
Italy, 579
aid program of, 402
communist party of, 12
in EEC, 404
U.S. relations with
missile base installations, 32, 76, 77, 237
MLF participation, 241, 247, 248, 391

Jackson, Barbara Ward, 107, 200, 202, 362
Jackson, C. D., 96, 126, 167
in development policy debate, 89–90
Jackson, Robert, 200
Japan, 10, 106, 206
Asian regionalism covering, 428
communist party of, 13
economic development of
future, 584
industrial power, 529, 566, 588
post-war recovery, 14, 15, 63
Japanese–American relations, 381, 494, 496
improvement of relations, 237
mutual defense agreements, 87, 585
U.S. national interest, 595–596
nonproliferation including, 381, 496, 564, 578, 580
Soviet overtures toward, 566
stabilization of, 529
in UN, 580
in World War II, 1, 2, 3, 6, 78
fiscal resources, 582
post-war occupation, 9
Southeast Asian occupation, 470, 600–601, 606
See also Okinawa
Jarring, Gunnar V., 179, 573
Jenkins, Alfred, 361
JOBS (Job Opportunities in the Business Sector), 342–343
Johnson, Lyndon B., xiii, xvii–xix, 236, 303–533, 575
arms-control program of, 377–390, 495
nonproliferation treaty, 369, 377–383, 390
test-ban treaty, 180
assessment of his administration, 526–533
alleged lack of sophistication, 366–368
by his critics, 167
hostility to his style, 531–532
impressive domestic achievements, 529, 530
as Commander-in-Chief, 310–311, 405, 435–525, 550–552, 601
conferences with S. Vietnamese, xviii, 453, 455–456, 457–458, 467–468, 509
future evaluation, 529–530
his Establishment opponents, 496
his popularity at home, 477–479, 481, 516, 527–528, 530, 532
national dialogue on the war, 484–490, 510–511, 519
political and military progress, 451–459
strain on U.S. political style, 501–503
U.S. troop mobilization, 427, 448,

463–464, 479, 508, 512–513, 519–520
watching S. Vietnam disintegrate, 432, 439–449
widening press opposition, 519
developing-nations approach of, 406–434, 571
aid programs, 402–403, 421–425, 430, 431
high-posture adventure, 411–415
low-posture exercises, 408–411
regional policy, xviii, 423, 426–432, 510, 527
domestic economy under, 313–335, 406, 528–529, 542
balance-of-payments problems, 395–397
employment rate, 315–316, 324–325
revolution in public spending, 327–328
rising prices, 529
table showing economic expansion, 314
tax increase, 520–521
legislative record of President, 149, 150, 328–332
domestic legislation listed by function, 330–332
as Majority Leader, 65, 71, 303, 366
military policy of, 305, 369
ABM development, 384–388
Soviet nuclear parity, 372–377
table of defense budget, 385
in national elections
1960 campaign, 127
1964 election, 333
withdrawal from 1968 contest, 311, 356–357, 482–483, 520–521, 529
national security affairs under, 168, 358–366
anticipatory meetings, 361–362
Tuesday lunch setting, 359–360
race problems encountered by, 310, 332, 334–351, 406, 477, 528, 530
development approach, 343–345
functional approach, 342–343
growth approach, 346
northern sector, 340–341, 350–351
southern sector, 338–340, 350
unpopular policy, 543
radical youth movement faced by, 352–356, 530
antiwar sector, 352, 497–500, 530
four critical factors, 353–355
his unpopularity, 545
political consequences, 355–357
succession of, 303–305
classic American style, 301–302
return to generational normalcy, 120
Texas Hill Country background of, 304, 337, 423, 531
as Vice President, 140, 158, 304–305, 366
Berlin visit, 232
report on Vietnam, 269–270
role in space policy, 181–182, 184
Southeast Asia tour, 269
west European alliances of, 310, 377–378, 391–405, 527
pressure on the dollar, 394, 397
trade policy, 397–399
U.S. troop reduction, 395–397
Johnson, U. Alexis, 239, 505
Johnston, Eric, 112
Joint Atomic Energy Committee, 75, 79, 239
Joint Chiefs of Staff, 161, 601
ABM program challenged by, 386
President briefed by, 172
Southeast Asia directed by, 359
focus shifted to Vietnam, 269
strengthening of, 71
White House liaison with, 514
Jones, Howard, 409
Jordan
crisis in, *see* Lebanon–Jordan crisis
guerrilla movement in, 571
in 6-day war, 416, 419, 571
Jorden, William, 232, 514
Jorden report (Dec. 1962), 278
July 26 Movement, 50, 102
Jury-trial provision (Civil Rights Act of 1957), 65
Justice and order, *see* Law and order

Kamel, Mostafa, 197, 415–416
Kasavubu, Joseph, 53
Kashmir, conflict over, 204, 206, 409
Kassim, Abdul, 36, 96
Katzenbach, Nicholas, 154, 362, 387
Keita, Modibo, 192–193
Kennan, George, 3, 76
explosive report on Latin America of, 164
Kennedy, Jacqueline Bouvier, 129, 197

Kennedy, John F., xviii–xix, 133–302, 415, 594
assassination of, 302, 332, 338
post-assassination literature, 125
assessment of his term in office, 296–302
constitutional issues faced, 299
heavy nuclear burden, 298
by intellectual community, 490–491
unfulfilled promise, 300–302
Atlantic defense alliances of, 234–250, 391, 392
control over MLF, 239, 246–247
nuclear asymmetry, 241
policy speeches, 235–236, 247–248
progress in relations, 236–237
U.S. forces in Europe, 226, 231, 236–237
U.S. military spending in Europe, 395
civil-rights program of, 151–159, 333, 337, 342
federal housing desegregated, 152
legislative program, 152–153, 154–155, 159, 332, 338
developing-nations strategy of, 185–207, 407, 426
evolution of program, 186–188
failure in Indonesia, 195
final press statement, 199
nations in crisis, 189–207
U.S. interests and responsibility, 185–186
domestic economic programs of, 136–150, 298–299, 406, 528
balance-of-payments problem, 136, 137, 147, 150
civil outlays, 148–150
labor policy, xviii, 122, 137–145, 299
six major steps, 137–138
tax-cut proposal, 134, 137, 138, 147
Johnson–Kennedy continuum, 361, 362–364, 526, 528, 530
appetite for reading, 363
bureaucratic coordination, 362
complexity of issues faced, 406–407
less-than-diplomatic language, 367–368
personnel attracted by Kennedy, 358
press conferences, 365
vocational programs, 542
work habits, 364
Johnson's relations with, 304–305
Khrushchev–Kennedy summit, *see* Vienna summit talks
Latin America policy of, 207, 208–220, 413
flexibility in Latin political life, 218
functional approach formulated, 256
"incompatibility" concept, 219–220
military strategy in Cuba, 209–210, 212, 213, 214
see also Bay of Pigs invasion; Cuba —missile crisis in
military/space objectives of, 160–184, 296–298
expenditures, 171–175, 182
manned space flight, 181–184
national security, 164–170
nuclear arithmetic favoring, 388–389
planning, 169–170
underground testing, 176, 179
nuclear diplomacy of
disarmament and arms-control goals, 176–181
test-ban treaty, 134, 298, 407
top-level talks, 228
outline of author's service under, xvii, 125
quality of the man, 125–129, 297
as Senator, 65–66, 117–118, 186
Indian aid debate, 106–107
speech praising Diem, 265
succession of, 111–129, 136, 264, 494
bipartisan consensus affecting, 116–118
campaign theme, 124
economic advice, 120–123
political style differences, 111
Vietnam involvement widened under, 264–295, 494, 501, 524
alternatives to engagement, 270–271, 502
Laos troop movements in relation to, 267–268, 269
military coup in S. Vietnam, 291–292, 293
number of U.S. combat deaths, 294
rationale for commitment, 294–295
research on guerrilla warfare, 265
violation of agreement ignored, 289–290
Kennedy, Robert F., 202–203, 356, 482
assassination of, 522
in Bay of Pigs defeat, 210–211, 213
diplomatic duties of, 194

African, 202
domestic, 158
Kennedy–Cooper Resolution (1959), 107
Kennedy Round trade negotiations, 392, 397–398, 403
Kent State tragedy, 352, 546
Kerner Commission, 341
Khe Sanh, battle of (1968), 461, 464–465, 518
journalists' analysis of, 519
Khmer Red organization, 554
Khrushchev, Nikita S., 15, 21, 265, 371
Berlin solutions of, 222, 231–233
Berlin Wall, 231–233
East German treaty, 83–84, 228–229
gamble for leverage, 253–254
China denounced by, 34
Cuban affairs and
account in his memoirs, 253, 256–257
Castro's politics, 49
Cuban revolution, 52
missile crisis, 177–178, 251–261, 263, 297, 388
de-Stalinization policy of, 15, 16, 21, 252, 260
détente with West sought by, 37–38, 82
developing nations viewed by, 86
on French Indochina War, 14
on Ho Chi Minh, 44, 49
industrial forecast of, xv, 55
failure, 57
Kennedy–Khrushchev summit, *see* Vienna summit talks
Middle East policy of, 35–36, 96
Nasser and, 196
nuclear policy of, 388
arms-control goals, 178, 179, 180–181
development program, 24–27, 76
two-power diplomacy, 228
political primacy of, 54
space program of, 182–183
status lost by, 252, 260–261
ousted from power, 370, 373
"Khrushchev at Bay" (Rostow), 251
Kiesinger, Kurt, 381, 397
Killian, James, 71, 112
Kim Il Sung, 420, 570, 606
King, Martin Luther, Jr.
assassination of, 151–152, 311, 522
new rioting occasioned, 338, 340
as antiwar leader, 479
demonstrations led by, 153, 155
Kissinger, Henry A., 224, 491
as author's successor, 365, 524
meeting with Le Duc Tho, 560, 561
Moscow visit of, 560
secret Peking mission of, 564
Komer, Robert, 205, 458
Kong Le, 47, 48, 109
Kontum, 559, 560, 562
Korea, 570
dialogue between two halves of, 570
Pueblo seized in, 410–411
South, 206, 371, 410–411, 529
Asian regionalism and, 427–428
officers' coup, 207
post-war rehabilitation, 475
unpopular regime, 225
U.S. troop reduction, 594
Korean War, 14, 15, 16, 37, 266, 290, 301, 559
congressional resolution on, 505
course of, 13, 14, 601
Establishment response to, 493–494
lessons drawn from, 88
as Stalin's adventure, 388
U.S. entry into, 164, 488, 493
Vietnamese analog to, 284, 482, 502
Korry, Edward, 431
Kosygin, Aleksei, 370, 390, 410
Middle East settlement and, 418–419
military program of, 372–373
on SALT Talks, 382–383, 387
Kozlov, Vasiliy Ivanovich, 84, 261, 370
Kristol, Irving, 490
Kubitschek, Juscelino, 99, 215
Ky, Nguyen Cao, 439, 454–458, 470, 555
election of, 456
Johnson's faith in, 455
military takeover by, 448
as puppet, 466
referendum pledged by, 452
Thieu–Ky electoral struggle, 555

Labor–Management Council, 138
Land Reform law, S. Vietnam (1970), 459
Lansdale, Brig. Gen. Edward, 119, 269, 447
request for his advice, 277, 278–279
Lansdale Report (1961), 264–265
Lao Dong Party
Central Committee of, 41
Third Party Congress, 42

Laos, 40, 44–49, 252, 265–268, 567
  airfields in, 275
  civil war in, 47–49, 109–110
  cease-fire sought for, 267–268
  contingency plans for, 506, 512, 513, 524, 551
  critical importance of, 116
  domino status of, 108–109, 496
  dual violation of its territory, 487, 489
  Establishment interest in, 494
  infiltration route through (Ho Chi Minh Trail), 42, 45, 47, 554
    activation, 44
    closing off, 285, 286, 288, 512, 561
    international agreement, 287–290, 448, 504
    invaded by S. Vietnam, 554, 555
    protection of corridor, 436
    rate of infiltration, 285, 288
  Kennedy–Khrushchev discussion of, 228
  as North Vietnamese target, 284
  underground headquarters in, 465
  undeveloped status of, 44
Laos Accords, *see* Geneva Accords (Conference) on Laos
Law and order, 311, 543–546, 574
  legislation to promote, 331
  as reaction to demonstrations, 352, 355
  See also Racial crisis—law-and-order response to
Lebanon–Jordan crisis (1958), 94–98
  French interest in, 79
  outline of, 95
  Sino–Soviet response to, 34–36, 94
Le Duan, 41, 43, 371
Le Duc Tho, 560, 561
Lee, Rear Adm. John M., 240
Lemnitzer, Gen. Lyman, 209, 214, 267
Lilienthal, David, 509–510
Lippmann, Walter, 364, 492
Little Rock crisis (1957), 66
Lodge, Henry Cabot, 197, 492
  as Vietnamese ambassador, 291, 294, 456, 510
    appointment, 291
Lovett, Robert A., 162, 165
Lublin Committee, 4, 5
Lumumba, Patrice, 53, 191

McCarthy, Eugene, 482, 496
McCarthy, Joseph (McCarthyism), 114, 354
McCloy, John J., 176, 397
McCone, John, 202
McDonald, David J., 141, 143
McGhee, George, 168, 169
  BNSP assignment of, 175
Macmillan, Harold, 74, 83, 203
  de Gaulle and, 79
  German policy of, 224, 230
  nuclear deterrence arrangements with, 242, 244–245, 247
McNamara, Robert S., 169, 175, 182, 209, 248
  administrative ability of, 161–162
  in Cuba missile crisis, 257
  defense budget of, 171–172, 173–174, 333
  missile program under, 378
    MLF arrangements, 239, 247
    nuclear arithmetic, 384–388, 389
    "Select Committee" on planning, 394
    Skybolt cancellation, 244
  as national security planner, 359, 360
  Vietnam policy of, 464, 506, 512
    bombing halt, 516
    mission to Vietnam, 290
    policy meetings with S. Vietnamese, 292, 453
    troop expansions, 448, 513
  World Bank headed by, 569
Malaya
  expansion of, 195
  guerrilla movement in, 13, 14, 119
Malaysia, 199, 496
  Asian regionalism and, 428
  formation of, 195
Manila conference on Vietnam (Oct. 1966), 458
Mann, Tom, 305
Mansfield, Mike, 396
Mao Tse-tung, 16, 21–24, 31, 588
  changing policy of, xv
  Cultural Revolution directed by, 372
  developing world viewed by, 86
  domestic economic problems of, 55–56, 57
  Great Leap Forward announced by, 32
  political–military strategy of, 13
  socialist ideology of, 21–22, 23, 24, 29
  Soviet deception of, 26
  on space race, 54
  study of his works, 265

Taiwan probe of, 36
U.S.–Soviet rapprochement and, 37–38
March on the Pentagon (Oct. 1967), 423
March on Washington (Aug. 28, 1963), 155, 406
Marines, U.S., 173, 278, 449
dispatched to Dominican Republic, 411–412
dispatched to Vietnam, 448
mobilized over Laos, 227, 267–268
pacification efforts of, 457
withdrawn from Okinawa, 558
Marshall, George C., 162, 165, 492
Marshall Plan, 11–12, 13, 17, 51, 339, 426, 493
secretariat for, 249
vision behind, 11
Mason, Edward S., 198
Matthews, Herbert, 100
Maurer, Ion Gheorghe, 434
Mayobre, Antonio, 415
Meany, George, 122
Medicare, 334, 342, 541, 542
Menshikov, Mihail, 230
Merchant, Livingston, 247
Meredith, James, 153
Mexico, 219, 582
Middle East crises, *see* Arab–Israeli relations; Lebanon–Jordan crisis; Suez crisis
Middle East Resolution (March 9, 1957), 94
Middleton, Drew, 230
Mikolajczyk, Stanislaw, 6
Mikoyan, Anastas, 51, 83, 288, 300
"Mikoyan, the Laos Agreement, and Continued Infiltration Into South Vietnam" (Rostow), 288–289
Military Affairs Party Committee, 451
Military technology (power)
growth of U.S., 1–2
See also Nuclear weapons; Space race
Millikan, Max, xviii, 89, 91, 106
Minh, Ho Chi, *see* Ho Chi Minh
Minh, Gen. Duong Van, 291–292, 555
"Missile gap," 25–26, 616–617
Missile technology, *see* Nuclear weapons; Space race
Mississippi, University of (Oxford), 153
MLF (Multilateral Force), 237–243, 245–250, 391–394
failure of, 248–250
list of participants in, 247
mode of promoting, 391–392
as object of Russian diplomacy, 378
proposal of, 77, 235, 239–242, 391
strong advocacy, 241
Mobutu, Col. Joseph, 53, 405
Model Cities program, 342, 343–345, 544, 591
federal spending on, 344–345
Mohieddin, Zakaria, 416, 417
Molotov, Vyacheslav M., 6, 12, 21
Monnet, Jean, 11, 80, 81, 362
Moon probes, 183, 628
astronaut training for, 71
cost of manned, 181
projected date for, 182
Morgenthau, Hans, 8
Moscow Conference (Nov. 1957), 28, 41
Moscow Declaration (Dec. 6, 1960), 34
Moyers, Bill, 305, 358, 507, 508
Moynihan, Daniel Patrick, 544
Multilateral Force, *see* MLF
Murphy, Robert, 95
Mutual Security Act (1958 amendment), 91
Myrdal, Gunnar, 155, 214

Nanterre *enragés*, 354
NASA (National Aeronautics and Space Administration), 71, 182
Nassau meeting (Dec. 1962), 244–246
Nasser, Gamal Abdel, 114, 169, 196–200, 570, 609
diplomatic accessibility of, 196–197
his role in Lebanon–Jordan crisis, 94, 96,
in 6-day war, 415–417
Gulf of Aqaba closed, 407, 415
Yemeni intervention of, 198–199
National Aeronautics and Space Administration (NASA), 71, 182
National Aeronautics and Space Council, 182, 184
National Alliance of Businessmen, 342
National Defense Education Act (1958), 71
National Goals, Commission on, 117, 118
National Guard, U.S.
in racial strife, 66, 153
violence of, against students, 356
National interest, 593–600, 605–611
defined, 605–607
in developing world, 596–597
dual Eurasian interests, 607–609

in Europe, 593–595
ideological interests, 607–610
military budget options in, 597–599
National liberation
of Vietnam, 41
wars of, 43
communist attitude toward, 24, 26–27, 54, 226
Cuban revolution as, 52
guerrilla warfare as, 87
research tools, 265
National Liberation Front (NLF) (South Vietnamese Communists) (Viet Cong), (VC), 42–43, 45, 448, 456–457, 524, 559
Allies press back rural dominance of, 458–459, 468–469, 515
Diem's overthrow affecting, 292
documents captured from, 450–451, 460, 462
formation of, 42, 44
increased mobilization of, 264, 271, 447
infiltration routes used by, 289
military and political capacity as eroding, 556
propaganda efforts of, 273
statistics on, 280
casualty figures, 445
troop ratios, 450
in Tet offensive, 460, 462–463, 466
in truce negotiations, 514
U.S. opinion influenced by, 515–516
in war's second stage, 449
National Policy Machinery, Subcommittee on, 166
National security affairs, 116–168, 169–170
reorganization of, 167
See also Johnson, Lyndon B.—national security affairs under
National Security Council (NSC), 73, 165–166, 167, 269, 359–366
atrophy of, 165–166
establishment of, 164–165
Executive Committee of, 257
Far Eastern affairs staff of, 514
Ghana project before, 202–203
informal meetings of, 358–360
interdepartmental papers processed by, 363
Planning Subcommittee of, 177
tasks of NSC special assistant, 364–366
National style, 600–604
future of, 603–604
history of, 600–602
Vietnam War straining, 501–503
NATO (North Atlantic Treaty Organization), 75–77, 115, 236, 527, 585, 601
budget for, 174
de Gaulle's stand on, 80, 310
French withdrawal, 394
Establishment interest in, 493
formation of, 13, 14
goals set for, 117
its role in East-West détente, 399–403
military command of (SHAPE), 407, 493
MLF within, *see* MLF
NATO Council (North Atlantic Council), 231, 401, 403
MLF project before, 240
NATO troop reductions, 395–397, 594–595
Warsaw Pact mutual reductions, 547–548, 563, 576
Paris summit meetings of
1957, 74, 75, 79, 92, 238
1960, 77, 238
1961, 239
1962, 242, 243
planners' club of (APAG), 236–237, 257
Russian posture on, 180, 377–378, 383
its questionable legitimacy, 226
serving U.S. interests, 593, 594–595
shift of NATO headquarters, 400
"NATO's Principal Political Function—Preparation for Settlement in Central Europe" (policy paper), 400
Negroes, *see* Racial crisis
Nehru, B. K., 423
Nehru, Jawaharlal, 107, 262, 407
in India–Pakistan conflict, 204, 205, 206
Netherlands, the
aid program of, 402, 403
Dutch New Guinea, 193, 194
MLF joined by, 247
New Deal, 113, 124, 328–329, 528
New Frontier, 120, 302
New Guinea (West Irian), 193–195, 561
New Left, 119, 352, 546
antiwar feeling in, 486, 499, 531
New York Economic Club, 134, 147

New York Times, The, 230, 244, 484, 516, 546
Ngo Dinh Diem, *see* Diem, Ngo Dinh
Nhu, Ngo Dinh, 276–277, 281–282
  in 1963 political crisis, 291–294, 455
    pagoda raids conducted, 291, 293
  pacification program under, 281
Nhu, Madame Ngo Dinh, 291, 292
Nigerian civil war, 567
Nitze, Paul, 169, 213, 233
Nixon, Richard M., xviii, 345, 537–576
  assessment of his term in office, 573–576
    conservative political phase, 574
    political advantages sought, 575
  developing-nations strategy of, 567–572
    awkward period, 569–570
    facing anti-Yankee nationalism, 568
    tables showing aid contributions, 568, 569
  economic programs of, 325, 537–543, 565–566, 574
    diffusion of power, 576
    dollar exchange rate, 588
    foreign aid, 567–570
    public spending, 540–543
    rising unemployment, 538, 539, 542, 544
    signaling U.S. weakness, 566
    wage–price policy required, 589
    weakening of the dollar, 539
    welfare reform, 541–542
  his foreign policy reviewed, 563–567
    criticism of policy papers, 563
    trade policy, 565–566
    visit to China, xv, 557, 565
  law-and-order contest under, 543–546, 574
  military and arms-control policy of, 546–550, 594
    chart showing military spending, 549
    chart of total armed forces, 548
  as political campaigner
    Kennedy–Nixon contest, 122
    1968 election, 355
    1972 campaign issues, 543, 574
    series of defeats, 85
  Southeast Asian War pursued by, 436, 458, 525, 550–564, 565, 576
    ambiguous policy, 552, 564
    chart of total armed forces, 548
    fiscal outlays, 547, 549, 589
    policy as political strength, 556
    resumption of bombing, 523, 560
    Vietnamization plan chosen, 550–551
    widening the war, 553–554, 555, 567
  as Vice President, 65, 96, 112, 115
    anti-Nixon demonstrations, 99
    debate with USSR, 84
Nkrumah, Kwame, 200–203, 650–651
  military coup against, 420
  nature of his reign, 200–202
NLF, *see* National Liberation Front
Nolting, Frederick, 290
Nonproliferation, *see* NPT; Nuclear diplomacy—nonproliferation objective of
Noronha, Reginald S., 191
North Atlantic Council, *see* NATO—NATO Council
North Atlantic Treaty Organization, *see* NATO
North Korea, *see* Korea; Korean War
North Vietnam, *see* Vietnam—North; Vietnam War
NPT (nonproliferation treaty), 369, 377–383, 389, 393, 433–434, 578–579
  Asian commitments linked to, 500
  preamble to, 579
  preliminary discussion of, 394
  signatories of, 578
NSAM 322, 393
NSC, *see* National Security Council
Nuclear diplomacy, 376, 377–388
  advances in, xv, 527
  nonproliferation objective of, 496
    conditions for achieving, 579–581
    NPT negotiations, 369, 377–384, 394
    U.S. China policy endangering, 564
    see also NPT
  nuclear arms control, 176–181
    bilateral agreement, 369; *see also* SALT Talks
    Moscow–Washington hot line, 181
    Soviet interest in, 34, 75
    as U.S. goal, 117
  nuclear blackmail, 15, 76–77, 230, 255, 261, 579
  nuclear test-ban proposals, 179–180
    disarmament linked to, 228
    inspection issue, 179–180
    1963 test-ban treaty, 134, 298, 407
    Russian, 32–33, 82–83
    treaty negotiations, 177, 180–181

Nuclear weapons, 24–27, 68–73, 172–175, 297–298
budget for, 172–174, 547
as Cold War issue, 15, 298
conservative approach to, 112–113
development goals for, 117
in Europe, 78–82, 234–235, 237–250, 391–394
Anglo–French asymmetry, 78–80, 82
arms control, 377, 379–382
German–Italian status, 241
mixed-manning demonstration (MLS), 393
removal of U.S. bases demanded, 394
Skybolt missiles, 243–244
U.S. missile bases, 32, 75–77, 79, 237–238
U.S.–European asymmetry, 594
see also MLF
ICBM development, 388
charts showing parity, 374–376
Soviet capability, 21, 22, 25–26, 55, 75, 223, 259
U.S. program, 69, 73
NSC 68 on, 165
peace in nuclear age, 610–611
as power base, 2, 18, 593–594
resumption of testing of, 176
Soviet advantage in, 69–70
strategic nuclear parity, 372–373
See also Antiballistic missiles; China—in nuclear club; Cuba—missile crisis in; Space race

OAS (Organization of American States), 103, 429
Cuban expulsion from, 218–221
future of, 583
reacts to missile crisis, 255–256, 258
U.S. failure to consult, 412–414, 415
OAU (Organization of African Unity), 431
OCB, *see* Operations Coordinating Board
O'Donnell, Kenneth, 134
OECD (Organization for Economic Co-operation and Development), 92, 236, 284, 585
Japanese membership in, 237
OEO (Office of Economic Opportunity), 342, 544
Okinawa, 237, 268, 558
Okun, Arthur M., 317, 322
"On How Much Flesh and Blood Can Stand: Laos and Vietnam" (Rostow), 506
Onassis, Jacqueline Kennedy, 129, 197
Open Housing Act of 1968, 338, 346, 350
Operation Head Start, 341
Operations Coordinating Board (OCB), 165–167
organization of, 165, 166
Organization for Economic Cooperation and Development, *see* OECD
Organization of American States, *see* OAS
Organization of African Unity (OAU), 431
Owen, Henry, 126, 177
as speech writer, 96, 235

Pacification program, 281–282, 286, 460
population status in, 439
slippage of, 464, 468
strategic-hamlet phase of, 281, 457
U.S. contribution to, 452, 457–459, 468–469
accelerated, 468–470, 482, 523, 550
alleged death of program, 519
change in U.S. mission, 551
military control, 459
Pakistan, 15, 87
development aid to, 88, 107
economic normalization, 597
India–Pakistan consortium, 91, 188
dismemberment of, 567
Indian conflict with, 204–206, 208, 651–653
Moslem–Hindu tensions, 205
1965 war, 371, 373, 407, 409–410, 422
1971 war, 562, 566, 570, 576
Khrushchev's view of, 225
Pantja Sila (Sukarno), 193
Paris, NATO meetings in, *see* NATO—Paris summit meetings of
Paris talks on Vietnam (1968–1972)
major agreements from, 522–524
negotiating base sought for, 469, 514–515, 521, 522
opening of, 311, 467, 479
resumed (1972), 560
Tet offensive linked to, 463, 467
as unsatisfactory compromise, 482
Vietnamization tied to, 550
Park, Chung Hee, 206, 410, 510, 570

Pastore, John, 66, 396
Pathet Lao (Laotian Communist party), 45–48, 266, 287
  control over, 45
  decrease in significance of, 524
  excluded from Laotian government, 46
Paulskirche statement (June 25, 1963), 247–248
Peace Corps, 206
  internationalization of, 305
  launching of, 188
  withdrawn from Indonesia, 409
Peace movement, *see* Antiwar movement
Peacemaking, responsibility for, 597, 610–611
P'eng Teh-huai, 33
Pentagon, *see* Defense, Department of
Perkins, Dexter, 7, 491
Pham Van Dong, 435
Philadelphia address (July 4, 1962), 235–236
Philippines, 88, 428
  guerrilla movement in, 13, 283, 493
  Vietnam conferences in, 458; *see also* Guam conferences on Vietnam
Phoui Sananikone, 46
Phoumi Nosavan, Gen., 47, 48, 109
  U.S. report on, 266
"Plan Six," 278, 506
Pleiku, 559, 560
Podgorny, Nikolai V., 370, 372–373
Point Four, 15, 105
Poland, 2, 3, 515, 601
  Declaration on (1945), 5
  provisional government of, 4–7
  rise of Polish nationalism, 16
  U.S.–China talks in Warsaw, 433
Policy Planning Council, xviii, 126, 175, 366, 400, 514
  author as chairman of, xvii
  Cuba policy designed by, 103
  Middle East policy formulated by, 96
  missile crisis considered by, 259
  regional planning of, 426, 504, 510
  Southeast Asia contingency plan of, 505
Political Congress, 454
Political Economy of Prosperity, The (Okun), 322
Politics and the Stages of Growth (Rostow), xvi
Pollution, *see* Ecology
Pompidou, Georges, 392
Population control, *see* Birth control; Pacification program
Porter, William, 458
Postan, M. M., 406
Potsdam Conference (Aug. 1945), 3, 5
  communique issued at, 10
Poverty program (War on Poverty), 305, 342, 406
  community action under, 345
  federal spending on, 343
  legislation governing, 331, 332
Pravda (Soviet journal), 196, 253–254, 261
  on Cuba missile crisis, 253, 254
Present at the Creation (Acheson), 167
Presidents of U.S.
  bureaucracy serving, 160–161
  See also Eisenhower Administration; Johnson, Lyndon B.; Kennedy, John F.; Nixon, Richard M.; Roosevelt, Franklin D.; Truman, Harry S.; Wilson, Woodrow
Proposal: Key to An Effective Foreign Policy, A (Rostow and Millikan), 89
Public Papers (Kennedy), 134
Pueblo, seizure of, 410–411, 522
Pugwash Conference (Moscow, 1960), 33, 34, 176, 617
  author's speech before, 577
Punta del Este, Charter of, 215–216, 217
Pushkin, Georgiy, 287–288
Pye, Lucian, 119, 273, 491

Quality, search for, 531, 588–592
  consensus required for, 590
  heavy tax burden and, 592
Quang Tri, 559, 560, 562
Quantico Panel report (June 1955), 72, 73
Quemoy–Matsu crisis (1958), 35, 521–522, 619

Racial crisis, 332–333, 334–351, 528
  African, 431
  black radicals, 353, 356
  civil-rights cause growing in, 332
  as "deepening schism," 347
  emergence of, 64–66
    civil-rights movement, 65
    school desegregation issue, 66
  law-and-order response to, 543–544, 574

inevitable backlash, 532
legislation to combat, 331–332, 338–340, 346
1963, 151–157, 299, 406–407
background, 152, 155–157
black nationhood sought, 157
catalytic events, 153–154
political promises in time of, 530
solution to ghetto crisis, 591
unforeseen scale of, 118–119
Vietnam interacting with, 479, 502
See also Riots
Radicals, *see* Buddhist activists; Fedayeen; New Left; Weathermen; Youth
Randall, Clarence, 88, 90, 202
Recession, economic
in 1950s, 60–63, 66–67
balance-of-payments sphere, 60–61, 115
cost-push inflation and, 112
expansion ending in, 62
price controls, 144
1970, 540, 546
Reischauer, Edwin O., 237
Reuther, Walter, 141–142, 316, 343
author's talk with, xviii, 140–141
Revenue sharing, 541, 542, 574
Revisionist debate, 7–8
Revolutionary Council, 209–210
Rickover, Adm. Hyman, 239
Riots, urban, 310, 311, 333, 530
police authority triggering, 350
reveal depth of race problem, 406
in succession of hot summers, 340
Washington burned during, 522
Rockefeller, Nelson, 72, 112, 126
in development policy debate, 88, 89
Rockefeller Panel reports (1958–60), 117
Rodríguez, Carlos Rafael, 51
Romania, 34, 567, 576
Roosevelt, Franklin D., 12, 124, 167, 299
administrative technique of, 168
Establishment and, 492, 494
Far East policy of, 606
as Johnson's model, 304, 333
power alliances of, 4–5
on U.S. troops in Europe, 226, 601
Roosevelt, Theodore, 124, 606
Rostow, Elspeth Davies, xiii, 215
Rural Reconstruction, Ministry of, 457
Rusk, Dean, 119, 161 163, 168, 175, 202, 255, 513
as administrator/adviser, 163
bureaucratic relations of, 161–162, 168, 235, 362
on Camp David discussions (Oct. 1966), 378
at foreign-ministers meetings, 231
with Gromyko, 232, 377, 378
Punta del Este, 218–220
Latin American diplomacy under, 218–221
Alliance for Progress, 216
Bay of Pigs, 209, 210
Cuba missile crisis, 258
on MLF, 239, 391
in national security operations, 366
his key position, 358
informal sessions attended, 359–360
at NATO conference, 245
on *Pueblo* incident, 411
senators' meeting chaired by, 396
Vietnam policy under, 488
author's advice, 504, 505, 506–507, 508
negotiating position, 521
policy meetings with S. Vietnamese, 292, 453
relation to view of Asia, 495
Russell, Richard, 396, 405
Russia, *see* Soviet Union
Russian Revolution of 1917, 586

SAC, *see* Strategic Air Command
Sadat, Anwar el-, 570–573
Saigon, 456, 459, 553
in 1972 offensive, 559, 560
pacification area around, 457
port of, 474
spoiling operations in, 452
Tet offensive against, 460, 464
university in, 473
Sallal, Abdulah, 198
SALT (Strategic Arms Limitation Talks), 377, 382–383, 389, 390, 557
ABM compromise affecting, 387–388, 563
announcement of, 369
future of, 599
opening of, 547
parity essential to, 373
Sarawak, 195
Saunders, Hal, 417
Schlesinger, Arthur M., Jr., xx, 168
in Bay of Pigs defeat, 210

Johnson's visit with, 303
revisionist thesis of, 7–8
Schlesinger, Arthur M., Sr., 574
Schoenbrun, David, 211
SEATO (Southeast Asia Treaty Organization)
creation of, 87
treaty establishing, 42, 43
Vietnam commitment basis, 486, 487, 501
SEATO Plan Five, 268
Second World War, *see* World War II
Segregation, *see* Racial crisis
Senate, U.S., 71, 186, 602
antiwar feeling in, 484, 496
civil-rights legislation before, 65, 152
Diem praised before, 265
Eisenhower's relations with, 366
Indian aid program before, 106–107
liberal members of, 303
NATO troop reductions advocated in, 396, 547–548
opposition to Kennedy in, 190
senators in steel negotiations, 142
test-ban treaty before, 180
Tonkin Resolution passed by, 489
Senior interdepartmental group (SIG), 362
SHAPE, 407, 493
Sharp, Adm. Ulysses S. Grant, 452
Shastri, Lal Bahadur, 409–410
Sheahan, John, 145
SIG (senior interdepartmental group), 362
Sihanouk, Norodom, Prince of Cambodia, 553
Sinai peninsula, 418, 419, 571
Six-day war, *see* Arab–Israeli relations—culminating in 6-day war
Skybolt missile program, 243–245
Smith, Bromley, 359, 360
Smith, Gerard, 103, 126, 240
Smith, Jerome, 158
SNCC (Student Nonviolent Coordinating Committee), 157
"Soft War, The," 283
Sokolovsky, V. A., 260
Sorensen, Theodore, 126, 149, 254
on Bay of Pigs, 214
on civil-rights policy, 159, 337
as speech writer, 187, 505
on Vietnam commitment, 295
South Korea, *see* Korea—South
South Vietnam, *see* ARVN; Danang; Hue; National Liberation Front; Pacification program; Saigon; Vietnam War
Southeast Asia, *see* Burma; Cambodia; French Indochina War; Indochina; Indonesia; Laos; Malaya; Malaysia; Thailand; Vietnam; Vietnam War
Southeast Asia Resolution (Aug. 1964), 486, 489
Southeast Asia Treaty Organization, *see* SEATO
Southern Manifesto (1956), 337
Souvanna Phouma, 46, 228
neutralist government formed by, 47–48, 109
rehabilitation of, 268
tax on infiltration corridor approved by, 489
Soviet Union, 2–18, 54–55, 369–389, 522
Allied aircraft buzzed by, 233–234
Cuban–Soviet relations, 51–52, 216–217
serendipitous for USSR, 51, 52
stepped-up arms shipments, 254
see also Cuba—missile crisis in
diffusion of power in, 585–588, 599
diminution of its control, 16–18, 561–562, 587
Russian history, 386
domestic economy of, 55, 56, 57, 73, 252, 595
Egyptian–Soviet relations, 15, 196, 570–572
burdensome Soviet presence, 570
future, 599
over 6-day war, 415
as emergent power, 2–3
European defense against, 238, 240–241
future of, 390, 599–600
Kennedy on Soviet strategy, 119
as Pakistan–India intermediary, 410, 562
policy changes in, xv, 370–371
role of, in Congolese turmoil, 190, 228
1960 revolution, 53
role of, in 6-day war, 415, 416, 417–419, 527
role of, in Vietnam War, 42–44, 45
armaments for Tet offensive, 460

Chinese role vs., 22–23, 43–44, 48–49, 371, 557
closing off infiltration route, 287–288, 289–290
initial commitment, 41
Laotian theater, 49, 267–268
Spring 1972 offensive, 557–562
U.S.–USSR dialogue, 376–377
U.S.–USSR nuclear contest, 377–389
arms-control talks, 176–181, 228; *see also* SALT
first-strike capability, 26, 27, 73
NPT treaty, 369, 377–383, 390, 579
missile development race, 68–70, 71–72, 73, 75–76
nuclear deception, 24–26
nuclear war games, 172, 175
strategic nuclear parity, 372–373
U.S.–USSR relations, 34, 54, 222–234, 373–390, 606
during Cold War, 4–15, 298
critical to Sino–Soviet diplomacy, 32, 36, 37–39
cultural exchange, 377
manned space flight, 182–184
over Middle East, 35
Nixon administration, 547, 557–562, 563–564, 566, 573
normalization, 309, 373, 527
NSC 68 report, 165
scientific cooperation, 169
second Berlin crisis, 229–233
strategic balance, 225–226, 253
U-2 spy incident, 82–83
see also Vienna summit talks
See also China, Communist—Sino–Soviet relations; Pugwash Conference
Space race, 181–184
alleged superiority in, 54
budget for, 171, 182
during Eisenhower's term, 68, 70–71, 181
first Sputnik launched in, 1, 18, 22, 68
See also Moon probes
Special Message to the Congress on Foreign Aid (March 22, 1961), 186–187
Spheres of influence, 8
Stages of Economic Growth, The (Rostow), xvi, 120
Stalin, Josef, 3–5, 16, 51, 69
Cold War diplomacy of, 4–5, 7, 8, 12–13
German disarmament policy, 10, 11
death of, 15
nuclear leverage, lack of, 388
Soviet power developed under, 3, 587
Stassen, Harold, 88
State, Department of, 10, 11, 162–164, 167
bureaucracy of, 163, 166
departments coordinated by, 167, 362
intelligence data from, 364
reorganization of, 168
See also Policy Planning Council
Steel price war (1961–1962), 142–145, 299
automobile prices, 141
social contract behind, 138
Stevenson, Adlai, 112, 490
in 1960 campaign, 127
Stimson, Henry L., 6, 492
Strategic Air Command (SAC), 75, 238
emergence of, 2
superiority of, 69
vulnerability of, 73, 172
Strategic Arms Limitation Talks, *see* SALT
Strategic hamlets, 281, 457
Strategic Studies, Institute for (London), 468
Strategy of Peace, The (Kennedy), 118
Strauss, Franz Josef, 399–400
Strout, Richard L., 543
Student Nonviolent Coordinating Committee (SNCC), 157
Students, radical, *see* Youth
Sudan, 572
Suez Canal, reopening of, 570, 572
Suez crisis (1956), 114, 256, 380, 609
Soviet–Egyptian arms deal and, 15
Suharto, Gen. T. N. J., 420
Sukarno, Prince, 192–196, 420
character of, 192–193
low-posture diplomacy with, 409
Peking alignment of, 407
Supreme Court, U.S., 338
1954 desegregation decision of, 64, 337
Nixon's appointments to, 545, 574
Symington, Stuart, 127, 396
Syria, 94
Jordan invaded by, 571
role of, in 6-day war, 416, 418
withdraws from UAR, 196

Taft, Robert, 541
Taiwan Straits crisis (1958), 35, 36–37
Tatu, Michel, 84, 223
on Cuba missile crisis, 255–256, 260
on Khrushchev's ouster, 370
Tax Reform Act of 1969, 542, 592
Tax surcharge, 318, 542, 574, 576
Taylor, Gen. Maxwell D., 161
as adviser on Vietnam, 269–271, 274–278, 456, 506
appointment, 268
coordinated advisory program, 280
McNamara–Taylor mission, 291
memos on U.S. choices, 270–271
Southeast Asia mission, 272, 274–277
Bay of Pigs inquest conducted by, 215
Test-ban proposals, *see* Nuclear diplomacy—nuclear test-ban proposals
Tet offensives
1968, 459–468 470, 495, 510, 516–521, 560, 562
aims, 460, 462–463
beginning, 410, 464
causes, 437, 459–460
influence on American public, 463, 467, 481–483, 502, 518–521
influence on Establishment, 495
test for nationalism, 476
1969, 311, 550
Thailand, 40, 88, 496, 567
Asian regionalism and, 428
defense of, 268
guerrilla movement in, 274, 488
Laos as buffer state for, 45
U.S. commitment to, 48
U.S. troop mobilization in, 268
Thang, Gen. Nguyen Chi, 457–458, 460
Thant, U, 195
Thermonuclear weapons, *see* Nuclear weapons
Thi, Gen., 454
Thieu, Nguyen Van, 439, 454–457, 471–472
election of, 456–457
noncompetitive race, 555
elections approved by, 455
military takeover by, 448
negotiating position of, 514, 515, 551
party system under, 510, 554–555
as patriot, 455
as puppet, 466
strengthening of administration, 556, 562
on troop withdrawals, 468, 523
Third World, 426, 567
Thompson, Sir Robert G. K., 280–281, 286, 519
Thomson, George, 416
Thorneycroft, Peter, 244
Thuc, Nguyen Dang, 509
Tito, Marshal (Josip Broz), 262
defection of, 13, 16, 587
Tonkin Gulf incident (Aug. 4, 1964), 370, 489, 507
Tonkin Gulf Resolution (Aug. 1964), 486, 489
Trade Expansion Act of 1962, 236
Trujillo Molina, Rafael, 103, 207
Truman, Harry S., 112, 113, 129, 505, 521, 601
Asia stabilized by, 529
assessed as leader, 193
Cold War diplomacy of, 5–6, 8, 10, 124
in Asia, 14
Point Four, 15
Truman Doctrine, 12, 13, 426
Establishment influence on, 493, 494
European unity encouraged by, 17
legislative record of President, 150
popularity of, 532
Tshombe, Moise, 53, 190–192
defeat of, 190
Tully, Grace, xx
Turkey, 12, 411
U.S. relations with, 169
defense alliances, 87
Khrushchev's view of, 225
missile base installations, 32, 76, 77, 237
MLF participation, 247
Russia threatened by U.S. missiles, 255, 258
Twenty-fourth Amendment, 152

U-2 flights, 25
international incident over, 84, 252, 632
Ulbricht, Walter, 16, 222–223
Unheavenly City, The (Banfield), 348–349
United Arab Republic, *see* Egypt; Syria
United Kingdom, *see* Great Britain
United Nations, 9, 164

arms-control proposals before, 176–177
Chinese admission to, 116, 428, 564
Security Council seat, 580
European Economic Commission of, 11, 16, 214
India–Pakistan cease-fire arranged by, 409–410
Indonesian withdrawal from, 371, 407
Khrushchev's visit to, 84
Middle East question before, 417, 418
crisis mediator, 573
1958 crisis, 95, 96–98
noninterference resolution, 98
Security Council Resolution (1967), 571
military presence of
Congolese, 190–192
Korean, 13
withdrawn from Sinai, 416
nonproliferation statement to, 382, 579
Southeast Asian affairs before, 370–371, 601
admission of Vietnam, 43
formation of Malaysia, 195
West Irian trusteeship, 194
UN fact-finding mission, 291, 292
United Nations Plan for Reconciliation, 191
United States in the World Arena, The (Rostow), xi, 119
central theme of, 300
on security and commitment, 212
United States Information Agency (USIA), 25
United States Steel, 144
Universalism, ideology of, 8
Uruguay, 219, 425
USIA (United States Information Agency), 25
U-2 flights, 25
international incident over, 84, 252, 632

Vance, Cyrus, 411
Vandenberg, Arthur, 9
Vanguard missile project, 71
Vantage Point, The (Johnson), 487, 514
Vichinsky, Andrei, 601
Vienna summit talks (June 1961), 49, 180, 182–183, 222, 223–228, 659–660
on balance of power, 225–226, 300
preparation for, 224
usefulness of, 227–228
Viet Cong, *see* National Liberation Front
Viet Minh, 40, 42, 228
Vietnam
North, 476
aligned with S. Vietnamese communists, 43
collectivization failure, 41
communist control, 40
domestic economy, 56, 57
Laos policy, 45–46
South, *see* ARVN; Danang; Hue; National Liberation Front; Pacification program; Saigon
Vietnam War, 40–49, 263–295, 429, 435–525, 599
battle statistics on, 438–445
captured weapons, 439, 440–441, 449, 464
casualty rates, 294, 464, 465, 467
casualty ratios, 280, 438, 440–441
effectiveness of bombing, 511
U.S. reliance on, 279–280
chronological summaries of
events leading to intensification, 448
five Johnson Administration phases, 438
1963 crisis, 290–292
"special warfare" phase, 266, 269
differing Sino-Soviet roles in, 22, 43–44, 49, 370–371
disintegrating South in, 135, 432, 439, 446–449
formulae for winning, 291, 448–449, 450, 457
four causes of, 42–43
future costs of, 591, 597–599
Korean troops in, 410, 559
modernization of S. Vietnam in, 470–475
as 1972 election issue, 557
North as aggressor in, 40, 41–42, 55, 371, 435–437
Cambodian interior, 554
drain on Northern economy, 57–58
encouragement of local dissidence, 284
infiltration of political and military cadres, 41, 44, 285, 504
question of legitimacy, 278
regular forces introduced, 310, 439, 447, 450, 507

Spring 1972 offensive, 556–562, 587
subject to debate, 487, 489–490, 502
use of monsoons, 559, 560
see also Tet offensives
peace talks on, *see* Paris talks on Vietnam
regional resistance in, 454
unpopularity of, 477–503, 515–516, 527–528, 532
atrocities and chemical warfare, 487, 489
attrition of American will, 435, 437, 450, 513
criticism from abroad, 396, 405, 527
Establishment split, 492–497
national dialogue, 484–490, 500, 510, 519
Nixon term, 555–556
transient U.S. presence, 429
see also Antiwar movement
U.S. attack on N. Vietnam in
bombing halt, 469, 480, 516, 521, 522–524
bombing raids, 371, 448, 464, 479, 509, 511–512, 560, 561
contingency plans, 278, 286–287, 505, 506, 507, 508
invasion contingency, 513, 551
mining harbors, 560, 561
naval strategy, 452, 560, 561
U.S. intensification of (1965–1969), 438–525, 550–556, 601
black soldiers, 152
charting the war's phases, 438–445
defense spending, 421
invasion of Cambodia, 352, 439, 546, 553
justification to come, 529–530
national security meetings, 358–359
nuclear gamble, 388
policy meetings with S. Vietnamese, xviii, 453, 455–456, 457–458, 468, 509, 515
spoiling operations, 452
substantial troop commitments, 427, 448, 463–464, 478–479, 508, 512–513, 519–520
U.S.–USSR dialogue, 377
U.S. involvement in (1956–1963), 264–295
advisory capacity, 108, 275–276, 278, 280
commitment, xix, 267, 295
Diem regime supported, 42, 56, 265, 271
first troop mobilizations, 268, 269
fiscal outlays, 315
Laotian theater, 45, 46, 47–48, 108–110, 116, 265–268
self-determination for South, 272–274
U.S. withdrawal from, 496–497, 556, 558
alternative to engagement, 270, 274
as cause of Spring 1972 offensive, 559
isolationist sentiment, 564
popular support, 478–480, 481–482, 487, 498
subject to negotiation, 514–515
timetables, 468, 480, 564
troop reductions, 472, 523, 546, 552
via Vietnamization, *see* Nixon, Richard M.—Southeast Asia War pursued by
VISTA (Volunteers in Service to America), 343
Volta Dam (Ghana), 202–203
Von Brentano, Heinrich, 236, 395
Vo-Nguyen Giap, Gen., *see* Giap, Vo-Nguyen
Voting Rights Act of 1965, 338, 544

Wage-price freeze, 539
Wage-price guideposts, 138–145, 316, 317, 320–323, 589, 640–641, 668–669
assessment of, 324–326
breakdown of, 145, 318, 320–322
pioneering of, 138–144, 298
reinstallation of, 538
rejection of, 537–538
Waging Peace (Eisenhower memoir), 59, 97
on Southeast Asia, 108–110
Wall Street Journal, The, 519
Wallace, George C., 154, 333
as conservative, 574
as law-and-order candidate, 355, 543, 545
War on Poverty, *see* Poverty program
Wars of national liberation, *see* National liberation—wars of
Warsaw, U.S.–China talks in, 433
Washington, March on (Aug. 28, 1963), 155, 406

Washington Post, The, 484, 519
Watts riot (Aug. 1965), 340, 406, 530
Weathermen, 356, 545
Webb, James, 182
Wessin y Wessin, Gen. Elias, 412
Westmoreland, Gen. William, 521, 552
  complexity of his task, 451–452
  contingency plans of
    invasion of North, 513
    troop expansions, 512, 513
  pacification under, 457, 459
  at security planning sessions, 358
  Tet offensive against, 464, 465–466
    additional U.S. troops requested, 519, 520
  on troop withdrawals, 468, 480, 551
  "victory" strategy of, 449
Wheeler, Gen. Earle, 481, 513
  ABM policy of, 386, 388
Wiesner, Jerome, 34
Wilson, Harold, 180, 409
  elected Prime Minister, 392
  MLF arrangements with, 392–393
Wilson, Woodrow, 124, 129, 299, 600, 609
Winter–spring offensives, *see* Tet offensives
Wirtz, Willard, 321–322, 323
World Bank (International Monetary Fund), 193, 202, 423
  aid programs financed via, 91, 99, 107, 568–569
  consortium arrangements of, 188, 197
  IDA of, *see* International Development Association
World War I, 290, 600
World War II, 1–5, 6, 215, 290, 493, 582
  de Gaulle's role in, 81
  demonstrating national style, 600
  Italian surrender in, 8, 9
  political effects of, 1–4, 596
  Russian weapons used in, 69
  SHAEF in, 17
  Supreme Allied Command in, 451–452
  Vietnam occupied during, 470

Yalta Conference (1945), 226, 601
Yalta Declaration on Liberated Europe (1945), 5, 7
Yemeni civil war (1962), 196, 198–199
Yew, Lee Kuan, 429
Young, Richard, 156–157
Youth, dissident (radical), 352–357, 530–531
  antiwar actions of, 352, 497–500
    author as favored target, 497
  black students, 352
  communist/anarchist influence on, 119, 354
  law-and-order backlash against, 545–546
  universal dissidence, 352, 355
  youth movement's origins, 119–120
Yugoslavia, 18, 286, 576
  as nonaligned nation, 225, 586
  nonproliferation involving, 379
  postwar development program of, 16
  role of, in Cold War, 12

Zorin, Valerian, 176